Of MEMORY, REMINISCENCE, and WRITING

OF MEMORY, REMINISCENCE, AND WRITING

On the Verge

DAVID FARRELL KRELL

Indiana University Press

BLOOMINGTON AND INDIANAPOLIS

The paper used in this publication meets the minimum requirements of American
National Standard for Information Sciences—Permanence of Paper for Printed
Library Materials, ANSI Z39.48-1984.
∞™

Manufactured in the United States of America

Library of Congress Cataloging-in-Publication Data

Krell, David Farrell.
Of memory, reminiscence, and writing : on the verge / by David
Farrell Krell.
p.   cm. — (Studies in continental thought)
ISBN 0-253-33193-5 (alk. paper). — ISBN 0-253-20592-1 (pbk. : alk. paper)
1. Memory—History. 2. Writing—Psychological aspects—History.
I. Title. II. Series.
BF371.K74 1990
153.1'2—dc20   89-46331
                                                                    CIP

1 2 3 4 5 94 93 92 91 90

The narrator of Edgar Allan Poe's "Ligeia," endeavoring to remember the quality of Ligeia's eyes: "There is no point, among the many incomprehensible anomalies of mind, more thrillingly exciting than the fact—never, I believe, noticed in the schools—that in our endeavors to recall to memory something long forgotten, we often find ourselves *upon the very verge* of remembrance, without being able, in the end, to remember."

Giordano Bruno, recording in *De umbris idearum* (1582) the image of the first decan of Gemini: *In prima geminorum facie, vir paratus ad serviendum, virgam habens in dextera. Vultu hilari atque iocundo.* ["In the first figure of The Twins, a man ready to serve, holding the verge in his right hand. His expression full of mirth and mischief."]

CONTENTS

PART TWO
ON THE VERGE

Acknowledgments

A number of passages of fiction have like old memories interrupted my train of thought throughout the book. Those responsible for these intrusions are as follows. In chapter 1: William Faulkner, *The Sound and the Fury*, first published in 1931; I am grateful to the Trustees of the Estate of William Faulkner and to Random House for their generous permission to reprint these passages. In chapter 2: James Joyce, *Ulysses*, first published in 1922; copyright renewed © 1984 and 1986; my thanks to the Trustees of the Joyce Estate and to Random House for their generous permission to reprint passages from *Ulysses*; one or two intrusions from Emerson's *Journals* have also occurred in chapter 2, as has a quotation from William Faulkner, *Light in August*, first published in 1932; again, thanks to the Trustees of the Faulkner Estate and to Random House for their generous permission to reprint. In chapter 3: James Joyce, *Finnegans Wake*, first published in 1939; copyright © 1939 by James Joyce; copyright renewed © 1967 by the Estate of James Joyce. All rights reserved. Reprinted by permission of Viking Penguin, a division of Penguin Books USA and by the Society of Authors, London. In chapter 4: Herman Melville, *Pierre: Or, The Ambiguities*, first published in 1852. In chapter 5: Edgar Allan Poe, "Ligeia," "The Fall of the House of Usher," and "The Pit and the Pendulum," first published in 1838, 1839, and 1843, respectively; along with two further intrusions by *Pierre*. In chapter 6: William Faulkner, *The Sound and the Fury*, reprinted with permission. Finally, in chapter 7: Robert Musil, *Der Mann ohne Eigenschaften*, Book II, Part III, first published in 1933 (translations my own).

I am grateful to Olive Lambert and Barbara Crawshaw for their generous and expert help in preparing the typescript and to John Sallis, Charles Scott, Jill Lavelle, Michael Hudac, and Marta Salomé for reading it.

For
Eunice Farrell Krell

Preface

This book has enjoyed a long and interesting death. I can see now that I will never write it and hence want to relate what it was supposed to have been. As well as I can remember.

When it was time for me to prepare a research proposal for my doctoral dissertation—in October of 1969—I submitted two of them. One involved Heidegger's reading of Nietzsche, the other promised some "essays in the phenomenology of memory." Even at that time the memory project would not stop proliferating, would not hold to a particular center, and my advisor suggested I stick to the presumably more clearly delineated topic. Which I have done now for twenty years.

Had I written about memory I might have told how, a year earlier, an astonishing discovery had come my way, quite by chance. In order to relax and settle down to sleep I began to write about some of the earliest recollections of my childhood, often mere images or vague sentiments devoid of context: my father hoisting me high over his head as I sat on the staircase; or playing by myself under a table with a fire engine; or bringing water to my earliest playmates and heroes, who came each week to collect the trash. My discovery was simply that in *writing* about these early memory images a vast store of remarkably detailed memories—in fact, an entire world of the most intense perceptions and feelings—began to unfold. I started to trace in the writing of these early memories, at first gropingly, though not without stylistic affectation, a world I assumed had been lost—no, that *had indeed been lost,* absent, "unconscious," call it what you will.

Such *writing* succeeded where no simple act of will or decision could. Succeeded in what? Who could say that these memory sequences were not eminent fictions? True, my mother, to whom I later sent a number of such sketches, confirmed them in various points of detail. For example, in one I was able to reconstruct the entire floorplan of the house I lived in until I was three, starting with that red engine under the dining table, the sun shining through the window at one end of the room, the stairway barely visible in the adjacent room. Such confirmations frightened rather than emboldened me: I did not want to be Borges' *Funes el memorioso,* laden to death with memories. Yet I did not need the confirmations to be disturbed by the power of these past presences that, far from being "haunting," as they properly ought to have been, were (as Husserl says) *leibhaft da,* bodily present, in flesh and in blood.

None of these things, I am sure, would have actually found their way into the dissertation. Instead, I planned to write about the failure of neurophysiological research to render plausible accounts of long-term memory; about the more fruitful psychoanalytic hermeneutic of memory and forgetting; and I would have focused on discussions in Husserl and Merleau-Ponty on time-consciousness and embodied memory. Yet behind all this brave science two

problems preoccupied me. First, the problem of the disparity between voluntary and involuntary memory; second, something I called the problem of memory and affirmation. About the first I wrote (I quote myself now, with apolo-
gies, inasmuch as my proposal, marked "First Choice," is before me as I write):

> How is it that I appear to be both slave and master with respect to my memory? For
> the most part I am fed memories, am thrown into them by the vicissitudes of my
> situation; my memory flow seems autonomous, almost schizophrenic, perpetually
> announcing to me my bondage to a past. At the same time, *I can* remember; that is, I
> am able to pursue a memory, fasten onto it, and interrogate it. I appear to be able to
> adopt a stance over and above the involuntary flow of memory. But what sort of "I"
> is this? What must my consciousness *be* in order to do such a thing?

It is fortunate that I never executed this plan, which began with a lie. Never did
I "pursue" a memory, much less "fasten onto it" and, philosopher-policeman,
"interrogate it." The writing that had opened up the dimension of memory to
me was never so cocksure, sustained, or confident. It was on the contrary so
vulnerable that after I resuscitated the plan to write about memory eight years
ago I had to look on while the project died under my hand. Died by a kind of
irony, an ironizing into which I slipped as soon as I had to deal with my earlier
memory sketches, a coyness by which I sought to protect myself from myself.
When I saw this inexpugnable irony, this paralyzing mockery in every line I
sketched, I realized that *On the Verge* would never be written. For it would
mean exposing and killing something that was my life. It was not simply that
these memories were "dear" to me, that I "cherished" or "embraced" them
nostalgically. They were both an *embarras de richesse* and an embarrassment.
And this was the *second* problem, the question of memory and affirmation,
which I had broached gingerly in my proposal in this way: "Memory has a way
of transforming any content into a wondrous appearance, bathing even the
most traumatic event in a soothing light, a yes-saying. To call this 'distortion' is
perhaps to miss part of the meaning of the phenomenon of memory. . . ." I
wanted that soothing light for my writing, but it turned out to be a darkness. A
darkness that irony and science could only disperse, never penetrate. No doubt
it was Nietzsche who had moved me: I wanted to oppose the affirmation of
eternal recurrence and *amor fati* to what Paul Ricoeur was calling "consent," a
word that seemed lukewarm and saccharine, whereas Nietzsche's was fire and
wine. Yet whatever that yes-saying might have been that guided my writing
twenty years ago, irony and a kind of anxiety organized a wake, raised a din,
and celebrated the untimely death of *On the Verge.*

Not that yes-saying is done. Only that through recurrence it has become
rather more wakeful. More *wakeful.* Silence for those "essays" in the "phenomenology of memory" and, above all, those "autobiographical" musings.
For the moment, a certain modest joy in these appendages, these bits of bone
and cartilage. *Disiecta membra* may have some merit on their own, on their
own give some pleasure.

                                                                    D. F. K.

Introduction

as though in order to begin writing one did not have to forget or otherwise suppress most of what *memory* and *reminiscence* have meant; as though the entire matter of memory, reminiscence, recall, recollection, revery, and repetition were not an endless overture arising out of an absolute past and capable of infinite development; as though one were not always *writing* on the verge of both remembrance and oblivion alike. On the verge?

The dictionaries tell a long tale of the word *verge,* derived from the Latin *virga,* feminine in form yet referring to the shaft of a Gothic column (now obsolete) or to one of the male organs (also obsolete) or to any number of (obsolete) cylindrical objects. *Virga* is a branch, seedling, or switch; then a rod or wand; later it is a symbol of office, much as the pen with which one writes is an emblem of the scholar and poet. To be "within the verge" is to be within the area of jurisdiction represented by the verger's scepter, *infra virgam hospitii nostri,* and soon *verge* comes to mean the precincts of a particular locale, its bounds or limits, and even the scope or range of a particular notion or category. More narrowly construed, the verge is the very edge, rim, or margin of that bounded space, its utmost limit; in this sense the word is used to suggest the end of a human life: "The mind was wandering, as it often does, on the dim verge of life." The sly Regan has both this and the political sense in mind when she admonishes King Lear (Act II, scene iv) as follows:

> O, sir, you are old;
> Nature in you stands on the very verge
> Of her confine: you should be rul'd and led
> By some discretion, that discerns your state
> Better than you yourself.

Finally, to be "on a verge" is to be on the extreme edge of a bluff, cliff, or abrupt descent of any sort. Washington Irving on the Alhambra at Granada: "In the center of this basin yawned the mouth of the pit. Sanchica ventured to the verge and peeped in." And not merely to be *on* it, since the verge is a brink "towards which there is progress or tendency." The verge anticipates and thus precedes "the point at which something begins." Something like a book, for example. Hence the familiar phrase "to be on the verge of," as Sir Benjamin Brody employed it in his *Psychological Inquiries:* "We are here on the verge of an inquiry which has perplexed the greatest philosophers."

As though the verge itself were not perplexing enough—rod, switch, pen, penis, precincts, realm, rim, and brink—there is a whole series of words to which it appears to be related. "To verge" is to skirt, circumvent, incline, or turn; to tend, descend, or veer off. All well and good. Yet *virga* is also discomfitingly close to both *vir* and *virgo*, and also to *virago*, not to breathe a word of potent *vis* or contagion *virus*. It seems to partake of all the opposites, as the following passage from the witches' sabbath in Nathaniel Hawthorne's "Young Goodman Brown" intimates:

> "And now my children, look upon each other."
> They did so; and . . . the wretched man beheld his Faith, and the wife her husband, trembling before that unhallowed altar. . . .
> "Welcome," repeated the fiend worshippers, in one cry of despair and triumph.
> And there they stood, the only pair, as it seemed, who were yet hesitating on the verge of wickedness in this dark wood.

Thus the verge is both the vertical measure and the horizontal measure, the boundary marker and the greensward within, both spindle of time and stretch of space; both woman and man; paper and pen; hesitation and wickedness. Yet before I surrender fully to the viewless wings of *The Oxford English Dictionary*   *Vultu hilari atque iocundo*   I would do well to recall the lesson of Ligeia's eyes   *I cannot, for my soul, remember how, when, or even precisely where*   and then to begin. Again.

Until the modern age the word *memory* extended across the vast verge of the Latin *memor,* "to be mindful," *mens,* "the mind," and all the words that display the Indogermanic roots *men-, mon-, mn-,* words related to thinking, intending, and being conscious or mindful in any way. When Chaucer wished to assure his reader or listener that Arcite did not die or even lose consciousness as a result of the fall from his steed all he needed to write was, "For he was yet in memorie and alyve" ("The Knight's Tale," 1. 2698). The sense of memory was so broad as to encompass both death and love: *hē mnēmē* is remembrance in general but also a record, memorial, or tomb; *mnaomai* means to turn one's mind to a thing but also to woo and to solicit favor. Even the medieval German word *minne,* which we remember thanks to the minnesingers and Tristan's ache of amorous love, derives from the sense of "having in mind." How paltry the word *memory* has become since then! We no longer hold it in memorie and alyve—and the present book is unfortunately no exception to the rule. It reduces the sense of memory to what contemporary psychology and neurophysiology call "long-term memory," that is, retention of persons, objects, or events from the distant past. Neither the acquisition nor retention of things we learn constitutes a part of the book, as though memory were not essential to the whole affair we call "education." Neither genetics nor immunology plays a part in it—as though I were certain that it is only mere metaphor at work when we assert that template RNA "remembers" or that the host "recognizes" its own and "rejects" the foreign invader, as though one could forget genes and all the body and write ghostily of memory and reminiscence. Moreover, so many of the writers and thinkers who have devoted themselves to memory find no place here; they remain forgotten, along with their particular questions.[1] And still the book tries to do too much.

Part One inquires into "Typography, Iconography, Engrammatology." It tries to show how the model for memory that has prevailed in Western thought from the Presocratics through modernity—the impressing of an imprint (*typos*) or the incising of a figure on the waxy surface of the mind or soul—seeks to solve the enigma of memory itself. That enigma has two aspects. First, memory appears to have both active and passive components or typographic styles. We remember without effort whatever "makes an impression" on us; but we can also "hammer something into our heads" in order not to forget. Passivity, however, most often prevails: Leopold Bloom may remember to pick up the soap for Molly, but he will also—in consequence of faulty mnemotechnic—forget to retrieve the housekey from the pocket of his discarded trousers. And whatever Bloom may do or not do on June 16, 1904, Blazes Boylan will be on his mind throughout the day and into the night. The common experience of memory as a faculty or power that we can exercise but also as a force that has a mind of its own seems to have shaped philosophical accounts of memory—as typography—early on. Yet typography is introduced to solve the enigma of memory under a second aspect. How do I know that what I am "now" remembering actually "corresponds" to what occurred in the past? What is the truth of memory? Whatever took place back then is (only as) past; it is bygone, irrecoverably absent; it is, as Heidegger said in one of his earliest lectures on time, *vorbei*. Yet my memory seems to put me in touch with such absent beings. At this instant, as I remember something far distant, what is it precisely that is present to me? Whatever it is, is it the same as what I once perceived or felt? Is it a copy or likeness derived from an original? Is it an *icon* of some now vanished presence? *Typography* proves to be in service to *iconography*. However, iconography itself proves to be a science of differences as well as likenesses. No *typos* can ever fully restore what one might have taken to be its "original."

What then about the *graphics* of both typo*graphy* and icono*graphy?* Impression or incision in memory is invariably described as a kind of *writing*, sometimes with illustrations, sometimes not. Memories are letters and words incised on a wax tablet or inscribed on a blank sheet of paper; they can be stored away, then retrieved at will and read at a later date. It makes little difference whether such inscription is being described by Socrates with a kind of childish delight or by a computer technologist taking a very grown-up pride in the achievements of his apparatus; it matters little whether it is Aristotle writing in terms of letters or Descartes speculating on tapestries of traces, threads, and nerve tubes; the contemporary neurophysiologist may even suppress all talk of engrams and appropriate the language of electrical circuitry and the micro-chip. Yet the problem remains one of encoding data, then storing, retrieving, and decoding it. Wax tablets, *tabulae rasae,* and even rude slabs or soft clumps of wax have a marvelous staying power. They are the hardest of hardware. Any account of memory and reminiscence must therefore try to say something about the convergence of typography and iconography in what I shall call *engrammatology:* discussion of the multifaceted role of *inscription* in memory processes—whether "passive" or "active," whether of reception or retrieval— will conduct us to the point where we shall have to ask whether writing is a metaphor for memory or memory a metaphor for writing.

I begin with Aristotle's *Peri mnēmēs kai anamnēsis,* "On Memory and Reminiscence," only then returning to Plato in search of clues concerning the mystery of mnemic presence: the presence of what is past, of what has passed, of what was, as presence of the imprints *(typoi),* likenesses *(eikones),* and inscribed letters *(grammata)* of memory. It soon turns out to be not so much an inquiry into the psychology of the mnemic faculty as a question concerning the *being* of beings, the ways in which (past) beings show themselves (now) in presencing. Such self-showing has everything to do with *time,* as one would expect in the case of memory and reminiscence, time and *images.* Images that show themselves *as* images of things that once were but now no longer are. Yet one may well doubt whether Plato and Aristotle succeed in accounting for the mysterious appearance in the soul of the impressed image or *typos,* an image that is held to be a likeness or *eikōn* of the thing now past, a likeness that is "read off" or "gleaned" from the image as though it were in fact a text composed of letters, *grammata,* a text that effaces itself before the full meaning and perfect (re)presentation of the past experience itself. Plato's *Theaetetus* introduces with panache the typography of images on the wax tablet of the soul, the gift of Mnemosyne, Mother of the Muses, to mortals. Yet in *Republic, Parmenides, Sophist,* and *Timaeus* the iconography of such images in wax comes to crisis. And the effort to encode and decode such icons by means of the syllables and letters of a text—in Plato's *Phaedrus, Cratylus, Philebus,* and again *Sophist* and *Theaetetus*—is fraught with difficulties of all kinds. Nor do Aristotle's treatises *On the Soul* and *On Memory and Reminiscence* resolve the aporias of typography, iconography, and engrammatology. However, none of this prevents that tripartite mechanism from becoming the prevalent model for memory and reminiscence from antiquity onward. Insofar as the theme of memory pervades western philosophical anthropologies, psychologies, theologies, and even cosmologies, the mnemic mechanism comes to have profound consequences for the history of metaphysics as "ontotheology."

In one way or another, typography, iconography, and engrammatology in the Platonic and Aristotelian philosophies implicate both the body and soul of mortal rememberers: memory and reminiscence, revery and recollection, remembrance and recall prove to be eminently psychosomatic. Whereas the traditional oppositional pairs activity/passivity, thought/sensation, mind/matter, and spirituality/corporeality impose themselves on virtually all accounts of memory, reminiscence, and writing from antiquity through modernity and into the present, that imposition never fully succeeds, is never fully convincing. If for Plato's *Cratylus* the body is the burial crypt and prison cell of the soul, it is also the hospice that protects and rescues the soul. Furthermore, it is the soul's semaphore—the signaller and giver of signs. Such signs, whether as typographic *vestiges* or engrammatological *notations,* are central to Augustine's account of the iconographic memory of the soul: the engrammatology of memory reverts willy-nilly to typography in the signs and spaces of the body, on which the soul's iconography thoroughly depends. On the far side of the mnemotechnical tradition, the tradition that preserves through the ages the hermetic art of "inner writing," Descartes' *Rules for the Direction of the Mind* also seeks to liberate the mind totally from its corporeal integument—that is to say, from an inherently "unstable" and "unreliable" memory, the weak reed of all cognition. Yet the typography, iconography, and engrammatology of sensation and intellection alike indicate that flight from corporeal memory to pure intuited presence in the mind is futile: if the analogy that is naturally suitable for both sensation and intellection is that of signet ring on wax tablet, whereby the reading of the resultant figures by the mind's eye ostensibly stands in iconic relation to a gleaning of the absent things themselves, then Descartes' distrust of memory—where that analogy has its ancient domicile—betrays the fact that the confidence in intuited presence, the confidence that undergirds an entire tradition, is chimerical. Thus Descartes' efforts to distill an "intellectual memory" from a grosser corporeal variety founded in the very trope that slips unobtrusively in and out of his texts on the body, the soul, and ideas: "I do not posit any other difference between the soul and its ideas than that between a piece of wax and the diverse impressions it can receive" (Letter to Mesland, May 2, 1644). If the soul is a waxen gland, then the ensouled creature is dead; it has, as Kierkegaard would say, merely neglected to wake up to that fact.

That the soul *is* a waxen gland wholly at the mercy of a mimetic typography is the lesson of Descartes' physiology, as elaborated in his *Treatise on Man.* An account of memory and reminiscence in Cartesian physiology is left to ponder the ultimate oxymoron of the system: the frenetic "animal spirits" reenact in microcosm the comedy of an impossible mimesis, a botched iconography, in which all hopes for the restoration of pure presence are dashed. Neither the "spirits" nor "little gland *H*" nor the nerve tubes leading to "region *B*" of the brain learn to decipher the figures that are stamped or woven there. Engrammatology fails, though again it is as if no one notices, no one remembers. Not even when Descartes demonstrates that the human being as such is a mimetic effect, an icon, a "type"—an automaton.

By rights, one ought to pursue the mnemic model of typography, iconography, and engrammatology through detailed readings of the British empiricists and the eighteenth-century French and nineteenth-century German materialists, mechanists, and epiphenomenalists. Yet even a brief look at Hobbes, Locke, and Hume, and an even briefer glimpse at David Hartley (through the critical eyes of Samuel Taylor Coleridge), will convince us of the staying-power of the ancient model for memory. In contemporary empirical and cognitive psychologies, neurophysiology, and biochemistry, as well as data-processing and information technology, the selfsame model perdures—even if wax has given way to magnetic tape or the floppy disc. That is why Coleridge's proto-phenomenological critique of Hartley's associationism still strikes us as relevant: we recognize in it the lineage that also produces the phenomenologies of Erwin Straus and Maurice Merleau-Ponty. These phenomenological accounts—whether of sensibility, perception, imagination, or memory—challenge the hegemony of typography, iconography, and engrammatology. They more than challenge it. Merleau-Ponty in particular finds himself on the verge of a new way of thinking about memory, one that is embedded in the lived body and the flesh of the world. He invokes what he calls the "hollow" (*creux,* related to our "crux" and "crucible") of "wild being," the hollow or clearing in visibility and in subjectivity as a whole, as though in distant reminiscence of Plato's *khōra,* the "receptacle of becoming," as elaborated in *Timaeus.* The hollow heralds the passing of an epoch of mnemic metaphysics. It marks the inception of a memory beneath the traditional ontotheological uses of recollection, a memory no longer in thrall to presence. Merleau-Ponty leads us to the very verge of a past that—as he says—has never been present.

At first blush, the Freudian typography of effraction or breaching, elaborated in the famous (or notorious) metapsychological venture of 1895, the "Project" toward a "Scientific Psychology," seems to conform to the traditional mnemic model. Yet the stakes here are undoubtedly higher than they ever were before. Effraction occurs, not on wax or in pallid automatons, but in the flesh of protoplasm; this more excruciating typography involves trauma, repression, enforced oblivion, bodily suffering, psychic misery, and the immanence and imminence of death. Freud's energetics of quantity-flow via breaching and his economy of resistance by means of contact-barriers confront a problem quite similar to that faced by Cartesian physiology: again and again the "Project" appeals to the very phenomena it is supposed to be explaining, presupposes what it claims to be accounting for. Worse, it makes its own *explanandum* utterly impossible. The mnemic typography of effraction requires that Freud distinguish between two types of neural systems, the one (ϕ) permeable and responsible for perception, the other (ψ) impermeable and so providing a matrix for inscribed memories. However, the very breaching of contact-barriers in ψ through the typography of effraction tends to reduce that system to ϕ—to the very perceptual system that ψ was called upon to supplement. Memory, the very life of the psyche, remains mysterious.

Freud's 1895 "Project," no matter how hastily sketched, no matter how faulty, is the highly complex culmination of typography, iconography, and engrammatology. Culmination and crisis. This becomes particularly clear in Freud's discussion of "quality signs" and "reality signs," by which the psychic system knows and remembers its parlous world. Such signs are the engrammatological hallmarks of his system. In the third and final part of his "Project," on the "normal processes in ψ," quality and reality signs assume the explicitly *linguistic* character that up to that point they had manifested only implicitly; they function as inscribed, incised, yet fundamentally written and read linguistic signs. Not surprisingly, these engrammatological tracings are said to be essential for "ego-formation," consciousness, and thought, all the traits of human subjectivity. Ironically, the engrammatological apparatus that

Freud thirty years later finds best suited to serve as an icon of psychic processes as a whole (especially the process that grants perdurant memory traces), namely, the famous "Mystic Writing Pad" of 1925, fails as dramatically as the 1895 "Project." Fails by reason of a *lapsus calami,* a slip of the stylus, a vicissitude of the verge, as Freud's *Notiz* on the mystic writing pad obfuscates the two things it most wants to bring to the fore by way of its "analogy." Which would suggest that Freud's is not a career advancing from physiology to grammatology but a sustained venture in engrammatology. But that—like all typographic, iconographic, and engrammatological matters—is a difficult story. Suffice to say that in the end psychoanalysis is not about the restitution and restoration of past glories: effraction or breaching is not the advance guard of a psychoanalytic Church Militant, but the embarrassed science of the vulnerability, exigency, and even calamity of an outraged life. A life that is ever on the verge.

Part Two of the present volume—for what I have described above is the movement of the three chapters of Part One—takes a second look at this life on the verge of memory, reminiscence, and writing. How does the *engrammatology* of memory and reminiscence relate to the *grammatology* envisaged more than two decades ago by Jacques Derrida?[2] No doubt, the thought of the *trace* of writing unites the two projects. Yet if the trace of grammatology pertains to a system of differences—and to differ*a*nce with an *a*—we may anticipate that Derrida's project will not be in service to anything like iconography. Indeed, if Derridean grammatology announces the closure of the metaphysics of presence, the mnemic model that promises to restore the presence of the past will itself be disengaged and set aside. That model nevertheless allows us to pose some questions concerning what Rodolphe Gasché calls the "quasi-transcendental" status of the Derridean notions of trace, arche-writing, arche-synthesis, and differance. Such questions come to a head in Derrida's invocation of "the absolute past," the past hinted at by Merleau-Ponty, as a past that "has never been present," the past of a radically irrecoverable pastness and passivity. To envisage such a past, however darkly, is to have experienced the failure of the traditional model for memory. To the extent that typography, iconography, and engrammatology characterize an essential operation in the Platonic text, the failure of the model spells the dissolution of what one might call "Plato's dream," the dream that by some pharmaceutical wizardry the noxious effects of writing can be neutralized, and the "good" scripture of reminiscence distilled from the "bad" script of texts.[3]

The doom of Plato's dream is doubtless a long time coming. One would have to examine the effects of the dissolution patiently in a whole range of texts, only a few of which will come to the fore here. Yet if inscription of memories in the soul brings to crisis the very distinction between the inside and outside of mind or spirit, we can anticipate that Hegel's *Erinnerung,* "interiorizing remembrance," will have to play an essential role on the verge of memory, reminiscence, and writing. On the verge of remembrance *tout court.* Whether in the mature system of the *Encyclopedia of Philosophical Sciences* or in the earlier *Philosophical Propaedeutics* and *Phenomenology of Spirit*, "interiorizing remembrance" seems to be both essential to the system and essentially anomalous there. *Erinnerung* occupies an impossible place in Hegel's thought of memory proper, *Gedächtnis*. Remembrance not only exceeds the system as a whole but also causes it to unravel. The fact that *Erinnerung* and *Gedächtnis* stand on either side of Hegel's account of language, signs, reading, and writing has something to do with their excessive, disruptive character. There can be neither a phenomenology nor a philosophy of the subject without *Erinnerung* and *Gedächtnis*. Yet *with* them there can only be a thinking that shatters confinements *without* ever achieving the vaunted freedom of the absolute. Absolute knowing—insofar as it rescues itself from total oblivion—remains on the verge.

If the mnemic dialectic of interiority and exteriority no longer dominates Martin Heidegger's thought, his thinking devotes itself nonetheless to commemoration. Such commemoration (*Andenken, Nachdenken, Gedenken*) commences with the fundamental ontology elaborated in his magnum opus, *Being and Time*.[4] In Heidegger's analysis of ecstatic-horizonal temporality, the one ecstasis of time that receives a novel name is that of the past—of which, Aristotle says, memory *is*. Whereas Heidegger accepts the traditional designations for future and present, he rejects altogether the notion of *Vergangenheit*, "the past," "the bygone." He analyzes instead what he calls the temporal ecstasis of "having-been," the *perfect* form, *Gewesenheit*. One might wonder whether his emphasis on what has been, *ge-wesen*, retains something of Hegel's insistence on essence, *Wesen*, and whether one ought to contrapose to both Hegel and Heidegger Nietzsche's forceful "It was." The imperfect, the imperfection of verging time, as opposed to time's perfection.

If *Gewesenheit* is the ecstasis of disposition and repetition, of the fundamental mode of mood, and especially the mood of anxiety, we will want to examine closely these less than perfect aspects of fundamental ontology. Something like a gap or chasm opens up in Heidegger's analysis of the temporal unfolding of anxiety; the attentive reader is suddenly stranded on the verge of that gulf. Anxiety is to provide a "hold" (*Halt*) for our essentially oblivious existence, an existence for which the forgetting of being is always more primordial than any remembrance of time will ever be. The gap that opens in the text and displaces the fundamental-ontological axis of (in)appropriateness (*Eigentlichkeit/Uneigentlichkeit*) will allow no hold whatsoever. Neither Heidegger's use of Nietzsche's *Use and Disadvantage of History for Life* on behalf of his own notion of "historicity" nor his own later meditation on Mnemosyne in "What Calls for Thinking?" can provide the hold he seeks. While memory gathers thought, the granting of what is to be thought withdraws. Heidegger's thinking early and late leaves us on the verge of withdrawal and expropriation, where nostalgia for the heartland and homeland of memory strives with letting-be. Letting *what* be? Nothing else than what is "bygone," the spurned passing by and away, the constitutive *Vorbei!* of human existence as perceived in Heidegger's earliest writings. But also the

Vorbeigang of divinity, the passing of "the last god." Nothing is more helpful in banishing nostalgia than Nietzsche's reminders, in the second and third treatises of *On the Genealogy of Morals*, concerning the painful prehistory of memory, the typography of punishment and incision. A typography, needless to relate, without icons or idols.

Can we say "yes" to such passing and such pain? Or must one remain on the verge even of affirmation? Not so much by withholding assent, even less by a begrudging refusal to engage, than by devoting oneself to a thinking of affirmation that is both suspicious of redemption and susceptible of yes-saying? A hesitant thinking that traces an experience of *mourning*, and the *default* of mourning, in the direction of *mirth?* The tonalities of laughter, from bitterness to mockery to potlatch, raise the variable music of such mourning. Pierre Klossowski's thinking of Nietzschean eternal recurrence as embodied, pulsional anamnesis and amnesia offers a point of departure for such thinking. Derrida's recent reflections on "impossible mourning," the promise of memory, and the double-yes of Joycean affirmation—an affirmation of life down to the very ashes—are its major way stations. Along with commemorations of both Hegel and Heidegger, who are not to be forgotten.

Affirmation leaves the recuperative and restorative machine of typography, iconography, and engrammatology to its own devices. It turns instead, as Nietzsche will always have anticipated, to the verge of musical ideas. Fragmented ideas, no doubt, of mirth and mourning, as though in order to begin

PART ONE

Typography, Iconography,
Engrammatology

(Stoop) if you are abcedminded, to this
claybook, what curios of signs (please stoop),
in this allaphbed! Can you rede (since We
and Thou had it out already) its world? It is
the same told of all. Many. Miscegenations
on miscegenations. . . .

For that (the rapt one warns) is what papyr
is meed of, made of, hides and hints and
misses in prints. Till ye finally (though not
yet endlike) meet with the acquaintance of
Mister Typus, Mistress Tope and all the little
typtopies. Fillstup. So you need hardly spell
me how every word will be bound over to
carry threescore and ten toptypsical readings
throughout the book

—James Joyce, *Finnegans Wake*

ONE

Slabs of Wax

Aristotle and Plato on Memory, Reminiscence, and Writing

as though the power of memory and our own efforts to remember could be neatly separated; as though the compulsion to recall could be purged, and the free play of revery safeguarded; that is the way the Philosopher begins.

Aristotle opens his treatise on memory by distinguishing between memory (*mnēmē*) or remembering (*mnēmoneuein*) on the one hand and reminiscing or recollecting (*to anamimnēskesthai*) on the other.[1] Memory as such he classifies as an affection or pathos; recollection or reminiscence he celebrates as an activity. Yet the grammar of the two verbs hardly supports Aristotle's distinction between passive memory and active recollection. "To remember" (*mnēmoneuein*) is not a passive but an active form, while "recollection" (*anamimnēskesthai*), presumably the active search for particular memories, is in fact passive—not even medial—in form.[2] "Recollection" or "reminiscence," at least in terms of grammar and etymology, is the passive form of the verb "to remind." Accordingly, recollection or reminiscence is a *being reminded;* it involves one thing *putting us in mind of another.* The prefix *ana-* may well mean "again," as Sorabji conjectures, so that *ana-mimnēskesthai* could mean "to be reminded again"; but it could also mean "up," "back up," "against," or even "throughout," suggesting the kinds of *motion* that Aristotle will later attribute to reminiscence.

However recalcitrant the grammar of these two verbs may be, Aristotle apparently wishes to distinguish *mnēmoneuein* and *anamimnēskesthai* as passive and active, respectively, the former an affection, the latter an undertaking. He insists that having a good memory is not the same as being good at recollecting, inasmuch as slow-witted persons *Can't you shut up that moaning and slobbering, Luster said* often have excellent memories, while the quick-witted and the good learners *Then I remembered I hadn't brushed my teeth* are better at recollecting. From the pedagogue's point of view, recollection clearly surpasses memory in value. Yet on what does its superiority rest? Why the association of memory with dull wits? We are put in mind of Faulkner's Benjy, thirty-three years old, moaning like a "loony" through the fence at the sound of the word "caddie," plunged back helplessly twenty-eight years to the Christmas when he was five years old, to the time when he had another name, a body not yet mutilated, and a sister named Caddy; lethargic, slow-witted Benjy, relying like a true primitive on his nose   *I could smell the bright cold . . . Caddy smelled like leaves.*   Slobbering, whimpering Benjy, confounding perception and memory, compressing present and past into one painful spectacle of emasculated presence, one protracted howl of dispossession   *Caddy smelled like trees in the rain.*   Benjy is the solitary inhabitor of memory; yet he never reminisces; he recollects nothing. If memory is pathos or affection, as Aristotle avers, then Benjy will become our symbol for absolute affection. For he is utterly pathetic.

MNĒME, LĒTHĒ

Yet what is the lethargy—from *lēthē*—that stupefies the inhabitor of *mnēmē?* In what does the dullness of dull wits consist? Or the alacrity of quick wits? What is presence of mind? Why is reminiscence or recollection associated with quick and vital presence, memory with a kind of lethargy and passivity? Such questions evoke what is perhaps the original icon or image of memory in our tradition—if it is proper to speak of an image as an original: memory is a *waxen surface* which, with greater or lesser resilience and elasticity, suffers the imprinting action of sensuous apprehending, "perception," and preserves traces of that action in the mind. Memory is, as we shall hear Socrates say in *Theaetetus,* "a good thick slab of wax" in the soul; and what we see, hear, smell, taste, feel, or even think are the signets, the styluses, the protruding edges of stamps and seals, the cutting edge of our experience.

Now, to be sure, the "objects" of mnemic experience in general, *ta mnēmoneuta,* are not of the present but of the past: *hē de mnēmē tou genomenou* (449b 15). As a neuter substantive, *to genomenon* (from *gignomai,* to come into being, be produced, come to pass) means "event" or "fact." Memory is of facts or events that have been generated or have come to pass; these facts and events are now, as we say, "past." We tend to understand the past as what is over and done with; but *ta genomena* present themselves much more forcefully than does something "past." They are what *has* come to *be.* Much later we will hear Heidegger insist on the perfect of the past: whatever is past *is* what *has* been *(ist gewesen).* At all events, says Aristotle, we cannot remember the future, which is "an object of conjecture or expectation." Nor to all appearances "is" remembrance "of the present" *(tou parontos),* which is grasped in perception or sensuous apprehending *(aisthēsis).* "No one could claim to remember the present while it is present [16: *paron hote parestin*]."

Commonplaces. Why does Aristotle bother to recount them? Because the problem of *time* is still a problem of *being* for him. If memory's objects are not of the present, what is it that becomes present, comes to presence, or presents itself when we remember? *Parousia* is not simply an empty chronometrical determination for Aristotle; it designates the presence of a thing or, as Sorabji himself suggests (67), the being of a being. Remembrance thus poses an ontological paradox and even "impasse," inasmuch as it allows what is past to become present *as* past, transposing us—sometimes faithfully, sometimes not—to what is no longer that which is, performing solo what both perception (*aisthēsis*) and thought (*theōrein, noein*) once accomplished, and perfectly assured of its own efficacious performance. Aristotle writes:

> But when one has knowledge and perception without their actual exercise [19–20: *aneu tōn energeiōn*] then one remembers; in the former case remembering one learned or thought a thing and in the latter that one heard or saw it or perceived it in some other way. For whenever a man actually is remembering he always says in his soul that he has heard, or perceived, or thought this earlier [*proteron*]. (449b 19–23)

Remembrance instigates a peculiar kind of presence. It "has" an object of perception or knowledge without activating perception or knowledge as such and without confusing past and present. For while remembering, a man tells himself that he is now present to something that was earlier. "Memory, then, is neither perception nor intellection, but a property or pathos of one of these, whenever time has elapsed." Here Aristotle describes memory not as a distinct faculty of the mind but as something that *aisthēsis* and *hypolēpsis* undergo, as an aspect of perception and thought marked by time. "All memory therefore occurs across time [29: *meta khronou*]," and only those creatures that have a sense of time—that is, of passage, lapse, rapture or *ekstasis*, as an *ek tinos eis ti*[3]—can be said to remember. They remember metachronically, that is, precisely by means of that awareness of time which underlies our experience as such. Yet that "common perception" of time also accounts for another crucial feature in Aristotle's account of memory. Aristotle underscores the importance of imagination and psychic "images" (*phantasmata*) in memory—as in thought (*noein*) itself. The psychic image is a pathos of the "common perceptual power" (450a 11: *tēs koinēs aisthēseōs*). The role of images in memory, plus the cognizance of time that we take in memory, time as a bounded magnitude, quantity, or how-much (*to poson hōrismenon*), and as a kind of motion (*kinēsis*), elevate memory—which at first seemed a mere aspect of perception—to the status of a "primary" perceptual power (12: *tōi prōtōi aisthētikoi*).[4]

Aristotle refers to the "common" perceptual power in *On the Soul* (426b 9ff.) and in *On Sleep and Waking* (455a 14ff.). It is that power which is able to discriminate (*krinein*) differences among the objects of various senses—between, for   *I could smell the bright cold*   example, "white" and "loud." It is also the unifying power by means of which one senses *that* one sees and hears at all. "For perception is one, and the paramount organ of perception is one [21–22: *mia aisthēsis, kai to kyrion aisthētērion hen*]."[5] This unifying power is "closely related" to the sense of *touch*, although it cannot simply be identified with that sense. The "primary" perceptual power to which memory is ascribed is apparently this same "common" or "master" perceptual faculty.[6] The ascription of memory to a common or master perceptual faculty that is itself highly reminiscent of touch is dramatically—or rhetorically—supported by the fact that in *On the Soul* (424a 18ff.) Aristotle employs precisely the same palpable metaphor for perception that he will employ for memory. Sense has the power to receive into itself the sensible forms (*tōn aisthētōn eidōn*) without the matter, "somewhat in the way wax receives the impression of the signet ring without receiving the iron or gold" of which the ring is made.

Having introduced the phantasm or mental image he regards as essential to the operations of memory, Aristotle now offers his famous formulation of the principal enigma of memory (450a 25ff.). Before we read that formulation, let us review the steps we have taken thus far. We began by noting Aristotle's effort to distinguish the passive and active powers of memory and reminiscence, respectively, even though the grammar of the verbs resisted his effort, inasmuch as a reminiscence seems to be a (passive) "being put in mind of something." Aristotle's motivation seemed to be a pedagogical one, favoring the active, recollective power and reflecting a certain antipathy toward the passivity and sensuousness of his slow-witted fellows, who are mired in a past. For such persons, as we anticipated, possess   *He went and pushed Caddy up into the tree to the first limb. We watched the muddy bottom of her drawers. Then we couldn't see her. We could hear the tree thrashing*   a muddy, earthy, gritty slab of wax in their souls. We then followed Aristotle to his definition of memory as "of the past" and posed in a preliminary way the question of the *presence* of the past, the cutting edge of experience, as it were, in our memories. What is at stake is the very being of the beings we have experienced. Aristotle's discussion of the power of memory in relation to the other powers of the soul—the "facultative" question as to whether memory is an aspect of perception and intellection, or perhaps a protoperception and unifying apprehension that allows us to be aware of time and to bask in the presence of images—should not be allowed to obscure the ontological import of Aristotle's inquiry. That memory occurs metachronically and kinetically through images has to do with the being of beings in time. Yet precisely that is the enigma.

Aristotle writes (450a 26–27): "One might be perplexed about how, if the pathos is present [*parontos*] but the thing in question [*pragmatos*] is absent [*apontos*], what is not present [*to mē paron*] is ever remembered." Aristotle's solution to the enigma, a solution anticipated in the very introduction of the *phantasmata,* is to conceive of the pathos or mental image that the soul perceives in memory "as being like a portrait" (29–30: *hoion zōgraphēma*). The word *zōgraphēma* derives from the root word for "living being," whether plant, animal, or human, but also of "figure" or, more generally, "work of art," and a nominative form of *graphō,* "to scratch or graze, mark or draw," "to represent by lines, paint, brand or inscribe," "to write, express with written characters." Inscription, marking by incision, is surely one of the earliest meanings of the word, as the various senses of the word *hē graphis,* (= *to grapheion*) suggest: embroidery needle, chisel, engraving tool, paintbrush, and stylus for writing on slabs of wax. Plato relies on the word *zōgraphēma* in *Cratylus* and

Philebus, as we shall see, for his principal clue concerning the mechanics of memory.

Whence this "portrait" of the absent being in question? The motion that took place in the soul and in the part of the body that has the soul, replies Aristotle, "inscribes a kind of imprint [30: *hoion typon*] of what is perceived, as people do who seal things with signet rings." Memory is the typography of *aisthēsis,* objective and subjective genitive. Thus the pathology of memory tries to determine the relative hardness or softness of what receives and harbors the imprint (450b 5: *to dekhomenon;* cf. *Timaeus,* 50b 6). If the quick-witted youth is too hygrotic, nothing will make an impression on him; and if the old fellow is too sclerotic, nothing will penetrate. Such sclerosis is Benjy's untimely fate: unlike his brother Quentin, whom we will meet in chapter 6, and who is all water   *And I could feel water again running swift and peaceful in the secret shade*   from birth to death, Benjy is rude red clay, molded, incised, more than circumcised, and baked hard   *You mean, he been three years old thirty years*   early on. However, typography does not finally resolve the principal enigma of memory, and Aristotle is constrained to repeat his question:

> But then if memory really occurs in this way, does one remember the pathos or that from which the pathos came to be? For if the former [the *pathos parontos*], we would be remembering nothing absent; if the latter [the *aph' hou,* thus the *apo* of *apontos,* the absent], how can we, while perceiving this [*pathos*], remember the absent thing, which we are not perceiving? If the pathos is like an imprint or trace [*typos ē graphē*] in us, why should the perception of this very thing be the memory of something else [*mnēmē heterou*] and not simply of itself? For in exercising memory one contemplates [*theōrei*] the pathos and this is what one perceives. How then does one remember what is not present [*to mē paron mnēmoneuei*]? For this would imply that one could also see and hear what is not present. (450b 11ff.)

There is a way, argues Aristotle, in which we actually do see and hear what is absent; he now proceeds to offer his most fully elaborated solution, bringing the first half of the inquiry to a conclusion (450b 20–451a 17). He describes the phantasm or mental image now postulated for memory as a figure sketched or painted on a panel, a figure that exhibits a fruitful ambiguity: the sketched or incised figure (*gegrammenon*) is, as it were, both an *objet d'art* (*zōion*) in its own right and a likeness or icon (*eikōn*) of a living being. In fact, the word *zōion* alone in this case embraces both senses of the ambiguity, inasmuch as it means both a living being and the figure or image one might draw or carve of such a being, its portrait or likeness. The *phantasmata* may thus be viewed, scanned, or "read" in two ways, either as objects of contemplation in their own right, as noemata and theoremes, or as portraits of something else. In the latter case, the phantasm is a kind of icon, a reminder or aid to memory (*mnēmoneuma*). Whenever the motion that is reminiscent of this "something else" actually occurs, the mind can observe the image either as autonomous—as a mere thought—or as an image in relation to an original. This either/or of our psychic scanning (*theōrein*) results in a common equivocation: we are often unsure in any given case whether what we "see" in our minds is actually a memory or not. Usually, however, we can enter into reflection, recollection, or reminiscence (*kai ennoēsai anamnēsthēnai*) and discover that we have heard or seen the thing in question earlier, and so escape equivocation. We do so escape when the autonomous image suddenly is seen in relation to something else (*hos allou*). To be sure, such shifting sometimes goes the wrong way: there exist people who are always beside or outside themselves—Aristotle cites the example of Antipheron of Oreus—who recount their wildest phantasms as though such things had actually taken place and were now actually being remembered. That is what happens each time a mere picture is thought to be a likeness, a sheer phantasm an icon. We do not know whether Quentin's remembered conversation with Jason Compson, Senior   *I have committed incest I said Father it was I*   refers to an event that actually took place; we are even incredulous that the recorded "confession" itself took place; and Robert Musil's Moosbrugger, who according to the prosecution has murdered and mutilated a young prostitute, recalls only how women passersby have always molested and insulted him; for the rest, he is rapt to the noises in the walls, in his clothes, and in his body. Luckily, Quentin and Moosbrugger, scanning all their phantasms as both/and, rather than either/or, are exceptions to the rule.

It is worth emphasizing once again the way in which Aristotle's picture of the portrait and image (curious doubling!) itself suggests a solution to the problem of image and original in memory. The phantasm, we said, *may be viewed as* either theoreme or icon, noema or mnemoneuma, whenever the *motion that is reminiscent of* the thing in question occurs. What about this viewing? And what sort of *kinēsis* is being thought here? The viewing is surely not some fortuitous "point of view," except perhaps in the cases of Antipheron, Quentin, Moosbrugger and, as we shall see, philosophers since Descartes. What is it that determines whether we see the pathos under its own aspect or in relation to an other? Surely, it dare not be a matter at our discretion? Must we not insist that all depends on how the imprint *shows itself* under its *own* motion? Is it not the radiance of the *typos,* no longer held in isolation but radiating outward with revelatory motion, that allows the true being of the absent entity to shine? However, whether the pathos looms in isolation and invites us to take it into our hands, slowly turning it to our rapt gaze; or slips unobtrusively into the moiling stream of irretrievable events; or, finally, as Aristotle hopes, whether it actually succeeds in retrieving by some inexplicable action at a distance a specific absent thing, person, or event, letting it radiate in full presence—no metaphor can say.

The aporia of memory as *iconography,* itself arising from the aporia of *typography,* compels us to ask: What is it that is present to us, the (mere) icon itself or that of which it *is* an icon? This question, in turn, opens onto a whole series of queries. What determines how we *see* the incised or painted graphics of memory? What enables us to *scan* or *read* the reminder or memorial in such a way that something else, something different, something original, becomes present? How can the *inscribing motion* be reminiscent of what has yet—precisely through its agency—to be remembered? What can have taught us to read and write before we remembered well enough to be taught anything at all?

Such questions are already on the very verge of what we might call *en-grammatologial* questions: What is the *self-showing* that underlies memorial *inscription?* What is the *presence* that we *read* in memory? Aristotle broaches some answers to these questions in the second half of his treatise—with his treatment of reminiscence or recollection.

ANAMNĒSIS

Recollections or reminiscences flourish, according to Aristotle, insofar as one *kinēsis* generates another and we find what we are trying to remember. *Kinēsis,* "motion," "change," "animation," "impulse," here means a gradual or perhaps quite sudden coming-to-presence or self-showing of an absent being that till now was *also absent from memory.*[7] Not even an icon of it was present to me. When a sequence of such motions or changes occurs, by either necessity or habit, a certain consistency, nexus, or node—the origins of what Dilthey, Heidegger, and Merleau-Ponty will much later call the *Zusammenhang des Lebens,* the "holding together" or cohesion of a life—is established. The method of recollection is to proceed either directly, as if by a shortcut, to one's goal; or more indirectly and painstakingly to the *penultimate* member of a series, in order to pass from thence on to the goal. We start out from the "now" (451b 19: *apo tou nyn*) or perhaps from something else, seeking something similar to or opposite from or connected with our starting-point. For the kinetic modes of the presencing of these things are sometimes the same as (*autai*), sometimes contemporaneous with (*hama*), and sometimes have a share in (*meros ekhousin*) one another, so that, if only we can find the proper starting-point, no more than a miniscule portion of what we wish to recollect will remain to be found.

Sorabji (97) refers to Meno's familiar paradox: How can we select a starting-point that is similar to, opposite to, or in some way connected with what we seek to recollect, unless we have in some sense already recollected it? "The answer," writes Sorabji, "is that one always knows some answer to the question, 'What are you seeking?' " Sorabji himself offers examples of temporal contiguity: I can remember what I did on Tuesday if I "go back" to Monday; I can remember where I put my hammer if I "recollect" where I put the chisel. Of crucial importance for Aristotle is this search (*zētein*) for a starting-point of the presencings (451b 30: *arkhē kinēseōs*) upon which the desired presencing will proceed. "For as the *pragmata* are related to one another in succession [*tō ephexēs*], so also are the *kinēseis.*" Often a person cannot recollect at first, says Aristotle; but, seeking, one finds. One generates (*ginetai*) many presencings, until one of them is followed by (*akolouthēsei*) the thing sought. What thing? The thing that is doubly absent: absent from presence, from the "now" of knowledge and perception, but also absent from present memory. We should therefore not be blasé about the double miracle of these generated presencings. Leaving aside for an instant the problems of the starting-point and the "penultimate" goal, which as we shall see in chapter 3 is a kind of supplementary starting-point, how do we explain the order of succession, this "following" of presencings? It ought to have a somewhat chastening effect on us to realize that in Heidegger's detailed analysis of Aristotle's treatise on time the word *akolouthei* expresses "the *apriori foundational nexus* of [temporal] motion" with regard to time as both a finite magnitude and a continuum; in other words, that the "following" of reminiscence or recollection derives from the "following" that constitutes time as such (24, 344–45). We should by no means expect to resolve such difficulties here; enough if we note that with memory and reminiscence we are everywhere in their presence. The sequence of motions or impulses that we are calling "presencings" is mysterious in the extreme, inasmuch as it seems to overcome from the inside, as it were, the double absence or exteriority of (unremembered) things:

> For remembering [*memnēsthai*] is the inherence of the power of presencings [or: the presence within of the power that excites changes; or: the potential existence in the mind of the effective stimulus or impulse—452a 10: *to eneinai dynamei tēn kinousan*]. And this in such a way that the man is moved [*kinēthēnai*] of himself and because of the motions that he has [*hōn ekhei kinēseōn*].

Yet we must now seek the starting-point, the *arkhē,* of all such motions or presencings. The best place to look, says Aristotle, is in the middle (452a 17: *to meson*). How can a starting-point be in the middle? Perhaps *arkhē* is not the "starting-point," conceived of as the initial point of a line-segment in homogeneous space-time, but the *ruling center* of a particular constellation of memories. The uncertainty of the manuscripts makes speculation on Aristotle's precise intention with "the technique of mid-points" in the series A B C D E F G H idle.[8] Perhaps the only matters to be stressed here are two: first, the *kinēsis* Aristotle intends to describe is not a linear movement from starting-point to end-point but a kind of back-and-forth movement from ruling centers to adjacent, contiguous memories; second, this back-and-forth movement itself ought not to be conceived of as a one-dimensional advance and retreat, since the contiguity of the members in any given triplet is not absolutely decisive. "It is possible to move to more than one point from the same starting-point, for example, from C to F or D." It is difficult to find any relation of "contiguity" between C and F, except that both are third in their respective sets of triplets. This example, which Aristotle introduces in order to show why when starting from the identical point we sometimes remember and other times do not, suggests that reminiscence or recollection is not inherently linear at all, and that the "series" A B C D E F G H is not a series in any mathematical or grammatological sense at all. At best, this constellation (not sequence) of memories can be described as formed by habit (*ethos*), a habit so ingrained that it is "already like nature" (452a 29). We can recollect quickly things we have thought of quite frequently; for just as in nature one thing occurs after another, so too in our exercise (*energeiai*) of recollection. "And frequency creates nature [30: *to de pollakis physin poiei*]." Our familiarity (with the things recollected) is already in accord with the self-showing movement of those things themselves. For just as there is an "earlier" and a "later" in all self-showing, so too in the setting-to-work of recollection. Repeated motions of presencing (what one might translate as *Wiederholung*) brings forth the self-showing itself. Nevertheless, the role of chance is greater in the realm of habit or *ethos* than in that of *physis*, "nature" as "upsurgence." (Even in the latter, of course, we find violent motion, *paraphysis*.) Hence in our efforts to recollect we are often diverted in false directions. Seeking a particular name, we stumble onto one that is only "like" it (*paromoion*). Reminiscence hovers in delicate balance between iconic likeness and (mere) eidoletic likeness; its self-showing (*physis*), even if we think of it as "second nature," is often enough an obfuscation or closing-off (*para physin*).

Aristotle now reverts to the subject of memory in general—even though it can hardly be said that his account of reminiscence has resolved its many paradoxes and puzzles—and reasserts the "great importance" of temporality for it (452b 7ff). In memory and reminiscence one must "know the time," either in units of measure or in some less definite way. Such knowing is analogous to the way we know magnitudes, namely, in proportion to one another. Memory is fully defined as the conjunction of the movements (of self-presencing, self-showing) that are related to things and the motion that is the lapse of time itself: "Whenever the movement of the thing and the movement of time [452b 24: *hē te tou pragmatos kinēsis kai hē tou khronou*] are engendered simultaneously [*hama ginetai*], then one is at work in memory [*tote tēi mnēmēi energei*]."

The delicate and mysterious conjunction of time and things in motion—which philosophers up to Husserl will rely on—is of course also a source of error in memory, perhaps *the* source of error. "For nothing prevents one from being deceived and believing that he is remembering when he is not." That is the sort of thing that happened to Antipheron of Oreus, and it happens also to Benjy of Oxford and Moosbrugger of Vienna. Their *Lebensuhr* or "clock of life" has run amok, scattering fragments of experience in all directions, or uniting them in bizarre concatenations. The distinction by which we order events occurring "at different times" suddenly ceases to cling to Moosbrugger's experiences "like a red ribbon tied in desperation about the throat of one twin," and his life is from hence permeated by an uncanny and thoroughly disruptive unity. "One can easily picture a human being's life as a flowing stream. However, the movement Moosbrugger perceived in his own life was the flow of a stream through a vast body of standing water: driving forward, the stream was also drawn back in eddies, and there the proper course of his life all but vanished."[9]

Moosbrugger's difficulty ought to give us pause. Reminiscence and memory function properly, says Aristotle, when the self-showing movement of the thing (*hē tou pragmatos kinēsis*) and the self-showing movement of time as such (*te . . . kai hē tou khronou*) are generated simultaneously (*hama ginetai*). Yet what is the self-showing movement of time itself? And how can anything be generated "simultaneously" with time? Not simultaneously *in* it but *with* it? Or does time loop back across itself every time we reminisce? Finally, let us remember what we read at the very beginning of Aristotle's treatise: memory is of the past, *tou genomenou*. Memory involves the *parousia* of *ta genomena*, not of things present in their presence, but of what has been. However, if we appeal to simultaneity of motion in time and in the self-showing of the thing, does not the entire structure of distance and distancings that Aristotle has been erecting collapse? Will not the *hama ginetai,* as necessary as it may be for iconography, wreck the distances opened up in time, from *pragmata* to *pathoi, pathoi* to *kinēseis, kinēseis* to the *arkhē kinēseōs,* and from the *arkhē* to the *eneinai dynamei tēn kinousan?*

At the close of his treatise Aristotle distinguishes recollection from memory by designating the former as a specifically *human* capacity (453a 5ff.). "The cause of this is that recollecting is, as it were, a kind of reasoning [*hoion syllogismos*]." Aristotle proffers two reasons for this. First, when recollecting, we *infer* (although Aristotle earlier said that we *sensed*) that we saw or heard or experienced this thing earlier (*proteron*). Second, recollecting is, as we have already seen, a kind of search (*zētēsis*); and the search is deliberative (*bouleutikos*), "inasmuch as deliberation is a kind of reasoning."[10] However, Aristotle's account abruptly shifts from the deliberative, ratiocinative, "syllogistic" nature of recollection to its corporeal essence, as though in a last-ditch effort to frustrate the next two thousand years of philosophical ontotheology. The search inherent in recollection seeks an image (*phantasmatos*); and the phantasmatic pathos within memory and reminiscence alike is profoundly tied to the body (*somatikos*). As evidence Aristotle refers to the annoyance we experience when we labor to recollect and yet   *without being able, in the end, to remember*   are unable to do so, an annoyance that is doubled—insult added to injury—when we stop trying and "recollect nonetheless." This sort of thing happens especially with melancholics   *We'll have to be quiet while Quentin is studying*   "who are most moved by *phantasmata*" and who are as powerless to stop recollection as anyone is to intercept a stone once it is thrown, even and especially when that stone will shatter the magic mirror   *there was another fire in the mirror*   of memory, destroying all nostalgia   *She ran right out of the mirror, out of the banked scent. Roses. Roses. Mr. and Mrs. Jason Richmond Compson announce the marriage of.*   The melancholic who is "rummaging and hunting" for something "moves that part of the body in which the pathos resides" (453a 23), and the movement proves to possess its own inertia, almost as though it were generating its own time. Those who are most susceptible to such motions are people whose "region of sensation" is most "fluid," (*hygrotēs*); once the fluid is agitated   *I could smell the curves of the river beyond the dusk and I saw the last light supine and tranquil upon tide-flats like pieces of broken mirror*   it does not cease "until the thing sought comes round again" and the movement can resume its straight course. Aristotle compares such agitations to pulsions resulting from fear and anger, which no countermovement seems capable of ameliorating, and to the curious pathos of a name or tune or saying   *She smelled like trees*   that runs through our heads and that we cannot shake. The agitations or disturbances that convulse a melancholic set the objects of recollection in a turbulent rotary motion; the motion does not abate until the object "sought" or rather fled "comes round again" (*rhaidiōs*) and "the self-showing pursues a straight course" (453a 26).

Aristotle ends on an even more dismal note. Dwarfish people cannot prevent the movements of their recollections from scattering   *and we stopped in the hall and Caddy knelt and put her arms around me and her cold bright face against mine. She smelled like trees*   and dispersing; they do not readily recollect "in a straight course" (453b 4: *euthyporein*). This perhaps ought to make us reconsider our earlier objections to the linear interpretation of recollection. Will not subsequent tradition appeal to the linearity of recollection, with fixed *arkhē* and *telos*, precisely in order to avoid the freakish back-and-forth motion of endless reminiscence? Recall those uncanny concluding words of Aristotle's treatise, on nature's natural dwarfs, the young and the old. Here it is not a matter of youth being too hygrotic, senescence too sclerotic. Both are now seen as fundamentally kinetic-metabolic, the former because they grow so rapidly, the latter because   *He knows more than folks thinks, Roskus said. He knowed they time was coming, like that pointer done. He could tell you when hisn coming, if he could talk. Or yours. Or mine*   they waste away.

TYPOS

If we want to know where Aristotle found his *typon* and *eikona*, as well as his graphics, as possible means of surmounting the ontological aporia of memory, we do not have far to look. Plato's *Theaetetus* had introduced both notions in ways the tradition would never be able to forget—ways it therefore would never be able to recollect freely and, as it were, head-on. *Republic, Parmenides, Sophist,* and *Timaeus* will prove to be further sources of Aristotelian iconography and engrammatology, and we shall turn to them as soon as we introduce a number of further details concerning the *typos.*

We remember that the Atomists, especially Democritus, were much occupied with the *typos* both in their "philosophy of nature" and in their "psychology," though they too inherited the notion from a hoary past. The word *ho typos* probably derives from—and at all events is related to—the verb *typtō*, "to beat, strike, or smite," in the sense for example of striking a coin. (The Greek word for hammer is *hē typas, hē typis*.) In Homer the noun *typos* refers to a blow or to the beat of horses' hooves, and by extension to the effects of such a blow or applied pressure: *ho typos* may be the impression made by a signet ring, the stamp on a coin, and an imprint or trace of any kind. It may be a figure worked in relief, a carved or modeled image, such as figures of Centaurs and Lapiths on a pediment frieze, a cast or replica formed in a mold, and even the hollow mold or matrix itself. Thus *ho typos* shares many of the equivocations we noted in the word *virga*, the verge. And no doubt one could easily expand typography to include *characterology* from Plato to Leibniz: *kharassō*, to sharpen, notch, furrow, scratch, or stamp, is perhaps a loan-word from the Hebrew *haraš*, to engrave; *kharax*, pointed stake, palisade, cutting, slip or graft, is also that cutting edge of an engraving. *Kharaktēr* (cf. *kharagma*) is both engraver, engraving tool, die or stamp, and the mark engraved, the impression, in one. Thus it comes to be associated with letters, and Plutarch can speak of *ho typos tōn kharakterōn*. As a replica, the characteristic *typos* may be quite exact, the "spittin' image" of an original—as children *Caddy's head was on Father's shoulder. Her hair was like fire, and little points of fire were in her eyes, and I went and Father lifted me into the chair too, and Caddy held me. She smelled like trees*   are sometimes said to be the *typoi* of a parent. Or, referring back to the matrix, the *typos* may be a pattern or model—indeed, an arche-type—capable of more or less exact duplication and iteration through many instances. For a later epoch, *ho typos* may be a form of expression or style, either as a general characteristic, approximate indication, and vague outline-sketch, or as a precise form with a specific function, for instance, a royal decree or legal summons. These are some, but by no means all, of the recorded meanings of the word.[11]

(A postscript on the verb *typtō*. During the games held in honor of the dead Patroklos (*Iliad* 23, 764), Odysseus races so close to Ajax that "his feet strike Ajax' footprints [*ikhnia typte*] before the sand can fall back into them." Yet perhaps the most striking appearance of the verb *typtō* has to wait for the *Tristrapaedia* of eighteenth-century England, which describes Tristram Shandy's early education:

Five years with a bib under his chin;
Four years in travelling from Christ-cross-row to Malachi;
A year and a half in learning to write his own name;
Seven long years and more τυπτω-ing it, at Greek and Latin. . . .[12]

But now I *typtō* my way back to Democritus and Plato.)

Aetius (I, 3, 18; I, 26, 2) ascribes to Democritus the view that necessity (*anankē*, whom we will also meet in *Timaeus* under the guise of *khōra*) operates according to "resistance" (*antitypia*) and "blows" or "collisions" (*plēgē*) of matter. He also recounts Democritus' doctrine that the atoms move through the unbounded "as the result of striking one another [*allēlotypia*]." Alexander of Aphrodisias reports Leucippus and Democritus' teaching that "the atoms move by mutual collisions [*allēlotypousas*] and blows." Theophrastus (*On the Senses*, 50–52) mentions an aspect of *atomotypia* that is particularly germane to the present topic: he attributes to Democritus the view that vision results from the formation of an image when "the compressed air between the eye and the object of sight is stamped [*typousthai*] by the object seen and the seeing."[13]

While only the barest trace of Democritean typography survives in Plato's account of vision (see *Theaetetus* 154a), the *typos* impresses itself powerfully on the Platonic account of memory. Memory is introduced in *Theaetetus* to refute the notion that knowledge is perception: we cannot say that when a man closes his eyes it is impossible for him to know anything. When Socrates begins to speak on behalf of Protagoras in a spirit of "fair play" (166), one of the first questions and replies he puts into Protagoras' mouth broaches the problem of mnemic *presence*. "Do you think you will find anyone to admit that one's present memory [*mnēmē pareinai*] of what was experienced in the past [*tōi hōn epathe*] is the same as what one formerly experienced, even though one is not now experiencing it?" No doubt the entire project of knowledge sustained over time hangs on this question, and the Protagorean reply is potentially devasting: "It is nothing of the sort" (166b 1–4). Much later in the dialogue (191cff.) the presence and the mechanics of the pathos in memory are discussed in greater detail, in the hope of proving Protagoras wrong:

> SOCRATES: Imagine, then, for the sake of argument, that our minds contain a slab of wax [191c 9: *kērinon ekmageion*], which in this or that individual may be larger or smaller, and composed of wax that is comparatively pure or muddy, harder in some, more liquid in others, and sometimes of just the right consistency.
> THEAETETUS: I'll imagine it so.
> SOCRATES: Let us call it the gift of Mnemosyne, Mother of the Muses, and say that whenever we wish to remember something we are seeing or hearing or even thinking in our minds we hold this wax under the perceptions or thoughts and imprint them on it [191d 6: *apotypousthai*], as we might impress the mark of a signet ring [7: *sēmeia ensēmainomenous*]. Whatever is so imprinted we remember and know as long as the little image [9: *eidōlon*] remains; whatever is rubbed out or has not succeeded in leaving an impression we have forgotten and do not know.
> THEAETETUS: Let it be as you say.

Plato's metaphor is of course subtly different from the later Aristotelian model. Socrates speaks of *wishing* to remember and of *holding* the waxen slab, gift of Mnemosyne, *under* what we intend to remember. Aristotelian *kinēsis*, the movement of presencing and self-showing, is far less subject to human will, except perhaps at the point where Aristotle says that granted the appropriate self-showing we may scan the engram *either* for its own sake *or* as a portrait of something else. Another difference is that Plato's discussion remains wholly within the context of Sophistic discourse: Socrates uses the metaphor not so much in order to explain what memory *is* as to show how false judgments are *possible*. If a man has the marks or signs (*sēmeia*) or little images (*eidōla*) of both Theaetetus and Theodorus imprinted in his soul, and if he sees the youth and the old man at a distance, he may, while trying to align the proper mark with what he sees, "like fitting a foot into its own footprint to effect a recognition," jumble the imprints, juggle the idols, and get the signs mixed up, "like a man who thrusts his feet into the wrong shoes." A rather pedestrian approach to false judgment, we may say, yet one that survives over centuries, as we shall see. Even though Socrates has preserved a certain amount of distance between body and soul in his construction, emphasizing that the slab of wax is

Mnemosyne's *gift,* not the great goddess herself in person but a sort of *eidōlon,* so that false judgment cannot actually be blamed on memory as such, he now develops a pathology of memory that scrutinizes the vicissitudes and frailties of the body. False judgment will be accounted for not by the soul's juggling of idols but by the quality of the waxen matrix of those lesser idols. *Theaetetus* 194c 4–195b 1:

> SOCRATES: . . . When a man has in his soul a good thick slab of wax, smooth and kneaded to the right consistency, and when whatever comes from the senses is stamped on these tablets of the heart—Homer's words hint at the soul's likeness to wax [i.e., *to kēr,* "heart," is reminiscent of *hē kēra,* "wax tablet"; Schleiermacher rescues the sense neatly by speaking of the ceraceous "marrow of the soul"]—then the signs [*ta sēmeia*] are clear and deep enough to last a long time. Such people learn well [d 3: *eumatheis;* cf. Aristotle, *On Memory,* 449b 9] and also have good memories, and in addition they do not interchange the signs of their perceptions but opine truly. These signs, being distinct and well-spaced, are quickly assigned to their particular places, which we call "beings" [*onta*], and such men are said to be wise. Don't you agree?
>
> THEAETETUS: Most emphatically.
>
> SOCRATES: But when a person has what the poet in his vast wisdom commends as a "shaggy heart" [cf. *Iliad* 2, 851 and *16,* 554: *lasion kēr,* a hirsute, manly breast], or when the slab is muddy or made of impure wax, or oversoft or hard, then matters stand in this way: the people with soft wax are quick to learn, but forgetful, those with hard wax the reverse. Where it is shaggy or rough, a gritty kind of stuff containing a lot of earth or filth   *Caddy took her dress off and threw it on the bank. Then she didn't have on anything but her bodice and drawers, and Quentin slapped her and she slipped and fell down in the water* the traces obtained are indistinct; as they are when the stuff is hard, for they have no depth. Impressions in soft wax also are indistinct, because they melt together and soon become blurred. And if, besides this, they overlap through being crowded together into some narrow little soul, they are still more indistinct. All such persons are likely to opine falsely. When they see or hear or think of something, they cannot quickly assign things to their particular places. Because they are so slow and sort things into the wrong places, they constantly see and hear and think amiss, and we say that they deceive themselves with regard to beings and are incorrigibly stupid.
>
> THEAETETUS: You speak as the best informed of men, O Socrates.

The stamps or seals (*sēmeia*[14]) of the signet ring are beings themselves, *ta onta,* in all their trenchant purity and clarity. Yet when they are stamped on human hearts—even the heart of a broadshouldered deepchested stronglimbed frankeyed redhaired freely freckled shaggybearded and generously hirsute Homeric hero, perhaps the heart of well-versed Odysseus himself—the resulting traces are marred and imprecise. Plato's jolly sideswipe at Homer should not be overlooked: the poet's "vast wisdom" is not equal to the epistemological sophistication and refinement of which Western man will be so proud, a sophistication he will embrace as his best defense against sophistry. Oddly, Plato himself does not seem so complacent, inasmuch as he has Socrates respond to

Theaetetus' praise by saying that he is disgusted with himself. For now he cannot explain how errors in unalloyed thought—for example, mathematical calculations—are possible. Apparently dissatisfied with both his sarcasm concerning the shaggy heart of perception and his buffoonery over memory getting its shoes on the wrong feet, Socrates pursues the question of what it means to possess knowledge. He is led to the second grand metaphor for memory, memory as the container of knowledge, and thence to truly monumental problems of iconography. However, before we follow Socrates into the birdcage, we ought to ask whether Plato's slab of wax has anything to do with Aristotle's and our own problem—the presence of the past.

Indeed it does. For the possibility of false judgment is the possibility of equivocation concerning presence. At 194a the words *parei, parousēi* appear, and they are contrasted with absence, *to tēs apousēs:* "Now, when perception is *present* to one of the imprints but not to the other; when [in other words] the mind applies the imprint of the *absent* perception to the perception that is *present;* the mind is deceived in every such instance" (my emphases). The matching of the trace or imprint with the living perception involves precisely the problem of the copresence of the present perception of that man there in the distance and the somehow "past" vestige or mark of that man in our memories. Indeed, as soon as we enter the cage Socrates will further define such copresence in terms of presence *at hand* (198d 7 and 200c 2: *prokheiron*).

Socrates and Theaetetus now take up (197bff.) the question of what it means actually to have *(ekhein)* rather than merely to be in possession of *(kektesthai)* knowledge. They are led to Socrates' second paradigm for memory, the aviary. While it presumably has nothing to do with typography, the aviary has everything to do with iconography. For those once wild birds are knowledges and ignorances, presences and absences, self-showings and obfuscations. Presuming that the second member of each of these pairs can be said to *be.*

SOCRATES: Now consider whether knowledge is a thing you can possess . . . without having it about you, like a man who has caught some wild birds—pigeons or what not—and keeps them in an aviary he has made for them at home. In a sense, of course, we might say he "has" them all the time [*aei ekhein*] inasmuch as he possesses them [*kektētai*], mightn't we?

THEAETETUS: Yes.

SOCRATES: But in another sense he "has" none of them, though he has got control of them, now that he has made them captive in an enclosure of his own; he can take and have hold of them [*labein kai skhein*] whenever he likes by catching any bird he chooses, and let them go again, and it is open to him to do that as often as he pleases.

THEAETETUS: That is so.

The crucial questions of course revolve about the difference between the two kinds of *acquisition* involved in learning (that is, capturing for the first time) and in recollecting (that is, grasping again the bird one already possesses), and the two kinds of *possession* of knowledge (one in which, we might say, knowledge is merely idling, the other in which what we have learned is explicitly "there for us"). Socrates inquires here with a view to the classic sophistic ploy, to wit, that mistaken judgments are not possible at all. Both Theaetetus and Socrates affirm that mistakes are readily possible, and that one often takes his pigeon for a falcon; but Socrates pushes the argument further—or, rather, the argument has its will of them, as Socrates has said earlier, "like a sailor trampling over seasick passengers." He, or it, proceeds (at 199d):

> In the first place, that a man should have knowledge of something and at the same time fail to recognize that very thing, not for want of knowing it but by reason of his very knowledge, and in the second place that he should judge that thing to be something else and vice versa—isn't that absurd, that when a piece of knowledge presents itself [epistēmēs paragenomenēs] the soul should fail to recognize anything and should know nothing?

Theaetetus tries to help by admitting some Birds of Ignorance into the aviary; catch hold of one and you are inevitably in error. Socrates objects that their rude critic will now have a hearty laugh at them—and at both of their metaphors for knowledge. He mimics the critic as follows:

> Are you going to tell me that there are yet further bits of knowledge *about* your bits of knowledge and ignorance, and that their owner keeps these shut up in yet another of your ridiculous birdcages or waxen slabs, knowing them as long as he possesses them, although he may not have them at hand in his mind [mē prokheirous ekhei en tēi psykhēi]? On that showing you will find yourselves perpetually driven round in a circle   *empty and blue and serene again as cornice and facade flowed smoothly once more from right to left; post and tree, window and doorway, and signboard, each in its ordered place*   and never getting any farther. (200b–c)

And so the two protagonists begin again, entering the third round of questioning concerning what knowledge is. We shall soon follow them, in a direction we shall have to call *engrammatological*, but not before dwelling awhile on, or in, the Platonic birdcage. As we noted, the image has at least a dual function, although its duplicity threatens to become boundless multiplicity. It is an image of memory, containing winged creatures of true knowledge, themselves images of true beings. The mnemic aviary is a likeness of likenesses, a treasury, vault, or chamber of icons. It will endure through the ages as Augustine's *cavus* and *thesaurus*, Hegel's pit, black as night, *eine nächtliche Schacht*, and as the multilayered Rome of Freud's *Civilization and Its Discontents*. Yet what can such containment and all hoarding of reserves be if memory is reduced to airy likeness? What *is* likeness? Or at least what is likeness *like?* one might ask   *Caddy smelled like leaves*   if only to hear the door of the cage slam shut.

EIKŌN

An *eikōn* is a likeness or image, portrait or statue, perhaps even a mirror-image. In Greek tragedy the word assumes the haunting sense of a specter or phantom; it possesses the numinous quality that emanates from every dark niche of every tiny Greek country church we stoop to enter today. And it is one of Plato's favorite words for one of his favorite themes, "likeness" being at issue in *Phaedo, Republic, Cratylus, Philebus, Parmenides, Sophist, Timaeus,* and perhaps everywhere else. Nor does Aristotle forget to use this word when he wants the soul to scan or read what is imprinted on it as a likeness of something else—the phantasm, we recall, being more than a mere *objet d'art.* Of the many Platonic dialogues that treat of likeness, I shall briefly consider only four—*Parmenides, Sophist, Republic,* and *Timaeus*—before taking up the final inquiry, the engrammatological, of the present chapter.

The problem of likeness (as of dissimilarity) and sameness (as of difference) recurs throughout the dizzying discourse of *Parmenides* (see 148a–b, 161a–b, and 165c–d for particularly vertiginous examples). Likeness in the strong sense of *homoiōsis* is in fact the first difficulty raised by the young and feisty Socrates, who here is made to defend that theory of separable *eidē* which the tradition has generally attributed to Plato himself. (Nowhere is the ascription of various opinions represented by personages in a dialogue to the author of the dialogues so hazardous, nowhere is the intentional fallacy so hair-raising in its consequences, as in the case of *Parmenides.*) "Do you not recognize," demands Socrates of the zealous (and jealous) Zeno, "that there exists just by itself a form of likeness [129a 1: *eidos ti homoiotētos*], and again another contrary form, unlikeness itself [2: *anomoion*], and that of these two forms you and I and all the things we speak of as 'many' come to partake [3: *metalambanein*]?" Socrates further asserts that such forms do not blend with their contraries, whereas things do, so that the meaning and the limits of "partaking" become crucial. In response to Parmenides' prodding, Socrates proposes that participation occurs on the basis of a kind of likeness—here not only in terms of *eikones,* images, but also the more abstract "likeness," *homoiōsis*—with the following devastating results:

> . . . O Parmenides, the best I can make of the matter is this—that these forms are as it were patterns [132d 2: *paradeigmata*] fixed in the nature of things [or: standing in the very upsurgence of things, *hestanai en tēi physei*]. The other things are made in their image [3: *eoikenai*] and are likenesses [*homoiotata*], and this participation [*hē methexis*] they come to have in the forms is nothing but their being imaged [4: *eikasthēnai*] upon them.
>
> Well, said Parmenides, if a thing is made in the image of a form [5: *eoiken tōi eidei*], can that form fail to be like [*homoion*] the image of it, insofar as the image was made in its likeness? Or is it possible that the like is like something unlike?
>
> That is impossible.
>
> And is it not quite necessary that the like must have taken up the one and selfsame [form] that it is like?
>
> Necessarily.
>
> But that in virtue of which like things are like, taking it up into themselves, is it not the form itself?
>
> By all means, of course.
>
> If so, it is not possible that something be like a form, or a form like something

else. Otherwise another form will always make its appearance over and above the first form, and if it too is to be alike, yet another. And there will be no end
The shapes flowed on   to this appearance of new forms if the form is to be like that which has taken it up into itself.
What you say is most revealing.
Hence it is not through likeness that the other things take up the forms; rather, we must look for another way of partaking.
Likely so.

Likely so: *Eoiken.* As lightheaded as the discussion may seem—because of the appearance of the *eidē* and the classic aporia of participation—it does show how difficult it will be for us to understand what we mean when we say that what we remember is *like* what once was. Aristotle's explanation—that we *see* or *read* the mnemic phantasm as an icon or likeness when we view it (in its presence) with a view to something else (in its absence), something different, hence *unlike*—will seem only more perplexing than before. An inquiry into memory as iconography must therefore confront the problem of likeness and difference with some perseverance—even if it should prove to be an exercise in futility.

Perhaps the most penetrating and yet most strikingly futile discussion of likeness occurs in the dialogue *Sophist.*[15] Here the Eleatic Stranger and Theaetetus seek to "capture" the sophist by distinguishing him from the genuine philosopher. The problem of likeness and difference arises as one of original versus imitation and authentic versus counterfeit. The Stranger and Theaetetus agree (at 234c) that the sophist is primarily an imitator of being and truth, one who exhibits idols or sheer phantasms in discourse (234c 6: *eidōla legomena;* 234d 1: *ta en tois logois phantasmata*). Their strategy for capture is to divide the art of idol-making (235b 8–9: *eidōlopoiikē*) according to two forms of imitation (*mimētikē*). One is the making of faithful likenesses (d 6: *eikastikē*), exemplified in those works of sculpture or painting in which the portrait preserves the proper proportions and colors of the person portrayed, the other the making of semblances (236c 4: *phantastikē*), as in colossal works which perforce distort proportions in order to make the portrait *appear to be* well-proportioned. However, the Stranger immediately recognizes the difficulty of this division: "Such 'appearing' [*to phainesthai*] and 'seeming' [*to dokein*] but not being [*einai de mē*]; and such gathering of something in discourse [*to legein*] which does not truly show itself [*alēthē de mē*]; all of this has always been and still is the greatest of aporias."[16] He is of course referring to the Parmenidean proscription of the utterance that nonbeing somehow *is* (*to mē on einai*), a proscription that the two will proceed to revoke. The Stranger demonstrates that to speak of nonbeing requires the use of the word "being" (nonbeing *being* unutterable) and of number (as being singular or plural). Yet to refrain utterly from speaking of nonbeing, hence to acquiesce in the putative impossibility of falsehood, is to grant the sophist an "impenetrable lurking place." For the sophist will demand   *What is it, Caddy said. What are*
you trying to tell Caddy   to know what an image or idol *is.* And it will be

useless to appeal to the examples of images in water or in mirrors, or to paintings and sculptures (as the Stranger has just done), for the sophist will always confine himself "to what can be gathered from discourse."

Theaetetus now bravely tries to define the *eidōlon* as "another thing made in accordance with something that shows itself without distortion" (240a 8: *to pros talēthinon aphōmoiōmenon heteron toiouton*). The Stranger demands to know what Theaetetus means by that other "thing"—which presumably also shows itself. The reply is that this other thing does not truly show itself but is only *like* the original (b 2: *eoikos*). Likely story. By *alēthinon* Theaetetus means a being that comes to presence truly in its being, *ontōs on*, but he has thereby consigned what is only *like* genuine self-showing to nonbeing, *ouk ontōs ouk on*, even though, as he insists, *as a likeness* the image comes to presence and is truly in being (11: *eikōn ontōs*). Yet the unsalubrious mixture of being and nonbeing remains, and the conversation now must turn to the perplexity of being (*to on*) as such, its unity *and* multiplicity, motion *and* change, sameness *and* difference. The conversation culminates in the discovery of dialectic, that is, the engrammatological blending or mixing of forms in discourse (251ff.), and the recognition that, as with the *grammata* of the alphabet, some forms will blend well together, while others will not (253). Being, motion, rest, sameness, and difference all pass in review, and the principal aporia receives a new shape: being *is not* (*ouk estin*), in the sense that "while it *is* its single self, it *is not* all that indefinite number of other things" (257a). To say *mē on* or to employ the negative *ou* is therefore not to assert the opposite of being (b 3: *ouk enantion . . . tou ontos*) but to indicate a particular aspect that is *different* from every other (*heteron monon*). Difference (*to thateron*) is therefore distributed throughout the language and the knowledge of being, however grave the impact of difference on iconography threatens to be.

Now (260cff.) the Stranger returns to the problem of likeness by asking whether "nonbeing" can be blended with belief and discourse. For if it can, falsehood is possible, "and idols and images and phantasies will be rampant" (260c 8–9). (Note the conflation of *eidōla, eikones* and *phantasia* here; however, if the twofold division of *eidōlopoiikē* into *eikastikē* and *phantastikē* is to be maintained, these would have to be carefully differentiated!) Referring tacitly to an earlier series of divisions in the dialogue, the Stranger now inserts the first division of image-making into another *preliminary* division, that of production (*poiētikē*) into divine and mortal kinds. The first is a production of selfsameness (*autopoiētikē*), the second a production of little images or copies (*eidōlopoiikē*). We are now occupied with the latter, of course, and have been throughout. However, this preliminary division is undercut by the admission that even divine production involves idols "which also owe their existence to daimonic contrivance" (266b 7: *daimoniai mēkhanēi*), idols such as dream images, shadows, reflections of light, and so on. The problem as to how such daimonic idols could be divided into likenesses and semblances remains unsolved, and it is at this juncture that the division of *eidōlopoiikē* into *eikastikē* and *phantastikē* is made. As though the genre "idol-making" could sustain a neat division into icons and phantasms! Be that as it may, *phantastikē* is then (267) further divided into two, a semblance produced by means of tools and another by means of the body itself, for example by the voice in mimicry or ventriloquism (*mimēsis*). *Mimēsis* or ventriloquism is further divided into two because some mimics are aware of the fact that they are imitating, others not. Thus *gnōsis*, knowing, distinguishes one kind of mimicry—*which is itself a division of* phantastikē. Thus "mimicry by acquaintance," ventriloquism proper (267e 1: *historikē mimēsis*), proceeds on the basis of knowledge (*met' epistēmēs*)! Now, the sophist cannot be said to have knowledge, so he must be located under "mimicry by conceit" (*doxomimētikē*), which is again severed in twain: one kind of ignorant mimic is utterly credulous, the other is suspicious of his own wisdom. The latter, the "ironic" mimic (268a 7: *eironikos*), also may be divided into two, the one preferring long orations before an assembly, the other firing off rapid arguments in private in order to force his opponents into contradiction. The former is less a ventriloquist than a demagogue and the latter is. . . . What? Or who? Wise man (*sophos*) or sophist (*sophistikos*)? Has anyone here seen Socrates?

Theaetetus's answer, which forces the entire discussion into a *Teufelskreis* or demonic circle, is that the short-winded ironic type is "a mimic of the wise man" (268c 1: *mimētēs . . . tou sophou*); he can be "truly described as in every way the selfsame existing sophist" (3: *touton . . . alēthōs auton . . . pantapasin, ontōs sophistēn*). Here all the words of *self-showing* (truth), *presencing* (being) and *sameness* (identity) are applied to the sophist—who nonetheless hides himself in *absence, nonbeing,* and *otherness.* His art is *enantiopoiologikē,* the art of making all discourse work against itself—in a word, making all discourse contradictory. The parentage or genealogy of his art: ironic, conceited mimicry, child of semblance-making, child of idol-making, itself a child of human production as *eidōlopoiikē.* What then is mimicry of the wise man? Is it likeness or semblance? Who *is* the mortal wise man? Is it the one who instigates all these divisions, the Stranger, the one Socrates thought might be a god, a master of *autopoiētikē* (see 216a)? To whom is such a "method" of binary division "congenial" (see 265a 2)? Perhaps at the end of the dialogue it is important to remember the Stranger's words at 259–260, words that conclude the long excursus on being and knowledge:

> Yet, good friend, the desire to separate everything from every other thing strikes a discordant note, and at all events pertains only to one whom the Muses have abandoned and who is utterly unphilosophical. . . . For the isolation of each thing from all the others amounts to the total annihilation of discourse, since discourse can come about only through a weaving together of forms, one into the other.

The one thing that is clear at the end of *Sophist* is that, just as we must have some idea of the meaning of being if nonbeing is to make any sense at all, so must we know what wisdom is and who the wise man is if we are to distinguish the sophist from him. The genealogy of the sophist, however, leaves the other side of the family tree wholly mysterious. Is there a *divine* production of idols?

What in either divine or mortal production constitutes the *likeness* of idols to originals? What is *eikastikē?* Or at least to what is it similar? What is mimicry by acquaintance, with knowledge? What is the quality of that ironic ventriloquism by which Socrates squeezes his interlocutors into corners of contradiction? These things await a discourse that weaves together rather than unravels. Perhaps the discourse of *Statesman,* or the silence of *Philosopher.* They wait long.

Yet presumably one of the above questions—the one our account of memory as iconography most needs to pose, namely, "What is *eikastikē?*"—has already been answered, if only in terms of the "likenesses" fabricated in painting and sculpture. The artist produces a likeness when he or she "reproduces in accord with the symmetry of the original [235d 7–8: *kata tas tou paradeigmatos symmetrias*] in length, breadth, and depth, and applies the appropriate colors." Contrasted with such production is that of the artist who executes "colossal" (e 5: *tōn megalōn*) works, and who must alter the proportions of the work in order to make it appear (to us mortals) to be well-proportioned. We might think of those two glories of Athens, Pheidias's gigantic sculpture of Pallas Athena and the temple that housed it, the Parthenon. Of the latter we know that each column was shaped asymmetrically and affixed to the porch at unequal intervals in order to evoke an illusion of equidistance. The "golden mean" of sculpture and of architecture is a human geometry, not a science of unearthly coordinates in empty, abstract space. Is the Stranger here insisting that colossal works of art are inferior likenesses and thus should be spurned in favor of works of which man is the pint-sized measure? Should Pheidias have stuck to "true proportion" and demanded of the Athenians that they wax to the stature of the statue in order to look on the goddess? In that case, *eikastikē* would be megalomania, oblivious of the difference between divine and mortal productions, perspectives, and proportions. Worse, the result of a megalithic artistry *without* the deliberate distortion of proportions which we call "perspective" would be even more disconcerting: a freak Pallas, massive in her nether parts, miniscule in head and arms. A kind of dwarf   *And folks don't like to look at a loony. Tain't no luck in it*   or little image—an *idol.* The Stranger himself recognizes the irony: If the artists of the colossal "wanted to render the self-showing symmetry of the beautiful" (235e 6–7: *tēn tōn kalōn alēthinēn symmetrian*), the result would be monstrous. If *alēthinē* is understood as exact and literal replication, then the measure of symmetry as such goes awry. The problem would then be to find a way to include mortals in the measuring, to remember them, without making man himself the measure. Yet the Stranger does not revert to the problem discussed at the outset of *Theaetetus.* Taking *alētheia* to be a mirror-image of some original, he asks rhetorically, "Do not the artist-craftsmen wave good-bye   *Keep your hands in your pockets, Caddy said. Or they'll get froze. You don't want your hands froze on Christmas do you*   to the true [236a 4: *khairein to alēthes*], and go off in search, not of the proportions of being [5: *ou tas ousas symmetrias*], but of those proportions that will really only appear to be beautiful [*alla tas doxousas einai kalas*]?" But, again, what is the alternative? Does the artist bid adieu to the self-showing when he makes his object *seem* as beautiful as its paradigm *is*? Even though Plato uses the word *kheirein* (principally) to mean farewell and dismissal, he is surely also aware of its Homeric sense: to greet, welcome, and rejoice in a thing or person who is now truly present and, as it were, at hand, *prokheiros*.[17] The question then would be whether the true—understood as what shows itself as it is—does indeed fare well precisely when the craftsman distorts proportions and shatters his celebrated but really rather silly mirror. For the art of mirroring is the sophistic art *par excellence*. In the tenth book of *Republic* the following memorable exchange between Socrates and Glaucon occurs (cf. *Sophist* 233e–234e):

> But now consider what name you would give to this craftsman.
> What one?
> The one who makes all the things that all handicraftsmen severally produce.
> A truly clever and wondrous man you tell of.
> Ah, but wait, and you will say so indeed, for this same handicraftsman is not only able to make all implements but also produces all plants and animals, including himself, and in addition earth and sky and the gods and all things in heaven and under the earth.
> A most marvelous Sophist, he said.
> Are you incredulous? said I. . . . Or do you not perceive that you yourself would be able to make all these things in a way?
> And in what way, I ask you, he said.
> . . . You could do it most quickly if you should choose to take a mirror and carry it about everywhere. You would speedily produce the sun and all the things in the sky, and speedily the earth and yourself and the other animals and implements and plants and all the objects of which we just now spoke.
> Yes, he said, the appearance [596e 4: *phainomena*] of them, but not, of course, the beings in their true self-showing [*tēi alētheiai*].

Here the artist-sophist is portrayed as altogether a mirror: his *eikastikē* is nothing else than *phantastikē*. He traffics in the purely phenomenal (in the restricted sense); his practice is sophistic, and it is impossible to see how a distinction between likeness and semblance could be maintained for such a practice. Yet it is even less possible to see what *mimēsis* has in common with "production," to see how one could "produce" with a mirror, unless Heidegger is right when he identifies the three kinds of production—the god producing the *idea,* the craftsman producing the thing, the painter producing the image—as a pro-ducing or leading forward into radiant outward appearance or profile, a bringing out of concealment and into presence. In the three "turns" of presencing only the degree of nondistortion differs; that is, in terms of our own discussion, only the symmetry varies, and it is essential that the modes of self-showing themselves be seen symmetrically, as being *like* one another.

> The more firmly we hold on to the selfsameness, the more significant the distinction must become. Plato here is wrestling with the conception of the varying *tropos,* that is, at the same time and above all, with the determination of that

"way" in which *on* [being] itself shows itself most purely, so that it does not portray itself by means of something else but presents itself in such a way that its outward appearance, *eidos*, constitutes its being. Such self-showing is the *eidos* as *idea*.[18]

Heidegger is also right to ridicule us for being "quick on the uptake" when we say that some kinds of production are "real" while others are "merely apparent." The problem of likeness, iconography, compels us beyond that handy distinction to the realm of unconcealment (*alētheia*) and upsurgence (*physis*) as such. The problem is to visualize "how the selfsame shows itself in various ways: three ways of self-showing; hence, of presence; hence, three metamorphoses of being itself" (182). Once we have seen what the three modes of presencing have in common, however, it is inevitable that the hierarchy be reestablished. The portrayed object shows an *idea* and a "thing," but shows both of them "in something else, in shades of color," something that muddies the radiance of pure showing.

What is decisive for the Greek-Platonic concept of *mimēsis* or imitation is not reproduction or portraiture, not the fact that the painter provides us with the same thing once again; what is decisive is that this is precisely what he cannot do, that he is even less capable than the craftsman of duplicating the same thing. It is therefore wrongheaded to apply to *mimēsis* notions of "naturalistic" or "primitivistic" copying and reproducing. Imitation is subordinate pro-duction. The *mimētēs* is defined in essence by his position of distance; such distance results from the hierarchy established with regard to ways of production and in the light of pure outward appearance, being. (185)

The artist's "position of distance" reminds us of those structures of distantiation that Aristotle erected in his analysis of memory—the distance of the "force within us" from the "source of motion," and of the latter from the pathos, as of the pathos from the things (*pragmata*) themselves. Yet the Platonic *hierarchy* here discussed by Heidegger is as mysterious as Aristotle's iconographic distantiations. To inquire into both adequately we would have to take up the question of *homoiōsis* once again, this time in the context of Aristotle's famous opening words in *Of Interpretation*, 16a 3–8. In chapter 4, below, we shall take up the *homoiōsis* of *pathēmata*, *pragmata*, symbols, and sounds—the entire machinery of iconography as engrammatology.

Finally, the discussion of *mimēsis* in Book Ten of *Republic* has consequences for the entire analysis of *eidōlopoiikē* in *Sophist*. Heidegger introduces the problem in this way:

What art produces is not the *eidos* as *idea* (*physis*), but *touto eidōlon*. The latter means a little *eidos*, but "little" not just in the sense of stature. In the way it shows and appears, the *eidōlon* is something slight. It is a mere residue of the genuine self-showing of beings, and even then in an alien domain, for example, color or some other material of portraiture. Such diminution of the way of pro-ducing is a darkening and distorting.

We are familiar with Plato's description of images in the central books of *Republic* (509e 1: *eikones*) as shadows or reflections in water. Such likenesses occupy the lowest sector of the divided-line, *eikasia* being the poorest form of knowledge, the penumbrous showing of things. Philosophic education is therefore understood as a clambering up the divided-line, as though it were the ladder of love, in order to nest amidst the Good, Beautiful, and True. Submerged are the compelling images of Plato's own text, the icon of the sun (509a 9), the image of the divided-line itself (533a 3), and the allegory of the cave. How out of place such icons are! we are likely to exclaim, as Glaucon does (515a 4), as soon as he and we see them *as* images, as soon as we remember that they are likenesses and simulacra rather than the things themselves. Yet it may well be that once we have diligently gone up and down the divided-line, and forth and back through these central books, it will become clear to us that all attempts to escape *eikones* are futile, that the forms themselves, the *eidē*, are figurines, *eidōla*, and that devotion to philosophy is inevitably idolatry.[19]

We have been pursuing for some time now the sources of Aristotelian typography and iconography in Plato's *Republic, Parmenides, Theaetetus,* and *Sophist*. Even in these dialogues the guiding metaphors of *eikōn* and *typos*, likeness, imprint, and coinage, are more than "epistemological" matters. Their function is primarily ontological, in that they have to do with structures of beings, their presencing and self-showing. Plato's *Timaeus*—the gossamer burlesque and cosmogonic midsummer night's dream that coined Western man's image of the universe and the self for two thousand years—tells us that the very *kosmos,* the universe of beings, is "a likeness of something" (29b 2: *eikōn tinos*); that in it the relationship of copy to original, image to paradigm, *genesis* to *ontōs on* obtains. Plato's *Timaeus*—and we will insist that *Timaeus* is a work of Plato's, even though Diogenes Laertius (VIII, 84) reports that Hermippus suggests that somebody else knows full well that when Plato went to Syracuse he purchased a Pythagorean tome from Philolaus of Croton's relatives and cribbed the entire *Timaeus* from it—insists that a discourse involving the *eikona* can only be *eikota*, "probable," "likely," not privy to the *logos* itself but "analogous," *ana logon* (29c 2). (Whether the homologous structure of *analogon* and *anamnēsis* is significant, whether the *ana-* in each case implies incessant motion and perpetual iteration rather than arrival at a fixed destination and perfect presence, are arresting questions—yet we will not stop for them.) How improbable and unlikely it all is, this comedy of Pythagorean loquacity and Socratic silence! How singularly odd the ostensibly iconic relationships are throughout![20] The most famous of these relationships is that of time and eternity, most famous because it is decisive for the *difference* between being and becoming as such. In fact, that difference cannot be expressed except through some tacit reference to time (or transiency) and eternity (or immutability), so that the icon-paradigm relationship is especially here caught in a curious circularity. Timaeus tells us that the Demiurge "considered that he would make a moving simulacrum of eternity" (37d 5: *eikō* [a poetic Ionic form of *eikōn*] ... *kinetōn tina aiōnos*). He thus ordered the heavens   *Then I looked at the fire again and the bright, smooth shapes went again. I could hear the clock and the roof and Caddy* in such a way that they yielded "a likeness [7: *eikona*] of eternity—which is at rest in One—in motion according to number." Thus the co(s)mic craftsman models motion on rest and number on unity. That circular motion should approximate rest, and that numbers— especially to a Pythagorean—should be accretions of monads, causes no astonishment. Yet that one of these should and could be the paradigm for the other, and that Rest and the One should be granted priority, these things resist every explanation. The circularity of ouranian divinities becomes the spiral of mortal interpretation.[21]

Yet the modeling or generating, fabricating or begetting of *time*—and it is difficult to distinguish the poietic from the generative powers of the craftsman-father, difficult to know whether here we have to do with *tiktō* or *tekhnē*—is not the only bewildering execution of a likeness by a likeness. Generated beings are everywhere imaged after eternal paradigms whose primary trait is that they are ungenerated. The immortal technician generates gods and things divine (*theoi, theon*) who are "neither immortal nor altogether indestructible" (41b 2). He then instructs these quasi-immortals to help him generate three classes of mortals. He specifically admonishes them that in their production of the mortal parts they are to "imitate" (41c 5) his production of them, and he insists on planting the immortal seed in mortals himself.[22] All this in a universe where like generates like! For the universe is a visible divinity modeled on the intelligible (92c 7: *eikōn tou noētou theos aisthētos*), so that, in spite of all the damage that differences and diseases and birdbrain astronomers can do, that universe remains one of a kind, perfectly monogenous (31b 3; 92c 9). Such is Timaeus' eloquence, tying the ties that bind—and blind.

What accounts for the slippage between paradigm and icon, the difference in rank between being and becoming? If the second is modeled on the first, what intervenes to make the copy inferior? What bitches the modeling? Such questions take us to the shaggy heart *and Caddy put her arms around me* of Timaeus' discourse, his "second beginning" at 48e, which proposes the "receptacle," *hypodokhē*, of becoming as a solution to the problem of the gap between the visible and the invisible. Whereas during the first part of his speech Timaeus of Locri has named only two kinds, first, a paradigmatic *eidos*, intelligible and eternally the same in being (48e 5–6), and second, an imitation (*mimēma*) of that paradigm that is visible and generated (48e 5–6), he now needs a third kind, a third *eidos* to embrace *Benjy, Caddy said, Benjy. She put her arms around me again. But I went away* the first two. It is difficult to find words for the third kind. Timaeus calls it "the receptacle of generation, a sort of nurse" (49a 5–6: *geneseōs hypodokhē . . . hoion tithēnē*). *Hypodokhē* means the reception or entertainment of a thing, its *Unterbringung* and *Unterhaltung*, or a means for admitting and harboring it. Timaeus has already mentioned that cup or mixing bowl (41d 4: *kratēra*) in which *the bowl steamed up to my face* the craftsman-father *Father took me up. He smelled like rain* blends the elements of soul that are destined for the universe and for mortals, and it is apparently something of the sort he now seeks for all becoming. However, the image shifts. It is not mere containment that is needed but something more supple and   *Versh's hand dipped the spoon in*   subtle. Something consisting of a material very much like wax. The receptacle must be "of a nature that receives all bodies" (50b 6: *ta panta dekhomenēs sōmata physeōs*), something like gold, which can be hammered, stamped, and coined in sundry forms. However, the receptacle must never abandon its own essence, even as it opens itself to all things; it must be "a natural recipient of impressions" (50c 2: *ekmageion*), set in motion and transmogrified by what enters into it, though untouched in its essence; it must embrace and release "imitations" of perdurant being (50c 5: *tōn ontōn aei mimēmata*). (*Ekmageion*, according to its second sense, means that on or in which an impression is made: it is the very word that was used earlier to describe the mnemic slab of wax at *Theaetetus* 191c 9ff. and 196a 3. *Timaeus* also employs several verbs derived from *typos*, designating the *mimēmata* [at 50c 5, for example] as *typothenta*, so that at crucial moments this dialogue too reverts from iconography to typography.)

Such then are the three *eidē* of Timaeus' second effort (50c–d): *that which is generated* (*to gignomenon*), that *in* which it is generated (*to d' en hōi gignetai*), and that *of* which the generated is a naturally derived resemblance (*to d' hothen aphomoioumenon phyetai to gignomenon*). The first may be likened to an infant, the last to its father, and the "in which" to its mother or to the mother's womb (50d 2–3: *to dekhomenon mētri*). Because she must entertain all traits, receiving them from without, the mother must be amorphous and altogether neutral   *Caddy smelled like trees. We don't like to perfume ourselves, Caddy said*   like the base of a perfume. Summing up what he has said so far, Timaeus concludes that the universal mother and receptacle of becoming   *Caddy smelled like trees in the rain*   may not be called earth, air, water, fire   *It was rising and falling on the walls*   or anything generated from these, and that she is "an invisible and characterless form which receives all things and which somehow participates in the intelligible in the most perplexing and baffling manner" (51a 4ff.). Of all aporias, the mother is most aporetic: an invisible *eidos* without form, she embraces all form and visibility; an *eidos* sharing in the intelligible, she defies all but the dreamiest of discourses. Matters only get worse when Timaeus (52a 8) tries to describe the "in which" as *khōra*, or more fully, *on to tēs khōras*, "being [or the self-showing presencing] that is eternally of the room." For it soon becomes clear that the slippage between paradigm and copy that prevents *that which* is generated from perfectly matching that *of* which it is a copy reverts to that *in* which the copy is generated. The last is said to be utterly characterless and neutral, yet we recognize here the source of that "veil of melancholy" that Schelling will find   *Then I saw Caddy, with flowers in her hair, and a long veil like shining wind. Caddy. Caddy*   draped over all nature. At the core of the shapeless receptacle lies some invisible and nameless

adversity   *I wasn't crying, but I couldn't stop*   that makes Timaeus
fear and despise the female parts.

The same extended metaphor that constitutes epistemology as a flight from
passivity to activity, from affection to action at a distance, as the dream of
perfect presence, makes ontology a flight from the female to   *I got undressed and I looked at myself, and I began to cry. Hush, Luster said. Looking
for them ain't going to do no good. They're gone*   the neutered male.
Which would mean that the tradition, for all its glorification of Mnemosyne,
who (as Heidegger will assure us) is a right mother, is not so much phal-
logocentric as it is gynephobic. And the phobia exacts its price. The failure of
Timaeus' discourse means the failure of iconography and of all ontotheology   *A door opened and I could smell it more than ever, and a head
came out. It wasn't Father. Father was sick there*   as such.

GRAMMATA

How we can have strayed so wildly on our course from typography to engrammatology I do not know. Let us abandon iconography to its crisis, at least
for a moment, and return at long last to *Theaetetus*, which now describes the
weaving (*symplokē*) of forms in terms of *letters*.

After the boorish critic has shooed Socrates and Theatetus out of the
birdcage (200d), our two heroes ask a third time what knowledge is. They
dress the birds as particles of knowledge compounded of "true belief" and
logos. The latter is composed of molecular names, any given *onoma* being a
collocation of unutterable and unknowable "elements of writing," the atomic
letters (202e). Knowledge is thus reduced to a hiss of the tongue—and a snake
devours all the birds. We are compelled to confront problems of grammatology, the science of letters, or, if the lessons of typography be remembered, of
engrammatology, the science of engrained or incised letters. The science of
letters conducts us willy-nilly to the realm of differance, *diaphora*, inasmuch as
a *logos* consisting of words and letters implies a hermeneutic of radical differences. At 209a 5 we read Socrates' astonishing words: *Logos de ge ēn hē tēs sēs
diapherotētos hermēneia. Logos* is essentially an account or explanation that
puts *the proper difference* into words; that is, in the present case, the *logos*
must explain how Theaetetus is *different* from Theodorus or, for that matter,
from Socrates. For it has already been ruled out that such difference could
reside straightforwardly in the differences among the syllables and letters of
their respective names.[23]

However, that is to anticipate the outcome of a long and difficult discussion. We must backtrack a bit. Socrates' dreamy discourse at 202a–c recounts
something he has heard, the hearsay, namely, that the primal elements (letters?)
of all things, the *prota stoikheia*, have no *logos*, no rhyme or reason, and
cannot be explained. For everything adduced to them would contest their
status as primal. They may have a name   *What is it, Caddy said. What*

are you trying to tell Caddy   but they can have no *logos,* since *logos* is itself woven of names. Theaetetus and Socrates now (202e 6) discuss the elements of writing proper, the *stoikheia tōn grammatōn,* syllables and letters. While the name *Socrates* can apparently be explained or calculated—that is, outfitted with a *logos*—as consisting of the syllables *Sō-kra-tēs,* and the syllable *Sō-* can be explained as consisting of the elements *S* and *ō,* Theaetetus understandably despairs of providing "the elements of an element." The "aphonic" sigma is not even a proper sound—it is, we said, the hiss of a serpent that threatens to devour all knowledge—and the omega, like the other six vowels, while "phonic," has no *logos.* Whether a single *idea* or *eidos* can be constructed out of such elements, or whether the "form" is a whole (*holon*) that somehow *exceeds* all its parts, is Socrates' question, a question he cannot induce Theaetetus to unravel in a way that will rescue the *difference* between whole and agglomerate. Yet whether the elements of *logos* are taken as syllables or letters ultimately makes no difference, according to Socrates (205e), perhaps because the two interlocutors (quite plausibly) insist on dividing rather than weaving.

It is doubtless time to let Theaetetus and Socrates go, and to bring this chapter to a close. For their effort to provide a hermeneutic of difference goes on and on, Socrates to Theaetetus, Theaetetus to Socrates, frogeye to frogeye, snubnose to snubnose, windbag to windegg, their circle dissolving to a final ironic identity: Theaetetus sets off for the battlefield where he will be infected with dysentery and mortally wounded—the dialogue began, we recall, with him *on* his shield—while Socrates heads for the law court to face the indictment of Miletus. Before we let them go, however, two details from the final part of their discussion may be remembered for our own purposes. The first of Socrates' efforts (at 206d) to define the *logos* that will ostensibly turn true opinion into knowledge brings us back to typography—if only ironically. Perhaps *logos* makes our thought transparent in nouns and verbs, says Socrates; by virtue of *logos* we stamp (3: *ektypoumenon*) our *doxa* onto the stream of words that flows through our lips. We can of course imagine the fate of this typography practiced on "streams" of "water," as on a "mirror," so reminiscent of the watery typography of writing that we are about to hear criticized in *Phaedrus* (276c 7–8). Learning to know and being able to remember the difference between Socrates and Theaetetus will require something solider, or at least more viscous. Socrates speaks:

> No, I imagine that Theaetetus will not be the object of opinion in me until this very snubnosedness has engraved and deposited in me [*ensēmēnamenē katathētai*] a memorial different from [*diaphoron ti mnēmeion*] all other cases of snubnosedness I have seen, and the same with everything else in your makeup. For if I should meet you again tomorrow this would cause me to be put in memory of you [*anamnēsei*] and to have a correct opinion concerning you.

However, before we agree—out of exhaustion—to countenance this regression to typography and iconography, we must give engrammatology three more brief chances to explain itself, chances of waxing complexity, as we shall see, in *Cratylus, Phaedrus,* and *Philebus.* The first is important for us as an explicit attempt to execute an iconography of names and the elements of names—since it is by reading the signs or marks imprinted on the wax slab of our souls that we remember, or hope to remember, the same. The second is vital because it conjoins the themes of memory and writing, although we will touch on it only cursorily here, taking it up once again in chapter 4. The third will show us how difficult it is to get a proper mixture—whether of pleasure or of letters—without memory.

In *Cratylus* Socrates and Hermogenes engage in the futile and comic effort to construct a mimetic theory of names, whereby names would imitate beings, as though names themselves were composed of syllables and letters that imitated the being of beings (424b 9–10: *hē mimēsis . . . ousa tēs ousias*). Their hypothesis is that the letters "resemble" things (424d 6: *kata tēn homoiotēta*). Socrates concedes that it seems "ridiculous" (425d 1) to search for such a resemblance, but he feels constrained to look for it, even if the search should prove to be not so much laughable as "hybristic" (426b 6). He then launches bravely into his physiology of phonemes—kinetic rho, sighing sigma, windy phi and psi, occluding tau, and liquid lambda—to the delight of Cratylus and to his own dubiety and discomfiture (428d 1–3): "Excellent Cratylus, I have long been wondering at my own wisdom. I cannot trust myself. And I think I ought to stop and ask myself, What am I saying?" Socrates and Cratylus can agree that both names and pictures or portraits are imitations of things, although in different senses, but the peculiar kind of likeness or image (*eikōn*) involved in either sense baffles them:

> SOCRATES: How is it now with one who imitates the being [*ousia*] of things in syllables and letters? Will it not be the same with him, that when he reproduces everything that is appropriate to the thing his icon will be fine—and in his case this is the name—but if he leaves something out or perhaps adds a touch he will still get an icon, but not a beautiful one? . . . (431b 2–7)
> CRATYLUS: Perhaps.

An image dare not differ too greatly from its original, for it would be a poor icon if it did. Yet ironically, or iconically, Socrates now insists that *perfect* likeness would in fact destroy the image-original relationship: unlike a number, to which addition or subtraction is fatal, and which thus cannot be "imitated" but only given originally, an icon dare not be conflated with its original, "it dare not reproduce every particular if it is to be an icon" (432b 1–4). What one must learn to see is "the extent to which icons fail to possess the same [*ta auta*] as that of which they are icons" (d 1–2).

We might interrupt at this juncture to note the consequences for the iconography of memory: memory and reminiscence can never be arithmetic, for, if they were, the self-showing of the remembered thing could not be distinguished from the original self-showing. Memory and reminiscence have to be engrammatological rather than arithmetical: the exigencies of iconography demand it. And thus the dream of a perfect division of *eidōlopoiikē* into *eikastikē* and *phantastikē* is a dream from which we must awaken. Every icon needs a touch of the phantasmatic about it, lest it thoroughly confuse past and present. But to return to *Cratylus*.

Socrates must now strike a compromise between the natural suitability and the conventional character of letters (435 a–d). Yet the compromise is an equivocation, indeed another "dream." Although Socrates encourages Cratylus to give up the search for beings in iconic names and to turn to *ta onta*, the self-showing presencings themselves, he momentarily forgets the objection he has just raised against Cratylus: "But if things are to be known only through names, how can we suppose that the givers of names had knowledge, or were legislators, before there were names at all, and therefore before they could have known them?" (438 5–8). When he sends Cratylus off with the injunction to seek not names but "far rather the things themselves from themselves" (439b 7: *auta ex autōn*), Cratylus can only rejoin that Socrates must do his part "to think more closely about these things." Socrates' part is not to play with names but   *His name's Benjy now, Caddy said. How come it is, Dilsey said. He ain't wore out the name he was born with yet is he. . . . Folks don't have no luck, changing names. My name been Dilsey since fore I could remember and it be Dilsey when they's long forgot me. How will they know it's Dilsey, when it's long forgot, Dilsey, Caddy said. It'll be in the Book, honey, Dilsey said. Writ out   to* name the things themselves. Yet Socrates has no access to the origin of the names uttered in his naming. His is not the god's vision and banquet, but the poor feast and meager reception of discourse, the restless search for being—which "name" itself implies: *onoma* is *on hou masma* (421a 10), "being for which there is a search." The name is that *self-showing* which we must *seek*.

Having mentioned the banquet, we ought to recall if only briefly that for Plato's *Phaedrus* the power to gather, tie, and weave by means of forms is nothing else than reminiscence or recollection (249c 2: *anamnēsis*). For Plato certainly as much as for Aristotle, reminiscence is not merely one among several powers of the soul; it sustains a privileged relation to the being of beings. The gathering and binding of philosophic discourse constitute the recollection of what our souls once saw before they took on human form. They are recollection of being (3: *einai*), which we once surveyed in the train of the god, gazing upward to the perfect presencing of all that comes to presence (4: *to on ontōs*). The philosopher's thought takes wing insofar as, to the full extent of its powers, it is "always mindful" (5: *aei . . . mnēmei*) of those presencings by virtue of which divinities *are* divine. Through devoted service to the means of remembrance, reminders or memorials (7: *hypomnēmasin*, cf. *hypomnēma*), the philosophic soul comes to proper perfection and attains its end (7–8: *teleous aei teletas teloumenos, teleos ontōs monos gignetai*). Yet, as we recall, devoted service to memorials or monuments is fraught with danger   *I was trying to say, and I caught her, trying to say, and she screamed and I was trying to say and trying and the bright shapes began to stop and I tried to get out. I tried to get off my face, but the bright shapes were going again. . . . But when I*

*breathed in, I couldn't breathe out again to cry, and I tried to keep from falling
off the hill and I fell off the hill into the bright, whirling shapes* and may
be closer to death than to life. Certainly such service is close to madness.
Remembrance is the fourth kind of *mania*, divine mania, most beneficial to
mortals, they say. As the philosophic soul gazes on beautiful things, it remembers what was once fully revealed (249d 5–6: *tou alēthous anamimneis-
komenos;* cf. *Meno* 81cff. and *Phaedo* 73d–eff.), and it sprouts wings. Like
Keats's sick eagle, however, it is unable to fly, and can only gaze longingly
upward. Yet even that is difficult: although each human soul must by nature
have already viewed beings as they come to presence, it is not easy for it to
remember (250a 1: *anamimneiskesthai*); to varying degrees, all are steeped in
oblivion (4: *lēthē*), and there are ultimately only a few human beings—such as
Er—in whom the remembrance itself remains sufficiently present (5: *to tēs
mnēmēs hikanōs parestin*).

Let me pause to note that here again it is the *parousia* or presence of the
mnemic by which its adequacy is measured. However much *anamnēsis* may
suggest the prolonged and laborious approach to memories, *mnēmē* itself remains that to which one must be *present*—even and especially if it reposes a
world away. All of which makes the service to reminders and memorials particularly uncanny. Even though these pages of Plato's *Phaedrus* have been
much on the contemporary mind of late, let us remind ourselves once again of
Thot's memorials, namely, the letters by which we write.

The god Thot proclaims to King Thamus of Egyptian Thebes the virtues of
his recently invented letters, *ta grammata*, devised as a kind of medicine for the
mind, in order to make it wiser and more capable of memory (274e 6:
mnēmēs . . . kai sophias pharmakon). King Thamus rejoins that the effect of
letters on the soul will rather be deleterious. They will induce oblivion (275a 2:
lēthē) and a neglect of memory (3: *mnēmēs ameletēsiai*).[24] Memory will be
debilitated if remembrance is provoked by means of an extrinsic confidence or
belief in the extraneous written word (3: *pistis graphēs exōthen*), which is
merely an alien imprint (4: *hyp' allotriōn typōn*), rather than by an intrinsic
effort of the soul to remember (*endothen autous hyph' hautōn*). Thot's remedy
is therefore an elixir not for remembering (5: *mnēmēs*) but for reminding
(*hypomnēseōs pharmakon*). As a hypomnesic, the letter produces only the
appearance of wisdom (6: *sophias . . . doxan*) but not true remembrance (*ouk
alētheian*). "True remembrance" is of course a pleonasm. The Greek word for
"true," as we have noted, means precisely what is rescued from oblivion, what
is remembered. Further, "remembered" is to be thought as "granted unconcealment," so that *sophias alētheian* suggests "wisdom that *shows itself* as
what it *is* in undistorted presence." Presencing is what is opened to view in
anamnēsis, namely, *to on ontōs*, the being of beings in the most perfect of its
"turnings."

Again we should pause, in order to remind ourselves how strange the story
or myth of *Phaedrus* is. Earlier on, the dialogue assured us that the only way a
mortal soul (as opposed to a god) could be ever mindful of those presencings

which are the gods' daily fare is through devoted service to memorials or reminders (*hypomnēmasin, hypomnēma*). Now we are told that mere memorials are not enough, and are even vitiating: we must aspire instead to the banquet itself. However, to Thamus' warnings one must pose a more carefully construed *typographic* question. If belief in the written letter is extrinsic, if its exterior, extraneous, and hence superficial *typos* or imprint is alien to the soul, how is it that memory itself—from the inside, as it were—can ever have been portrayed typographically? Does not the cutting edge of the *typos* itself confound outside and inside right from the start?[25]

Socrates himself goes on to discuss the notorious disadvantages of the written word, so reminiscent of a mute portrait, disadvantages every reader of the Platonic dialogues has come to know: its obstinate refusal to answer questions, a refusal that is only aggravated by its promiscuity (inasmuch as the taciturn text flaunts itself at anyone who cares to ogle it). Yet, insolent as they may appear to be, the written letters are actually helpless orphans: "If they are insulted or unjustly maltreated, they always need their Father's help; for by themselves they do not know how to protect and help themselves" (275e 4). He concludes with an extended metaphor: Writing will be the philosopher's form of *play*, though certainly not the object of his devotion, while his *labor* will be dialogue. Writing will be a kind of puttering about in the garden; dialogue will be serious, scientific agriculture. Never will writing be the philosopher's earnest pursuit (276c 7: *ouk ara spoudēi*), for it is absurd to write in water (*en hydati grapsei*: recall the effort to stamp imprints on the stream of words flowing from a mouth in dialogue), absurd to sow inky seeds through a reed (8: *speirōn dia kalamou*), inky seeds of impotent words (*logōn adynatōn*). For such printed words can neither help themselves by means of speech (9: *logōi*) nor competently instruct others in the matter of self-showing proper (*hikanōs talēthē didaxai*). Such competency would of course depend utterly on the compelling *presence* of the being of beings in the philosopher's memory; the competency (*hikanōs*) of the philosopher is a certain sufficiency of presence—as indicated above (250a 5: *hikanōs parestin*).[26]

However harsh the condemnation of orphan writing may have seemed just now, Socrates soon gives ground in a strange, if playful, way. The man of knowledge will sow seed in the child's garden of letters, will write solely for the sake of play (276d 1–2), and yet such play will not be utterly mindless. For it will assemble a store of treasures, reminders (3: *hypomnēmata thesaurizomenos*), for the sake of old age, inasmuch as old age tends toward forgetfulness (*eis to lēthēs gēras*). And this playful puttering in the garden will fill the man of knowledge with joy when he sees what he has sown flourishing quietly there (5: *phyomenous apalous*), as though the written word did have an upsurgent life all its own. While others indulge in merry games at drinking parties—not that drinking parties cannot offer occasions for fecund play of their own kind—the philosopher will pursue fruitful play in *logoi* and in telling stories about things like justice.

Which leaves only the materials in *Philebus* which I promised to relate—

briefly, in order then to summarize and come to a conclusion, or at least a close. Perhaps I can best introduce these final materials by referring to Aristotle once again, as I did at the outset, albeit this time to his treatise *On the Soul*. For there he tells us most clearly what is at stake in the preference of (putatively active) *anamnēsis* to (ostensibly passive) *mnēmē*. Aristotle states:

> Mind [*nous*] in the passive sense is such [namely: something that has both matter and maker in it] because it *becomes* all things [*panta ginesthai*]; but mind has another aspect in that it *makes* all things [*panta poiein*]; this is a kind of positive state like light; for in a sense light makes potential colors into actual ones. Mind in this sense is separable, impassive, and unmixed [*ho nous khōristos kai apathēs kai amigēs*], since it is essentially an activity [*ōn energeiai*]; for the agent [*to poioun*] is always superior to the patient [*tou paskhontos*], and the originating principle [*arkhē*] to the matter [*tēs hylēs*]. (430a 14–25)

The active, productive mind alone is "undying and eternal," and thus capable of existence apart from the body. Yet for all its supremacy the active mind, as we embodied mortals know it, is limited precisely in its knowledge of self in the presumably superior state of separation. In a parenthetical remark Aristotle explains that "we do not remember" (23: *ou mnēmoneuomen*) anything at all of what the mind experiences in separation, because active mind receives no impressions, is *apathes*, while passive mind (*pathētikos*) is perishable. An odd situation results. While burdened with the body and its senses, phantasms, and fate, the active mind feasts almost uninterruptedly on impressions; when at last it is free to enjoy its essential nature wholly without interruption at the divine banquet, the purely active mind is perfectly and literally *apathetic*. Separation of soul from body may be fulfillment or frustration: we simply do not remember.

Yet if for *Plato* knowledge is remembrance, this particular incapacity to remember would appear to be devastating. Or, on the contrary, that very incapacity might account for the omnipresence of *myth* in Plato's dialogues wherever memory and reminiscence—not to mention writing—are in question.

In the middle of *Philebus* (33dff.) memory and recollection are defined in terms of body and soul, respectively, that is to say, in terms of the distinctness of soul from body. Socrates calls *mnēmē* the preservation of *aisthēsis*, and distinguishes from it *anamnēsis*, which retrieves the soul's experiences "without the body, in and for itself" (34 b 7: *aneu tou sōmatos autē en heautēi*). The purpose of this distinction, Socrates insists, is to teach us about "the pleasure of the soul apart from [c 6: *khōris*] the body," and thus the nature of the soul's isolate desire. Yet such separation proves to be fatal to desire and pleasure alike, for here remembrance and the body are and must be intimately related. And not only here. For when we consider the typography, iconography, and engrammatology of memory, *mnēmē* too, for its part, is as much a matter of the soul as of the body.

At 38e 12 Socrates compares the soul to a book (*biblios*). In the book of the soul, memory, sensations, and the affections "inscribe discourses" (39a 3: *graphein . . . logous*). Thus the soul contains an "internal scribe" who "writes" the soul's experience (6–7: *grammateus grapsēi*), sometimes truly, sometimes falsely. Socrates also detects the presence of a *second* artist-craftsman in the soul, "a painter [b 6: *zōgraphon*] who comes after the writer and paints in the soul icons of these discourses [6–7: *tōn legomenōn eikonas toutōn graphei*]." Thus the graphics of the soul (and not merely of the body) include the incising of both words and pictures: there is a sense in which we can "see icons in ourselves [c 1: *eikonas en autōi*] of what we have previously believed or said." Both the writing and the portraiture that transpire within the soul point to the *intrinsic mediation* of the body on which the soul depends. Just as in the effort to seek unity in the many and a manifold in the one—that is, the effort to make sense of the interconnections between forms and things—it is the *intermediates* that count (see 16c), so here as well Socrates and Protarchus find themselves *en mesōi*, in the middle, "in between." It is always a matter of mediation and measure, of a *mixture,* as Socrates later says, that exhibits the *metron* and symmetry (64d 9). Thus Socrates demonstrates to Protrarchus that pleasure requires at least a momentary *memory* of pleasure. The honey of pleasure must be mixed with the salubrious water of intelligence, insight, or thoughtfulness (61c 6: *phronēsis*), the water—we must add—being drawn from the fountain of Mnemosyne. As the two men begin to mingle honey and water for the sake of the good life, Socrates invokes the aid of two gods, Dionysos and Hephaestos, who may have something to do with mixtures, the latter forging links of steel, the former binding with ribands of love. And in their search for intermediates and interconnections, the interlocutors are no doubt remembering what the dialogue has said about letters, *ta grammata.* For in his account of intermediates and the in-between (*ta metaxy*), Socrates chose as his prime example the letters of the alphabet and their relationship to the infinite possibilities of sound:

> The unlimited variety of sound [*phōnē*] was once discerned by some god, or perhaps some godlike man; you know the story that there was some such person in Egypt called Thot. He it was who originally discerned the existence in that unlimited variety [*en tōi apeirōi*] of the vowels [*ta phōnēenta*]—not in the singular but in the plural—and then of other things which, though they could not be called articulate sounds, yet were noises of a kind [i.e., the consonants]. There were a number of them too, not just one; and as a third class he discriminated what we now call the mutes [*aphōna*]. Having done that he divided up the noiseless ones or mutes until he got each one by itself, and did the same thing with the vowels and the intermediate sounds [*ta mesa*]. (18b 6ff.)

The sounds intermediate between sounding letters or phonics (vowels) and silent letters or aphonics (mutes) are the consonants. We recall the subsequent tradition—extending at least from Rousseau through Saussure, and including Schelling, for whom consonants in the creative Word pronounced by God represent the principle of darkness and gravity[27]—that disparages consonants as marks of death, as eminently thanatological signs. Remarkably, Plato's Socrates here identifies the consonants as beings that are not independent and yet are not nothing; he locates them precisely in the intermediate position of genesis and of mortality. But to return to the tale of Thot:

In the end he found a number of all these things [i.e., phonics, mutes, and conso-nants] and affixed to the whole collection, as to each single member of it, the name "letter" [*stoikheion*]. It was because he realized that none of us could ever get to know any one of the collection all by itself, in isolation from all the rest, that he conceived of "letter" as a kind of bond of unity, uniting as it were all these sounds into one, and so he gave utterance to the expression "art of letters" [*grammatikē tekhnē*], implying that there was one art that dealt with the sounds.

The letters are thus elements, *stoikheia,* each with its proper identity, yet bound to the whole collection; the *grammatikē tekhnē* treats of the entire manifold of commingled sounds. Understandably, Philebus and Protarchus complain early on about Socrates' "roundabout methods" and the seeming irrelevance of all this. Yet, as we have just seen, the doctrine of the intermediates—between the one and an indeterminate number, between sound and silence—in fact proves highly relevant to the discussion of the soul's plea-sure and desire, both of which require memory and reminiscence. Yet let us be a friend to Philebus—and stop here.

If we now look back on this meandering chapter we can discern five stages on our way thus far. In the first, we saw how Aristotle wished to distinguish active reminiscence from passive memory, and we wondered at the ostensible lethargy of memory proper. For the objects of memory and reminscence alike are past. Thus the "presence" of such objects in memory quickly emerged as the central enigma. Aristotle associated memory with the "common" and "paramount" perceptual power by virtue of which memory knows both time and images, *phantasmata.* And just as protoperception seemed to relate closely to touch, so did both time and images touch on memory—as a signet ring touches sealing wax. Yet typography alone failed to resolve the ontological aporia of memory—the presence of *typos* to *pathos,* and *pathos* to *pragmatos.* Typography therefore issued onto iconography. The phantasm or imprint is an icon of the absent thing. Yet the icon can function only by virtue of some *motion* by which we can eventually either see the icon under its own aspect or "read" it as referring to an other. With this reference to reading we found ourselves on the verge of en-grammatology: the *typos* is an *engram,* an inscribed or incised letter, element, or portrait, purporting to be an *icon.*

In the second stage we examined the sequence of kinetic presencings in reminiscence, *anamnēsis,* a sequence that is neither strictly linear nor (except in pathological cases) entirely circular. A number of problems arose concerning the search for an *arkhē kinēseōs,* that is, for a "tonic" for the whole series of musical movements that would bring us to the desired end of remembrance. For even "natural" self-showings can be distorted by *paraphysis,* and every icon can turn out to be a "mere likeness," *paromoion.* In the end, the major difficulty with Aristotle's boldest solution to the enigma of recollection or reminiscence—the simultaneous generation (*hama ginetai*) of the *pragmata* and of time as such—was not that it failed but that it worked too well: even if we restrict the sense of time to mean the time-of-the-*pragmata,* the expression *hama ginetai* appears to close all the distances. Yet memory and reminiscence are *of the past* and require the distance that will prevent their collapse into perception and intellection. Aristotle's treatise, while it sets the pace for investigation into memory for the next two millennia, fails to clarify the enigmas it so deftly reveals. What is the *typos,* such that it can be an *eikōn* of the things themselves, whose presence—whose very being—we read from the *grammata* engraved on the wax slab of the soul? At this point we set off in search of the imprint, icon, and engram in Greek philosophy prior to Aristotle.

Our third step took us to some likely sources of Aristotle's typography and iconography in the Greek Atomists and in Plato's *Theaetetus.* The latter is perhaps the classic source of those slabs of wax, produced no doubt in one of the back rooms of the Platonic pharmacy. Yet the problem arose of the relation of those traces in the wax which Socrates himself calls idols, not icons, to the beings or self-showings of the past. Socrates' efforts to blame it all on the wax—a substance that is depressingly gritty and filthy   *Caddy was all wet and muddy behind, and I started to cry and she came and squatted* in the common mortal—will not distract us from the aporia of presence/absence in memory. Socrates himself advances from the typographic slab to the aviary in order to get closer to the mysterious presence, *parousia,* and the being-at-hand, *prokheiros,* that would guarantee a perfect grasp of beings in *epistēmē.* Yet this second grand metaphor for memory, the properly iconographic metaphor, also fails—for the reason we usually associate with the "Third Man argument" in *Parmenides.* While this likeness of a container of likenesses has a certain seductive charm, such that it has made its mark on the Occidental mind for centuries, likeness itself remains mysterious. As though the question *What is? ti esti; quid est?* were not itself implicated in the problematic *presence* of memory, we asked of several Platonic dialogues the question *What is likeness?*

Our fourth step—actually a series of rather wearying iconographic excursions into four dialogues—resulted in the following difficulties:

(1) The "likeness" of two things, conceived of in *Parmenides* as the participation of those two things in some form of "likeness," participation *by* "likeness," became stranger than ever.

(2) All talk of "likeness," according to *Sophist,* had to be interrupted by a full discussion of dialectic, which weaves the forms. Such weaving (*symplokē*) would have to eschew the oppositional thinking of being/nonbeing (or absolute presence, absolute absence) by paying heed to multiple *differences.* It is precisely *mimēsis* that will not submit to capture in the binary divisions of the Stranger's diacritical method. Weaving on the verge of the loom—and not stamping, printing, or painting icons—will be the art.

(3) The critique of the artist-of-the-colossal in *Sophist* reminded us that *mimēsis* cannot be the straightforward mirroring of self-showing (*vide* Book Ten of *Republic*); nor does the use of iconography in the central books of *Republic* cause us to cherish the illusion that at some point images will be left behind forever and perfect self-showing attained.

(4) The botched icons and bitched generations and fabrications of Plato's *Timaeus* demonstrated the failure of all efforts to rescue presencing from becoming and transiency; the need to conjoin kinds, to interweave them, here found its most perfect parodic expression.

By this time—that of our fifth step—the futility of the question *What is likeness?* became apparent, and we undertook an approach to engrammatology by way of Plato's *Cratylus, Phaedrus,* and *Philebus,* remembering that *Theaetetus* describes the weaving of *eidē* in terms of *letters.* Yet it was far easier to say what such letters cannot be than to explain why an account of memory and reminiscence persistently has recourse to them. Our fifth step took us through a discussion of *logos* in *Theaetetus* as a hermeneutic of "proper difference" and even of *différance.* Yet that hermeneutic had less to do with syllables and letters as such than with typography—the imprinted memorial that would allow Socrates to remember Theaetetus and not to believe he was looking in a mirror. In waxing desperation we turned to *Cratylus,* where a kind of death knell of iconography sounded: an icon can never possess the same (*ta auta*) as that of which it is an icon, no matter what Timaeus' Demiurge may have dreamt; and the Stranger's dream of distinguishing sharply between the production of likenesses and the production of semblances also evanesced. We then turned to *Phaedrus,* which first invoked *hypomnēsis* not in order to disparage it but to laud it as devoted service to all the means of remembrance, service that conducts the philosophic soul to its fitting end—which is to be ever mindful of the divine. Only then did we proceed to the familiar condemnation of writing precisely as *hypomnēsis,* as "extrinsic" and "external" to the soul, that is, as disruptive of the soul's "sufficient presence to memory." We then asked about the relation of outside to inside, of absence to presence, and wondered whether the typography of memory—now taken in its full engrammatological import as the soul's own *writing,* which it can *read*—does not from the outset frustrate any such condemnation. The *typos* confounds outside and inside, absence and presence, from the very beginning. That is its brief. That is its cutting edge. And so it seems that writing is of memory and memory of writing before there is writing in the usual sense—since time immemorial, as it were.

These results will not be surprising to readers familiar with the early work of Jacques Derrida. In chapter 4 we will have occasion to take up the notions of *trace* and *arche-writing,* and the somewhat later notion of *dissemination,* seeing in them crucial implements for weaving a discourse on memory, reminiscence, and writing. Perhaps it is necessary to reinvent the Derridean wheel—and the loom and the verge—in order to be struck by the vast amount of time that had to elapse before engrammatology could flourish. If memory is of writing, why do Plato and Aristotle, askers of all the questions that need asking, fail to inquire into the essentially scriptural parentage of *typos, eikōn,* and *grammata?* Certainly the child's garden of graphics depicted in *Phaedrus* does not stake out such an inquiry. *Philebus* offers us tantalizing bits of such an investigation, as do *Theaetetus, Sophist,* and *Cratylus.* If the only way to weave forms with forms and forms with things is through the science of interconnections and intermedi-

ates, then the *means* and *mediation* of letters, their eminently mortal status in-
between, becomes crucial. The Derridean analysis of "good" and "bad" writing,
which we shall also take up in chapter 4, tells us what is essential here: as long as
the urge to separate soul from body prevails—interiority from exteriority, life
from death, spirit from sensuality, nourishment from offal, vociferation from the
gorge, speech from writing—and as long as Western metaphysics ignores Aristotle's warning and tries to remember or to conjure the divine banquet of the
soul's splendid isolation, no explicit engrammatology is possible. Schelling, who
resisted the urge to separate only to fall afoul of the tradition's insistence on an
ultimate and total scission (*die endliche gänzliche Scheidung*),[28] spins out the
dream in his *Stuttgarter Privatvorlesung* of 1810; and since it is a memorable
dream about memory by memory for memory   *Then the dark began to go
in smooth, bright shapes, like it always does, even when Caddy says that I have
been asleep*   I feel no compunction about reproducing it here. In the course
of his oneiric speculations on the afterlife, the life of the soul in splendid isolation, Schelling writes:

> One question is: What will it be like as regards the power of memory [*Erinnerungs-
> kraft*]? Remembrance will not of course extend to everything possible, inasmuch
> as a just man even here would give a great deal in order to be able to forget at the
> right time [*zur rechten Zeit vergessen zu können*]. There will be a kind of forgetful-
> ness, a Lethe, but with a different effect: when the good arrive there they will have
> forgetfulness of everything evil, and thus of all suffering and pain; the wicked, on
> the contrary, will have forgetfulness of everything good. And further, it will surely
> not be the power of memory we possess here; for here we must first *interiorize*
> everything [*alles* innerlich machen], whereas there everything *is* already interior.
> The phrase "power of memory" is much too weak to capture the sense. One says
> of a friend, a beloved with whom we were of one heart and one mind, that we
> remember them from within [or are inward with them: *man erinnere sich ihrer*];
> they live perpetually within us; they do not have to enter our heart of hearts
> [*Gemüth*]; they are already there. And thus will remembrance be in the afterlife.

You can always spot the Blessed: they are the ones with the complacent,
inane grins on their faces. It is of course the Damned who are more troublesome, like the Birds of Ignorance: because their power of remembrance has
nothing to which it can contrast its malevolence, because their remembrance is
either so interior that it too enjoys the intimacy of its beloved or so exterior
that no pain of dispossession can make the slightest impression on it, the
Damned sport precisely the same grin. *Il faut*   Carry Maury up the hill,
Versh   *imaginer Sisyphe heureux*.

Waxen Glands and Fleshy Hollows

The Body of Memory from Descartes to Merleau-Ponty

Plato's *Philebus* has implicated both *psykhē* and *sōma* body-and-soul in the graphics of memory. Earlier, *Theaetetus* devised a second model for memory beyond typography—the aviary—which was to account for memory and knowledge ostensibly without the action of the body, so that the space of the cage would be purely psychic, not somatic, space. The thoroughgoing mixture of body and soul in *Philebus* now finds support in a famous passage in *Cratylus* (400b 8–c 10) that has to do with the body, enclosure (as in a cage), and signification. The following passage will serve as our new point of departure:

> HERMOGENES: But what shall we say of the next word?
> SOCRATES: You mean *sōma* [body, *Körper*].
> HERMOGENES: Yes.
> SOCRATES: That may be variously interpreted, and still more variously if a little permutation is allowed. For some say that the body is the gravemound [*sēma, die Gräber*] of the soul, which is thought to be buried in the present now [*en tōi nyn paronti*]; or again, because the soul signals by means of signs through the body [400c 3: *dioti au toutōi* sēmainei *ha an* sēmainēi *hē* psykhē], it is rightly called the index [*sēma*: Schleiermacher translates *sēmainei* as *begreiflich machen*, *sēma* as *Greifer* and *Griffel*—the soul makes everything graspable, and so the *sēma* (gravemarker, memorial, monument) is the "grasper," "gripper," and *Griffel*, that is, a writing stylus made of slate, designed for slateboards, or a sketching pencil of some sort (from *grapheion*, instrument for writing, but with allusion to the Old High German *grifan, greifen*: "to grasp"]. Most likely the Orphic poets were the inventors of the name, because the soul for some reason is paying penalty and thus has this enclosure [*peribolon*], so that it may be preserved [*sōizetai*], which enclosure is the very image of a prison [*desmōtēriou eikona*]. And that is what the body is for the soul, until it has paid penalty, precisely as the name *sōma* implies [Schleiermacher translates, ingeniously, *der "Körper," ihr* Kerker], without our having to change a single letter [*hen gramma*].

Socrates' "etymology" of the word *body* (the quotation marks are necessary, inasmuch as this series of deductions may be as risible as those involving the soul, as Socrates himself concedes, and all of this more buffoonery than philosophy) begins and ends with that cairn or heap of stones which is the original crypt, both burial site and pathmarker, the earliest *herm*. The enclosures of crypt and prison that it opens up make room for *signification* as such. Strange tomb, curious prison! It "rescues" and "preserves" mortals as well as inhibits them; and it is only "by means of it" that the soul can signify with signs. If the original sign is a memorial or monument, we can expect that the whole question of memory, reminiscence, and writing will involve a hermeneutics of body and soul—as well as a meditation on mourning—as no other question will. And the *space* of the living body will not be so readily distinguishable from the space of the mourning soul, whatever Christian ontotheology may have hoped. The theme of the body of memory, and the body-space of memory, will take us from *Cratylus* and Augustine's *Confessions* to the classic art of mnemotechnic, and from thence to modernity, with its waxen glands— and fleshy hollows.

AUGUST MNEMOTECHNIC

On our way to modernity and the waxen glands of memory, we might tarry in the spaces that so fascinated and affrighted Augustine   *FROM THE FATHERS It was revealed to me that those things are good which yet are corrupted which neither if they were supremely good nor unless they were good could be corrupted. Ah, curse you! That's Saint Augustine*   and mnemotechnicians both before and after him.[1] We shall tarry as Augustine rushes through them ("And so I shall go on," *transibo ergo*) in his search of his lord and father, a search that in fact elaborates a written memorial to his mother—that formidable mother, that right mother, as Heidegger will say, in the garb of a woman but altogether virile in her faith (IX, 4 and 13). Augustine's passion to transcend ("I shall go beyond") the body and the "birdlime of concupiscence" that the mothersmilk of his faith threatens to become, his mad dash ("through all these do I scurry and flit," *discurro et volito*, X, 17) in search of the father who will deign to make him a eunuch for the sake of the kingdom of heaven (II, 2 and VIII, 1), is certainly germane to our theme— *Timaeus* has taught us that—but we shall merely linger in the spaces. They are many and vast, and Augustine's invocations of them awesome: *in campos et lata praetoria memoriae*, in the fields and spacious palaces of memory . . . *ubi sunt thesauri innumerabilium imaginum*, where are treasuries of numberless images . . . *de receptaculis . . . grandis memoriae recessus et . . . secreti atque ineffabiles sinus . . . aula ingenti . . . penetrale amplum et infinitum . . . remota interiore loco, non loco . . . et miris cellis . . . tan remota et retrusa quasi in cavis . . . quasi venter . . . de ventre cibus ruminando.* "Great is the power of memory, a terrifying thing it is, O my God, a profound and infinite multiplicity; and this is the soul, and this am I myself. So what am I, O my God? Of what nature am I? Various, manifold in its ways is this life, and staggeringly immense" (X, 17).

Augustine distinguishes three kinds of treasures hidden in the folds and sinuosities of memory, in the hope of stumbling across a fourth. Behold these caverns full of things generated (*rerum generibus*) through either (1) images, (2) self-presence, or (3) notions and notations. The first are the imprints of all corporeal things, all sensations, images (as Book XI, chapter 18 says) "implanted in the mind like vestiges as these things passed through the senses." Such vestiges or footprints we recognise as the *typoi* discussed in chapter 1: Augustine's ambulatory typography generates the first class (the lowest class) of objects in the mind. The second class (by no means second in order of rank, however) comprises the objects of all the arts and sciences, generated not by vestiges of preterite time but by *praesentia* as such. If the treasures we glean through study of the arts and sciences are vestiges of anything, then it is of eternity—*in aeterno . . . totum esse praesens* (cf. XI, 13: *celsitudine semper praesentis aeternitatis*). The genesis of such things generated in the mind is perforce mysterious, inasmuch as they are icons of ungenerated being: they occupy the time that "can no longer be divided into even the most minute parts of a moment," the time of the instantaneous *aleph* that has no space (XI, 15: *Praesens autem nullum habet spatium*). Presence in the spaces of memory is a presence that has no space: this is a further aspect of the mysteries of iconography and engrammatology, and we shall have to return to it. The third sort of being that is generated in memory (not at the top of the list, but certainly not at the bottom either) comprises the affections of the mind (*affectiones animi*); these are generated through *notiones vel notationes*. *Notio*, from *nosco*, "to get to know something," is of course the "notion" or "concept" of a thing. Yet Augustine immediately writes *vel notationes*, "or characters," that is, written marks incised on tablets of multicolored wax. The affections of the mind—by means of which I can remember in equanimity either joy or sadness—thus explicitly involve engrammatology. Augustine no doubt wants to resist the cutting engram and its ceraceous matrix, and stresses that these affections revert to a power that is *the mind's own*, "since the mind is one thing, and the body another" (X, 14). A certain "ridiculous simile" occurs to him, however, and he cannot resist noting it at least notionally: memory of the mind's affections is like "the belly of the mind," "ruminating without tasting." Such Augustinian rumination would disembowel the mind, just as the power to remember joy joylessly would core the heart, and just as the power to think a tune without moving tongue or lips would disgorge the voice from the throat.[2]

Yet any such radical distinction between memorious mind and body is impossible, for two related iconographic reasons. First, the *time* of the second class of objects (those of the arts and sciences) is strangely distended in such a way as to encompass all three kinds: future and past times have being and *are* only insofar as "wherever they are, they are not future or past *sed presentia*" (XI, 18). Thus there are three times, as it were, *praesens de praeteritis, praesens de praesentibus*, and *praesens de futuris*. All three times are in the soul, *in anima*, the third being "expectation," the second intuition, while the first is *memoria*. Yet we do not find three kinds of *praesens de praeteritis* corresponding to the three classes of objects generated in memory *per imagines, per praesentiam,* and *per notiones vel notationes.* Why not? Because being and presence are one. And why are being and presence one? Because there is no iconography *(per praesentiam)* without engrammatology *(per notiones vel notationes),* and no engrammatology without typography *(per imagines).*

Which brings us to the second reason for the impossibility of a radical distinction between reminiscent mind and the memorious body. Whenever past events are narrated truly, writes Augustine (XI, 18), it is not the things themselves that memory proffers, inasmuch as these are past, "but words conceived on the basis of the images of these things," *sed verba concepta ex imaginibus earum.* The *res ipsae,* as they pass through the senses, affix or imprint their verbal footprints or vestiges in the mind. The *verba concepta* are precisely *notiones vel notationes:* our notions are notations, marks of presence themselves present insofar as they have been typed in the soul by means of words. Iconography mediates typography and engrammatology, yet each of these two reverts to the other without cease. Just as the "I think" is an "I gather" *(cogito/ cogo),* precisely as a gathering into presence at hand (X, 11: *tamquam ad manum posita . . . quasi ad manum posita),* so are *notatio/notio* and *nosco/ noto* related. Notion is notation, knowing a noting, and noting (N.B.) an inscribing or imprinting. Of what? Of *verba concepta,* "words" (the third kind), conceived *ex imaginibus* or *per imagines* (the first kind), themselves vestiges of things past that are *present* (the second kind, which is more kin than kind: *per praesentiam, ad manum posita adesse).* Thus the inscribed image encroaches on the ostensibly pure presence of objects of the arts and sciences, as well as on the notions and names that affect the soul; encroaches on them because the *typos* marks and effects the presence of them all. In the far-flung fields and spacious quarters, the receptacles, recesses, and sinuses, the vast courts, ample and unending *ouvertures,* in the cells and in certain secret caves, in the glens and dens and caverns, the cubicles and sanctuaries, in the rumbling belly of the mind, there is nothing unmarked by time and space and linguistic signs. Which is why Augustine would actually be scandalized if he succeeded in finding the father lurking there, even though there is nowhere else for him to hide, "and I did not find you outside of memory" (X, 24). "But where do you lodge in my memory, lord, where do you abide? What sort of chamber have you fabricated for yourself? What kind of sanctuary have you constructed for yourself?" (25). "And so where did I find you? . . . Place there is none; we go backward, we go forward, but place there is none" (26).

Augustine wanders from place to place in search of signs. He finds himself caught up willy-nilly in the discourse of mnemotechnic, notes Frances Yates, even though he would like to banish this vain art, the orator's "art of memory," from his memorial.[3] Perhaps that art can serve our own inquiry as a kind of bridge, or staircase, from Greek antiquity to rationalist-empiricist modernity— or, to alter the image, as a metamorphosis of Socrates' waxen slab of the heart to Descartes' ceraceous pineal gland.

Mnemonics or mnemotechnic   *What a mnice old mness it all* *mnakes!*   has as its legendary sire the lyric poet and epigrammaticist Simonides of Chios (556–468 B.C.), although its known sources are all Latin: the pseudo-Ciceronic *Ad Herennium,* Cicero's *De oratore* and *De inventione,* and Quintilian's *Institutio oratoria. Ad Herennium* designates memory as the treasure-house (*thesaurus*) of inventions (20), a word that we recall in Plato and Augustine and that we shall find again later in Aquinas and in Locke.[4] Treasure-house of inventions? What sorts of inventions? Coins and coinages of one sort or another; or perhaps figurines or icons cast in a mold; all transformed now into rhetorical tropes or figures of speech. The fundamental strategy of mnemo-technic is   *I presume you shall have remembered what I will have taught you on that head? . . . Stop twirling your thumbs and have a good old thunk. See, you have forgotten. Exercise your mnemotechnic. La causa è santa. Tara. Tara. (aside) He will surely remember*   to memorize a sequence of places (*loci*) and to insert images (*imagines*) into them, visual images that are strikingly reminiscent of what is to be remembered. *Ad Herennium* calls them *formae, notae,* or *simulacra,* and compares their installation in the *loci* of memory to a kind of inner writing: " 'For the places are very much like wax tablets or papy-rus, the images like the letters, the arrangement and disposition of the images like the script, and the oral delivery is like reading' " (49–50). Further, it advises that the images be active, animated, vital, vivacious: *imagines agentes.* These agent images must be "novel" and "striking" if they are to be effective *typoi.* They must be highly visual, emotional, colorful, and dramatic: a street brawl *PRIVATE CARR (loosening his belt, shouts) I'll wring the neck of any fucking bastard says a word against my bleeding fucking king. . . . I'll do him in, so help me fucking Christ! I'll wring the bastard fucker's bleeding blasted fucking wind-pipe!*   would do nicely—"a striking scene in every sense of the word," Yates observes (25; 29). Such intense visualization indicates that mnemotechnic is bound up with both painting and poetry, as *Philebus* suggests: Plutarch attri-butes to Simonides the remark that painting is silent poetry, poetry painting that speaks (42–43). Perhaps the passage that most induces Yates (50) to align the classic art of memory to the general Greek model for memory, the wax slab, is Quintilian's confirmation of the equation *loci* = wax, *imagines* = letters *Fresh air helps memory. Or a lilt. Ahbeesee defeegee kelomen opeecue rustyouvee doubleyou*   in *Institutio oratoria XI,* ii, 32–33, a confirmation so strong that it tends to *replace* the equation altogether or *reduce* it to its original form. The student of rhetoric should, according to Quintilian (40), "learn a passage by heart from the same tablets on which he has committed it to writing. For he will have certain tracks to guide him in pursuit of memory, and the mind's eye will be fixed not merely on the pages on which the words were written but on the individual lines, and at times he will speak as though he were reading aloud. . . ." Hegel (see chapter 5, below) will not forget this key coun-sel   *On the doorstep he felt in his hip pocket for the latchkey. Not there. In the trousers I left off. Must get it*   of Quintilian's.

Not a word about the many mnemotechnic systems that confirm the en-grammatological tradition of "inner writing" in memory—Martianus Ca-pella's *De nuptius Philologiae et Mercurii* in the fifth century (64), Peter of

Ravenna's fifteenth-century *Phoenix, sive artificiosa memoria* (119ff.), or the Dominican mnemonic systems of Johannes Romberch and Cosmas Rossellius (122ff.)—nor any discussion of those Renaissance Neoplatonist transformations of mnemotechnic   *Mnemo?*   into an occult or hermetic
I say so. I say so. E'en so. Technic   science, such as Giulio Camillo's famous "memory theater," which has become so significant for contemporary architecture, or Ficino's translation of the *Corpus Hermeticum* (135ff.); nor, finally, even a hint of Lull's natural, material logic, or Giordano Bruno's encyclopedic mnemonics in *De umbris idearum . . . Ad internam scripturam* (199) and his invocation to memory in *Cena de le ceneri* (300: "And thou, Mnemosyne mine, who art hidden   *I could go home still: tram: something I forgot. Just to see: before: dressing. No. Here. No*   beneath the thirty seals and immured within the dark prison of the shadows of ideas, let me hear thy voice sounding in my ear"); but straight on into the seventeenth-century search for a method. Or, rather, at this point I shall abandon altogether Yates's account of the influence of the art of memory   *But the recipe is in the other trousers. O, and I forgot that latchkey too*   on the *ars combinatoria, characteristica,* and *calculus* of Bacon, Descartes, and Leibniz (35ff.), and proceed directly to Descartes' account of memory and recollection. For while the art of memory was keeping alive the engrammatological tradition of "inner writing," the "writing in the soul" of Plato and Aristotle, the typography of memory was preparing to reassert itself in a striking way.

DESCARTES

Descartes' various accounts of memory, when read in the sequence in which he wrote them, appear to take us farther and farther from typography, iconography, and engrammatology.[5] For his accounts of memory after the *Regulae* (ca. 1628) and the *Traité de l'Homme* (ca. 1633–34?) emphasize a *second* power of memory that would be housed in the understanding alone, an "intellectual memory" in isolation from the body. However, that second memory preserves traces of the first, very much as in the case of Augustine, and thus exhibits the typographic, iconographic, and engrammatological structures dominant since antiquity.

In Rule Three of the *Regulae ad directionem ingenii* (44–45/X, 369–70) Descartes concedes that a long chain of deductions can be held fixed in one mental gaze or act of intellective vision, so to speak, only if in some sense they are *remembered*. The danger of this concession is that it grants hostages—of full presence in intuition—to the fortunes of a weak and vacillating memory. His promulgation of *enumeratio*, by which we are able to run through the series of linked deductions again and again in order to make the linkages as present to our minds as possible, aims to counteract the otherwise doleful dependence on memory. Rule Seven (57–61/387–92) elaborates the practice of enumeration—which he here also calls *induction*—in some detail. Descartes reiterates the difficulty of recalling the entire route of a complex deduction, and reports:

> To remedy this I would run over them from time to time in one continuous movement of the imagination, so that while it was intuitively perceiving each thing it would pass on to the next; and this I would do until I had learned to pass from the first to the last so quickly that no stage in the process was left to the care of memory [*nullas memoriae partes reliquendo*], but I seemed to have the whole in intuition before me at the same time. This method both relieves memory, diminishing the sluggishness of our thinking [*ingenii . . . tarditas*], and enlarges our capacity of mind.

Descartes' example in Rule Seven is apt—perhaps a bit too apt: if I wish to make some deduction concerning all the classes of corporeal things, I can expect a long enumeration, whereas if I wish to prove that the rational soul is not in any way corporeal, "I do not need a complete enumeration." The method proves to be an ingenious (or ingenuous) corroboration of the matter—the nonmaterial matter of remembrance in the *ingenium*.

A further example of enumeration occurs in Rule Twelve (75/410–11), where the crucial issue of a (complete) inventory of the elements of cognition arises. Descartes' enumeration, which "appears" to him "to be complete and to omit nothing to which our human powers can apply," begins with the intuited *presence* of what is present, and proceeds to two derivative forms of cognition: "First, that which presents itself spontaneously [*id . . . quod sponte obvium est*]; secondly, how we learn one thing by means of another; and thirdly, what deductions one can draw from each thing." Presence dominates the hierarchy of cognition, and spontaneity founds the order and assures the success of enumeration.

Rule Eleven (73–75/407–10) reiterates the fact that the certitude of a complex deduction "depends to some extent on memory," and that *enumeratio* is therefore designed to reduce the role of memory in reasoning as much as possible: ". . . I pass so quickly from the first to the last that practically no step is left to the memory, and I seem to view the whole all at the same time." (One wonders of course what Socrates would have made of this oneiric "seem to"!) Meanwhile, Descartes proceeds to summarize the first part of his projected tripartite treatise in Rule Twelve (75–89/410–30), which provides a synoptic account of the four principal powers of the mind—understanding (*intellectus*), imagination, sensation, and memory. The account of sensation is a classic of typography. Descartes writes:

> Let us then conceive of the matter as follows: all our external senses . . . properly speaking perceive in virtue of passivity alone, precisely in the way that wax receives an imprinted figure [*figuram*] from a seal. And it should not be thought that all we mean to assert is an analogy between the two [*Neque hoc per analogiam dici putandum est*].

As far as sensation is concerned, typography is neither a model nor a metaphor, neither an allegory nor an analogy. The figure impressed is no mere figure of speech. Descartes forcefully excludes such shadows of presence. Typography is literal: "We ought to conceive [*sed plane concipiendum*] that the way in which the exterior figure of the sentient body is really modified by the object is entirely the same as the way in which the shape of the wax's surface is altered by the seal." "The exterior figure of the sentient body. . . ." Before any impression occurs, the sensing body has a figure, *is* a figure, a waxen figure that receives the imprint of *other* figures. And not merely "as it were."

The second stage in the cognitive process that Descartes is describing is the conveyance of the impressed figure of the object to the *sensus communis*. Yet the terms in which he portrays the conveyance shift slightly. Descartes now emphasizes the external sense's being moved or stimulated (*movetur*); it is in fact that movement which conveys the figure to the common sense faculty at the very instant of its impression. In the following way:

> It is in exactly the same manner that now, as I write, I recognize that at the very moment when the separate characters are being written down on the paper, not only is the lower part of the pen moved, but every motion in that part, no matter how slight, is simultaneously transmitted to the whole pen. All these diverse motions are traced in the air by the upper end of the pen, although I do not conceive of anything real passing [*etiamsi nihil reale . . . transmigrare concipiam*] from one extremity to the other. Now, who imagines that the connection between the different parts of the human body is slighter than that between the ends of a pen, and what simpler way of expressing this could be found?

Yet this simplest way, leading so quickly and effortlessly from typography to engrammatology, invoking the sympathetic motions of the verge itself, is perhaps too simple, too quick. There is something odd about the way it reverses the direction of its attention, from the characters traced in ink back up the quill to the tip of the feather, instead of proceeding in the direction of the inscription, advancing to the incision and thus exhibiting depth-through-the-matrice. At all events, the mysterious third stage of the cognitive process is now reached, whereby the figure of the body is both affirmed and denied—the stage of imagination and memory. Oddly, the text now reverses directions once again, from feathery engrammatology back to incisive typography:

> Thirdly, we must believe that the *sensus communis* has a function like that of a seal, impressing on the fancy [*phantasia*] or the imagination, as though on wax, those very figures and ideas that come uncontaminated [*puras*] and without bodily admixture [*et sine corpore*] from the external senses. Yet this fancy is a genuine part of the body [*veram partem corporis*], of sufficient size to allow its various parts to assume various figures distinct from one another, and to let those parts become accustomed to retaining the impressions for a considerable time. In the latter case we have what is called memory.

Memory retains over time the sense-impressions that are conveyed to the *phantasia*, which is thoroughly corporeal; the impressions themselves, however, are now purged of all corporeal admixture. A conundrum. Yet why does Descartes revert to the wax/signet model when describing the action of the *sensus communis* on the *phantasia,* thus abandoning the purer breezes stirred by the top tip of his quill? Surely, in order to rescue for imagination and—above all—for memory the *selfsameness* of the figures eventually remembered and those impressed on the surface of the exterior sensibility. The entire cognitive process would grind to a halt at the point where our assurance—our certitude—concerning the identity of the figures, the perfect efficiency of iconography, began to waver. Descartes now (in step four) reverts to the figure of the pen or quill, the figure of the verge, in order to show how airy fancy can itself influence the nerves and the senses, can itself reverse the direction of the movement; in so doing, he stresses that such reversal is independent of the power of reason. We shall soon follow him in that direction, but not before completing the series with the fifth step.

"Finally, fifthly, we must think that the power by which we are properly said to know things is purely spiritual, no less distinct from every part of the body than blood is from bone, or hand from eye." A troubling equation, or analogy of proportion, one that enumerates the noncorporeal nature of intellection in terms of two corporeal differences. That blood is bred in the bone   *What's bred in the bone cannot fail me to fly / And Olivet's breezy—Goodbye, now, goodbye!*   and that hand and eye are engaged in a long-standing contract—one hinted at by Descartes himself when he chooses to fix objects in the cognitive *gaze* with the cooperation of the writing *hand*—Descartes here ignores. Yet when he introduces the *ingenium,* seal and wax again come out on the table, this time however strictly by way of analogy in a looser sense, analogy as mere figure of speech:

> It [the mind] is a single entity [*unicamque esse*], whether it receives impressions from the common sense simultaneously with the fancy, or applies itself to those that are preserved in the memory, or forms new ones. . . . In all these operations this cognitive power is at one time passive, at another active, and resembles now the seal and now the wax. Yet the resemblance on this occasion is only one of analogy, for among corporeal things there is nothing wholly similar to this faculty.

Let us not pause to wonder about a single entity that can be passive as well as active, wax as well as seal, and which, although it constantly has to do with the wholly corporeal fancy, is itself wholly spiritual. And let us note only in passing that the resemblance by way of analogy—the analogy of the figure, the figure of the analogy—expresses itself in and as the very same typographic resemblance that earlier spurned analogy—the literal wax and seal, seal and wax. Let us abandon this early work of Descartes after noting one final use of writing in enumeration, a use that explicitly implicates memory.

Rule Sixteen (107–11/454–59) urges the researcher, who can attend to only one thing at a time, not to try to *remember* matters that do not require immediate attention; these matters, represented by highly abbreviated symbols (*per brevissimas notas*), are to be committed to paper as written notes. Writing thus serves as a substitute, and not merely as a supplement, for memory. Writing *by hand* rescues the mind's *eye* from excessive strain. For memory seems to be a power "created by nature for this very purpose," and writing is its corresponding art.

> But because this faculty [i.e., memory] is often unstable, and in order to obviate the necessity of expending any part of our attention in firming it up while we are engaged in other thoughts, the art of writing [*scribendi ars*] was most opportunely invented. Thanks to this resource [*cujus ope freti*], we confide nothing at all to memory, but, liberating our imagination to receive the ideas occupying us at present, we trace on paper [*in charta pingemus*] whatever ought to be preserved, employing the most abbreviated symbols. . . .

Although writing by hand corresponds to the mental power of memory, the highly abbreviated written note liberates the imagination and spurns the shaky reed of memory: ". . . we confide nothing at all to memory." And Descartes adduces the following lines several pages later, in the rule's penultimate paragraph: ". . . none of those things that do not require perpetual attention ought to be committed to memory if we can set them down on paper, lest any part of our mind be distracted from the object that is present to our thought by some superfluous recollection." If the invented art of writing is more a substitute for than a supplement of memory, it is because memory itself is a supplement of intuition, and intuition the putative interior (non)space of pure presence.[6]

In Descartes' correspondence a dozen years after the composition of the *Regulae* we find several detailed references to "intellectual memory."[7] Such a notion is in fact a natural development of the position in the *Regulae,* by which Descartes asserts the radical difference between cogitation and the complex of imagination, memory, and sensation. And it is fraught with all the difficulties of the initial position. In the letters of 1640 to Meyssonnier and *What was the name of that priesty looking chap was always squinting in when he passed? . . . Pen something. Pendennis? My memory is getting* Mersenne, Descartes admits that the seat of intellectual memory, the pineal gland—to which we shall soon wend our way—must somehow suffer those "convolutions" or "folds" that one finds on the cerebral surface, like figures impressed on a waxen surface. Such convolutions account for the mind's disposition to remember with the help of guidelines, tracks, or traces, which he here compares to folds in a sheet of paper. And yet any such convolutions or corrugations in the pineal gland or *conarium,* however necessary *What reminiscences temporarily corrugated his brow? Reminiscences of coincidences, truth stranger than fiction* to account for mnemic conservation and the anamnesic process, mar the surface of the gland: Descartes does not doubt that those who suffer the largest number of folds on the surface of the gland are the most dull-witted, bestial, bedazzled, and benumbed of humans (1067, 1070: *hébété, grossier*). Conservation of impressions inhibits the reception of new impressions, so that Descartes will have to worry about the conservation of the spirituality of this waxen gland or, in Véronique Fóti's apt words, "the virginal purity of the *conarium*" (76). Precisely how difficult the preservation of that purity will be Descartes indicates in these astonishing lines to

Mersenne (1071), which postulate not only an intellectual memory ensconced in the pineal gland but also a somewhat grosser sort of memory within the convolutions of the brain, a handy sort of memory located in the luthier's digits (cf. 1067), and also "what one might call *local memory* outside of us, in the manner that when we have read a particular book, not all the elements [*espèces*] that can help us to remember what is in it are in our brains; but that there are also several [such elements] in the paper of the particular copy we have read [*il y en a aussi plusieurs dans le papier de l'exemplaire que nous avons lu*]." The paper itself, on which *we* have written nothing, to which *we* have committed no sorts of reminders by way of abbreviated symbols, nonetheless possesses—as Quintilian well knew—*mémoire locale*. At this point, the point at which the power of memory is externalized beyond the outermost exterior of the sentient body, Descartes hastens to revert to "yet another memory" besides the one which "depends on the body," a memory "altogether intellectual, which depends on the soul alone" (1071; cf. 1083).

In his reply to "Hyperaspites" in August of 1641, Descartes recounts that process of corporeal memory by which "cerebral particles" produce "a trace" in the brain. Once that account has drawn to a close, he refrains from using the word *remember* at all when it comes to matters purely intellectual: *Des choses purement intellectuelles, il n'y a pas de souvenir à proprement parler. . . .* However, as Descartes will soon indicate, "properly speaking" is what we seldom do. He now (1131) predicates of those purely intellectual things the *timelessness* that would remove them utterly from the realm of memory, asserts it in backward fashion: ". . . but the first time that they [purely intellectual things] present themselves to the mind [*se présentent à l'esprit*] they are thought every bit as much as the second time [*aussi bien que la seconde*]." Yet that apparent *timelessness,* which seems   *I wanted then to have now concluded. . . .* *But tomorrow is a new day will be. Past was is today. What now is will then morrow as now was be past yester*   to allow us to confuse or conflate second and first presentations to the mind, immediately points back to a corporeal relation—that of language, of *names*. Intellectual things are "allied with certain names which, being corporeal, cause us to remember again [*ressouvenir*] the things themselves." Yet there would be much to say on this point, writes Descartes, and his letter is "not the place" for it. Oddly, Descartes employs the same abnegation in his 1644 *Principles* (I, 74, cf. 44), where it is a matter of discussing the relation of memory, speech (*parole*), and the human proclivity to error. It is apparently *never* in place to discuss language and names, even when memory reminds us of it constantly. We shall have to wait for Hegel's account of names in the "hierarchy of transition" from sensation to thought, considered in chapter 5, below. Yet we can bring this brief account of Descartes' even briefer accounts of "intellectual memory" to a close by considering his letter to Père Mesland, written on May 2, 1644.

After invoking the piece of wax and its impressed figures as his simile for the sole difference between the soul and its ideas—"I do not posit any other difference between the soul and its ideas than that between a piece of wax and the diverse impressions [*figures*] it can receive"—Descartes again attempts to elaborate his distinction   *Why was the chant arrested at the conclusion of this first distich? In consequence of defective mnemotechnic*   between bodily and spiritual memory (1164–5). Memory of material things depends on the "vestiges" (what Augustine knew—and left—as "footprints") these things leave in the brain; memory of intellectual things "depends on some other vestiges, which perdure in thought itself." The latter constitute an altogether distinct "genre," one that no comparison with corporeal beings in space can capture, as Descartes' letter demonstrates when it lets the remainder of the paragraph (on corporeal memory) hang suspended on the phrase *au lieu que:* ". . . whereas, contrariwise, the vestiges on the brain take it on themselves to move the soul in the same way that the brain had moved the soul previously, thus causing it to remember something; in altogether the same way that the folds in a piece of paper or linen cause them to be more readily folded the way they were folded earlier than if they never had been folded thus." Yet these curious references *volens nolens* back to corporeal memory, the inability of intellectual memory to express itself in any other way than parasitically, incarnately, should perhaps make us more willing to consider corporeal memory at greater length. Whereas Descartes' "mature philosophy" appears to disdain it, corporeal memory, as we shall see, has its own seductions.

Although the *Treatise on Man,* written in French, first appeared posthumously in 1664, Descartes had already formulated his thoughts on human physiology prior to the 1637 *Discourse on Method,* as he himself relates in a letter to Père Mersenne dated 23 November 1646. The fifth part of the *Discourse,* on "physical questions," bears many notable resemblances to the *Treatise.* Both betray a debt to William Harvey's inspired mechanics of general circulation, *De motu cordis* (1628–29), although   *A pump after all, pumping thousands of gallons of blood every day. One fine day it gets bunged up: and there you are. . . . Old rusty pumps: damn the thing else*   for Descartes the heart itself is not a pump but the kettle it had always been in traditional physiologies. Harvey's mechanics of circulation is present in full force, however: Descartes' favorite images for human physiology prove to be the artificial fountain, the mill, and the clock, with its weights and wheels, spindles and verge. Except that the body's organs themselves tend to be almost waxlike in substance: *Je suppose que le corps n'est autre chose qu'une statue ou machine de terre* (807/XI, 120).

The *Treatise,* most likely composed in 1633–34, remains incomplete, and yet its mechanical torso casts a shadow across the centuries to come—Malebranche was certainly not the last to be captivated by it. On its penultimate page Descartes writes, "Before I proceed to a description of the rational soul. . . ." Yet his automaton functioned so ingeniously *without* the contrivance of a rational soul   *The machines clanked in threefour time. Thump, thump, thump. Now if he got paralyzed there and no-one knew how to stop them they'd clank on and on the same, print it over and over and up and back. Monkeydoodle the whole thing. Want a cool head*   that most rational souls of the eighteenth, nineteenth, and twentieth centuries were perfectly willing to let the *Treatise* end where it in fact ends. In the body of Descartes' text, to be sure, some space is reserved for the rational soul, which is like the *fontenier* who sits at the place where all the pipes of the fountain meet, adjusting their valves to the tempo of royal *Water Music* (815/131). The rational soul, when it wills something (854/179), causes the gland to lean in this or that direction, or else it scans the surface of the gland, "considering" the forms and images that play on its surface (852/177). What truly inspires Descartes however is the vast repertory of activities in which the body can engage independently of *l'âme raisonnable*. The repertory opens with the circulation of the blood and the distribution of the animal spirits, and does not end even with acts of sense-perception, imagination, and memory. Nothing like a complete account is possible here, where it is simply a matter of tracing the typographic, iconographic, and engrammatological physiology of memory.[8]

There is one aspect of this "mechanical torso," the fragmentary text of Descartes' *Treatise on Man*, that one dare not overlook at the outset; namely, the fact that it is a *fiction*. The opening words of the text, *Ces hommes*, are in fact the first words of the eighteenth chapter of the text entitled *The World, or Treatise on Light*. The sixth chapter of that treatise begins as follows: "Permit your thought then to exit from this world awhile, in order to come to see another altogether novel world, which I shall bring to birth in its presence within imaginary spaces [*que je ferai naître en sa présence dans les espaces imaginaires*]" (AT, XI, 31). And the thirteenth chapter, on light, ends as follows: "Thus one must recognize that the men of this new world are of such a nature that when their eyes are pressed in such fashion . . . etc." (97). "These men" at the opening of the *Treatise on Man* are thus (in the words of Charles Adams and Paul Tannery) inhabitants "of this artificial world, which Descartes is constructing whole and entire in imaginary spaces, and not in the real world where we live" (iv). The text itself is therefore a kind of automaton, a simulacrum or icon of the "real" world in which "we" "live," a mere contrivance. Unless of course the real world for which Descartes was writing, the world of ecclesiastical and court authority, was itself a world fabricated of fictions, so that only a "fiction" could exercise the freedom of truth. Or of "truth." At all events, the text and its novel tale are mimes, reminiscences, icons, and hypomnesics rather than embodiments of the full presence of objects themselves in memory as such. It would be ironic if, as we begin to read the text, we forgot this cardinal (fictional) aspect.

The arteries that transport blood from the heart to the brain in "these men" divide off "into an infinity of tiny branches"; these branches or threads "compose" in some unexplained way nerve-fibers, "tissues stretched like tapestries at the base of the brain's convolutions." (These tapestries may be inspected in Descartes' Figure 24 [Plate 1], to the left of the letter G.) The most vital, forceful, and subtle parts of the blood are free to circulate among the "concavities" of the brain itself—for the brain is like a vast, multichambered cavern or mineshaft in the earth. There the particles of the blood yield "a

Fig. 24.

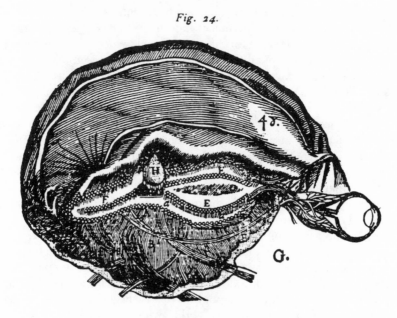

PLATE 1

certain quite subtle wind, or rather, a very lively and pure flame, to which the
name *animal spirits* has been given." The animal spirits, introduced in late
antiquity by Erasistratus of Chios, confirmed by Galen, and omnipresent until
Harvey, hovering ever in a state of agitation, "gather   *This morning the
remains of the late Mr. Patrick Dignam. Machines. Smash a man to atoms if
they got him caught. Rule the world today. His machineries are pegging away
too. Like these, got out of hand: fermenting*   about a certain tiny *gland*
situated at about the middle of the substance of the brain, at the very entrance
of its concavities." (It later proves to be important for Descartes' account that
the gland is slightly off-center, being positioned only at "about" the fulcrum of
the brain.)[9] Here a vast "network" of tubes enables the most subtle parts of the
blood, those containing the spirits, to flow *into* the pineal gland itself. The
gland (labelled *H* and visible in all the illustrations in Figures 27, 28, and 29
[Plate 2] may be imagined as "an abundant well-spring" *from* which the animal spirits are able to stream   *EXIT BLOOM Begone! he said. The
world is before you.—Back in no time, Mr. Bloom said, hurrying out*   to
all the portions of the brain. Itself the form of a flame, the *conarium* receives
and dispatches the tinier flames of the spirits in perpetual Pentecost. Having
arrived at the appropriate regions of the brain, the animal spirits penetrate the
pores of the brain's substance, passing from them into the nerve tubes and
thence to all the organs, limbs, and muscles of the body. The pores of the brain
are like "intervals" between adjacent threads of the cerebral tapestry. These
subtle spirits enter them, "always looking back at [or "facing": *regardant;* see

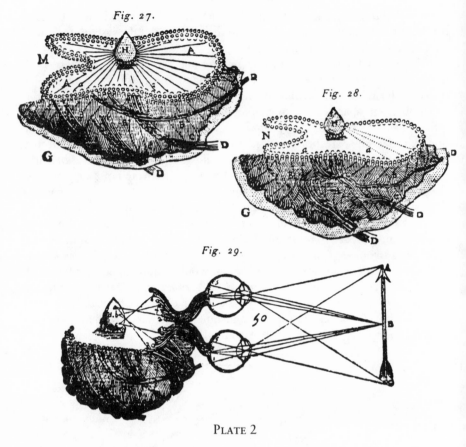

Fig. 27.

Fig. 28.

Fig. 29.

PLATE 2

844/170; cf. *regardent,* 851/176], the gland" which is their "source." They are "readily able to turn hither and thither toward the diverse points of this gland," Descartes assures us, although he does not explicitly relate what it is they are looking for or at. It is as though they were awaiting a signal of some kind, a somatic/semantic signal. Be that as it may, the "very delicate threads" of the tapestry, into whose interstices, pores, or intervals the spirits pour, converge, and interlace in the region labelled *B* (see Descartes' Figures 24 and 27 on Plates 1 and 2), where memory has its seat; the longer threads, along which the spirits wend their way, proceed to region *D,* nearer the exterior surface of the brain (see Figure 27), and pass from there to all the parts of the body.

At this point I should pause to observe that it is not always easy to link up or distinguish between Descartes' tubes and pores, avenues and intervals: the animal spirits threaten to evaporate into the entire inner space of the body.[10] It is as though Cartesian physiology were not careful enough about its intervals, as though a faithful graphic illustration of the system would look something like a staircase painting by Albers or Escher, or like a Gestaltist puzzle, where the lines ambiguously comprise both figure and ground. The importance of *interval* and *difference* in Cartesian physiology is not restricted to the pores of the brain tissue, however, but extends to the very core of the system, the pineal gland and its parties of animal spirits.

Gland *H* is the seat of both *imagination* and the *sensus communis.* Both faculties belong to the five "interior" sense faculties listed by Avicenna, which traditionally possess a peculiar power of discrimination, an ability to distinguish differences, as we saw in chapter 1. This *sensus communis,* which Aristotle calls the "common," "primary," "ultimate," or "master" perceptual power, orders the perceptions of the five senses precisely by "sensing that they are different" (*On the Soul,* 426a 14); it allows a creature to sense *that* it is sensing in general; supplies images for thought; senses the lapse of time; and presumably senses the differences among all these sensible activities. Aquinas (*Summa theologiae,* I, q.78 a.4 ad 1, 2) distinguishes the *sensus communis* from the *sensus proprius,* attributing to the former a peculiar kind of "discernment." The "proper" inner sense of any given exterior sense cannot differentiate among the objects of the various senses; neither vision nor taste is able to distinguish white from sweet, an ability that would require discernment or even cognition. "Thus it is necessary that a *discretionis iudicium* pertain to the common sense, to which are referred, as to a common term, all sensuous apprehensions," a referring that is handsomely illustrated by the figure from Reisch's *Margarita philosophiae* (see Plate 3).

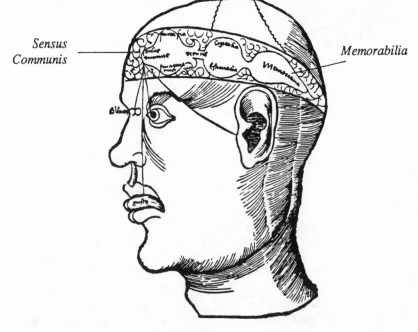

PLATE 3

Corresponding to its differentiating function, the pineal gland in Descartes' physiological system possesses a differentiated structure. It is composed of "very soft material," perhaps (as we might imagine) the consistency of wax in a very warm chamber; its material is not embedded firmly in the substance of the brain but is attached to it solely by delicate, pliable arteries. The force of the blood propelled through these arteries by the beat or heat of the heart holds the gland in approximate balance, like a flame dancing on a candlewick. The elastic arteries enable the gland to incline first in one direction, then another, 360° in a circle, spilling the animal spirits in the particular direction they are to pursue, toward this or that region of the brain (see Figures 27, Plate 2, and 25, Plate 4).

What actually causes the gland to tip in different directions? Descartes cites two causes in addition to the altogether mysterious influence of the rational soul, here bracketed from his account. The second is an exterior—albeit not extrinsic—cause, to wit, the action of objects imprinted on the senses in perception. The first is an intrinsic cause, that is, one that operates entirely within the

Fig. 25.

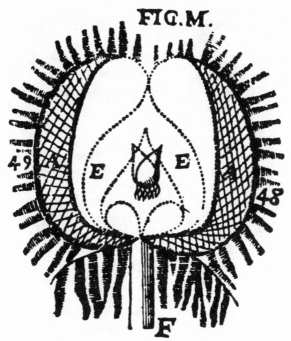

PLATE 4

circuitry of blood and brain, tube and interval; namely, the "difference" in force encountered among the parties of animal spirits bursting from the gland. The animal spirits, Descartes stresses, are "almost always different in some respect" (854–55/180). Difference—and I am tempted for the second time to write the word as differance in Derrida's sense, with a pineal a—dominates the system dynamically (in the hydraulic standing or leaning of the gland), topographically (in the gland's position slightly off-center as well as in the intervals among the threads of substance in the tapestry of the brain), and energetically (in the gradients of force empowering the animal spirits). The sheer distinction between internal and external causes implies the most striking difference of all, inasmuch as it enables gland H to be the seat of both imagination and the *sensus communis*. Nevertheless, sense-perception does win the upper hand in Descartes' mechanical system, for reasons inherent in the typographic dispositive itself. What "ordinarily" causes the gland to move is "the force of the object itself" on a given sense organ, the sense organ in turn "acting on" the apertures of the appropriate tubes leading to the brain. If these tubes may be compared to   *HOW A GREAT DAILY ORGAN IS TURNED OUT*
"the *porte-vent* in our church organs," then sensible objects in the external world are "like the organist's fingers" (841/165). The little man, the homunculus who normally serves as the mascot of the immanent rational principle, is now catapulted *outside* the body and the mind *into* the world where we live. (Presuming for a moment that Descartes' fiction has *something* to do with the world where we live.) The organist and fountaineer, the little man   *DIMIN-ISHED DIGITS PROVE TOO TITILLATING FOR FRISKY FRUMPS*
who now plays upon the sense organs of the body, is banished from the body's interiority, is marked and branded   *the one handled adulterer*   by the chronic practice of typography.

Vision may serve as an example. Objects strike (*frappent*)[11] the eye. More specifically, rays of light press upon selected points of the eyeball; they then "trace at the rear of the eye a figure that corresponds to the figure of the object" (see Figure 35, Plate 5 for this and the following stages). Sundry threads of optic nerve tissue transmit this figure to the brain tubes upon which the threads open and are thus "also able to trace the figure in the interior surface of the brain." At this juncture the animal spirits sally forth from those points of the gland that are inclined toward the tubes in question, that is to say, the points that "face" or "look at" the tubes toward which the gland is now leaning. Precisely when or how, by whom or by what, the gland is inclined remains unclear: at times Descartes describes the gland as inclining in a particular direction in order to cast the animal spirits to the proper region (854/179); at other times he describes the spirits' departure from the gland as a gratuitous "heading toward" the requisite tubes, their spontaneous egress "attracting" the gland, drawing it in their jetstream, as it were (863/188). Whatever the case, in sense-perception it is the object at hand (the organist's or fountaineer's hand) that initiates the motion of the spirits and the gland, via the sense organ and nerve tubes, until the animal spirits "trace a figure" corresponding to the

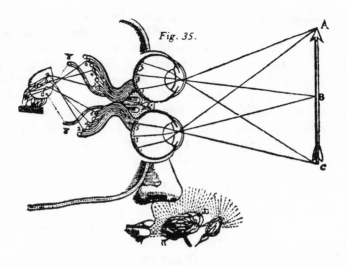

Fig. 35.

PLATE 5

figure at the rear of the eye, which is the figure of the object, onto the "interior surface" of the brain—that is, "on the surface of this gland." Sense-perception itself is thus multiple typography and iconography, and it ushers in a new kind of engrammatology.

We should pause a moment at this "interior surface," this outside-inside, that is the surface of *la petite glande*. Iconography is possible only through the maneuver of this impressive yet impossible interiorization. For the slab of wax must now produce an *inner* writing. It will not do simply to pass from the waxen slab to the inner spaces of the aviary and cavern. The slab itself must be transported to the inside; the *surface*, exposed to the roses and arrows of outrageous fortune, must now become an *inner* surface; only through such doubling or duplication of surfaces will iconography and engrammatology succeed. The little gland, so very reminiscent of a candle flame, is in fact the most porous of waxes, allowing the animal spirits ingress and egress, just as its surface was imported from outside to inside. The gland is in fact very much like the foetus in Mother Mnemosyne's womb, that most startling outside-inside, which Descartes here briefly invokes. Images perceived by the mother, because they are borne by the blood to all the parts of her body, may "sometimes" be impressed on the brain and the very limbs of the foetus "by certain actions of the mother" (852/177). Descartes declines to account for this iconography within the matrix, however, even though it promises to illumine a goodly portion of the mysteries of eternity and alterity; he "contents" himself with an account of how images "are impressed in the interior part of the brain marked B, which is the seat of *memory*."[12]

We shall follow Descartes' account in the direction of memory proper as soon as we remind ourselves of one further iconographic point. As in the texts of Aristotle, Plato, and Augustine, so here with Descartes, it is always a matter of the *présence des objets,* or rather, of the transference of that presence to the presence of their traces within us, which is a transference by blows. Descartes insists that imagination too, and not merely the presence of objects—and, to be sure, the rational soul as well—can effect the presence of ideas. Yet we shall see how iconography reverts to typography, regardless of the "several causes" Descartes wishes to reinstate. And if one should ask where the new kind of engrammatology has disappeared to in all this, I can only wonder whether it will emerge in Descartes' account of reminiscence. First, however, *memory.* Descartes writes:

> Think of it in the following way. After the spirits emerge from gland *H* (Figure 29), having received there the impression of some idea, they pass thence by the tubes 2, 4, 6, and tubes similar to them, into the pores or intervals among the tiny threads that compose this part *B* of the brain. The spirits have the power to enlarge these intervals somewhat and to bend and variously deploy the tiny threads they encounter on their paths, according to the diverse ways they move and the diverse apertures of the tubes along which they pass. The result is that the animal spirits trace there too the figures that correspond to those of the objects. They do not always do so here as easily or as perfectly at the first stroke as they do on the gland *H,* but little by little they get better and better, as long as their action is robust and long-lasting, or is reiterated several times. That prevents these figures from being readily erased, and conserves them there in such a way that by virtue of them the ideas that were formerly on the gland are able to take shape there once again long afterwards, without requiring the presence of the corresponding objects. And in this *memory* consists. (852/177–78)

It is clear that not only the sense organs, the tubes, and the gland receive impressions, but so also in some way do the animal spirits themselves. Whether the animal spirits are stamped passively, or whether they somehow actively *see* and *scan* the figure on the gland to which they always turn their gaze, as if awaiting a sign; whether in other words the animal spirits are more spectating spirit   *A typesetter brought him a limp galleypage. He began to check it silently. Mr. Bloom stood by, hearing the loud throbs of cranks, watching the silent typesetters at their cases*   than branded animal; whether the spirits *need* the gland at all   *the obedient reels feeding in huge webs of paper. Clank it. Clank it. Miles of it unreeled*   in order to see or to be impressed, inasmuch as they themselves have transmitted the figures there in the first place; whether the gland needs *them,* since it clearly has the impression in its possession—all these are arresting questions. The spirits' power to enlarge the intervals and to weave the threads into a picturesque tapestry is hardly surprising; what seems odd is that they should require these threads to work on, and that their tracings should not always succeed at the first stroke. Since they have already transmitted the figure from the sense organ to the gland, they are surely capable of remembering it well enough without weaving the threads, or well enough to weave them expertly. (Capable of *remembering* it! What am I saying?) The animal spirits in any case should prefer the gland as a medium, and stick with it, as it were, rather than messing about with the rest of the brain. Figures and images are easier to apply to the gland and more perfect in the execution. Higher quality wax. Less grit. *Why* the spirits should head for region B (not *how* they do so, since clearly they remember the way), and why they should toil away at their own artistic education, typtoing at it seven long years and more—these things too remain enigmatic. That the gland's future recollections depend on the images woven by animal spirits in the Ghobelin of memory is indisputable. Yet why the spiriting animal spirits should have to depend on the animal apparatus at all is not clear.

Descartes therefore illustrates. With an image. Not to be forgotten. He writes (853/178) that the animal spirits have the power "to form certain passages" in brain tissue "which remain open" after sensation has ceased. Even if these passages should close they leave "a certain disposition" in the slender threads of the brain by which the route can be reopened. (This "disposition" will return to trouble us later.) Descartes appeals to the image of *puncture* or *perforation* (see Figure 30, Plate 6), a particularly violent yet strikingly efficient form of typography. Even after the punch or stamp is removed —*Muchibus thankibus* the tiny holes in the stretched canvas drumhead perdure; or, if they seal over again, the canvas still bears stigmatic traces of the holes and a "disposition" to reopen them. There is doubtless something odd about this image, both its canvas and its punch. Canvas is normally used for painted portraits, such as Franz Hals's likeness of the haughty philosopher, or for *objets d'art* of some kind. Yet here a punctuated pattern appears, not exactly a paint-by-numbers canvas guaranteeing a standardized image, but something very much like it: a sort of child's sewing

Fig. 30.

PLATE 6

card. Or do the holes indicate that this model for memory is a kind of sieve? A sieve, Socrates would have said, for milking billy goats.

Let us now scan the entire series of figures reproduced in Plates 1–6, unless we already remember them well enough: the highly complex threads, tissues, and tubes of the brain, the pineal flame at its heart, the enthroned gland bowing regally in all directions to its court; the flame now like the bud of a bursting thistle, the *conarium* in dehiscence; the almondshaped flame pondering whether to sniff roses or take the measure of an arrow; the gland, having made up its mind, now all eyes (and memory) for the arrow; and finally, as though the arrow had sown dragonseed, the punch, the punch to the brain. Note the graceful hand that wields it as though it were a verge. Are these the fountaineer's or organist's digits? Digits of external objects? Digits of the gland? Or is it the laced cuff of the animal spirits themselves? Perhaps it is the gentle hand of   *MEMORABLE BATTLES RECALLED*   Plato, winning by subversion and irony the Battle of the Ancients and Moderns? In any case, the hand manipulates the instrument that *impresses* or *inscribes* mnemic images on the brain. The problem of the *retrieval* of those images nonetheless remains. How do we get from the holes back to the stamp? How do we get from the stamp to the presence-at-hand of the hand itself, in order to beat it to the punch, as it were? How does Descartes account for reminiscence and recall?

In the *Treatise on Man* accidental or involuntary recall alone receives treatment; recollection as such, as we shall see later, is taken up in article 42 of the later *Treatise on the Passions of the Soul*. Gratuitous or involuntary recall, dependent on neither the rational soul nor external objects, occurs as follows:

> For the rest, it must be said that when gland   *K.M.R.I.*   H leans to one side, due solely to the force of the spirits, without the rational soul or the external senses contributing to its motion, the ideas that take shape on its surface proceed not only from the inequalities encountered among the small particles [or "groups": *parties*] of these spirits—inequalities that cause the differences among the humors, as was said above—but also from the impressions of the memory. For if the figure of a particular object is impressed much more distinctly than any other at the region of the brain toward which the gland now happens to be leaning, then the spirits that are headed there cannot fail to receive the impression. It is in this way that things past occasionally return in thought as if by accident, without the memory of them being excited by any object that touches the senses.

Here the spirits' egress from the gland—an exodus that is always differential in its ejaculatory force—causes the gland to incline toward the memorial region. There the spirits that (for whatever reason) tend toward this part of the brain receive an impression. And here Descartes' account ends. Yet it must be that the animal spirits *return* to the gland—unless their looking back to it can communicate telepathically, televisually—in order to transmit to it the received mnemic image. And why did the spirits sally forth from the gland in the first place? They were clearly on their way somewhere   *Wait. . . . Remember. . . . I am almosting it*   when archaic impressions distracted them and then sent them on their way with useless baggage. Gratuitous remembering is the animal spirits' forgetting what they are about. Such oblivion leads Descartes   *in order to exercise mnemotechnic . . . he remembered by mnemotechnic*   quite naturally to castigate those people who daydream and allow their fancy to wander nonchalantly through the halls of memory; they absorb impressions higgledy-piggledy in the palimpsest of their minds, in this way producing all the monsters that populate myth and legend. Waxen glands, for all the marvels they produce, are prone to moral turpitude, lassitude, lethargy, and benumbment.

Descartes now reverts to the theme of "disposition," reaching that point in his account where the *supplementary* or *substitutive* nature of the typographic apparatus—which is both essential to and superfluous for Descartes' account—compels far larger questions, questions of anthropology and ontology. We cannot stay to elaborate them, but let us at least read the following passage, perhaps the most disarming of a disarming treatise:

> Yet the effect of memory that seems to me most worthy of consideration here consists in this: even if there be no soul in this machine [*sans qu'il y ait aucune âme dans cette machine*], it [this machine] can [*peut*] naturally be disposed to imitate all the movements that true men, or rather, other similar machines, will make in its presence.

It is a particular *effect of memory* that informs the Cartesian anthropology, at least in the *Traité de l'Homme*, as such. Which effect? The effect of *mimēsis*. The production of an imitation so iconographically perfect   *Nightmare from which you will never awake*   that the difference between true human beings and automatons can be reduced to an *ou bien:* true men, "or rather," other *machines semblables.* The sameness or similarity of the other machines rests on that "natural disposition" toward imitation in them all.[13] The iconography of memory is hence not limited in its effects: it stamps machine and man alike, banishing the soul to the subjunctive mood of mere hypothesis, provided only that the movements to be imitated occur in the machine's presence, *en sa présence.* It is not the apparatus of memory that succumbs to the logic of the supplement but *the soul itself*—and those idols of the soul, the animal *spirits,* who although they *try* to read and speak   *Sllt. The nethermost deck of the first machine jogged forward its flyboard with sllt the first batch of quirefolded papers. Sllt. Almost human the way it sllt to call attention. Doing its level best to speak. That door too sllt creaking, asking to be shut. Everything speaks in its own way. Sllt*   are themselves mere instruments of waxen *mimēsis.*

We therefore dare not close before reintroducing the rational soul and voluntary memory by grace of article 42 of the *Treatise on the Passions of the Soul,* where there may be, we speculated, some hope of encountering engrammatology. No doubt we shall reintroduce the rational soul, the scanner of icons and reader of signs, only to be compelled to bid it adieu once and for all.

Art. 42. *How we find in our souls the things we want to remember.*
Thus when the soul wants [*veut*] to remember something, the will causes the

gland—by inclining successively to different sides—to thrust [*pousse*] the spirits toward different parts of the brain, until they come across [*rencontrent*] that part where it finds the traces left there by the object it wants to remember. For these traces are nothing other than this, that the pores of the brain, by which the spirits have formerly followed their course because of the presence of this object [i.e. *présence* in some former, actual sense-perception], have by that means acquired a greater facility than the others in being opened once more in the same way by the spirits that approach them. Thus the spirits, coming in contact with these pores, enter into them more easily than into the others, by which means they excite a particular movement in the gland, which represents the same object to the soul and causes it to know that this is what it wanted to remember.

There is some reason to wonder whether the soul is not indeed the mere supplement of a powerful mimetic operation over which it has no control. How does the soul cause the gland to lean? Does not the differential ejaculation of the animal spirits function sufficiently as a cause? And are not these spirits themselves wholly at the mercy of the distended pores over whose disposition to *be* differentially open the spirits have no say? How do the animal spirits "excite" the gland telepathically? What interior or exterior surface *of* the gland (—does it have an interior surface? does any surface of the body become interior? does mimesis achieve the miracle of an outside become inside?) can receive a *typos* or *engram* for the soul's spectation, its scanning or gleaning, when the soul itself is sitting *in* the gland? Finally, must we not say that there is something topsy-turvy about all this? If the will wills to remember, why does it cause   *Poor, poor, poor Pyrrhus*   the gland to spill in all directions? Because the will does not know what it wants to remember. Why does the gland—which ought to know better—allow itself to be bullied? Because it does not know   *Pyrrhus, sir? Pyrrhus, a pier*   what the will wills to remember. Why do the spirits run amok, hoping for the encounter of their dreams but ready to fall   *Yes, yes. They went under. Pyrrhus, wished by an oracle, made a last attempt to retrieve the fortunes of Greece*   into any pores that will gape for them? Because they do not know what the will wills to remember. Why must the news of their random movements, their tumbling into intervals, when conveyed back to the gland, retrace the representation of the absent object? Because the animal spirits still do not know and they never will know, even when they are fully present to the traces of the remembered objects, what the will wills to remember. It is the gland that will read their frenetic motions and re-present them—the same gland that helplessly tipped and spilled its contents an instant ago. And now all these inept automatic creatures who live their lives backwards   *He stayed in his walk to watch a typesetter neatly distributing type. Reads it backwards first. Quickly he does it. Must require some practice that. mangiD kcirtaP. Poor papa with his haggadah book reading backwards with his finger to me*   will "cause" the soul "to know" what it "wills" to "remember." The soul now joins the ranks of all these mechanical stumblebunnies. Presumably it is now content. But in the rough and tumble it marks the waxen pallor of its once lambent flesh.

HOBBES AND LOCKE

Away then from these Continental confusions! Away to England, which is less bemused, more sober and stern, though every bit as faithful to the ancient lessons of typography, iconography, and engrammatology. Away then once more to Shandy Hall:

> Pray, Sir, in all the reading which you have ever read, did you ever read such a book as Locke's *Essay upon the Human Understanding?* – Don't answer me rashly – because many, I know, quote the book, who have not read it, – and many have read it who understand it not; – if either of these is your case, as I write to instruct, I will tell you in three words what the book is. – It is a history. – A history! of who? what? where? when? Don't hurry yourself. – It is a history-book, Sir, (which may possibly recommend it to the world) of what passes in a man's own mind; and if you will say so much of the book, and no more, believe me, you will cut no contemptible figure in a metaphysic circle.
>
> But this by the way.
>
> Now if you will venture to go along with me, and look down into the bottom of this matter, it will be found that the cause of obscurity and confusion, in the mind of man, is threefold.
>
> Dull organs, dear Sir, in the first place. Secondly, slight and transient impressions made by objects when the said organs are not dull. And, thirdly, a memory like unto a sieve, not able to retain what is has received. – Call down Dolly your chamber-maid, and I will give you my cap and bell along with it, if I make not this matter so plain that Dolly herself should understand it as well as Malebranch. – When Dolly has indited her epistle to Robin, and has thrust her arm into the bottom of her pocket hanging by her right side; – take that opportunity to recollect that the organs and faculties of perception, can, by nothing in this world, be so aptly typified and explained as by that one thing which Dolly's hand is in search of. – Your organs are not so dull that I should inform you – 'tis an inch, Sir, of red seal-wax.
>
> When this is melted and dropped upon the letter, if Dolly fumbles too long for her thimble, till the wax is over hardened, it will not receive the mark of her thimble from the usual impulse which was wont to imprint it. Very well: If Dolly's wax, for want of better, is bees-wax, or of a temper too soft – though it may receive, – it will not hold the impression, how hard soever Dolly thrusts against it; and last of all, supposing the wax good, and eke the thimble, but applied thereto in careless haste, as her Mistress rings the bell; – in any one of these three cases, the print, left by the thimble, will be as unlike the prototype as a brass-jack.[14]

When Descartes surrenders his second lump of wax to Locke, the wax of the second of his *Meditations,* surrenders it because it fails to retain any imprint and because he can think just as well or ill without it, the great English philosopher holds it once again to the firelight of reason, feeling the Softness and Warmth of its secondary properties. Locke need not employ the wax after the crude manner of Socrates; by now the slab of wax has itself become the very stamp and sign of cognition. Everywhere in the *Essay Concerning Human Understanding*[15] we encounter impressions—*Ideas* imprinted or stamped on the soul either by sensation or reflection. To be sure, the typography is more attentuated than it used to be. For example, the understanding "deepens" a child's impressions concerning the operations of its own mind (II, 1, §8), and it is difficult to see how such reflexive "deepening" could occur by mere punctilious repetition of the imprinting action. Further, even straightforward perception itself requires that impressions "reach" the mind and "be taken notice of within" (II, 9, §3). One wonders whether such "notice" depends on *notio* or *notatio* in Augustine's sense, or on Aristotelian *theōrein*, the very "scanning" or "reading" of a *typos* as an engrammatological *eikōn*. Whatever the case, neither the sense organs alone nor the combined apparatus of neural conduits and animal spirits can account for perception. Impressions—better, impulses— must be conveyed from without "to their Audience in the Brain, the mind's Presence-room (as I may call it)" (II, 3, §1). "Audience": the royal reception wherein the mind deigns to hear and entertain the suits of its subjects. "Presence-room": the chamber or receptacle occupied by the monarch who will read, scan, or in some other way heed all other beings that attain to presence, *parousia*.

There is much however in the *Essay* that will not jibe with our tristrapaedic notions of British Empiricism, and this is nowhere more striking than in Locke's treatment of memory and retention. Precisely why it is that the *Essay* here achieves its profoundest pathos—there are passages on memory and retention which despite Locke's proscription of eloquence are little short of threnody—I am unable to say. Memory is second in importance to perception in an intellectual creature; yet its mysteries elevate it to the very highest rank as an object of inquiry. The principal enigma remains the Aristotelian-Platonic-Augustinian aporia of the presence of what is past or absent; the principal image of mnemic space remains the neo-Hellenic and medieval *thesaurus* or treasury-house. "*This is Memory,*" writes Locke, "which is as it were the Storehouse of our *Ideas.*" He continues:

> For the narrow Mind of Man, not being capable of having many *Ideas* under View and Consideration at once, it was necessary to have a Repository, to lay up those *Ideas,* which at another time it might have use of. But our *Ideas* being nothing, but actual Perceptions in the Mind, which cease to be any thing, when there is no perception of them, this *laying up* of our *Ideas* in the Repository of the Memory, signifies no more but this, that the Mind has a Power, in many cases, to revive Perceptions, which it has once had, with this additional Perception annexed to them, that it has had them before. And in this Sense it is, that our *Ideas* are said to be in our Memories, when indeed, they are actually no where, but only there is an ability in the Mind, when it will, to revive them again; and as it were paint them anew on it self, though some with more, some with less difficulty; some more lively, and others more obscurely.

Memory serves as a repository for ideas that have ceased to be anything, a storehouse whose stores are nothing stored nowhere. *Loco, non loco.* Call it then a faculty or power in the mind to revive perceptions, to limn them anew (typography as restoration of old monuments) and then tag them, date them, by means of a second perception. Such restorations vary in degree of successful execution. Some are "more lively" than others, the revivification or restitution to living presence achieving or being achieved by a higher degree of verisimilitude. Verisimilitude? To what should the restoration—which, after all, is each time a novel construction—approximate? Apparently memory *is* a storehouse, not simply of lackluster copies, but of originals? Thus, in modern guise, the Aristotelian dilemma of the present *pathos* and *typos* of a past and absent being. Yet even if we were to grant Locke that   *At the housesteps of the 4th of the equidifferent uneven numbers, number 7 Eccles Street, he inserted his hand mechanically into the back pocket of his trousers to obtain his latchkey*   memory is more construction than conservation, and so engage ourselves to the project that has shaped much of the history of empirical psychological research into memory, will we be content to say that memory is an ability in the mind "when it will" to revive memories? Is Locke himself so certain of his voluntarism? Let us recall   *Was it there? It was in the corresponding pocket of the trousers which he had worn on the day but one preceding. Why was he doubly irritated? Because he had forgotten and because he remembered that he had reminded himself twice not to forget*   the key "pathetic" passage in the *Essay,* of which Sterne's sieve is a ludic reminder. Locke reflects (II, 10 §4) on the difference in the degree of perdurance of memories and on the universal tendency of impressions to fade. Some impressions are produced in the senses only once; others, though produced repeatedly, fall on a heedless or distracted mind, "as in Men, intent only on one thing, not setting the stamp deep into itself." Bodily illness occasionally debilitates the mind, which then has not the strength to hold impressions. "In all these cases, *Ideas* in the Mind quickly fade, and often vanish quite out of the Understanding, leaving no more footsteps or remaining Characters of themselves, than Shadows do flying over Fields of Corn; and the Mind is void of them, as if they had never been there." Total effacement of vestiges of the past, eradication of entire periods of one's own history, is therefore eminently possible. Echoing footsteps that leave no prints, reverberating to silence; clouds and birds flitting over the landscape as shadows, never alighting. Decay of impressions, argues Locke, is in fact the rule:

> The Memory in some Men, 'tis true, is very tenacious, even to a Miracle: But yet there seems to be a constant decay of all our *Ideas,* even of those which are struck deepest, and in Minds the most retentive; so that if they be not sometimes renewed by repeated Exercise of the Senses, or Reflection on those kind of Objects, which at first occasioned them, the Print wears out, and at last there remains nothing to be seen. Thus, the *Ideas,* as well as Children, of our Youth, often die before us: And our Minds represent to us those Tombs, to which we are approaching; where though the Brass and Marble remain, yet the Inscriptions are effaced by time, and the Imagery moulders away. *The Pictures drawn in our Minds, are laid in fading Colours;* and if not sometimes refreshed, vanish and disappear. How much the Constitution of our Bodies, and the make of our animal Spirits, are concerned in this; and whether the Temper of the Brain make this difference, that in some it retains the Characters drawn on it like Marble, in others like Free-stone, and in

others little better than Sand, I shall not here enquire, though it may seem probable, that the Constitution of the Body does sometimes influence the Memory; since
we oftentimes find a Disease quite strip the Mind of all its *Ideas,* and the flames of
a Fever, in a few days, calcine all those Images to dust and confusion, which seem'd
to be as lasting, as if graved in marble. (§5)

The miracle of memory, resurrecting the past and rescuing it from the
ravages of time and death, pales before a decay against which even print proves
helpless; the deaths of our children, the irreversible evanescence of our own
youth; Ralph Waldo Emerson burying in quick succession his wife Ellen, his
brother Charles, his son Waldo; the mind itself   *The least differences in
intellect are immeasurable. This beloved and now departed Boy, this Image in
every part beautiful, how he expands in his dimensions in this fond Memory to
the dimensions of Nature!*   looming as a tombstone without inscription
or graven symbol, devoid of letters and images; the final irony of the ancient
sōma-sēma, the body as tomb and engraved sign, subtly altered in that all the
once legible tracings are effaced. Even marble tombstone—the most durable of
waxes, one would think, the most heavenly material for glands—burns   *I
comprehend nothing of this fact but its bitterness. Explanation I have
none, . . . only oblivion*   to calcareous ash. Even the hardiest of memories
reduces, as Locke writes, "to dust and   *Rudy!*   confusion."

As Locke proceeds to discuss active reminiscence (§6) his text exhibits a kind
of upswing; yet the more sober and even somber tone soon reasserts itself.
Memory *can* retain certain ideas, namely, "those that are *oftenest refreshed,*" the
putative "original Qualities of Bodies" such as solidity, extension, figure, and so
on. Reminiscence, which is not so much *painting* the ideas anew as *viewing* them
again, although engrammatological viewing means *reviving* them, whatever
such typographic revivification can mean, Locke describes as follows:

§7. In this secondary Perception, as I may so call it, or viewing again the *Ideas,*
that are lodg'd *in* the *Memory, the Mind is oftentimes more than barely passive,*
the appearance of those dormant Pictures, depending sometimes on the Will. The
Mind very often sets it self on work in search of some hidden *Idea,* and turns, as it
were, the Eye of the Soul upon it; though sometimes too they start up in our Minds
of their own accord, and offer themselves to the Understanding; and very often are
rouzed and tumbled out of their dark Cells, into open Day-light, by some turbulent
and tempestuous Passion; our Affections bringing *Ideas* to our Memory, which
had otherwise lain quiet and unregarded. This farther is to be observed, concerning
Ideas lodg'd in the Memory, and upon occasion revived by the Mind, that they are
not only (as the Word *revive* imports) none of them new ones; but also that the
Mind takes notice of them, as of a former Impression, and renews its acquaintance
with them, as with *Ideas* it had known before. So that though *Ideas* formerly
imprinted are not all constantly in view, yet in remembrance they are constantly
known to be such, as have been formerly imprinted, *i.e.* in view, and taken notice
of before by the Understanding.

Mind then may be more than merely passive, may assert itself in a willful
search, setting itself to work by turning its inner eye—the escutcheon of spirit

having as its armorial bearing *Esprits animaux en regardant*—toward some hidden memory. Locke anticipates that the hidden memory has always already been unearthed, so that the eye can shine upon it; he presupposes that the search for an *arkhē kinēseōs* and the whole series of movements of presencing that Aristotle took pains to describe have always already taken place. At all events, active reminiscence is given short shrift in Locke's account. For a kind of passive, second-order perception now asserts its rights. Occasionally remembrances emerge "of their own accord," as though they had a mind of their own. Often our passions or affections rouse them. And in each case, Locke concludes, now following Aristotle quite closely, reminiscences give or show themselves as ideas that "have been formerly imprinted." Indeed remembrance "constantly knows" the pastness of its memories, even when such memories have long been forgotten, long been unknown.

Sections 8 and 9 of the *Essay*, to which I shall refer only in passing, demonstrate the importance of memory "in an intellectual Creature," but also its precariousness. We may lose ideas completely to oblivion, or not find them quickly enough when we need them, the second defect proving almost as crippling as the first. And in Locke's view there is no "intellectual memory" that could conveniently cancel time and make each intellection the first of its kind, its virginity renewed by some mysterious lustration. Indeed, his account ends by ascertaining a third defect of memory, if a fate can be called a defect. Whereas God and his angelic hosts can be present to "the whole Scene" at once, mortals—as Hölderlin's Empedocles discovers—are fettered by the law of succession. Even Blaise Pascal, that "prodigy of parts" and monster of memory, who, "till the decay of his health had impaired his memory, . . . forgot nothing of what he had done, read, or thought in any part of his rational Age," was condemned to the straits of succession. Whereas the angels may enjoy "one Picture" encompassing all their past knowledge, a capacity that would be "no small advantage to the knowledge of a thinking Man," human beings confront the inevitable dispersion of their knowledge in sundry spaces and times. However, even though we doubtless share memory with the lower animals, who remember in virtue of "traces in their Brains" (§10), and even though the advantage of having everything present in one picture seems almost palpable, there is something in Locke's account that is so resolutely and unabashedly mortal that one wonders whether the disadvantages of the seraphic "one Picture" were not every bit as palpable to him. How would a prodigy not merely of Parts but of the Whole fare? Locke will not have had the advantage of being able to recall Luis Borges' Ireneo Funes—"Funes el memorioso" (1942)—and yet he may have anticipated something of Funes' fate. Which is, one must say, bound to be funereal. A prodigious memory is perhaps a prodigal memory, Locke suggests in his remarks on language:

> But it is beyond the Power of humane Capacity to frame and retain distinct *Ideas* of all the particular Things we meet with: every Bird, and Beast Men saw; every Tree, and Plant, that affected the Senses, could not find a place in the most

capacious Understanding. If it be looked on, as an instance of a prodigious Memory, That some Generals have been able to call every Soldier in their Army, by his proper Name: We may easily find a Reason, why Men have never attempted to give Names to each Sheep in their Flock, or Crow that flies over their heads; much less to call every Leaf of Plants, or Grain of Sand that came in their way, by a peculiar Name. (III, 3, §2, cf. 1, §3)

The memorious general is of course Cyrus of Persia, as reported in Pliny's *Natural History,* the very book that Funes is studying at the moment of his collapse. Funes' fall and subsequent paralysis   *la inmovilidad era un precio minimo*   embody the condition of his mind, burdened now by implacable perception and memory   *esa rapsodia de voces inconexas . . . , el vertiginoso mundo de Funes . . . , la presion de una realidad tan infatigable.*   Unable to gather his perceptions, unable to *think*—that is to say, as Nietzsche reminds us in "On Truth and Lie in a Nonmoral Sense," unable to *forget differences*—Funes describes his condition to the narrator of the tale in three remarks that rise in a crescendo of fatal self-understanding:

> He told me: *I alone possess more memories than all human beings have had since the world became the world.* And also: *My dreams are like the wakefulness of the rest of you.* And also, toward dawn: *My memory, sir, is like a garbage-dump.*

Having no power to resist the incessant hammering of the world, no capacity to parry the blows of numberless *typoi,* Funes is less an immortal than a pummeled witness of mortality. Unto his own predictable end, which we might telescope in the following extracts:

> His own face in the mirror, his own hands, each time they surprised him. Swift relates that the emperor of Lilliput discerned the movement of the sweep hand; Funes discerned continually the silent advances of corruption, of cavities, of fatigue. He noted everywhere the progress of death, of humidity. He was the solitary and lucid spectator of a world that was multiform, instantaneous, and all but intolerably precise. . . .
> Ireneo Funes dies in 1889 of pulmonary congestion.

These hardly triumphant accounts of memory in Locke and Borges, emphasizing mortality and decay, should perhaps induce us to remember Hobbes—for whom memory is *decayed sense.* Recollection of Locke's great predecessor reveals that Sterne's satire of the sealing wax is perhaps better directed at him. Sensation, imagination, and memory all move within Hobbes's Galilean universe, move within what we might think of as modern, not Hebraic, "Galilean turbulence." For sensation   *What? Where? I can't remember anything. I remember only ideas and sensations*   in Hobbes is in fact highly reminiscent of the state of nature, which is a state of siege. External bodies "press" upon the appropriate sense organs and, through the network of the nerves, penetrate to the citadel of heart and brain. Having well-nigh breached the walls, the external body "causeth there a resistance, or counter-pressure, or endeavour of the heart, to deliver itself."[16] Because the endeavor to resist presses outward, as though to expel the invader, "it seemeth to be some matter without." "And this *seeming,* or *fancy,* is that which men call *Sense.*" Neither the body nor the soul is therefore actually comparable to a slab of wax, since the erstwhile signet-ring is now merely brandished as a mailed fist and makes its impressions through action at a distance   *He rushes towards Stephen, fist outstretched*   on cowed flesh. One is reminded of Kafka's *In der Strafkolonie,* although the Hobbesian pummeling produces no excruciating incision or script, no legible law, and only makes us see stars. Such bruising yet ethereal impressions are caused by "divers motions," several of which Hobbes now enumerates: "And as pressing, rubbing, or striking the Eye, makes us fancy a light; and pressing the Eare, produceth a dinne; so do the bodies also we see, or hear, produce the same by their strong, though unobserved, action." We are reminded too of Democritean *antitypia,* although the   *SOPHIST WALLOPS HAUGHTY HELEN SQUARE ON PROBOSCIS. SPARTANS GNASH MOLARS. ITHACANS VOW PEN IS CHAMP*   action in Hobbes seems even more violent than in the world of the Greek. Typography has become bombardment. Even after the external object is removed and the all-clear siren wails, the motions induced in us continue, "as we see in the water, though the wind cease, the waves give not over rowling for a long time after" (I, 2). Hobbes defines *imagination* as this "decaying sense," especially when the word *sense* (which is *fancy*) is emphasized. "But when we would express the *decay,* and signifie that the Sense is fading, old, and past, it is called *Memory.*" Imagination and memory "are but one thing, which for divers considerations hath divers names." Thus Hobbes appears to demolish the ancient aporia of memory, that figment of "Aristotelity," inasmuch as only memory's *reference* to the past and to absence plays a role in his account, not the *presence* of that reference. At the same time, all activity, scanning, reading, and regarding seem to have ceased in the inertial world of external motion; all is passivity; all resistance is eventual acceptance of inflicted punishment, as body and mind suffer at the hands of whatever in the belligerent world places them under siege.

However, a less violent typographic simile emerges in Hobbes's third chapter, on "Mentall Discourse," a simile we would have to call engrammatological, no matter how unadorned it seems. "All Fancies are Motions within us," Hobbes begins, in a familiar vein, "reliques of those made in the Sense." These motions of imagination and memory proceed in the precise *order* they had in sensation. They do so by virtue of the "coherence of the matter moved, in such manner, as water upon a plain Table is drawn which way any one part of it is guided by the finger." The power of this icon in Hobbes's text—the finger drawing water in a rivulet across a smooth tabletop—establishes the plausibility of the explanation while simultaneously concealing the engrammatological problem. The lines of Hobbes's own text work on the limpid, lymphoid reader by capillary action and cohesive attraction: they induce in the reader the obedient motion of all the water that ever spilled on tabletop, so that all he or she can do is adhere and follow. It is as though Hobbes were introducing the typographer's mark called "the fist" or "index", the fist   ☞

to pummel the reader with Hobbesian motion and the index ☞ to draw and fix the reader's attention—much in the way Sterne uses the fist or index in *Tristram Shandy* (II, 12) to draw the reader's attention to the gentle humanity of Uncle Toby, the Military Man, Knight of the Mailed Fist, who would not hurt a fly. Yet Hobbes's icon also effectively suppresses the question as to how spilled water can be read and retraced back to our earlier experience. No use reading over spilled water. That such mnemic motions must be *read* is clear from Hobbes's own remarks on "Speech" in chapter four. He begins with an iconographic regress from *Printing,* which, "though ingenious," is "no great matter," through *Letters,* which are a "profitable Invention for continuing the memory of time past," to *Speech,* "consisting of *Names* or *Appellations,* and their Connexion," which is assuredly divine in origin. Hobbes's interpretation of letters is in the classical grammatological tradition that we shall be discussing in chapter 4, inextricably tied to the mnemotechnic and anamnesic traditions. Not only do the letters in some general way "continue" the memory of time past by monumentalizing it; they are our way to remember "the divers motions of the Tongue, Palat, Lips, and other organs of Speech." "Divers motions," as though tongue, lips, and larynx were themselves external bodies pressing on the heart and brain, mimicking sensation and sense. The letters, reminiscent of the motions of the organs of speech, enact at a second level, mimetically, remembrance of decaying sense.

Most intriguing in Hobbes, as in Locke (see *Essay* II, 2, §2ff.) is the iconographic and engrammatological interpretation of speech itself. The "first use of names" or appellations, writes Hobbes (I, 4), "is to serve for *Marks,* or *Notes* [recall Augustine's *notio/notatio*] of remembrance." Locke (*Essay,* III, 2, §1–2) calls spoken words "sensible Marks of *Ideas*" which function for "the Assistance of their own Memory" or "*for the recording of our own thoughts* for the *help* of our Memories, whereby, as it were, we talk to our selves . . ." (9, §2). For both Hobbes and Locke, *spoken* names are *written* records, that is, memorials or monuments lodged or erected in memory. Memory is linguistic through and through; moreover, it is scriptural, as though spoken names were, prior to all speech, a kind of originary writing. Yet since the motions of the organs of speech are somehow reminiscent of the motions induced in us by the world of (fancied) invading external bodies, motions that unerringly produce the index of sense, the full sense of Hobbesian memory is engrammatological. What remains unclear is the relation of those two levels of motion—speech and sensation—between which memory is caught. The metaphor of motion, or the motion of *metapherein,* from state of siege to index on tabletop, receives no further treatment in *Leviathan,* since metaphor for Hobbes, as for Locke, is an abuse of speech. Hobbes excoriates metaphor with the help of a brilliant simile: "Metaphors, and senseless and ambiguous words, are like *ignes fatui;*[17] and reasoning upon them, is wandering amongst innumerable absurdities; and their end, contention, and sedition, or contempt" (I, 5). Hobbes therefore chooses Perspicuous Words, transparent terms, those that submit to calculation and accountancy (= *ratio*). Yet to insist on submission, on the capitulation of language, is to forget the motions of both fist and index, both the Galilean world and words. The world of Galilean turbulence is too busy warding off attack to be mindful of the provenance of such a *ratio:* its modernity consists in what a much later thinker will call "the high-velocity expulsion of Mnemosyne," inasmuch as "modern man . . . puts all his stock into forgetting as quickly as possible."[18]

COLERIDGE, ERWIN STRAUS, AND MERLEAU-PONTY

It would be possible to trace in detail the typography, iconography, and engrammatology of memory from Descartes, Hobbes, and Locke through La Mettrie, Holbach, and David Hartley into the mechanistic and epiphenomenalist philosophies of the nineteenth and twentieth centuries, up to our own day. Possible, yet time-and-space-consuming.

Hume's *Enquiry Concerning Human Understanding* (1748) and *Treatise on Human Nature* (1739), while doubtless philosophical milestones in their own right, would only corroborate the iconographic and typographic traditions.[19] (Coleridge tells of his surprise at finding how reminiscent *Hume's* account of association is of *Aquinas's* commentary on *Aristotle's* treatise on memory in the *Parva naturalia.* He then tells us of the discovery in Hume's library of a copy of the *Parva naturalia* "swathed and swaddled" inside a copy of Aquinas's commentary! A story that suggests in scullery-maid fashion the continuity of ancient typography, iconography, and engrammatology.) In the *Enquiry* (II, 11) Hume argues that memory can "mimic" and "copy" perceptions, although neither memory nor imagination achieves "such a pitch of vivacity" as even the dullest perception attains. In the earlier *Treatise* (I, 1, §1) Hume appears to adopt wholeheartedly the typographic model for impressions of "all our sensations, passions and emotions, as they make their first appearance in the soul"; yet he later (I, 3, §5) insists that the "ultimate cause" of impressions must remain an open question. At all events, memory (I, 1, §3) "repeats our impressions" in such a way that the resulting object is "somewhat intermediate betwixt an impression and an idea"; if an idea, then one that is considerably more "lively and strong" than any idea of the imagination. "When we remember a past event, the idea of it flows in upon the mind in a forcible manner; whereas in the imagination the perception is faint and languid, and cannot without difficulty be preserv'd by the mind steddy and uniform for any considerable time" (9). A second difference is of course that memory "is in a manner ty'd down" to the *order* of the original perceptions in a way that imagination is not. Indeed, Hume calls it the "chief exercise of the memory" to preserve the "order and position" of the simple ideas. The *engrammatological* character of memory, that is, the relation of impressions to those "marks" of spoken or written language, appears to be considerably less present in Hume than in his forebears—a fact that might be of importance for Hume's scepticism.

Perhaps two reminders by way of indirection and opposition will compensate for the lack of any further detailed historical tracings—first, Coleridge's refutation in his *Biographia literaria* of David Hartley's "associationism" and then in more recent times Erwin Straus's and Maurice Merleau-Ponty's criticisms of the prevailing neurophysiological models for both perception and memory. Each of these, and certainly all of them taken together, will push the engrammatological question to the point where the dominant models for memory will find themselves on the verge of collapse. In the following chapter we shall find Freud occupying that very verge.

Coleridge replies to David Hartley's *Observations on Man* (1749) in the fifth and sixth chapters of his *Biographia literaria* (1817).[20] In the tradition extending from Locke and Boyle to Joseph Priestley, Hartley had developed an intriguing alloy of mechanistic psychology and deistic philosophy. Both of his principal psychological and philosophical themes, sense perception and the "association of ideas," appealed to "vibrations" and "vibratiuncles" in the medulla oblongata as their ultimate explanatory point of reference. While embracing Malebranche's "occasionalism" and Leibniz's "preestablished harmony," thus avoiding the full consequences   *Wait. Five months. Molecules all change. I am other I now*   of the mechanist philosophy, Hartley had nonetheless attempted to explain all the operations of the mind in terms of these mechanical vibrations. Coleridge was in fact an admirer of Hartley's—he had named his first child, born in 1796, David Hartley Coleridge—while resisting the mechanistic tendency of all his mentor's ideas. In the fifth chapter of his *Biographia literaria* Coleridge inveighs against Hartley's Hobbesian and Cartesian background and takes up the banner of Aristotle's theory of association as developed in *On the Soul* and *On Memory and Reminiscence*. Aristotle's theory, Coleridge affirms, makes no use of "particles propagating motion like billiard balls" or "nervous or animal spirits . . . that etch and re-etch engravings on the brain." Such mechanistic models do not rank as hypotheses; they are not mere "suppositions"; they are rather "suffictions," *hypopoiēseis*. Fictions superimposed or foisted on the phenomena, on what Coleridge calls "the circumstances of *life.*" Fictions beyond the Cartesian fiction. "From a hundred possible confutations," writes Coleridge (166–67), "let one suffice."

> According to this system the idea or vibration *a* from the external object A becomes associable with the idea or vibration *m* from the external object M, because the oscillation *a* propagated itself so as to re-produce the oscillation *m*. But the original impression from M was essentially different from the impression [derived from] A: unless therefore different causes may produce the same effect, the vibration *a* could never produce the vibration *m:* and this therefore could never be the means, by which *a* and *m* are associated. To understand this, the attentive reader need only be reminded, that the ideas are themselves, in Hartley's system, nothing more than their appropriate configurative vibrations. It is a mere delusion of the fancy to conceive the pre-existence of the ideas, in any chain of association, as so many differently coloured billiard-balls in contact, so that when an object, the billiard-stick, strikes the first or white ball, the same motion propagates itself

through the red, green, blue and black, and sets the whole in motion. No! we must [i.e., would have to] suppose the very same force, which *constitutes* the white ball, to *constitute* the red or black; or the idea of a circle to *constitute* the idea of a triangle; which is impossible.

Coleridge now proceeds from Hartley's theory of association to the neural mechanism undergirding it. He rejects forthwith the vocabulary of "habits" and "dispositions" in questions concerning the nerves, however unavoidable that vocabulary becomes whenever we try to relate mechanistic theory to everyday experience, to "the circumstances of *life*." The "nerve" itself, far from supplying an Archimedian point for psychology, proves to be *Archimedes. I have it! My memory's not so bad* a fiction. Coleridge compares the "nerve" (and one must wonder whether the situation would change at all if he spoke of "neural states," much beloved in contemporary analytical philosophical discussions) to "the flint which the wag placed in the pot as the first ingredient of his stone-broth, requiring only salt, turnips, and mutton, for the remainder!" Even if we grant the existence of atomic nerves, however, two alternatives emerge. Either the nerve is restricted to one vibration, one idea, in which case the "propagation" required by association creates an anarchical situation of purely arbitrary concatenations; or the nerve is capable of several vibrations, and it becomes impossible to say why at any given time precisely this or that vibration is preferred to the others. Were the mechanistic psychology of associationism true, Coleridge concludes, "our whole life would be divided between the despotism of outward impressions, and that of senseless and passive memory." The lordly law of mechanical association "would itself be the slave of chances" (171).

Coleridge's critique of psychophysical mechanism is one of the grandparents of contemporary phenomenological and "humanistic" psychological critiques. Both are unmistakably of the lineage of German Idealism, which never succumbed to the allures of the machine *But I, entelechy, form of forms, am I by memory because under everchanging forms* and which preferred to cultivate links with ancient Greek, Cabalistic, and Gnostic thought. Both of these traits are clearly visible in Maurice Merleau-Ponty's and Erwin Straus's phenomenological critiques of mechanistic neurophysiology—if only because the neurophysiologies to which they are responding are themselves direct descendants of Hartley's, Hobbes's, and Descartes' mechanistic conceptions of sensation and memory. Before taking up their critical analyses, we should therefore try briefly to characterize contemporary neurophysiology as a culmination of the typographic and iconographic tradition, a tradition that founders in the rough seas of ancient engrammatological problems.

The neurophysiologist tries to determine what sorts of biochemical changes occur in and among the neurons of the brain during various stages of the memory process. His or her guiding question is how perceptual experience is consolidated and conserved, whether by means of "traces" or "engrams" in the cerebral cortex, by "reverberating circuits" of neurons there, or by "protein synthesis" (through RNA) within individual neurons supported by surrounding glia cells. No one can gainsay the advances made in the technical penetration of the neuron and its molecular constituents. Even where results are disputed (as in transfer-of-training studies, in which injections of RNA or homogenate extracts of brain tissue from trained animals seem sometimes, though not consistently, to transmit learning to untrained ones), the insights gained are impressive. Whatever criticisms follow, the fact remains that neurophysiology has helped to demonstrate in a convincing way that the rememberer—like the painter of whom Valéry and Merleau-Ponty speak—always "takes his body with him" when he remembers. How that living, working body is to be described remains the bedeviling problem.[21]

Merleau-Ponty's criticism of reflex theory, worked out almost fifty years ago in *La structure du comportement*, to a surprising extent still applies to neurophysiological research into memory phenomena—with some minor qualifications. For example, it would have been impossible fifty years ago to hear a researcher assert that behavior theorists "all seem agreed" that the two principal elements of the classical reflex arc, stimulus and response, are to be regarded as "inextricably tied together," viewed as "two continuously interacting factors in a continuous process."[22] Whether contemporary neurophysiology always remembers this self-imposed limitation is doubtful, however, since in practice it usually begins by asserting the existence of "an" electrical impulse leaping from the axon of one neuron to the dendrites of another. A second area where progress in conception seems to have been made, although again its impact on laboratory practice seems doubtful, is that of "localization." Neurophysiologists today are more receptive to the notions of "structure" and "form" with regard to the central sector of the nervous system, and are likely to consider strict localization of functions in specific parts of the brain more a trap than an itinerary for research.[23] Nevertheless, Merleau-Ponty's description in *La structure du comportement* (22) of neurophysiology's general approach to the organism remains all too relevant in the case of current research into memory:

> The functioning of the organism is analyzed by proceeding from the periphery to the center; nerve phenomena are conceived on the model of discrete stimulations which are received at the surface of the organism; the discontinuity of these sensory terminations is extended into the interior of the nervous system, so much so that the functioning is finally represented as a mosaic of autonomous processes which interfere with and correct each other.

To be sure, neurophysiology no longer relies exclusively on the models of classical physics and mechanics in the tradition of La Mettrie's *Homme machine* (1748) and Descartes' *Traité de l'Homme*, models which, at the time Merleau-Ponty wrote, were already "obsolete" thanks to quantum mechanics and relativity theory. To what extent the notions of separate sectors of space and time, atomic units of matter, and linear causality through contiguity persist in neurophysiological theory and practice remains a disturbing question—

hence the quotation marks or "scare-quotes" around the word "obsolete." The prevailing models nowadays are those of data-processing (information theory, feedback mechanisms, cybernetics), artificial intelligence, cognitive science, electronics technology, and, strange though it may sound, business management. The seventeenth- and eighteenth-century French and English models have been superseded by twentieth-century American ones. No matter what their nationality, researchers tend to define memory in terms of "registration" or "encoding," "retention" or "storage," and "retrieval." Just as an earthquake "registers" (typographically) on the Richter Scale, so are "selected sensory data" that have been reduced (iconographically) to a "code" registered (engrammatologically) in the nervous system. Such encoded data are "filed and stored for later use." Finally, and most mysteriously, "we" can rummage through those files in response to a "call" for "specific information," read or scan their contents (engrammatology reverting to iconography translating back to typography), retrieve what "we" are looking for, and (presumably) lay it on the desk of the Chairperson of the Board of Directors of the Mind. (If my readers should think it accidental that the model of office management is employed throughout neurophysiological research, let them apply to any government agency or to industry for funds to carry on such research: the predominance of the business model reflects the omnipresence of business investment in all contemporary scientific research; and any account that would neglect altogether the social-critical aspects of such research regresses to the status of what Marx called "German Ideology.") With respect to the processes of encoding and storing these novel mnemic icons in the brain, models of electronics technology and data-processing take over. The ten to twelve billion neurons of the human brain and the network of over 4×10^{12} synaptic connections among them are described as a "wiring pattern." (Transistorized circuitry and microchip technology will of course already have made all talk of "wiring" obsolete.) Then a theoretical attempt is made, regressing to classical physics, to reduce each neuron, or at least each synapse between the axon and dendrites of any two neurons, or at the very least one chemical transmitter in the vesicles of the dendrites, to the reception of only one type of "electrical nerve impulse." To explain various "patterns" of memory, as of perception, some sort of "interaction" among the atomic units is then postulated.

It is important to stress the imaginative character of such hypotheses based on models built on metaphors incised on wax tablets—less hypotheses, as Coleridge insisted, than *hypopoiēseis,* "suffictions"—and to identify the places where such a constellation appears to answer questions that the research itself cannot even properly pose. For instance, the path of impulses that effect perception of light—forgetting for a moment that the eye directs itself towards the reception of such impulses, so that all talk of "effecting" is really a subterfuge—has been traced as far as the sensory cortex of the brain. At that point even the simplest neural impulse vanishes into what researchers with a taste for classical literature call "the labyrinth," those with a more highly developed culinary sense, "a mass of spaghetti." Needless to say, the paths of

the sundry impulses that must be postulated in cases of higher-order perception, thought, imagination, and memory are even less penetrable. The lack of
direct or even indirect observation by means of electron microscopy, micropho-
tography, and so on does not prevent the neurophysiologist from assuming that
the "encoding" process depends on two factors: *which* synapses transmit the
impulses, and *how much* activation occurs. In other words, specific localization and quantification remain the typtopical guidelines for research even when
new models and metaphors appear to replace the old, when the wax turns to
steel, plastic, or silicon. Nevertheless, the nature of neural activation, the type
of circuitry established among neurons, and the kind of change instituted
within the neuron or in the glia cells remain unsolved mysteries. One wishes
that the candor shown by researcher K. S. Lashley back in 1950 were more
common among neurophysiologists in our own day of public-relations opti-
mism: after reviewing the neurophysiological evidence for memory, Lashley
(cited by Pribram: 7) concluded that memory was really quite impossible. If we
focus now on the engrammatological phase of recall or "retrieval," where the
enigma of memory and reminiscence comes to the fore, we may be inclined to
agree with him.

For the model of memory based on the conception of typographic sensation, starting at the periphery of the nervous system (with receptors being
activated by some sort of external stimulation) and moving toward the cerebral
cortex (on the heels of electrical impulses), the phenomenon of recall—the fact
that I *can* remember—is the most riddlesome of all. Because the model functions on the basis of external stimulation, the researcher must appeal to an
invasion by similar or identical electrical impulses in order to account for
retrieval. Thus in D. O. Hebb's model for memory the "reverberating circuit"
(shades of Hartleyan "vibratiuncles" and Hobbesian "rowling waves"!) of any
given memory-content is declared to be "self-exciting" and closed; nevertheless, the circuit is set in motion typo-iconographically by the influx of identical
or at least similar sensory data. Everyday experience does of course provide
instances of such remembrance triggered by sensation. The night Joe Christmas
breaks into Miss Burden's kitchen and locates by smell and touch a bowl of
food which he then begins to bolt down, the combination of smell, touch, and
taste induces in him remembrance of his puritanical stepfather:

> *I'll know it in a minute, I have eaten it before, somewhere. In a minute I will* memory
> clicking knowing *I see I see I more than see hear I hear I see my head bent I hear the
> monotonous dogmatic voice which I believe will never cease going on and on forever
> and peeping I see the indomitable bullet head the clean blunt beard they too bent and
> I thinking How can he be so nothungry and I smelling my mouth and tongue
> weeping the hot salt of waiting my eyes tasting the hot steam from the dish.* "It's
> peas," he said, aloud. "For sweet Jesus. Field peas cooked with molasses."[24]

And yet to say that recall always depends upon sensory input is to deny what
our experience also shows; namely, that Joe *can* think back to that indomitable
bullet head even in the absence of field peas. Neither he nor we are wholly at

the mercy of external stimuli when we remember. However, because the power of revery or reminiscence to bring those images back is inconceivable in terms of the prevailing model, the phenomenon is shunted aside in favor of what ostensibly can be more easily explained. Pribram's admission that the customary model for memory consolidation and storage possesses "no satisfactory mechanism for information retrieval" is surely correct. Moreover, it exposes the bankruptcy of his own appeal to "computer programming" (61).

The difficulty in conceptualizing recall or retrieval, in accounting for mnemic *output* rather than neural *input,* arises from the dilemma we observed at the heart of the Cartesian account of memory. Descartes' theory of "memory traces"—that is his term, we remember, so that it is no recent invention—and the neurophysiology descended directly from that theory presuppose what they wish to explain as "retrieval." That is the basic lesson of the critical portions of Merleau-Ponty's phenomenology of perceptual behavior, and it is a lesson that would bear repeating in a phenomenology of memory.[25] An implication for our pursuit of the sciences is that conceptual models often confound research at the very point when they appear to be most helpful, since they have a way of suggesting that research already knows what it has not yet even properly asked. The neurophysiologist says that after sensory experience has been registered, encoded in the neurons, and stored in the filing cabinets of the cerebral cortex, "we" can, upon demand, search for and retrieve the desired information. Who desires and demands? Who is the Chairperson of the Board? Who serves as his or her retrieving "we"?

In his contiguous papers on "Remembering and Infantile Amnesia" and "Memory Traces,"[26] Erwin Straus insistently poses the question of the "we" who read or scan the engrams. At least initially there is no question of altering in any fundamental way the terms of the traditional engrammatological aporia: "The trope of the engram belongs, it seems, to the archetype of interpretation" (59). Among Straus's objections to the trope is one that restates the Aristotelian aporia, which Straus later identifies as "the fundamental problem" of a phenomenology of memory (62, 77). It involves the mysterious co-presence in the mind of *typos* and *eikōn*—in modern dress:

> In fact, how could a memory image welded to a trace represent anything of the past? At the moment of sensory stimulation the impression was actual; with the activation of a trace, a memory image should become actual; impression and image each has its own particular place on the line of physical time. This certainly poses a formidable problem to any theory of traces: an engram, though generated in the past, functions in the present; and, in accordance with the theory, the corresponding memory image must be present. Taken in isolation, an engram cannot represent another thing. Belonging exclusively to the present, it cannot represent the past.

We shall in a moment confront the related problems of the time-line and representation, the latter of course to be taken quite literally as the problem of re-presentation. Straus provides two striking images of the typographic neurophysiology of memory: it is as though goods were being stored in a warehouse, or guests lodged in a metropolitan hotel, without anyone "keeping a record" of what, who, or where they are (63). What is missing from such accounts is a certain ill-defined yet irrefragable "continuity" in the personal existence of the one doing or suffering the remembering; what is missing is the "nexus" that Heidegger (after Dilthey) and Merleau-Ponty (after Heidegger) called the *Zusammenhang des Lebens*. (See chapter 6, below.) The continuity, cohesion, or coherence of a life, according to Straus, resides in the capacity for a gleaning or gathering, perhaps a very general sort of *reading*. And yet in "the modern interpretation of the engram," from Hobbes to the present, "the reader is eliminated" (77). In the "dynamic trace theory" of Hobbes, our awareness of the past is reduced to a passing sensation; the *of* in the phrase "awareness *of* the past" is now a purely subjective genitive, and the remembered qualities are soon to become "secondary qualities."

In his critique of contemporary neurophysiological trace theory—a theory more miraculous than the story of Lazarus's resurrection   *Knocking them all up out of their graves. Come forth, Lazarus! And he came fifth and lost the job*   inasmuch as it purports to be a description of natural events—Straus (96) distinguishes three stages. First, a trace or engram, defined as "the more or less lasting alteration of the nervous tissue," is engraved or impressed. Second, in preparation for the eventual reawakening of the trace, the trace itself is placed in cold storage and thus made to disappear: "What has happened is undone." Third, the impression is struck once again in retrieval, the trace drawn once more. In this "magical physiology," the cycle of engrammatological miracles goes on ceaselessly. It is perhaps the second phase, however, the temporary obfuscation of the trace (which Straus compares to a footprint in the snow, a "vestige" in the literal Augustinian sense), that is most miraculous.

> However one may imagine the reactivation of a trace, it can only begin to have effect where the impression had ended, i.e., to stay with the example of the foot-print, deep at the bottom of the impression. A trace, from the physiological or physical point of view, cannot return to the starting position by itself. . . . Its reactivation needed a preparatory process by which the "more or less lasting changes" would become erased, so to speak, and had then to reproduce themselves by themselves (97).

In Straus's own slipping into the imperfect tense ("Its reactivation needed . . .") the imperfection of the model is marked. In this "ping-pong game of misinter-pretations" nothing is won except by ruse, inasmuch as the explanation every-where makes secret appeals to what it is supposed to explain. Straus's recapitu-lation highlights two such subterfuges: first, the iconographic belief and confi-dence that the perceptual image and the mnemic image are as identical as two prints produced by the same typographic plate; second, an unending confusion concerning the plate itself as both signet and image, both cutting edge and primal print, such that the reactivation can be thought to occur by virtue of an alternation of self-effacement and "a kind of phosphorescence" (98). Whether the stimulus is portrayed in terms of closed or open circuitry, that is to say, whether it is held to be exposed to other external stimuli or to interference from other regions of the brain, the identical problem remains. How does one explain the way in which a trace could ever find its way back　　　*Been walking in muck somewhere*　　　from its final to its initial state, find its way back without losing contact with that final state, "so that it swings back there," the sole of the boot raising the crushed snow or squished muck only to depress it again? We shall not linger over Straus's proposed solutions to these dilemmas in what he calls "The Phenomenology of the Trace" (83–90). Let it suffice to note three things that he reserves for the "long preparatory work" that will have to precede "a new physiological theory of meaning" (99).

First, any effective theory of the trace must be able to make manifest the *course and flow* of past events by going back, as it were, beyond the discrete units of the preterite to the *pluperfect* tense in which their history is written.

Second, such a regress would have to establish something similar— although the comparison here is mine—to what Heidegger in sections 17 and 18 of *Being and Time* calls the *Verweisungszusammenhang* and *Bewandtnisganzheit,* the nexus or node of references within a significative whole.

Third, the significative whole of constituted memory would itself have to be scanned by something like a gleaning consciousness: "Traces must be read." But this means that the functioning of traces does not *found* memory; rather, the *reading* of traces *presupposes* memory (98–99). Memory must therefore be a constituent of the global phenomenon of being-in-the-world.

Straus does not himself appear to be fully convinced that *phenomenology* as such will be able to guide and undertake such research. We have already heard him invoke the "long preparatory work" that he deems essential. His "Conclusion" ends with these words: "Should we ever regain the clearing in this forest of problems, then we will have returned from our long wandering not with a new answer but with a new kind of questioning" (100). That new kind of questioning, at least as far as the phenomenological tradition is concerned, is perhaps to be found less in Husserl than in Heidegger (discussed in chapter 6, below) and in Merleau-Ponty, to whom we shall now turn.[27] However, lest by now we have lost hold of the aporias and enigmas of memory and reminiscence—and after delving into so much detailed material, never mind how superficially, there is every reason for our having forgotten them—we may find it useful to invoke a straightforward and powerful hypomnetic. Even though Jean-Paul Sartre's discussion of temporality in *Being and Nothingness* is perhaps the least memorable of his long work, his presentation of the classical problem of memory is matchless. He would forgive us for following the advice he himself proffered: after hearing him pose the problems we shall turn to Merleau-Ponty's efforts to redefine—if not resolve—them. "Them," I say, putting the "aporias and enigmas" of typography, iconography, and engrammatology into a cautionary plural, even if, as Straus has shown, *the* problem since Plato and Aristotle is the *presence* in memory of the *past*. Sartre writes:

All theory of memory implies presuppositions concerning the being of the past. These presuppositions, which have never been elucidated, have obscured the problem of memory [*souvenir*] and that of temporality in general. Once and for all we must pose the question: What is the *being* of a past being [or a being past: *un être passé*]? (. . .) We say that the past is no longer [*n'est plus*]. From this point of view it seems that one would want to attribute being to the present alone. This ontological presupposition has engendered the famous theory of cerebral traces: since the past no longer is, since it has foundered in nothingness, the continued existence of our memory [*souvenir*] depends on the *present* modification of our being; it will depend, for example, on an imprint presently marked on a group of brain cells. Thus all is present: the body, the present perception, and the past as a trace present in the body. All is *in act,* inasmuch as the trace does not have virtual existence *qua* memory [*souvenir*], but is altogether an *actual* trace. If the memory [*le souvenir*] is reborn, it is in the present, in consequence of a present process, namely, the rupture of protoplasmic equilibrium in the cell group under consideration. Psychophysiological parallelism, which is instantaneous and extratemporal, is there in order to explain how this physiological process is correlative to a strictly psychic yet equally present phenomenon: the appearance of the memory image in consciousness. The more recent notion of the *engram* adds nothing to this, but only adorns this theory with pseudo-scientific terminology. Yet if all is present, how explain the *pastness* [passivité] of remembering; that is to say, the fact that in its intention a consciousness that reminisces [*se remémore*] transcends the present in order to aim at the event back there where it *was*.[28]

One way of describing Merleau-Ponty's philosophical project as a whole would be to say that the phenomenologist endeavored to show that the "we" cited earlier can effectively *transcend* the present, though never by free-floating anticipations of the future or wistful absorption in the past. The "we" can be neither mechanism's bundle of responses nor transcendental philosophy's homunculus hovering in the mind. Commenting on Descartes' *Dioptrique* in a working note of September, 1959, Merleau-Ponty asks: "*Who* will see the image painted in the eyes or in the brain? There must in the end be a *thought* of this image—Descartes himself realizes that we always posit a little man inside man, that our objectifying view of our body always obliges us to search *farther* inside [*plus au-dedans*] for this *man who sees,* whom we thought we beheld beneath our eyes."[29] Merleau-Ponty is fully aware that homunculus' position is impossible: shooed out into the world in order to be the organist's or fountaineer's digits—the digits of the *objects* that press on the senses—he is then chased back into the machine so that his own digits can sketch, paint, punch, and weave, his own eyes read, so that "our" soul can cognize.

Yet what he [Descartes? homunculus? both?] does not see is that the primordial vision at which one must arrive cannot be the *thought of seeing* [pensée de voir]—This thought, this unveiling of being which ultimately is *for* someone, is once again the little man in man, but this time compressed to a metaphysical point. Because in the end we only know of that vision which pertains to a composite substance, and it is this subtilized vision that we call thought—If being is to unveil itself, it will be in the face of a transcendence and not an intentionality, it will be brute being caught in the shifting sands [*l'être brut enlisé*], a being that reverts to itself [*qui revient à lui-même*]: it will be the *sensible* hollowing itself out [*qui se creuse*]—

The dwindling, shifting punctuation of the note reflects the unfinished character of the thought—eking out for itself a kind of hollow. Yet we dare not stamp Merleau-Ponty's as simply one more type or icon in the en-grammatological tradition, as though the "primacy of perception" ever meant to provide a final fixed abode for homunculus. The *creux* or hollow Merleau-Ponty has in mind as the site of transcendence, a site caught forever in brute immanence, has everything to do with memory: *se creuser la tête* means to make a great effort to recall something, to reflect intensely (*Robert*). This hollow in the flesh is not an engram in the wax slab or waxen gland, nor a container for catching birds and icons; it is on the verge of a very different kind of thinking. Merleau-Ponty uses the word *creux* in (at least) two crucial places late in chapter four of *The Visible and the Invisible*, "The Intertwining—The Chiasm" (VI, 193, 198), to indicate a pit or hollow that opens of itself in the otherwise too solid flesh of the world, a concavity that allows there to be visibility; he also uses the word to designate "a certain interiority, a certain absence, a negativity that is not nothing" in the otherwise too crystalline flesh of ideas. Nor is this pit or hollow—the immemorial cavern of memory from Augustine through Hegel—absent from Merleau-Ponty's earlier work. His *Phenomenology of Perception* invokes it (again, at least) twice in the chapter on "Temporality," identifying a hollow within the ecstatic subject, the hollow "where time is made."[30] Thus the hollow *under the sacred rooftree, over the bowls of memory where every hollow holds a hallow, with a pledge till the drengs in the Salmon House* has everything to do with memory.

While exposing the constructivist fallacy or "experience error" in the accounts of perception in classical psychology and neurophysiology—which borrow from perceptual experience the very elements they use to "construct" such experience, elements such as "association" and "the projection of memories"—Merleau-Ponty is led to a kind of gap or fissure that allows him to pose what he calls "the true problem of memory":

It is a matter of understanding how, by its own life, and without transporting complementary materials within a mythical unconscious, consciousness can with time alter the structure of its landscapes—how at each instant its former experiences are present to it in the form of a horizon which it is able to reopen, if it takes that horizon as its theme, in an act of reminiscence [*remémoration*], but which it can also leave "at the margins," from which point it grants to the perceived a present atmosphere and significance. A field always at the disposal of consciousness and which, for that very reason, encompasses and envelops all its perceptions, an atmosphere, a horizon or, if you will, a series of given "montages" that assign to it a temporal situation—such is the presence of the past which renders possible the distinct acts of perception and reminiscence. . . . To remember [*se souvenir*] is not to restore under the gaze of consciousness a tableau of the self-subsistent past; it is to ensconce oneself in the horizon of the past and to unfold little by little the perspectives contained there until the experiences bounded by that horizon are, as it were, lived anew in their temporal place. (PP, 30)

Yet this field "always at the disposal of consciousness" becomes increasingly problematic in Merleau-Ponty's *Phenomenology*. The capacity to live the past "anew" is not only limited by the present perspectives of consciousness but also radically dependent on what might be called "an immense Memory of the world" (PP, 84), to which our own memories constantly appeal. Our access to that mysterious capital Memory, itself reminiscent of what Descartes called *local memory,* is less a matter of consciousness than of the lived body, which is our anchorage in the world. It is perhaps more properly reminiscent of the memory in the luthier's fingers, not grasping the punch but plucking the strings, dancing a Gavotte. In his chapter "The Body as Expression, and Speech" (PP, 211), that access to memory—with considerable help from Proust—receives its finest expression in Merleau-Ponty's work: "The role of the body in memory is understood only if memory is not the constituting consciousness of the past but an effort to reopen time, starting from the implications of the present, and only if the body, being our permanent means of 'adopting a stance' and of thus fabricating for ourselves a range of pseudo-presents, is the means by which we communicate with time as well as space." At this point in his text (211) Merleau-Ponty inserts these famous lines from the "Overture" to *Swann's Way,* the overture to Combray and to Proustian recollection as such:

> . . . when I awoke like this, and my mind struggled in an unsuccessful attempt to discover where I was, everything would be moving round me through the darkness: things, places, years. My body, still too heavy with sleep to move, would make an effort to construe the form which its tiredness took as an orientation of its various members, so as to induce from them the direction of the wall, the position of the furniture, in order to piece together and give a name to the house in which it must be living.[31]

Here we have perhaps the finest creative interpretation of those words from *Cratylus* with which we began: the body rescues and preserves the soul by signaling to it, or giving it signs, granting it an index on the world. Without the body the sleep of the soul is long. Merleau-Ponty continues to cite the Proust passage as follows:

> Its memory, the composite memory of its ribs, knees, and shoulderblades, offered it a whole series of rooms in which it had at one time or another slept, while the unseen walls kept changing, adapting themselves to the shape of each successive room imagined, whirling madly through the darkness. [Merleau-Ponty deletes a number of lines, then takes up the thread.] . . . My body, the side upon which I was lying, loyally preserving from the past what my mind ought never to have forgotten, brought back before my eyes the glimmering flame of the nightlight in its bowl of Bohemian glass, shaped like an urn and hung by chains from the ceiling, and the chimneypiece of Sienna marble in my bedroom at Combray, in my great-aunt's house, in those far-distant days which, at the moment of waking, seemed to me to be actually there without my representing them precisely.

The human body and its memory, the body as lived rather than the pallid cadaver with waxen glands or volatile paraffin ones, remain for Merleau-Ponty the secret guardian of that "thickness," "opacity," and "depth" in the hollow (*creux*) that both limits and guarantees our being in the world. And Proust remains for him the exemplary witness of those "musical ideas" that resist capture and reduction to pure presence. The lived body and its memory serve as the sentinels of what at the conclusion of his chapter "Sensation," which traditionally might have concluded with the sharp, snapping report of punch perforating taut canvas, Merleau-Ponty quietly invokes as "an original past, a past that has never been present" (280). *Un passé qui n'a jamais été présent.* With that phrase (which we are accustomed to attribute to Levinas and Derrida, but not to Merleau-Ponty) we find ourselves at the closure of the tradition I am calling typographic, iconographic, and engrammatological, and on the verge of something quite new and difficult to think. Nor should Merleau-Ponty's reference to "an *original* past" deceive us. "My" possession of "my" time, writes Merleau-Ponty at the outset of his chapter "Others and the Human World," is "always deferred," *toujours différée* (398). The "originary past" is a matter not of possession but of "opacity" (403). If there is a past for us, it is only as an "ambiguous presence"; we experience its *ouverture* precisely as an opening upon "this opaque mass" (418). Existence "assumes" its past, whether by accepting or rejecting it, so that we are always, as Proust says, "perched on the pyramid of the past" (450). And yet such a perch offers no bird's-eye-view either of the world around us or of our own past, so that if the pyramid seems to elevate us to that "atmosphere of time" which we call "eternity" (451) it will be important to remember the precariousness of our foothold (475). The sentiment of eternity, nourishing itself on time, is hypocritical (484). Thus the cohesion of a life is not perfect pyramidal equilibrium, with each declining plane supporting the others, the apex formed by their interrupted fall pointing beyond itself into lovely blueness. It is not a matter of perches but of difficult and sometimes dangerous descents:

> But the continuous interlocking of fields of presence, by which this access to the past is itself guaranteed to me, is essentially characterized by the fact that it can only be effected little by little and step by step. Each present, because it is by its very essence of the present, excludes juxtaposition with other presents; even in the far-distant past I can embrace a certain period of my life only by unrolling it afresh according to its own proper *tempo*. (483)

That "my" past, the past of my body and its memory, its hollow in being, has its own time and tact, its own *tempo*, is perhaps one way to characterize those musical ideas of Proust's *Recherche*. If we recollect a moment longer and in somewhat greater detail Proust's famous *mémoire involontaire*, it may well lead us to the verge of Merleau-Ponty's hollow, that *creux* or crucible of time and space which *Timaeus* calls *hypodokhē*, *kratēra*, and *khōra*.

So much emerges from the fragrance of that cup of tea and taste of madeleine—not simply the contents of the four final pages of the "Overture" but the whole of Combray, the entire narrative that follows. That fragrance and taste, renewed at the end of "Combray," open onto the story of "Swann in Love." Fragrance and taste are not facts sought out by intelligence; Proust compares them to Celtic burial grounds of moments once lived.[32] It is not intelligence or even sense that calculates their pastness. Rather, the emotional incandescence of the emergent memories themselves, pulsing on a wave of *jouissance,* yields whatever "real presence" the past may yield up; and the sheer *hasard* of our crossing those burial grounds again, that is, of our encountering the objects, odors, noises, and cracked pavements where they hide, determines whether or not this "resurrection" prophesied by a "magical pact" will in fact occur. Thus the narrator of *Remembrance* portrays a familiar section of Paris but confesses himself unable to contribute to it an "element" he has "long lost": ". . . the feeling that makes us not merely regard the thing as a spectacle but believe in it as in a being without equivalent . . ." (50/66). The upsurgent wave of joy—the *arkhē kinēseōs*—marks not the end but the onset of the search. For however much the narrator of *Recherche* and the theoretician of *Contre Sainte-Beuve* disparage the intellectual search, it is intelligence itself that must confirm its own inferiority and attest to the eminence of "instinct" or "sensibility." Hence the narrator carefully arranges a mise-en-scène for the possible recurrence of the flood of recollections that accompanied "the first mouthful"; he alternates highly disciplined repetitions of effort with periods of rest and recuperation. That said, for all his pains there is no telling whether or when the directives will succeed. At first, and for long stretches, nothing. Then: "I feel something start within me, something that leaves its resting-place [*qui se déplace*] and attempts to rise, something that has been embedded like an anchor at a great depth; I do not yet know what it is, but I can feel it rising slowly; I can measure the resistance, I can hear the echo of great spaces traversed [*j'entends la rumeur des distances traversées*]" (35/46). The narrator anticipates that it is a "visual memory" on the rise, an "image" somehow linked to the fragrance and the taste of tea and madeleine, wedded to them, but not, we might add, incised or inscribed typographically and iconographically in them. The image is at first wholly without contours, "and I cannot distinguish its form, cannot invite it—it being the one possible interpreter—to translate me to the evidence of its contemporary, its inseparable paramour, the taste of cake soaked in tea" (35/46). As he pens the words *inséparable compagne,* the narrator—if it is the narrator who is writing—finds himself on the verge, the absolute suspense and suspension of the memory that may or may not be mounting. Clearly, the narrator or writer who appears to wield the verge as pen or plume, though never as scepter, is not wholly in control. He is like the dreamer of whom Merleau-Ponty says (PP, 196), "*La verge du rêveur devient ce serpent.*" "Now that I feel nothing, it has stopped, has perhaps gone down again into its darkness," the narrator continues. Hence the repeated, bootless efforts. "Ten times over I must essay the task, must lean down towards it." It is thus not a matter of windlass and spike and the old heave-ho, but of inclination, straining, and above all, waiting. He struggles only against the inveterate faintness of heart (*lâcheté*) that urges him to quit the verge, shoo the serpent, and assume the rounds of dailiness. Waiting. Vigilant. "And then suddenly [*tout d'un coup*] the memory returns" (36/46). Not simply "the memory" returns, but the whole of Combray. It seems incredible that so much can arise from so little, and we are perhaps wise to remember all the writer's ruses—since the verge is as much stylus as it is snake and abyss. Proust's *Remembrance of Things Past* stands there, itself a work of art as much as a memorial. We are perhaps suspicious of Proust's Celtic burial ground and his mystic resurrection.

> But when from a long-distant past nothing subsists; after the beings are dead, after the things are broken and scattered; alone, more fragile, but with more vitality, more unsubstantial, more persistent, more faithful, the smell and taste of things remain poised a long time, like souls, ready to recall; waiting, hoping, amid the ruins of all the rest; ready to bear unfalteringly, in the tiny and almost impalpable drop of their essence [*goutelette presque impalpable*], the immense edifice of recollection. (36/47)

The lip of the narrator's teacup is itself a curved porcelain crater, a verge gathering the vapors that quite by chance ensure the cohesion of a life—or at least the cohesion of a work of art. The rim of that verge marks the *ouverture* upon Combray, the Combray that *was*. "And just as the Japanese amuse themselves by filling a porcelain bowl with water and steeping in it little crumbs of paper which until then are without character or form, but, the moment they become wet, stretch themselves and bend, take on colour, differentiate themselves . . . , so in that moment . . . the whole of Combray . . . sprang into being, town and gardens, from my cup of tea" (36/47–48). The question of course remains as to what this oriental amusement, so imbued with gardens and flowers and writing, involves. All the cunning and discernment of the writer wielding the verge, no doubt; and all the patience and helplessness of the one who waits upon the verge. It would be foolish to think that we could ever simply opt for one rather than the other. Perhaps memory itself works as do those authors to whom Merleau-Ponty refers when he says that they begin to write their books without knowing what they will put in them.[33]

The duplicity of the verge gradually emerges in the final chapters of Merleau-Ponty's *Phenomenology* and throughout *The Visible and the Invisible*. The hollow in being where time and space are made is formed by dehiscence and explosion (PP, 480, 487). The "now" of time is no more than a synthesis of transition, and time itself is as much ecstasis as coherence. The "field of presence," in which alone, according to Merleau-Ponty, I can find my way back to a past time, is not monolithic. A crack or fissure, *une fêlure interne* (PP, 515), reminiscent of what Heidegger in "The Origin of the Work of Art" calls *der Riss*, invariably marks that field.[34] Time is (ambiguously) both the cycles of the body's organic functions and the surge and thrust (*jaillissement:* PP, 517) of my personal existence. My lived body is both center and diffusion, both personal existence and "double anonymity," that is to say, an anonymity arising from the "generality" of a shared intercorporeal world but also from the very "individuality" of my existence (PP, 512). Perhaps the most telling evidence of such anonymity, as of the ambiguity that haunts every field of presence, occurs in what Merleau-Ponty comes to call "the problem of passivity." He invokes that problem in the *Phenomenology of Perception* in the context of a discussion of Husserlian "passive synthesis" and Heideggerian ecstasis (487–88). In the first place, what we call *passivity* is not an "alien reality" imposed on us by some causal action "from the outside." Rather, it is an *investissement*, the very situation of our being, "which we recommence perpetually." Passivity is the "acquired" spontaneity of our existence: Merleau-Ponty does not shy from the oxymoron of an acquired spontaneity, "this monster," which Sartre confronts but forthwith rejects (489). Indeed, the problem of passivity that lies at the heart of the phenomenology of temporality poses the ultimate challenge to any dialectical philosophy. Or, as we shall say in chapter 5, any *hyperdialectical* philosophy.

That at least is the theme of Merleau-Ponty's "Monday Course" in 1954–55, a theme that reemerges in his chapter "Interrogation and Dialectic" in *The Visible and the Invisible*.[35] The problem of passivity—of sleep and dreamlife, the unconscious, and memory (*la mémoire*), all of which testify to the *acquired* spontaneity of existence—is the ultimate obstacle for modern metaphysical reflection. This is not to deny what he says elsewhere, namely, that once one is "installed" in such reflection and proceeds to reduce sleep, the unconscious, and memory to the subject's constituting consciousness, these cease to be obstacles to reflection. And it remains true that even outside the philosophy of reflection the subject is not utterly undone by these obstacles: the subject is not a mere link in that causal chain which the natural sciences assume to be cosmic order. Here as elsewhere Merleau-Ponty is bound to navigate the straits between mechanism and intellectualism, although this of itself tells us nothing about his relation to typography, iconography, and engrammatology, inasmuch as that tradition has bridgeheads on both shores of these straits.

Perceptual experience displays "a genre of being with respect to which the subject is not sovereign, but without its being imprisoned in it" (R, 66). "Perceptual experience" here of course has an expanded sense, not simply because it includes memory (memory was included from the start, even by classical psychology), but because Merleau-Ponty now wishes to elaborate an "ontology of the perceived world" beyond the realm of "sensuous nature." The course thus tries to understand how consciousness can be "inspired by a past that apparently escapes it" and how it can "finally reopen an access to the past" (R, 66–67). Passivity—also to be understood as a sense of "pastness"—becomes possible for consciousness insofar as consciousness "realizes a certain gap [*écart*], a certain variant in a field of existence that is already instituted, a field that is already behind us" (R, 67). Such realization is not Husserlian *Sinngebung*, a term that is exhausted in and by the chapter "Temporality" in the *Phenomenology*, but an operation at once more technical and more playful. The "weight" of this field of existence, "like the weight of a *volant*, comes to play a role precisely in those actions by which we transform it." The *volant* may be (and here I eliminate all but a few of its many meanings) a shuttlecock in a game of badminton, veering in mid-air both according to its own center of gravity and in response to the blow of the racquet; or the slanted blade or "wing" of a windmill, turning on the oblique, slantingly; or a sort of "fly-wheel" in a piece of machinery, or the strange rotating butterfly that operates the chimes of a clock; or the steering wheel of a car; all of which combine weight and motion—a sort of acquired spontaneity—in order to assure to a given operation a measure of equilibrium; or, perhaps stemming from this last sense, a "reserve" or "margin" of play that one might gain. (See VI, 257, where Merleau-Ponty speaks of philosophical reflection as an essentially limited reflexivity, calling it a "prolongation of the *volant* of the body.") At all events, if it is a shuttlecock, our existence is not designed for high-altitude thinking; if a steering wheel, not designed for infinite manipulation; if a reserve, one that constantly feeds motion. Living is not primarily "giving a meaning" to things and "imposing significations" on events. It is rather a "vortex of experience that is formed with our birth at the point of contact between the 'outside' and the one who is called upon to live it" (R, 67). Merleau-Ponty places the "*dehors*" in quotation marks, precisely in the way Heidegger writes "*draussen*" in section 13 of *Being and Time,* presumably for the same reason: the subject is *always already* on the "outside," even when it appeals to its "sphere of immanence."

Turning specifically to memory, Merleau-Ponty notes that phenomenology of memory is "idling," in neutral gear, inasmuch as the fundamental aporia of "conservation" versus "construction," which I touched upon in my remarks on Locke, can be neither resolved nor circumvented. Memory seems to be construction insofar as we can read or scan only those "representations" that consciousness has put there—that is, translating into the language we have been using, engrammatology allows us to construct *each time as though for the first time* the icon typographically impressed there. Yet memory seems equally to be conservation, inasmuch as the icon is read or scanned *hōs allou,* with a view to something else, something that *was.* Thus even if memory were construction, notes Merleau-Ponty, there would have to be another memory behind the constructivist one, measuring the value or verisimilitude of its constructions; constructivist memory would have to have access to "a past freely given and in inverse proportion to our voluntary memory" (R, 72), which is perhaps what the "immense Memory of the world" was to have granted. Now comes the decisive statement of the course summary: "The immanence and the transcendence of the past, the activity and the passivity of memory, can be reconciled only if we refrain from posing the problem in terms of representation." If "representation" here means the entire process according to which an *eikōn* is typed into the wax slab of the soul, or an engram incised in the waxen glands of the Cartesian *machine de terre,* then Merleau-Ponty is calling for nothing less than an end to the tradition of typography, iconography, and engrammatology. That he is calling for such an end is corroborated by the remarks in his "Monday Course" that follow.

Not even *the present* is an object of representation or *Vorstellung,* Merleau-Ponty insists, so that the parousial underpinning of the tradition is itself undermined. The present, as a *field* of presence, a field of *existence,* is "a certain unique position of index for being-in-the-world." Our relations with it, and thus with the past as well, can be attributed only to "a postural schema that possesses and sketches out [*détient et désigne*] a series of temporal positions and possibilities." We might pause to wonder whether the "detaining" and "designing" of the postural "schema" can successfully resist traditional inscriptions, which do not have their power for nothing. Merleau-Ponty tries to resist slipping into the marks and traces of the metaphysical—that is, parousial— past by attributing the postural schema to the lived body. It is the body that enables us to respond to the silent questions "Where am I?" and "What time is it?" These questions, cited by Paul Claudel as queries posed and answered by the body, Merleau-Ponty reiterates in "Interrogation and Dialectic" (VI, 140). The reiteration is indicative of the fact that the problem of passivity or acquired spontaneity opens onto the most general questions of Merleau-Ponty's later philosophy. A phenomenology of passivity would deceive itself, he warns us at the conclusion of the résumé, if it simply persisted in playing off against one another the positive and negative poles of dialectical philosophy. It is a matter not of reconciling opposites but of causing the traditional categories to tremble; it is a matter not of "supplementary clarifications" but of a new way to philosophize. The consequences for the question at hand, memory, are as follows: the alternatives of construction and conservation and the representational thinking on which both are based must fall away, as must the apparent evidence of the very word *memory.* Remembering is not the contrary of forgetting. "True memory" is found at the *intersection* of remembrance and oblivion, "at the instant where the memory returns which was both forgotten and preserved by our forgetting," *à l'instant où revient le souvenir oublié et gardi par l'oubli* (R, 72). That instant of intersection *is* the verge—presuming that one could find it and name it while being on it. On the verge, remembering and forgetting are "two modes of our oblique relation to a past that is present to us only by the determinate emptiness it leaves in us."

"Both forgotten and preserved." "Determinate emptiness." "Acquired spontaneity." We are left with these paradoxes and flights of hyperdialectic. If Merleau-Ponty expatiates on them at all it is in that same "Monday Course" of 1954–55.[36]

> Even when I appear to renew myself, it always happens through an application of my past, my earlier history. I am passive when I move myself and am active even when I am subjected to events. Passivity is bound up with our proper being.
>
> Yet how is it with the problem of memory? Memory is the irruption of other things in us. Of course, memory is often conceived as conservation. However, because of the very dimension that is proper to it, i.e., the past, it is utterly impossible that this past should be a diminished, debilitated, and pallid being, preserved somewhere in consciousness.
>
> The past is no longer. Yet it is no mere meaning. For it is neither a weakened being nor a nothing nor a not-being. It is being-that-has-been, a modality of being, of that being which while separated from the present remains nonetheless in

contact with the present. A theory of memory demands that one repeat from top to bottom the analysis of the present.

If the present becomes past, this by no means happens by virtue of a weakening of the present time. For it is through the body that we have access to the past. How does one remember an earlier bodily state and an earlier mode of being? My present body possesses variations that I may realize in the future; the earlier modes of my embodiment become the history of my current being in the world. The body schema implies that my body is currently polarized by particular attitudes and modes of behavior. That is true with regard to both space and time. Thus the past cannot be deduced, inasmuch as it cannot be grasped. It is encompassed by the present, "I can." One can actualize the past, but one cannot realize it. Thus the body assumes the role of a mediator in memory. Time is read off from the body because time incorporates itself in the body, is sedimented there: the body appears as temporality, sedimentation, temporalizing, corporeal mediation between me and the past. Thus the earlier problem is transformed: it is no longer a matter of memory as conservation of images, memories; just as little is it a matter of the transcendental faculty of memory. Here the experience of a memory that is returning from oblivion stands at the center. It appears that thanks to this conception we may be able to overcome the problematic alternative between a consciousness that conserves and a consciousness that constructs the past. For we bring both concepts into positive interrelation, and we say that through forgetting the past is present [*durch das Vergessen ist die Vergangenheit gegenwärtig*]. This of course presupposes a new philosophy. . . .

There is no way we can linger here with this "new philosophy," which is more interrogation than dialectic, more a holding-at-a-distance than an approximation (VI, 137–38). Again Merleau-Ponty invokes the word *creux,* the hollow or "free space" that both enables interrogation and prevents its perfect fulfillment. Merleau-Ponty's reflection itself becomes increasingly memorious of mortality, not because he will have died while engaged in it, but because it is the very "unrolling of our life," our life *en train de vivre* (VI, 140), Coleridge's "circumstances of *life*." Nor can we follow Merleau-Ponty along the *via regia* of his reflection into "The Intertwining—The Chiasm," past its various cairns and pathmarkers: the element of flesh, the doubling, dehiscence, invagination, and "quilting" or "clustering" (*capitonnage*)—each of these serving as a signpost toward "a differentiation that is never fully achieved," an ultimate "reversibility." Let it suffice to remember that the "absolute truth" of reversibility, the flesh of the world, is for Merleau-Ponty not a termination or even an approximation but—as he was fond of saying—the index of a problem. Not the index that imperiously draws spilled water across a tabletop, but the index that points unwaveringly to the ambiguous semaphore that is the human body. Which Merleau-Ponty always remembers never to forget.

We began the chapter by inquiring into the spaces of memory's graphics, whether reputedly psychic or somatic. Plato's *Cratylus* and *Philebus* encouraged us to insist that somatic space remains crucial for all graphics, even when the soul is said to be emancipated from that space. Precisely because the pristine sign is the herm, a gravemarker, it is the *living* body that salvages the soul and that signals. Perhaps it is also that which grants the signs of memory, reminiscence, and writing.

Augustine's caverns of memory and mind are dreams of a presence devoid of somatic space. Thus the three dimensions of time reduce to one *praesentia*, and *praesentia* corresponds to one of the three classes of objects in the memory, to wit, those of the arts and sciences, perfectly interior, occupying "no space." However, only by a series of typographic, iconographic, and engrammatological maneuvers can all three classes of objects be subsumed under presence—the presence that is proximate to the absent father (I, 4: "most hidden and most present"), as close as Augustine will get to the father, the father who receives all the maternal accolades (IV, 1: "sucking your milk") and who is approached in speech (X, 1: *ideo loquor*) and above all by wielding the verge (X, 1: *in stilo*).

A brief excursus on the art of memory and its long-standing tradition of "inner writing" brought us to Descartes. We examined his not altogether successful distinction between two powers of memory, the corporeal and the intellectual, finding that from the period of the *Regulae* onward the identical engrammatological and figural model served both. Nor was it simply a matter of the identical model prevailing: rather, the crucial problem proved to be communication from the outside to the inside, exterior to interior, superficies to depth, no matter whether the memory in question was said to be wholly intelligible, wholly corporeal, or a mixture of both. As the ready substitution of writing for memory in the *Regulae* suggested, writing is remembering and reading the essential form of reminiscence.

In the *Treatise on Man,* that fiction which in its account of memory tries to get on *without a reader,* the animal spirits, the *petite glande,* and the soul must nonetheless retain the power to scan and glean images. They must retain the power of *regard,* even if such a power resists description as a mimetic effect of the machine. The soul itself appears as a mimetic effect, and that means an effect of memory, so that memory in Descartes' mime seems to exercise the most powerfully reflexive and perhaps even disseminative effect. It becomes impossible to tell which is the most expendable item in Descartes' model for memory: the *animal* spirits, the animal *spirits,* the cerebral tapestry of region *B,* the nerve tubes, the intervals, the rational soul and its "will," or the gland. An account that seems to presuppose at each stage what it means to explain, if indeed strategies of fiction can be said to cloak the will to explain, Descartes' impressive *machine de terre* nonetheless survives across the ages. Perhaps the most intriguing aspects of the machine—this Rube Goldberg of memory and reminiscence—are the series of barely adumbrated *differences* that go into its making. The explanatory power of the contrivance resides less in its perfect centeredness, identity, and selfsameness than in differences (1) as identified by the *sensus communis* within the gland, (2) in texture or substance between the tissues of the brain and the gland itself, (3) between the bilateral nature of every other part of the perceiving-remembering machine and the monogenic gland,

(4) in the gland's slightly off-center, highly mobile situation in the brain, and (5) in the variable ejaculatory force and vitality of the parties of spirits. Yet these very differences threaten to demolish the machine—for example, by making it impossible to distinguish nerve tubes from intervals, so that the animal spirits may rarify and evaporate to the surface of the body, the exterior surface, inasmuch as the porous skin can hardly be expected to contain what penetrates the taut weft of the brain. If not only the fountaineer's digits but also the spirits themselves are spilled, catapulted to the outside, this machine will meet oblivion. It will be the death of us. Or at least of "these men."

We took up Hobbes's and Locke's conceptions of retention as faded sensation and fading memory, respectively, noting the latter's tragic sense and the former's siege mentality. It is no doubt the Galilean-Hobbesian account that prevails in later empirical-scientific accounts of memory. Before proceeding to these, however, we paused to remark on the mimetic-mnemonic nature of *letters* in the doctrines of them both. Each develops an eminently engrammatological account of retention, privileging the role of archival "marks" or *typoi* even when it is speech he is discussing. By way of transition, we recounted Samuel Taylor Coleridge's spirited refutation of David Hartley's associationism.

That refutation anticipates the fundamental thrust of later phenomenological and humanistic-psychological criticisms of the theory of engrams and traces. Contemporary neurophysiology remains typographic, iconographic, and engrammatological, however much its models for memory may have altered. The problem of recall or retrieval proves to be the stumbling block of such theories, which first do away with the "reader" in order to be wholly empirical, then reintroduce "him" in order to explain how "we" remember. Erwin Straus shows how trace theory can preserve its explanatory power only by the double maneuver of self-effacement and repetition through "phosphorescence." Merleau-Ponty in his *Structure of Behavior* and *Phenomemology of Perception* demonstrates the ways in which neurophysiology and empirical psychology consistently presuppose what they claim to explain.

However, Merleau-Ponty became important for us less for his criticisms of traditional accounts of memory than for his own venturing to the verge of a new kind of thinking. To which, no doubt, we shall have to return repeatedly. His invocation of a "hollow" in visibility and in subjectivity, a kind of space where time is made, and from which we—unlike Augustine—do not dream of escaping; his depiction of the past not as a tableau but as a horizon, margin, or atmosphere of my present; and his insistence that one can approach one's past only step by step, little by little, like those fledgling weavers, the animal spirits, in accord with a *tempo* not of one's own choosing—these were the first rudiments of a new way to think about memory and reminiscence. And it had something to do with both writing and the body's efforts to reopen a past time, the body and the writing serving as guarantors and as limits of my access to the past. In his most radical reflections on the lived body as a hollow in being, a hollow not only of perception but also of memory, Merleau-Ponty gestured toward the idea of a *past that has never been present*. And when elaborating the problem of passivity he called for the abandonment of what Heidegger analyzes and decries as *vorstellendes Denken,* "representational thinking." Reminiscence would not be the scanning or reading of representations; memory would not be their coinage in the psyche through typography, iconography, and engrammatology. Are we on the verge of discovering what they *would* be?

Our inquiry into waxen glands and fleshy hollows has led us to the verge. Yet we shall take a detour, a circumscription or circumnavigation about the rim, before confronting the question of the verge. We shall now raise the question—already prompted by Descartes, Hobbes, and Locke, and especially by contemporary phenomenology—concerning the relation of memory, reminiscence, and writing to the economy of the organism's life-death as elaborated in Freudian psychoanalysis. That detour may in fact prove to be the most direct route *by a commodius vicus of recirculation back* along the rim to the theme of the verge "itself."

THREE

Wax Magic

Freud and the Typography of Effraction

In many ways Freud's 1895 "Project" toward a scientific psychology represents a monstrous regression.[1] In it the seasoned neurologist struggles to elaborate and defend a point of view he himself has already abandoned. His early neurological studies of aphasias had convinced him that function and dysfunction were not strictly localizable in any cerebral topography and that the most one could speak of were certain *dynamic* centers in the brain (24–25; 185–86; 374). Moreover, his earliest work on hysterical symptoms had persuaded him that no mechanics could account for the highly differentiated susceptibility of patients to this or that specific somatic disturbance. Ernst Kris (30) cites Freud's 1893 article, "*Quelques considérations pour une étude comparative des paralyses motrices organiques et hystériques,*" which argues "that hysteric paralysis 'acts as though there were no such thing as brain anatomy' " and that the vulnerability of patients to paralysis resides in " 'a particular circle of representations' " rather than in a localizable lesion or breach in the cerebral order. Little wonder that not long after Freud completed the sketch toward a scientific psychology (in autumn of 1895) he confessed to Fliess that he no longer understood the state of mind he was in when he wrote it (Letter 36; 145). As though it had been composed in a hypnoid state. And yet it remains the case that this monstrous regression, empowered by the energetics of Helmholtz and Fechner, Brücke, Meynert, and Exner, never lost its attractive power for Freud, no matter how disruptive that energetics proved to be of his own most hardwon insights—the primary process, repression, the sexual etiology of neurosis, the talking-cure, and so on.

In this chapter it cannot be a matter of the larger picture of Freud's gradual and never finally accomplished abandonment of an energetics of the psychic mechanism.[2] However, if Freud increasingly appeals to the model of *writing and reading* in his theory of the psyche, as Derrida has convincingly shown, and if that model is thought to alter though not altogether surrender the *mechanics* of typographic imprint and trace, then an inquiry into the Freudian adventure is unavoidable for our investigation. If memory since time immemorial is typography, iconography, and engrammatology, and if these three pertain since time out of mind to writing, then Freud's effort to reach an understanding of both writing and the psyche beyond them will have epoch-making consequences. That epochal turn is reflected in Derrida's apparently modest reformulation of a single question in the introductory pages of "Freud and the Scene of Writing" (ED, 297/199): "Not whether the psychism is really a kind of text, but: What is a text, and what might the psychical be, such that it can be represented in a text?" An ancient question, incised in waxen tablets; a modern question, jotted down in the most abbreviated symbols as a supplement (to) memory; a question that no longer allows us to presume either that writing is a metaphor for memory and reminiscence or that memory and reminiscence are figures of writing. It is the question we shall pursue in a reading of the 1895 *Psychologie* and of a later text, the 1925 *Wunderblock*, the "mystic writing pad," the final waxen wonder of the West.

Yet at the outset it is worth emphasizing the importance of the question of memory for psychoanalysis as such and as a whole. At the risk of simplemind-edly rehearsing things all the world knows by now, some initial and altogether general remarks about the centrality of memory in psychoanalytic theory and practice may be in order. For psychoanalysis takes memory to be the source of both the *malady* with which it is concerned and the *therapy* it proffers.

MEMORY, MALADY, AND THERAPY

Psychoanalysis did not spring full-grown and armor-clad from the head of Freud. Each of its theoretical and practical features developed incessantly dur-ing a career that lasted half a century. Yet one of its earliest and most enduring traits was the significance of memory for it. During the first of his introductory lectures "On Psychoanalysis," delivered at Clark University in Worcester, Mas-sachusetts in 1909, Freud italicized the following sentence: "*Our hysterical patients are suffering from reminiscences.*"[3] He explained that whatever com-plaints hysterics might have, a facial tic, chronic nausea, numbness in the limbs, the complaints could be regarded—a purely physiological, "medical" cause having been excluded—as vestiges of remembrance. Freud called them *Erinnerungssymbole*, "symbols of rememberance." Hysteric symptoms symbol-ize one or more traumatic events in the patient's past life, often from early childhood, events of which the patient is perfectly unaware, that is to say, which he or she cannot remember. Freud compared these symptoms to monu-ments or memorials—like ancient herms, serving as both burial crypts and pathmarkers—that affect the patient in a mysteriously persistent and overpow-ering way. Freud had visited London a few days before his ship sailed for America and had gone to see "Charing Cross" and "The Monument." The tourguide explained that "The Monument," which had no more revealing name than that, was to remind Londoners of the devastating fire of 1666; "Charing Cross" was erected during the thirteenth century by one of the Plantagenet kings, for there the coffin of his dead queen had touched down during the funeral procession. Very moving, says the tourist. Yet what would the tourist think if a passerby were to pause at Charing Cross or The Monument and then suddenly collapse in paroxysms of grief, utterly unable to move from the spot and take up his or her daily routine? That is what happens to hysterics, Freud explained. Some monument of the past that has no remembered significance cripples them in the present.

In an anonymous article published in 1904 ("*Die Freudsche Psychoanalytische Methode*")[4] Freud notes that very early in his treatment of hysteria and compulsive neuroses he made an observation that was "determinative" for psychoanalysis. When patients tried to recount their case histories they were often stymied by insuperable barriers that prevented their recollecting when and where it all started. "There is no case history of neurosis," Freud was led to conclude, "without amnesia of some sort." Yet not the purely passive amnesia we might suffer after an accident: when he encouraged his patients to concentrate and apply themselves in order to recall these events that were forgotten or distorted beyond recognition, they resisted actively with every cunning art at their disposal. They assured him it was a matter of no consequence, changed the subject, "forgot" to show up for their next appointment. Freud speculated that the amnesias themselves resulted from a force that was still at work in the patients. He called it *Widerstand*, resistance, and attributed it to *Unlustgefühle*, feelings of displeasure (or as we usually translate it, *unpleasure*) that were instituting an enforced oblivion. Nietzsche had in the second treatise of *On the Genealogy of Morals* hypothesized an "active forgetfulness." Freud called it *Verdrängung*, repression. Yet, paradoxically, he attributed neurotic symptoms to the *incompleteness* of the amnesia, the *failure* to achieve total forgetfulness, the ultimate *futility* of resistance. In one of his earliest cases, that of Miss Lucy R., Freud was driven to conclude that although "forgetting" was actually intended and wished, it was "always only *apparently* successful."[5] He was compelled to recognize, as he put it, *eine unvermutete Treue des Gedächtnisses*, a fidelity of memory far greater than anything one could have anticipated. That fidelity made people sick. Freud believed it might also cure.

In 1893 Freud and Breuer published their "preliminary report" on the "psychic mechanism of hysteric phenomena." Two years later—the very year of Freud's sketch toward a scientific psychology—their *Studien über Hysterie* incorporated the "preliminary report" as an introduction to five detailed case histories (one by Breuer, four by Freud), a theoretical discussion by Breuer, and concluding observations "toward the psychotherapy of hysteria" by Freud. The first and last sections of the book established memory as both the mainspring of the hysteric mechanism and the principal tool of the therapy. In their preliminary report Breuer and Freud attributed their interest in hypnosis to the fact that a normal interview with hysteric patients could not elicit information on the etiology of the symptoms. The etiology involved events they "really could not remember." Hypnosis proved to be one way "to awaken the memories of that time" in which, after an incubation period, the symptoms first began to appear. To rouse such memories was not merely an academic exercise in recall; it implied nothing less than the disappearance of the symptoms that had somehow sprung from dormant "reminiscences." The

authors italicized the following passage, and Freud reprinted it in his concluding comments:

> For we found—at first to our very great surprise—that the particular hysteric
> symptoms vanished without further ado, and without recurring, when we were
> able to awaken to full clarity remembrance of the occasioning event, when at the
> same time we were also able to call to wakefulness the accompanying affect, and
> when the patient portrayed the event in the greatest possible detail and put the
> affect into words. (SH, 9–10; 204)

Here Freud and Breuer emphasized four aspects of the therapy. First, the
symptoms result from an *Erlebnis,* or from a series of traumatic experiences,
which the "ego-consciousness" of the patient no longer remembers; if the
analyst succeeds in restoring remembrance of these events in the patient, the
symptoms will vanish like pacified ghosts. Second, such remembrance must
come to pass as an intense affective or emotional experience, the traumatic
events being recovered "in as lively a manner as possible," virtually tugged into
their *statum nascendi,* the state in which they ought to have been experienced
the first time. Third, the pathogenic events must be portrayed in minute detail,
the analyst aiding the patient in the process of microscopic remembrance by
relentless interrogation. Fourth, the patient must give utterance to the affect,
must speak it out.

However, in the same preliminary report the two therapists contend that
memory is also responsible for the *formation* of the symptoms in the first place.
They stress, to repeat, that "for the most part, hysteric patients are suffering
from reminiscences," that is to say, from *unknown* memories, as though memories do not have to be remembered in order *to be,* indeed as though the most
potent memories are those we *forget,* those that (as Merleau-Ponty says) are
guarded and preserved by oblivion, so that Being and Thinking are not at all
coterminous. Such unremembered reminiscences do not erode with the passage
of time; they retain their affective force, or such force retains them. Their force
is accounted for by the fact that the patient cannot repulse or even react to
(*abreagieren*) the original event in a way that might expend the emotional
energy the event had summoned. If the emotional reaction is obstructed, the
affect remains linked to the reminiscence, the reminiscence imprisoned in the
affect, as it were. Such unremembered reminiscences, which the patient is
unable to associate with the rest of his or her conscious life, Freud and (especially) Breuer ascribe to an abnormal state of consciousness, which they call
"hypnoid." These reminiscences are dissociated from consciousness in a way
that *more than parallels* the way in which a patient's ego-consciousness is
dissociated during hypnosis. Here the very language betrays the interlacing of
disease and cure: hypnosis is the therapy for hypnoid malady. Freud underscores the same interrelation of malady and therapy in his 1893 address to the
Viennese Medical Association: "The effort to learn the occasioning factor of a
symptom is simultaneously a therapeutic maneuver" (StA 6, 20).

When the affective charge of such dissociated or hypnoid reminiscences reaches a certain threshold, it produces more or less chronic hysteric symptoms by virtue of what Breuer and Freud call a "conversion into the somatic" (SH, 127). The essence of psychotherapy is the countermanding of somatological conversion: if unremembered reminiscences yield the somatic symptom, then reminiscences remembered dissolve it. Freud and Breuer conclude: "It is by now comprehensible how the method of psychotherapy here presented heals. *It cancels the effects of the representation that was not originally 'abreacted' by enabling its pent-up affect to be released by means of talk and by bringing the representation to correction by means of association*" (SH, 18). The spoken word—much more than a sign signifying a signified—reasserts its rights in the domain of the symbolic: symptoms or "symbols of remembrance" are disbanded and the reminiscences behind them reappropriated as memories proper. The latter, no longer dissociated, are brought home. They can now be corrected by means of a kind of dialogue with one another, in which each remembrance understands itself as a perspective, as one associated with others.

In the two to three years that intervened between the preliminary report by Breuer and Freud and the latter's concluding remarks, "Toward the Psychotherapy of Hysteria," Freud distanced himself from hypnosis and from the Breuerian "cathartic method" and achieved fundamental insights into the sexual etiology of neuroses. These shifts in point of view and new insights need not concern us here, but one point merits our attention. Freud describes his replacement of hypnosis with the method of "enforced concentration": the analyst requests that the patient lie back, close his eyes, and concentrate, assuring him he *will* remember what must be remembered, and so "compels" the patient to remember. Such compulsion, *Drängen,* on the analyst's part counteracts the patient's tendency to repress, *Verdrängen,* the pathogenic representations. Once again, in *Drängen* and *Verdrängen,* we discern the interpenetration of malady and therapy.

Perhaps it is unnecessary to go into greater detail—although Freud's descriptions of enforced concentration, the procedure of laying a hand on the patient's forehead or temple in order to overcome resistance (the procedure itself mirroring the "conversion into the somatic"), the threefold layering of repressed material, the roots of a general theory of the unconscious, as well as of "transference" in the therapeutic situation, all make the concluding chapter of *Studien über Hysterie* one of the classics of psychoanalysis. Yet for the sake of my own theme let me now summarize. An event or series of events that are shocking and painful to an individual occur; he or she cannot, for one reason or another, react to them, move *away from* them, as it were. A powerful emotional charge adheres to a reminiscence or representation of the event and causes it to be unrememberable, inaccessible to consciousness, ostracized from the realm of the "I think," but by no means powerless. At a certain critical point, enacting some mysterious symbolism, miming the event, the body "remembers." With the conversion into the somatic we reach the heart of the interlacing of disease and cure. As symptoms, or bodily interpretations of the repressed event, these iconographic "symbols of remembrance" constitute the first stage of genuine recollection and recovery. True, without the tic, the nausea, the numbness in the extremities, the patient would not need a doctor; but now that he does, the doctor needs those symptoms as herms or signposts, else he or she has nowhere to go in search of help. Beginning with those engrammatological clues the analyst labors week after week to negotiate a reconciliation and repatriation. That can be achieved when the patient is able to recollect the repressed events in vivid detail and put those remembered events and the feelings attached to them into the words and gestures of dramatic speech.

Thus Freud's famous "talking cure." It rests on the confidence that there is something in the patient which, in spite of all resistance, wants to *express itself* and *to know*. In chapter 5 we shall say the same of *spirit* in Hegel's *Phenomenology*. Freud encourages the analyst to have faith in the ultimate fidelity—and also the benevolence—of memory: no matter how recalcitrant a particular remembered scene may be for a nascent analysis, no matter how absurd and contradictory, it will find its place when the analysis is complete, that is to say, when the symbols of remembrance have been recovered in genuine remembrance. However, is not such dramatic recollection and catharsis of emotion dangerous? Should not the sprite be kept in the bottle? In an address to his dubious medical colleagues in 1905 Freud assures them that the remembrance induced by analysis cannot cause more emotional and somatological damage than the amnesia. If the unremembered reminiscence is *thanatos,* remembrance is *eros,* and *eros* will prevail.

Why that is so, Freud is never able to explain to his own satisfaction. This is not the place to rehearse his various attempts at a solution. The secret of the talking cure runs deep. Just how deep Freud suggests in a late work, *The Future of an Illusion,* where in a fully positive sense he invokes the psychoanalyst's "god," *unser Gott,* Logos (StA 9, 187). *The Future of an Illusion* appears in 1927, the very year in which Heidegger's *Being and Time* challenges the ontotheological interpretation of the being that "has *logos.*" We will not follow Freud's *Future,* however, but will turn back now to the 1895 project toward a scientific psychology.

QUANTITY

The "Project" is not without abortive developments, inconsistencies, reversals, and contradictions; it is not without *imperfection,* this regressive monster. Again and again the text allows the *imperfect tense* to interrupt the narrative flow of   *You may never know in the preterite all perhaps that you would not believe that you ever even saw to be about to. Perhaps*   the present, such interruption suggesting that sketches toward a scientific psychology are already relics of the past. Composed precipitately in the late summer and autumn of 1895, it shows three parts: the first (undated) provides a "general plan" of a neural theory of mental behavior based on a quantitative conception of excitation and discharge; the second (dated September 25) offers a "psychopathology" of hysteria, based (tenuously) on the general neural theory outlined in part one; the third (dated October 5) attempts to describe "normal psychic processes," especially conscious thought, memory, and language behavior. The first part shows twenty-one sections, the second six, the third only one, although it readily falls into four parts.

The overarching scheme of the "Project" emerges in a remark Freud makes to Fliess on May 25, 1895: "Two intentions torment me: namely, to see how a doctrine of psychic function takes shape when one introduces quantitative observation, a kind of economics of neural energy [*eine Ökonomik der Nervenkraft*]; and, secondly, to carve out of psychopathology the gain [*Gewinn*] for normal psychology" (129). The economics prove to be problematic, the gain meager, even though the 1895 "Project" will continue to inform the metapsychological treatises from 1915 to 1923. Preeminently occupied with "pathological defense" mechanisms, laboring over the psychotherapy of hysteria, and having scarcely begun the sketch, he writes to Fliess about it on August 16 as though it were a sin of the past: "It was a curious business, this ϕψω. . . . To put it briefly, I've chucked in the whole alphabet, and I try to tell myself that it is of no interest to me whatsoever" (133). And a dozen lines later: "The psychology really has become a cross. . . . I wanted no more than to clarify defense, but explained something right out of nature [*mitten aus der Natur heraus*]. I had to work through the problem of quality, sleep, memory [*Erinnerung*], in short, all psychology. And now I'll have no more of it." Curious imperfection, this system finished before it is begun, this "cross." The following discussion will overlook the repetitions in Freud's text and will focus on its frustrations, especially as regards the specific topic of memory (*Gedächtnis*) and remembrance (*Erinnerung*).

The "intent" of Freud's sketch is to provide a psychology for "natural science," based on material parts (neurons) and their quantitatively determined states. Two fundamental states emerge, "activity" and "rest," fresh from Plato's *Sophist;* activity is distinguished from rest by "quantity," that is, quantities of force subject to the laws of motion. Freud does not pause to ponder what one of those basic states ("rest") can be in a universe of Galilean turbulence, but does concede that his efforts join those of many other researchers (he is thinking perhaps of Sigmund Exner's 1894 system), and that "similar attempts are common these days" (379). Indeed, one of the sketch's insuperable problems, a problem shared by all such systems, will be that quantity alone fails to account for several aspects of mental and emotional life that are of crucial importance to the budding psychopathologist (aspects such as *repression,* destined to be the cornerstone of psychoanalytic theory), so that at a very early stage in the argument Freud will have to appeal beyond quantity to quality.

In the first section of Part One Freud elaborates "The Quantitative Conception" as his "First Principal Proposition." In direct contradiction to what Josef Breuer will soon claim in their collaborative *Studien über Hysterie,* Freud asserts that the psychopathology of hysteria and compulsive neurosis, with its appeals to highly charged stimuli, substitutions, conversions, and discharges, implies a general conception of neural excitation in terms of "quantities in flux" (380). Thus it "seemed" "not unjustified" to try to generalize these findings. "Neural inertia" is the first such generalization. In their structure and development neurons betray this primal fact: they endeavor to void quantity (*sich der Quantität zu entledigen trachten*). That there are fundamentally *two* neural systems, the sensible (afferent) and the motor (efferent), reflects the fundamental structure of reflex behavior, to wit, the *intake* and *discharge* of quantities of energy. Thus the neural systems are inheritances of our protoplasmic past, or as Freud will later suggest, are in macrocosmic relation to the microcosm of one-celled animal life, with the surface of the cells exposed to excitations from the external world. The primary function of the neural systems is to transfer sensible excitation to the motor apparatus in order to reduce excitation and dispel stimulus through flight. Such "flight stimulus" occurs along neural pathways that by virtue of some mysterious "secondary function" come to be "preferred and preserved" avenues of discharge (381).

This fairly straightforward account of quantity intake and discharge is soon disturbed by the phenomenon of indigenous, endogenous stimulation, that is, excitations occurring within the organism that are bound up with hunger, respiration, and sexual reproduction. The "exigency of life" (*die Not des Lebens*) cannot be resolved by mere flight but only by specific changes in particular conditions in the "outer world," such changes necessitating the expenditure of considerable energy. The proper calamity of life, life's destitution or needful condition (*Not*), is that it must quit the Nirvana of zero-excitation, abandon the paradise of inertia, and settle for the halfway house of Fechnerian "constancy." The neural system

> must come to accept a reserve [*Vorrat*] of quantity [Q = exogenous excitation], in order to satisfy the demands for specific action. However, in the way the system does this, the perdurance of the same tendency shows itself. For it is modified into a striving at least to maintain the quantity [Qἠ = endogenous excitation] at the lowest possible level and to defend itself against its increase; that is to say, to keep it constant.

Freud now applies the rubric "secondary function" to the modified striving to maintain a modicum of endogenous energy as a reserve for specific action designed to alleviate the exigency of life.

Freud's "second principal proposition" (in fact the last such proposition, since he drops the term *Hauptsatz* from the title of subsequent sections) develops his "theory of neurons" (382). The nervous system consists of a series of distinct though similarly constructed neurons. The neurons come into contact with one another only indirectly through the mediation of "foreign mass," absorbing a "quantity" of energy that flows along certain favored routes (*Leitungsrichtungen*) in the dendrites and discharging energy along the cylindrical axon. Freud notes the "abundant divergences" of the dendrites and their "various calibers," that is to say, the *difference* in the thickness of these cell processes; such difference reflects morphologically a differentiating function soon to be described. Neurons can at one time be "occupied" or cathected by fixed quantities of endogenous energy, and at another time be "empty." Neural inertia expresses itself in the "streaming" of quantity from dendrites to axon. "Thus the single neuron is the icon [*Abbild*] of the entire nervous system, with its duplex construction, the axon serving as its organ of discharge."

Let us bypass this curious iconography of the nervous system and its neural components and proceed to Freud's more detailed account of the secondary function. It requires that the flow of quantity be interrupted, that the homology of neuron and nervous system be somewhat restricted, or perhaps that the adherence of both microcosm and macrocosm to the principle of inertia be put into question. The *storing* of quantity, which the secondary function requires, compels us to suppose that the point of contact between the axon of one neuron and the dendrites of the next is in fact a barrier (*Kontaktschranke*). As Derrida recognizes (ED, 298–99), the hypothesis of *contact barriers* (influenced perhaps by Foster and Sherrington's work two years earlier on the "synaptic gap") is essential to Freud's sketch. The first justification of such a supposition is that it allows him to conceive of the conduction of energy through highly differentiated rather than undifferentiated types of protoplasm: the capacity to conduct quantities of energy is differential, and it is to be accounted for by a "differentiation in protoplasm." However, such differentiation in protoplasm itself accounts for "a better capacity for the advancing *via mala, hyber pass, heckhisway per alptrack: through landsvague and vain, after many mandelays* of further conductions" (383). We soon realize that one never bypasses iconography: the paradoxes of original and copy—also fresh from Plato's *Sophist*—prevail even here in speculations on the neural structure and function *guide them through the labyrinth of their samilikes and the alteregoases of their pseudoselves* of this complex slab of quantity we call the human body. And where we find iconography we may be sure that typography and engrammatology will not be wanting. Freud now recounts the second justification of the theory of contact barriers, the one that clarifies the relevance of all this for memory and thus for the psyche as a whole.

A principal property of nerve tissue is memory [*das Gedächtnis*], that is, quite generally, the capacity to be changed for the duration [*dauernd*] by events that occur but once [*einmalige Vorgänge*]. This is in striking contrast to the behavior of matter that allows the motion of a wave to permeate it and then reverts to its former state. Any psychological theory worthy of the name must provide an explanation of "memory." Now, every such theory comes up against the difficulty that on the one hand it must assume that after excitation the neurons are in a different state than before, while on the other it cannot deny that new excitations generally confront the identical conditions of reception that earlier excitations confronted. Hence the neurons should be both influenced and unchanged, without bias. An apparatus capable of this complicated achievement lies for the moment beyond our powers of invention; we rescue ourselves by ascribing the perdurant influence via excitation to one class of neurons, and contrariwise the immutability, that is, the freshness required for new excitations, to another. In this way the current practice of segregating "perception cells" from "remembrance cells" came to be; however, it is a practice that has been coordinated with nothing else and that cannot itself appeal to anything else.

The imperfect tense (*So entstand . . .*) suggests the imperfection of the ascription, which remains an anomaly (*die sich aber sonst in nichts eingefügt hat*), perhaps what Coleridge called a suffiction (*und selbst sich auf nichts berufen kann*). Nevertheless, the theory of duplex (and even tripartite) construction in the neurons is the mainstay of psychoanalytic theory (see chapter seven of *The Interpretation of Dreams* and the whole of *Beyond the Pleasure Principle*).[6] And it forms the backbone of the 1895 sketch, as we shall now see, with Freud's depiction of the φ, ψ, and ω neurons.

The contact-barrier theory, having unearthed "this way out," "this loophole" (*diesen Ausweg*), now asserts that there are two classes of neurons: the permeable, which allow endogenous quantity to pass through them "as though they possessed no contact barriers," so that such neurons revert to their prior condition; and those neurons that are relatively impermeable, which bring their contact barriers to bear in such a way that energy flows only with difficulty, and only in part, through them (384). By suffering transformation to another state, such impermeable neurons grant us "*a possibility of portraying memory.*" Permeable neurons serve perception but are incapable of retention; impermeable neurons are the "bearers" of memory and of psychic processes in general. Freud designates the latter accordingly as the ψ neurons, the former, more mysteriously, as the φ neurons. (Or perhaps the designation ψ is more mysterious: Plato's *Cratylus*, at 427a, aligns *phi* and *psi,* identifying both as windy consonants requiring "great expenditure of breath," so that the stoppage of flow by "contact barriers" and the possibility of retention, the possibility of a psyche that will not expire, remain the aporias.) In any case, Freud does not for the moment take up the conundrum that perception is neither a psychic process in general nor an accomplishment that is inherently capable of retention, so that it is difficult to see how anything perceived is ever remembered. Nor does he comment on the further conundrum—to which he nevertheless explicitly draws our attention—that the ψ neurons, as they become better and better conductors across their contact barriers, become less and less impermeable and thus more and more similar to the neurons they were invented to supplement. The condition of the contact barriers is itself determined as a degree of "breaching" or "effraction" (*Grad der Bahnung*). "*Memory is portrayed* [dargestellt] *by means of the breachings at hand among the ψ neurons.*" Memory is thus a power of showing the way, *eine wegweisende Macht,* that "prefers" one path to another (*Wegbevorzugung*), ensuring that the resistance offered by the sundry contact barriers will be a differentiated resistance. One is reminded of the differentiation of the intervals and pores into which in Descartes' suffiction the animal spirits tumble. "*Memory would be portrayed by virtue of the differences* [Unterschiede] *in the breachings among the ψ neu-*

rons" (385). Breaching or effraction itself operates according to a twofold factor, to wit, "the magnitude of the impression," *die Grösse des Eindrucks,* and "the frequency of the recurrence of the same impressions," *die Häufigkeit der Wiederholung.* Here too, in this first explicit reference to *catastrophes and eccentricities transmitted by the ancient legacy of the past, type by tope, letter from litter, word at ward, with sendence of sundance* typography, to the *Ein-druck* that was sure to come, we find a further reminiscence of the Cartesian account: the *robust* and *repeated* punctilious action of the journeyman weavers assures the retention of differentiated memories in region B of the brain.

Freud again rehearses the fundamental trait of neural inertia. If the system strives to keep the amount of stimulus as low as possible; if it only reluctantly makes way for the secondary function by which the exigency of life requires and receives its reserve of quantity, the secondary function in turn requiring an increase in the number and variety of impermeable (ψ) neurons; then the *breachings* that facilitate the flow of quantity can readily be seen as "*in service to the primary function.*" Breaching must therefore be seen as a partial reversion to an earlier state, prior to the exigency of life. Derrida is therefore entirely right *Add lightest knot into tiptition* to stress that "life is already menaced by the origin of the memory that constitutes it, and already menaced in the effraction [*le frayage*] it resists, the breaching that it can contain only by repeating it" (ED, 301/202); and he is also right in seeing the 1895 "Project" (as psychoanalysts such as Ernst Kris have also seen it) as the seedbed of Freud's mature notion of the economy of life-death *O foetal sleep! Ah, fatal slip!* in the repetition compulsion of *Beyond the Pleasure Principle.* However, to return to the 1895 sketch, such breachings in any single neuron are multiple, and one can readily imagine that all the reserved energy flows in one specific direction rather than in another, thanks to differences in the "paving" of its various avenues. Freud here appears to abandon the microcosm/macrocosm model according to which the axon or *Abfuhrorgan* of any given neuron is singular. As the network of contact barriers and breachings grows, the economy *Shop! Please shop! Shop ado please! O ado please shop. How hominous his house, haunt it? Yesses indeed it be!* of life-death becomes supremely complex.

Granted such complexity, it is easy to see that Freud can hardly be expected to explain *everything.* "In what breaching otherwise consists is a question we shall not discuss."[7] And yet the entire theory (or fiction) stands (or falls) with the account of a differentiated typography that tends to erase the difference between the neural systems as such. One might suppose that the contact barriers themselves somehow *absorb* endogenous quantities of energy; yet Freud assures us that the quantity "left behind" by the breaching itself is expelled, discharged "precisely in consequence of the breaching, which of course makes [the neuron] more permeable." In other words, breaching itself requires the *perdurant presence* of quantity, even though its sole function is to *let quantity pass.* Which is a way of saying that breaching and the preferential path appear to presuppose precisely what they are meant to account for—*both to presuppose it and to make it utterly impossible.* After posing the additional problem as to whether the magnitude and frequency of impressions need be equal, whether $3\ Q = 1\ Q\acute{\eta} \cdot 3$ (he will later, at 395, reflect on the strength of the latter half of the equation, as *periodicity,* and then, at 405, assert the likelihood of the supremacy of the first half), Freud concludes by conceding: "All this must be held in reserve [*vorbehalten bleiben*] for later adaptations of the theory to psychic facts." There is no end of psychic facts, however, hovering in the wings and awaiting their cue.

In the third section, "The Biological Standpoint" (387–90), Freud reasserts his confidence in the duplex theory of neurons to account for retention and fresh reception, even though he himself has shown how the putative differences in breachings tend to reduce the two systems to one and thus to destroy the theory's explanatory power. That his hypothesis betrays something of "the gratuitousness of the *constructio ad hoc*" (387) he   *Prospector projector and boomooster giant builder of all causeways woesoever, hopping offpoint and true terminus of straxstraightcuts and corkscrewn perambulaups, zeal whence to goal whither, wonderlust*   freely concedes. Nothing in the histology of his times supports such a duplex morphology. (See note 8, below). Freud therefore pursues the question in general "biological" terms; that is to say, in terms of the *genealogy* of the duplex system, its possible morphogenesis or "development."

"From the outset," the nervous system exhibits two functions, as we have seen: it receives stimuli from the outside and endeavors to discharge the resulting endogenous excitation. The exigency of life (hunger, respiration, reproduction) intervenes in the discharge process, however, compelling the system "toward further biological development." Let us pause a moment to ponder the curious intervention of *die Not des Lebens.* If the nervous system "from the outset" possesses two functions, then what becomes of the distinction between primary and secondary functions? We recall that the latter term shifted in its sense and application, from the general discharge of quantity in the motor system (the efferent system) to the general accretion of quantity as an endogenous reserve for exigent life. One might wonder, from a "biological" point of view, if there ever was   *But really now whenabouts? Expatiate then how much times we live in. Yes?*   at "the outset" a primary system without a secondary system, an outside without an inside, a neural inertia, quantity flow without a reserve; one might wonder therefore whether the secondary function is not every bit as original, "from the outset," as the primary function, whether indeed that primary function taken by itself could have anything to do with life. What was life   *Don't forget! The grand fooneral will now shortly occur. Remember*   before it became need?

Freud now (388) hypothesizes that the φ neurons are to be found in the spinal gray matter, the ψ neurons in the gray matter of the cerebrum proper. The latter manifest no direct links with the periphery of the body, and thus no links with the outside world, but merely serve the sympathetic nervous system.[8]

Yet the hypothesis ψ-φ is so close to being a "sci-fi" hypothesis, so exposed to the charge of arbitrariness (*Willkür*), that Freud now pursues another "way out." Because it is ultimately the (differential) quantity of excitation that produces the breachings, one may transfer the differentiating factor from the *morphology* of the neurons themselves to their *topology*. "A difference of essence is replaced by a difference in destiny and milieu" (389). The permeability or impermeability of neurons thus would depend on the quantity that reaches them in their environment. If the φ neurons have to do solely with the periphery of the somatic system, the ψ neurons with the endogenous, visceral system, then one may assume that the peripheral system is exposed to the quantities that exceed the threshold of the contact barriers of the (φ) neurons there, and that the level of excitation in the endogenous system—whatever the vicissitudes of life—does not exceed the threshold, so that accretion of quantity can occur in the central (ψ) neurons. If we were able merely to change the locale and the network (*Topik und Verbindung*) of the two sets of nerves, their structural permeability or impermeability would correspondingly change.

The fact that the external world, the world of the organist's fingers and the lacecuff punch, serves as "the origin of all large quantities of energy," the fact that in the world of Galilean turbulence we are exposed to "mighty, powerfully moved masses that propagate their motion," leads plausibly to this shift from a protoplasmic to a topical   *Tip. Take Tamotimo's topical. Tip*   account. The very first exigency of life would be to neutralize typography by absorbing and discharging large quantities. On the periphery, the frontier between life and death, topography would master typography. All would be permeability—without permutation, without memory. The psyche, the system of ψ neurons, would be purely supplementary, *nachträglich*. Yet Freud quickly dashes this illusion. For the system of ψ neurons is in fact, as we anticipated, necessary from the outset. It receives quantities of energy from *two* sources, namely, from inner-corporeal excitation *but also from the φ neurons themselves*. Life, it seems, must be in the world. Freud is now concerned to show that these quantities of stimulus, though double in terms of their source, are actually smaller in magnitude than those in the φ system. The fact that the histology of nerve cells indicates a basically homologous structure in all such cells suggests that endogenous stimulation is of the order of magnitude of intercellular exchange generally—hence, presumably, weaker than in the case of the peripheral φ system.

Freud therefore returns to "The Problem of Quantity" (390), particularly with regard to the φ system. The fact that neurons are not directly exposed to the outside world, that they terminate in sundry cellular formations, implies that quantity (from the outside) is always (from the outset) dampened, tempered, or reduced. The nerve-end apparatus is thus a *shield* against quantity, a screen that allows only "quotients" or fractions of the original force to penetrate. (Such shielding apparatus would not be necessary in the endogenous sphere, inasmuch as excitation would already have been filtered down to the proper intercellular or intracellular level.) A general theory of the nervous structure would therefore have as its central concept *Abwehr*, defense; and Freud   *wiv his defences down during his wappin stillstand*   introduces two further *Ab-* words to express this pervasive notion of apotropaism and aversion. "The structure of the nervous system may thus serve to *withstand* [Abhaltung], may serve to *discharge* [Abfuhr] endogenous quantity (Qἡ) from the neurons" (391). The several subsystems of the overarching nervous system may therefore be viewed as increasingly refined filters designed to hinder the passage of quantity. The secret of their efficacy is difficult to discern; the clear signal of their failure is the pathology of pain, *der Schmerz*. Freud will return to that pathology once again five sections later, with *Das Schmerz-erlebnis* (404–5). And we too shall have to take up the theme of pain later in Part Two of the present volume, especially in chapters 6 and 7.

Yet pain has its   *Whose dolour, O so mine!*   own mystery. For it is perfectly confluent with stimulation in general. Just as the principle of principles for neurology is neural inertia or "flight from stimulus," *Reizflucht,* so the principle of neuropathology is "flight from pain," *Schmerzflucht*. Except that here it is difficult to know how to translate *Reizflucht* and *Schmerzflucht*. Is it flight *from* stimulus and pain, or the flight and coarsing *of* these things? In other words, how does one distinguish between neurology and neuropathology when *pathos,* as typography, perforation, puncture, penetration, and effraction, is the very mechanism and the norm? Only by postulating a quantity in excess of the φ threshold, and thus *a fortiori* in excess of the ψ threshold, a quantity whose invasion in effect levels the ψ neurons to φ neurons, smashes all contact barriers, equalizes all differential thresholds, and institutes a stasis   *Approach not for ghost sake! It is dormition!*   more than reminiscent of death. Pain is "the most domineering of all processes," as Freud will repeat in the 1914 "Narcissism" essay and the 1923 *The Ego and the Id* (StA 3, 49; 294), even though it consists of nothing more than an enhancement of quantity, nothing more than more. One is reminded of Aristotle's arguments in *On the Soul* and *On Sense* (413b–414a; 421a; and 435a) that the sense of touch, whose metaxy is the flesh (*hē sarx*), is in fact the primary sense, since if stimulation of the sense of touch is enhanced to a critical point the organism dies. As though struck down by the Hobbesian mace. Pain strikes like lightning, writes Freud (392), leaving in its path a breach that may destroy the contact barrier altogether, so that future stimulation of ψ will flow without resistance, as though it were φ. And yet. Could lightning ever strike twice—would it ever *have* to strike twice—in the same place? The place, the impossible *topos,* of life-death? What is the *quality* of such lightning?

QUALITY

A breach opens in Freud's own text with the introduction of "The Problem of Quality." Why quality at all in a psychology dedicated to quantity? Whatever the reply, and whatever the precedents in the "School of Helmholtz," we may suspect that, once it gapes, the breach of quality will not heal; Part Three of

Freud's sketch will peter out in the very course and flow of his account of quality—with questions of consciousness, hallucination, thought, speech, and memory. Let us therefore follow Freud's text with particular care now (392–93), even though we will soon have to move more quickly.

> Up to now we have left undiscussed the fact that every psychological theory, in addition to its efforts on the side of natural science, must also fulfill another significant requirement. It should explain to us what we know in the most enigmatic way by virtue of our "consciousness"; and because our consciousness knows nothing of the suppositions we have employed throughout—quantities and neurons—a theory should also account for this ignorance of ours [*dieses Nichtwissen*].
>
> We immediately become aware of the presupposition that has hitherto guided us. We have treated psychic processes as things that can do without this knowing undertaken by consciousness, as things that exist independently of such knowing. We are quite prepared not to find the particulars of our suppositions corroborated by consciousness. If we do not allow ourselves to be deceived in this regard, our being so prepared follows from the presupposition that consciousness provides neither complete nor reliable knowledge of neural processes; the latter are from the outset to be regarded in their full scope as unconscious, as though they are to be disclosed like any other item of nature [*wie andere natürliche Dinge zu erschliessen*].

Why does Freud bother with these platitudes? What rises to disturb him—which disturbs so few disciples of the *Traité de l'Homme*? Is it not as though a reversal in what Hegel will have called the "experience of consciousness" occurs here, a primal reversal; as though precisely at this breach something like a phenomenology of spirit were on the verge of instigating itself once again? The next paragraph of Freud's text (393) informs us of the nature of the disturbance: if neurons function and quantities flow without our being conscious of them, if they can *dispense with* consciousness and *dispose of it*, then they must somehow have *disposition over* consciousness, both producing and exceeding it. Into which system then is consciousness to be mustered, integrated, ordered, or reduced (*einzureihen*)? Freud does not hesitate: "But then the content of consciousness [*der Inhalt des Bewusstseins*] is to be integrated into our quantitative ψ processes." Why into the endogenous, psychic, mnemic system? And *how*, inasmuch as consciousness is introduced via quality, and not quantity? Freud will not always decide for the ψ system. In fact, containment of consciousness will soon call for a major revision in the binary structure of the theory. For there is a kind of difference in and about consciousness that resists both typography (contact barriers, effraction) and topography (difference in destiny, milieu).

"Consciousness gives us what we call *qualities*, sensations [*Empfindungen*] that in their vast multiplicity are *otherwise* [*die in grosser Mannigfaltigkeit anders sind*] and whose being *otherwise* [*und deren Anders*] is distinguished by relationships with the external world" (393). The reiterated *Anders* is odd both grammatically and lexically. Its oddness reflects something of importance for the differential theory Freud is trying to develop. "In this otherwise there are sequences, similarities, and such-like; there are, properly speaking, no quantities in it." In the being otherwise of consciousness, in abundant and multifaceted relationships with the outer world, the theory of quantitative energy-flow proves to be all but irrelevant. Why the flagging confidence, when up to now Freud has been perfectly willing to speculate and soar, his text itself coarsing   *as highly charged with electrons as haphazards can*   like quantity? Freud does not say, but poses other questions instead: "One might ask, *how* do qualities originate, and *where* do they originate?" He is not confident that answers will come easily: "These are questions that require the most solicitous investigation, questions we can here take up only in a rough-and-ready way." He elaborates the topological question as follows:

> Where? Where do qualities originate? Not in the external world. For according to our natural-scientific view, to which psychology too is here to be subjected [*unterworfen werden soll*], outside there are only masses in motion, nothing else. Perhaps they originate in the φ system? What inclines us in that direction is the fact that qualities are bound up with perception [*Wahrnehmung*]; yet this contradicts everything else that is to be rightly claimed for the seat of consciousness in the superior levels of the nervous system. Well, then, in the ψ system. An important objection rises against this, however: in perception the φ and ψ systems are both active, working with one another; there is, however, a psychic process that occurs exclusively in ψ, to wit, reproduction or remembrance, and this in general terms is *without quality*. Remembrance establishes *de norma* nothing of the special kind of perceptual quality. Thus one is encouraged to suppose that there may be a third system of neurons, perceptual neurons, as it were, that are coexcited whenever we perceive, though not whenever we reproduce [in memory]; the states of excitation undergone by the system of perceptual neurons produce the various qualities, which are *conscious sensations*. (393)

The place and function of this third neural system, the W system (= *Wahrnehmung* or perception, transliterated [presumably by Freud himself] misleadingly as the ω [omega] system), shift and oscillate, bedeviling Freud's psychology over decades.[9] Why, we must ask, is quality attributed to perception, and not to memory? Why is memory banished from quality, and thus from consciousness? Is it merely the Hobbesian, Humean notion of memory and imagination as faded, lackluster perception, perception devoid of "such a pitch of vivacity," that induces Freud to associate quality solely with perception? At all events, and no matter what may have induced him, can a theory that divorces perception and memory satisfy?

Freud acknowledges that the demands of quantitative science impose themselves on the *description* of conscious qualities that he is now assaying to provide. Yet rather than being abashed by such an imposition, he endeavors to take advantage of the entanglement of method in the matter in order to produce a kind of deduction, a *Regeldetri* or "golden rule" that will find the unknown *fourth* where *three* are given. "For whereas science has posed for itself the task of leading our sensible *qualities* collectively back to *external quantity*, we can expect of the structure of the nervous system that it will consist of contrivances [*Vorrichtungen*] that transform external *quantity* into quality, whereby the original tendency toward the obstruction of *quantity* again appears to be victorious" (394). Freud depicts the nerve-end apparatus as a series of shields, umbrellas, or filters that gradually decrease the amount of penetrating quantity. Initially, he places the perceptual system—and hence consciousness—at the most interior level, as Diagram 1 (mine, not Freud's) indicates. By the time endogenous quantity reaches the perceptual system it should be excluded as much as possible (*möglichst ausgeschaltet*); it should be transformed into pure quality. Yet the system as depicted confronts "an enormous difficulty," a difficulty that arises at about the place where "memory" meets "consciousness and quality": if permeability allows the influx of quantity, and if the system is already essentially or virtually impermeable, then it becomes difficult to see how the W system could account for the ephemeral stream of consciousness, the rapid alteration and flux of its content, and the

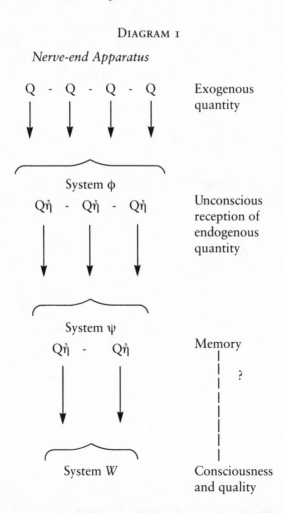

DIAGRAM 1

Nerve-end Apparatus

seamless transition from one perceived quality to another contemporaneous quality. Only "full permeability" and "complete *restitutio in integrum*" will do for perception. Perceptual neurons, like the organs of perception, thus can have nothing to do with memory. Yet where could such full permeability and total effraction stem from, if not from quantity? The introduction of perceptual quality and conscious sensation entails a crisis of typography: if quantity is effectively filtered out by the φ system, what possible *antitypia* could connect perception with the external world?

No doubt it is this crisis that will instigate the change in Freud's account which he reports to Fliess in letter 39, dated January 1, 1896. Put most simply, what Freud suggests here is that the W system be intercalated between the φ and ψ systems. Further, φ is now said to transmit its *quality* to W. The latter is now represented as transmitting neither quality nor quantity to ψ. Indeed, how could it do so when ω neurons are defined as having the capacity for only the "most meager quantitative cathexis"? Mysteriously, the W system is said to "incite" (*anregen*) the ψ system, with no real transmission of quantity. (One recalls Descartes' expression *nihil reale transmigrare* in the *Regulae*.) Freud doubtless senses the continuing crisis: "I don't know whether you can understand this gobbledygook," he writes to Fliess (153). The letter goes on   *I don't understand. I fail to say. I dearsee you too*   to discuss consciousness in general, as well as a "secondary, artificial consciousness" that advenes as a supplement to the ψ system, a consciousness that has to do with "linguistic association." However, the third part of the "Project" will also take us there, and so we return to Freud's *Entwurf*.

For the moment, Freud sees "only one way out," and that is to revise thoroughly his basic assumptions about endogenous quantity flow. The revision here (395) takes the form of introducing a "temporal nature" into such quantity. It is not as painful an introduction as it might seem, if we remember that *t* is a factor in almost all laws of mechanics. However, it is not time as such that Freud   *now and then, time on time again, as per periodicity*   introduces, but *periodicity*. No doubt Fliess's fixation on the functions of *periods* in the lives of both male and female human beings helps to breach Freud's "way out." Periodicity would account for a motion within and among neurons that no contact barrier could resist. Even though the W system would be incapable of taking up and passing on to ψ even endogenous quantities, it would be subject to "*periods* of excitation." Affection by periods, requiring a modicum of quantity, would constitute "the fundament of consciousness."

Whether and how periodicity alters the fundamental conception of neural inertia remains a crucial question. Was not quantity from the outset conceived as periodic, that is, as occurring in relatively discrete and differential bursts of energy, reminiscent perhaps of those foraying parties of animal spirits? And what are we to make of an incitement or excitation (*Anregung/Erregung*) that would not function as a typographic impressing? Are we not, even with periodicity, still locked within a typographic system of the crudest sort? Freud only makes matters worse when he expands the notion of periodicity in order to embrace the ψ system as well, arguing that it is here merely "without quality" or "monotonous." He broaches the urgent question, however, when he reverts to the issue of the origin of differences (*Verschiedenheiten*) among the periods. For the system has been differential from the start, whether the origin of differences was attributed to sundry nerve systems, varying thicknesses of the axons, contact barriers, breachings, quantities, destinies, or milieus.

Freud now shifts his theater of operations from the nerve-end apparatus to the various sense organs themselves; the action of these he depicts by means of an inversion   *and everthelest your umbr*   of the protective umbrella. Sense organs function rather as *sieves*. They allow only particular *periods* of stimulus to pass. They somehow communicate periodic difference (*diese Verschiedenheit*) to the neurons by way of "analogous" motion. (Recall Descartes' eventual embrace of feathery *analogy* for cognition—also in the *Regulae*.) These "modifications" (presumably not structural alterations but periodic motions, a kind of neural Morse Code) pass through the φ system to the ψ system and on to the perceptual system. (Only later, as we have noted, will *W* be sandwiched between φ and ψ.) There, well-nigh free of quantity, these periodic motions "produce conscious sensations of qualities." Now, even though the periodic motions pass through ψ, they leave no traces (*keine Spuren*), so that perception is not reproducible *as such*. Freud will return to this last quandary (e.g. at 419 and 444), which we have already had occasion to mention, the quandary that makes it impossible for us to conceive how anything perceived could ever be remembered. Although it is certainly difficult to depict periodicity as such, the sieves or filters   *now that I come to drink of it filtred, a gracecup fulled of bitterness*   that are organs of sensation might be portrayed as in Diagram 2.

The breach in Freud's "Project" expands with his account of "Consciousness," closely tied to the sensation of qualities in perception. Here Freud seeks to demonstrate that consciousness is not a psychic process as such, that it occurs outside the ψ system. Whether or not memory can ever be regained for consciousness, or consciousness for memory, remains the burning question. Surely, we can attain satisfaction only when memory, perception, and consciousness are fully integrated, though not conflated.[10]

Freud has by now (396–97) identified consciousness with the perceptual system, but he complicates that system by adducing to it the paramount qualities of pleasure and unpleasure. The latter, *Unlust*, at first seems to correspond to what was earlier identified as pain. Yet both intense pleasure and excruciating pain diminish the zone of potentially perceived qualities, which is always a "zone of indifference" with regard to *Lust* and *Unlust*. After providing a detailed résumé of "the functioning of the apparatus" (397–400), Freud reasserts the inexplicable yet essential capacity of the nuclear neurons, that is, the central nervous system, to be both fully effracted, fully "paved," and highly resistant—thus capable of retention. No distinction between quantity and periodicity, no account of "intermittence" and "summation," no appeal to the "defenseless exposure" of the ψ system to quantity as the "*trigger* [Triebfeder]

Diagram 2

Sense Organs

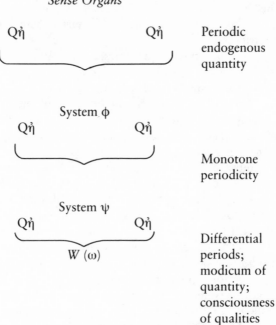

Qἠ   Qἠ   Periodic
                                  endogenous
                                  quantity

System φ
Qἠ   Qἠ

                                  Monotone
                                  periodicity

System ψ
Qἠ   Qἠ
        W (ω)   Differential
                                  periods;
                                  modicum of
                                  quantity;
                                  consciousness
                                  of qualities

of the psychic mechanism" will dissolve the paradox. Nor will the introduction of two new terms destined to designate the source of power (*Antrieb, Macht*) for all psychic activity, terms for which the sketch has not adequately prepared the reader: "We know this power to be the *will* [*der* Wille], the descendant of the *drives* [Triebe]" (402). If philosophy is Freud's initial goal, for which medicine is the detour, the regnant philosopher appears to be Schopenhauer. As we have always known (see *Jenseits*, StA 3, 259). Except that the words *Wille* and *Trieb* will survive Schopenhauer to dominate the entire tradition of *Lebensphilosophie* from Dilthey, Nietzsche, Driesch, and Scheler up to a very unwilling Heidegger.[11]

Yet no such appeal to possible "influences" will aid us in following the giant steps Freud now takes in portraying "the experience of satisfaction" (402–4), not *Lust* but *Befriedigung*, "pacification," in the face of calamitous life, a life of will, compulsion, and drive. Compulsion, *Drang*, seeks discharge in the motor system. If such discharge produces only "internal" changes such as shifts in mood, cries, or the innervation of blood vessels, the surge of the compulsion will not be checked. Cessation of the stimulus in ψ can occur only by virtue of *an intervention in the outer world,* instigation of a specific action that brings on nourishment or reaches the sexual object. To be sure, the infantile human organism is incapable of direct interventions to supply itself with nourishment; it relies on "an experienced individual" to provide "*help from the outside* [fremde Hilfe]." Thus the "internal" changes rejected above actually fulfill "the supremely important secondary function of *making oneself understood* [Verständigung], and the primordial helplessness of the human being is the *primal source* [Urquelle] of all *moral motives.*" Freud allows us no time to catch our breaths but proceeds   *If I lose my breath for a minute or two, don't speak, remember!* ... *It's thinking of all* ... *I'll begin again in a jiffey* ... *How well you'll feel! For ever after*   to an even more fateful deduction. The experience of satisfaction through foreign aid, as it were, the checking of compulsion through the specific actions of benevolent persons in the outside world, has the most telling consequences for the further development of the individual. Satisfaction, the achievement of inner peace, occurs by way of a cathexis (or "occupation," *Besetzung,* a term introduced already in the second section of Part One)—not merely a discharge. Cathexis of an *object perceived as essential* to the discharge of unpleasure. Through the operation of association by contemporaneity a cathexis is established that proves to be every bit as important as the effraction that allows for the discharge of distressful quantity: a breaching is established "between two mnemic images," that is, presumably, between the *Erinnerungsbildern* of the situations "before" and "after" the experience of satiation. Further, a breaching is established between this pair of images and the nuclear neuron to which the compulsion—given the exigency of life—will inevitably return. As the compulsion or wish (*Wunsch*) is activated, the already established breaching will lead to the image of the remembered object, *das Objekterinnerungsbild.* That image is of course an icon, the particular icon   *You were dreamend, dear*   associated with satiety, the cessation of hunger and the achievement of peace. At long last memory and perception are to be linked! Freud forges the link, enacts the primordial iconography of memory, as follows: "I do not doubt that this activation of the wish at first produces the same thing that the perception does [*zunächst dasselbe ergibt wie die Wahrnehmung*], namely, an *hallucination.*"   *Sonly all in your imagination, dim. Poor little brittle magic nation, dim of mind!*   Should the motor nervous system swing into action, should the infant head turn and the groping mouth begin to suck, suck air, "disappointment will not be wanting [*so bleibt die Enttäuschung nicht aus*]." Which makes it easy to see   *I said are you there here's nobody here only me*   why a return to the "experience of pain" is necessary. When in Freud's sketch toward a scientific psychology, typography becomes iconography, the result is delusion and torment, a wretchedness on the verge of outrage.

Once we have caught our breath, now realizing why it was vital for Freud to protect W from ψ, we do well to press Freud on these mnemic images that originate in perception and terminate in hallucination. Does mere quantity produce them, or quality, or some sort of periodic mixture of both? What precisely is the relation of Freudian iconography (if that word can be retained when it is purely a matter of *phantastikē*) to typography? And will there be no sign, no reading, no engrammatology, to rout the phantasms?

The mnemic image also comes to play a role in the experience of pain (404–

5). Pain cannot be *equated* with unpleasure, yet the unpleasure sensed in W and the tendency to discharge (because of an overload in ψ) are doubtless associated through breaching with "a mnemic image of the object that excites pain." It is the action of this image that calls forth quantity, not in order to discharge it via the motor system, but by way of detours (*auf Umwegen*) to key it into a *power affect*. This mechanism now captures Freud's imagination. "Key neurons," "*Schlüsselneuronen*," instrumental to the release of pleasure and unpleasure in the efferent (motor) system, hence to sexuality, involve the cathexis of mnemic images. Freud does not pause to comment on this *Besetzung von Erinnerungen* (405, lines 1–2), a catachresis that wreaks havoc with his efforts to distinguish quality from quantity. Indeed, mnemic images themselves, connected not by effraction but by some subordinate "circuitry" (*die ψ -Leitungen*), will soon begin to behave like little quantities, even though as early as 1891 it was clear to Freud that "representations" could not be encapsulated in "cells" (see StA 3, 165–66). There also seems to be some confusion as to whether the image produces the affect, or the affect the image, even though it is here a matter of *re-production* and thus activation of cathected images as such. In an outrageous reversal, the icons themselves now function as *typoi*. The "key neurons," stimulated by the excess of quantity in ψ, *a quantity itself released by the cathexis of memories*, mediate between "mnemic image" and "affect unpleasure." Pain has opened a "superb breaching" to them. Pain will be the engrammatological power. Yet who is there to "read" pain?

Freud will soon introduce the ego (406–8), but only by way of further clarification of *Affekt*, "affects and wishful states," *Wunschzustände* (405–6). Affects and wishful or desirous states complement the pair *pain* and *satisfaction* and constitute the four fundamental psychic *Erlebnisse*. Affect, produced by a sudden release of quantity in ψ, is, as we have seen, closely associated with pain; it will not surprise us (thanks to the art of *Regeldetri*) that satisfaction or pacification relates closely to wishful states produced by *summation* or the gradual accretion of small quantities in ψ. Affect and wish are of supreme importance for the psychic process, writes Freud; they supply the "motives" for that process as such. "Out of the wishful state there arises immediately an *attraction* toward the object wished for or its mnemic image; from the experiences of pain there results a repulsion, a revulsion against cathexis of the inimical mnemic image." Freud's prosopopoeia with regard to the psychic motives indicates the incipient unfolding of a primal drama, a primal scene: "These [motives] are primary *desirous attraction* [Wunschanziehung] and primary *defense* [Abwehr]."

In spite of the fact that the two prior discussions of pain ought to have made description of the defense mechanism less laborious than an account of desirous attraction, the latter will be dealt with quite readily, whereas the former will eventually destroy the entire project. Desirous attraction is consequent upon an excess in the cathexis of a "friendly memory." Craving or desire (*der Begierdezustand*) involves an excess beyond what any mere perception of the object would produce. The excess in quantity in turn produces "an especially good breaching" in the ψ system between a nuclear and a "mantle" neuron nearer the periphery, in the pallium. Desire *moves*.

"It is more difficult to explain primary *defense* or *repression*," emphasizes Freud, writing the crucial word *Verdrängung* here for the first time and adding, by way of apposition, "the fact that an inimical mnemic image will be abandoned by cathexis as soon as possible." (Kris notes that Freud later, at 430, distinguishes between primary defence and repression, as he does much later, in the 1915 essay on "Repression," between flight from pain and repression [StA 3, 108].) Perhaps the difficulty can be seen, however darkly, in the awkward phrase "will be abandoned by cathexis," *dass ein feindliches Erinnerungsbild so bald als möglich von der Besetzung verlassen wird.*" What can it mean to abandon a memory? And how does cathexis come to don the mask of agency and the subject? What *is* cathexis? Heretofore it has meant the occupation of neurons by quantity; it entered into Freud's account so long ago and so lubriciously that we have scarcely noted or noticed it. Yet if the fundamental tendency of the nervous system as a whole is *discharge* of quantity, we should perhaps puzzle over it even after Freud has introduced the fundamental revisions of quality and periodicity.

Periods were introduced as a process of energic *induction*, the *appropriation of* and *filling with* quality. Quality entered on the scene as that final sifting of quantity that gets through to the W system. *Besetzung* was first employed in a new sense beginning with the section on "Consciousness" (397), in the context of pleasure and unpleasure: "Pleasure and unpleasure would be the sensations of their own cathexis [*wären die Empfindungen der eigenen Besetzung*], of their own level in W [*des eigenen Niveaus in W*], whereby W and ψ represent in a certain way containers that communicate with one another." To what does the word *eigen*, "own," refer in these phrases? Perhaps to sensation of the qualities pleasure and unpleasure *as the original auto-affection?* An auto-affection, we remember, that reduces the zone of perceptual qualities. Reduces them to the *essential* motives or *Erlebnisse*.

The economy of cathexis in the W neurons as developed in the final lines of the section on consciousness (397) is far from pellucid. It will be necessary to "introduce the 'ego' " if we are to make any sense of cathexis as auto-affection. In the meantime, Freud can only appeal to the model of flight from pain, which is merely analogous to primary defense and even farther removed from the pressing issue of primary repression, whose very name suggests the auto-affection of unpleasure. Primary experiences of pain are brought to an end by defenses consisting of simple reflex actions. Yet Freud complicates such simple action by introducing a kind of semaphore, a kind of engrammatology. Inasmuch as signals and signs will become increasingly important in the 1895 sketch, we ought to let the drama unfold, even though the personifications employed now seem truly comic. "The emergence of another object in the place of the inimical one was the signal that the experience of pain was over." Thus the hand stops hurting as soon as the object "water" emerges in place of "fire," because, as Freud will now say, the hand is biologically instructed, *biologisch belehrt*. The ψ system thus endeavors to "reproduce" the image of the state that signals cessation of pain. Freud argues that biological learning too can be traced back to mechanical principles and quantitative moments, forgetting for the nonce those revisions of the theory that have already forced themselves on him. "In the case at hand, it can readily be the increase in endogenous quantity always accompanying the cathexis of inimical memories that compels us toward an increase in discharge activity, and thus toward a flushing away of memories too [*zum Abfluss auch von Erinnerungen drängt*]." With the coupling of compelling memories and the root of repression, *Drang* and *Verdrängung*, Freud's "Project" enters a new phase—

"THE INTRODUCTION OF THE 'EGO'"

The ego is an "organization" in the ψ system, an organization of neurons in the nucleus or kernel (*des Kernes*) of that system. Such neurons are *continuously* cathected by endogenous quantity and thus constitute reserves (*Vorrat*) needed to effect changes in the outside world. Freud offers the following perfunctory account of the ego's function (an account that remains nonetheless relevant for *Beyond the Pleasure Principle* [1920] and *The Ego and the Id* [1923]): "While it remains necessary for the ego to strive to surrender its cathexes along the path of satisfaction [*auf dem Wege der Befriedigung*], this can happen in no other way than by influencing the repetition of painful experiences and affects [*die Wiederholung von Schmerzerlebnissen und Affekten*] in the manner now to be described, which can generally be designated as *inhibition* [Hemmung]" (407). The principal mechanism of inhibition—the influencing of repetitious, painful experiences—is "lateral cathexis," *Seitenbesetzung*, a manner of "sidetracking" a quotient of quantity. Freud's sketch in Diagram 3 illustrates this complex inhibitory influence.

DIAGRAM 3

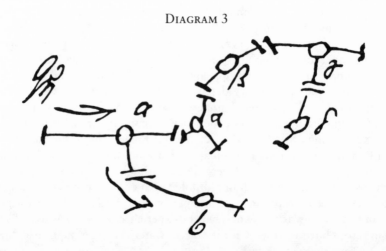

Here the lower arrow actually indicates the *normal* path of a quantity of endogenous energy (that is, one that has already passed through the filter of the φ system) from neuron *a* to *b*. That normal path represents "psychic primary processes," to which Freud will soon turn. The ego exists precisely in order to inhibit that process by diverting a quotient of quantity, and eventually perhaps all of it, from *b* to α (alpha). It is intriguing that the sidetracking indicated here actually follows straight-line motion in the diagram, from *a* to α, so that lateral cathexis is actually *preferred* to what is otherwise called *primary*. Inhibition, writes Freud, is "a decisive advantage for ψ" (408). That advantage becomes clear in the following narrative: "Let us suppose [*Nehmen wir an*] that *a* is an inimical memory [*eine feindliche Erinnerung*]. . . ." Never mind the question as to how tube-station *a* of the neural Metro can be said to *be* a memory: let us grant that a certain iconography has translated the mnemic image (*Bild*) into protoplasm, that a certain typography has become amalgamated with topography. Let us suppose further, writes Freud, that *b* is "a key-neuron for unpleasure." The awakening (*Erweckung*) of *a*, that is, the activation of the inimical memory image leads directly (*a→b*) to the release or parturition (*Entbindung*) of unpleasure. Key-neuron *b* might well have remained quiescent had it not been for the awakening of *a;* its unpleasure would have had no goal, and, *zwecklos*, its full burden would not have fallen on the system. However, the lateral cathexis α-δ, which is nothing else than the ego-organization, comes to play a major inhibitory role now that the icon *a* has been stirred to wakeful life. The release of unpleasure will be "slight," thanks to that rescue organization; the neural system will be "spared" (*erspart*) the "development and discharge of quantity."

Yet how does α know—yes, *know*—when to step into the breach? How is the ego-organization alerted to the imminent awakening of *a*? Where does the switchman sit? Or the *fontenier*? Now that the lace cuff graces the hand of the ego—what Augustine called "the hand of my heart," the hand that repulses unwanted memories—and now that the hand of the ego operates the sidetracking mechanism, a special sort of *signaling system* will have to be brought into service. For only if some signal makes the ego *aware* (aufmerksam) of the imminent reoccupation (*die ankommende Neubesetzung*) of *a* and *b* can the ego exert itself. The signaling system proves to be the crucial contribution of the ego in both the "primary process and secondary process in ψ" (409–11). Freud will return to it in the third and final section of his project, "Attempt to Portray the Normal Processes" (443).

Two outrages menace the psychic system. First, vulnerability (*Hilflosigkeit*) and the resultant damage (*Schaden*) enter on the scene when in *desire* (*im Wunschzustande*) the "object-memory" is recathected in a situation where "satisfaction must perforce remain in default—inasmuch as the object is not at hand *in reality* [*nicht real vorhanden*] but is only present in fantasy-*representation* [*nur in Phantasie*-Vorstellung *vorhanden ist*]" (409). The icon is *prokheiros*, at hand, as the vestige of Theodorus, "gift of god"; yet it may very well be snubnosed Theaetetus, or even Socrates, that I see. *False judgment is possible.* And in the primary process, where craving itself conjures the *hallucination* of pacification, all but inevitable. "ψ is initially incapable of making this distinction [between *reale Vorhandenheit* and fantastic representation, *phantastikē*], because it can only work according to the sequence of analogous states among its neurons." The system therefore needs "from elsewhere a criterion for distinguishing between *perception* and *representation* [Wahrnehmung *und* Vorstellung]."[12]

The second outrage to befall the psychic system, the impending reoccupation of an inimical memory-image, can be averted only if the system is made aware of it. The system can prevent (*vorbeugen*) the release of unpleasure only if it inhibits the reoccupation sufficiently ahead of time (*zeitig genug*). Such inhibition, effected by the lateral occupation of the ego-organization, needs a sign, *ein Zeichen,* or what the "Two Principles" calls "a system of *marks*" (StA 3, 19). The iconography of memory images will require a revamped engrammatology, one that will avert and divert cathexis rather than simply restore (hallucinatory) presence. If such engrammatology fails, if the signal is not forthcoming, the result will be "staggering unpleasure and excessive primary defense." (Freud's mention of *primary* defense here must make us ask whether the process we are now discussing, that of signal and sidetracking, is primary or secondary; it seems likely that lateral cathexis is a secondary process, "primary process" being reserved for discharge of quantity; yet we will no doubt have cause to return to this theme more than once.)

In order to avoid "biological damage," the psychic system must prevent both excessive "wish cathexis" and the occupation of "inimical memory images," especially when the latter arise not from the external world but from associations within the system itself. In other words, hallucination is possible in cases of trauma as well as pleasure, and is in both cases harmful, inasmuch as it seduces (*verlockt*) the system into excessive discharge. The solution in both cases "is a matter of a sign [*ein Zeichen*] to distinguish perception [which for Freud is virtually always *true* perception, *Wahr-nehmung*] from remembrance (representation)." Freud is asking for a sign that will pass between ψ and W. Pass between them as readily as a period. *In hoc signo* Freud will emerge victorious with a scientific psychology securely in hand. Whence such a sign? "It is probably the perceptual neurons that yield this sign, the *reality sign.*" With every perception of the external world, a qualitative excitation occurs in the perceptual nervous system. "News" of that discharge of excitation reaches ψ. (It appears that the diagrams of both the nerve-end apparatus and the sense organs are now placed on their heads, the umbrellas and sieves inverted once again, so that system W now stands at the top.) "*News of the discharge of W(ω) is therefore the seal of quality, or reality sign, for ψ* [das Qualitäts- oder Realitätszeichen für ψ]" (410).

We ought to pause in order to underscore the anomaly. The very first axiom of a scientific psychology is "the quantitative conception" (380–81); and now "reality," that is, contact with the "external world," a world which, scientifically considered, is nothing but quantity, proves to depend on the communication of quality, not quantity. *Quality is more real than quantity.* Yet the *commu-*

nication of quality itself depends on the quantity of excitation, whereby the decisive factor is the cathected ego-organization. The latter alone "*makes possible a criterion for distinguishing between perception and remembrance*" (410). Without following all the ins and outs of the mechanics of the qualitative signal, we may allow Freud to summarize as follows:

> The cathexis of desire [*Wunschbesetzung*] to the point of hallucination [and] the full development of unpleasure [*die volle Unlustentwicklung*], which brings the full exertion of defense with it, we shall designate as *psychic primary processes;* by contrast, those processes that a sound cathexis of the ego makes possible and that represent a moderating influence on the above, we shall call *psychic secondary processes.* As we see, the condition of the latter is a correct application of the *reality sign,* an application that is possible only by means of the inhibiting action of the ego [*bei Ichhemmung*]. (411)

With the "sound cathexis of the ego," we are not far from what the *Traumdeutung* will call the "probing labors of thought" (StA 2, 569). The next three sections of the 1895 psychology focus on "Cognitive [*Erkennende*] and Reproductive Thinking," "Remembering and Judging," and "Thought and Reality" (411–19). We shall limn their contents only in the broadest strokes, since Freud himself will bring us back to them in Part Three. Yet even these broad strokes will have to delineate the bizarre terrain between primary and secondary processes, the no-man's-land of *Regeldetri,* neural syntax, identity, and the teat   *in our mutter nation*   of the breast, to which Freud now leads us.

Inhibition by the ego, that is, the sidetracking and binding of excessive quantity streaming from an excessively desired icon in ψ, allows hallucination—which is the natural condition for man, man's initial state of nature—to come to an end. Inhibition enables us to know or recognize (*erkennen*) that the craved object may well be unreal, *nicht real,* that is, not truly present at hand, *ou prokheiros.* Presuming that it is the *hand* that craves, although it is not. Freud projects three possible situations: (1) total coverage (the Husserlian notion of *volle Deckung* is perfectly apt here) between the memory image cathected by desire and a perception; (2) partial coverage, a far more "interesting" situation in that it calls forth genuine labors of thought, *Denkarbeit;* and (3) total dysymmetry, which leaves us with nothing to say or think or do. About the first we need only remark that while it served as the *Limes* of Husserl's dreams, which were from start to finish dreams of *volle Deckung,* Freud finds it of no "biological interest." It does provide an opportunity (taken by Ernst Kris) to present a passage from a much later text, "*Die Verneinung*" (1925; StA 3, 375–76), that provides a context for the entire discussion of the "reality probe" that is *Denken.*

> The first and most proximate goal of the reality probe [*Realitätsprüfung*] is therefore not to find an object in real perception that corresponds to the one represented but to *find it again,* to convince oneself that it is still at hand. A further contribution to the estrangement [*Entfremdung*] between the subjective and the objective arises from another capacity of our thinking faculty. The reproduction of perception in representation is not always its faithful retrieval [*Wiederholung*]; it can be

modified by omissions and transmogrified by the fusion of diverse elements. It is the task of the reality probe to oversee [*kontrollieren*] how far these distortions go. One realizes however that it is a condition for the institution of the reality probe that objects have gotten lost, objects that once provided real satisfaction.

It will thus always have been a matter of loss and alienation, of the primary outrage we saw impending some pages back. It will always be a matter of retrieval with distortion and after frustration. It will be, under the best of circumstances, a calculation of the damage done, an estimate of losses, a salvage operation, a "repetition of painful experience." The vigor of the 1895 sketch and all its bravura flights of physiologic fancy cannot conceal the deprivation or annul the outrage.

What is it that gets "covered" when desire and perception only partly coalesce? "It is . . . time to remember," writes Freud, "that perceptual cathexes are never cathexes of individual neurons, but always of complexes" (412). The meeting of desire and perception, through breaching, occurs complex to complex. If the cathected *desire* can also be represented as neuron *a* joined by effraction to neuron *b*, the cathected *perception* may be represented as neuron *a* joined by effraction to neuron *c*, as follows:

$$N(a) + N(b) = N(a) + N(c)$$

The problem is of course to establish the equality, validate the equal sign. However convincing *Regedetri* may be (recall that Freud employed it in "The Problem of Quality" in order to invert the umbrella of the nerve-end apparatus into the sieve of the sense-organ apparatus; that is to say, in order to take science's project of reducing perceptual quality to measurable quantity as the inverse of the structure of the nervous system, which filters   *down the scales, the way they went up, under talls and threading tormentors, shunning the startraps and slipping in sliders, risking a runway, ruing reveals* quantity in order to perceive quality), no apodictic or adequate equation seems possible. It is far more commonly the case that the "reality sign" corroborates only a partial dovetailing of complexes. Even that part is questionable, as we might imagine. How is the identical neuron *a* known to be involved in the cathexis of both desire and perception? Freud will fall back on the principle of identity (*a* = *a*), and yet nothing in the "sieve" diagram allows us to assume that a *neuron* can travel back and forth between systems ψ and W. To be sure, some sort of transport will be necessary in addition to the energetic effraction and circuitry discussed so far, some other sort of wandering, some passing of signs or engrams, a kind of news network. For the moment, Freud is content to assert that comparison (*Vergleich*) is possible within a whole range of perceptual complexes where neuron *a* prevails and then to analyze or dissect (*zerlegen*) the perceptual complex in which *a* remains stable as *b* "varies." And he does not shy from an even more astonishingly unabashed use of *Regeldetri*:

Language [*Die Sprache*] will later propose the term judgment [*Urteil*] for this analysis [Zerlegung] and will uncover the similarity that actually exists [*tatsächlich vorliegt*] between the nucleus of the ego and the constant perceptual component, and between the transitory cathexes in the pallium and the inconstant component; language will call neuron *a* the *thing* and neuron *b* its activity or property, in short, its *predicate*. (412–13)

Iconograpy and engrammatology here perform their most dazzling classical maneuvers, and the clumsy typography of breachings appears to be effectively sidetracked. Neuron *a* now embraces (1) the constant component of an entire range of perceptual cathexes somewhere on the frontier between W and ψ; (2) the nucleus of the ego, the subject, both as the subject-pole of the thinking process and as the grammatical subject of sentences; and (3) the thing, *das Ding*, also as the subject of propositions. Neuron *b* is now declared to be a component of the W complex, its variable component, whereas earlier it was identified as a component of the *Wunschbesetzung*, the cathexis of desire, or even as a depot of unpleasure. Neuron *b* is already traveling, already shifting, far more than neuron *a*; it has established by ruse a kind of identity that surely will fail to withstand even the most charitable reality probe. And what happened to neuron *c*, which was supposed to be the variable constituent of W? Neuron *c* will return in a moment, for it too is shifting. Yet let us not be distracted by the wanderings of *b* and the temporary disappearance of *c* to the point where we lose sight of the audacious character of Freud's thinking in the passages we are examining now. The thesis of Jacques Lacan, to the effect that the unconscious is structured as a language, seems quite tame in comparison with Freud's: Freud is suggesting that *the entire neural and psychical system is structured as a language,* that there is a protoplasmic or neurotopological syntax, a grammar of flesh that will ensure, among other things, the identity of things themselves and of subject and object, and ultimately of thought and being.

Freud declares judging, *Urteilen*, to be a process in ψ. We must be astonished by that as well, inasmuch as everything about reality seemed to depend on W, the perceptual system. Yet perception will prove to be anything but pure. As the very title of this section, "The Thinking that Recognizes and Reproduces [*Das erkennende und reproduzierende Denken*]," suggests, we are here precisely at the limits of ψ and W, where the one system passes, *must* pass, into the other. For Freud, as for Hegel and Hölderlin before him, *Urteil* is *Ur-Teilung*, the primal diremption and *ordeal* of the psyche. Judgment is first made possible by the inhibition produced by the ego-organization, without which every idol would be an icon, every image an original, every phantasm a phenomenon, every tremulous being an instance of full presence. Now that judgment is *possible*, it is "called forth" by the dissimilarity (*Unähnlichkeit*) between the desirous cathexis of a particular memory image and a perceptual cathexis that is similar to it (*ihr ähnlich*). How the similarity and dissimilarity confront one another, or rather, how the one calls forth a judgment upon the other, is a question that might send us scurrying back to *Theaetetus* and *Sophist*. Unlike *b*, however, we shall not scurry but hold our ground and continue reading. For we do not yet know the proper object of Freud's iconography. What *is* the object of desire? What constitutes the identity $a = a$?

One can analyze the process further: if neuron *a* coalesces [in the coverage of complexes], but neuron *c* is perceived instead of neuron *b*, the work of the ego [*Icharbeit*] pursues the connections of this neuron *c* and causes [*lässt*] new cathexes to emerge by force of the quantity streaming along these relays, until access to the missing neuron *b* is found. As a rule, a dynamic image [*Bewegungsbild*] results, coming into operation between neuron *c* and neuron *b;* with the reactivation of this image by means of an actually executed movement, the perception of neuron *b*, and thereby the sought identity, is produced. (413)

The next sentence of Freud's text—and we shall read it, since nothing about the "movement" of "judgment" is clear as yet—begins with a Z.B., *Zum Beispiel*, "For example." It will be Freud's *sole* example of a cathected desire, dynamic image, judgment, and perception coalescing. "For example, the desired mnemic image is the image   *Lowly, longly, a wail went forth. Pure Yawn lay low. On the mead of the hillock lay, heartsoul dormant mid shadowed landshape*   of the mother's breast and its   *lashbetassled lids on the verge of closing time, whiles ouze of his sidewiseopen mouth* nipple in full front view   *languishing as the princeliest treble treacle or lichee chewchow*   and the first perception is a lateral view of the same object without the nipple." The cathected memory image of desire and the initial or primary perception are related as full front view (remembered, not seen) to lateral, partial (perceived, not now remembered) view. "In the child's memory [*Erinnerung*] an experience may be found, an experience it had accidentally while   *Yawn in a semiswoon lay awailing and (hooh!) what helpings of honeyful swoothead (phew!)*   sucking, that with a certain turn of the head the full front image is transformed into the lateral image." The primal interiorization, quite contingent in its details yet absolutely essential as a scene, which is the scene of life's exigency, *die Not des Lebens,* the scene of desperately needed reserves and incipient ego-organization, involves the metamorphosis of full moon to new moon, no moon, and back again, as we too now shall see. "The lateral image now in view leads to a movement   *One seekings*   of the head; a first attempt shows   *Not the lithe slender, not the broad roundish near the lithe slender, not the fairsized fullfeatured to the leeward of the broad roundish but*   that its opposite must be executed, and the perception   *indeed and inneed, the curling, perfectportioned, flowerfleckled, shapely highhued, delicate features swaying to the windward of the fairsized fullfeatured*   of the full front view is achieved."

Such seeking and finding presuppose a nascent yet already efficient ego-organization. No amount of differentiated breaching or circuitry can account for it. For it is teleological, dominated by an aim, *einem Ziel.* All perception is tendentious. Like Husserl's *Leermeinen,* or empty intending, Freudian perception is preview and retrospect at once. "The aim is to return back to the missed neuron *b* and to trigger the sensation of identity, that is, the moment in which only neuron *b* is cathected—the moment when the itinerant cathexis steers home [*einmündet*] to neuron *b*" (414). Neuron *b*. Neuron *b*reast. Neuron Benjy. Whereas neuron *c* allows only a fixed pattern of breachings (by association) to occur in and as primary process, neuron b permits of various constellations of cathexis in the secondary process of reproductive thinking (*des reproduzierenden Denkens*), guided always by pain and unpleasure along its *via negativa* until it homes in, homes in on and into the mouth, where b *einmündet*.

Although Freud does acknowledge the possibility of a "pure act of thought," one that seeks pure identity without the ultimate goal of the return to neuron b, reproductive thinking in his view has an eminently "practical purpose" and "a biologically defined end." The need to cognize is the need to restore, to find one's way back. Again, Freud's schematic remarks on interiorizing remembrance (*erinnern*), awakening of memories (*wecken, wachrufen*), and judgment baffle, while his illustration strikes home. "Let us suppose that the object that provides the perception is similar to the object, a *fellow human being*" (415). We will not pause to note the remarkably speedy progress of the neophyte ego-organization, which has passed from a needy turn of the head to full-blown subjectivity and intersubjectivity. "The theoretical interest [in our fellow humans] can then be explained by way of the fact that *such* an object is simultaneously the first object that satisfied us [*das erste Befriedigungsobjekt*]; more, it is the first inimical object as well as the sole aiding power; it is therefore in our fellow human beings that man comes to know." *Am Nebenmenschen lernt darum der Mensch erkennen.* Freud recounts the way in which the other's gestures are read in my own body, the other's cry by my own remembered cry. He declines to enter into further detail, summarizing "Remembering and Judging" as follows:

> Let us be content to fasten onto the following point: it is the original interest in producing the situation of satisfaction that has produced *reproductive reminiscence* [*das* reproduzierende Nachdenken] on the one hand and *judging* [Beurteilen] on the other. The latter is a means to get from the real, given, perceived situation to the desired situation. Here the presupposition remains that the ψ processes are not uninhibited, but transpire in an active ego. The eminently practical direction of all thought-work would thereby be demonstrated. (416)

Finally, with "Thought and Reality," we are brought to the final phase of Part One of the 1895 project, which brings Freud to the place where he will have to begin in earnest: the place where dreams are made and analyzed. Expanding on the earlier, empty sense of identity, $a = a$, Freud now declares the "end and aim" of all thought processes to be "the establishment of a *condition of identity*, the transposition of a cathected endogenous quantity originating from outside [*sic*] to a neuron cathected by the ego" (416–17). The attempted fusion, or confusion, of inside and outside gives us pause: the cathected quantity is identified as endogenous Qἡ, thus as a part of the ψ system; and yet Freud specifies that the quantity "originates from outside." What has become of the peripheral system? What has become of quality, which relates the psyche to the outside world? Also dubious is Freud's neat distinction between two fields of operation for thinking: "*Cognitive* or *judgmental* thinking searches for identity [of the quantity deriving from the outside world] with a corporeal cathexis [*Körperbesetzung'*]; *reproductive* thinking searches for the identity [of such quantity] with a psychic cathexis (one's own lived experience)" (417). There is something uncanny about this division into bodily and psychic fields— when the psyche was to have been explained strictly in terms of quantity. Freud reinstates the traditional mind-body dualism in the very project that should have abolished that dualism forever. Yet there is no doubt that with lateral cathexis in system ψ and consequent ego-organization, something like subjectivity and an appropriate experience (*Ereignis*) that is irreducibly and properly one's own (*eigenes*) will not be far behind.

Such a reinstatement is no doubt crucial for the kind of "reality" Freud has in mind—the reality of personal history, in particular a sexual history characterized by latency or retardation till puberty, a history that the dynamic image of our corporeal being does so much to influence. The capacity for the imitation of movements and even for compassion with another's suffering points to a primitive or primary judgment based on pure association. Judgment in such cases is actually the *primary process,* and our later capacity for judgmental thought a modification (*Ermässigung*) of that process. We must recognize the later capacity as secondary, rooted in the earlier mimetic tendency. Freud now explicitly identifies the process of judgment as involving an integration of system φ and the "internal news" provided by ego cathexis. The discharge of quality invading from the outside leaves a certain residue, presumably in and for system W (perception), and Freud reverts to the things we perceive in the world in a sentence equal to any Wittgenstein ever penned: *Was wir Dinge nennen, sind Reste, die sich der Beurteilung entziehen.* "What we call things are residues that withdraw from judgment" (418). So much for the realism we confronted some pages earlier: the thing is no longer the stable neuron a beset by variable qualities; the thing itself, as Hegel would say, slips away. The reality sign is the mark of a certain withdrawal or pulling out, a remainder of quantity that cannot be either discharged or internally bound. The process of thought remains a cathexis in ψ, codetermined by lateral cathexis. And thought about things? Secondary process is a repetition (*Wiederholung*) of the original discharge in the ψ system "*on a lower level, with lesser quantities.*" The *binding* of excessive quantity in lateral cathexis, while crucial for that repetition, does not alone fulfill the iconographic function; that is, binding alone does not enable us to retrieve the residues that withdraw from discharge. Thinking must satisfy "another condition" (419). "It dare not alter in any essential way the effractions created by the primary processes, otherwise it falsifies the traces of reality [*die Spuren der Realität*]." What traces? We last saw them in Freud's discussion of periodicity, where the sifting and filtering of quantity to perceptual quality in the sense organs was discussed. Or *did* we see *Spuren* there? Certainly the *word* appeared, but only in a negation: "The propagation of quality cannot be maintained [*Haltbar ist diese Qualitätsfortpflanzung nicht*]; it leaves no traces [*sie hinterlässt keine Spuren*]; it is not reproducible" (395). Whence then the traces of reality that dare not be falsified? When did the things—these residues and remainders in withdrawal—ever march augustly through the soul in order to leave vestiges of their footfall? When we turn to Part Three of the "Project" it will be purely in order to search out the origin of these impossible traces. Freud already appears to be so sure of them—these traces of reality that his metapsychology never surrenders (see StA 3, 19, 134, 147, 210, 235, 289)—that he is prepared to entertain a secondary set of vestiges, those of the thought process itself. For it is indubitably the case, *unzweifelhaft*, as Descartes well knew, that the process of thought "leaves durable traces." How else explain the fact that the second time we go over something in thought—for example, in what Descartes called *enumeratio*—we expend significantly less energy? Freud now elides the two thoughts: in order not to falsify reality we need "special traces," "indicators" (*Anzeichen*) for our thought processes, indicators that constitute a "thought-memory" (*Denkgedächtnis*). And he makes a promise to which we shall hold him: "We will later hear by what means the traces of thought processes are distinguished from those of reality."

The final trinity of sections in Part One, "Primary Processes—Sleep and Dreams," "Dream Analysis," and "Dream Consciousness," conducts Freud to the very threshold of psychopathology. Here as well, only the broadest strokes. For our own engrammatological purposes, Part Three is, or at least promises to be, the decisive part.

Primary process in ψ occurs either as pain (penetration by exogenous quantity) or affect (endogenous quantity released by effraction); secondary process, modifying the primary, occurs by virtue of reproductive thought alone. Reproductive thinking, essentially a kind of memory, involves a transposition of endogenous quantity from the ego to a mainline cathexis by means of a "thought-interest" that is proportional to "affect-interest." Whether or not there are primary processes in ψ that do not require "attention" (*Aufmerksamkeit*) is now the question. Even though Freud says that such a question is to "remain open" (420), there is no doubt that what will be called the "psychology of the unconscious" hinges on it. For the iconography that is now to be established in the "similarity" between the mechanisms of psychoneurosis and normal dream function, as Ernst Kris notes (420 n. 1), will be "rediscovered" in 1899 by Freud, with the *Traumdeutung*, as the *via regia* of psychoanalytic theory and practice.

What in the 1895 "Project" is the relation of dream-work to thought-work? Are ego-organization and the transposition of endogenous quantity in secondary process involved in the same way in both thinking and dreaming? In spite of our (wholly justified) desire to paint in broad strokes, we shall once again have to follow Freud's text quite closely here. "It is an important fact that every day we have before us, during sleep, ψ primary processes that have gradually been biologically suppressed in ψ development." Every word here will prove to be important: that we have *alltäglich*, every day, every twenty-four hours, with every cycle of waking and sleeping, *vor uns*, before us, where "us" may well not be the ego-organization in the sense of perceptual consciousness but where "we" will still have some sort of access to "it," *alltäglich während des Schlafes*, during sleep, "it" or "them" being ψ-*Primärvorgänge*, processes involving the release of quantity as affect by way of breaching, processes *wie sie in der ψ-Entwicklung biologisch allmählich unterdrückt worden sind*. The "biological development" of ψ referred to here is presumably phylogenetic, not ontogenetic: the gradual suppression of certain processes over aeons of time, a suppression necessary for species development. So that something like *Unterdrückung*, oppression and suppression—not yet "repression," *Verdrängung*—would be the primary nature of primary process: the primal mystery. "A second fact of equal significance [is] that the pathological mechanisms that are disclosed by the most minute analyses of psychoneuroses possess the greatest similarity to dream processes." However significant this fact, its reminiscent cycle will not bring it back, its *rhaidiōs* will not fully revolve, until four years have passed in Freud's life. As though the iconography of dream and neurosis will itself have to suffer *Unterdrückung*.

And sleep? The scene of primary process brought before us every night of every day? The child sleeps as soon as the exigency of life disdains to torture it further with hunger, wet, and chill; nods pacified at the breast, *an der Brust*. The adult *post coenam et coitum*. "Condition for sleep is thus the *decrease of endogenous charge in the ψ nucleus*, which makes the secondary function (reproductive thinking) superfluous. In sleep the individual enjoys the ideal state [*Idealzustand*] of inertia, disburdened of the reserve of endogenous quantity." For pages and pages there has been no mention of inertia, *Trägheit*, pillar of the quantitative hypothesis. Sleep alone restores it to us. When we awaken, reserves agglomerate in the "ego," and so "we may surmise that it is discharge of the ego [*Ichentladung*] that conditions and characterizes sleep." Thus it becomes "immediately clear" that here (with *Ichentladung*) we have "the *condition for psychic primary processes*."

However, what is not immediately clear is the relation of vigilant *Ichhemmung* to the *Ichentladung* of sleep. We were careful to translate the former, not as inhibition *of* the ego, but inhibition *by* the ego. Ego-organization and lateral cathexis were introduced in order to sidetrack quantity that is bound for cathexis in a traumatic or excessively desired mnemic image, bound in either case for pain and unpleasure. If we now translate *Ichentladung* as anything else than discharge *by* the ego, if we let the ego sink into oblivion, how will we find peace and satiety? Or is it the case that once the ego has done its work of deflection it can—indeed must—be dispensed with? "Whether with adults in sleep the *ego* completely disburdens itself is uncertain." The phrase *sich vollständig entlastet* suggests that the ego is the subject (if not the agent) and by no means simply the object of the disburdening. Once needed in order to prevent the most damaging excesses from occurring in the primary process, the ego-organization is perhaps now to be (temporarily) retired. And in this context, yet another sentence for Wittgenstein: "From the peculiarities of sleep many things are to be derived that do not suffer surmise" (421). *Aus den Eigentümlichkeiten des Schlafes ist manches zu entnehmen, was sich nicht erraten lässt*. Without going into these peculiarities, among which are "quantity signs" (not *quality* signs), which would conduct us to the sacred precincts of hypnosis and psychotherapy, let us state the paradox that Freud confronts: If sleep is initiated by closure of the sense organs and cessation of attention, if system ψ calls a halt to "ϕ impressions" and interrupts the otherwise relentless typography of *Eindrücke,* the psychic system nevertheless remains fully occupied during sleep with the most chaotic play of images, an iconography beyond your wildest dreams, on call in the stillest of nights.

Freud isolates six points of "Dream Analysis" for discussion (422–24), then proceeds to the final topic of Part One, "Dream Consciousness" (424–26). After noting (1) that dreams dispense with motor discharge and (2) that their bizarre logic derives from association, he emphasizes (3) their *hallucinatory* character. Dreams are every bit as lively (*lebhaft*) as perceptions are; furthermore, they are possessed of a consciousness (as point six will reiterate) and they command belief. Freud here reminds us that the "primary remembrance" of a perception is itself hallucinatory until ego-inhibition "teaches us never to cathect W so that it can by regression be transposed to ϕ" (423). The only thing that seems to help prevent this regression, apart from the *unidirectional streaming* of quantity from ϕ to ψ, and not from ψ to ϕ, is language—the operation of *signs.* "One closes the eyes and hallucinates, opens them and thinks in words." (4) The "purpose and meaning" of dreams is wish-fulfillment, even if hallucinatory, a supposition that further corroborates Freud's conviction "*that the primary wish-cathexis* [Wunschbesetzung] *was also hallucinatory in nature*" (424). (5) Dreams tend to follow already breached patterns of quantity flow, so that they cause little pain or biological damage; that means that unlike other primary processes in ψ they are subject to "a bad memory," *das schlechte Gedächtnis,* and are often quickly forgotten. Finally (6), consciousness provides quality (that is, the quality normally associated with sense-perception) for these hallucinations, this fact implying "that consciousness is not bound to the ego," inasmuch as the ego is "disburdened" in sleep. Not a word here about the *reality sign,* for it too is missing from dream-life. Consciousness can be an ingredient of every ψ process, and Freud explicitly warns us not to equate primary processes with "unconscious" processes. While Freud's reflections in chapter seven of *Die Traumdeutung* will doubtless differentiate much more sharply the senses of "consciousness" and "unconscious," tipping the balance in the direction of the latter, the final remark of this section—"*Two hints of inestimable importance for what follows!*" (the only phrase in the entire text that appears in *italic* rather than spaced type)—will wear well throughout the career of psychoanalysis: "If one interrogates consciousness when a memory of the dream is preserved [*bei erhaltenem Traumgedächtnis*] about the content of that dream [*Trauminhalt*], the result is that the significance of dreams as wish-fulfillments is covered over by a series of processes—all of them found in neuroses—characterizing the content's pathological nature." "Dream consciousness" is above all discontinuous, and its "missing links" all turn out to have a "sexual chemistry," as in the exemplary case (for *Die Traumdeutung*) of the dream of "Irma's injection." The (quite literal) sexual chemistry (propyltrimethylamin) does not enter consciousness, but is displaced. Yet what can such displacement mean, when consciousness itself is displaced from the ego? Is displacement only the substitution of one quantity for another? At the abrupt close of Part One of his "Project," the end of the "General Plan" for a scientific psychology, Freud finds himself cast back onto the shoals of a problem by now quite familiar: "The psychic sequence in dreams thus occurs in accord with quantity (Q) [that is to say, *exogenous* quantity]; yet it is not quantity that decides whether or not the sequence becomes conscious" (426). The riddle of the missing links will be the enigma of primary repression; and no purely quantitative theory will be equal to it.

SIGNS

For the sake of my own inquiry into typography, iconography, and engrammatology, which has all but vanished in the technicalities of Part One of the 1895 psychology, let me discreetly circumvent Part Two, "Psychopathology" (427–38), even though the *sexual* character of neuroses has everything to do with *quality*, the nodal enigma of Part One. I shall also thereby circumvent the themes of the deferral or retardation (*Nachträglichkeit*) of puberty (essential to the import of periodicity for individual development), resistance, and repression—the very knot of the enigma (432). Further, these psychopathological themes all revolve about the fact that in neurosis a certain *memory* (not a perception: 436) releases sexual energy, a certain *memory trace* fools the ego-organization and inflicts unpleasure on the system (438). In short, it is *not* discreet to overlook the role of memory in psychopathology, or of psychopathology in memory processes, inasmuch as the most irascible problems of Part One here come to a head. The entire arc described by psychoanalysis may be seen as having its springboard in these few pages of the *Entwurf*. Yet rather than dream of doing them justice here, let me proceed to Part Three, "An Attempt to Portray the Normal ψ Processes" (439–66). Even here I shall forego a thorough account, approaching the final segment of Freud's "Project" with certain specific questions in mind:

(1) Does Freud compel the tradition of typography, iconography, and engrammatology to a critical point, at which the relation of *writing* and *psychism* (as memory) becomes radically undecidable?

(2) Does Freud successfully resolve the traditional typographic-engrammatological difficulty—that the "impermeable" memory neurons must be both "influenced" and "unchanged" at once, simultaneously breached and unbroken, visited and virginal in one?

(3) Once the notion of quality has been introduced, once it has forced its way into Freud's account for essential reasons, can the quantitative project be rescued?

(4) Can periodicity (the foundation of consciousness) and/or lateral cathexis (the foundation of ego-organization) step into the breach, as it were, in order to unify perception and memory?

(5) Does Freud ever explain how the signaling system functions, the system of *Zeichen* by which, for example, the ego-organization interrupts and side-tracks the cathexis of an inimical memory image?

(6) Does the successful integration of φ, ψ, and W come about only with the *dynamic* image, an image that allows perception to guide behavior in such a way that the goal of *desire*—neuron *b*—is attained?

(7) However it may function dynamically, is it not the *sign* alone that has commerce with both ψ and W, so that engrammatology (understood as the reading of signs) is the only hope for an integration of memory and perception?

The bulk of these questions we shall no doubt let slip into oblivion. Yet there is a certain trajectory to them, culminating in the question posed several pages back: Whence the traces of reality, *Realitätsspuren,* whence the signs and signals of reality, *Realitätszeichen,* that thinking must respect? Of what *type* are these traces?

Part Three, "An Attempt to Portray the Normal ψ Processes," sets out to fulfill Freud's second global intention—to reap the rewards of psychopathology for a universal or general psychology, a psychology that would be a detour to philosophy. The text consists of four unnumbered and untitled sections. The first (439–51) poses the problem of the reality sign or quality sign in the two instances that are critical for the ψ system, primary defense against threatening unpleasure and the search for real (not hallucinatory) satisfaction. The second (451–54) is devoted to the relation of linguistic signs to the reality signs of thought, the third (455–61) to the relation of such linguistic signs to memory as such, and the fourth (461–66) to three varieties of possible error in thought processes.

In the first section of this final part of his project Freud attempts to sketch a theory of attention (*Aufmerksamkeit*) that will unite quality and quantity. Whatever vestiges of reality-testing remain in Freud's later writings, these speculations on attention will not long survive. *Die Traumdeutung* will search in another direction, as will the 1911 "Two Principles." (See also "The Unconscious," StA 3, 151, including note 1). Yet, for the moment at least, "The attention mechanism is not to be circumvented" (450). For it is the decisive exertion of the so-called secondary processes, in which a constantly cathected mass of neurons (the ego-organization) exercises some sort of influence on more transitory cathexes.

> If I have on the one hand the ego and on the other W (perceptions), that is, cathexes in ψ by φ (from the external world), then I need a mechanism that causes the ego to follow the perceptions and to influence them. I find this mechanism in the fact that, according to what I have presupposed, a perception always excites ω [a perceptual neuron] and thus yields quantity signs [*Quantitätszeichen abgibt*]. (438)

Earlier it was sufficient to discuss breaching in terms of quantity flow; now (presuming we do not have here a slip of the pen) it is to be a matter of quantity (not quality) *signs.* Why? Presumably because perception from the outset required the supposition of quality rather than quantity. Quantitative psychology can enter the realm of perception only if it borrows from quality its signal character, only if it becomes a psychology of quantity *signs*. To be sure, whether and how the (quantity) sign can be *read* remains the difficulty. Freud continues: "More precisely, the perception excites consciousness in W (consciousness of a quality), and the discharge of perceptual excitation will deliver the news to ψ, this news being the selfsame quality sign. I proffer the supposition that it is these quality signs that cause ψ to be *interested in* the perception." Such *interest* on the part of ψ, where alone *memory* is possible, is what Freud means by *Aufmerksamkeit*. "Attention" therefore should serve as the missing link between perception and memory. Yet he concedes from the start: "I find it difficult to explain its emergence mechanically (automatically)." He will try to understand it "biologically," and that means in terms of the genesis and development of the entire system, the entire narrative of need, craving, expectation, frustration, and ephemeral fulfillment. The principal biological justification of secondary processes (such as thinking and remembering) is that they assist in restoring the real presence of the desired object—above and beyond its presence in hallucination. "Biological experience has taught us that this representation [of the desired object] dare not be so strongly cathected that it can be confused with a perception; it has taught us to defer the discharge until the quality signs emerge from the representation as proof that the representation is now real, is now a perceptual cathexis" (440). Freud is perfectly aware that such signs pose a challenge to the quantitative effort as a whole. Yet he cannot dispense with them. For it is a matter of knowing which perceptions are the "correct" ones (441), that is to say, the ones that can be brought into iconographic accord with particular cathexes of remembrance.

If quality (quantity?) signs arise from *perception*, who or what can actually bring them into accord with mnemic images? Freud now appeals to the excitation of certain *motor* neurons (443) as a way of communicating the news, *die Nachrichtung*, to system ψ. (Such "news" may perhaps best be understood as a *supplementary direction* [*Nach-richtung*] of excitation; yet at the end of the line, Erwin Straus would remind us, one finds oneself appealing to an "attentive" gleaning of "the news.") Past lessons in engrammatology should have prepared us for the particular area of motor activity that Freud will now summarily invoke:

> *Linguistic association* fulfills this purpose. It consists in connecting ψ neurons with [motor] neurons that serve representations of sounds [*Klangvorstellungen*] and that themselves have the most intimate association with linguistic motor images [*motorischen Sprachbildern*]. These associations possess two advantages over all the others: they are circumscribed (few in number) and they are exclusive. The excitation always proceeds from acoustic image [*Klangbild*] to word image [*Wortbild*], and from the latter to discharge. Hence if the memory images are of such a kind that a partial stream can pass from them to the acoustic images and motor word images, then cathexis of memory images is accompanied by news concerning discharge, such news being the quality signs, and thereby the conscious-

ness signs, of memory. Now, if the ego has already cathected these word images, and if it has prior to that cathected the perceptual-discharge images, then it has fabricated the mechanism that steers the ψ cathexis toward the memories that emerge in the flow of quantity. This is *conscious, observational thinking.* (443–44)

A host of doubts and difficulties arises here. One would have to confront all these notions with the linguistics of Saussure—and indeed the linguistics of Plato's *Philebus* (18b–c), which emphasizes the unlimited variety (*apeiron*) of sounds—not only in the case of the acoustic image as such but the closed or circumscribed order of such images, as well as their specificity and exclusivity.[13] One would also have to think forward to Lacan's "L'instance de la lettre dans l'inconscient, ou la raison depuis Freud" (1957), which rests on the irresolvable ambiguity of "ultimately differential elements" composed by "laws of a closed order."[14] One would also have to come to terms with the fact that the famous "talking cure" of psychoanalysis—*unser Gott,* Logos—hinges on the kind of mechanism described here. Problematic of course is the identification of such a mechanism with *conscious,* even "observational" thought. Yet it is of supreme engrammatological importance that both memory and thought processes are seen to rely on breachings as tracings (*Bahnungen als Spuren:* 444) that are intimately bound up with language; and further, that such language, while at first identified as speech ("Innervation of speech is originally a valve-like effective discharge for ψ"), soon glides from *Klangbild* to *Wortbild* to *Erinnerungsbild,* bearing thither on traces of language the stamp and seal, the *typos,* of perceptual quality. Freud's phonocentrism—like that of Hobbes and Locke—advances to the (r)uses of writing, a reliance upon writing   *It stays in book of that which is*   even sooner than Derrida supposes (ED, 297, 303/200, 204).

I shall not trace in any detail the account of speech innervation developed here by Freud (444–46), but only confirm that its trajectory, from the cry (*Schreinachricht*), through the phoneme (*Laute*), to the imitative tendency of onomatopoeia is classically phonocentric. And like all classic phonocentrisms, Freud's speculations contain a hidden reference to something like writing. For the binding of quantity in the ego, the achievement of high cathexis with relatively little streaming, is itself a highly charged writing. A writing that marks the *genesis* and *genealogy* of the I—the laborious rise of the ego being   *In the ink of his sweat he will find it yet*   for Freud the event that is "most obscure" (448).[15]

After reiterating his conception of the ego as a network of neurons at the core of the psychic system, a network cathected more or less stably, *konstant,* Freud now speculates on its genesis from the (precarious) experience of satisfaction. Satisfaction or pacification involves the association of "a perception (the desired image) and a dynamic index." The apposition or equation of perception and desired image, *Wahrnehmung* and *Wunschbild,* of course begs the entire question of how the former could ever have become the latter—presuming that *Wunschbild* and *Erinnerungsbild* are at least sometimes synonymous. For perceptions cannot be retained. Or, at least, they leave no traces in ψ apart from linguistic traces, hardly the traces of use to an infant in search of the moon. Not only is the communication between W and ψ now being presupposed, but the ego-organization itself is being asked to organize its own transit authority and its own banking system. Freud writes:

> In the repetitive state of craving, in *expectation,* the education and development of this nascent ego takes place. It first learns that it dare not occupy [*besetzen*] the dynamic images [*Bewegungsbilder*] in such a way that discharge follows, as long as certain conditions have not been fulfilled on the part of perception. Further, it learns that it dare not occupy the desired representation beyond a certain degree, because it would then deceive itself in hallucinations. Yet if it respects these two barriers and turns its attention to the new perceptions, it has some prospect of attaining the desired satisfaction. Thus it is clear that the barriers that prevent the ego from occupying the desired image and the dynamic image beyond a certain degree are the grounds for storing endogenous quantity in the ego; they require the ego, so to speak, to translate such quantity in certain amounts to the neurons it is able to reach.

It is of course the threatening unpleasure (*Unlustdrohung*) that does the real educating in this innercity school of hard knocks. The primary biological legacy is primary defense (*die primäre Abwehr*), its complement the law of biological attention: "*Whenever a reality sign emerges, cathexis is to be extended to the cathected perception at hand and contemporary with it*" (451). Reality signs are signs of quality. And signs of quality are the text to be attended to. Yet both the threatening and the promising signs are highly mysterious, and no perfunctory appeal to speech and to the dynamic image associated particularly with speech (see the 1891 aphasias monograph) will solve the riddle of their origin. That origin lies in their aboriginal repetition, *Wiederholung,* in a schooling that will always already have to have taken place. "How *primary defense,* nonoccupation thanks to the threat of unpleasure, can be portrayed mechanically, this I really cannot say" (450). Freud owes us this one: *Ich gestatte mir von jetzt an . . . schuldig zu bleiben.* Although it is said to be an account of the origin of quality signs in perception, this debt is nonetheless a debt of memory, of traces of *Erinnerung* in *Gedächtnis.* For quality signs can be kept only in a thesaurus.

Freud's truncated speculations on linguistic quality signs and their relation to reality signs in thought—"*the supreme, most secure form of cognitive thought process*" (453)—do not bring us any closer to the origin of signs. Nor does the third section of Part Three do so; in fact, it makes the function of quality signs more perplexing than ever. Yet here Freud has more to say about *Gedächtnis* and *Erinnerung,* and again we will want to follow him closely. The fourth section, on the possibility of error (*Irrtum*) in thought, a possibility that would inevitably lead us back to *Theaetetus,* we shall forego in favor of this third section, drawing on the fourth only when it aids our final effort to understand signs, signals, seals, and traces in the 1895 *Entwurf.*

Although Freud celebrates *theoretical* thought as thinking in which "unpleasure plays no role" (464), so that such thought is possible only when memory processes are "bound" to the ego-organization; and although his description of *critical* or *probative* thought sounds like nothing less than a portrait of the analyst as a young man; there is no doubt but that *practical* thinking is for him the "origin" and "ultimate goal" of all thought processes, the process of which all the others are offshoots (461). Another word for *practical,* to be sure, is *biological.* Freud once again tries to clarify the path that leads from a particular perception (W) back to a desirous representation or *Plus-Vorstellung* (+V). How is it that lateral cathexes do not consistently sidetrack and divert the pathway between perception and memory image? Surprisingly, Freud's answer to this question (455) will take us back to Aristotle's account of reminiscence. If neuron *d* is contiguous with +V; if (in Aristotle's words) *d* is that penultimate point to which the proper *arkhē kinēseōs,* the dominant source or starting-point of self-showing, must guide us; if the final move to +V occurs at that point on its own; then how is it that the effraction or breached pathway from *a* to *b* to *c* need not necessarily be followed step-by-step? How is it possible to get directly from *a* to *d?*

Let us pause and marvel a moment at Freud's Aristotelianism. Why does Freud not speak of a *Bahnung* that would take us ("we" for the moment being endogenous quantity) all the preferential way to +V? He has not hitherto shied from referring to mnemic images (*Erinnerungsbilder*) when, properly speaking, it is a question of neurons; so that it cannot be out of embarrassment in the face of these icons embedded in protoplasm. Why for that matter do both Aristotle and Freud trust in that "association," that intimate *Wahlverwandtschaft,* between *d* and +V? In chapter 1 we puzzled over the sufficiency of movement to the penultimate goal of remembrance; perhaps Freud's Aristotelianism is profound enough to solve that puzzle.

It is sufficient to move to the penultimate image in a sequence of reminiscences because the *ultimate* image and the *origin* of the series, the *arkhē kinēseōs,* are in fact selfsame. The movement in both the Aristotelian and Freudian cases is not linear but circular, not in the sense of a melancholic *Teufelskreis* but in the sense that the very choice of what Aristotle calls "the right starting-point" itself guarantees the success of the movement, if guarantees there are. The efficacy of that choice, in Aristotle's account, is difficult to explain. In Freud's, it is hard to see how lateral cathexis can be played off against effraction in this way. (Indeed, Freud confuses himself with Husserl yet again: modification of effraction or breaching, he says, *liegt . . . im Belieben des Ich* [455], as though the ego can, "whenever I like," alter an established breaching.) The exertion required would neatly account for "difficulties in thinking," *Denkschwierigkeiten* (456), but it would hardly explain successful association.

In this connection, Freud casts doubt on the role heretofore assigned to quality signs. He now says that they are "not indispensable" in processes of practical thought, even though they do "secure and fix" these processes. Later (464) quality signs will be reinstated, at least for *cognizing* and *critical* thinking, which "awaken" to such signs, or summon those signs themselves to vigilance (*Wachrufung aller Qualitätszeichen*); but for the moment, in *practical* thinking, where W should pass "quickly" to the dynamic image that will get us closer to + V, who can take the time to call for seals of approval? "Wherever the sequence leading from a certain perception to particular goal-cathexes has already repeatedly occurred and is stereotyped by memory breachings [*durch Gedächtnisbahnungen stereotypiert ist*], there is seldom any occasion for awakening the quality sign" (456). The breachings of perception and memory (perception *to* memory) that we have been laboring to understand are now so thoroughly effracted that their typography is in stereo, solid state. Now the specific action called for by the dynamic image appears to negotiate perfectly well on the basis of the fixed breaching from W to + V and back again. Never mind the possibility that + V may be so excessively desired   *I am highly sheshe sherious*   that W proves   *He war*   to be more *w*anted and *w*ished-for than w*ahrgenommen*. Never mind   *My lips went livid from the joy of fear*   the likelihood of outrage. "During the sequence, this dynamic image was cathected only in a bound way [that is to say, in full cooperation with the ego, the binding power], and the thought process took its departure from a perception (W) that was pursued purely as memory image [*Erinnerungsbild*]; because of these facts, the entire thought process can achieve its independence from expectation and reality; it can progress to identity with no alteration at all" (457). The thinking and the identity in question are, we must remember, *practical*, so that the new-found independence of the thought process must make us wonder. Have the old aporias really been solved while our backs were turned? So it would seem. Freud continues:

> It is now time to qualify an assertion made earlier [at 444 in Freud's text] to the effect that a memory of thought processes is made possible only by quality signs, because otherwise the traces [*Spuren*] of those processes could not be distinguished from the traces of perceptual breachings. What we must still insist on is the fact that our *memory of reality* [*das* Realgedächtnis] dare not properly speaking be modified by any thinking about it. On the other hand, it is undeniable that when we think about a particular theme we leave behind traces extraordinarily significant for later reflection, and it is extremely doubtful whether only the thinking that occurs with quality signs and consciousness does this.

I interrupt here to note the rather unexpected turn in Freud's thought. It is not that quality signs are now to be dispensed with, and the only possible criteria for distinguishing hallucination and reality abandoned. It may rather be that the quality signs always were too close to cognitive thought, too close to "pure" thought and consciousness, to have served as such criteria. These seals of approval, these pathfinders and *Wegweiser*, are a dream that *practical* thinking does not, cannot, take time to dream. But to return to the passage: "Thus there must be thought breachings—and yet the original associative paths dare not be obliterated. Because there is only one kind of breaching, one might suppose, the two conclusions are incompatible." We are thrust back upon the aporia that arose countless pages—and many centuries—ago. Effractions are *einerlei*, of a single kind. How is it possible for them to permit a retracing in practical thought that does not cover over the original breachings? And yet is it possible to conceive of such thought as leaving no traces of its own?

Freud's reply, based on the level of excitation in the breachings, a level that is presumably higher in thought processes than in primary associations (—although, unless our memories betray us, Freud earlier [at 418] insisted that the level of excitation in thought processes was generally quite low, just as endogenous quantity is significantly lower than exogenous quantity), is hardly convincing, and he proffers it perhaps only halfheartedly. What remains indisputable is that "memory consists in the breachings [*in den Bahnungen*]" (458). Freud can only appeal to the level of excitation that occurs in them, or to the "threshold value" he has introduced into the contact barrier (454), as though $Q\dot\eta$ had not itself from the outset been differential in its "value," and as though the entire system of breachings had not from the outset been radically dependent on quantity flow. However, just as in Part One Freud appealed to *periodicity* in order to account for differences in breaching, so now a certain temporal dimension reasserts itself in his text. It will once again be a matter of subsequent returns and augmentings, of retracings over time, of *Nachträglichkeit*. The account is hardly clear, but let us follow it closely. For we are now at the end. Last chance to collect on that debt.

In addition to cognitive and practical thinking there is "a reproductive, *remembering* thinking," which is not entirely absorbed in practical thought (458). Such *erinnerndes Denken* in fact serves as an essential mediator between the practical thinking that follows the wiles and ways of primary process and the probing, critical thinking that analyzes with full consciousness. As mediator, *erinnerndes Denken* has the capacity to reverse directions: "It pursues a given thought process in the opposite direction, as it were, back to a perception, once again under [the condition of] goallessness, as distinct from practical thinking; and on its pursuit it takes advantage [*bedient sich dabei*] of a large range of quality signs." Such mediation is of course a   *Well, we have frankly enjoyed more than anything these secret workings of natures* miracle. Or a kind of magic. In a unidirectional system of quantity flow, where even the news flows only one way, whence in all the world this *Rückverfolgung*? If the hypothesis of quantity flow plus lateral cathexes is unable to account for what Freud will soon call *Rückströmung* (460), what is this strange power of memorative thinking, a thinking that hovers somewhere between consciousness and the unconscious? Is it the prototype of what Freud in *Die Traumdeutung* will call the preconscious, *das Vorbewusste*? Whatever the case, this capacity to radiate stereophonically in both directions, to inside and outside at once, is crucial in *Erinnerung;* we shall see that capacity come to the fore once again—in Hegel's philosophy, discussed in chapter 5, below.

In its regress to *W*, remembrance or reminiscence meets up with certain "mediative members," *Mittelglieder*. They were introduced in the final section of Part One, "Dream Consciousness," to explain how the sexual chemistry of "Irma's injection" evaded detection. Sexual chemistry *is* the middle member (425). As the mediator between cathected desire and hallucination, the middle member is always "what remains to be disclosed." It is something very much like a quality sign, a sign that is not read, yet not altogether identical to such signs. "In this pursuit back, the process stumbles across middle members that have up to now been unconscious, having left behind no quality signs; they are members whose quality signs emerge after deferral [*sich nachträglich er-geben*]." The *Mittelglieder*—reminiscent of the *Mittelwesen* of the ancients, such as daimons or hermaphrodites, who communicate between realms nor-mally segregated from one another, or those intermediates that Socrates (again in *Philebus*) is looking for both in pleasure and in speech—are in fact traces (*Spuren*) that the thought sequence has left behind, vestiges that are *not yet* quality signs, not yet, but only *nachträglich*. Quality signs often serve as the indicators of commencement and termination, the start and finish (= *arkhē kinēseōs?*) of a particular stretch of the way, a stretch one would otherwise never disclose. Yet once launched on that stretch, thought encounters these strange middling creatures. Or encounters them at the end, in the form of *results*. "Whatever the case, the reproducibility of thought processes far ex-ceeds their quality signs; the latter are made conscious by deferred action, although it is perhaps more often the result of the thought sequence that leaves traces rather than the stages of that sequence."

Freud now cites one of the possible mishaps that may beset thought processes—that an instance of "practical thought with cathected goals" leads to the release of unpleasure—lest his account appear too elegiac. If a memory releases unpleasure it is apparently because the perception to which it is tied (let us not ask how) produced the same unpleasure or pain. Such perceptions summon a great deal of attention, less because of their quality signs than merely on account of the "reaction" they provoke; that is to say, they are associated with exertions or expressions of affect and defense. The destiny of such memory images is that their repetition at first awakens affect and unpleasure quite intensely. Yet "with time" they lose this malignant capacity (459). At first such intense and lively images preserve their "sensuous quali-ties" but when they lose their effective power they become Hobbesian-Humean memory images. Such loss of affective strength eventuates when they become "bound," tethered by and to the ego-organization. When a thought sequence crosses the path of an as yet *unbound* memory image, the latter's quality signs, "often of a sensuous nature," come to the fore, along with the consequent sensation of unpleasure and tendency to discharge. All this releases a certain affect—one that is liable to interrupt the thought sequence.

Yet what is time, asks Freud, that it should *weaken* the affective charges of images that are still too lively to be called *Erinnerungsbilder* proper? There is as yet no sign of Freud's later conviction concerning the timelessness of the unconscious, and yet Freud himself is certainly aware of the anomaly of time's action:

> What is it that transpires with those *reminiscences* that are capable of affect [*affektfähigen* Erinnerungen] up to the point when they became *bound* [gebändigt *werden*]? It is not plausible that "time" debilitates the repetition of their affective capacity, inasmuch as this moment [i.e., time] otherwise contributes precisely to the strengthening of an association. It must be the case that something occurs in "time," with the repetitions, that effects this subjugation; and this can be nothing else than the fact that a relation to the ego or to ego-cathexes assumes power over the reminiscence.

Because painful experiences leave traces of excessive φ quantity and produce a hypertrophied breaching in the direction of unpleasure, they require the ego's robust and repeated exertions in binding, the "repetition of painful experiences," until the path to unpleasure is effectively blocked. These traces of excessive φ quantity—as yet unbound—in fact account for the power of hallucination over the ψ system:

> The fact that the reminiscence [*die Erinnerung*] exhibits an hallucinatory character for such a long time also demands its own explanation, one that will be significant for our conception of hallucination as such. Here it is plausible to suppose that this capacity for hallucination, along with the capacity for affect, are indications of the fact that the ego-cathexis has not yet exerted any influence on the reminiscence, that in this reminiscence the primary directions of discharge and the full process, or primary process, have the upper hand. (460)

Hallucination is in fact the dark side of that mysterious backflow of reproductive or reminiscent thinking, *Rückverfolgung*, discussed a moment ago. Hallucination requires a regressive streaming of quantity, a *Rückströmung*, from ψ to φ and W. The backwash occurs because of excessive quantity cathected in particular memories formed by an unusually strong effraction, memories not yet sufficiently inhibited (or, as the *Studien über Hysterie* will say, not yet sufficiently *associated*) by the ego. Such inhibition or binding by the ego would seem to be the proper result of the mediative thought of reminiscence, and yet Freud—confusing himself now with Nietzsche—equates it with forgetting (*Vergessen*):

> Now at long last it will be possible to occupy the painful reminiscence in such a way that it exerts no backward streaming and can give birth only to a modicum of unpleasure. Now it is bound, indeed by a thought-breaching [*Denkbahnung*] so strong that the latter exerts a lasting impact, exercising an inhibitory effect even in later repetitions of the reminiscence. Through desuetude, the path leading to the release of unpleasure will gradually augment its resistance. For breachings are subject to gradual ruination (oblivion) [*Verfall (Vergessen)*]. Only then is this reminiscence a bound reminiscence, a reminiscence like any other.

Properly speaking, what is "forgotten" is not the lively reminiscence but the effraction connecting it to unpleasure. Even though the breaching itself was never "remembered" as such, Freud now equates its waxing resistance with forgetting, oblivion. Even more ironically, such oblivion is what transforms a hallucination into a proper memory. It is also worth noting that Freud here identifies the reminiscence as a *painful* one, whereas earlier it was a wish-cathexis, an excessively desired icon, that spawned hallucination. The shift is important inasmuch as the inhibiting or binding of excessive wish-cathexis is what earlier called for signs of quality and reality.

Freud now (461) discusses the "signal" that primary thought-defense reads in order to evade unpleasure. Yet the sign of reality, the only sign that can prevent frustration and outrage, continues to elude him and us. Although Freud explicitly invokes both *Realitätszeichen* and *Qualitätszeichen,* their operations remain utterly mysterious. The debt is still outstanding.

WAX MAGIC

At the end of this long and tortuous path—an effraction with multiple contact barriers, lateral cathexes, regressive flows, and irruptions of unpleasure—Freud's text can hardly satisfy us. It did not satisfy him. What began as crucifixion ended as a burlesque of delusion, *eine Art*   Could you wheedle a staveling encore out of your imitationer's jubalharp, hey, Mr Jinglejoys? *Wahnwitz* (Letter 36 to Fliess; 145). It doubtless fulfilled Freud's need to integrate the flood of new materials and novel insights that were about to sweep him from neurology to the exotic shores of psychoanalysis. And there is no question but that completion of the task induced in him a distinct euphoria. Two weeks after composing Part Three, Freud to Fliess:

> In one energetic night of the week now flown by, at that precise degree of inflicted pain [*Schmerzbelastung*] that in my case produces the optimal conditions for cerebral activity, the barriers [*die Schranken*] suddenly lifted, the blinders fell away, and one's gaze encompassed everything from details on neurosis to the conditions of consciousness. Everything seemed to fit everything else, the gear-wheels meshed, one got the impression that the thing was now actually a machine, that it would soon be running on its own steam. The three systems of neurons, the free and the bound states of quantity, the primary and secondary processes, the main tendency and the compromise tendency of the nervous system, the two biological rules of attention and defense, the quality signs, real[ity] signs, and thought signs, the state of the psychosexual cluster—the sexual condition of repression, ultimately the conditions of consciousness in its perceptual function—it all passed muster [*alles stimmte*] and it still does today! Of course, I can hardly contain my delight. . . .
>
> All other sorts of neurotic corroborations [*sic*] come pouring in. The thing [*die Sache*] is really true and genuine. (Letter 32; 139–40; cf. ED, 306 n.1/329–30 n.8)

However, no amount of *neurotischen Bestätigungen* could sustain Freud's mania or overcome the doubts that riddle the 1895 *Psychologie.* If only five weeks later the euphoria has succumbed to sarcasm concerning the odd system he has "hatched," this duckbilled platypus of a scientific psychology, the endeavor remains impressive, even awesome. It would no doubt be salutary to trace the progress of this hybrid—the progress of typography, iconography, and engrammatology, the progress of *Finny. Vary vary finny!*

philosophy—in a whole series of later works, beginning with letters 39 and 52 and proceeding to chapter seven of *Die Traumdeutung,* the 1911 "Formulations Concerning the Two Principles of Psychic Occurrence" (StA 3, 17–24), chapter four of *Beyond the Pleasure Principle* (1920), and all of *The Ego and the Id* (1923). Yet we shall follow the advice of Ernst Kris (185 n. 1) and the example of Jacques Derrida by turning exclusively to the brief 1925 text, *Notiz über den "Wunderblock,"* "Note on the 'Mystic Writing Pad' " (StA 3, 365–69). Our purpose in doing so will be to see how the aporias of the 1895 "Project" culminate in the crisis of engrammatology—a crisis in which writing must serve as the metaphor for perception and memory but can no longer serve as a "known" providing a magic explanation for something "unknown." That crisis will cause Derrida's question to resonate once again: "What is a text, and what might the psychical be, such that it can be represented by a text?" (ED, 297/199).

"If I distrust my memory . . ." begins Freud, almost three decades after the 1895 "Project" (StA 3, 365). Such distrust aligns him with philosophers of almost all persuasions, even the Platonists, and most certainly the Cartesians. "If I distrust my memory—we know that the neurotic distrusts his to a conspicuous extent, but the normal person too has every reason to do so—I can supplement and secure [*ergänzen und versichern*] its function by making for myself a written note [*eine schriftliche Aufzeichnung*]." Freud wishes to focus on the *plane* or *surface* [Fläche] on which such jottings might be made, although it is the possible depth or interiority of such a *res extensa* that interests him—as it interested Hegel before him. Such a plane surface with depth-potential represents "a materialized piece of the apparatus of remembrance," which is in fact "invisible within me." The great advantage of such a plane surface is that it preserves inscriptions without distortion, so that they can be "reproduced" (the quotation marks are Freud's, inasmuch as reproduction here is simply a reading) any time I like, *nach Belieben.*

Use of such technical apparatus (recommended, we recall, in Descartes' *Regulae*) has in the past necessitated following one of two procedures. One could choose either a permanent writing surface, such as a sheet of paper, or a readily erasable surface, such as a blackboard. The advantage of the former was that when one covered a sheet of paper with notes jotted in ink the result was a "durable *memory trace,*" *eine 'dauerhafte* Erinnerungsspur.' Of course, the concomitant disadvantage was that the receptivity of the surface was soon exhausted: once the sheet was fully inscribed one had to set it aside and take up another, thus running the risk of becoming what the Germans call *verzettelt,* bewildered among countless bits and scraps of paper, or the risk of being burdened with an archive of papers even when one is no longer interested in the theme recorded on them. The free and untrammeled spirit in us was disgruntled.

Freud's complaint is not identical to Socrates' (or King Thamus') in *Phaedrus*, but it is surely related. Freud does not bemoan the *exteriority* of the indelible written trace as such; the exteriority of the durable and immutable trace is precisely its advantage. Yet the piling up of useless records is no doubt reminiscent of the ancient complaint that the written text gapes at us and refuses to engage in dialogue. Chalk and blackboard have the advantage of being "limitlessly receptive"; I can erase the board and fill it again with fresh traces—I do not need to replace the board with another. The obvious disadvantage is that here a permanent trace is not possible, or at least not likely. Once the board is full I must make a decision about what will have to go, a decision about what in the future will never interest me again. The archivist in us is struck with horror. Freud concludes: "Unlimited receptivity and maintenance of perdurant traces—these seem to exclude one another in the devices we substitute for our memory; either the receptive surface has to be renewed or the recorded note obliterated" (365–66). Unlike the technical apparatus that serves to augment our senses when they suffer some deficiency (apparatus such as eyeglasses, hearing aids, and telescopes), both writing-paper and chalkboard are insufficiently mimetic of the faculty they are meant to supplement. Although memory traces are not immutable, they certainly do perdure; and yet there always seems to be room for the reception of more traces. Can a new device, a novel *aide-mémoire,* be found?

Freud reminds his readers of his surmise in *Die Traumdeutung* that the dual function of memory in fact relies on a dual system—two distinct "organs of the psychic apparatus." He does not mention the 1895 sketch, which began with abashed speculations on such a duality, or the even earlier reflections by Josef Breuer in this regard; nor does he pause over the bizarre juxtaposition of "psyche," "organs," and "apparatus," the dual or multiple catachresis of traditional philosophical anthropology. The first such system, the perceptual-conscious system, in which we descry the evolution of systems φ and W from 1895, is capable of receiving perceptions but not of maintaining perdurant traces; the latter arise in " 'memory systems' deposited behind" the perceptual-conscious system (*kämen in dahinter gelegenen 'Erinnerungsystemen' zustande*). He calls the "inexplicable phenomenon" of consciousness, which originates *in place of* perdurant traces, an insight attained in *Beyond the Pleasure Principle* (1920), although we know that the ground for it is prepared already in 1895 (*Anfänge,* 392–97). Freud now introduces—"unveils" would be the wrong word—the recently marketed *Wunderblock,* the miraculous writing pad, as an aid to memory far better suited than either paper or chalkboard to emulate the structure and functions of both perception and memory. The mystic writing pad promises to be a more faithful icon of the psyche. True, Freud does not publish his *Notiz über den "Wunderblock"* on such a writing pad, no matter how miraculous, nor is it recorded that he prepared his text on it; he no doubt preferred the less renewable but far more durable method of publication in a printed journal and then in his typeset *Gesammelte Werke.* Nevertheless, Freud's account of the icon is so finely wrought, so lucid and precise, that we may be confident that he at some point actually wielded such a pad, just as we may trust that Husserl had a tone-producing machine on his desk all the while he was composing his lectures on internal time-consciousness.

To be sure, the editors of the *Standard Edition* indicate that Freud's account is flawed, and we ought to take a moment to clarify the defect. Derrida records the remark of Freud's editors (ED, 330 n. 1/331 n. 28), appended to the following sentence in the *Notiz:* "If one wants to destroy the note one has jotted down, it is sufficient to lift the composite cover sheet by its unattached lower edge gently [*mit leichtem Griff*] from the wax pad." The *Studienausgabe* of Freud's works, which I have before me as I write and which contains the editorial material of the *Standard Edition,* contains the following editorial note: "The manner in which the cover sheet is lifted from the wax pad is somewhat different in today's 'mystic writing pads,' but this alters nothing in the principle" (367 n. 1). The introductory note to which we are then referred (364) tells us that "today's" mystic writing pads, sold under the brandname " 'Printator'-*Dauerschreibblock*," achieve the separation of cover sheet and waxen matrix by means of a concealed lever or slide—one no longer lifts the composite cover sheet but moves the lever from left to right or right to left in order to efface the text. Derrida spurns the editors' apologetics and writes: "We are tempted to think that Freud botches his technical description else-where as well for the sake of his analogy." He declines to point out these places. Certainly there is nothing in today's *Printator* that cancels Derrida's own principal point: the machine still requires *two hands* for its operation.

Surely, we have a right to be a bit bemused by the editors' intrusion and Derrida's temptation. Surely, Freud cannot be held responsible for the fact that technical improvements have altered the implement itself, rendering his description in one or other respect obsolete. Who can control what is tossed onto the market? Who would want to halt technical progress? Progress—even if the greatest source of *pleasure* in the apparatus, the gentle grip of thumb and index lifting ever so slowly the shiny clear and the dull gray sheets from the sticky tablet, the crackling sound of text on the verge of obliteration, the line of text or illustration disappearing an instant *before* the separation seems to occur, vanishing like water once spilled on tabletop, like a stream flowing back to its source—even if all that pleasure is dashed. But enough of pleasure. Science.

There does seem to be one minor infidelity in Freud's description, which neither the editors nor Derrida pinpoints, an infidelity that does not arise from technical progress but mars the description of even the original *Wunderblock,* and precisely in the region where science releases the greatest pleasure. Freud has by now described the resinous, waxy subsurface of the tablet, the matrix that will both provide the dark line of text and retain the impressions made by the stylus even after the text has been erased. He finds the dual cover sheet, consisting of a celluloid upper layer and a far more delicate "wax paper" beneath, "more interesting" (367). The infidelity occurs precisely with regard to the point in which Freud is most interested—*Interesse* being the word he used in 1895 to describe the mechanism of attention, *Aufmerksamkeit,* the mechanism that allows ψ to influence W and φ. "This sheet is the more interesting component of the little apparatus. The sheet itself consists of two layers, which, *except at the two horizontal edges,* can be separated from one another [*die ausser an den beiden queren Rändern voneinander abgehoben werden können*]" (367; my emphases). Now, in any mystic writing pad that has ever found its way into my hands, and they are legion (the pads, not my hands, which are two, and eminently capable of slips), I have never seen the two sheets attached to one another at both top and bottom. Rather, the laminating celluloid folio and the dull, delicate undersheet are joined together only at the *top* of the device, precisely where the two leaves   *Lispn! No wind no word. Only a leaf, just a leaf and then leaves*   are attached as a unit to the pitchlike subsurface of the matrix. Freud's infidelity will not affect the principal use of the pad as an analogy for perception and memory, but it will make one of his most precious discoveries impossible. However, let us follow Freud's further description of the pad's function—it will be impossible to capture the beauty of Freud's prose   *But there's a great poet in you too*   in any translation, so that such translations should themselves work mystically and quickly vanish:

> One employs the mystic writing pad by carrying out the writing [*Aufschreibung*] on the celluloid laminate of the wax tablet's coversheet. For such writing we require no pencil or piece of chalk: the writing does not consist in the delivery of material to the receptive surface. We have here a return to the way in which the ancients wrote on tablets of clay and wax. A pointed stylus notches the surface, whose depressions yield "script" [*Ein spitzer Stilus ritzt die Oberfläche, deren Vertiefungen die "Schrift" ergeben*]. (367)

The magic of the writing pad at first seems to consist in the fact that it too is a regressive monster, a throwback to the most primitive style and stylus of typography. Here script is produced as the *profundation* of a surface, whose *relief* effects the separation of light from darkness. And it is the darkness that is read, the darkness that articulates. We may therefore expect that the subsurface of pitch will come to play a role in the yielding of light to dark. Yet the magic of the writing pad is no mere regression:

> With the mystic writing pad, the notching does not occur directly, but by mediation [*Vermittlung*] of the coversheet that lies over it. At the places where it touches down, the stylus presses the wax paper undersheet onto the wax tablet; furrows become visible on the otherwise smooth, pale gray surface of the celluloid
> *With pale blake I write tintingface*   as darkling script.

At this point Freud describes the erase-function of the pad, and here the editors (and Derrida) make their interventions. Freud notes that once the composite coversheet is raised and the furrows and depressions eliminated (yet *are* they eliminated?) no restoration of the traces occurs when the upper sheets again come into contact with the pitch. "The mystic writing pad is now script-free and ready to receive new jottings." Of course, the pad functions so far precisely as a blackboard does when covered with writing and then erased.

Freud interrupts his description with this brief paragraph: "The minor imperfections of the device naturally hold no interest for us, inasmuch as we only wish to pursue its approximation to the structure of the psychical perceptual apparatus." Never mind the optimistic juxtaposition of "psychical" and "perceptual," *des seelischen Wahrnehmungsapparats;* although it would be good to know whether and how ψ and W are juxtaposed, particularly with regard to ϕ. Never mind that, because we now arrive at   *You will tell me some time if I can believe its all. You know where I am bringing you? You remember?* the consequences of that imperfection that is not the machine's but Freud's. An imperfection that impairs the second of the three "analogies" outlined by Derrida (ED, 331–32/224–25). Freud writes:

> If one cautiously lifts the celluloid laminate [*Zelluloidplatte*] from the wax paper at a time when the pad is covered with writing one sees the script every bit as clearly on the surface of the wax paper itself; one might ask why the celluloid laminate of the coversheet is necessary at all. Experiment then shows that the thin paper would easily be creased or torn were one to write directly on it with the stylus. The celluloid laminate is thus a protective covering [*eine schützende Hülle*] for the wax paper, designed to withstand [*abhalten*] damaging influences from the outside [*schädigende Einwirkungen von aussen*]. The celluloid is a "shield against stimulus" ["*Reizschütz*"]; the layer that is properly receptive of stimulus is the paper. (367–68)

Freud can now reveal the legend or key to the analogy. He refers to chapter four of *Beyond the Pleasure Principle* as the source of his notion that "our psychical perceptual apparatus consists of two layers, an outer protection against stimulus, designed to reduce the magnitude of the oncoming excitations, and a surface behind it [*Oberfläche dahinter*] that is designed to receive stimulus, the system W-Bw [perception-consciousness]." Yet we could translate the entire structure of *Beyond* into the terms found already in *Die Traumdeutung* (StA 2, 512–17, 583–86 passim), where each system appears, one "behind" the other; and we could trace various aspects of that earlier system back to the 1895 "Project," its ϕ, ψ, W, its umbrellas and sieves, contact barriers, cathexes, and breachings. We shall forego such translations in order to note the fact that Freud's "experiment," the one by which he would separate "cautiously" the two layers of the system perception-consciousness, cannot be executed. For he has sewn the two leaves at both horizontal rims of the pad, at both top and bottom, so that only the composite can "with a gentle grip" be removed from the pitch of memory.

A mere slip of the verge, no doubt. Scarcely affecting "the principle." Yet it suggests that the relation of ϕ to W remains problematic. In letter 39 to Fliess (January 1, 1896; 153), we recall, Freud first intercalated ω between the ϕ and ψ neurons, in such a way that ϕ would communicate its quality (but only a modicum of its quantity) to ω, while the latter communicated neither quantity nor quality to ψ but only "stimulated" or "incited" it by directing unbound psychic energies. (At this point   *Which route are they going? Why?*

Freud made his reference to *Kauderwelsch,* "gobbledygook.") By attaching φ and W at both ends Freud now makes it impossible to see how excessive quantity can be filtered to the point where only refined qualities can arise (in consciousness); but that also means—although it would take many further steps to demonstrate these things—that it becomes impossible to isolate the primary process in ψ and even to envisage the calamity of life, impossible to identify inner need and outer reality, impossible to read the quality signs that might put an end to hallucination.

Let us see whether the third analogy—that involving memory proper, the waxen subsurface or substrate of the mystic writing pad—fares any better. For: "The analogy would not have much value if it did not lend itself to being pursued farther" (368). Freud returns to his description of the function of the magic writing tablet at the point where the composite cover sheet has been raised and the text effaced. "Yet it can be readily determined that the perdurant trace of what was written [*die Dauerspur des Geschriebenen*] on the wax tablet itself remains preserved, and that in suitable lighting it is legible [*bei geeigneter Belichtung lesbar*]." Freud's tablet, the one he has now in front of him on his desk, must of course be new; otherwise the pitch would have been furrowed and carved to a dull, undecipherable, Hegelian gray on gray, like the pineal gland *d'un hébété.* Yet let us not spoil *Freud's* pleasure so quickly:

> Thus the pad provides not only an ever-renewable receptive surface, like a black-board, but also perdurant traces of the written text, like the usual paper tablet. It solves the problem of how to unite the two accomplishments by distributing them *to two separate conjoined* [sic] *components or systems.* But that is very much the same way in which—according to my supposition, mentioned above—our psychic apparatus fulfills the perceptual function. The layer that receives stimulation—the system of perception and consciousness—forms no lasting traces; the groundwork of remembrance [*Erinnerung*] originates in other contiguous systems.

The two separate, conjoined systems are of course perception-consciousness and memory; we shall ignore the implication that perception-consciousness is also attached at both ends to the shield φ. Separate, conjoined. Conjoined when script actually appears, separate when script is erased. Yet does that mean that everything perceived is recorded in memory? When the systems are conjoined, laminated to one another, celluloid to wax paper, wax paper to wax tablet, wax to wax, are not all perceptions ipso facto memories? And when separation occurs, even with a gentle grip, does not perception, deprived of memory, cease to function? In 1895 the two systems were so effectively separated that it seemed as though nothing perceived could ever be remembered; in 1925 it becomes difficult to see how anything perceived could ever be forgotten. Granted propitious lighting.

What about the two systems in separation? What about the propitious lighting of pitchlike memory? Freud is about to raise with a careful grip the composite coversheet, in order to examine the illumination of memory traces. As he begins to raise it the reader senses that Freud's *Notiz* is about to obliterate itself: "It need not disturb us that the perdurant traces of the jottings received by the mystic writing pad are not employed in any way [*nicht verwertet werden*]; it suffices that they are at hand [*es genügt, dass sie vorhanden sind*]." At issue is the presence at hand, *prokheiros, Vorhandensein*, of traces. Typography. To the question as to whether or not they can be read, whether or not typography will advance to engrammatology, Freud feigns indifference. Even though the only reason for preferring the advanced technology of the mystic writing pad over the stoneage method of slate and the modern paper pad is the fact that under suitable lighting the written trace in the pitchlike substratum of the *Wunderblock* can be read, *lesbar ist*. Freud raises the cover sheet even farther; one hears the dry crackling sound; it is almost a hiss:

> Of course, the analogical relation of such an auxiliary apparatus to the paradigmatic organ has to come to an end somewhere. To be sure, the mystic writing pad cannot also "reproduce" the script from the inside [*von innen her*] once it has been eradicated; it really would be a mystic writing pad if it could achieve this in the way our memory [*Gedächtnis*] does.

Freud now restates the terms of the analogy, adjudges it "not entirely far-fetched," and seems to be on the verge of expunging the whole as a passing fancy, a caprice. We are no doubt disappointed. For the second time now. The traditional engrammatological problem is the inability to account for the *reading* of the incised letters in memory. If Freud should acquiesce in the failure of his analogy—or his machine—to "reproduce" the written text *von innen her,* then he is surely telling us no more than *Phaedrus* has taught us, and his career as a philosopher will have been exceedingly short-lived.

We shall take up this question of mnemic reproduction and interiority in later chapters; yet two comments from Derrida's "Freud and the Scene of Writing" may be considered at this juncture. The first exhibits the essential continuity of Freud's mystic writing pad with earlier typographic systems, while the second points to the abyss that underlies or undermines the depth or *profondeur* of all such systems. Derrida writes:

> The multiplicity of layered surfaces in the apparatus abandoned to itself is a complexity that is dead and without depth. Life as profundity pertains solely to the wax of psychical memory. Freud thus continues to contrapose, as Plato does, hypomnemic writing to writing *en tēi psykhēi*, itself woven of traces, empirical reminiscences of a truth that is present outside of time. With that, separated from the psyche's ability to respond, the mystic writing pad, as a representation abandoned to itself, reverts once again to Cartesian space and Cartesian mechanism: *natural* wax, the exteriority of the *aide-mémoire*. (ED, 336/227)

Yet what about those furrows inscribed in the substrate, the in-depth relief of the system "behind," where suitable light penetrates in order to cast the shadows *Sole shadow shows* in the interior depth of the rune? What happens after Freud has raised the composite coversheet fully?

Let us observe that the *profundity* of the mystic writing pad is simultaneously a profundity without fundament [*fond*], an infinite referral [*renvoi*], and a perfectly superficial exteriority: a stratification of surfaces whose relation to self, to the inside, is only the implication of another equally exposed surface. It unites the two empirical certitudes that constitute us: that of infinite depth in the implication of meaning, the unlimited envelopment of the actual, and simultaneously that of the membranous essence of being, the absolute absence of underpinnings [*l'absence absolue du dessous*]. (ED, 331/224)

We shall not now pursue Derrida's anatomical tracing of that membranous or pellicular essence, which expands the scene of writing beyond the apparatus of the dead machine to encompass society, the world, and history. For Freud does *not* erase the whole text—indeed, granted suitable lighting, he cannot do so.   *What has gone? How it ends? Begin to forget it. It will remember itself from every sides, with all gestures, in each our word. Today's truth, tomorrow's trend. Forget, remember!*   The most daring of Freud's analogies, the third and last, which we have been introducing for several pages now, is yet to come. It involves the illumination or limning of script, "the becoming visible of script and its disappearance with the incandescence [*Aufleuchten*] and passing away [*Vergehen*] of consciousness in perception" (368). We will want to follow this final analogy most closely, the analogy that should account for the liaison—the hyphen—within the system *W-Bw*, inasmuch as the introduction of consciousness *cum* perceptual quality into a putatively quantitative psychology proved both absolutely necessary and inevitably fatal to the 1895 system. "I confess that I am inclined to push the comparison even farther," writes Freud at the outset of his third analogy.

With the mystic writing pad, the script vanishes each time the intimate [*innige*] contact between the paper that receives the stimulus and the wax tablet that preserves the impression is canceled [*aufgehoben wird*]. That coincides with the notion I developed long ago, but till now have kept to myself, concerning the mode of function in the psychical perceptual apparatus.

The editors of the *Standard Edition* interrupt (StA 3, 369 n. 1) in order to indicate that the secret Freud is about to reveal has actually slipped out in *Beyond the Pleasure Principle,* and that it appears "in germ" at the end of section 19 of the first part of the 1895 *Entwurf,* "Primary Processes—Sleep and Dreams" (see *Anfänge,* 421 and pages 137–40, above). The secret will involve the troublesome notion of "attention," *Aufmerksamkeit,* as a quantity from ψ that goes to meet (in the neurons of the pallium) the invading sensations in ϕ. Sleep (but also hypnosis) would be the counterstate to such wakeful perception. The question we posed earlier involved the possibility of a primary process in ψ that would not require *Aufmerksamkeit,* the possibility for example of dream-work, and thus the very possibility of a path for psychoanalysis beyond mere ego-psychology.

Freud now elaborates his third analogy in the *Notiz* (369): "I adopted the supposition that cathectic innervations are dispatched into and withdrawn from the fully permeable system W-Bw [perception-consciousness], and that this occurs in rapid periodic thrusts [*in raschen periodischen Stössen*] from within [*aus dem Inneren*]." These periodic thrusts will not surprise us: periodicity was introduced early on in the "Project" as one of the first devices to account for the perception of qualities and thus the origins of consciousness (*Anfänge*, 395; pages 122–23, above). As the inversion of umbrella to sieve, periodicity was to be the fundamental mode of communication between ϕ and ψ, accounting for our perception rather than merely our pain; yet even the inversion did not succeed in allowing thoroughgoing communication, did not allow perception to leave *traces* that are reproducible in memory. The juxtaposition of *cathexis* and *full permeability* retains its mystery to the end.

Although the thrusts of periodicity do not surprise us now, something else surely must: the thrusts emerge *aus dem Inneren*, "from within." Yet once the shields have been inverted and become filters, is not all quantity flow endogenous, is not all "within"? Freud's topical-tropical vagueness is disturbing, to say the least. It is true, as Derrida remarks, that an important *temporal* dimension is being opened here for writing and for the psyche—perhaps the dimension in which the two can no longer be readily distinguished. "Freud, reconstructing an *operation,* cannot reduce either time [as Descartes does when he demands to know the *truth* of the wax] or the multiplicity of its sensible layers" (ED, 332/225). Yet by this time we may rightly insist on more specificity with regard to these psychic innards. Who or what releases these periodic thrusts? And whence? Freud continues: "As long as the system [W-Bw] is cathected in this way, it receives the perceptions that are accompanied by consciousness and relays [*weiterleitet*] the excitation further to the unconscious memory systems; as soon as the cathexis is withdrawn, consciousness is extinguished and the system's efforts come to a standstill [*ist sistiert*]." Why the *plural,* unconscious memory systems? What sort of relay is it that connects ϕ and ψ, via W? What is the meaning of that *Anregung* Freud introduced in his letter to Fliess in order to distinguish W from ψ, that is, in order to prevent a general theory of quantitative excitation (*Erregung*) from conflating the permeable and impermeable systems? And precisely how is cathexis withdrawn? Has the mystery surrounding *Ichentladung* been dissolved? What is the relation of such cathexis-withdrawal to inhibition by the ego, the sidetracking of quantity in and by the ego-organization? Is it the ego that is responsible for the periodic thrusts, or is it consciousness? Or are both ego and consciousness themselves outcomes of periodicity?

None of these questions, even after thirty years of intense psychoanalytic practice, has been resolved by the time of the *Notiz.* Although later in 1925, in the article on "Negation" (StA 3, 376), Freud will attribute periodic thrust to the probative action of the ego (an attribution in conformity with the *tendency* of the 1895 "Project," in which the introduction of the ego is of central importance), here in the *Notiz* he attributes typographic thrust to the pitchlike substratum of the psyche, to memory and the unconscious. "It is as though the unconscious were to stretch out feelers into the external world by means of the

W-Bw system, feelers that are quickly retracted after they have gotten a taste [*verkostet haben*] of its [i.e., the external world's] excitations." The pseudo-podic unconscious is that single-celled microcosm of the nervous structure as a whole that we entertained many pages ago. The "inner," *das Innere,* of the structure is here neither consciousness nor the ego but the unconscious, the unconscious as memory: a cavern, pit, or shaft darker than any script. "I would have the interruptions that occur from the outside in the case of the mystic writing pad [i.e., the gentle grip raising the composite coversheet from the waxen subsurface] come about [in *W-Bw*] by means of the discontinuity in the stream of innervation; instead of an actual [*wirklichen*] cancellation of contact, my supposition would call for the periodically recurring impassivity [*Unerregbarkeit*] of the perceptual system."

Two cycles of periods mesh here, the cycle of feeling-thrusts by the unconscious, employing *W-Bw* as a means, and the cycle of periods of nonexcitability in general, presumably in sleep. A general period of (possible) activation of *W-Bw* would be further punctuated by (actual) activation of perceptual feelers, feelers that as *means* belong to *W-Bw* but whose origin and end (*arkhē kinēseōs*) is the unconscious. And in the meshing of these two cycles, *time:* "I further surmised that this discontinuous *modus operandi* of the system *W-Bw* underlies the genesis of the representation of time." According to Derrida, such temporality *as* spacing (*espacement*) would mean far more than the horizonal discontinuity   *Where are we at all? and whenabouts in the name of space?*   in any chain of signs; it would mean "writing as interruption and reestablishment of contact among the diverse depths of psychic layers, the exceedingly heterogeneous temporal stuff of psychic work [*travail psychique*] itself" (ED, 333/225). The genesis of temporality in turn would produce "the differentiated duration and depth of a scene" (ED, 333/225). That scene encompasses the performance by multiple personae of a miraculous writing. Freud's concluding sentence:

> If one conceives of it in this way—that while one hand covers the superficies of the mystic writing pad with writing [*während eine Hand die Oberfläche . . . beschreibt*] another hand [*eine andere*] periodically raises the coversheet of the pad from its wax tablet—that would be a pictorialization [*Versinnlichung*] of the way in which I would want to represent to myself [*mir vorstellen wollte*] the functioning of our psychical perceptual apparatus.

Derrida's preoccupation with the two (or more) hands that operate the apparatus is no mere whimsy. *Eine Hand* clearly belongs to us. Us, who? Let us say, us the ego-organization, although even this steady hand, the writing hand, relies on the periodic thrust of feelers extended by the unconscious for whatever will become script. More troublesome is *eine andere.* We can insert the word *Hand* because of the feminine gender: *eine andere* is not the bizarre adverbial *anders* that emerged earlier with the problem of quality (*Anfänge,* 393; see page 119, above). The word that causes the difficulty is the indefinite article *eine.* Another. *An* other? Hand? Does Freud refrain from writing *die andere* because there is yet a *third* hand at play? Thus a *second* person? A *Nebenmensch?* How many hands would *W-Bw* take, if we remember that its substratum is a totally different system, separate, though conjoined?

A hand across the top to hold the pad firmly in place.

A hand to guide the red wooden stylus across the celluloid shield.

And while that hand is trying to write, trying to preserve the intimate contact between perception and memory, *a third hand* to introduce discontinuity—not merely the discontinuity of blancs in the line of writing but a discontinuity of depth; a profound *temporal* interruption, the instauration of time and alterity as such. The scene of the tablet's functioning, the scene of wax magic, will have to become rather more complicated.

Cette machine ne marche pas   are you spraken sea Djoytsch?
toute seule. Its *maintenance*, its main-taining by hand and holding by presence, the presence of the "now," *maintenant,* its presence at hand, *prokheiros,* in the "now" is inordinately complex (ED, 334/226). Indeed, "the ideal virginity of the now [*du maintenant*] is constituted by the work of memory." The implication is that it will not be possible to isolate *W-Bw* from the unconscious, or even to distinguish clearly between the functions of perception-consciousness and memory or the states of consciousness and unconsciousness, as *The Ego and the Id* freely concedes. Derrida writes:

> Thus traces produce the space of their inscription only by giving themselves the period of their effacement. From the origin, in the "present" of their first impression, they are constituted by the double force of repetition and effacement, legibility and illegibility. A machine for two hands. . . .

A machine for two hands, *eine Hand* and *eine andere.* Perhaps we should think of hands as human beings, such as farmhands or sailors at sea, all hands on deck, where the demands are so excessive   *Sea, sea! Here, weir, reach, island, bridge. Where you meet I. The day. Remember!*   that one never has enough hands on hand to get the job done.

> A machine for two hands, a multiplicity of instances or of origins—is this not the originary relation to the other [*le rapport à l'autre*] and the originary temporality of writing, its "primary" complication: originary spacing, differance, and efface-ment of the simple origin; the moment we cross the threshold [*dès le seuil*], a *polemos* of what one stubbornly insists on calling "perception"? . . . One must be many in order to write and even in order to "perceive."

The closure of pure perception—and perhaps perception became impure forever with Merleau-Ponty—is the closure of typography. The multiplication of hands, as of cycles and periods, makes the presence at hand of all the icons of iconography a presence riddled by multiple absences. Engrammatology, executed on a magic writing pad, is no longer incision, storage, and retrieval of perceptions. The magic writing pad itself becomes one of the layers   *I'm getting mixed*   that effect the magic: "The subject of writing is a *system* of relations among the layers: of the mystic writing pad, of the psychical, of society, of the world" (ED, 335/227). Both less and more than a system, a holding together   *How small it's all!*   that is from the outset discontinuous. Freud's mystic writing pad is in fact (part of) the primal scene: "At the heart of this scene, the punctual simplicity of the classical subject *Loonely in me loneness*   cannot be found" (ED, 335/227). The punctuation that punches, stamps, and coins the subject, the violent inscription of breaching or effraction, the "metonymy boundlessly at work on the same metaphor" in Freud's work, serves as a silent and concealed exergue for the whole of "Freud and the Scene of Writing," which culminates   *When we come in the presence*   in a series of questions concerning genitality and the repression of writing. Without following these questions concerning prohibition, censorship, interdiction, and primary repression in both the Freudian and Derridean texts, we ought at the end to remember   *So. Avelaval. My leaves have drifted from me. All. But one clings still. I'll bear it on me. To remind me of. Lff!*   the outrage that in the 1895 *Entwurf* organizes the scene of desire, unpleasure, and tenuous satisfaction.

With Freud it is never a matter of gloriously efficient breachings, perfectly punctual effractions, and guaranteed tracings. Both the "Project" and the "Note," and all the systems to which they are responding, are markedly vulnerable. Menace is the scene   *For our netherworld's bosomfoes are working tooth and nail overtime: in earthveins, toadcavities, chessganglions, saltklesters, underfed: nagging firenibblers knockling aterman up out of his hinderclutch*   of life, exigency its daily fare. If restitution and restoration are everywhere sought   *mememormee!*   it is only because loss is everywhere found.

PART TWO

On the Verge

Past and present and future are not disjoined
but joined. The greatest poet forms the consis-
tence of what is to be from what has been
and is. He drags the dead out of their coffins
and stands them again on their feet. . . . he
says to the past, Rise and walk before me
that I may realize you. He learns the lesson. . . . he places himself where the future becomes present. The greatest poet does not
only dazzle his rays over character and scenes
and passions. . . . he finally ascends and fin-
ishes all. . . . he exhibits the pinnacles that no
man can tell what they are for or what is
beyond. . . . he glows a moment on the ex-
tremest verge.

—Walt Whitman, *Leaves of Grass*

Of Tracings without Wax

The Early Work of Jacques Derrida

as though such questions had not been confronting us before we even dreamt of beginning; as though we could elude them by evasion and, yes, a highly developed sense of oblivion; questions such as these: What does *memory* mean in and for the history of metaphysics, in which being means "presence" or "coming to presence"? Does it not always and everywhere mean preservation of the past as of a bygone present? Does not metaphysics conceive of *reminiscence* as an act of "recollection" in principle capable of restoring to full presence what is now absent? And will not recollection of presence always have demanded a certain kind of *writing* as its translucent medium?

The prevailing models for memory in the epoch of parousial metaphysics—which is the only epoch we know, even if we suspect that we are living in the age of its closure—share the same basic structure. Whether it be Socrates' slab of wax, Descartes' waxen gland H, or the neurophysiologist's computer storage depot, the models for memory are, I have argued, *typographic, iconographic,* and *engrammatological.* Typographic: persons, objects, and events make their mark on the mind, impressing their characteristic signs as presences which—if all goes well—will remain on call for *re*call at will. Iconographic: because these persons, objects, and events are now absent, hence "are" "not," their presence in and to the mind must be accounted for by means of a certain likeness. Engrammatological: because likeness or verisimilitude itself announces a fatal incommensurability or difference, a gap in both time and space between the (present) image and its (absent) original, the icon is from the outset translated into a medium that effaces itself and promises to close all the gaps—the medium of inscribed letters, letters of the phonetic alphabet.

In the present chapter I shall look more closely at phonetic writing as Derrida analyzes it in his early texts, especially *Of Grammatology* and *Dissemination.* It will of course be impossible to do justice to these rich analyses, and I will be turning to them only in order to become clearer about the "situation" of memory, reminiscence, and writing in our time. For, as we begin to remember the prevalent models for memory and the ubiquitous goal of presence, the entire constellation of memory, reminiscence, and writing shifts and breaks into motion, altering ancient patterns of meaning forever. If such a shift or alteration can be said to have a destination, the telos of its movement would be *the verge*. To be *on* the verge is to tend to presence principally in the modes of absence, evanescence, failure to remember, and oblivion. A script at the limits of legibility, the opacities of a vagrant spirit, a temporality of mortal transience, and an affirmation without nostalgia are the verger's only sources of light: in this chapter, the writing of memory and the memory of writing; in chapter 5, Hegel's impossible location of interiorizing remembrance (*Erinnerung*) in the thinking memory (*Gedächtnis*) of spirit; in chapter 6, Heidegger's and Nietzsche's reflections on the imperfect "It was" of perfect time, the imperfection that mars "having-been" or *Gewesenheit;* and in chapter 7, the possibility and necessity of double affirmation through memory as mirth and mourning.

In each case, to be on the verge is to be anywhere but at the center or origin of memory, reminiscence, and writing. Nostalgia for that font and source permeates the idealist, empiricist, positivist, and phenomenological projects of philosophy. What happens to philosophy if and when that nostalgia evaporates? Typography, iconography, and engrammatology are the mechanisms of that nostalgia, and their passing is the passing of philosophy. However, passing, as we shall see in chapter 6, is undecidably passing *by* and passing *away*. If we do happen to live in a time of transition, a time of what Heidegger calls *Übergang*, then we will not be too quick to say down what verge philosophy is now hurtling. For *Übergang* may be more than merely a temporary plight of mortals "today"; "going over" may be mortal downgoing, *Untergang*. While everywhere on the brink of such statements—both about our times and our mortality—I will concentrate on memory, reminiscence, and writing, and so tarry a while longer on the verge. In this chapter by considering matters of *script*, the *absolute past*, and what one might call *Plato's dream*.

SCRIPTURE, SCRIPTION, SCRIPT

Trace and differance, the two principal designations of what Derrida calls *arche-writing* and what I shall here variously call *scripture, scription,* and *script,* do not lend themselves to a systematic account. All the more reason to admire Rodolphe Gasché's rigorously systematic description of them, which I shall use here as an initial orientation.[1]

According to Gasché, trace and differance are but two of the five infrastructures or graphematic structures of deconstruction, the three others being supplementarity, iterability, and the "re-mark." Whatever else it might be—and its structure is highly complex—the trace expresses "an originary nonpresence and alterity" at the heart   *So perfect to Pierre had long seemed the illuminated scroll of his life thus far, that only one hiatus was discoverable by him in that sweetly-writ manuscript. A sister had been omitted from the text*   of all systems of expression (191). Pure ideality of meaning, pure self-presence as such, both require and enable infinite repeatability. "I can repeat, as often as I like," Husserl is fond of saying in his descriptions of *Wiedererinnerung*. Yet infinite repeatability of a self-identical unit of meaning depends in a bedeviling way on several series of differences. "Indeed, for an ideal entity to repeat *itself,* it must be able to intimate *itself* in contrast to an Other from which it is different" (192). Theaetetus is *not* Socrates is *not* Theodorus is *not even* snubnosedness, and the *typos* or *eikōn* of the nose that will enable us to remember any one of them *as* one of them will rely in an ultimately unaccountable way on an infinite series of differences. "In short, the arche-trace must be understood   *In their precise tracings-out and subtile causations, the strongest and fieriest emotions of life defy all analytical insight*   as the fold of an irreducible 'bending-back,' as a minimal (self-)difference within (self-)identity" (192).

Such a "fold" or "bending-back" may remind us of the classic criticism of the engram by Coleridge, Erwin Straus, and Merleau-Ponty. In order for the engram to do its work it must efface itself, like a footprint vanishing from the snow; it must eradicate itself (in order to preserve the surface) yet reintroduce itself at the will of the tracker or "reader" of the prints. Moreover, the problem of the virginal surface of snowscape or pineal gland or writing pad is not merely one of the gradual accumulation of marks, not merely a problem of crowding or excessive corrugation; the engrammatological dilemma is there with the very first mark or imprint, already there with the supposition that there can be a "very first" pristine mark. The bending-back of which Gasché writes is actually a *doubling* that does not follow the iconographic model of image and original. In support of what Plato's *Cratylus* has taught us, Gasché writes:

> Because a mark acquires the ideal identity necessary to its iteration as the mark of something other than itself only to the extent that it is constituted by what it is not, the totalizing semic mark must also inscribe or insert within itself the differential structure of the mark, that which makes the mark possible. The mark must thus be marked, or re-marked, by its own mark (march, margin). Since in its irreducible duplication it must include a reference to what it is not, inserting something heterogeneous to itself in itself—namely, what demarcates it as a mark—the mark also names the space of inscription of the marks, what holds them together and separates them, what makes them resemble and differ from one another. . . . The re-mark is thus *more* than the totality of the marks and more than the totalizing concept of the mark; in addition it is what makes that totality possible. . . . The trait by which the mark becomes doubled, however, is an undecidable trait, one that constitutes a limit to the (conceptualizing or representing) reflection of the limits or margins of the mark. . . . (219–20)

This last point is perhaps the most difficult   *The metaphysical writers confess, that the most impressive, sudden, and overwhelming event, as well as the minutest, is but the product of an infinite series of infinitely involved and untraceable foregoing occurrences*   of all, and Gasché attempts to clarify it by the following:

> The re-mark is an essential limit to all coinciding reflection or mirroring, a dou-
> bling of the mark that makes all self-reflective adequation impossible. For struc-
> tural reasons, there is always more than totality; the extra valence added by the

delegate of the asemic space of diacritical differentiation of the totality of semes
always—infinitely—remains to be accounted for. (221)

However impenetrable such "asemic space" may seem, the doubling of the
mark, less a doubling than a kind of fission or ceaseless internal division and
differentiating, is actually something that has confronted us from the outset.
The doubling in question is not a replication of simples but a duplex relationship   *This romantic filial love*   between the simple (what Plato calls
the *eidos*) and its simulacra, the icon and the idol (*eikōn, eidōlon*). Better, it is
the duplicitous relation of the simulacra to the self-showing or perfect presence
of the *idea*. The duplicitous simulacrum embodies what Gasché (226) calls a
"subtle excess of truth and ontology," an excess in the sense of an exceeding or
transgressing of bounds. Thus the straightforward logico-metaphysical opposition of truth and untruth founders. What we are asked to entertain here is "a
simulacrum *without an ultimate referent. . . .*" The originary duplicity of the
simulacrum "initiates but also displaces the metaphysical opposition of original and copy, and the copy of a copy, into a completely different field" (227).
The "field" in question is of course not a field at all but a declivity, a
slippery slope, a verge. We set foot on it whenever we   *seemed to entertain some insane hopes of wedding this unattainable being*   try for example to distinguish as Aristotle does an activity (such as reminiscing) from a pure
pathos (such as involuntary remembering); or whenever with Aristotle we
designate the waxy surface as the "original image" of memory; or when we try
to understand the *sensus communis* as a sensing *that* one senses; or when the
word *being* doubles in that curious phrase, "the being of beings," here meaning
the mysterious presence of what is past in our memories, the being of beings *in
time;* or when we gaze on the *zōgraphēma,* which is in some bizarre sense a
"living portrait" of a living being, both an object in its own right and   *It
is an excellent likeness, my child*   an icon of an Other; remembering that
the word *zōion* itself, without the supplement of the *graphēma,* operates according to the selfsame duplicity (living being/likeness); or when we recall
Aristotle's suggestion that the mind can scan or glean (*theōrein*) doubly; or
when we bring to mind the happenstance that Aristotle's account of the portrait itself doubles as a portrait of the phantasms of the mind, an image of
images that are themselves duplex; or, more negatively, when we consider that
the explanation in terms of phantasmata only redoubles the enigma of memory,
inasmuch as *both* the object *and* its portrait are absent from memory before it
remembers; or when we recall that the motion followed by recollection is
pursuit (*akolouthei*) of time's own motion, but that such pursuit is not perfect
in the case of reminiscence, inasmuch as false directions are always possible,
and that for every *physis* or upsurgent self-showing there is a *paraphysis* or
"obfuscation," for every genuine *homoiōsis* also a *paromoion,* a mere likeness
of likeness; or the curious doubling of body and soul in memory, in that
remembering seems to be both syllogistic inference and a profoundly incarnate
pathos; or, finally, the curious doubling in the Aristotelian pathology of the

elderly—nature's natural dwarfs—who in their very wasting away are both sclerotic and metabolic.

No doubt we would encounter Plato—the apostle of *eidos* and apostate of *eidōla*—just as often on the verge. Plato's *typos* and *karaktēr* are themselves as duplicitous as *virga,* "the verge," inasmuch as they suggest that *in* which, *by* which, and *of* which a stamping occurs—matrix, marker, and modeled image in one; remembering that infinite duplication and iteration are what the entire typographic process is about; whereby both the wax slab and aviary images involve an iteration of likenesses rather than an introduction of beings themselves; so that it may be either comforting or disconcerting to note that the iconography of memory lies at the heart of the fundamental aporia of Platonic participation (of form and form, as of being and form); which is to say, the aporia of the *being* of beings; this odd doubling leading to the duplicity of sophist and philosopher, of self-showing in an Other, presencing as a kind of absence and nonbeing; or to the duplicity of the megalithic artist who imitates the goddess perfectly and shows her to be a gigantic midget; whence Heidegger's insight that *mimēsis* is precisely what neither artist nor craftsman achieves, even if the craftsman is the divine father of all; given what he has to work with—a duplicitous receptacle   *a reverential and devoted son seemed lover enough for this widow Bloom*   and mother of all becoming. Letters too, *ta grammata,* are not without their own duplicities. In *Theaetetus* and *Sophist* they appear as perdurant elements in the flood of speech, as the alogical atoms of logos. For Hobbes and Locke as well, letters have a perdurant, atomic character: the sounds that produce names and perspicuous words are from the outset *marks* or *notes* of *memory,* as though the sounds doubled as letters before being sounded, and as though (as Quintilian would have affirmed) speaking were a kind of *reading.* However, by reminding ourselves of the importance of letters in accounts of knowledge and memory, accounts that are essentially engrammatological, we approach—more directly now—Derrida's *Of Grammatology* and *Dissemination.*

The most general theses of grammatology illuminate the destiny of what I have been calling typography, iconography, and engrammatology. If the phonetization of writing dissimulates its own history, that dissimulation facilitates the search for a medium so transparent that it appears to preserve the full presence of what is absent or past; however, if the history of metaphysics ascribes to the logos of *living* language the origin of *truth,* repressing writing and expelling it from the sanctuary of truth, then the fate of typographic and iconographic memory will be the fate of truth as such; if the very scientificity of science is bound up with the logocentrism of our tradition, then the experience of what I am calling the verge will not leave untouched the spheres of knowledge and science. Further, if the dissimulation of the process of phonetization is failing in our time; if phonematic or glossematic language finally reveals itself—in its very emphasis on the tongue, voice, hearing, sound, breath, living dialogue, genuine communication, speech acts, and so on—as "the guise or disguise of a premier writing" (G, 16–17/7), then script cannot be a simple supplement, and the supplemental relationship of *writing* to memory and reminiscence is drawn into a kind of turbulence. Finally, if it is the full *presence* of living speech that grants to the living word its privileged place in the history of metaphysics, then the enigma of memory—the *presence* of the *past*—will perhaps serve as the crucible or mortar of that tradition. If typographic inscription in the mind seems the only way to account for the iconographic presence of the past, memory seems to be the scene both of crisis and of supreme fulfillment for logocentrism. Crisis, inasmuch as the incised mark alone, rather than the stream of words flowing from the mouth, guarantees a hold on meaning; fulfillment, inasmuch as the engrammatological reading or scanning of the incised marks appears to restore both the virginity of the matrix and the full presence of what was absent.

I cannot offer here an account of the enigmatic phenomenon of the *s'entendre-parler,* hearing and understanding oneself while speaking, which is so central to Derrida's argument in both *Voice and Phenomenon* and *Of Grammatology.*[2] However, let me pose the obvious question to that analysis: Does not the very crisis of logocentrism in the prevailing models for memory and reminiscence, which do not repress writing but appeal blatantly to it, indicate a flaw in the Derridean depiction of the *s'entendre-parler?* If the principal enigma of memory is resolved always and everywhere in our tradition by an appeal to marks, signs, notations, and text, is not scription rather than speech the privileged place of presence?

Like most obvious questions, the one I have just posed stops short, fails to remember. For the success of engrammatology always necessitated the *reading* of memorious marks, signs, notations, and text, which of themselves were marks of oblivion, mere hypomnemics. And the secret of this success was well-kept. How did the reading, the retrieval, function? How did it work? Did it not work by translating the incised icons back into the cutting edge of presence itself? And is there anything in the foregoing account that suggests that it is something other than presence, interiority, absolute proximity to being, and self-affection that accounts for the miracle of memory?

When Derrida presents that text from Aristotle's *Of Interpretation* (I, 16a, 3ff.) that cried for attention in chapter 1 but never got it, a text made crucially relevant by Heidegger's discussion of it in "The Way to Language," there can be no doubt about the relevance of grammatology for engrammatology. Aristotle identifies the sounds emitted by the voice (*ta en tēi phōnēi*) as symbols of the affections of the psyche (*tōn en tēi psykhēi pathēmatōn symbola*), and written words (*ta graphomena*) as symbols of those sounds. If memory and reminiscence involve the presence of such *pathēmata* in the mind, as they do, it will not be irrelevant to engrammatology that "the voice, producing the *first symbols,* has a rapport of essential and immediate proximity with the soul" (G, 21–22/11). As premier productress   *the low melodies of her far interior voice hovered in sweet echoes in the room*   of signifiers, the voice cannot be one signifier among others. "Between being and the soul, things and the affections, there would be a relation of translation or natural signification;

between the soul and the logos, a rapport of conventional symbolization" (G, 22/11). Even if the voice is not itself pure transparency, and even if speech differs from one nation to the next, voice and speech are as intimate with phenomena as any signification can be. Aristotle writes:

> Spoken words are symbols of affections in the soul, written words are the symbols of spoken words. And just as written letters [*grammata*] are not the same for all peoples, neither are spoken sounds [*phōnai*]. Yet the affections in the soul, of which these are preeminently the signs [*sēmeia prōtōs*: Derrida translates: *sont immediatement les signes*], are the same for all men, as are the things [*pragmata*] of which those affections are the likenesses [*homoiōmata*].

Iconography proper pertains to the things themselves, the *pragmata*, as they are captured typographically in the impressions or affections of the soul, the *pathēmata*. The latter constitute the universal language, the original text, the script and scripture of human experience. One must therefore stress more than Derrida does that neither spoken nor written words conform perfectly to such likeness. Engrammatology—can it ever be equal to the task of iconography? More important, Derrida seems to restrict the attribution of *preeminent* signification to the spoken word, whereas in Aristotle's text the *tauta* probably refers to both spoken and written *sēmeia*, both speech and writing. Heidegger certainly reads the phrase that way: he translates *hōn mentoi tauta sēmeia prōtōs* as "*Woven indes diese (Laute und Schrift) erstlich ein Zeigen sind . . . ,*" "Yet that of which these [sounds and writing] are in the first instance a showing. . . ."[3] Not only the relegation of both writing and speech to a secondary status should be stressed here, but also Heidegger's translation of *sēmeia* as *das Zeigende,* the showing. Because I stressed the importance of self-showing in my reading of Aristotle's *Of Memory and Reminiscence,* I am perhaps justified in stressing here the inadequacy of both writing and speech to such showing: no system of signs seems equal to the self-showing of either the things themselves in sensuous apprehension or of the affections (*pathēmata*) in the soul's interior life. Nevertheless, two points argue against my reservations: first, in the opening lines of the passage Aristotle unequivocally subordinates writing to speech, the latter symbolizing the *pathēmata,* the former symbolizing speech, and thus perduring at a second (or third) remove from the things themselves; second, Heidegger himself never doubts the priority of speech in Aristotle's "classic construction," and his whole undertaking in "The Way to Language" is to put in question the *lingua* of language, our glossary and glossolalia, our *Mund-art,* the way we dialecticians mouth the words of language. In short, one must doubtless be cautious when affirming "the absolute proximity of the voice and being," remembering that our tradition is not so much phonocentric as *sigocentric* (from *sigein,* to maintain silence); the philosophic voice has always been the voice that keeps silent, as Socrates tells us in *Sophist* (at 263e; cf. *Theaetetus,* 189e–190a): "Thinking [*dianoia*] and discourse [*logos*] are the same, except that what we call thinking is the dialogue [*dialogos*] within the soul which the soul has with itself [*pros autēn*] and which comes to be without sound [*aneu phōnēs*]." The Western tradition is *aneuphonic* rather than phonocentric. And yet Derrida is right to suggest that writing has always seemed noisier to the tradition than speech: the scratch of the verge is generally   *He will not be called to; he will not be stirred. Sometimes the intent ear of Isabel in the next room, overhears the alternate silence, and then the long lonely scratch of his pen. It is, as if she heard the busy claw of some midnight mole in the ground*   more disruptive of interiority than the warbling throat. *Interiority* is the issue, an interiority that obviously has to do with remembrance as interiorization (*Er-Innerung, Innerlich-machen*); the issue is not some sort of contest between speech and writing, in which the proximity of voice and being would be matched against Sacred Scripture or Descartes scribbling at the hearth. "Script" or "scription," *écriture* in Derrida's sense, is *exteriority* as such, whether in written or spoken form: "The exteriority of the signifier is the exteriority of writing [*écriture*] in general, and we shall try to show . . . that there is no linguistic sign prior to writing" (G, 26/14). If matters should seem otherwise, Derrida argues, it is because of a certain "metaphorical mediation" by which script insinuates itself into the heart of being as the very voice of God: ". . . scripture [*écriture*] of the truth of the soul, opposed by *Phaedrus* (278a) to bad script [*mauvaise écriture*] (to scription [*écriture*] in the 'proper' and current sense, 'sensuous' writing, 'in space') . . . ":

> . . . everything that functions as a metaphor in these discourses confirms the privilege of logos and founds the "proper" sense thus given to writing: a sign signifying a signifier itself signifying an eternal truth, eternally thought and spoken in the proximity of a present logos. The paradox to which one must pay heed is thus the following: natural and universal scripture, intelligible and nontemporal scription, is thus named by metaphor. Sensuous script, which is finite, etc., is designated as writing in the proper sense; it is thus thought to be on the side of culture, technicity, and artifice: a human procedure, the ruse of a creature incarnated by accident, or of a finite creature. (G, 26–27/14–15)

"Natural" writing here shares none of the *Natürlichkeit* before which Hegel shudders in awe and horror; "natural" here has nothing to do with nature   *I never knew a mortal mother. The farthest stretch of my life's memory can not recall a single feature of such a face*   but everything to do with the demiurge and father, the lord of the logos. The father's is the universal, intelligible scripture, which is *nontemporal, atemporal.* His is the realm of the pure signified, wholly present in the time of a breath or the blink of an eye, which leaves no *trace* (G, 31/18). Yet how could such "natural" scripture serve the typography, iconography, and engrammatology of memory and reminiscence? If the pure signified leaves no trace, can it ever have been the object of memory? Or, to ask it the other way around, starting from our (finite) experiences in this (finite) world: What has the deconstruction of pure ideality into *trace* and *differance* to do with our remembering and forgetting of persons, things, and events in the world? How does Derrida's thought of the trace affect the traces of typography, iconography, and engrammatology?

A first reply arises during Derrida's genealogical account of the "usurpation" (in the eyes of Rousseau and Saussure) of speech by writing. It is in fact the *durability* and *duration* of the mnemic trace, inscription as "the durable institution of a sign" (G, 65/44), that makes it so seductive for the typographic tradition; the excellence of the *typos* and its impressed mark resides precisely in its simulation of eternity or permanent presence. Yet if this is so, the typographic tradition gives the lie to phonocentrism and makes a nonsense of the imputed "contamination" of living language by script. "To explain the usurpation [of speech by writing] by means of the strength of *duration* [durée] in script and by virtue of the *hardness* [dureté] of substance in script—is this not to contradict outrageously what is otherwise affirmed concerning the oral tradition of language, which is said to be 'independent of writing, and fixed in an altogether different manner'?" (G, 60/41). The hardness of the mnemic trace is of course a sometime thing: not a thinker in the West who has not stressed the difficulties in getting the verge just right—the verge as both the cutting edge of the stylus and the waxen matrice. Hardness in and of itself implies lethargy and oblivion: Benjy. Which would suggest why memory is the crucible—or perhaps the Achilles heel, and even the jugular—of the metaphysics of presence. If writing is the evil, transgression, violence, sacrilege, and incest   *they were wont to call each other brother and sister*   committed against the mother tongue, or what Thoreau identifies as the *father* tongue, then memory and reminiscence will have been the scene of such wickedness. In the midst of wistfulness and nostalgia, reports of treachery and death. If script haunts language "as its premier and most intimate possibility" even after it has been banished beyond the frontiers of interiority (G, 64/44), so does memory haunt knowledge and every ontotheological security as their inexplicable shadow.

A second reply to our question arises during Derrida's most explicit account of the trace, in "The Outside ⊁ the Inside," as being somehow *prior to typography.* "Before even being given over to incision or engraving, to the sketch or the letter, to a signifier generally referring back to a signifier signified by it, the concept of *graphie* implies the agency of the *instituted trace,* as the possibility common to all systems of signification" (G, 68/46). Both typogra*phy* and icono*graphy* presuppose the *graphie* as such—if one can retain the phrase "as such," which itself relies on the *typos* and *eikōn* of graphematics, which of course one cannot. For the deconstruction of graphematics discloses "the absence of an other, transcendental present," an absence that "presents itself" as "an irreducible absence within the presence of the trace" (G, 68/47). The graphic trace thus marks a relation to "the other" of being. "One must think the trace prior to the being [*avant l'étant*]" (G, 69/47). And: "The field of being, before being determined as a field of presence, is structured by the diverse possibilities—genetic and structural—of the trace" (G, 69/47). Thus the field of scriptive being, like the field of existence as Merleau-Ponty writes of it, is for Derrida a certain "hollow" (*creux*)   *doth not the Scripture intimate, that He holdeth all of us in the hollow of His Hand?—a Hollow, truly!*

in being, a hollowing-out (*se creuser*) of being. For Merleau-Ponty, the hollow of being is *temporality* as such; the hollowing action is *temporalization*. In Derrida's quasi-transcendental account of the trace as arche-writing and arche-synthesis, three items are pervasive: in addition to (1) "language as *écriture*" and (2) "the structure of the relation to the other," one must also consider (3) "the movement of temporalization" (G, 69; 88/47; 60). Temporalization and temporising, both in the hollow of *différance* as differentiation and deferral, are no doubt central to any inquiry into memory.[4] I shall therefore turn to the question of temporalization after making two more replies to the question concerning the relevance of grammatology for engrammatology.

The third reply deepens and perhaps even supersedes the account of the *graphie*. For the very *possibility* of the trace, as relation to an otherness, refers us to *play* rather than to the work of graphematics. "One could call *play* [jeu] the absence of the transcendental signified, as the infinite expansiveness [*illimitation*] of play; that is to say, as that which causes ontotheology and the metaphysics of presence to tremble" (G, 73/50). If script, scripture, and scription constitute "the play in language," such play resonates in the debate between Thot and King Thamus in *Phaedrus,* to which we shall return in the final part of the chapter; as the *"play of the world* [jeu du monde]," such play would also have to be discussed in terms of the Heraclitean *Aion,* Nietzschean "world-play, the ruling," the Heideggerian play of being, in which humanity is the stakes, and Eugen Fink's "play as cosmic symbol" (G, 73–74/326 n. 14). Here it can only be a matter of seeing that the duplicities that disturb the smooth functioning of iconography arise precisely from such oscillation or play. The oscillation within verisimilitude, which is always equally dissimulation, disturbs both the *icon* and the *graphie* that would serve it. "Before being or not being 'noted,' 'represented,' or 'figured' in a '*graphie*' [now placed in scare-quotes], the linguistic sign implies an originary writing" (G, 77/52). If oral language   *in a voice that seems to come from under your great-grandfather's tomb*   already belongs to such scription, the pure presence it dreams of approximating is lost forever. The project of a perfect restoration of the past in active remembrance, through the combined efforts of typography, iconography, and engrammatology, thereby founders. Again, it is not a matter of "rehabilitating" script during or after the epoch of phonocentrism, or even of reversing the order of dependence in the linguistics of speech and writing; rather, it is a matter of recognizing that there never was a pure presence uncontaminated by the exteriority and instability of a system of signs, no icon that was ever preserved intact, no cutting edge that ever wholly mastered the matrix. No doubt, the "new concept" of *arche-writing* continues to "communicate with" the "vulgar" sense of script. Writing, in the quotidian sense, "could only impose itself historically by the dissimulation of arche-writing [objective genitive, in the first place, subjective genitive if one takes seriously, as one must, arche-writing as the complicity of origins (G, 140/92)], by the desire for a speech that repels its other, its double, and labors to reduce its difference" (G, 83/56). And that difference "cannot be thought without the trace" (G, 83/56).

This third reply conducts us to the "field of transcendental experience" *If man must wrestle, perhaps it is well that it should be on the nakedest possible plain* on which the hardest grammatological battles are fought (see G, 89–90/60–61; 95–96/65–66). Why the *possibility* of the trace leads Derrida to that field is clear, if we recall that after Kant every question of condition-of-possibility is a transcendental question. What the transcendental *passage* (*parcours:* G, 90/61) can be, as passage to an ultra-transcendental text, a passage that leaves a certain trace in its wake (*sillage*), without which the ultra-transcendental text would be virtually identical to a text on the hitherside of such a passage, I cannot say. Except that if the *necessity* of such a passage is also the necessity of an *erasure* (". . . the value of the transcendental *archie* ought to let its necessity be felt before allowing itself to be erased"), then the text of deconstruction cannot and does not appeal to any of the traditional processes of typography, iconography, and engrammatology. "The trace is not only the disappearance of the origin; here—in the discourse in which we are engaged and according to the passage [*parcours*] we are following—it means that the origin has not even disappeared; that it was only ever constituted in the return of a nonorigin, the trace, which thus becomes the origin of origin" (G, 90/61). Trace is thus thought, not as a constituted difference or system of differences, but as the very movement *as of ambiguous fairies dancing on the heath* of differentiation, as "*pure* movement":

> *The (pure) trace is differance.* It does not depend on any sensible plenitude, whether audible or visible, phonic or graphic. On the contrary, it is the condition of these things. Although it *does not exist,* although it is never a *present-being* outside all plenitude, its possibility is *de jure* anterior to everything we call a sign (signified/signifier, content/expression, etc.), concept, or operation, whether motor or sensible. (G, 92/62)

In this outer stratosphere of deconstructive abstraction, where we rejoin Rodolphe Gasché's meditation, the trace appears to be untouched and untouchable—form of forms, entelechy of entelechies, the very "formation of forms." Yet precisely here (G, 92/63) Derrida reminds us that the pure movement of differance, with an *a,* is also "the being-imprinted of the imprint," *l'être-imprimé de l'empreinte*. While I cannot pursue the consequences of such an imprint for Derrida's analysis of the acoustic image, or comment on his insistence on a kind of "phenomenological reduction" by which the distinction between "appearing sound" and "the appearance of the sound" will be saved, this reintroduction of the imprint transposes a kind of typography to that transcendental field of experience. The reintroduction of the imprint has the effect of *relocating* the entire discussion of textuality and of tying typography to an explicit *engrammatology*. I have elsewhere criticized the following passage as having introduced an arche-limbo into grammatology,[5] and yet it now seems that I must dedicate—*si l'on peut dédicacer l'archi-limbo d'entre deux pages, en vol, United*—considerable space to it here:

... one should recognize that it is in the specific zone of this imprint and this trace, in the temporalization of something *lived* [*d'un* vécu] which is neither *in* the world nor in an "other world," which is no more sonorous than it is luminous, no more *in* time than *in* space, that differences appear among the elements, or rather, produce these elements, cause them to surge forth as such, and thus constitute *texts*, chains and systems of traces. These chains and these systems can sketch themselves out [*se dessiner*] only in the web of this trace or imprint. The unheard difference between the appearing and the to-appear (between the "world" and the "lived") is the condition of all the other differences, all the other traces, and *it is already a trace*. This last concept too is absolutely and *de jure* "anterior" to every *physiological* problematic concerning the nature of the engram or *metaphysical* problematic concerning the meaning of absolute presence, which the trace thus sets about decoding. *In effect, the trace is the absolute origin of meaning in general. Which amounts to saying once again that there is no absolute origin of meaning in general.* (G, 95/65)

Here trace and imprint are named side by side. Yet not in order to submit the thought of the trace to typography in any traditional sense. Once again *temporalization* of the lived is designated as the essential site of the transcendental trace; once again, after Kant and Heidegger, the importance of temporalization for a quasi-transcendental inquiry can hardly surprise us. The limbo of such quasi-transcendence, demarcated solely by a series of neither/nors and no more thises than thats, beyond the bounds of sonority and visibility, time and space, beyond the world and even "the elements," beyond the *stoikheia* of the ancients, beyond the stuff of the world and the letters of the alphabet, is to be the (impossible) site of the to-appear (*l'apparaître*) of all these things; better, the site of the difference between their participial appearing (*l'apparaissant*) and infinitival to-appear; as though Derrida were thinking here the Heideggerian *ontological difference* between the participial *Seiendes* and infinitival *Sein*, a difference Derrida explicitly relegates to an order that is posterior to the order of the trace of differance; and almost as though he were committing what Merleau-Ponty calls "the experience error," borrowing from the experience of space, time, text, and world the elements behind the elements by which one would then *construct* and *explain* experience in transcendental terms. Yet if the unheard, unheard-of difference is *already a trace*, grammatology would pass through this transcendental domain without leaving permanent traces. Derrida here tries for the first time explicitly to distance himself from the physiology of the engram—so vigorously criticized by Sartre and Straus. If the trace is called an imprint, it is not in order to establish through engrammatology the readable presence of a past. If the trace itself sets out to decipher or decode the sense of absolute presence, it is not in order to release the decoded meaning from the storage depot of a programmed memory to an engrammatological scanner. Rather, deconstruction opens onto the problem of passivity and "the absolute past." To which we shall turn after a fourth and final reply to the question of the relationship between grammatology and engrammatology.

The fourth reply instigates a plunge from the outer stratosphere of transcendence to what is perhaps the most elemental and elementary level, the level indicated by the reference we have just heard to the "physiological" engram. One of Derrida's most important themes and theses in *Of Grammatology* is the opposition of "good" and "bad" writing, and the relation of each of these to human corporeality. "Good" writing, the scripture of spirit and heart, is united to the voice and breath; hearing and understanding itself at once, its signifying is apparently transparent, effacing itself before "the things themselves." "Bad writing" is tied to the extraneous and extrinsic, to excrescence and viscosity, to technique and artificiality, and is "exiled in the exteriority of the body" (G, 30/17). To be on the verge requires—as we heard Merleau-Ponty say of the painter, quoting Valéry—that we take our bodies with us when we remember. Or that our bodies remember to take us with them.

That the verge of memory and the hollow of human embodiment are intimate with one another has become manifest by this time, especially through waxen glands and fleshy hollows, and with the same doubling and duplicity that we saw in classic typography, iconography, and engrammatology. For example, in *Philebus'* search for a salubrious mixture, a mediation between body and soul, pleasure and memory; thus putting into question the dream of a simply psychic, purely interior, totally disembodied space for memory; or in *Cratylus'* "prison" of the soul, the body, which is as much hospice as jail, however, and the soul's sole indicator or signifier (*sēma/sōma*); the same duplicity emerges willy-nilly when Augustine defines the space of the soul as a space of nonspace (*remota interiore loco, non loco*); the capacious nonspace of perfect presence (*Praesens autem nullum habet spatium*); or in that strange duplicity by which our *notiones,* including the *verba concepta* that enable us to glean a being as being of the past, are *notationes;* so that Quintilian could take the ancient icon of memory to be the mnemotechnic original—urging his students to be guided by the tracks on the wax tablet until they become like tracks in the mind, and remembering like reading; or in the duplicity of *phantasia* in Descartes' *Regulae,* "imagination" being typography, "as though on wax," and yet putatively uncontaminated by bodily admixture; as also when Descartes tries to segregate soul from body by enumerating the corporeal differences of blood from bone (forgetting the ceraceous marrow of Homeric typography) and eye from hand (forgetting what he himself is doing—presuming that he is here *writing*); or the way in which convolutions or "folds" in the brain's surface are the very traces of memory, whereas the same marks on the pineal gland are denigrated as ruts, marks of bestiality; or the way in which for Descartes the innermost power of the soul and the most external and extrinsic sheet of paper can *both* be said to possess "memory"; or the way in which homunculus, the little man inside man, is required to be both inside the mind and outside among the world's objects; or the very duplicity by which the *surface* of the gland functions as an *inner* surface, imitating the figures of the figures of the figures of objects in the *outer* world; or the ultimate duplicity of the mimetic machine, the human being, the creature that is itself no more than an effect of memory; which would of course mean that it is equally an effect of oblivion, this frenetic soulless machine that has forgotten what it is, believes it is an animal or an angel.

No doubt Derrida would urge us to be cautious about taking "bad writing" as the "elemental" level, the level that would found or explain all the others—trace, differance, play, and so on. Indeed, there are moments in *Of Grammatology* when human embodiment is specifically relegated to an order of lesser transcendental dignity, an order posterior to the trace and derivative of it. If script sullies the soul by   *I say, my pretty one! Dear! Dear! young man! Oh, love, you are in a vast hurry, ain't you? Can't you stop a bit, now, my dear: do—there's a sweet fellow*   allowing something extrinsic to irrupt within, if it is a kind of "sin," defined as "inversion of the natural relations between soul and body in passion," then it is by no means a "simple analogy" we are confronting here. Rather:

> . . . *écriture,* the letter, and sensuous inscription have always in the Western tradition been considered to be the body and the matter that are exterior to spirit, the breath, the word, and the logos. And the problem of soul and body is doubtless derived from the problem of writing to which it seems—inversely—to lend its metaphors. (G, 52/35)

The "order of implication," as Derrida likes to say, is quite clear: the problem of *écriture* takes its "*metaphors*" from the body-soul distinction; but this is an "inversion" of the proper order, inasmuch as the problem of scripture, scription, script comes first. No doubt the entire issue of metaphor would have to be reawakened here—the issue of that unwritten history in which divine scripture and human script are opposed—in order to make sense of Derrida's own claim. Is writing in the immediate, current, "proper" sense merely *thought* [G, 27/15: *elle est alors pensée*] to be on the side of civilization, technology, and artifice? Is it merely *thought* to be "a human procedure, the ruse of a being incarnated by accident"? Derrida qualifies his analysis in the following way: "Thus it is not a matter of inverting the proper sense and the figural sense; it is rather one of determining the 'proper' sense of *écriture* as metaphoricity itself" (G, 27/15). Human embodiment is embodiment of the voice that hears and understands itself speaking, as of the face, eye   *his eyes fixed upon the girl's wonderfully beautiful ear*   and hand that enter into a sort of "contract" or "transaction" in reading and writing (G, 125–27/84–86; 407–9/288–90).

While one can sympathize with Derrida's desire to neutralize the "propriety" of the *corps propre,* the lived body, one's "own" body, by scare-quotes (G, 407/288); and while one also wishes to avoid if at all possible the mechanist, technological, or teleological vocabularies that would make of the human body a metaphysical substance and substrate (G, 126/85); it is inevitable and indeed a welcome inevitability that one return to Merleau-Ponty's notion of a corporeal *habitation* in the world (G, 126/85), of an "inscription in speech and inscription as *habitation,* always already situated" (G, 410/290). Whereas human embodiment and metaphoricity may occupy the very same niche in grammatology's order of implication, the tension between them does not diminish. Even in our own time of endless preoccupation with metaphor in literary criticism, linguistics, structural anthropology, and psychoanalysis, who is equal to the thought that metaphoricity is the fate of that creature incarnated by accident? If the very oxymoron of "creature *accidentally* incarnate" can be written without a flinch or a jolt, what hope have we for "metaphoricity"?

It is therefore hardly surprising that the quasi-transcendental dignity or priority of metaphoricity over embodiment cannot be sustained in *Of Grammatology* itself: Derrida's own genealogy of Saussure's terror in the face of "the tyranny of the letter" necessitates his observation that such a tyranny "is at bottom [*en son fond*] the mastery of the body over the soul" (G, 57/38). The wickedness of bad writing, the source of its repression in the epoch of metaphysics, is the wickedness   *betraying pander to the monstrousest vice*   of embodiment. Innocence itself, in the form of Pope Innocent III, cited by Nietzsche in *On the Genealogy of Morals* (ZGM II, 7; 5, 303), catalogues the scurrilous improprieties of the body: ". . . impure procreation, nauseating nourishment in the womb, squalidness of the matter from which the human being develops, horrid stench, excrescence   *in ambiguous pursuit of strange young women*   of spit, urine, and filth." Not to mention ink, even by way of analogy or *Quit thy analogies; sweet in the orator's mouth, bitter in the thinker's belly*   of metaphor.

THE ABSOLUTE PAST

These four replies ought to convince us of the relevance of Derridean deconstruction and grammatology for what I have called the mnemic tradition of typography, iconography, and engrammatology. However, are there no critical consequences of the latter for the former? Does the Derridean "trace" altogether escape the seductive grooves and notches of the mnemic tradition? The very quasi-transcendentality, queasy transcendentality, of grammatology once again gives us pause, as does the (altogether "natural") focus on temporalization. Both themes, transcendentality and time, hand in hand, arise from nowhere else than the metaphysics of presence. Here there can be no question of "escape," as Derrida himself repeatedly reminds us. Memory reminds and   *His face was wonderful to me. Something strangely like it, and yet again unlike it, I had seen before, but where, I could not tell. But one day, looking into the smooth water behind the house, there I saw the likeness—something strangely like, and yet unlike, the likeness of his face*   remains.

Even though he defines the trace as pure movement or *kinēsis* without existence in the field of present-being, Derrida does not shy from speaking of the "originary" or arche-synthesis that is realized by it. "Without a retention in the minimal unity of temporal experience, without a trace retaining the other as an other in the same, no difference would do its work and no meaning would appear" (G, 92/62). "Retention," "minimal unity of temporal experience," "its work," and "meaning" suggest that the agenda of the trace—its

programme, as Derrida says—is a familiar one   *Pierre Glendinning, thou*
art not the only child of thy father; in the eye of the sun, the hand that traces
this is thy sister's; yes, Pierre, Isabel calls thee her brother—her brother!
after Kant, Hegel, Husserl, Heidegger, and Bergson.[6] And after two millennia
of typography, iconography, and engrammatology, which are all about the
work of retention, minimal unity, an other *in* the same, and (remembered,
recollected, recuperated) meaning. Retention of minimal unity: a *hold* on the
one: is this what grammatology hinges on? By what sort of hinge, what sort of
retention, and of what sort of past? A past absolved from presence and the
present, a past that never was present, as Merleau-Ponty says—what can that
be? How can one ever have remembered it, even if only to point toward its
withdrawal? Such questions will no doubt recur when we remember the
thinker of the absolute and the thinker(s) of withdrawal. "Absolute"? "Past"?

"Absolute past" is of the time and tension of the hinge, *la brisure* (G, 96–
108/65–73). Yet if the portal of Derridean grammatology hinges on it, and it
does, then the door is lifted from the jamb, the entire frame of entry and exit
undone. All that is left for us to say is that thought on the hinge—which is both
difference and articulation, fragment and jointure, breach and pocket, wound
and fold—moves on the thought of time and time's spacing. "Origin of the
experiences of space and time," begins Derrida (G, 96/65), as though forgetting
that the (*non*)*origin* of origin has just now been envisaged; "this writing of the
difference, this weave of the trace permits the difference of space and time to
articulate itself, to appear [*apparaître*] as such in the unity of experience," as
though forgetting that the participle-infinitive distinction (*Seiendes-Sein*) is, as I
have already noted, the eminent ontological distinction, wholly ensconced in
the question of being as the presence of the present; "(of a 'same' ['*même*']
lived on the basis of a 'same' body proper)," as though the "same" underlay
difference in the way that substance underlies accidents and as though the lived
body, one's own body, *le corps propre*, could be such an origin. As though
forgetting his own objections to Merleau-Ponty.

Yet the thought of the hinge is one of articulation rather than substance,
articulation "before" substance, tracings without wax. "Such articulation thus
allows a graphic chain (whether 'visual' or 'tactile' and 'spatial') to adapt itself,
possibly in a linear fashion, to a chain that is spoken ('phonic,' 'temporal')."
Whether in Saussurean linguistics a graphic chain can be said to adapt itself to
a spoken word, or vice versa, need not detain us here. The more important
point is that the "psychic imprint," which is the "lived appearing" (*apparaître
vécu*) of language as such, points to a temporalizing synthesis in which, as we
have seen, the imprint is irreducible. That the Saussurean psychic imprint (in
the form of acoustic and verbal images or concepts) cannot readily be distinguished from the physiological, and that the model for both is the traditional
mnemic model of typography, iconography, and engrammatology, is indicated   *Most miraculous of all to Pierre was the vague impression, that*
somewhere he had seen traits of the likeness of that face before   by the
following passage from Saussure's *Course*, which Derrida does not cite:

It is by the functioning of the receptive and coordinative faculties that imprints [*empreintes*] are formed in the speaking subjects, imprints that turn out to be sensed as the same in all [or: are notably the same in all; *qui arrivent à être sensiblement les mêmes chez tous*]. How must one represent this social product so that language might appear perfectly disengaged from the rest? If we were able to embrace the sum of verbal images that are stored up [*emmagasinées:* a word that appears throughout Bergson's *Matière et mémoire*] in all individuals, we would be touching on the social relation that constitutes a particular language [*la langue*]. It is a treasury deposited [*un trésor déposé*] by the practice of speech in subjects. . . .[7]

The storage-house and thesaurus of memory, with all its "psychic imprints," is of course essential to the functioning of languages and of language as such. "Essential" here means irreducible and in some sense unbudgeable, "passive." Speech itself is originarily passive, notes Derrida (G, 97/66), "but in a sense of passivity that no intramundane metaphor would be able to communicate." Once again we run up against a fateful and fatal metaphoricity that is older   *Fate had separated the brother and the sister, till to each other they somehow seemed so not at all*   than both the tenor and vehicle of any given metaphor. Once again we confront the pastness and passivity that so occupied Merleau-Ponty toward the end of his life, a passivity profoundly related to the genesis of space and time in the "hollow of being." As we shall see in chapter 6, it preoccupied Heidegger as well.

"Such passivity," continues Derrida, now reaching the point that is central to our own inquiry, "is also the relation to a past, to an always-already-there that no reactivation of the origin would be able to master fully and reawaken to presence." It is not merely a question here of the historical past, or of a social backdrop, or of the genesis of a given milieu or a particular language. "This impossibility of reanimating absolutely the evidence of an originary presence," Derrida now writes, with the pen of a phenomenologist and quasi-transcendentalist, "thus would take us back to [*nous renvoie à*] an absolute past [*un passé absolu*]." The "impossibility" of evidence, the "impossibility" of the restoration or restitution of originary presence "would" conduct us back to an absolute past. Why the subjunctive? Presumably because it is difficult to see how "impossibility" can "conduct us" anywhere. Such a past would in effect be as absolutely unattainable as an "absolute beginning with the absolute."[8] Strangely, perhaps unaccountably, Derrida takes this impossibility as an authorization: "It is this that authorizes us to designate as *trace* that which does not let itself be summarized in the simplicity of a present." Such an authorization has its price or its forfeit. Derrida must challenge the way in which Husserlian phenomenology treats as equal partners the traces of retention and protention: by privileging protention and anticipation in this way—for it is a spurious equality—one risks "effacing the irreducibility of the always-already-there and the fundamental passivity we call *time*." Derrida does not take up the admittedly captious question   *In the strange relativeness, reciprocalness, and transmittedness, between the long-dead father's portrait, and the living daughter's face, Pierre might have seemed to see reflected to him, by visible and uncontradictable symbols, the tyranny of Time and Fate*   that I shall now pose: By insisting on the "irreducibility" of a "fundamental" passivity, does one not stress the "always" and the "there" of "always-already-there," and is not such insistence itself a trace of the typotopographical tradition? The appeal to time as a "fundamental" passivity, the passivity that founds being or serves as the horizon of its meaning or the condition of its possibility, should at least betray the fact that it is not easy to draw traces without wax.

It is precisely this issue, less specious than it might seem at first, that Derrida now confronts, one that has everything to do with the verge: If the trace were to conduct us back to an absolute past, it would be in order to "oblige us to think a past that one can no longer comprehend in the form of modified presence, as a past present [*un présent-passé*]." The absolute past is neither a present perfect nor an imperfect, neither a *passé simple* nor a *passé composé*, all of which would be forms of tensed past-present or present-past. The absolute past defeats our grammar and our (en)grammatology. Strictly speaking, and thinking *rigoreusement*, "the absolute past that is retained in the trace [*qui se retient dans la trace*] no longer merits . . . the name of 'the past'." The absolute past is *retained* in the trace; yet such absolutely mysterious retention   *Now Pierre began to see mysteries interpieced with mysteries and mysteries eluding mysteries; and began to seem to see the mere imaginariness of the so supposed solidest principle of human association*   does not yield up a recuperable present-past. The absolute past does not *stand*, does not *hold*, as does Heidegger's *Gewesenheit*, "having-been," to be discussed in chapter 6. Thus both historic having-been (the perfect) and fresh retention (the just-now), both the Heideggerian and the Husserlian phenomenological pasts, undergo erasure, "especially inasmuch as [*d'autant plus que*] the strange movement of the trace announces as well as [*autant que*] recalls: differance differs and defers [*la différance diffère*]."

Strange movement. Perhaps the very movement Aristotle attempts to descry and describe as *anamnēsis*, starting from an *arkhē kinēsiōs* and advancing to a mid-point or penultimate point, whether that motion be linear or circular or an even more bizarre spiral-like combination of the two. Perhaps that spiral motion, from ruling center to a series of wandering satellites in the constellation, better suits the movement of the trace than the image of furrow and wake (*sillage*), which always seems to be written in wax rather than on water. Yet however much we are meant to focus on the strange motion of the trace, rather than on the substance of its retained mark, however diligently we try to think   *the nominal conversion of a sister into a wife*   of tracings without wax, it will not do to abandon typography altogether. That the *logos* is a *typos*, an imprint, is an essential concomitant of the new thought of passivity; that this imprint is the "scriptural resource of language," indicates that *logos* is not a creationist activity, "the replete and continuous element of divine speech" (G, 99/68). However much Derrida emphasizes the difficulty of the thought of finitude, and however much he takes finitude to be essentially bound up with the psychoanalytic economy of life-death   *What was it to be dead? What is it to be living? Wherein is the difference between the words Death and Life?*   rather than a Nietzschean or Heideggerian discourse on the death of God, there can be no doubt that "the hinge of language" in Derrida attaches to a whole series of discourses in contemporary philosophy that resound with intimations of mortality. At one point in his text (G, 101/69), Derrida writes that "signification takes shape only in the hollow [*creux*] of differance," thus going to join *volens nolens* the thought of Merleau-Ponty. Thus Derrida cannot ascribe to Levinas and Heidegger alone the thought of "a past that never was and that never can be lived . . . in the form of presence" (G, 103/70); as we saw in chapter 2, that very thought is at the heart of Merleau-Ponty's approach to the atmospheric past in *Phenomenology of Perception*. A further (unspecified) reference to the Merleau-Pontian hollow occurs precisely at the point in the lecture on "Differance" where Derrida introduces the notion of a radical past:

> Differance is what brings about the fact that the movement of signification is possible only if each element that is said to be 'present,' appearing on the scene of presence, is related to something other than itself, preserving to itself the mark of the past element and allowing itself from the outset to be hollowed out [*se laissant déjà creuser*] by the mark of its relation to a future element. The trace is related no less to what one calls the future than to what one calls the past; it constitutes what one calls the present by its very relation to what is not it—absolutely not it; that is to say, not even a past or a future as modified presents.[9] (M, 13/13)

As intimations of mortality, all these discourses devote themselves to overcoming the concepts, categories, and structures they themselves employ. Derridean thought of the trace is, to say the least, no exception. Yet before taking up the explicit question, Why the word *trace*, why a word so impacted in the mnemic metaphysics of presence? It would be well for us to diverge a moment from the realm of grammatology to the scene of psychoanalysis. For it is here, as we have indicated, that in Derrida's view the discourse of (in)finitude is undone; and it is also here that my own doubts concerning the transcendental framework of Derridean deconstruction meet their most direct response.

A persistent theme in "Freud and the Scene of Writing" is that Freud's own conceptual apparatus is again and again undone by what it goes to confront. Psychoanalysis deconstructs the metaphysics of presence without ever confronting it directly, as though by magic, and Derridean deconstruction pursues psychoanalytic discourse   *He held her tremblingly; she bent over him, toward him; his mouth wet her ear; he whispered it*   both to dismantle it and to enter under its spell. That spell arises from the psychoanalytic devotion to something like an absolute past. I shall intervene only in those few moments of the "Scene" where the "spacing" of time is discussed in a way that is directly relevant to the quasi-transcendental structure and auto-deconstruction of the trace.

"That the present in general is not original but reconstituted, that it is not the absolute form, fully alive and constitutive of experience, that there is no purity of the living present—such is the theme, so formidable for the history of metaphysics, that Freud calls on us to think by means of a conceptuality that is unequal to the thing itself" (ED, 314/212). The reconstituted character of the present is the sole Freudian thought that resists total absorption into traditional metaphysics and contemporary science. Communications between the unconscious and consciousness, through the portal of the preconscious, or between id, ego, and superego, are not mere translations of a text established and "archived" once and for all. Nor is the communication between perceptual consciousness and the world "outside" the straightforward inscription of an unchanging text, whose original form could be established by a Hobbesian or Cartesian plumbing of the mind. Rather, all such communications revert to a circulation of "psychic energy" and even a kind of "psychic writing" that in some sense is prior to mundane writing. Of course, that "in some sense prior" is what gives us all our trouble: we ought to fear matching Freud's inadequate conceptuality with inadequacies of our own, inadequacies that hide in phrases like *une conceptualité inégale à la chose même,* or *la possibilité de l'écriture,* or above all in the prepositional phrases "prior to" and "on the basis of" that structure our own inquiry. A certain awkwardness should mar discourse on transcendental or queasy quasi-transcendental structures, a certain transcendent gawkiness should here be our only grace. In a rare instance of transcendent gawkiness, Derrida's own text (ED, 315) betrays the difficulties and dangers that infest the verge of the absolute past: he begins a parenthesis in mid-sentence and closes the sentence long before finally closing the parenthesis—after nine further lines of text. The parenthetical point is abstruse, and I will not be able to discuss it fully here:

> The "objectivist" or "mundane" consideration of writing teaches us nothing if we fail to refer it to a space of psychic writing (one would say transcendental writing, were one, with Husserl, to see in the psyche a region of the world. Yet as this is also the case with Freud, who wants at the same time to respect both the being-in-the-world of the psychical, its local-being [*être-local*], and the originality of its topology, which is irreducible to any ordinary intra-mundaneity, it is perhaps necessary to think that what we are describing here as the work of writing [*travail de l'écriture*] effaces the transcendental difference between origin of the world and being in-the-world. Effaces it while producing it: milieu of the dialogue and the misunderstanding between the Husserlian and Heideggerian concepts of being-in-the world).

Here the paragraph ends—tantalizingly, parenthetically, transcendently awkwardly. It does not help to add Merleau-Ponty's name to that milieu and its dialogue, not without a full discussion. Let it suffice for the moment to cite the labor and travail, work and passion, agency and suffering of the trace, the travail of scription, which undoes *while* producing: *efface en produisant.* What does the trace efface? Not "itself," but the "transcendental difference" between the *genesis* of the world in and for a constitutive-transcendental phenomenology of consciousness and our *being* in-the-world in and for an existential-fundamental ontology of Dasein. However, if the "transcendental difference" between genetic phenomenology and ontology of Dasein erases itself in the self-production of the trace in psychic scription, does not the "self-production" of the "trace" become as problematic as the difference it eradicates? It is not clear to me *how* the "transcendental difference" between the Husserlian project of, say, a phenomenology of internal time-consciousness (see note 27 of chapter 2, above) and the Heideggerian analysis of ecstatic temporality (discussed in chapter 6, below) establishes or inscribes itself; it therefore remains a *lucus a non lucendo* to speak of the effacing of such a difference, especially by a "psychic writing" in which scription performs the transcendental function while the psyche remains as fugitive as it ever was for both phenomenology and fundamental ontology. Scription, which is in-the-world, offers no short route to the world that is *sought* by phenomenology and fundamental ontology. Deconstruction unsettles those projects, and perhaps undoes them forever, but it does not dissipate the enigmas they went to confront. How odd it would be if we thought that deconstruction could be a simple substitute for either project, as though Derrida had never put into question the logic of the supplement.

What is the status of the psychic scription on which psychoanalysis—for all its inadequate conceptuality—depends? What the foregoing chapter failed to elucidate after considerable labors   *The girl moved not; was done with all her tremblings; leaned closer to him, with an inexpressible strangeness of an intense love, new and inexplicable*   I cannot here utter in a word. Derrida is at least concerned to show that the site (*lieu*) of psychic inscription is inherently unstable; whether one is occupied with the earlier or the later topology of the psyche, scription is never the mere "displacement of significations in a limpid, pregiven, immobile space," never the "white [*blanche*] neutrality of a discourse" (ED, 316/213). As we saw in the preceding chapter, effraction is "rupture and irruption *making their way* (*rupta, via rupta*)," opening up for the first time, as it were, form and matter, space and time—indeed, "procuring a reversibility of time and space" (ED, 317/214). The word *reversibility* signals the transcendental function of psychic scription, as does the reference to the *work, workings,* and *worked* nature of the psychic travail that produces the mysterious *Erinnerungsspur* or "mnemic trace." Derrida emphasizes "the *itinerant* work of the trace, producing and not merely traversing its route," the trace that—like William Carlos Williams's *saxifrage*—clears its own path, *se fraye elle-même son chemin* (ED, 317/214). However, if in *Of Grammatology* (G, 90/61) Derrida suggests that transcendental passage is a *parcours* that leaves no durable marks, then one may wonder why the (mere) *parcours* is not enough for the transcendental trace, which here is made to "produce." And yet the travail of the self-producing trace also points to its own undoing in the retardation of *Nachträglichkeit* not only of psychosexual development but of psychic writing as such. The primitive scene is a scene of scription, not a tableau or an archive; the transcendental scene is one of trac*ings*—not trac*es*—without wax. Those tracings would require that we read Freud's remarks concerning the atemporality of the unconscious in the way that Heidegger reads Kant: the putative atemporality of the deepest stratum of psychic life may rest on an inappropriate, "vulgar" sense of time; just as one may have to abandon the *Nacheinander* of the Kantian transcendental analytic for the *Wiederholung* of the *question* of time as the horizon of being, so one may have to abandon the "atemporality of the unconscious" for the *impossible-unthinkable-unsayable* of "the absolute past."

Over the face of Pierre there shot a terrible self-revelation; he imprinted repeated burning kisses upon her; pressed hard her hand; would not let go her sweet and awful passiveness. *Nachträglichkeit* and a kind of silent, spacing *periodicity* would displace the *Nacheinander* of time, letters, quality signs, reality signs, and all such durable traces in wax:

> What is proper to writing, as we have indicated elsewhere, is (in a difficult sense of the word) *spacing* [espacement]: the diastem and the becoming space of time, along with the deployment, on an original site, of significations which linear consecutivity and irreversibility, passing from point-of-presence to point-of-presence, can only tend to repress, and which to a certain extent they fail to repress. Especially in the writing we call phonetic. The collusion between it and the logos (or the time of logic) that is dominated by the principle of noncontradiction—the fundament of the metaphysics of presence in its entirety—is profound. Now, in all silent or not purely phonic spacing of significations, concatenations are possible that no longer conform to the linearity of logical time, or of the time of consciousness or preconsciousness, or of the time of "verbal representation." The frontier between the nonphonetic space of writing (even in "phonetic" writing) and the space of the scene of dreams is uncertain. (ED, 321/217)

We shall therefore soon pass to the scene of dreams; if not to the Freudian scene, then to the backroom of Plato's dream. Yet not before putting (or pushing) the question of reversibility. If the *irreversibility* of phonic or phonetic script, proceeding punctually from instance to instance, is undone in a scription that is essentially *reversible* in terms of the spacing of time and timing of space, *reversible* in a sense even more radical than that of the Hegelian dialectic of space-time (discussed in chapter 5, below); if *reversibility* is the mark of the trace in its transcendental employ, as the mark of what a phenomenology of embodiment would call the flesh   *they changed; they coiled together, and entangledly stood mute*   of the world; then why would one insist on retaining traces of the trace? With or without wax?

"Why the *trace*?" asks Derrida (G, 102/70). "What has guided us in the choice of this word?" There can be little doubt that part of the answer to this question lies in the powerful impetus of the engrammatological tradition of memory and reminiscence itself. Yet question and answer alike are displaced here, and even out of place: "If words and concepts attain their sense only in concatenations of differences, one can justify one's language and choice of terms only from within a topic and an historical strategy." Such justification does not dream of ever being "absolute and definitive." Absolute justification is absolutely passé, vanished in a *passé absolu*. If justification and evidence are dreams of proximity, immediacy, and presence, deconstruction is a removal to the outside, a movement *of* the outside, *espacement*, even in that place where interiority seemed to be sovereign and where absence itself seemed to be a witness to the veritable being of the past—the topos of memory. "If the trace, the arche-phenomenon of 'memory,' which must be thought prior to the opposition between nature and culture, animality and humanity, and so on, pertains to the very movement of signification, signification is *a priori* written, whether or not it is inscribed in one form or another in a 'sensuous' and 'spatial' element that one would call 'exterior'." Traces remain emblems of exteriority, to repeat, whether with or without wax.

> Arche-writing, premier possibility of speech, then of 'graphie' in the narrow sense, birthplace of the 'usurpation' denounced from Plato to Saussure, this trace is the opening [*l'ouverture*] of the premier exteriority in general, the enigmatic relation of the living being to its other, as of an inside to an outside: spacing. The outside, the "spatial" and "objective" exteriority that we believe we know to be the most familiar thing in the world, familiarity itself, would not appear without the *gramme; without differance as temporalization; without the nonpresence of the other inscribed in the meaning of the present; without the relation to death as the concrete structure of the living present. (G, 103/70–71)

The opening of this first or premier exteriority will soon take us to Hegel's dialectic of interiorization/exteriorization, the very mystery of *Erinnerung* and *Gedächtnis,* which we shall examine in the following chapter. For it is the dream of spirit from Plato onward, Plato's dream, that grammatology is so rudely disturbing—no doubt by the creaking and bumping of its hinge unhinged: "That the signified is originarily and essentially (and not only for a finite and created spirit) trace; that the signified is *always already in the position of the signifier;* such is the apparently innocent proposition wherein the metaphysics of the logos, of presence and consciousness, must reflect *écriture* as its death and its resource" (G, 107–8/73).

PLATO'S DREAM

Derrida suspects that Plato's theory of writing is "more subtle, critical, and disquieted [*inquiète*] than the theory that presides over the birth of Saussurian linguistics" (G, 50–51/33–34). We might therefore begin to consider Plato's dream   *I will know what* is, *and do what my deepest angel dictates.—The letter!—Isabel,—sister,—brother,—me,* me—*my sacred father!—This is some accursed dream!*   by noting some of the places in *Of Grammatology* where the discussion of *Phaedrus* comes to the fore, only then turning to Derrida's detailed account in "Plato's Pharmacy," where the disquiet mounts. Finally, I will intersperse some remarks from a recent essay by Derrida on *khōra* in Plato's *Timaeus,* where dream and disquiet merge.[10]

Derrida cites *Phaedrus* when it is a question of explicating the exteriority of both signifier *and signified* in script. Plato's Socrates seems to deny such exteriority when he invokes, through "a metaphorical mediation," scripture of the truth in the soul, as opposed to "bad writing."[11] Thus the entire problem of metaphoricity, of "script as metaphoricity itself," is at issue in Derrida's reading of *Phaedrus.* The wickedness of script proves to be its operation of *contami-*

nation, precisely through the mechanism of this metaphoricity: if Saussure believes language to be an internal (phonemic) system, he nonetheless decries the fact that "notation" (shades of Augustine   *for thee, thy sacred father is no more a saint*   and Quintilian!) is superimposed on it. "Scripture's malady comes from the outside (*exōthen*), said *Phaedrus* (275a) long ago" (G, 51–52/34). Hence the dour tone of condemnation   *Unutterable that a man should be thus!*   in Saussure's Genevan *Cours,* the Calvinist rhetoric of irruption, corruption, sin, and defilement betraying a certain continuity   *Now look around in that most miserable room, and at that most miserable of all the pursuits of a man*   with the Platonic tradition. Writing is the invasion of an inside by an outside, a demonic incursion, a devilish inversion of the "natural" relationship of submission to the magisterial soul by the servile body—or, rather, by a body waxing rebellious and passionate. It is here that Derrida asserts the priority of the *scriptural* metaphorics over the metaphorics of *embodiment,* even though the implosion of vehicle and tenor in metaphoricity "itself" would make such an order of implication quite untenable. More troubling than such an unjustified and unjustifiable hierarchy is the suspicion that "tracings without wax" might dream of suppressing the body or subjecting it to the ostensibly more fundamental structures of scripture; for such orders of implication within a deconstructed metaphoricity are perhaps contaminated in unforeseen ways by the very metaphysics of pure (disembodied) presence that it desires to put in question.

Toward the close of Derrida's "theoretical matrix" (Part I of the *Grammatology*), in the context of "the complicity of origins," Plato's *Phaedrus* again enters the discussion (G, 139/91–92). To the entire complex of logo-phonocentrism, linearism and ethnocentrism, metaphysics of presence and alphabetic script, Derrida poses a series of questions that arise from his reading of *Phaedrus* and the other dialogues. These sundry related centrisms he gathers under the rubric *heliocentrism,* concerning which he asks:

> Why should speech have been "eclipsed" in the West by script? . . . And is it not necessary to meditate on this heliocentric concept of speech? As well as on the resemblance between the logos and the sun (whether as the good or as the death that one cannot look in the face), or between the logos and the king or father (the good or the intelligible sun are compared to the father in the *Republic* at 508c)? What must script be in order to menace this analogical system in its secret and vulnerable center? What must script be in order to signify the *eclipse* of that which is *good* and that which is *father?* Is it not necessary to stop thinking of script as the eclipse that comes to interrupt and obfuscate the glory of the word? And if there is some necessity of eclipse, must not the relation of shadow and light, script and speech, itself appear otherwise?

Finally, in the context of Rousseau's *Essay on the Origin of Languages,* in the final chapter of the *Grammatology* (G, 413/292), Derrida invokes *Phaedrus* once again. Here it is a matter of disclosing the way in which graphic illustration and representation in general never fully achieve what I have been calling iconography—the restoration of full presence through the identity of image and original. "The original possibility of the image is the supplement: that which is adjoined without adjoining anything [*qui s'ajoute sans rien ajouter*], in order to fill a void that demands filling in something that is already replete [*pour combler un vide qui dans le plein demande à se laisser remplacer*]" (G, 412–13/292). The (il)logic of the supplement manifests itself not only in Rousseau but also as early as Plato's *Phaedrus:*

> Script as painting is thus at one and the same time the *malady* and the *remedy* in the *phainesthai* [the "to-appear" of things] or in the *eidos* [their aspect, outward appearance, form]. Early on, Plato says that the art or technique (*tekhnē*) of writing is a *pharmakon* (a drug or tincture, whether salutary or noxious). And what is disquieting about script is already felt in its resemblance to painting. Script is *like* painting, like the *zoōgrapheme* that is itself determined (in *Cratylus*, 430– 432) within the framework of *mimēsis*. Resemblance is disquieting: "I think that what is really quite terrible in writing, Phaedrus, is also the fact that it truly resembles painting (*zōgraphia*) a great deal" (275d). Here painting, zoography, betrays being and speech, words and things, because it fixes them [*les fige*].

Such fixing or fixating is ambiguous   *Scarce know I what I have written*   and we ought to pause over the ambiguity before proceeding to "Plato's Pharmacy." The whole point of *typography* is to *fix* imprints   *She looked fixedly in his face, and stood rooted*   in the soul; *iconography* can succeed only if the image is figured   *She tossed her ebon tresses over her; she fixed her ebon eyes on him*   on the original; and *engrammatology* can flourish only if the letters or elements are scanned so closely   *Isabel eyed him fixedly*   that the mind is *fixed* on them. Such holding, figuring, and fixing in the waxen tablets of soul, on the gland, or in the neuron mark the very achievement of the process. What has Plato to complain about? How can script, fixed and firm like the laws of a city, be bad?[12] Derrida paraphrases the reply of Thamus, king and judge, a reply we have already heard in chapter 1 and which we shall have to reconsider here: "It's [i.e., script's] scions take the form of living beings, but when one questions them they no longer reply. Zoography has brought death in its train. Script does the same. No one is there, and certainly not the father, to respond to interrogation."

As we enter the strange world of Plato's apothecary (the one who occupies the *apotheca*, "storehouse") we will want to remember the themes touched on thus far: the exteriority of signification and of the signified as such, which putatively makes script deleterious; the metaphorical mediation by which scription appears both outside and inside the soul, "bad writing" penetrating or contaminating the soul, "good writing" dwelling within as the voice and breath of the divine word; the interlacing of the scriptural metaphor with the entire metaphorics of soul and body, in spite of the apparent supremacy of the former metaphorics over the latter; the heliocentrism of speech, the paradoxical eclipse of speech betraying the secret vulnerability of the solar father; and the supplemental character of all representation and illustration, their disquieting function as resemblance through fixation of images taking us back to the ambiguity of "good" as opposed to "bad" writing, scripture *versus* script, living word haunted by cadaverous text. Yet because the chambers of Derrida's and Plato's *Phaedrus* are so vast and so artfully constructed   *From eight o'clock in the morning till half-past four in the evening, Pierre sits there in his room;—eight hours and a half!*   I will focus on a small number of points: first, typography and weaving, the mnemic and dialectical arts, the two principal arts of philosophy; second, iconography and genealogy, the paternal-filial relation of speech and writing; third, engrammatology and pharmacology, as realms of supplementation, contamination, and complicity; fourth, Derrida's dream.

(1) If mortar and pestle are the apothecary's emblems, those of the philosopher are the tools associated with typography and weaving—the signet and the loom, both employing the "verge." Derrida selects as his motto for "Plato's Pharmacy" a dictionary entry on the word *kolaphos*. Among its meanings (blow on the cheek, slap, peck, and so on), not surprisingly, are the typographical senses of notching, engraving, and marking. We know the word today as the publisher's colophon. Related to it is the word *glyph* (cf. *Griffel*, *grapheion*), to scratch a surface, hollow it out (*creuser*). The cutting edge and the hollow are but two sides of the same coinage—which is coinage as such. Both the hollowing tool and its matrice are touched by the verge, are on the verge; both are on the verge of *being* the verge.

Because *Sophist* and *Statesman* (251ff. and 277ff.) consistently define dialectic as the art of weaving, it is natural that Derrida   *Here surely is a wonderful stillness of eight hours and a half, repeated day after day. In the heart of such silence, surely something is at work. Is it creation, or destruction?*   should at the outset of Part I of "Plato's Pharmacy" introduce textuality, textile, weave, web, and a part of the loom that produces these: *histos*, "anything set upright," especially the mast or spur of a ship, the beam of a vertical loom, or the sail or web itself, even a spider's web. One of the meanings of *histos* that Derrida cites is: "III. *baguette, verge*" (D, 73/65). Just as the verge of a loom or mast of a ship is nothing without its glistening woven stuff billowing in the wind, what Homer calls *histia leuka*, hollowing out as a kind of cosmic bowl or receptacle, so is the apothecary's pestle nothing without the crater-shaped mortar.

This profusion or confusion of escutcheons, armorial bearings, and guild symbols is in fact an essential part of the pharmacology that will challenge traditional typography. For the *pharmakon*, rather than being any identifiable and reliable substance, is itself the antisubstance par excellence; it is "that which resists every philosopheme, exceeding them indefinitely as nonidentity, nonessence, nonsubstance, and for that very reason furnishing them with the inexhaustible adversity of its base and its absence of base" (D, 79/70). Already we are quite close to the "third kind" of Plato's *Timaeus*, the unintelligible and nonsensuous *khōra*, the baseless base of paradigms and beings. For it is the verge as hollow and matrix   *the devouring profundities, now opened up in him, consume all his vigor*   that will pose insurmountable problems for typography and engrammatology. Derrida emphasizes the importance of the ambiguity of the *typos*, as both the cutting edge of the *eidos* and the graphic imprint: the type is not only the graphic character but also "the eidetic model," and the cutting edge itself also appears to share in the traits of the matrice it means to inscribe. It is as though the *typos* itself were always already a trace—a problem that will return in Derrida's discussion of *Timaeus* (D, 184/159). It is as though typography itself mixes the contrary values (good/bad, true/false, essence/appearance, and so on), which derive their entire value from being held in separation from one another; mixes them all precisely insofar as it fails to preserve the inside/outside distinction on which all opposition depends, insofar as it fails to preserve pure interiority and exteriority. The *typos* cuts both ways:

> If script, according to the king and under the sun, produces the inverse of the effect it claims to produce; if the *pharmakon* is nefarious; that is because . . . it is not of this world [*pas d'ici*]. It comes from down below, is exterior or foreign to the living, which is right here inside, foreign to the *logos* as *zōon* that it claims to aid or supplement. The imprints (*typoi*) of script this time do not inscribe themselves, as hypothesized in *Theaetetus* (191ff.), in a hollow *within* the wax of the soul [*en creux* dans *la cire*], thus responding to the spontaneous and autochthonous movements of psychic life. Knowing that he can confide or abandon his thoughts to the outside, to the vestibule [*à la consigne*], to physical, spatial, and superficial marks that one lays out on a tablet, the one who has at his disposal the *tekhnē* of script will come to rely on them. He will know that he can absent himself without the *typoi* ceasing to be there, that he can forget them without their ceasing to serve him. They will represent him even if he forgets them; they will sustain his speech even if he is not there to animate them. Even if he is dead. Only a *pharmakon* can retain such powers, power over death, no doubt, but also in collusion with it. Thus *pharmakon* and script always involve a question of life and death. (D, 119/104–5)

Yet if incised letters threaten verdant life with stony death, if the life within is put at risk by a certain pallid exteriority,   *Builds Pierre the noble world of a new book? or does the Pale Haggardness unbuild the lungs and the life in him?*   it is nonetheless true that script mimics memory in its very *typos*— *Elle mime en son type la mémoire* (D, 120/105)—to the extent that it is impossible to preserve the truth of memory from its simulacrum, genuine remembrance from the *aide-mémoire*, inside from outside. The monument of death   *He is learning how to live, by rehearsing the part of death* and the musty archive mushroom within the soul itself. "The space of script, space as scription, opens in the violent movement of this supplementation [*suppléance*], in the difference between *mnēmē* and *hypomnēsis*" (D, 124/109). Yet the difference is itself intrinsic to memory: "The outside is already *in* the work of memory" (D, 124/109). Typography is the dangerous supplement of effraction within memory itself. Even before memory lays itself low with letters, it suffers the violence of the trace. Typography *is* pharmacology, from the outset. And even though Plato will quickly turn to his second trade, the art of weaving; even though he will prefer dialectic to grammar and typography; even though he will insist that living speech is a psychic *graphie* without effraction, a writing in the soul for purposes of demonstration, education, transmission, and especially unveiling and uncovering (*alētheia*); such weaving will nevertheless want its warp and weft *to perdure*, and the verge of the loom will be driven hard. Precisely because life is ephemeral and eminently vulnerable, it needs the supplement of forms and laws engraved in stone. If script is the flower of evil, that flower is nonetheless carved in granite. Does not Plato's Socrates, for all his devotion to life, prefer perdurant death? Presuming that Plato's Socrates, looming behind, is not himself a flower of script.

Such a presumption cannot of course be sustained. Not only because of the postcard that depicts *Socrates* writing at the behest of *Plato*, but for reasons developed in *Timaeus*, with its *khōra*. To be sure, *Timaeus* is all about typography. Derrida emphasizes that fact throughout his essay, referring to "these *types* of translation . . . , hermeneutical *types*," and to the receptacle that "*seems to receive* these types" (269); to "these known types of being, recognized or, if you prefer, *received* by philosophical discourse" (270), and to the *khōra*, which "does not have the characters of a being" (271); to the "immense history of interpretations and reappropriations" that "superimpose inscriptions and reliefs, giving form to it [i.e., *khōra*] by impressing types there" (272); to "every ratiocination of the philosophical *type*," or "*ontological* type," which is at once "defied and taken up again by the very thing that gives place to it" (273); to the inability to assign *khōra* to either *mythos* or *logos*, inasmuch as it is neither a philosopheme nor "a fable of the mythic type" (275); and to the "structure of pre-inscription and of typographic prescription" (277–78) in Plato's dialogue. Furthermore, *Timaeus* is also about Socrates, who seems as malleable and resilient as *khōra* itself. Socrates is of many kinds, though not quite sophistic imitator, not quite poet, not quite the philosopher-statesman he is always desirous of addressing. Yet his being many types threatens the operation of typography as such: "Socrates effaces himself, effaces in himself all types, all genres, including that of the men of image and simulacrum whom he feigns to resemble . . ." (281). Right from the start, the strange affinity of Socrates and *khōra* is expressed in a series of motifs one might call "*typomorphic*." The Socratic type, which is of course a mélange of types and no specific type at all, anticipates the sequence of types to be imprinted on the choric *ekmageion* or *porte-empreinte*, "this material that is always ready to receive the imprint"; the Socratic nontype thus anticipates the ambiguity of the imprinted relief (*ektypōma*) on the stamp or signet itself, and hence cannot be typed as father or mother or even infant. In his innocence and duplicity he is all three at once. Which makes it difficult to presume anything about that flower of script we call Plato's Socrates.

(2) If typography and weaving are matters of life and death, they verge on the scene of succeeding generations, of genealogy and the family. A strange scene of kinship as well as kingship, father and son, father and sun, solar paternity and divinity; Derrida calls the scene of the pharmacy *basileo-patro-helio-theological* (D, 154/134). Generation and genealogy, kinship and descent, are matters of passage from like to like—hence matters of *iconography*. How-

ever, just as typography is hollowed out from the inside by its own meta-phorics, so is the icon continually displaced by its simulacra, lost among idols. The very myth of writing, its Egyptianism, discloses the distance of every icon from its original. The father *logos* is the father *of* the *logos*. Even if god-the-king-who-speaks (D, 86/76–77) is a father who spurns   *I will be impious, for piety hath juggled me, and taught me to revere, where I should spurn*   the *pharmakon* of writing, the *origin* of the *logos* is *his own* father in turn; a certain *anachronism* infects the line of descent, such that "the logos is a son," indeed, a son who would be destroyed "without the *presence* and the present *attendance* of his father" (D, 86/76–77). Without the paternal logos to answer   *When Pierre was twelve years old, his father had died, leaving behind him, in the general voice of the world, a marked reputation*   for him, the son is mere scription and silence. He is an orphan, and perhaps a parricide as well. Viewed from the position of King Thamus, who holds the scepter and verge in his own right hand, writing is not only wretched but also treacherous and treasonous. The son's misery   *Let the ambiguous procession of events reveal their own ambiguousness*   is ambiguous:

> . . . the orphan's distress, to be sure; for the orphan not only needs to be helped by a presence but also needs that help transported to him and brought to his aid. Yet in lamenting the orphan one also accuses him—and writing—of pretending to distance himself from his father, emancipating himself from his father with an air of complacency and self-sufficiency. From the position of the one who holds the scepter, the desire of writing is indicated, designated, and denounced as the desire to be an orphan, the desire of patricidal subversion. Is not this *pharmakon* criminal? Is it not a poisoned gift?

The duplicity of the son—scription as both scripture and script—thus repre-sents what Derrida calls "genealogical rupture and remoteness from the origin" (D, 83/74). The myth of scription is thus scription of the myth: repetition without knowledge. And the duplicity of sons   *his father's shrine seemed spotless*   is an inherited duplicity, the duplicity of the father *logos*. Sons are the *typoi* or spitting images of their fathers   *for Pierre was not only his father's only child, but his namesake*   if what the fathers spit is seed or ink. Whether in Egyptian, Assyrian, or Babylonian myths of scripture, scrip-tion, and script, the oppositions that dominate those myths find themselves undone by duplicities within the Platonic text. Speech and writing, life and death, father and son, master and servant, first and second, legitimate son and orphan bastard, soul and body, inside and outside, good and evil, seriousness and play, day and night, sun and moon (D, 96/85)—all suffer a certain conta-gion or contamination across the line of each binary opposition. In spite of Hegel's insistence in *The Philosophy of Right* (§140f.) that Plato's Socrates is ironic toward persons   *majestically and holily walked the venerated form of the departed husband and father*   but never toward ideas, the Platonic text is worked by what Derrida calls "a subversive dislocation of identity in general" (D, 97/86). Amon-Re, the father of Thot, is the hidden or eclipsed sun, the enucleated eye and egg of history.[13] There is no eye that can read engrammatologically the icon of the origins, inasmuch as the grapheme is the origin and possibility of *logos* as such (D, 100/88). Thus Thot, like Hermes Psychopompos, is both the patron of writing and the god of the dead: he is the monument   *Blessed and glorified in his tomb beyond Prince Mausolus is that mortal sire, who, after an honorable, pure course of life, dies, and is buried, as in a choice fountain, in the filial breast of a tender-hearted and intellectually appreciative child*   or mausoleum of the father. The dead one too identifies himself as the god: he is Thot, il est Thot   *Thrown into that fountain, all sweet recollections become marbleized; so that things which in themselves were evanescent, thus became unchangeable and eternal*   er ist Thot (D, 104/92). The Platonic text too, not only the Nietzschean,[14] is thus marked by ob-sequence, by which the generations themselves and all genealogies are displaced:

> The system of these characters elaborates an original logic: the figure of Thot is set in opposition to his other (father, son, life, speech, origin or orient, and so on), but in supplementing it. That figure joins and opposes by repeating or replacing [*tenant lieu*]. At the same time, it takes shape, takes its form precisely from that which it simultaneously resists and for which it substitutes. Hence it opposes itself, passes into its contrary; this messenger-god is thus a god of absolute passage between opposites. If he had an identity—but he is precisely the god of nonidentity—it would be that *coincidentia oppositorum* to which we shall soon once again have recourse. Distinguishing himself from his other, Thot also imitates him, makes himself his sign and representative, obeys him, conforms to him, replaces him, if need be by violence. He is thus the other of the father, the father, and the subversive movement of replacement. The god of writing is thus simultaneously his father, his son, and himself. He does not allow himself to be assigned a fixed place in the play of differences. Cunning [*rusé*], ungraspable, masked, a plotter and trickster like Hermes, he is neither a king nor a jack; he is rather   *Like knavish cards, the leaves of all great books were covertly packed*   a sort of joker, a deployable signifier, a wild card, putting some play into play [*donnant du jeu au jeu*]. (D, 105/92–93)

As phantasm and simulacrum, scription cannot possibly serve the iconography   *In this shrine, in this niche of this pillar, stood the perfect marble form of his departed father; without blemish, unclouded, snow-white, and serene*   of which it nevertheless makes us dream. *Eikastikē*, precisely because it is mimetic, can only be good by being bad. "Imitation responds to its essence and is what it is—imitation—only by being flawed in some particular point; or, rather, by being in default" (D, 160/139). This, we recall, is the lesson of *Cratylus*. Imitation, no matter how efficiently typographic, is essentially   *and again, and again, still deep and deeper, was stamped in Pierre's soul the cherished conceit, that his virtuous father, so beautiful on earth, was now uncorruptibly sainted in heaven*   iconoclastic. And essentially patricidal:

> What is the father? we asked above. The father is. The father is (the lost son). Writing, the lost son, does not reply to this question, she is scripted [*elle (s') écrit*]:

(that) the father is not; that is to say, is not present. When it is no longer a lapsed speech of the father, writing suspends the question *what is?* which is always, expressed tautologically, the question "what is the father?" and the answer "the father is that which is." (D, 169/146)

Parricidic script   *The stabbed man knows the steel; prate not to him that it was only a tickling feather*   is thus parasitic script   *one little bit of paper scratched over with a few small characters by a sharpened feather* in which parasite and host remain not only inseparable but also indistinguishable, so that the very metaphoricity of scription and its division into "good" (inscription of scriptural truth in the soul) and "bad" (extrinsic and effractive script) is dispersed. Dispersed   *his father no more a saint, and Isabel a sister indeed?*   or disseminated:

> According to a scheme that will dominate all Western philosophy, a good writing (natural, living, knowing, intelligible, interior, speaking) is opposed to a bad writing (artificial, moribund, ignorant, sensuous, exterior, mute). And the good can be designated only through the metaphor of the bad. Metaphoricity is the logic of contamination and the contamination of logic. Bad writing is, with respect to the good, like a model of linguistic designation and a simulacrum of essence. . . . [Thus] the conclusion of the *Phaedrus* is less a condemnation of writing in the name of present speech than the preference for one kind of writing over another, for a fecund trace as opposed to a sterile one, for a generative sowing of seed (because deposited in the inside) as opposed to a sowing that is scattered outside in pure loss: the risk of *dissemination.* (D, 172/149)

Dissemination inevitably invokes the co(s)mic family scene of *Timaeus,* with the demiurgic father who *looks to* (and hence himself *is not*) the paradigms, the monogenic son who should be the very icon of his father, and the form   *but also the subtler expression of the portrait of his then youthful father, strangely translated, and intermarryingly blended with some before unknown, foreign feminineness*   of the wandering cause, the matrix and receptacle of becoming, in whom the difference between son and father—the lapse or slippage from pure being to corruptible becoming, the lapse from good demiurgic scripture to bad matricidal script—unfolds: the familial scene is   *Ah, fathers and mothers! all the world round, be heedful—give heed! Thy little one may not now comprehend the meaning of those words and those signs, by which, in its innocent presence, thou thinkest to disguise the sinister thing ye would hint. Not now he knows; not very much even of the externals he consciously marks; but if, in afterlife, Fate puts the chemic key of the cipher into his hands; then how swiftly and how wonderfully, he reads all the obscurest and most obliterate inscriptions he finds in his memory; yes, and rummages himself all over, for still hidden things to read*   the place and space of *khōra.* *Khōra,* broached by "a bastard reasoning," is neither *logos* nor *mythos* as such, nor a hybrid scion of both. The customary rhetorical opposition of proper-versus-metaphorical sense fails in and through such discourse. Here a kind of anachronism interrupts all succession or order of implication. *Khōra* anachronizes the questions of being and

essence, anachronizes the self-presencings or showings on which all iconography
would depend. Anachronizes them by anticipating everything that future interpretations will say of *khōra:*

> With *khōra itself,* if at least one can speak of this *x* which must never have any
> proper determination, whether sensible or intelligible, material or formal, and thus
> no self-identity. *Everything happens as if* the coming history of interpretations of
> *khōra* had been written in advance, that is, prescribed, *reproduced and reflected in
> advance* in a few pages of *Timaeus* "on the subject" of *khōra* "itself." (272)

Because the cosmos is itself a sensuous icon of the intelligible paradigms,
discourse about it can only be *likely:* mythical discourse *plays* with the image,
plays with verisimilitude, just as the beings we encounter in the world are
"iconic beings," modeled on the forms, hence "like" them (282). Just as the
living memory of the Athenians is exiled in the graphic vestiges of the Egyptian
archive visited by the poet and lawgiver Solon, so is the being on which becoming is said to have been modeled   *The old mummy lies buried in cloth on
cloth; it takes time to unwrap this Egyptian king*   encrypted in an ancient
script. It will have been the *engrammatological* script of all traditional memory
systems.

(3) Yet if engrammatology is pharmacology, the ancient script will never
have been pure, never originary, but always contaminated, complicit with opposition. The effort to distinguish extraneous hypomnesis from interior anamnesis, however essential, however necessary, is a failed effort. A futile effort. A
dream.   *It is all a dream—we dream that we dreamed we dream.*
Plato's dream.

It is a dream of wars fought against the sophists, themselves Socratic *eidōla,*
who are taken to be icons of the master. Whereas the sophists employ memory
in order to fuel their mechanical, lifeless elenchus, relying on an endless recurrence of blows by lethal monuments, Socrates' Plato treasures reminiscence as
the gentle (re)productive unveiling of pure presence. Duped by the sophists'
endless procession of spurious arguments, the men of Athens will execute the
original rather than the copies—execute it not by art but   *the dark hemlock hath no music in its thoughtful boughs*   by hemlock. Invasion by the
extraneous is breach of justice and violent death. Yet if life itself is such invasion, must not Socrates' Plato (as we have already asked) opt for death
*Therefore, never more will I play the vile pigmy, and by small memorials after
death, attempt to reverse the decree of death, by essaying the poor perpetuating
of the image of the original. Let all die, and mix again!*   rather than *this*
life?

> The outside is already *in* the work of memory. Evil insinuates itself in the self-
> revelation of memory, in the general organization of mnemic activity. Memory is
> essentially finite. Plato recognizes this in attributing life to it. As in the case of every
> living organism, he assigns, as we have seen, limits to it. For a memory without
> limits would not be memory but the infinity of a presence to self. Thus memory
> always already needs signs in order to recall the nonpresent, to which it necessarily

relates. The movement of dialectic testifies to it. Memory allows itself to be contaminated by its premier exteriority, its premier supplement, *hypomnēsis.* Yet what Plato *dreams* of is a memory without signs. (D, 124/109)

Why the dream? Because the very ideality of the *eidos* depends on its iterability, the perfect repetition of the same. Such repetition in turn requires a doubling, a supplementation. Yet the doubling suggests that the original lets itself be *typed* (D, 125/109: *puisse lui-même se faire 'typer'*), lets itself be represented by a signifier, and even by the signifier of a signifier. Plato's dream is always   *in the warm halls of the heart one single, untestified memory's spark shall suffice to enkindle such a blaze of evidence, that all the corners of conviction are as suddenly lighted up as a midnight city by a burning building, which on every side whirls its reddened brands*   on the verge of nightmare. "Thus, even though writing is exterior to (interior) memory, even though hypomnesia is not memory, it affects and hypnotizes memory from the inside. Such is the effect of this *pharmakon*" (D, 125/110). That is the nightmare.

How is one to explain memory's *susceptibility,* its exposure to the ill effects of drugging, hypnosis, and bedazzlement, if not by conceding that these exterior threats are always already at work on the inside, that the game is rigged? How fight the concession, fend off the nightmare, except by the mythologic of the dream? Here Derrida recollects Freud's famous "reasoning of the kettle" in *Interpretation of Dreams,* in which the logic of his own dream, "Irma's injection," is exemplified (D, 126/111; Freud, StA 2, 138–39). The young doctor protests his innocence by way of a comic overdetermination (which merits repetition in his study of *Witz*):

> The entire plea—for this dream is nothing else—reminds one intensely [*lebhaft*] of the self-defense of the man who was accused by his neighbor of having returned a kettle in a damaged condition. Number one, he had returned it undamaged; number two, the kettle already had holes in it when the neighbor lent it out; and number three, he never borrowed a kettle from his neighbor. But all to the good: if only one of these three lines of defense can be made to stick, the man will have to be declared innocent. (StA 4, 61 and 191)

Derrida extends the logic of the dream—the logic of the kettle, *kratēra,* bowl, or receptacle—to the engrammatology of memory and reminiscence:

> (1) Writing is rigorously exterior and inferior to living memory and living speech, which are accordingly intact. (2) Writing is harmful to them because it stupefies them and infects their very life, which would be intact if it were not for writing. There would not be gaps [*trous*] in memory and in speech if there were not writing. (3) Besides, if one has resorted to hypomnesia and writing, it is because living memory is finite, because it already had gaps in it before writing left its traces there. Writing has no effect on memory.

The very overdetermination of the logic of the kettle, in which each explanation supplements the other by destroying it, suggests that only the thinnest sheet separates the surface   *far as any geologist has yet gone down into the world, it is found to consist of nothing but surface stratified on surface. To*

its axis, the world being nothing but superinduced superficies   of hypomnesia from genuine anamnesia. Very much like the vulnerable middle surface
of the mystic writing pad, which adheres to the waxen substratum of the system
but communicates with the outermost surface as well, thus linking memory
and perception. Yet the "invisible thickness" of this frayable sheet functions
more as unifier than as segregator. If "perception" stands for what cannot be
remembered, for unlimited effraction and hence oblivion, then unification is in
fact a contamination or complicity. "At one blow, the unity of this sheet, of the
system of this difference between signified and signifier—is it not also the
inseparability of sophistry and philosophy?" (D, 127/112). A profound complicity also between the most intransigent of sophisms and the most inflexible
of laws. If legislation (*nomothesia*) requires that the laws be inscribed and fixed
in letters (*en grammasi tethenta: Laws* VII, 793b–c); if in other words laws are
"engrammatical" (the only near-appearance of "engrammatology" in "Plato's
Pharmacy," to my knowledge); then the infiltration of hypomnesia inside the
walls of the City of Memory has always already begun. The machinery of the
law, effraction, is already bitched by a breaching of the law, by infraction.
Precisely as the mechanism of the most primitive memory, the memory that
calamitous life must fabricate if it is to avoid starvation, rests on the most
intense and lively hallucination.   *Pierre, the lips that do now speak to
thee, never touched a woman's breast; I seem not of woman born.*   When
cathected desire, dynamic image, and judgment coalesce, the result may be a
vision or an envisagement, a miracle or a mirage, the rising sun or the vanishing
moon, fool's fire. Depending on a certain *accidental* turn of the head.
*The brightest success now seemed intolerable to him, since he so plainly saw,
that the brightest success could not be the sole offspring of Merit; but of Merit
for the one thousandth part, and nine hundred and ninety-nine combining and
dovetailing accidents for the rest.*   Depending on a quality that leaves no
traces, but only impossible indicators or signs. The logic of the dream advances
inexorably through a series of complicities—anamnesia and hypomnesia, legislation and engrammatology as pharmacology—en route to what *Timaeus* calls
"the nurse of becoming."

     The essence of the *pharmakon* is that it has no stable essence, no proper
character; "it is in no sense of the word (whether metaphysical, physical,
chemical, or alchemical) a *substance*" (D, 144/125–26). Far from being
monoeidetic, the *pharmakon* is aneidetic. Which is to say that the *eidos* "itself"
is complicit with this medicine whose effects are far from being simple. If there
is an *eidos* of the *pharmakon* at all, it occupies a strange place:

> It is rather the anterior milieu in which differentiation in general is produced, along
> with the opposition between the *eidos* and its other; this milieu is *analogous* to the
> one that later will be reserved—after, and in accord with, a philosophical
> decision—for the transcendental imagination, this "art concealed in the depths of
> the soul" [Kant, *Kritik der reinen Vernunft*, B 180], which cannot simply be
> relegated to either the sensible or the intelligible, to either passivity or activity. The

milieu-element will always be analogous to the mixed-medium. In a certain manner, Plato thought and even formulated this ambivalence.

Nowhere more so than in the *hypodokhē*, the "receptacle" of *khōra*, which itself involves manifold forms of hypomnesia. *Khōra* is actually a kind of chiasm, as the letter *khi* (χ) in both *hypodokhē* and *khōra* betrays: it is—as Merleau-Ponty too would have said—the scene of "double participation in the distinct regions of soul and body, of the invisible and the visible" (D, 145/127). If the *pharmakon* is "the movement, the place, and the play" of difference, the differance of difference, *khōra* is the inaccessible nonplace   *for though the young lady might have been very beautiful, and good-hearted, yet no one on this side of the water certainly knew her history; and she was a foreigner; and would not have made so suitable and excellent a match for your father as* your dear mother afterward did   of that movement, that play. It is the world of dreams. For example   *Look again. I am thy real father* Plato's.

The *programme* of *khōra*, somewhere between *mythos* and *logos*, not readily identifiable with either of these taken in isolation, *can* be apprehended—if only in a dream (*fût-ce en rêve*). Which is precisely what Timaeus says of this third kind, "which we behold as in a dream" (52b 3: *oneiropoloumen bleptontes*), and of which "we have only this dreamlike sense" (b 7–c 1: *oneirōxeōs*). That dreamlike sense, far from being an inadequate *logos* or a pure *mythos*, is *the reason your father did not want his portrait taken was, because he was secretly in love with the French young lady, and did not want his secret published in a portrait*   our only access to the inaccessible. And it is an access through a series of fictional receptacles, each one contained in yet another, like Chinese boxes or   *Look, again, I am thy father as he more truly was*   Russian Babas. Except that there is no end to them, no end or bottom at which one would find "the philosophy-of-Plato" (287). It is not simply a matter of renouncing the abstraction of "Platonism," and rejecting the securities of scholarly or philological asceticism; it is a question of the strategy of examining the fictions *Consider this strange, ambiguous smile, Pierre; more narrowly regard this mouth. Behold, what is this too ardent and, as it were, unchastened light in these eyes, Pierre?*   one by one. And just as *Symposium* is a monument of memory, a multiple retelling, so is *Timaeus* a concatenation or a telescoping series of fictions: (1) the text of *Timaeus* itself, which begins, "One, two, three—but where is the fourth, my dear Timaeus?"; (2) the discussion of the preceding day, often identified with the text we call *Republic;* (3) its résumé by Socrates; (4) young Critias' recounting the tale he has already told the others the day before, on their way home; (5) the tale as told by Solon to Critias' grandfather when the latter was only ten—for Solon was a friend of Grandfather Critias' father, *I am thy father, boy. There was once a certain, oh, but too lovely young Frenchwoman, Pierre. Youth is hot, and temptation strong, Pierre, and in the minutest moment momentous things are irrevocably done, Pierre; and Time sweeps on, and the thing is not always carried down by its stream, but may be left stranded on its bank; away beyond, in the young, green countries, Pierre. Look again*   Critias' great-grandfather Dropides; (6) Solon in turn is relating a discussion he had with an Egyptian priest of Sais—for Solon is a *Lehrling zu Sais*—who recounts (7) the myth of Phaethon, son   *Probe a little, Pierre. Never fear, never fear. No matter for thy father now. Look, do I not smile?—yes, and with an unchangeable smile*   of Helios, and (∞) the tale of Athens and Atlantis. The last-named tale is preserved *in writing* in the archives of the temple of Neith. This *emboîtement* of written fictions is recounted by Critias at 26b–c, at which point the tale of Atlantis is postponed in order that Timaeus can recount the creation of the universe. Thus the entire discourse of *Timaeus* is punctuated, articulated, and scanned   *Once upon a time, there was a lovely young Frenchwoman, Pierre. Have you carefully, and analytically, and psychologically, and metaphysically, considered her belongings and surroundings, and all her incidentals, Pierre?*   by a series of returns, moving farther and farther back in time to a kind of absolute past, a time "before." These returns are altogether *necessary*, and are about nothing else than necessity, *Anankē*, prior to all the oppositions of philosophy. It is a dreamlike discourse (293) whose origin is always indefinite, postponed, "confided to a responsibility that is ceaselessly adjourned, without a fixed and determinable subject":

> From relating to relating the author distances himself increasingly. The mythic utterance thus resembles a discourse that has no legitimate father. Orphan or bastard, it is thus distinguished from the philosophic *logos* which, as *Phaedrus* says, must have a father who replies—for him and about him. This familial scheme by which one situates a discourse will be found at work when we are situating—if one can still put it this way—the site of all sites, that is, *khōra*. (291)

Such scansion backward, and such packaging of discourses one in another as a kind of bottomless reflection or *mise en abyme*, is a matter of constraint *and* play in the Platonic text. The apothecary occupies a backroom, "an *arrière-boutique* in the penumbra of the pharmacy" (D, 147/129), no doubt overlooking the garden where his homeopathic herbs flourish, as in Hawthorne's noxious text, "Rappaccini's Daughter"; it is here—in the *apotheca*, if not in the garden—that the philosopher plays, constrained only by language   *Consider; for a smile is the chosen vehicle of all ambiguities, Pierre*   and by the things themselves, his textual "operations" proceeding "prior to the oppositions between conscious and unconscious, freedom and constraint, voluntary and involuntary, discourse and language." What Plato produces—or Socrates, wielding two verges, with Plato behind him—is anything but a Platonic *corpus* or lexicon. "In a word, we do not believe that there exists, strictly speaking, a Platonic text, closed in on itself, with its inside and its outside" (D, 149/130). If *Sōkratēs-pharmakos* speaks with the voice of the father, and Plato writes only after Socrates' death, in order to expiate the father, transgressing the law of Thamus and thus repeating the patricide, that voice and its death are inextricably mixed in the dialogues. "The containment [*emboîtement*] of scenes is abyssal. The pharmacy has no foundation [*fond*]"

(D, 170/148). In no strong sense can it in fact be the voice of the father: Socrates is midwife rather than sire and is "in a relation of supplementation from father to son" (D, 177/153). As for Plato, if it is he who writes, "the scene is complicated: condemning writing as the lost son or parricide, Plato conducts himself as a son who is *writing* this condemnation, thus expiating and confirming the death of Socrates" (D, 177/153). Plato may dream of tracings without wax, but he dreams in black ink.   *Here, then, is the untimely, timely end;—Life's last chapter well stitched into the middle; Nor book, nor author of the book, hath any sequel, though each hath its last lettering!—It is ambiguous still.*

(4) John Llewelyn, in *Derrida on the Threshold of Sense*, presents two texts from Derrida's *La Carte postale* that indicate in a telling manner the extent to which Plato's dream may be anyone's. For example   *Look again. I am thy real father*   Derrida's.

> Me, I am a man of my word [*un homme de parole*]. I have never had anything to write. When I have something to say I say it, or say it to myself. *Basta*. You are the only one to understand why I have found it absolutely necessary to write precisely the opposite—when it is a matter of axiomatics—of what I desire, of what I know my desire to be, in other words, you: living speech, presence itself, proximity, the proper, the keep, and so on. Of necessity I had to write topsy-turvy—and in order to give myself up to Necessity.[15]

And several pages later:

> I have understood that it was you. You have always been "my" metaphysics, the metaphysics of my life, the "verso" of everything I write (my desire, speech, presence, proximity, the law, my heart and my soul, everything I love and that you know before I do)

At the back of "Plato's Pharmacy" (D, 195/169)   *A rickety chair, two hollow barrels, a plank, paper, pens, and infernally black ink*   after having explicated the graphics of supplementarity and its doublings, repetitions, and reversals, including what he calls (whether or not in memory of Merleau-Ponty) "original reversibility," Derrida presumably instructs the printer to set a series of points—too many for an ellipsis or a time-line—to serve as a kind of curtain separating the pharmacy proper from the *apotheca* or *thesaurus*, the backroom where elixirs are mixed and tinctures concocted.   *Is there then all this work to one book; which shall be read in a very few hours; and, far more frequently, utterly skipped in one second; and which, in the end, whatever it be, must undoubtedly go to the worms?*   "After having closed the pharmacy, Plato retired, sheltered from the sun. He advanced a few paces into the shadow, toward the fund of reserves [*vers le fond de la réserve*], hunched over the *pharmakon*, decided to analyze."

"Because we are beginning to write, write in a different way," says the *Grammatology* (G, 130/87), "we should re-read in another way." In *what* way, it is perhaps too soon to tell.   *Two books are being writ; of which the world shall only see one, and that the bungled one.*   At any rate, in such a way that traces are not taken to be *typoi* and *eikones* fixed for engrammatological decipherment. "In the viscous liquid, quivering in the depths of the drug, the entire pharmacy was reflected, repeating the abyss of its phantasm."

In what follows the verb tenses change from perfect and past to the present, inasmuch as the analyst is apparently present to the phantasm at hand. "And so the analyst knows how to distinguish, between two repetitions." Why the comma appears where it does, as though to bar the word *distinguish* from its direct object and to open the *between* in such a way that it encompasses the analyst and all his know-how, no one can say. Nor why, at the bottom of the page (D, 196/170), the same thing occurs in multiple iterations: "He knows how to distinguish, between two repetitions." And yet again: "It would be necessary to distinguish, between two repetitions."   *The larger book, and the infinitely better, is for Pierre's own private shelf. That it is, whose unfathomable cravings drink his blood; the other only demands his ink. But circumstances have so decreed, that the one can not be composed on the paper, but only as the other is writ down in his soul.*   At all events, between these two repetitions of the repetition, the mood is set. And it is subjunctive.

He would like to isolate the good repetition from the bad one, the true repetition from the false one.

Again he hunches over: each repetition repeats the other [*elles se répètent l'une l'autre*].

Holding the *pharmakon* in one hand, his calamus in the other, Plato transcribes the play of formulae while murmuring to himself. The closed space of the pharmacy amplifies immeasurably the resonance of his monologue. His immured words hurtle themselves into the corners of the room, some words disintegrate, fragments of phrases separate off, disarticulated members circulate among the passages, are fixed for the time of a single turn, translating one another; they rearticulate, repercuss, contradict, tell tales, return like responses, organize their exchanges, protect themselves, institute an internal commerce, take themselves to be a dialogue. Replete with meaning. An entire history. All philosophy.

Plato's analysis is here interrupted by a series of blows, strokes, beats, or *coups*—the diabolical concussion   *With the soul of an Atheist, he wrote down the godliest things; with the feeling of misery and death in him, he created forms of gladness and life. For the pangs in his heart, he put down hoots on the paper. And every thing else he disguised under the so conveniently adjustable drapery of all stretchable Philosophy*   that brings illness and death (*pharma* being according to at least one etymology [D, 151 n. 54/132 n. 59] related to *frapper*); the counterstroke or antidote that neutralizes the diabolical blow; a forceful stroke or an impotent one, such as writing in water, or a toss of the dice; a peripety or sudden turn in the fortunes of characters in a play (*coup de théâtre*)—culminating in the typographic blow with which "Plato's Pharmacy" began: "... *kolaphos* ... *glyph* ... *colpus* ... blow ... glyph ... scalpel ... scalp ... *khrysos*, chrysolite, chrysology...." Having returned Dionysius' adulterated gold, his filthy lucre, Plato is now in search of the Philosopher's Stone, dreams of the purest gold. The sound of words, like hammer blows, distracts him.

> Plato stops up his ears, in order better to hear himself speaking, better to see, better to analyze.
> He knows how to distinguish, between two repetitions.
> He is looking for gold. . . .
> It would be necessary [*Il faudrait*] to distinguish, between two repetitions.
> —But each repeats the other once again; each substitutes itself for the other. . . .
> —Not at all: they do not replace one another, since they all join up. . . .
> —That's just it. . . .

These bits of detached monologue, *disiecta membra* bouncing off the walls, aligning haphazardly, between two repetitions of writing, as though in dialogue. Meanwhile, all the while, silently moving, the apothecary's verge, the inky reed or calamus in paths untrodden, whoever you are holding me now in hand, the base of all metaphysics, recorders ages hence, roots and leaves themselves alone, trickle drops! my blue veins leaving! here the frailest leaves of me and yet my strongest lasting, I dream'd in a dream, we two boys together clinging, one the other never leaving, what think you I take my pen in hand to record?

> That still has to be noted. And this Second Letter will have to be finished:
> ". . . Think this over and take care lest some day you rue having unwisely divulged your views. The best safeguard will be to learn by heart instead of writing. For it is impossible for what is written not to be disclosed. That is the reason why I have never written about these things, . . . and why there is no written work by Plato, and never will be. What people call his works are the works of a Socrates become young and magnificent once again. Farewell. Do as I say. As soon as you have read and re-read this letter, burn it. . . ."

Plato's dream, writ large, is never to have written. Never to have written is best for man, ancient wisemen say. And second best? To dream of the Egyptian priests of Neith guarding in their archive what ancient wisemen have written is best for man. To dream of a Socrates become young and robust again, a Socrates producing works, a Socrates (as one translator of the Letters has it) "embellished and modernized."[16]

To dream that the purest thinker of the West should also be the thinker who wrote the most and best of all. To dream that one's own writing could vanish in flames   *Steadfastly Pierre watched the first crispings and blackenings of the painted scroll*   without a trace, or that the only tracings left would be without wax, would be no more than ashes. To dream that these ashes would glow in the memory of man, glimmer   *for one swift instant, seen through the flame and smoke, the upwrithing portrait tormentedly stared at him in beseeching horror*   in the innermost cavities of the heart where nothing extrinsic intrudes, would perdure and never smolder, never never be lost.

—I hope this doesn't get lost. Quickly, a double . . . graphite . . . carbon . . . re-read this letter . . . burn it. There there is ash. [*Il y a là cendre.*] And now it would be necessary to distinguish, between two repetitions. . . .

The night passes. In the morning, knocks are heard at the door. They seem to be coming from outside this time, these *coups*. . . .

Two knocks . . . four. . . .

—But it may be a residue, a dream, a morsel of a dream, an echo of the night . . . this other theater, these *coups* from the outside. . . .

.   .   .   .

No attempt at summary. But where do tracings without wax leave memory and reminiscence? If typography, iconography, and engrammatology *show themselves* to be the dream of perfect recuperation of a past in the present, oneiric restoration or restitution to full presence, then what will memory, reminiscence, and writing be for us without them? Us?

No doubt, I have been on the verge of such questions   *Pierre, when thou just hovered on the verge, thou wert a riddle to me; but now, that thou art deep down in the gulf of the soul,—now, when thou wouldst be lunatic to wise men, perhaps—now doth poor ignorant Isabel begin to comprehend thee* from the very outset. It is time to confront more directly the consequences of the passing of the dream both for the metaphysics of memory and the memory of metaphysics.

Hegel's *is* a metaphysics of memory in an unheard-of sense, and I shall now take up the themes of memory and remembrance in his mature system (in the *Encyclopedia of Philosophical Sciences*) and in his "introductions" to it, or to the first part of it (in the *Philosophical Propaedeutics* and *Phenomenology of Spirit*). Heidegger's thought too is in memory of metaphysics, and what-has-been plays an unparalleled role in his career early and late (unless Hegel be that parallel). Chapter 6 will thus take up again what we have heard Derrida call the "absolute past," interrogating Heideggerian *Gewesenheit* with the help of Nietzsche's imperfect thought—of time and its "It was." Finally, in chapter 7 I will turn to a number of Derrida's most recent writings in order to revert from the memory of metaphysics to what will very much look like a renewed metaphysics of memory. Yet it will merely be an idol or "slight" image, by no means an icon, of metaphysics; for it will have been a matter of asking what happens after the Platonic letter is burned (by Plato himself); after the Hegelian pyramid sinks into its own internal shaft (as Hegel himself, in spite of himself, bears witness); and after the Heideggerian gathering of time and being (as Heidegger himself reminds us) disperses   *And here it may be randomly suggested, by way of bagatelle, whether some things that men think they do not know, are not for all that thoroughly comprehended by them; and yet, so to speak, though contained in themselves, are kept a secret from themselves? The idea of Death seems such a thing*   to mirth and mourning.

Between two repetitions. Outside. On the verge.

FIVE

Of Pits and Pyramids

Hegel on Memory, Remembrance, and Writing

It may prove necessary to remember that the words for memory and remembrance in Hegel's philosophy—*Gedächtnis* and *Erinnerung*—recollect the whole of his thought, so that they can scarcely be treated adequately as an isolated subject. *Gedächtnis* is reminiscent of *Gedanke, Denken,* of the thought and thinking as such. For Hegel, thought is the very form philosophy takes. *Erinnerung,* which he occasionally writes as *Er-Innerung,* calls to mind not only a particular faculty or power of spirit but the *method,* the fundamental *way,* of all things on, above, and below the Earth—the way of interiorization. Virtually every object that enters the philosopher's ken, whether of nature, society, culture, morality, or logic, serves to remind him or her of memory and remembrance. Each is metonymic-mnemonic of the whole; each is on the verge of *being* the whole. Yet if that is so, the movement of interiorization must come full circle, *and thus must turn outward,* without absolute beginning or end.

Nevertheless, every inquiry must start somewhere. I shall start by summoning up those brief sections of the *Encyclopedia of Philosophical Sciences* (third edition, 1830) that invoke remembrance and memory explicitly: §§452–54, "Die Erinnerung," and §§461–64, "Gedächtnis."[1] Of course, it would be fatal to begin by forgetting the *situation* of these sections. The first thing to keep in mind about their situation is what separates *Erinnerung* from *Gedächtnis,* namely, the matter that occupies §§455–60. These six sections dwell on the imagination (*die Einbildungskraft*) as productive of images or icons, and especially on the kind of fancy that produces *signs.* Hegel's most explicit references to language, speech, and writing in the *Encyclopedia* are lodged between interiorizing remembrance and memory. Both *Erinnerung* and *Gedächtnis* verge on writing: they are supremely engrammatological. I will therefore have occasion throughout to recall Derrida's essay on Hegel's semiology, "Le puits et la pyramide," which we might translate as "The Pit and   *I saw the lips of the black-robed judges. They appeared to me white—whiter than the sheet upon which I trace these words. . . . I saw them fashion the syllables of my name; and I shuddered because no sound succeeded*   the Pyramid."[2]

Yet before placing interiorizing remembrance, sign-making fancy, and memory in the context of Hegel's "Psychology," I shall take a preliminary look at

Erinnerung elsewhere in the *Encyclopedia:* (1) in Hegel's logic, specifically, his treatment of cognition; (2) in his geology and biology, the study of inorganic and organic nature; and (3) in the final sections of his philosophy of spirit, under the heading "Philosophy." After this preliminary glance at interiorizing remembrance at various junctures in the system of the *Encyclopedia,* I will turn to Hegel's "Psychology," presumably the proper place of both remembrance and memory when viewed as aspects of intelligence. One particular image of interiorizing remembrance, an echo of inorganic nature reverberating in a well, pit, or mineshaft, will claim our attention. After a detailed examination of *Erinnerung* and a brief glimpse at imagination and the sign-making fancy, I shall proceed to *Gedächtnis,* productive memory, which exhibits affinities to thought itself, *der Gedanke, das Gedachte.* The precise relationship of memory to interiorizing remembrance and to thought will prove to be problematic: memory will turn out to be profoundly interior and extravagantly superficial—both spiritual and mechanical—at once. Furthermore, memory will prove to be subordinate to the movement of interiorizing remembrance, which itself becomes increasingly difficult to locate in Hegel's system. As though it were lost at the bottom of that echoing shaft. Much later in the chapter—since every inquiry must end somewhere—I will descend into the pit of Hegel's system, seeking the genesis of *Erinnerung* in his *Phenomenology of Spirit.*

THE SITUATION OF *ERINNERUNG* IN HEGEL'S SYSTEM

The whole of remembrance, imagination, and memory is memorialized in the *Encyclopedia's* third part, "The Philosophy of Spirit," first division, "Subjective Spirit," third section, "Psychology," first subdivision, "Theoretical Spirit," §§445–68. Memory, and especially interiorizing remembrance, are obviously matters of firsts and thirds for Hegel, beginnings and ends, precisely because their function is to rescue seconds, that is, midpoints, mediations, and differences. For this reason *Erinnerung* in particular everywhere surpasses its situation in the "Psychology," appearing throughout Hegel's account of the philosophical sciences at decisive junctures. Only a small selection of those junctures is recollected in what follows, one for each of the *Encyclopedia's* three major parts: (1) logic, (2) philosophy of nature, and (3) philosophy of spirit.

(1) A number of items in the "Introduction" to the *Encyclopedia* and in the "Preliminary Conception" of its first part, "The Science of Logic," might be remembered here, but I shall pass over them in silence and proceed to the third part of the logic. Whereas the first part of the logic presents the doctrine of being (or thought in its unmediated state) and the second part the doctrine of essence (or thought in its reflected and mediated state), the third part unfolds the doctrine of the concept as the actual grasp of the idea (or thought "*in its having returned to itself*" and in its fully developed being-with-itself). Here the idea expresses itself in the moments of life, cognition, and absolute idea.

In spite of what I said a moment ago about firsts and thirds, the movement of interiorizing remembrance proceeds most noticeably in the second moment: cognition (*Erkennen*) constitutes the process and progress of the idea and of reason itself in the mediation of difference. In its coming to know itself the idea cancels and surpasses the onesidedness of both subjectivity and objectivity in their limited and limiting senses: it surpasses vacuous subjectivity by taking up into itself, as its own content, the world that is in being; it overcomes alien objectivity—the existent world viewed as a mere aggregate of contingencies and insignificant details—by means of the *interiority* of the *subjective* (§225: *das* Innre *des* Subjektiven). Yet cognition appears under two guises. Hegel employs the title *Erkennen* twice in his schema, the narrowly epistemological sense being subordinate to cognition broadly conceived, that is, conceived in such a way that *willing* pertains to it. Surprisingly, interiorizing remembrance plays a vital role in the latter. Willing achieves for subjectivity the return to self of a spirit that is simultaneously "the *interiorizing remembrance* of the *content* into itself" (§234). Hegel also describes this return as *Erinnerung* of "the presupposition of theoretical comportment," namely, the presupposition that the *object* is the proper truth and substance of theoretical inquiry. If it were not for such remembrance, subjectivity would be ceaseless contradiction and dispersion, the sheer frustration that results when what should be (*Sollen*) is separated from what is (*Sein*). The speculative or absolute idea (the third division in which the concept and logic as a whole culminate) thus depends on an interiorizing remembrance that is not purely theoretical but also practical. If the dialectical method in logic is not to be mere extrinsic form, it must be interiorized as "the soul and the very grasp [*Begriff*] of the content" (§243). Thought thinking itself dare not forget. It must freely remember its own *life*, its first moment and inception. Logic yields gracefully   *but then, all at once, there came a most deadly nausea over my spirit*   to the philosophy of nature. Hence it is odd that when philosophy of spirit rises from the ashes of nature and retrieves the notion of *Erkennen*, remembrance is reduced to the theoretical sphere. Its importance for practical spirit—for the will—appears to be forgotten.

(2) Philosophy of nature traces the *biography* of interiorizing remembrance. It is a life-story told from the outside, from a position of alienation, seeking interiorities everywhere. Remembrance plays a particularly striking role in this grandest of "seconds," the realm of exteriority and difference *par excellence*. Here again but a few reminders, from two domains of Hegel's "Organic Physics," to wit, the pre-organic stage of geological nature, and vegetable life.

Geological nature is the "processless immediacy" that life presupposes as its condition (§338). Nevertheless, however much geological nature may now appear to be without process, it is in fact full of gaps and openings, passages across boundless reaches of time from outside to inside and back again, rifts and shifts caused by ruptures and eruptions of all sorts. All these have to do with *Erinnerung*. "The *interiorizing remembrance* of the idea of nature into itself, on the way toward subjective and even more toward intellectual vitality, is the

Urteil in itself," that is to say, not merely "judgment" but, literally, a primordial sundering, *Ur-teilung*, the "ordeal" of the idea in its self. The initial outcome of this primeval sundering, which all life in its immediate totality presupposes, is the globe of planet Earth, the very figure of organism. (Perhaps the very figure engraved by Matthäus Merian for the "second emblem" of Michael Maier's *Atalanta fugiens*, 1618, "Nutrix ejus terra est [His nurse is Earth]," the figure reproduced here as Plate 7.) Yet the formation of this global presupposition, Hegel reminds us, is ineluctably past (§339). Its process is lost in the mists of geological time—which during the eighteenth and nineteenth centuries receded steadily beyond the reaches of both knowledge and faith. In his epochal *Theory of the Earth*, first published in 1788, then expanded in 1795, James Hutton proclaimed of geological nature that ". . . we find no vestige of a beginning,—no prospect of an end."[3] As though analysis of geological nature, the infinite presupposition of life, were identical to the analysis of mind itself as Wordsworth described it in "The Prelude" (Book II, lines 228–33):

> Hard task, vain hope, to analyse the mind,
> If each most obvious and particular thought,
> Not in a mystical and idle sense,
> But in the words of Reason deeply weighed,
> Hath no beginning.

PLATE 7

The irretrievable geological past of Earth's radically exterior sidereal nexus implies certain dramatic consequences for terrestrial life: subsequent physical organization does not evolve from a unified seed or kernal poised in its husk; on the contrary, its point of departure is *already an outcome.* Hegel (§340) uses the word *Ausgang* when referring to that organization, *Ausgang* meaning both outcome and point of departure. In this way the proto-stage of geological nature serves as a paradigm of vegetable life, in which reproduction is so much the essence that it becomes impossible to say where one individual stops (outcome) and another begins (point of departure). M. J. Petry translates *Ausgang* as "egression."[4] Yet such originary egression implies that physical organization is nothing less than primal differ*a*nce (spelled with a pyramidal "A"), a nonorigin, a foregone conclusion, as it were, that nevertheless will not yield up its secrets to philosophical science.[5] *Sidereal Earth remains a presupposition.*

The outcome and point of departure of geological nature involves the mediation of two (or three) principles, namely, granite and limestone. (*Three* when one considers that limestone or chalk is the neutral base of an already reduced binary distinction.) Such stony principles are not utterly without process, however, and they continue their lapidary, titanic labor of aeons. The granite principle develops partly as massive chunks of solid rock and partly as more highly determined differentiations in myriad mineral moments, "the metals and the oryctognostic objects in general." (Oryctognostic: from *oryktos,* related to digging or mining, and *gnōsis,* knowledge, hence having to do with the science of minerals and fossils.) Granitic development eventually "loses itself in mechanical stratifications and in alluviums devoid of immanent configuration," its power to form exhausted, and proceeds, as it were, by rote. The neutral principle—expressed in all forms of calcium carbonate—now intervenes. Its first productions are "the less imposing formations on the flank,"[6] that is to say, those lower ranges identified by Johann Gottlob Lehmann in 1756 as *Flöz-Gebirge,* fletz formations or stratified mountains extending laterally (*zur Seite:* as though the chalky ranges were the lateral cathexis of spirit) from the massive granitic ranges. The still later productions of alkali earth, containing the remains of ancient sea creatures and yielding coal, marble, and limestone, are what the leading Neptunist of his time, Abraham Gottlob Werner, describes in 1787 as "alluvial mountains." Hegel denigrates these last as jumbled forms, concrescences yielded by an "extrinsic mixture" of the two principles. It is of course in these less sublime chalky mountains, the stratified and the alluvial, and not in the granitic ranges, that caverns and their monstrous crystallizations appear. Lehmann's *Investigation into the History of Stratified Mountains* (1756) cites the changes wrought in such fletz mountains by cataclysms and contingencies of all kinds—earthquakes, deluges, tidal waves, and so on—in the following words: "Changes even took place in the interior of the earth. For, wherever the waters acted upon soluble earths and minerals, such as limestone mountains, they were able with little difficulty to dissolve these and to carry away the dissolved parts, thus creating caverns, sink holes, canyons, etc."[7]

What is the upshot of Hegel's "organic physics" of "geological nature" for an account of interiorizing remembrance? The mediating process of the granitic and neutral principles remains *vergangen*, bygone, altogether out of reach, as a kind of absolute past. Especially the second and third sets of mountains, the stratified alluvials—mineralogically the most heterogeneous and paleontologically the richest, veritably embedded with monuments of crustaceous life, the delight of all spelunkers—Hegel derides and abandons. He quits geology, which in his *Philosophical Propaedeutics* he equates with "extinguished process," for biology and anthropology.[8] Because it is the *outcome* of a merely "presupposed past," and because it has its sidereal nexus *outside* itself, the terrestrial globe proves to be the ultimate oxymoron—Hegel calls it the "crystal of life" and the "organism of the prostrate Earth." Precisely as outcome, Earth serves as a point of departure; it is fructified and vivified in its seas. The caverns and pits of the calcareous, alluvial past, themselves the immemorial wash of time, the vast burial vaults of an absolute past, are abandoned for the amniotic environment of myriad single-celled animals. Sidereal Earth, its rock and chalk, hills and hollows, pits and lodes, is left behind in the ebbtide of spirit. As if forgotten. On the verge of remembrance.

Of interiorizing remembrance in vegetable and animal life there would be at least as much to relate. Yet vegetable life—with its roots, branches, leaves, buds, and seeds—fails to produce truly individualized plants. Its avatars assimilate nourishment in a relatively simple, nonmediated way; they cannot budge from their place; and they reproduce in a fashion that bars our knowing where the process itself begins and ends—

> O chestnut-tree, great rooted blossomer,
> Are you the leaf, the blossom or the bole?

The sole interiority of plants is expressed in the channeling of some of its cells into the tender inner parts designed for plant circulation, as opposed to the durable woody fibers of the exterior. Yet the incipient "return into itself," the phloem and xylum of vegetable life, achieve no real measure of "self-feeling" (§347). Such life too is left behind and forgotten, presuming that spirit leaves anything behind other than its lifeless sidereal presupposition.

The interiority of *animal* life in all its variegated forms and their general modes of assimilation, reproduction, and generation is of course far more complex and profound. Yet it would lead us too far afield to recall these matters in any detail here. Of greater moment is Hegel's "Anthropology," even if by referring to it I invade "Philosophy of Spirit" ahead of schedule. The very notion of "psyche" or "soul" results from an essential interiorizing (§401: *innerlich machen; erinnert werden*) of what is simply "found" in "sensation," a faculty that humans share with animals. Throughout his "Anthropology," Hegel plays on the relationship of the words *das Gefundene*, "what is found," and *die Empfindung*, "sensation," both of them formed on the verb *finden*, "to find." The embodiment of spirit in man is expressed in man's interiorizing remembrance of what (in sensation) seems to have been merely found outside him. Hegel's "Psychology" focuses on this interior way of spirit, and I shall turn to it after one final example of *Erinnerung* at crucial junctures in the *Encyclopedia*—this time at the very end of the book (§§572–77), where Hegel defines "Philosophy" as such.

(3) It is the very existence and essence of "Philosophy," as discussed in the closing sections of the *Encyclopedia*, to remember. The very movement that constitutes philosophy comes to grips with itself—although coming to grips with a movement might well threaten both the movement and the grip—by unceasing retrospection with regard to its knowledge. Hegel begs his hearers to remember (*so mag noch dies darüber erinnert werden*) that philosophy respects concrete, determinate unity alone and does not countenance empty, abstract, thoughtless agglomeration (§573). Philosophy does not establish extrinsic connections and identities; it is the esoteric, not exoteric, study of God, identity, cognition, and the concept. The self-thinking idea is universality that is tried and tested, proved and preserved, a universality that recalls its own beginnings in the realm of logic and its proper odyssey through the realm of nature (§§574–75). Absolute spirit, as eternal progression and development of the idea, is as much activity as result, and the proper name of its activity is *interiorization*. Hegel remembers at the end to cite that moving paean to autonoesis—self-thinking thought—in Aristotle's *Metaphysics* (XII, 7), autonoesis being the divine *arkhē* and apotheosis of interiorization.

So much for a very general and admittedly impressionistic determination of interiorizing remembrance in the vast circles of the *Encyclopedia* as a whole. Let me begin again, trying this time not to forget   *Long suffering* *had nearly annihilated all my ordinary powers of mind*   so many details, so many differences.

THE PSYCHOLOGY OF *ERINNERUNG* AND *GEDÄCHTNIS*

"Psychology" studies the various faculties of subjective spirit, such as intuition, representation, and memory, in order to liberate the concept from immediacy and extraneous (as opposed to interiorized) determination. It scrutinizes the dialectic that is at work in spirit as such. The content of that dialectic is both being-in-itself and spirit's own being: Hegel establishes the two poles of the dialectic as *das An-sich-seiende* and *das Seinige,* just as earlier in the *Encyclopedia* (§20) and even in the *Phenomenology* he juxtaposed subjective "opinion" and the intended "universal" (*die Meinung, das Meinige, das Meinen,* and *das Allgemeine*).

Spirit's way is theoretical inasmuch as it posits the determinations of reason as its own, making them subjective; practical inasmuch as it strives to liberate the determinations of will from their subjectivity, positing them as in-itself. We are now to consider the theoretical segment of spirit's way, even though in the "logic," as I have noted, remembrance is found to play a crucial role in spirit's practical development. (Would we not have expected remembrance to play a predominately theoretical role in the logic, whereas the "philosophy of spirit," which is both "objective" and "subjective," would be the place for remembrance as *will?* The opposite is the case. It seems as though philosophy of spirit has forgotten what logic already attained, as though dialectical philosophy were not really perfect progress but a ceaseless slipping back, like a spider trying to make its way up a slippery limestone wall.) Be that as it may, for subjective spirit interiorizing remembrance is a matter of the theoretical life, a matter of intelligence. *Die Intelligenz*—by no means mere "intellect," *Verstand*—finds itself initially determined from outside itself; specifically, in sensation. Its activities, functions, faculties, or powers are organized in a *hierarchy of transition* wherein all ostensibly alien determinations come to be grasped as its own. Such transition (*Übergang*) constitutes cognition (*Erkennen*). "The concept of cognition has proved to be intelligence itself, the certitude of reason; and the actuality of intelligence *is* cognition itself" (§445). (No distinction is made now between the broader and narrower senses of *Erkennen*.) Hegel anticipates the moments in the cognitive hierarchy of transition as "intuition, representation, interiorizing remembrance, and so on" (§445). Yet his structuring of the moments by no means places remembrance and memory on an equal footing with intuition and representation. The outline of the hierarchy looks like this:

  α) Intuition [*Anschauung*, §§446–50]
  β) Representation [*Die Vorstellung*, §§451–64]
    1) Remembrance [*Die Erinnerung*, §§452–54]
    2) Imagination [*Die Einbildungskraft*, §§455–60]
    3) Memory [*Gedächtnis*, §§461–64]
  γ) Thinking [*Das Denken*, §§465–68]

The apparent subordination of interiorizing remembrance, imagination, and memory to representation would hardly be worth noticing if we did not recollect the disparagement of *Vorstellung* throughout Hegel's lectures on aesthetics, religion, history of philosophy, and philosophy of history—indeed farther back than the *Phenomenology* itself, in the "early writings." Representation is a fallen form of thought, a merely extrinsic reflection ignorant of contexts; it is thought sullied by intuition and sensation. In the *Phenomenology* Hegel abjures *Vorstellung* as a "piddling" form of consciousness, as natural and vulgar as can be.[9] Yet throughout the *Encyclopedia,* and in the *Phenomenology* as well, interiorizing remembrance plays a role that could never be reduced to piddling importance. *Erinnerung* occupies a special—if ambiguous and fugitive—place in Hegel's thought as a whole. I shall try to locate that place. The difficulty is that remembrance seems to be more the movement of transition itself than any moment of the hierarchy. Hence it seems perpetually out of place; it is always as though spirit were on the very verge of it. But let me begin at the beginning of the hierarchy of transition, with intuition.

Spirit in the form of intuition remains caught up in a fabric of inarticulate feelings and sensations. Hegel calls it spirit's "muffled weaving," *sein dumpfes Weben,* a phrase he has already used in the "Anthropology" to characterize sensation (cf. §400).[10] The German word for fabric, *Stoff,* reminds us of even earlier stages in spirit's development, for example, of the stuff of vegetable nature (cf. §345). In intuition the determination of spirit remains extrinsic to it, as a determination of embodiment or abstract immediacy. Although feeling appears to be immediate and thus "the most present [*präsenteste*] form, as it were, in which the subject comports itself toward a given content" (§447), such presence proves to be limited to isolated particularity, to the stuff of embodied existence. Yet even in primitive sensation, muffled and inarticulate as it may be, spirit sets off in the interiorizing direction it will continue to follow until it finds itself weaving the forms. Hegel identifies that direction as attentiveness or alertness (*die Aufmerksamkeit*), the very category that will be so important for Freud's attempt to portray the normal psychic processes, to which he (Hegel) immediately appends the phrase "active *remembrance*" (§448: *die tätige* Erinnerung). The upshot is that interiorizing remembrance cannot be fixed as that specific moment of representation which is *subsequent to* intuition— indeed, we have not yet arrived at the moment of intuition proper, are only now arriving there, thanks to the unscheduled intervention of interiorizing remembrance. *Erinnerung* is functioning even before it has come to be, work- ing its effects in the hierarchy of transition from sensation to thought even before its moment has come. Or have I   *By long suffering my nerves had been unstrung, until I trembled at the sound of my own voice*   simply neglected to recall that Hegelian "moments" are never truly isolable, certainly not as points on a line-segment, one succeeding upon another? Perhaps the freedom of motion displayed by *Erinnerung* within cognition is to teach us something about dialectical thinking in general? It is almost as though the spider *must* slip back down that slippery slope in order to remember what she is about. However that may be, I note for now the prescience and ubiquity of active remembrance, which makes manifest to intelligence the fact that what- ever it feels itself to be determined by is in fact its own, *des Seinigen,* and hence has the quality of being, *des Sein-igen.* The crucial role played by interiorizing remembrance after its debut in intuition is described in section 449 as follows: "Intelligence, as this concrete unity of the two moments [namely, both its attentiveness or inner alertness and its feeling of being outside itself], indeed, remembered immediately in itself within the fabric that is outside, and in its interiorizing remembrance in itself being plunged in being-outside-itself, is *intuition.*" In section 450 the dialectic swings back to the side of interiority, the favored side, the side of origins and eventual ends: "Intelligence directs its attention just as essentially toward and against its own being-outside-itself and is an awakening to itself in its very immediacy, its interiorizing remembrance into itself in such immediacy; in this way intuition is the concreteness of the fabric and of its self; intuition is *its own,* so that it no longer needs to find its content.—"

Under the heading *representation,* the second major stage in the hierarchy of transition, Hegel's analysis continues to define the interiorizing remem- brance that has not yet been thematized but is already at work "as remembered [or: internalized] intuition" (§451). Representation occupies the midpoint between the unmediated exteriority of a bemused intelligence that finds itself determined by some alien objectivity and the mediated interiority of an intelligence that is free and that thinks. As this midpoint, *Vorstellung* is still onesidedly subjective, inasmuch as what is its own remains conditioned by immediacy and is not yet its own proper way to be (*das Sein*). Intelligence proceeds to interiorize its intuitions, positing itself *as* intuiting, catching itself looking at things, as it were, and thus seeing itself through the magic of reflection. In this way it simultaneously cancels the sheer subjectivity of interiority, "in itself externalizing it from itself [*in ihr selbst ihrer sich zu entäussern*]." In its "*own externality*," representation comes "*to be in itself.*" Yet because representation "begins" with intuition and its fabric of sensations, its activity "is still burdened [*behaftet*] with this difference." Representation remains embroiled in synthesis, while pure thought of the concept will move freely in "concrete immanence."

Precisely at this point Hegel's explication of *Erinnerung* proper begins, as though interiorizing remembrance might be expected to liberate intelligence from its syntheses and foreign dependencies. Yet how could *Erinnerung* perform such liberation without forgetting what it had already done in and for intelligent intuition? The liberation has to do with *icons* or *images* in the interior space-time of intelligence. "Remembering-interiorizing at first as intuition, intelligence posits the *content* of the *feeling* in its interiority, in its [intelligence's] *own space* and its *own time*" (§452). Such positing of content and reduction of space-time result in an image, *Bild*. (Inserted into Hegel's text immediately prior to the word *Bild* is a double-alpha, pointing forward to a double-beta and double-gamma in sections 453 and 454, respectively. *Erinnerung,* however much it encroaches on *Einbildungskraft* right from the start, occurs in and as three specific moments, which I want to trace with some care. All three moments have to do with the fate of the content of intuition in representation.) In the first moment of *Erinnerung* the image achieves a measure of freedom from the immediacy and particularity of the intuition; it is "arbitrary" or "contingent," inasmuch as it has been isolated from the "external" space and time that shaped its unmediated context. Yet what are space and time, that they can *be* outside *and* inside? If "interior" space and time are arbitrary (*willkürlich,* subject to the freedom that spirit is ever seeking), how is the content of intuition to be remembered in its particularity and individuality? Or does *Erinnerung* require that some aspects of intuition be forgotten and fall into oblivion? Is there something like what Nietzsche calls *active forgetfulness* at work in it?

This would be the place for a detailed recollection of Hegel's "Mechanics" of space and time. That mechanics rejects the Kantian interpretation of space and time as forms of intuition and substitutes for it a whole series of negations. The dialectic of space-time involves movement from the unmediated exteriority of space to the interiorities of point, line, plane, and of time itself as abstract subjectivity. Time therefore has everything to do with finite consciousness

Looking upward, I surveyed the ceiling of my prison. . . . In one of its panels a very singular figure riveted my whole attention. It was the painted figure of Time

as he is commonly represented, save that, in lieu of a scythe, he held what, at a casual glance, I supposed to be the pictured image of a huge pendulum, such as we see on antique clocks. . . . I fancied that I saw it in motion and hence interiorizing remembrance, though not with the idea in and for itself, not with spirit as such, which is *But what mainly disturbed me was the idea that it had perceptibly* descended eternal. One would here be on the sliddery surface of the innermost vault of Hegel's ontology—the relation of eternity to time, being to nothing, for-itself to in-itself. A veritable abyss of problems, swathed in darkness. I therefore return to the immediate context, advancing to *Erinnerung* in its second moment (§453), avoiding that breach from which there would be no escape.

The image or *Bild* is itself transitory, *vorübergehend,* inasmuch as intelligence comprises the time and space, the *when?* and *where?* of the image. For intelligence is not only the "consciousness" and "existence" of its determinations; it is also their "subject," their "in-itself." Interiorized and remembered in intelligence, the image no longer *exists* as such. It is, Hegel says, *"unconsciously preserved," bewusstlos aufbewahrt,* in intelligence. Yet what can it mean that the image is transitory? The entire tradition of philosophy has devoted itself to demonstrating the durability of the eidetic icon. What sort of icon is it that is transitory? An imprint in oversoft wax, hygrotic typography, a *failed* iconography, a loss of presence. The image is no longer existent, *nicht mehr existierend.* It no longer "stands out," its cutting edge has lost its contours, there is no relief. And yet. The icon is *preserved.* Like the soul incarcerate. And preserved *unconsciously,* unbeknownst, *unbewusst.* An engram as yet unread in a book as yet unopened.

Something very strange is happening here in the second moment (ββ) of the image. Whereas interiority has heretofore been identified with a kind of attentiveness or awareness, with the vigilance of a spirit that is *present to itself,* and contraposed to an exteriority that is ultimately impenetrable, muffling, and alienating, interiority itself is now said to be infected with darkness. Obscurity encroaches on the lucid self-presence of intelligence itself. There are things of which intelligence—itself the hallmark of consciousness—is not yet or no longer conscious. When Hegel says that intelligence is the "subject" and the "in-itself" of its determinations, this now means that it is *subject to* images *in themselves.* The emphatic words *bewusstlos aufbewahrt* reflect the paradox that Locke phrased so well—"that our *Ideas* are said to be in our Memories, when indeed, they are actually no where. . . ." These same words, "unconsciously preserved," now release a series of "Remarks" (to §453) as cryptic as any Hegel ever penned:

> To grasp intelligence as this shaft dark as night [*diesen nächtlichen Schacht*], in which a world of images and representations infinite in number is preserved, without their being in consciousness, is on the one hand the universal requirement in general of grasping the concept as concrete, as for example one grasps the seed in such a way that it contains *affirmatively,* in *virtual* possibility, all the *determinations* that come to *existence* only in the development of the tree. It is the inability to

grasp this universal, which is concrete in itself and yet which remains *simple,* that has occasioned the preservation of particular representations in particular *fibers* and *places;* what is different is essentially to have but one individualized spatial existence.—But the seed emerges from the existing determinations only within an other, in the seed of the fruit; only in this way does it come to *return* to its simplicity and come once more to the existence of being-in-itself. However, intelligence as such is the free *existence* of *being-in-itself* internally remembering itself in itself in its development [*die freie* Existenz *des in seiner Entwicklung sich in sich erinnernden* Ansichseins]. Intelligence is thus to be grasped on the other hand as this *unconscious* shaft, that is, as the *existing* universal in which what is different is not yet posited as discrete. Indeed, this *in-itself* is the first form of universality that presents itself to representation.

A shaft or pit deep in the earth, and a tree with its seed, fibers, and shaft of trunk: it is pointless to complain about Hegel's catachresis, since for him all nature is a mixed metaphor—he seeks the determinations of the concept wherever he can find them. Not that such finding could or should have anything to do with sensation, *Empfindung.* Yet the fact that philosophy of nature, and especially geology and biology, are remembered here in some detail has to do with the peculiar *Ohnmacht der Natur* which is not so much "impotence" as a swooning or sinking into the oblivion of unconsciousness. A swoon and oblivion that will pass. For such unconsciousness preserves images. *The unconscious preservation of images in intelligence itself,* acting as a kind of subliminal text, *preserves the images of unconscious nature,* its pits and its plants. Perhaps we ought not forget these images of intelligent nature too quickly. Perhaps these are the images of natural intelligence, images that are therefore indistinguishable from originals, icons that are paradigms, or at least presuppositions.

Hegel calls intelligence in its capacity to preserve images unconsciously "a shaft dark as night" or "nocturnal   *the blackness of darkness supervened; all sensations appeared swallowed up in a mad rushing descent of the soul into Hades. Then silence, and stillness, and night were the*   pit," *diesen nächtlichen Schacht.* The word *Schacht* is a mining term equivalent to the English *shaft.* The *Oxford English Dictionary* defines the latter as "a vertical or slightly inclined well-like excavation in mining, tunneling, etc., as a means of access to underground workings. . . ." Thus the cognate "shaft" is perhaps to be preferred to the word "pit," which goes back to the Latin *puteo,* "to emit an offensive smell"—the Romans used the word *puteus* for a ditch, drain, cloaca, or cess-pool. However, *pit* does have two dubious advantages: first, it signifies a hole or cavity in the ground, "formed either by digging or by some natural process," whereas a shaft is most likely to be manmade; second, a pit can also be "a deep hole or chamber in which prisoners are confined," and the thought of images imprisoned   *I put forward my arm, shuddered to find that I had fallen at the very brink of a circular pit*   in a subterranean cell dark as night, while incorrigibly romantic, may not be altogether out of place. Hegel's adjective *nächtlich* is foreboding: the dark of night is the absolute negation of light and hence of all manifestation, even of selfhood (see §§275–79).

We remember that planet Earth—herself an outcome, sidereal egression, and bifurcated point of departure—is not yet a self-contained seed; she is pitted with petrous differences, cavities that (presumably) contain no germ of life. It is significant therefore that Hegel immediately shifts the imagery of interiorizing remembrance away from the geological *Ausgang* toward vegetable life. The seed embraces in itself the concrete universal, contains all the determinations of the individual plant as virtual possibilities. We recall that the inadequacy of vegetable interiority lies in its failure to produce a genuine individual self as a simple unity. Instead, the plant is merely fixed in one particular place, changing and developing solely in the specialization of its fibers. Its ceaseless return to self in fertilization and reproduction remains bound to abstraction, exteriority, and otherness. Thus the glory of phototropic vegetable life is rooted in inglorious detritus and debris. Whereas Hegel's contemporary, Schelling, counters every "womanly lament" with fervent affirmations—"All birth is birth from darkness into light; the kernel of seed must first be plunged deep in the earth and expire in gloom in order that the more beauteous figure of light [*Lichtgestalt*] loom and unfold along the beams of the sun"—Georges Bataille, in our own century, merely exposes the hinterside of romantic fervor when in "The Language of Flowers" he drags the figure of light back into the mire—

> Flowers themselves, lost in this immense movement from earth to sky, are reduced to an episodic role; to a diversion, moreover, that is apparently misunderstood: they can only contribute, by breaking the monotony, to the inevitable seductiveness produced by the general thrust from low to high. And in order to destroy this favorable impression nothing less is necessary than the impossible and fantastic vision of roots swarming under the surface of the soil, nauseating and naked like vermin.[11]

As opposed to all this, Hegelian intelligence *exists*, that is, develops and unfolds, standing out as a being on its own; intelligence is being-in-itself freely internalizing itself, remembering its self. Yet intelligence is in-itself only "on the one hand," *einerseits*, and a onesided existence would be abstract, hence no real existence at all. "On the other hand," *andrerseits* (and now Hegel returns to his own point of departure, abandoning the seed for the geological scission, the rift in which the seed will be planted), intelligence is "this *unconscious* shaft," a pit *existing* or *insisting* as the universal whose other or difference is not yet individualized or discrete. The image of the pit or shaft, as an existent in-itself, is not yet sure of its imagic *content*. We arrive at the third moment (γγ, §454) of the image in remembrance, which is also an image *of* remembrance—an iconographic reflexivity not to be forgotten.

The "abstractly preserved image" requires for its true existence an existent intuiting. What we actually call *Erinnerung* is the relation of the image to an intuiting whereby each individual intuition conforms to the universal and to representation as such. Intelligence is now interior to and intimate with itself (*sich innerlich ist*), recognizing the content of any sensation or intuition as "*already its own*" and therefore tried and true, *preserved* (*bewährt/aufbewahrt*).

Hegel portrays such intimacy—and as readers of *Theaetetus* we will not be surprised by this—in terms of possession: "The image, which in the shaft of intelligence was only its property [*Eigentum*], is with the determination of exteriority now also in possession [*im Besitze*] of that exteriority. Hence the image is at the same time posited as distinguishable from the intuition and separable from the simple night in which it was at first plunged." In this third moment the image or icon presumably escapes from the night in which all cows are black; it is scooped out of the pit and released to the exterior, which intelligence now not only owns but also occupies. Intelligence proves to be the power that dispenses, exteriorizes, expropriates (*äussert*) and, as we shall see, ex-presses (*ausdrückt*) what is its own, its property. The interiorizing movement of remembrance hence must retain and even culminate in a movement of exteriorization. The supposition that it now does not need an extrinsic intuition to do this would testify to its sovereignty (*Gewalt*). The synthesis of an interior image with its remembered existence is representation proper, *das Vorstellen*. And yet these closing words of *Die Erinnerung* are wholly mysterious: how understand the curious *doubling* by which the intimate, interior icon (*des innerlichen Bildes*) and interiorized existence (*mit dem erinnerten Dasein*) are synthesized? how identify the icon inside with some remembered existence? how recuperate the contingencies of the outside in necessitous interiority? To be sure, we have reached the threshold of *Vorstellung* proper, in which "the inner also has in itself the determination of being able to be *posed* before intelligence [*vor die Intelligenz* gestellt *werden zu können*], to have its existence in intelligence"; yet whether such pre-position or posing before can be wholly interior *in* intelligence remains entirely questionable. Precisely when, where, and how does representation slough off those traits that always arouse Hegel's scorn? And where *Erinnerung* is concerned, would not sloughing off amount to a kind of amnesia and primal repression?

The second major moment of representation, imagination, cannot detain us now. Yet we dare not forget that it is here that the procession of images from the shadowy shaft supplies intelligence with a stockpile (*Vorrat*) of images and representations over which it has free disposition. (And we ought to note in passing the similar structure and function of *Vorrat* in Freud's 1895 "Project": the lateral cathexis of ego-organization places a reserve of quantity—sometimes indistinguishable from mnemic images—at the disposal of the nervous system.) Intelligence now makes connections and associations among images as their proper content dictates, repatriating them, as it were. Those images drawn from the shaft of night and into the light of day are not the mere banalities of a life history, however, inasmuch as reason itself is here at work. Reason's images, fabricated by the "sign-making fancy" of reproductive imagination, are signs, *Zeichen*, soon to become *words* and *names*. As always, no iconography without engrammatology. In the sign-making fancy, says Hegel, "intelligence is not the indeterminate shaft" (§457). For the kind of imagination that produces signs— for example, in the writing of a nonfictional text, such as a lecture course, and perhaps in the writing of a fictional text as well—the image of the pit   *My cognizance of the pit had become known to the inquisitorial agents*—the pit, *whose horrors had been destined for so bold a recusant as myself*—the pit, *typical of hell and regarded by rumor as the Ultima Thule of all their punishments. The plunge into this pit I had avoided by the merest of accidents* is destined to be abandoned. Abandoned not for the pyramid (which it must nonetheless pass through) but for the workshop (*Werkstätte*) of spirit as reason. A workshop outfitted with machines *There was something, however, in the appearance of this machine which caused me to regard it more attentively* which, as we shall see, are mnemonic word-machines.

Yet I am moving far too quickly: although we do not want to be detained I must recall the order of steps or stages in the hierarchy of transition—here the transition of the content from pictorial images to significant words. I shall follow the path indicated in the *Encyclopedia,* not that of the *Propaedeutics* (§§150–53), which, with its treatment of sleep and dreams, premonitions and hallucinations, natural sympathy and spiritism, delirium and insanity *and then all is* madness—*the madness of a memory which busies itself among forbidden things* is far more complex. The role of imagination in the account of representation in the *Encyclopedia* may be reduced to the following five stages, the first three involving the play of *association,* the last two requiring the labor of *reason.*

First, an association or relation of images occurs, "the play of a thoughtless representing" (§455).

Second, the gradual formation of general or universal representations by virtue of the contiguity of similar images begins. The attractive power or affinity of such icons for one another derives from intelligent subjectivity, as interiorizing-remembering, which examines their content and asserts itself as the source of universality (§455).

Third, intelligent association is recognized as subsumption under a universal, a (relatively) free connecting of images according to their proper content or sense. Such subsumption is the work of fancy, or the symbolizing, allegorizing, and creatively poetic imagination—still bound to what it has found in sensation, however, and thus still synthetic (§456).

Fourth, play becomes labor, as we encounter the sudden assertion of reason. *Vernunft* does not merely synthesize but appropriates (*aneignen*) what is found; it simultaneously determines its own concrete intuition of self as "in being." In such assertion reason is active and expressive, *productive* of its intuitions. It makes signs (§457). Fancy is thus the true midpoint between what is found and what is reason's own, of being and universality, not by way of extrinsic synthesis but as concrete individuality. In sign-making fancy intelligence is no longer "the indeterminate shaft" but "concrete subjectivity" (§457). We might express the matter fittingly by gracing Hegel's geology with a phrase of Nietzsche's: with intelligence as fancy forming signs, we exit from the calcareous shaft onto "the granite of spiritual fate."

Fifth, for intelligent reason the *word* is "properly the worthiest kind of externalization of its representations" (§459). Precisely in the way Augustine appeals to *verba concepta* as both related to sensuous vestiges and yet radically distinct from them, Hegel puts all his faith in *names*. The dignity of the word, as a *name,* consists in the simplicity or univocity of its significance, its syllables, its letters, and its resonance.

These five steps within *Einbildungskraft* take us *Down—certainly, relentlessly down!* to the core of Derrida's "Le puits et *Down— still unceasingly—still inevitably down!* la pyramide." I cannot reproduce Derrida's analysis in any detail here, although Hegel's semiology is crucial for the matters of interiorizing remembrance and memory. Before proceeding to Hegel's account of memory proper, it would be well to recall hastily some of Derrida's principal findings.

(1) If metaphysics—Hegel's metaphysics included—determines being as presence, the sign can only be passage to a *lost* presence; the sign must be provisional and subsequent, even when it takes the form of a spoken word or name. The sign is a *supplement* subservient to the process of an *Aneignung* that is more re-appropriation than appropriation pure and simple, more an infinite return than a return to or by the infinite.

(2) Such reappropriation by grace of signs therefore remains mysterious, if not entirely futile, inasmuch as the status of the sign is determined as much by loss and absence as by appropriation and presence. The pyramid, Hegel's symbol for the sign (§458), contains its own obscure shafts, multiple shafts *Deep, deep, and still deep and deeper we must go, if we would find out the heart of a man; descending into which is as descending a spiral stair in a shaft, without any end, and where that endlessness is only concealed by the spiralness of the stair, and the blackness of the shaft* in which intelligence inevitably finds and loses itself. Early in "The Pit and the Pyramid" Derrida writes:

> A path—we shall follow it—leads from this pit of night, silent as death and resonant with all the powers of voice that it holds in reserve, to that pyramid removed from the Egyptian desert and looming suddenly out of the sober and abstract fabric of the Hegelian text, constituting there the stature and the status of the sign. The natural source [i.e., the pit] and the historical construction [the pyramid], each in its own way, remain silent. The enigma is that, in accordance with the trajectory of onto-theology, this path remains circular: the pyramid again becomes the pit it will have been all along. (M, 88/77)

The nocturnal pit can never be abandoned, all hierarchies of transition notwithstanding. To desire to ascend out of it is to surrender dialectic and to lapse into something approximating absolute oblivion.

(3) In Hegel's semiology the sign proves to be both production and intuition. In fact, it conjoins in itself all the binary oppositions of metaphysics: interiority/exteriority, spontaneity/receptivity, intelligibility/sensibility, sameness/otherness, and so on. The pyramid itself proves to be an eminently ambiguous sign/symbol: a monument built for the living as well as for the dead, testifying to mortality and immortality alike, representing the containment of the foreign soul of significance *and breathing with greater freedom, I turned my glances to the pallid and rigid figure upon the bed.*

Then rushed upon me a thousand memories   but yielding up no more than an embalmed corpse or   *By vast pains we mine into the pyramid; by horrible gropings we come to the central room; with joy we espy the sarcophagus; but we lift the lid—and no body is there!—appallingly vacant as vast is the soul of a man!*   opening onto an empty vault.

(4) The standard Hegel applies to the phonetic sign, by which he gauges its superiority over all other types of signs, is the degree of arbitrariness (*Willkür*—actually a more perfect freedom of the will, as envisaged in practical philosophy) and the mastery or domination (*Herrschaft*) it permits. The demands of freedom and dominion require a kind of hidden maneuver: the sign succeeds by effacing its own spacing in the text, obliterating its *espacement*, obscuring its own exteriority; and by obfuscating the *temporisation* of its own sound and voice. Such obfuscation occurs in the privileging of the *name*, the *concept*, that is to say, in the preference for the mineral deposits of logic over the detritus of nature.[12]

Derrida himself reminds us of the importance of Hegel's theory of signs for the determination of both *Erinnerung* and *Gedächtnis:* he notes that in the "Philosophical Encyclopedia" of the *Propaedeutics* (to which we shall soon turn) it is not productive imagination but productive memory, *das produktive Gedächtnis* (§156), that serves as the medium of interiorization and the source of language (M, 101/87). It is for this reason that in the *Grammatologie* (G, 41/26) Derrida exalts Hegel for his "rehabilitation" of thought as the "*productive memory* of signs," acclaiming him "the last philosopher of the book and the first thinker of writing." Yet Hegel's semiology is also constricted by its commitment to the nominative character of language, its naming function, which Wittgenstein's *Philosophical Investigations* describes as the most primitive and childlike function of language. In Hegel's privileging of the name, and in that hidden maneuver by which the sign conceals its embodiment, the formalism that Hegel criticizes in Leibniz and in all mandarin mathematical thinking reasserts its privilege. The commitment to the name is essential to what Hegel will now assert of memory proper, *Gedächtnis* (§461–64), namely, that it is the transition to conceptual thought itself. Section 459 closes by weaving a tapestry of intelligence, speech, memory, and thought: "The mediation of representations by means of the less sensuous element of tones is further manifested in its peculiar essentiality for the following transition from representation to thought—the memory." And the final section on imagination (§460) insists on the importance of the *name* in such mediation:

> The name, as a connection of the intuition that is produced by intelligence with its significance [*Bedeutung*], is at first a *single* transitory production; and the connection of the representation as something interior with the intuition as something exterior is itself *extrinsic*. Internalizing remembrance of this exteriority is *memory*.

Thus *Gedächtnis* too is thoroughly subordinated to *Erinnerung:* memory is the interiorizing remembrance of names (as significations). Interiorizing remembrance clearly remains at work *after* its moment has been fully explicated, just as it entered on the scene *prior to* its proper moment. Dialectical negotiation of outside and inside can itself find no fixed abode in the system. Intelligence as thinking memory (*Gedächtnis*) "runs through the same activities of interiorizing remembrance" which Hegel has discussed earlier, except that now its intuition is of a word, not a sensation. In fact, Hegel directs us back to sections 451 and following, in order that we may recapitulate the steps of *Erinnerung*, making the proper substitutions and bringing the parallel to its full stature and status. Again three moments are identified, double-alpha through double-gamma. Because such repetitions are in fact microcosms of the grand repetition, the macrocosm that finds its end only in a reinstatement of the beginning, we should follow Hegel's counsel. Let us banish the fear that when we arrive *the second time* at section 461 we will once again have to shuttle back to sections 451 and following, returning *in infinitum*, unable to *read* the musical sign for repetition ‖: 451–461 :‖ just once and then get on with it, outside of it, beyond it. It would be necessary to distinguish, between two repetitions. . . .

When double-alpha first appeared, it was as a symbol inserted immediately before the italicized word *Bild*. One step removed from the sensuous stuff of intuition, the image or icon was said to occupy its own space and time, the space-time of intelligence. Yet that occupation was itself transitory, *vorübergehend;* it slipped out of existence and into the noctural shaft, *bewusstlos aufbewahrt.* Now, in the first section of *Gedächtnis* (§461), we find a repetition of that removal and slippage, a repetition with a difference.

> —αα) By means of this interiorizing remembrance, intelligence now elevates the *single* connection—that connection which the sign *is,* which makes the sign belong to intelligence—to a *universal,* that is, to a perdurant connection. The latter is a connection in which name and meaning [*Bedeutung*] are tied to one another objectively for intelligence; it makes the intuition which the name is at first into a *representation,* so that the content, the meaning, and the sign are identified, are one representation, and the representing is concrete in its interiority, with the content as its [the representing's] existence.—The memory that *retains* names.

Rather than removal, elevation; rather than slippage, connection and binding. In this repetition of double-alpha it is identity that prevails, as singularity passes to universality, to the tie that b(l)inds.

In the realm of representation (as opposed to intuition) the sign is a name, and the name is the thing: *Der* Name *ist so die* Sache (§462). So saying, we arrive at double-beta. Above (§453), double-beta introduced the transitory character of the image and its unconscious preservation. Obscurity invaded intelligence itself. The image became virtual possibility, one among an infinite number, one in an entire world of representations. And intelligence became on the one hand *unconscious,* undeveloped, simple, not yet existent, and on the other hand an existent *shaft,* in-itself, a kind of proto-interiority opening up a space-time for representation. Now, in section 462, double-beta stands as a symbol and perhaps even a simulacrum of *reproductive* memory: "*Das* ββ) reproduzierende *Gedächtnis.*" Reproductive memory recognizes the matter in the name, the name in the matter, "without intuition and image," *ohne Anschauung und Bild*. Rather than unconscious preservation of the image that announces itself as transitory, cancellation of the image, iconoclasm; rather than the shaft, a neutralization of the inside-outside distinction. "The name, as *existence* of the content in intelligence, is the *exteriority* of intelligence itself in itself [*die Äusserlichkeit ihrer selbst in ihr*]; the *interiorizing remembrance* of the name, as of the intuition produced by it, is at the same time the *exteriorization* in which intelligence within itself posits itself [*in der sie innerhalb ihrer selbst sich setzt*]." Intelligence may rattle off a string of names by sheer association, and yet if they are *names* it is no mere rattling: "It is in names that we *think*."

Just as the first double-beta introduced us to the "Remark," one of the most cryptic, so does the repetition of double-beta bring us to an extended "Remark," one that will bring us back to the very verge of the shaft. Here Hegel describes in detail—and criticizes as superficial and silly—the ancient art of mnemotechnic, which employs *loci* and *imagines agentes*, thus relying on extrinsic connections between its standardized tableaux and the variable contents to be remembered. The result of mnemotechnic is that things are not truly learned by heart. To recite *auswendig*, to churn out, requires that one learn *inwendig*, that is, that one turn inward, interiorize the material to be learned, and then draw it forth "out of the deep shaft of the ego." The shaft, let it be noted, is no longer the pit of representational intelligence but the wellspring of concrete subjectivity or ego; no longer black as night but profound; no longer the obscure source of numberless pictorial images but the ancient thesaurus into which significant names are introduced and withdrawn again *at will*. The shaft no longer preserves something *found* in experience, no longer contains the *Gefundenes* of *Empfindung*, but produces spirit's own word. Spirit gives itself   *In the deepest slumber—no! In delirium—no! In a swoon—no! In death—no! even in the grave all* is not *lost. Else there is no immortality for man. Arousing from the most profound of slumbers, we break the gossamer web of some dream. Yet in a second afterward (so frail may that web have been) we remember not that we have dreamed. . . . Amid frequent and thoughtful endeavors to remember, amid earnest struggles to regather some token of the state of seeming nothingness into which my soul had lapsed, there have been moments when I have dreamed of success; there have been brief, very brief periods when I have conjured up remembrance which the lucid reason of a later epoch assures me could have had reference only to that condition of seeming unconsciousness. These shadows of memory tell, indistinctly* the shaft.

Which brings us now to the final moment, the repetition of double-gamma. Earlier, double-gamma introduced section 454, the place where intelligence took full possession (*Besitz*) of the icon that heretofore was solely its property (*Eigentum*). Double-gamma thus entered on the scene in the first instance as a repetition, a replaying of the struggle in *Theaetetus* to differentiate *hexis* from *ktēsis*. The shaft dark as night began to resemble more and more the aviary.

The door of which, we remember, slammed shut. We ourselves introduced double-gamma some pages back by noting that this third moment of the image in remembrance—remember that αα, ββ, and γγ are moments of *Erinnerung* first of all, that only by repetition do they become moments of *Gedächtnis*— was also an image *of* remembrance that we ought not allow to fade from memory. Double-gamma was therefore the moment in which intelligence took full possesion of its intuition, recognizing the *content* of every intuition as "*already its own.*" This recognition entailed a release of the image from the shaft of intelligence to the outside: double-gamma was a moment of externalization, and as such the culmination of interiorization. Now, in section 463, the double-gamma introduces the *penultimate* moment of memory, not the *final* moment (§464), the final moment being the accession to *thinking.* Perhaps because it is only the penultimate moment of *Gedächtnis,* we find in the repetition of double-gamma the most perfect of repetitions: here too the third moment is one of exteriorization, of release to the outside; here too that movement to the outside is held to be the culmination of interiorization—"this supreme *Erinnerung,*" Hegel says of *Gedächtnis* γγ. That movement has to do with the connection of names and their significations or meanings—an explicitly *extrinsic* connection that will secure the inner heartland of thought.

True memory preserves not images—these have all been set free—but the interiority of intelligence itself. Hence its superiority over intuitive imagination. It seems we will have no difficulty in leaving both intuition and representation behind as we repeat the three moments of *Erinnerung.* The question of course ‖: ? :‖ is whether we will be able to leave *Gedächtnis* behind as we repeat the moments of *Erinnerung* and so move *toward* memory, true memory, thinking memory itself. Oddly, the supreme interiority of memory, of *Erinnerung* in *Gedächtnis,* is manifested in the ability of intelligence to poll-parrot a merely existent, wholly extrinsic series of names at its discretion. For this shows that even extreme abstraction, even free-floating signs, can be interiorized and then externalized mechanically at will. What spirit has made its own, namely, words bereft of all significance, now simply flows forth as something in process of being found, as *ein Gefunden-werdendes.* Never mind the reemergence of sensation (*Empfindung*) here, never mind the continuous muffled weaving. Mechanical memory testifies to the profound objectivity and perdurant significance of intelligence.[13]

Intelligence is the active identity "*for itself*" of the exterior objectivity and significance of names; the identity "*in itself*" of these things is nothing less than reason, *Vernunft.* "In this way, *memory* is the transition to the activity of the thought." It is the transition, needless to relate, in which the hierarchy of transition itself comes to its end. The thought no longer *has* a meaning; it *is* the meaning. The thought *exists* as the *interiority* of subjectivity: this is the ultimate, not the penultimate, moment of memory: the *arkhē kinēseōs.* The German language itself, Hegel remarks, betrays the genuine affinity of memory and the thought, *Gedächtnis* and *Gedanke.* Yet it remains one of the most difficult tasks of a philosophy of spirit "to grasp the status and significance of

the memory and to come to grips with its organic connection with thinking."
In spite of all the interiorizations at play in Hegel's treatment of memory
proper, Hegel concludes that *Gedächtnis* is "only the extrinsic way, the
onesided moment, of the *existence* of thinking" (§464). In the activity of
thinking itself, intelligence is recognitive, *wiedererkennend;* it recognizes all
intuition as its own. Thoughtful intelligence knows "that what is *thought, is;*
and that what is, inasmuch as it is a thought, only *is for it;* the *thinking* of
intelligence is *having thoughts;* they are the content and object of intelligence"
(§465). Thinking itself advances through sundry stages and culminates in the
moment when intelligence "appropriates" whatever immediately determines it,
taking "full possession" of "its property" (§468). The metaphorics of appropriation is confirmed in the *Rechtsphilosophie* (1820) when Hegel defines the
essential moment of property, that is, taking possession (*Besitzergreifung*), in
terms of interiorizing remembrance, *erinnern* (see §50 and especially the hand-
written notes to §57; 7, 125). Thinking accomplishes the final negation of
immediacy, whereby negation *for itself* recognizes its role in determining all
content. Thinking, "as the free concept," is now free   *For the moment, at*
least, I was free   in terms of content. Such intelligence, Hegel concludes,
bringing us   *Free!—and in the grasp of the Inquisition!*   finally to
the realm of *practical* spirit, is *the will.* Thus ends Hegel's account of theoretical spirit, seat of memory and witness to the infinitely repetitious interiorizing
movement of remembrance.

ERINNERUNG AND *GEDÄCHTNIS* IN THE *PHILOSOPHICAL PROPAEDEUTICS* OF 1808

Even though the "Philosophical Encyclopedia" of the so-called *Propaedeutics*
(4, 9–69) is from an editorial point of view (606–9) a highly problematic text,
it is tempting for a number of reasons to turn back to it at this point. First, a
number of transitions and developments in the later *Encyclopedia* are much
more clearly expressed here. Second, a number of significant variations emerge
in the earlier text, especially with regard to imagination (*Einbildungskraft*) and
memory (*Gedächtnis*). Third, and most generally, the character of Hegel's
doctrine of memory in terms of the threefold structure we have in Part One
called typographic, iconographic, and engrammatological here appears in its
clearest outlines.

   Let me begin with the third point, the crucial one for my own enterprise.
When we take a rather more distant, less sharply focused look at the Hegelian
system as we find it   *I have said, that I minutely remember the details of*
the chamber—yet I am sadly forgetful on topics of deep moment; and here
there was no system, no keeping, in the fantastic display, to take hold upon the
memory   in the *Propaedeutics,* its contours stand out in bold relief. The
discussions of feeling (*das Gefühl:* 4, 43: E, §§399–408) and intuition (*die*
Anschauung: cited in the *Propaedeutics* as the first topic of *Erinnerung,* 4, 44;
E, §§446–50), betray the fact that feeling, sensation, and intuition in the

system are conceived *typographically*. All are forms of affection, affection by stuff, pure contingency, and hence violence and violation. The essential mediation of *antitypia* is what Hegel calls representation, *die Vorstellung* (4, 43–53). In the *Propaedeutics*, as in the *Encyclopedia*, the essential powers of representation are interiorizing remembrance, imagination, and memory. Taken together, as representation, these powers prove to be *iconographic*. True, section 143 of the earlier work explicitly denies that the interiorized representation of *Erinnerung* is "a comparison of two individual intuitions" (46). "The *self-sameness* that I recognize is on the one hand the identity of the *content* of the representation; on the other hand I recognize in my current intuition *my own* identity with myself; or I remember *myself* in that representation (*erinnere mich in ihr*]." Nevertheless, the discussion of "subsumption" in the very next section is classically iconographic: "In interiorizing remembrance the image of a past intuition or representation is summoned by a present one, an intuition or representation that was the *same* [*die* nämliche *war*] as the present one." The long and difficult discussion of preservation and connection in the *Encyclopedia* will not have been in vain: *Vorstellung* is iconography. Finally, at some point (and the point shifts between imagination in the *Encyclopedia* and memory in the *Propaedeutics*) the iconography of representation is bound to become *engrammatology*, an explicit reflection on the semiotic character of memory and reminiscence. The first words of "C. *Das Gedächtnis*" in the *Propaedeutics* are: "The *sign* in general" (51). Hegel recognizes that *mnēmē* and Mnemosyne are invariably hypomnemic, that they involve signs and signals that must be scanned, gleaned, or read. Thus the "situation" of Hegel's principal treatise on language, speech, writing, and reading is a situation on the frontier of remembrance and memory, in the domain of productive memory, imagination, or reproductive memory; that situation is so far from being accidental that we must see it as the culmination of a tradition—the end of the book and the verge of writing.

In what ways does the *Propaedeutics* depart significantly from the later system, and what difficulties in our reading of the *Encyclopedia* does it help to resolve? The "Science of Spirit," Part Three of the *Propaedeutics,* comprises and compresses what the *Encyclopedia* will distinguish as "Anthropology" and "Psychology." The most immediate expression of this compression is the fact that in the earlier work (but compare Hegel's 1820 *Philosophy of Right*, §4 [7, 48]) *feeling,* rather than intuition, constitutes the first moment in the hierarchy of transition that is "intelligence." The function of representation is clearly marked: its three moments (interiorizing remembrance, imagination, and memory) are to grant *Gefühl* an object, transforming fleeting feeling into the stable content of something felt (§134; 4, 43–44):

> Only in representation does one have an *object.* The stages of representation are as follows: 1) intelligence *remembers* [or *interiorizes* itself: *sich erinnert*] by generally separating itself from the content of the feeling; 2) intelligence *imagines* [or *informs* in itself: *sich* einbildet] this content, retaining it without its object, summoning it forth and connecting it freely from out of itself; 3) intelligence takes from the

content its immediate significance and gives it another significance and connection in *memory*.

Yet the distribution of tasks within these three moments of intelligence is not identical in the earlier and later systems. The most intriguing shift, one to which Derrida has already drawn our attention (M, 101 n. 6/87 n. 15), is the location in the *Propaedeutics* of much of the discussion concerning language and signs in *memory* rather than in imagination. Yet one can see why the "summoning" and "connecting" of contents (in imagination) will eventually involve language as much as the "taking" and "giving" of meaning and connection (in memory).

A second, less noticeable shift involves elusive *Erinnerung* itself—the "motor" of the system in all its transitions, everywhere and nowhere at once. In the *Propaedeutics* the major rubrics are feeling, representation, and thinking. The moments of the second, as we have just seen, are remembrance, imagination, and memory. However, when Hegel comes to outline the contents of *Erinnerung*, placing the numbers 1, 2 and 3 before its essential moments (see §§135, 138, and 143), he identifies them as:

1. intuition
2. representation
3. interiorizing remembrance

The first two correspond to the two initial *major* rubrics in the *Encyclopedia's* hierarchy of transition, the second rubric, "representation," being the parent rubric of *Erinnerung* in the mature system; the third, remembrance, occupies the place that the *Encyclopedia* will reserve for thinking, *Denken*. In the *Propaedeutics* the moment of remembrance is both the first moment of representation and the third moment of itself. *Erinnerung* is thus the onset and the culmination of transition, the double-alpha and double-omega of the system.

The liberation of intuition from its space and time to a space-time interior in and intrinsic to intelligence is in the *Propaedeutics* (§§136–42) discussed in far greater detail. Hegel's references to the Kantian forms of intuition make the stakes of that liberation far more perspicuous here than in the *Encyclopedia*. That it is a liberation from imprisonment becomes clear in a parenthetical remark to section 137: "Things are imprisoned by this determinateness in time and space; they are imprisoned by one another according to their determinations; they are in the universal dungeon." Remembrance as representation will sever the cincture of their particularity (*Bande ihrer Einzelheit:* §142) and release them, not to the outside, but to a more profound interiority, the perfectly unobstructed vista   *With how vast a triumph—with how vivid a delight—with how much of all that is ethereal in hope did I feel, as she bent . . . that delicious vista by slow degrees expanding before me, down whose long gorgeous, and all untrodden path, I might at length pass onward to the goal of a wisdom too divinely precious not to be forbidden!*   of pure self-presence. Although the shaft dark as night does not gape in the *Propaedeutics* (the "universal dungeon" is a misnomer inasmuch as universality is precisely what things that are locked in space and time lack), there is one moment (§140) when we see it begin to yawn:

> The intuition, transposed to the *ego*, is not merely image; it becomes *representation in general*. It is not simply that the intuition taken up into interiority perfectly corresponds with the immediate intuition; rather, the intuition is emancipated from its context in space and time, removed from it. It is an existence [*Dasein*] that is *sublated* [aufgehobenes], that is to say, as much *nonexistent* [nichtseiendes] as *preserved* [aufbewahrtes].

Of the major variation in the two treatments of *Einbildungskraft* I will say nothing here, except to note that when Hegel excises a large chunk of imagination it will have to be filled by material from *Gedächtnis*. What Hegel eliminates, and later transposes from "Psychology" to "Anthropology" (see E, §404ff.   *My memory flew back (oh, with what intensity of regret!)*   ), are three astonishing paragraphs, equal to anything in Kant's *Anthropology*, on dreams   *I revelled in recollections*   and visions, somnambulism, madness   *Now, then, did my spirit fully and freely burn*   and delusion. A tangle of profuse images   *Sommer: Vergissmeinnicht*   will be cleared from the text in order to make room for the discussion of language and signs. That it is *Bilder* that will have to be cleared away, "stripped off" and subtracted rather than sublated, is no accident. For memory sacrifices and assassinates images for the sake of words. Nowhere in the tradition is the move from iconography to engrammatology so stark in its violence: "The image is slayed [*ertötet*], and the word stands in for [*vertritt*] the image" (§159; 4, 52). Predictably, it is the spoken word that performs the iconoclastic act   *(what marvel that I shudder while I write?)*   and dashes the disordered images   *I stirred not—but gazed upon the apparition. There was a mad disorder in my thoughts—a tumult unappeasable*   of the sensuous world of space and time (§159; 4, 52): "Speech is the slaying of the sensuous world in its immediate existence, the becoming sublated of that world to an existence that is a clarion call   *And now slowly opened the eyes of the figure which stood before me*   reverberating in all representational creatures." Iconolastic speech is thus an aggravated typography, a kind of superlative *hypertyposis*, which one might contrast to Kantian *hypotyposis*.[14]

Can we now, if only as a moment of relief, remember sufficient of what has gone before to attempt something like an overview of both Hegelian systems of *Erinnerung* and *Gedächtnis*? And can we combine with such an overview an attempt at interrogation?

In Hegel's distinction between *Erinnerung* and *Gedächtnis* we confront a memento of the traditional distinction between activity and passivity, even though *Gedächtnis* is always on the verge of active thought. Also in perfect conformity with the tradition is Hegel's privileging of activity over passivity, interiority over exteriority, self-presence over alien objectivity, freedom over both accident and constraint, necessity over contingency. Yet passivity continues to mar *Gedächtnis:* all the purgings of an ever-active interiorization cannot wipe away the stain of sensuousness, the mark of dependence, the blows of typography that—however crucial they may be—offend the spirit. *Erinnerung* exceeds *Gedächtnis* as such. It is omnipresent in dialectic as the very movement in which all other functions, faculties, and activities of spirit are but particular gestures, including the gesture of egress. It is by virtue of the vagabondage of interiorizing remembrance in the hierarchy of transition that memory can be the transition to thought. *Erinnerung* as such however remains dark. Plato's aviary and Augustine's spacious fields, theater, and thesaurus of memory have become a pit where every trace testifies to loss and not recuperated presence; to an absolute past and not a present; to a granitic and *cryptic* presupposition and not a concrete proof; to a cavernous gap and not a spheric seed; to unannealed difference and

The fearful difference quickly increased   not to identity. In Hegel's *Erinnerung* we find but the barest trace of the sensuous engram, the *typos,* as such. To scatter that trace Hegel posits the sign in reproductive memory or imagination—not in internalizing remembrance but in a faculty he would rescue from the pit and its pendulum and transfer to the perdurant pyramid. Mausoleum of meaning. Metronome of eternity. Yet the rescue and the transfer remain suspect inasmuch as memory reverts to *Erinnerung,* as indeed thought itself does. The sign, word, and name—the sources of universality and the resources of reason itself—are after all *found,* just as an image or a sensation are found, inscribed in stone or ululating in the throat. The inscribing instrument and the throat itself are verges of pyramidal signs. Does Hegel actually enter the shaft of such signs, the pit of the pyramid itself? Does he descend into its depth and risk losing himself in the receding origins of interiority and of language? Or does he not hesitate on the rim of the shaft of remembrance, on the brink of the pit of the sign, suffering there a kind of vertigo   *"Death," I said, "any death but that of the pit!" Fool! Might I not have known that* into the pit *it was the object of the burning iron to urge me?*   that makes him "shrink back" (as Heidegger says of other thinkers in different yet not unrelated contexts) and grasp at a logic that *seems* firmly rooted, confident all the while that he has already made the descent, that he is now truly present to the deepest strata of experience? How very odd it would be if Hegel failed to remember the verge as such, the verge of remembrance, which is the permanent topic and typical tool of his thought. Yet how *could* Hegel lose himself, how *could* he let go, if the concept (*Begriff/ begreifen*) has its grip on   *An outstretched arm caught my own as I fell, fainting, into the abyss*   or is itself somehow gripped by the superficies of language and memory, so that dialectic can surrender everything but its determinate object, its grip? Hegel's thought remains a matter of the grasp, of production and technique—mechanical dialectic *mining* the depths rather than freely exploring them without a thought to reserves. His is the philosophy of the granitic presupposition, all seed ensconced in the protective husk and hull of the absolute. It does not peer patiently down the shaft, much less overcome all prohibitions and inhibitions and descend into it. And what it does not condescend to see it cannot remember. "It does not *see* the foundationless play [*le sans-fond de jeu*] on which (the) history (of meaning) is erected."[15]

Yet a cautionary word is called for. Hegel gives a name to thinking memory and a local habitation. To *Erinnerung* he gives an image, one over which he hardly has free disposition, an image he cannot slay with words. What in fact constrains Hegel to introduce into his system *diesen nächtlichen Schacht?* The only possible answer is that Hegel responds to the call of the blackness of darkness. True, he does not swoon; he equips himself with lights. He is wont to forget the image by transmogrifying it into an icon owned by the ego. Yet the simple, ineluctable happenstance of his having found the image, or of its having found him in the course of the writing or lecturing, preserves the element of *Empfindung* that Hegel would otherwise suppress. And why should we object that he merely preserves the element *unconsciously,* preserves it in his *text,* as long as the shaft comes to gape, as long as Hegel's hearers and readers come to stumble onto the very verge of it? To interiorize something that remains obstinately outside and resists all incorporation—contingency, adversity, language, the past—is to remain subject to perpetual egress. *Erinnerung* requires, and is, *Entäusserung.* It is—dare we say it?—dialectical. "Dialectical" in the sense indicated negatively by Merleau-Ponty when he says that dialectical truth, as truth "in act," ceases to be such as soon as it "separates itself from its becoming, or forgets it, or relegates it to the past."[16]

When we remember carefully enough we are displaced from all centers, removed from all interiors. When it is truly reminiscent and not merely recollective or appropriative, Hegelian dialectic is *ecstatic,* no matter what centripetal plans Hegel himself may have had for it. The eccentric, ecstatic dialectic of *Erinnerung/Entäusserung* comes into play more dramatically in Hegel's *Phenomenology of Spirit* than in either the *Encyclopedia* or the *Propaedeutics,* however, so that this chapter will come to a close only after it ushers in *the deep and dark tarn at my feet closed sullenly and silently over the fragments of* a brief examination of the beginning and the end of Hegel's *Phenomenology.*

ER-INNERUNG IN THE *PHENOMENOLOGY OF SPIRIT*

It may seem preposterous to turn now to the last chapter of Hegel's *Phenomenology of Spirit,* as though all the preceding chapters posed no problems for me and I were prepared to finish reading the book before I began—with a flourish of absolute self-assurance. *Das absolute Wissen,* "Absolute Knowing," *is* the title of the last chapter. Yet anyone who has taken pains to follow any of the earlier stages in the phenomenology of spirit knows that absolute knowing is never a matter of being cocksure. Hegel ends his book not with a flourish but with a sober, if not somber, reflection on interiorizing remembrance. He does not fail to remember the travail of the phenomenologist who tries to recollect the experience of consciousness and the protracted historical development of spirit. He does not fail to remember that each new phase of that experience and that history has as its herald negation and inversion—the insight that what we thought we knew is not true, or at least that it is not the whole story, an insight that each time we have it turns us upside down. It is as though one can only *verge on* the true, measuring absolute knowing against absolute commencement, presupposition, and ignorance.

Before turning to the final chapter I shall refer briefly to the Introduction, where the method and goal of phenomenology are treated. Here Hegel   *A cadaverousness of complexion; an eye large, liquid, and luminous beyond comparison.* . . . *The now ghastly pallor of the skin, and the now miraculous lustre of the eye*   designates the phenomenological science of the experience of consciousness as "self-accomplishing skepticism." The theme of skepticism dominates the entire Introduction. Yet one must distinguish among at least three kinds of skepticism.

First, there is a thoroughly unschooled and timid sort of skepticism that despairs of ever bridging the gap between consciousness and the absolute, the latter understood as the things in themselves as they are essentially. Viewing knowledge as an implement or a medium that invariably distorts whatever it touches or mediates, such skepticism is unmanned by its fear of error—which, Hegel says, is actually fear of the truth. Such fear must be overcome if philosophy is to get underway at all. Sufficient to overcome such timorous skepticism is the fortitude Hegel invokes in his famous opening remarks in 1817 to his Berlin students, to wit, "*courage in the truth, belief in the power of spirit.*"

Second, there is a kind of skepticism, identified as a specific moment in the history of thought and in the experience of consciousness, that has a good deal of history and experience behind it and has already attained to the dimension of self-consciousness. Such skeptical self-consciousness entertains no illusions about knowledge as an "implement" or "medium" inadequate to the absolute. It comprehends the necessity of dialectic. Yet it is "*absolute dialectical restlessness,*" and its self-consciousness is but "a purely accidental confusion, the vertigo [*Schwindel*] of a perpetually self-generating disorder" (PG, 156–57). Consciousness of self here finds itself enmeshed in contradictions; it is at once its own master and its own slave. Such skepticism sees double, is itself a duplicate consciousness. And it is unhappy.

Historical skepticism is much more reminiscent of the self-accomplishing skepticism of phenomenology—the third kind—than is hesitant, pusillanimous skepticism, precisely because of the role interiorizing remembrance plays in both. Although Hegel's account of Hume in his *Lectures on the History of Philosophy* (20, 275ff.) is perfunctory, the detailed and sympathetic treatment of Sextus Empiricus there (19, 367ff.) reflects Hegel's own passion for self-accomplishing skepticism—and for remembrance—in the *Phenomenology*. He describes classical skepticism's surrender of objectivity and truth, its sacrifice of all stable content, as "complete remembrance" (*die vollkommene Erinnerung*) and as "internalization" (*die Innerlichmachung: 19,* 404). Complete interiority is the abyss of self-consciousness, infinite subjectivity as infinite abstraction, crying for the concreteness of the Christian revolution. Yet the parallel is too close for comfort: the disappearance of all objective content, the resulting "confusion" when all meaning begins to move, stoic indifference or ataraxia poised on the brink of absolute listlessness, and even anorexia   *The writer spoke of acute bodily illness—of a mental disorder which oppressed him—and of an earnest desire to see me . . . with a view of attempting . . . some alleviation of his malady*   all seem as much a part of phenomenological as of historical skepticism.

It is especially difficult *for us* to make the transition from historical to self-accomplishing skepticism, since skepticism in the form of *suspicion* is the hallmark of our own frazzled age—even if we should want to smile good-naturedly on Jean-Paul Sartre's insistence that "human reality" is "by nature an unhappy consciousness with no possibility of surpassing its unhappy state."[17] Yet the fate of every effort to read Hegel's *Phenomenology* depends on one's trying to make the transition, or trying to remember one's already having done so. Phenomenology of spirit, as science of the experience of consciousness, is the presentation (*Darstellung*) of knowledge that comes to appear (*des erscheinenden Wissens*). It retraces the way taken by "natural consciousness," which advances toward "true knowledge" through various stations. These stations constitute the sequence of consciousness' own configurations or shapes (*Gestalten*). Phenomenological presentation is a way of doubt, even desperation, inasmuch as the natural consciousness whose path it is retracing experiences again and again the untruth of appearing knowledge; yet the phenomenological observer knows that this is the route consciousness must take if it is to assume the form of science. Such phenomenological presentation, secure in the truth of the essential untruth of appearing knowledge, is "self-accomplishing skepticism." *Self-accomplishing* means that skepticism, impelled by determinate negation, which is always a *result* and which always produces a *new object* for testing, progresses to a point where the necessity of its passage and of all the sundry stations is granted. At that point it is no longer necessary for knowledge to go out beyond itself. At that point, presumably, natural consciousness and phenomenological consciousness will have coalesced. Before it arrives at that point consciousness is torn out of itself and dies a death; indeed, many deaths. It remains unsatisfied with its progress to this or that station, is ill-at-ease with all constraint and restriction, impatient to surpass all limitation. "Hence, consciousness suffers from a violence that spoils its own limited satisfaction, and this violence stems from consciousness itself" (PG, 69). While consciousness is caught up in such violence or turbulence, anxiety in the face of truth may return, struggling to retain the object that is about to evanesce. Nothing quells such anxiety, not even the inertia of thoughtlessness—"the thought troubles thoughtlessness, and its restlessness disturbs the inertia." The turmoil of dialectic proceeds unabated.

What has remembrance to do with such skepticism? The phenomenologist observes and records the stations of the experience of consciousness, then presents them, re-presents or recapitulates them, as it were. The very first stage of such observation and presentation, "Sensuous Certainty," may serve as an example.

Sensations seem to be immediately certain to consciousness. Consciousness simply *finds* itself in *Empfindungen* and among the objects that press upon it here and now. (We know that this typographic starting point will not vanish altogether from Hegel's mature system.) Yet when natural consciousness looks at this certainty more closely, putting it into words, it becomes intimate with the fact that such certainty is mediated: the sensations are certain through me, as I am (somewhat) certain through them. Consciousness now suffers its first inversion. A new object emerges as the embodiment of the true, one that requires us to take up the theme of perception and the "thing" as such. The movement of inversion, the commencement of dialectic, does not require philosophical lucubration or even a great deal of phenomenological scrutiny. Hegel insists that consciousness *naturally* experiences the thrust of negation as soon as it expresses itself about sensuous certainty. What then is the phenomenologist for? Hegel replies:

> It becomes clear that the dialectic of sensuous certainty is nothing other than the simple history of its movement or of its experience. . . . Hence, natural consciousness itself always advances to this result, to what is true in sensuous certainty, and makes it a part of its experience. However, natural consciousness always forgets the result straightway and begins the movement all over again. (PG, 86–87)

As historian of the experience of consciousness, the phenomenologist possesses an essentially *reminiscent* and *ruminative* consciousness. He or she is possessed of a kind of double consciousness, one that sees itself seeing and *remembers* its having done so. It is this retentive consciousness that Hegel defines as self-accomplishing skepticism. Phenomenological consciousness remains mindful of the "for us" of things, of the movement of inversion that constitutes experience. Yet unlike the fainthearted, halting skeptic, the phenomenologist remains mindful also of the emergence of altered forms of the true, of new objects for consciousness. By virtue of his or her ability to retain and recapitulate in detail the dialectic of experience, the phenomenologist is a kind of therapist, curing the amnesias of natural consciousness. To undertake a cure of natural consciousness, the phenomenologist must let it undergo its inversions, accepting each exhibited result—the fruit of determinate negation—as relevant. Yet at every crucial point in the cure he or she must exercise the authority that is always vested in the one who sees and has seen, that is, the one who has reached the place   *The vault in which we placed it (and which had been so long unopened that our torches, half smothered in its oppressive atmosphere, gave us little opportunity for investigation) was small, damp, and entirely without means of admission for light*   where semblance and exteriority fall away, "where appearance is the same as essence" (PG, 75). The phenomenologist is the monster of memory who *shows* and *presents*. And the only thing that can prevent effortless ascent into absolute dogmatism is the readiness of the phenomenologist to *remember*. Relentlessly. Monumentally.

How are we to conceive of the point where skepticism is accomplished, where remembrance becomes absolute knowing, where appearance equals essence and itinerary becomes system, where all the stations will have been

visited and all the configurations of consciousness contemplated? Is it a point
of imperturbable calm and perfect sanity, untroubled by haunting recollections
of pain and turmoil? The sweet contentment of oblivion—Stuttgart Heaven—
would be, not self-accomplishing skepticism (note that the participle is present,
not past) but perfect nihilism, as Nietzsche describes it in a note jotted down in
the autumn of 1887 entitled "The complete nihilist":

> The nihilist's eye . . . is unfaithful to its memories—it lets them drop, lose their
> leaves. It does not prevent their fading to that corpselike pallor which debility
> drapes over what is distant and past. And what the nihilist neglects to do for
> himself he neglects to do for mankind's entire past—he lets it drop.[18]

Absolute knowing must therefore be something else, something more akin to
remembrance than forgetfulness. What *remains* of reminiscent absolute knowing? What remains *after* absolute knowing remembers? Absolute?

Absolute. The dictionary says: loosened, absolved, free—that is, free from
interference, connection, relation, comparison, and dependence. The *Oxford
English Dictionary* cites James F. Ferrier's *Institutes of Metaphysic,* published
twenty-five years after Hegel's death, as follows: "Whatever can be known (or
conceived) out of relation, that is to say, without any correlative being necessarily known (or conceived) along with it, is the known Absolute." Yet is the
"known Absolute" what Hegel means by "absolute knowing"? Absolutely not.
For absolute knowing is the *nexus* of all known or conceived relations, the never
fully realized totality of dependencies, comparisons, connections, and interfer-
ences that make up the experience of consciousness and the history of spirit. The
key words in Hegel's final chapter all suggest such interference and mutual
dependence: *die Entäusserung des Selbstbewusstseins,* the need, on the one
hand, for self-consciousness to go outside itself for its objects, the need that
appears as the culmination of *Erinnerung* in the mature system; *die Nichtigkeit
des Gegenstandes,* the experience that, on the other hand, without a consciousness to apprehend and comprehend it, the object is nothing; and *die Bewegung
des Selbsts,* the realization that it is neither boundless fascination with objects
outside nor total captivation by my identity inside that defines spirit, but the
ceaseless and no doubt violent movement between these two poles of experience.

In his final chapter, after discussing the identity of substance and subject,
Hegel defines absolute knowing as "the final configuration [or shape: *Gestalt*]
of spirit" (PG, 556). Absolute knowing is the configuration in which content
and form coalesce and perdure as *Begriff,* the actual grasp of the concept. The
appearance of spirit, grasped conceptually, is accomplished science. Had Hegel
wished to end his book with a lordly gesture, he would have stopped here. He
did not. He could not. He had just   *In the manner of my friend I was at
once struck with an incoherence—an inconsistency*   defined science as
"spirit . . . *appearing* to consciousness." Hegel himself   *His voice . . .
that leaden, self-balanced, and perfectly modulated guttural utterance*
emphasizes the present participle *erscheinend* and reintroduces a distinction
where all had seemed firmly grasped identity. Spirit *appearing* to conscious-

ness? *Whose* consciousness? *Appearing?* When? Where? And how is it with "spirit"?

The third moment of the final chapter (PG, 557) begins with the concession that absolute knowing does not *exist* until it appears "in time and actuality." It comes to exist at the point where experience itself becomes the proper object of and for consciousness; that is, the point where experience is recognized as substance and substance is understood as spirit's becoming what it is in itself. Substance, recognized as the experience of spirit's coming to be, is "the circle that goes back into itself, presupposing its beginning and attaining it only in the end" ‖: PG, 559 :‖. At the point where Hegel contemplates the closure of the circle he introduces the word *Erinnerung*, inasmuch as end and beginning are joined in remembrance. He writes:

> Because its [that is, spirit's] perfection consists in *knowing* perfectly well what it is, knowing its substance, such knowing is its *going into itself* [Insichgehen], in which spirit abandons its existence and commits its shape [*Gestalt*] to remembrance. With its going into itself, spirit sinks into the night of its self-consciousness, but its vanished existence is preserved in that night; and its surpassed existence—the prior one, but now born anew from knowledge—is the new existence, a new world and a new shape of spirit. (PG, 563–64)

The preserving night into which self-consciousness sinks will not be unfamiliar to us. The shape of consciousness is now a shade: the word *Gestalt* is redolent of ghostly shapes and shades (recall the apelike *gespenstische Gestalt* of Mahler's *Das Lied von der Erde*). Vanished from existence, self-consciousness is nevertheless preserved. Where? Hegel describes the existence of spirit in space and time as passage through "a gallery of images" (PG, 563). These images—if we remember ahead to the *Encyclopedia*—will have been removed from the roughhewn pit and eventually set up in the exhibition hall; the pyramid in which self-consciousness is preserved will have been reconstructed in the workshop or *apotheca* of a museum. Such surpassed existence may therefore not be genuinely ecstatic or eccentric, in spite of our desire earlier to have it so, inasmuch as it remains within walls that are always familiar and reassuring. Spirit's existence is said to be consummated— although it is destined for nothing else than a "new" existence—when spirit commits its shape to interiorizing remembrance, *Erinnerung*. It is high time we took a closer look at this word, the crucial sign/symbol of Hegelian philosophy.

Erinnerung possesses four structural parts, corresponding to its four syllables: *Er-in(n)-er-ung*. *Er-*: a verbal prefix meaning to initiate a process that will bring something about. *In-*: a preposition *in*dicating that something *in*habits or *in*heres or dwells *in*side or with*in* an *in*terior. This little preposition, which apparently cannot be defined without overt or covert reference to itself, as though *in* were itself the absolute presupposition of all preposition, is the heart of the word *Erinnerung*. It lies at the core of Hegel's own etymological interpretation of remembrance. While discussing Platonic *anamnēsis* in his lectures on the history of philosophy (19, 44), Hegel appeals to the pristine sense of *Erinnerung* as *Sich-innerlich-machen*, "to make oneself interior," and as *Insichgehen*, the word that appears in the final pages of the *Phenomenology*, "to go into oneself." He calls such active interiorization the "profoundly thoughtful sense of the word," inasmuch as it locates the universality that cognition seeks within a conscious spiritual interior. *Er-:* now indicating the comparative form, or perhaps a pseudocomparative form, since the adjective *innere* has no simple form. By this reading, *Er-inner(e)-ung* has but three parts, and conforms to a quite general pattern, verbal-adjectival-nominal, as in *Ent-schuldig-ung*. In English too the words *inner* and *interior* are both comparative in form, meaning "more or further inward," "situated more within." A suggestion of ineluctable process, one that never quits the comparative for the superlative: interior, yet never utterly intimate, never innermost, so that what appears to be absolute—altogether "in"—never escapes comparison and relation with-"out." Finally, *-ung:* the nominalization of the verb, naming (as one of the names of reproductive memory) the process of intensified interiorization.

The verb in question is *sich erinnern an etwas:* to make oneself (for the verb is *reflexive*) interior, *more* interior—

by going out to something else—

inasmuch as the preposition *an* takes the accusative and expresses motion toward. Although it is true that especially in the age of Goethe and Hegel the syntax of the verb is in flux, occasionally not reflexive and often taking the genitive or dative rather than the accusative, the reference to something with-"out" is constant.

On the last page of the *Phenomenology* (although not only there: see PG, 524), Hegel hyphenates the noun, writing it as *Er-Innerung*, in order to stress that all the icons in the gallery traversed by spirit   *his very ancient family had been noted, time out of mind, for a peculiar sensibility of temperament, displaying itself, through long ages, in many works of exalted art*   are now recognized as being spirit's own productions. They portray what spirit *in itself* is eternally, but which it has come to know *for itself* only through its sojourn in time. In the project of remembrance, spirit must begin afresh and educate itself all over again, without prejudice or advantage, "as though all that had gone before were lost to it, and as though it had learned nothing from the experience of earlier spirits" (PG, 564). In the Preface (PG, 11), Hegel depicts the moment at which extraneous preoccupation with results, conclusions, and generalities *ends* and thinking *begins* not as remembrance but as a self-forgetting; like Lucinde giving herself over to Julius' mouth and ardor, or

Julius surrendering to the snowscape of Lucinde's breasts and the tropics of Lucinde's thighs, the phenomenologist remembers when to give, live and let live, forget: *in ihr [der Sache] zu verweilen und sich in ihr zu vergessen, . . . sich ihr [hingeben].*[19] Yet any given avatar of spirit *does* possess an advantage over its predecessors: it now begins its education "at a higher level." Remembrance preserves (*aufbewahrt*) as though in a mineshaft or cavern the experience of spirit's forebears. Thus preserving, remembrance is ever the (more) interior, *das Innre,* "indeed the higher form of substance." "Higher" of course means "ever deeper," and depth is measured by the ever-expanding breadth of (exterior, though not extrinsic) experience. Spirit's interiority perdures in the comparative form and does not beguile itself with superlatives. We would also have to write it as *Erinn-Er-ung* if we wanted to do justice to dialectic. Spirit never escapes   *He was enchained by certain superstitious impressions in regard to the dwelling which he tenanted, and whence, for many years, he had never ventured forth*   from the gallery of images. If its existence in that gallery is not ecstatic, it is nonetheless uncanny.

The founding of that gallery is mysterious, and so is each image contained in it. Each remembered portrait, each family likeness, and each dawning recognition testify to spirit's submersion in time, submission to what at least *appears* to be outside itself, and subjection to the task of remembrance. *Erinn-Er-ung* is itself an *Entäuss-Er-ung:* to *go* farther inside implies that spirit *is* farther outside; or, if the words "inside" and "outside" no longer make sense, we must at least say that spirit remains in the presence-absence of its unequal icons. It is no consolation if what spirit remembers proves to be its own handiwork, an icon from its own studio workshop. For it is precisely the newly established identity and ascription that make the quondam estrangement all the more terrifying. In the last lines of the *Phenomenology of Spirit* Hegel   *His countenance was, as usual, cadaverously wan—but, moreover, there was a species of mad hilarity in his eyes—an evidently restrained hysteria in his whole demeanor*   employs two words to describe the science of knowing that appears in history: *Erinnerung,* interiorizing remembrance, and *Schädelstätte,* the place, not of the workshop, but of the skull, Golgotha.

Viewed from the point of view of contingent existence, the organization of spirit's realm is *history;* from the point of view of its conceptualized and actually grasped structure, such organization is the *science* of knowing-that-appears. History and science together constitute "the remembrance and the Golgotha of absolute spirit." The conjunction *and* is crucial in both phrases. For if spirit comes to grasp itself as becoming, and if its comprehension is not abstract and bloodless, then it must remember that it has not always grasped; the goal exceeded its reach for aeons of time and for each well-preserved avatar of spirit; it was anxious and afraid and unhappy, its life was one of restlessness and turmoil; and all of this was necessary. Why?

As long as history and science remain two "sides" of the organization of spirit's realm, dialectic is stillborn and spirit grasps nothing of its life. If in its history spirit *did* suffer, then as science it *still does.* If time and spatial extension revert to the self of spirit, then even after the translation to inner space and time spirit will be ever on the verge of remembering the *when?* and *where?* of its own experience, while the *why?* will continue to elude it as a kind of malady that began long ago (or even now) to seal its fate   *We replaced and screwed down the lid*   intractably. Spirit not only *is* history (as science), but also *has* a history, and that is its destiny: in remembrance teleology and archeology coalesce.

Natural consciousness forgets straightway. Phenomenological consciousness, as absolute knowing, that is, knowing that must always begin again to compare, tries to remember. Is there some kind of exigency, breaching, resistance, primary repression, or trauma that would account for the tendency of natural consciousness to forget, a tendency that Hegel's *Phenomenology of Spirit*, as far as I can see, does not explain? If such resistance or repression be attributed to feelings of unpleasure, themselves emanating from an experience of profound anxiety, indeed, anxiety in the face of the truth, what is it in truth that has so traumatized consciousness? Perhaps Schelling seeks that primal injury when he speculates on the "will of the ground" in God's personal nature, a ground that is in him yet different from him, the resulting bifurcation issuing in "a source of sadness," a "veil of melancholy" that cloaks all nature and all life.[20] Perhaps Herman Melville is in chase of that vulnerability when in *Moby-Dick* he has Ahab say:

> To trail the genealogies of these high mortal miseries, carries us at last among the sourceless primogenitures of the gods; so that, in the face of all the glad, haymaking suns, and soft-cymballing, round harvest-moons, we must needs give in to this: that the gods themselves are not for ever glad. The ineffaceable, sad birthmark in the brow of man, is but the stamp of sorrow in the signers. (Chap. 106)

Perhaps Heidegger—to whom we shall now turn—points to the still undisclosed trauma in spirit's experience when he asks of Hegel near the conclusion of *Being and Time* (§82b): "How is spirit itself to be understood when we say that it is fitting for it to fall into . . . time?" Perhaps Jean Hyppolite points to it when he refers to Hegel's *Phenomenology* as the "true Oedipus tragedy of the entire human mind."[21] Finally, another friend of Hegel's student days, Hölderlin, surely touches the wound when he meditates on spirit's Golgotha, its having plunged into time, the matrix of memory and mortality:

> But the gods have enough
> Of their own immortality, and if
> The celestial ones need one thing
> It is heroes and men and
> Whatever else is mortal. For, since
> The most blessed of themselves feel nothing,
> It must be—if such a thing
> May be said—that in the names of the gods
> An Other feels for them;
> They need him. . . .[22]

And in the first draft of a poem called "Mnemosyne," a name Hegel preserves in and for productive memory:

> ... The celestial ones
> Cannot do everything. For mortals
> Alone attain to the abyss. So it turns
> with them. Long is
> The time. Yet the true
> Is what happens.[23]

To accompany Hegelian thought to the verge itself   *my brain reeled as I saw the mighty walls rushing asunder*   would mean to experience the bipolar dialectic of interiority/exteriority as irreparably shattered. The *in* of *Erinnerung* would designate, not the centripetal presencing of *spirit,* but the series of displacements we call *world.* We would be forced to retreat from the gallery and its workshop to the pyramid and the pit, recognizing our situation on the verge as one of radical exposure and vulnerability. For we are never truly so much *on* the verge as to be *in* it: we do not occupy it as a vantage point. We experience it as a withdrawal and a decentering, a ceaseless slipping back, or at best as a transition *without* hierarchy, in that very realm where we thought dwelled the lord of the demesne, the Substance who would be Subject.

The *in* or *innere* of *Erinnerung* as interiorization can no longer be appropriated and "held in" by the system, can no longer be *In-halt.* Determinate "content" is the stepping-stone for the transition from dialectical to speculative thought, from negative to positive rationality and affirmative science in Hegel's system (E, §82); yet precisely this *Inhalt,* as content or reserve, the property of thoughtful intelligence, is depleted by the incessant action of displacing *Erinnerung-Entäusserung.* Wherever the comparative form prevails, no capital accumulates, no stockpile looms. "Thus the dialectician is always one who 'commences.' "[24] Without appeal to the "higher level," without the ruse of greater profundity. Even the ostensible progress from images to words, pictures to names, *Erinnerung* to *Gedächtnis,* and memory to thought, proves to be illusory: to think is to recall the images conjured by the words and tracings of the text in perpetual irruption and interruption; to think is to scan the icons and idols invoked by the language that found Hegel. Not in order to secure them in fixating recollection but to plumb—gingerly—their cavernous depths. Without lights.

Our response to the call of the blackness of darkness is not exhausted by anything we have read or written here. We are still on the verge of discovering what each of these strains of Hegel's thought and strands of Hegel's style *I shall ever bear about me a memory of the many solemn hours I thus spent alone with the master of the House of*   did not forget to remember.

Of Having-Been

Heidegger and Nietzsche on the Time of Remembering and Forgetting

Heidegger reminds us that to think is to remember that our thinking has always already forgotten what it has been and what it might become. Preposterous. Perverse. Plausible. Persuasive. In this chapter I shall examine a handful of texts on having-been, remembrance, and oblivion: passages from *Being and Time* (1927) and from the Marburg lecture courses of the 1920s that are ancillary to it, including the lecture delivered on July 25, 1924, to the Marburg theologians, "The Concept of Time." After several brief references to Nietzsche's works, I shall then turn to the first part of Heidegger's 1951–52 lecture course, "What Calls for Thinking?"

Why insist on the verge of having-been? Because having-been, *Gewesenheit*, is the one "ecstasis" of human temporality that resists the usual name we assign it as one of the three dimensions of time: if the future, *Zukunft*, is the *primary* ecstasis, happily lending itself to existential-ontological analysis by designating "what is to come," *das Zu-künftige;* if the present, *Gegenwart*, is more dubious, inasmuch as it seduces us to an eminently inappropriate, merely theoretical dimension of our being-there; the past, *Vergangenheit*, has to be abjured altogether as precisely what human existence *never* is, not when alive, not even when dead. For the dimension we call the past, the dimension of which memory according to Aristotle *is*, Heidegger seeks and finds a new word: *Gewesenheit*, a nominalization of the past participle, the perfect participle *gewesen*, as in the expression *ich bin gewesen,* "I have been."

However, must one not push the question harder? Why does Heidegger disdain the imperfect? Why bypass the past in order to insist on having-been? Does having-been promise to rescue the essence, *Ge-Wesen*, of being? Would not the promise of such a rescue make Heidegger's thinking a mere reminiscence of Hegel, a monument or souvenir of spirit? If Heidegger indeed spurns the imperfect and imperfection of time, time and its "It was," does that not mean that—despite his long and intense preoccupation with Nietzsche—Nietzsche's experience of time remains closed to Heidegger? Such questions are no doubt precipitate. I shall try to read a bit before taking up any of them.[1]

FORGETTING BEING

The impasse we find ourselves in, writes Heidegger in the opening pages of *Being and Time,* arises from the same perplexity as that experienced by the Eleatic Stranger and Theaetetus in Plato's *Sophist.* "The designated question has today been forgotten ..." (SZ, 2). "Today," whether in 400 B.C. or 40 A.N. (*Anno Nietzscheani*), the question of the meaning of being *ist in Vergessenheit gekommen,* has come or gone into oblivion. The perfection of our tradition consists in its having always already forgotten its matutinal question. However, that the tradition has to be dismantled, destructured, and scrutinized betrays the fact that an incipient remembrance is now at work: Heidegger too can feel the anchor at the bottom of the sea break loose, can feel it rising, can almost imagine, though not yet fully descry, the distance traversed. A certain resistance is at work in Heidegger—or a counterresistance—opposing perfect oblivion. Later we will hear him call it *counterruinance.* He is not without need, not *unbedürftig;* complacency (*Bedürfnislosigkeit*) is the last thing one would attribute to him. Yet the legacy of the tradition is a prevailing and apparently all-consuming complacency. All access to the "original experiences" that once served as the sources of our philosophical concepts and categories appears to be effectively blocked. Phenomenology is the discipline that would shatter complacency and grant access to what-has-been.

Well, then, what has been? Above all else, to repeat, a forgetting and a complacency that are all but perfect. Against oblivion and all other creature-comforts Heidegger seeks in that questioning being he calls *Dasein* or "being-there" a provisional answer to the question as to how "something like being" can be understood—and that means remembered—at all. His discipline will require of him that he not foist any given concrete "idea" or "ideal" of existence onto being-there, that he let the structures of human existence show themselves of themselves as they are "at first and for the most part" in their undifferentiated state. His discipline will exact of him remembrance of how it is with being-there.

Well, then, how is it? He cites Augustine's treatise on memory (*Confessions,* X, 16; SZ, 43–44): "But what could be closer to me than I myself?" Augustine finds that the answer "must be": "Surely it is I who toil here, and that in which I toil is myself: I have been made to be stony soil for myself, and I am dripping with sweat." Heidegger does not pause to wonder at the fact that Augustine is tilling the stony soil of a cavern black as night; does not mention the perfervid search for a father or the massive monument to a mother. For Augustine is one of the proto-phenomenologists, the other being Aristotle. Their discipline should teach us to resist the tendency of what is at first and for the most part our quotidian lot: flight in the face of our ownmost being, escape into average dailiness, forgetting our being-there   *June 2, 1910 When the shadow of the sash appeared on the curtains it was between seven and eight o'clock and*

then I was in time again, hearing the watch   as such, the tendency to exist
inappropriately, *uneigentlich.*

Yet what if the discipline of remembrance and our resistance to the way in
which we at first and for the most part exist were themselves spawned by a
particular ideal of existence; what if discipline and resistance were the most
unsubtle and pervasive forms of conceptual *foisting,* rather than a phenomenological *letting come* to the fore? What if the very opposition of appropriate and
inappropriate modes of existence were the imposition of a familiar yet highly
particular possibility of an all-too-human existence; what if the Augustinian
legacy were itself precisely that proclivity to flight and forgetting? It would be
foolish to suppose that these doubts do not rise in and for Heidegger himself.
They loom not only after *Being and Time* but also precisely in the very construction of that text. And they are more than mere doubts: they are perhaps better
described as the *chasms* into which every reader of *Being and Time* has to
plummet, even though every page in that book has a number and we read
complacently from one numbered page to the next from the beginning to the
end.[2]

In section 13, "Exemplifying being-in in a founded mode: knowing the
world," which is the second half of the very brief chapter that tries to grasp the
global phenomenon of being-in-the-world before it is analyzed into its component parts, Heidegger says something strange about forgetting (SZ, 62). If
knowing the world is a founded (not a founding) mode of being-in-the-world,
being-there is always already "out there" in the world; it is never encapsulated
in an "inner sphere" (such as transcendental subjectivity) from which consciousness might sally forth and to which it would return with epistemic booty.
Even when I am merely brooding in my cavern or my cage I am no less
"outside" among beings in the world than when I am "grasping" something in
an originary way "inside." "Even the forgetting of something, in which every
ontological relating [*Seinsbeziehung*] to what was previously known is apparently extinguished, must be grasped *as a modification of the original being-in,*
and so in the same way must all deception and every error" (SZ, 62; the
emphasis is Heidegger's). One is reminded of the way in which Heidegger in his
logic courses always has recourse to the revelatory character of errors and
mistakes: only when we are deceived do we take the trouble of asking what is
true, what *is.* What Heidegger in *Being and Time* calls *ursprüngliches In-Sein,*
"original being-in," is thus the seedbed of all *originäres Erfassen,* "originary
grasping": all theoretical behavior and every thematizing, including that of
Heidegger's own fundamental ontology, springs from something that goes before, something prior, something forgotten and concealed, of which it is a mere
modification.[3] Which would mean, as we have just heard, but do not yet
comprehend, *that remembering is a modification of some sort of proto-
forgetting,* and not the other way around. While the discipline of phenomenology may pride itself on its originary grasping, our pristine state of oblivion is
actually closer to the origin of human being. Why must that be remembered,
remembered above all else? And *how* can it be remembered in a way that

remains true to the oblivion that characterizes *being-in* (which is not merely, not preeminently, *knowing*) the world?

I cannot summarize here the structure and movement of Heidegger's existential-ontological analysis of Dasein. *It was Grandfather's and when Father gave it to me he said, Quentin, I give you the mausoleum of all hope and desire. . . . I give it to you not that you may remember time, but that you might forget it now and then for a moment and not spend all your breath trying to conquer it.* I shall instead make four insertions into the *second* division of that analysis, "Dasein and Temporality," which is itself a reprise of the provisional analysis of quotidian Dasein in Division I. Division II inquires into the most appropriate possibility of human existence viewed originally and as a whole. My four insertions will be into (1) section 65, "Temporality as the ontological meaning of care"; (2) section 68, "The temporality of disclosedness in general," and especially (3) section 68b, on the temporalization of "disposition," *Befindlichkeit;* and (4) sections 73–76, on "having-been" as the historicity of Dasein.

(1) We remember that *time* is to be the horizon on which the meaning of anything resembling *being* will loom. What will claim our attention is the *temporalization* of a resolute openedness that somehow runs ahead, *eine vorlaufende Entschlossenheit;* an openedness that does not so much anticipate death as let it come to the fore in all its overwhelming power; and thus the temporalization of *anxiety,* which serves as the portal to that openedness; inasmuch as *ent-schlossen* means not tightfistedly resolute but opened up, unlocked. We have every right to be bemused about how such a *temporal* analysis will answer all the questions that have accumulated in sections 53, 58, and 64, concerning freedom unto death, willing to have a conscience, guilt, and steadfastness of self; and how it will resolve all the methodological quandaries portrayed so brilliantly, so ruthlessly, in sections 45, 61, and 63, on the possible being-a-whole of finite Dasein, on ontic attestation and ontological conceptuality, and on proper access and adequate originality. Heidegger girds his loins at the outset of section 65, "Temporality as the ontological meaning of care," by summoning the "unbroken discipline" of a "gaze" that will "understand existentially" the whole of Dasein's appropriate being without dispersion or distraction (SZ, 323): *Im unzerstreuten, existenzial verstehenden Blick. . . .* That unblinking *Blick* will of course have everything to do with the moment, *der Augenblick,* in which there-being twists free from oblivion and remembers who it is. Yet how will such a gaze differ from the insistent gape of theory? How will such a moment or blink of an eye differ from the traditional phenomenological presentification that in Heidegger's own view is egregiously inappropriate? What happens when we gird the loins? *Because no battle is ever won he said. They are not even fought. The field only reveals to man his own folly and despair, and victory is an illusion of philosophers and fools.*

Why do we do, or claim to be doing, *fundamental* ontology? What does it mean to remember being, to recover and reiterate a forgotten question?

In the present context of memory, reminiscence, and writing, I shall focus on the temporal ecstasis of having-been. And yet something *like* the perfect comes to the fore even in the structures of future and present. If the future "lets" Dasein "arrive at itself," if it is *Sich-auf-sich-zukommenlassen* (SZ, 325), such arrival involves an ecstatic recoil of Dasein back onto itself. The *zu* is a *zurück*. The name Heidegger chooses for the instant of ecstasis, the temporalizing of existence in each ecstasis as such, is *Entrückung*, "rapture." Its seizures are not unidirectional. They move not merely forward into some linear future but also backward. *Rücken* is in fact two words, with two apparently distinct origins: *der Rücken*, "the back," *zurück*, "behind" (the English word "ridge" is a member of its family); and the verb *rucken* (or *rücken*), "sudden movement" (the English verb "to rock" is apparently related to it). The "sudden movement" of ecstatic temporality is not simply a forward leap into future possibilities; it is simultaneously a movement back or recoil to that from which Dasein is thrown. The sudden rocking movement of time, *Ent-rückung*, is a kind of whiplash effect by which the wave of the future bends back over itself even as it tosses its crest ahead, as though the force behind it were too strong for simple progress. It is almost as though time itself confronted that *Trägheit* or neural inertia that is the cornerstone of Freud's "scientific psychology." The horizon formed by the raptures of temporality, the upon-which of projection, is thus both all-encompassing and inherently unstable; like Zarathustra's disconcerting avenue of the future it returns *as past* to the gateway "Moment." We can summarize Heidegger's account of the temporal ecstases simply by repeating that the futural *auf-sich-zu* is simultaneously an *auf-sich-zu-rück*, a rocking back or recoiling of time.

Whatever difficulties might attend the ecstatic analysis of future and present—and they are legion—let me focus on having-been in section 65. For here the forward-thrusting brunt of the wave, the resolute openedness that runs ahead (*die vorlaufende Entschlossenheit*) reverts to the force that is always already behind it. Heidegger writes: "The openedness that runs ahead understands Dasein in its essential being-guilty. Such understanding implies that being-guilty is taken over existingly by *being* the thrown ground of a nullity" (SZ, 325). Here he reminds us of the essential steps taken in section 58, "Understanding the call [of conscience], and guilt." That section is to demonstrate in a "self-interpretation" of our being-there and by means of "ontic-existentiell attestation" the possibility that Dasein can *be*—and can be *interpreted ontologically as*—a whole. The passage continues: "But taking over thrownness means that Dasein should properly *be* in the way *it already in each case was*. And taking over thrownness is possible only if futural Dasein can *be* its ownmost 'how it already in each case was'; that is, can *be* its 'having been' " (SZ, 325–26). In this mysterious passage, the imperfect *was* undergoes a metamorphosis to the perfect *having-been*. Where there was *was*, there shall have been the perfect, *Gewesen*. *Present* perfect, as the text goes on to specify: "Only to the extent that Dasein in general *is* as I *am* having-been [*ich bin-gewesen*] can it come to itself futurally by way of coming *back*. Properly futural Dasein *is* properly *having been*." *Eigentlich zukünftig* ist *das Dasein eigentlich* gewesen.

The English translation has to fracture the perfect tense, *ist gewesen*, into a third-person present indicative of *to be* and a perfect participle employing the auxiliary *to have*. Yet Heidegger is here struggling to express the *unity* of time's temporalizing in and as Dasein. There never was a time of being-there that was not simultaneously futural and always already perfect. More radically, futural time itself, *to* which I come, is that time *back* to which I have always already come. The order of implication, the transcendental order of a priori propositions of a priori temporal science (as Heidegger elsewhere calls fundamental ontology), is forcefully stated: only insofar as (*insofern*) Dasein is at all, and that means is at all as *present perfect*, can it precisely in its running ahead into an open future come (back) to itself. That Dasein *ist gewesen* means that it exists *zukünftig . . . zukommend . . . zurückkommend*. To arrive at a future necessitates coming back onto oneself, *auf sich selbst zurück*, as one has been. Yet at the very end of the passage Heidegger shifts the emphasis back to the future, as it were, in order to shore up his thesis concerning the inappropriateness of the present and the primacy of the (finite) future:

> Running ahead into one's uttermost and ownmost possibility is the understanding retrogression [*das verstehende Zurückkommen*] to one's ownmost having-been. Dasein can properly *be* having-been [again the translation shatters the German phrase "*gewesen* sein," in which the italicized *sein* is heard both as an auxiliary and as the infinitive] only insofar as it is futural. Having-been springs in a certain way from the future.

Here the order of implication is reversed: rather than understanding *zukommen* on the basis of a *zurückkommen*, futurity is now made the basis for all coming back. Whether the *entspringen* ("springing from") to which Heidegger appeals here involves the *degeneration* he will soon invoke (SZ, 334: "The ontological origin [*Ursprung*] of the being of Dasein is not 'slighter' than that which springs from it; rather, it towers over it in power from the start, and all 'springing from' in the field of ontology is degeneration") is an arresting question. Such "springing" will no doubt occupy us from now on. Yet we should be on guard about these leaps, springs, and somersaults in the direction of wonted origins. For something can be *original*, resisting all derivation from everything else, and nonetheless be *manifold*. The ontologist who insists on tracing everything back to some "primal ground" or *Urgrund* (SZ, 131) should not study the ways of time. For precisely here Heidegger will insist that all talk of "springing from" is out of place, that the ecstases are equally original, "equiprimordial," *gleichursprünglich* (SZ, 131, 329, 350). The upshot is that the "situation" of being-there can scarcely be demarcated by the language of "springing from," the language of derivation, order of implication, or transcendental condition of possibility. Yet no other language stands at Heidegger's disposal, so that the genesis of the perfect ecstasis can only be described as follows: "Having-been springs from the future in such a way that the future that has been [*die gewesene . . . Zukunft*] (better, that is having-been [*gewesende*]), releases the present from out of itself" (SZ, 326). The gravity of the crisis in the language is felt as soon as Heidegger tries to distinguish the vulgar understanding of temporality (which "springs from" an "inappropriate temporality" and which thus has "its own proper origin," *ihren eigenen Ursprung*) by saying that it is *abkünftig*, "derivative." What is the difference between *abgeleiteten*, *abkünftigen*, and *entsprungenen* temporalities or ecstases? How can the vulgar understanding of time have its proper origin in inappropriate temporality and yet be derivative "without gaps" (*lückenlos*) of "original and proper temporality"? If all "springing from" is degeneration in the field of ontology, and if the equiprimordiality of the temporal ecstases makes it impossible to derive one from the others, can fundamental ontology sustain the derivation of inappropriate from original temporality? The derivation of the time of forgetting from the time of remembering? And if the time of forgetting were, as Heidegger has suggested, the more original time? Or if, as seems more likely, the derivation of the two were radically undecidable? Would not Heidegger's derivation be as bewildering as the Demiurge's "generation" of quasi-immortals and mortals, or his iconography of the "moving image of eternity," that is, time? For Heidegger these questions stand and fall with the possibility of showing that resolute openedness and fully appropriate care as a whole are "but a modality of temporality" (SZ, 327). The *unity* of the structure of care would have to become visible in the temporalizing of temporality as such. As though (the time of) forgetting and remembering were *one*, and these two phenomena thoroughly indistinguishable. As though not only the particular *souvenir* were guarded by oblivion, as Merleau-Ponty says, but also remembering as such. As though remembrance could only be on the verge.

Again Heidegger emphasizes that neither future nor having-been can be understood in terms of the not-yet-present or no-longer-present of some thing   *Then I could hear the watch again*   at hand. And again the ecstatic analysis makes all derivation   *The hour began to strike* problematic. While the *primary* sense and direction of existentiality is futural, the primacy of having-been seems to be more primary than the primacy of the future: "Only because care is grounded [*gründet*] in having-been can Dasein, as the thrown being which it is, exist" (SZ, 328). Dasein "finds itself" always and only as thrown *factum*. Its disposition to be, *Befindlichkeit*, is always as having-been. "The primary existential sense of facticity lies in having-been." Thus the very *finitude* of original temporality rests on the odd alternating current of future and perfect, and not on the future alone. The futural *Auf-sich-zu* exists as "the impassable [*unüberholbare*] possibility of nullity" (SZ, 330). It exists ecstatically not so much as an opening but as closing, *schliessen*, inasmuch as the ability to be of Dasein is perfectly circumscribed. Such closing and closure will soon induce Heidegger to write of remembering and forgetting.

The impassable possibility is the futural possibility of being a nullity. How is the impassability of *death* related to the possibility that emerges from having-been—the ontological possibility of recovery, reprise, repetition? How do *Unüberholbarkeit* and *Wiederholbarkeit* abide one another? That is the question

I shall now take up, turning to section 68, "The temporality of disclosedness in general." Yet it is important to note that Heidegger's detailed analysis of the temporality of disclosedness itself constitutes a repetition (*Wiederholung*) of the existential analysis as a whole, indeed a "more original repetition"; the "tasks" implied in this more original repetition themselves "spring from" temporality itself. The title of section 66 is "The temporality of Dasein and the tasks springing from it that relate to a more original repetition of the existential analysis." At the end of that section (SZ, 333), Heidegger concedes that the repetition now to be undertaken may well itself need to be repeated in terms of *Sein* as such and in general; he will repeat this warning at the very end of the book (SZ, 437) as a way of introducing what was to have been Division III of Part One, "Time and Being." Even though the scope of such "repetitions" expands and dilates beyond all possibility of containment, I am interested here precisely in the closure-of-horizon that impassability (*Unüberholbarkeit*) implies: let me contract my own inquiry quite sharply, focusing solely on one aspect of repetition, namely, its relation to the *anxiety* in which we confront the possibility of nullity, the possibility of an oblivion that is total.

(2) In the opening paragraph of section 68 Heidegger stresses that the various "structural moments" of disclosedness—understanding, disposition, falling, and discourse—are to be traced back to "the *one* temporality" (SZ, 335), regardless of what he may have written earlier concerning the "proper origin" of inappropriate temporality (SZ, 326). Indeed, that one temporality shines through each of the structural moments (such as understanding, discussed first in 68a) with each of its ecstases. Thus the temporal elaboration of *Verstehen* involves not only the future ecstasis but also the present (both as the appropriate moment of vision and as inappropriate presentification) and having-been as well. The analysis of having-been, which we are now to pursue in the direction of anxiety, here introduces—in a way one could not have anticipated—phenomena normally associated with remembering and forgetting.

Having introduced *Gewesenheit* into the analysis of understanding, Heidegger writes:

> The proper coming-to-itself of the openedness that runs ahead is at the same time [*zumal*] a coming back to one's ownmost self, thrown into its individuation. This ecstasis [i.e., having-been] makes it possible for Dasein, resolutely open [*entschlossen*], to take over the being that it already is. In running ahead, Dasein *fetches* itself *again* [holt *sich das Dasein* wieder], carries itself *forward* into its ownmost ability to be [*in das eigenste Seinkönnen* vor]. (SZ, 339)

The inextricability of the temporal ecstases, especially of future and having-been, here manifests itself in the monstrous neologism and oxymoron *sich vor-wieder-holen*. Again something of the rocking motion of *Entrückung* or rapture comes into view. Repetition is not simply the taking up of something past. To fetch back again is to carry existence foward. This is the *appropriate* way for Dasein to be. However, Dasein usually *forgets* its having-been (shades of

Hegelian natural consciousness!) and, instead of conducting itself forward to its ownmost possibility to be, fritters its life away in a wholly inappropriate present. The passage continues:

> We call the proper *being* of having-been [*das eigentliche Gewesen-sein*] *repetition.* Yet inappropriate self-projection upon possibilities drawn from the things we take care of and presentify is possible only because Dasein *has forgotten* itself in its ownmost *thrown* ability to be [*dass sich das Dasein in seinem eigensten* geworfenen Seinkönnen vergessen hat].

The last phrase is of course ambiguous. Has Dasein forgotten itself inasmuch as it has neglected its ownmost, thrown being-able-to-be? Or has it forgotten itself precisely *in* that being thrown, in such a way that oblivion *is* precisely its *ownmost* way to be? To insist on such ambiguity would no doubt be perverse—the former sense is surely the one Heidegger would want us to glean from the phrase. Yet can we be altogether clear here about what forgetting and remembering might signify? If in section 13 Heidegger desired to subordinate forgetting to the global phenomenon of being-in, oblivion now seems to assume an uncanny preeminence:

> Such forgetting is not nothing, nor simply the lack of remembrance [*Fehlen von Erinnerung*]; rather, it is a proper, "positive," ecstatic mode of having-been. The ecstasis (rapture) of forgetting is characterized by a disengagement *in the face of* one's ownmost having-been, a disengagement that is closed off to itself. This occurs in such a way that the disengagement in the face of . . . ecstatically closes off that which it faces and thereby at one and the same time closes off itself.

In this passage—whose every phrase resists translation—the ecstatic analysis broaches a repetition of the analysis of anxiety. Forgetting is no mere lack of remembrance. It is an "own," *eigener,* a "positive," and even an "ecstatic" mode of having-been. This *doubling* of the perfect ecstasis of *Gewesenheit* into remembering and forgetting ought to give us pause: having-been, itself an ecstasis of temporality, has the further ecstatic modes of remembrance and oblivion. Heidegger focuses on the latter. He attaches to it the word *Entrückung,* which always and everywhere describes the instantaneous movement of temporalization as such; yet if there is "rapture," *Entrückung,* in oblivion, there is surely also "rupture," "evasion," *Ausrücken,* an abrupt turning away or—as I have rendered it here—*disengagement.* From what? *Ausrücken* ecstatically closes off, *verschliesst,* that which faces it, obfuscates its *Wovor* or projected horizon, and thereby occludes itself.

We should be astonished at this ecstatic closure. Virtually everywhere else in *Being and Time* and in the Marburg lecture courses *ecstasis* is taken to be the horizon of *disclosure,* the opening up of beings in general.[4] Whatever *appears* to close off proves to be a horizon, an *Umschluss* rather than a *Verschluss,* a frame of reference rather than a stockade or barricade. Why on this page (SZ, 339) do we have to trace a zigzag line from *verschliesst* ("closes off") to *"erschliesst"* ("discloses" in quotation marks) and back to *verschliesst* (see lines 15, 25, 30)? No doubt the closure and its obfuscated *Wovor* have to do with anxiety: the structure of the "in the face of which" (*Wovor*) is central to the analyses of anxiety in sections 40 and 68b, to which I shall soon turn. But only after completing the reading of section 68a. I broke off at the following point (SZ, 339): "*Oblivion* [Vergessenheit] as inappropriate having-been herewith relates to one's own thrown *being* [Sein]; it is the temporal sense of the manner of being [*Seinsart*] in accord with which at first and for the most part I have—*been.*" Once again, only a pun on the German *bin* and the English *been* seems to capture the perfect of the original: *zunächst und zumeist gewesen—* bin. I *am* having *been* (in my average everyday existence) *oblivious* of my own (thrown) being. No wonder the question of being has to be not so much repeated as fetched forward, and that the very sense of such a *question* will have to reawaken! Yet how reawaken, and from what, if oblivion is its *own, positive, ecstatic* mode of having-been? Oblivion seems to be the ground on which alone being can rise; yet if oblivion be perfect, how can anything rise? "And only on the basis [*auf dem Grunde*] of such forgetting can the presentification that takes care of things and readies itself for them *retain* [behalten] those beings unlike Dasein that we encounter in our environment. To such retaining there corresponds a not-retaining, which represents a 'forgetting' in the derivative sense."[5]

We can perhaps now understand why section 66, on the repetition of the existential analysis, closes by insisting that the being of Dasein "first receives its comprehensive ontological transparency in the horizon of the clarified being of beings unlike Dasein . . ." (SZ, 333). And why Heidegger's lecture courses immediately after *Being and Time* try to reinterpret the very first existentials— those relating to the beings that are "handy" (*zuhanden*) or "at hand" (*vorhanden*) around us. For both ways of taking up beings unlike Dasein appear to be rooted in oblivion. Section 68a concludes by emphasizing the *closure* and *oblivion* that infect perfect having-been, releasing from it a present that can only be a falling, an utterly inappropriate drifting, if not a foundering:

> Just as expectation is possible only on the basis of readiness [*Gewärtigen*], so is *remembering* [*die* Erinnerung] possible only on the basis of forgetting, *and not the other way around.* For in the mode of oblivion [*Vergessenheit*], having-been "discloses" ["*erschliesst*"] primarily the horizon into which [*in den hinein*] the Dasein that is lost in the "externality" of the things it takes care of can remember itself.

Here a classic model of the inside/outside opposition appears, qualified only by a set of "scare-quotes." Dasein is at first and for the most part lost, forlorn, and abandoned to the outside of an external, extrinsic, and superficial world, a world of things "unlike Dasein." Against such "*Äusserlichkeit*" Dasein will struggle to find a horizon *into which* it can *interiorize* itself: *sich erinnern kann.* Only the quotation marks rescue the passage from what would be total surrender to the ontotheology of the inward journey, the Hegelian voyage into interiority; the *raison d'être* of Heidegger's existential analysis of being-in-the-world, as the fundamental ontology of Dasein, hangs entirely on those scare-quotes. Or does the accusative *in den hinein* perhaps suggest that

Dasein can "interiorize" only by advancing into the world of its concerns in a new way? The problem then would be *how* this new way through oblivion would "disclose" itself, and *why* the scare-quotes about "disclosure" are needed. The passage—and with it section 68a—ends thus:

> Forgetting-presentifying readiness [vergessend-gegenwärtigende Gewärtigen] is a proper ecstatic unity. In accord with it, inappropriate understanding temporalizes with regard to its temporality. The unity of these ecstases closes off proper being-able-to-be; it is consequently the existential condition of the possiblity of vacillating occlusion [*Unentschlossenheit*]. Even though the inappropriate understanding that takes care of things is determined by the presentifying of what is taken care of, the temporalizing of understanding is nevertheless fulfilled primarily in the future.

Precisely how the future can rescue Dasein from the closure of an inappropriate present, itself oblivious to and cut off from the past; precisely how the perfect possibility of occlusion can be countered or resisted; precisely how *this* occlusion differs from the closure of horizon experienced in an *appropriate* confrontation with the *finite* future; precisely how the ecstatic unity of a disengagement in which we are exposed to everything that can be presentified can be broken, so that the oblivion that closes off our *proper* being will yield to a remembering, to a new and resolute advance through oblivion *out into* the world—none of this, to say the least, is clear. Rescue and remembrance seem *unlikely*.

(3) In section 68b Heidegger turns to the temporality of disposition or *Befindlichkeit*, "how we find ourselves to be." It may be worth noting that his reprise of the fundamental structural elements of being-in reverses the order in which they originally appeared: in Division I Heidegger discussed *Befindlichkeit* first (see §§29–30), presumably because mood is a more original and more comprehensive kind of disclosure than understanding. Why does the temporal reprise begin with the narrower form of disclosure, to wit, understanding? Has the tendency to theory and conceptual comprehension in Heidegger's ontological analysis engineered a reversal of priorities? An unthematized reversal, to be sure. However that may be, Heidegger reaffirms the "far more original" disclosure of the *thrownness* and *facticity* of Dasein in disposition, mood, or attunement (*Stimmung*). Precisely what these have to do with *time* is obscure. It is insufficient to say that they come and go in time, but neither can some sort of deduction or schematism derive dispositions and moods from the ecstases of time. However, the one demonstration that will have to succeed if the ontological analysis is to proceed at all is that of the difference between *fear* and *anxiety*. If anxiety is the *founding disposition* of existence, temporal analysis should once again be able to distinguish it from fear (as the provisional analysis did in §§30 and 40). And it should also be able to show us how the *closure* within oblivion of our appropriate ability-to-be is shattered—by the temporalizing of temporality itself and as such.

The very temporality of fear is inappropriate, inasmuch as it snags, forcing us to remain fixed on some present being that confronts and threatens us.

"Its [i.e., fear's] existential-temporal sense is constituted by a self-forgetting [*ein Sichvergessen*]: the confused disengagement [*Ausrücken*] in the face of one's own factical ability to be . . ." (SZ, 341). We may be surprised to see the existential structure of *forgetting* being introduced in the context of disposition, whereas earlier it seemed (quite plausibly) to pertain to *understanding*. Or will we allow references to the *totality* of the care-structure, the *global* phenomenon of being-in-the-world, and the *unity* and *equal originality* of the ecstases to allay our suspicions? At all events, Heidegger (342) cites Aristotle's reference to fear as *tarakhē*, something that oppresses and confuses us. Such oppression, *Gedrücktheit*, is a depression or dulling of the senses, a confusion that causes one to lose one's head and to forget. "Confusion is grounded in a forgetting." Oppression and confusion close off (*verschliessen*) Dasein's thrownness. Caught in a house ablaze, Dasein will lose its head and grab the handiest and most banal things, carrying them to safety. Its proper having-been is blocked in a confused presentifying. Fear is just another way of slamming the door in the face of what-has-been (26, 267). In anxiety, on the contrary, Dasein is brought back to its ownmost ability to be. That in the face of which and that about which Dasein is anxious are coextensive; they "cover" one another perfectly, and the being that "fulfills" the *Wovor* and *Worum* of anxiety is Dasein itself as being-in-the-world. Yet what is the *temporality* of this most phenomenological moment   *The quarter hour sounded. I stopped and listened to it until the chimes ceased*   in fundamental ontology? "Anxiety becomes anxious about naked Dasein, thrown into uncanniness. It brings us back to the pure 'that' of our ownmost, individualized thrownness. Such bringing back does not have the character of a disengaging forgetting; yet neither does it have the character of a remembering." Here Heidegger distances himself from any straightforward counterposing of oblivion and remembrance, outside and inside, alienation and recuperation. The analysis becomes considerably more intricate.

> However, just as little does anxiety already imply a taking over of existence into resolve by way of repetition [*eine wiederholende Übernahme der Existenz in den Entschluss*]. Rather, as opposed to that, anxiety brings us back to thrownness *as possible-repeatable*. And in this way it unveils *also* the possibility of an appropriate being able to be. Such being able, in repetition, with repetition as futural, must come back to the thrown "there." *The specific ecstatic mode of having-been, which constitutes the disposition of anxiety, brings us to confront repeatability.* (SZ, 343)

Vor die Wiederholbarkeit bringen: to bring face-to-face with or to cause to confront the recoverability or repeatability of having-been. This is the proper, appropriate relation of Dasein to its *Gewesenheit*. How does it temporalize? In a way that parallels and yet is opposed to forgetting. If *Vergessen* was earlier designated as a proper (*eigener*), "positive," ecstatic mode of having-been (SZ, 339, lines 11–12), *Wiederholbarkeit* is now attributed to the "specific" ecstatic mode of having-been, the mode of temporality that "constitutes" anxiety. How

does anxiety temporalize, anxiety   *And Father said That's sad too, peo-*
ple ... cannot even remember tomorrow what seemed dreadful today
instead of fear, anxiety enabling and opening up an appropriate relation to
having-been?

Anxiety temporalizes as a kind of *hold*, not on things, and not as *In-halt*,
but on one's insurmountable possibility both to be and not to be. Anxiety
temporalizes as a hold on the impassability (*Unüberholbarkeit*) of death. Anxiety temporalizes as recovery of what is forgotten in everyday preoccupations
and even in exceptional moments of fright—recovery of the utter nonrecover-
ability of Dasein in death. Yet the temporalization of anxiety, as the hold on
this slipperiest of all amalgams, *Wiederholbarkeit/Unüberholbarkeit*, will resist
phenomenological depiction. Indeed, a gap will open here (on page 344 of *Sein
und Zeit*) that the remainder of the book will persistently fail to bridge or close.
It is perhaps the deepest of those chasms Heidegger refers to in his Schelling
book (see note 2, above), those gullies into which every attentive reader must
plunge. Plummeting, falling without hold, the reader will perhaps experience
fear: limitless possibilities for distinguishing anxiety from fear, the appropriate
from the inappropriate, the ownmost from the alien, will hurtle confusedly by.
None of them will grant a hold. The attentive reader of *Being and Time* will
therefore experience something like animal fear in the gorge that threatens to
swallow SZ, 344.

Anxiety presumably temporalizes as a *hold* on the ecstasis of having-been, a
grip on the thrownness of factical Dasein. Such a hold *makes* anxiety *present*.
However, even though the appropriate *Gegenwart* of anxiety is *held*, "it still
does not of itself have the character of the moment [*Augenblick*] that temporalizes in resolve [*Entschluss*]." Rather:

> Anxiety only brings us into the mood of a *possible* resolve. Its presence [*Gegenwart*]
> holds the moment when anxiety itself alone is possible, holds the moment *poised for
> the leap*.

> Die Angst bringt nur in die Stimmung eines *möglichen* Entschlusses. Ihre Gegenwart
> hält den Augenblick, als welcher sie selbst und nur sie möglich ist, *auf dem Sprung*.

Anxiety induces a mood or attunement in which resolute openedness becomes
possible. In anxiety, the glance of an eye or moment of vision in which Dasein
confronts its mortality is possible, yet not actual. When does the eye truly see?
When does mortal vision penetrate into the open? When does the moment of
mortality lunge? When do mortals remember no longer to forget?

Anxiety arises from being-in-the-world as thrown being-unto-death. Yet
how does its rise   *And maybe when He says Rise the eyes will come
floating up too, out of the deep quiet and the sleep, to look on glory. And after a
while the flat irons would come floating up*   temporalize? "The future and
present of anxiety temporalize from an original having-been in the sense of a
bringing back to repeatability." And yet, as we have seen, having-been releases
both oblivion and resolute reprise. How then does temporalization release the
latter rather than the former; how in the thick of oblivion does it induce recov-

ery? How does ecstatic temporality achieve what no mere "choice" of "will" could ever achieve? Or does ecstatic analysis rest on a suppressed yet massive voluntarism and decisionism? At the top of SZ, 344 we heard that anxiety "only brings us into the mood of a *possible* resolve." Toward the bottom of the page, on the far side of the gorge we will never escape, we hear:

> But anxiety can properly arise only in a resolutely open Dasein.

> Eigentlich aber kann die Angst nur aufsteigen in einem entschlossenen Dasein.

Anxiety makes resolute openedness in the face of thrown being-toward-death possible; anxiety can properly arise however only in a Dasein that is already resolutely open. This is not in any obvious sense a hermeneutical circularity. Nor is it a mere ambiguity in the exposition. It is an indication of the happenstance that *anxiety does not temporalize,* or that it is *always only on the verge* of temporalizing. The analysis of ecstatic temporality will not support the binary opposition of appropriateness/inappropriateness upon which the whole of *Being and Time* is constructed.[6]

Heidegger's analysis terminates in a profusion and confusion of ecstases: "Although both modes of disposition, fear and anxiety, are grounded primarily in a *having-been,* their origin with a view to their own temporalizing in the totality of care differs in each case." How the *origin* of a temporalizing can differ from its *ground* is obscure. "Anxiety springs from [*entspringt*] the *future* of resolute openedness. . . ." Yet the future of a *possible* resolute openedness, as we have just seen, awaits the hold that anxiety alone can bring. Anxiety, for its part, will never spring from any future if it is not already poised to leap. The resolute openedness that runs ahead will be manacled by an infinite series of readinesses. And, at all events, is not all *Entspringen* in the field of ontological analysis degeneration? Heidegger will soon thematize this leaping-from (SZ, 347–48), but it will be difficult to see in it anything more than "a waxing oblivion" (SZ, 347, line 6 from the bottom).

The final irony: even if anxiety were able to temporalize, even if by keeping a stiff upper lip or an unlocked heart a resolutely open Dasein were able to influence time in its proper unfolding, the result might be less edifying than one might imagine. Almost equidistant between the impossible verges of SZ, 344, between anxiety-as-possible-resolve and resolve-as-possible-anxiety, appear the words *benommen, Benommenheit,* "dazed," "benumbed," "bedazzled," and their corresponding nominatives. They are used to describe the peculiar power of anxiety to shock human beings into remembrance of their proper uncanniness. Heidegger writes:

> In the peculiar temporality of anxiety, by which anxiety is grounded originally in having-been, with future and present temporalizing out of it alone, we find confirmation of the possibility of the might [*Mächtigkeit*] that makes the mood of anxiety so exceptional. In it Dasein is fully brought back to its naked uncanniness and is benumbed by it [*zurückgenommen . . . benommen*]. Yet this benumbing not

only *takes* Dasein back out of its *"worldly"* possibilities but also *gives* it at the same time the possibility of an *appropriate* ability to be.

The dual action of *Benommenheit* takes *(nimmt)* and gives *(gibt)* Dasein its possibilities. Its emphatic *giving (gibt, geben)* mimics the very granting of time and being. *Ereignis* dazzles. Yet who is *Ereignis* for? For beings *like Dasein*. Which beings are icons of Dasein? Two years after the publication of *Being and Time*, in a lecture course in which Heidegger struggles to distinguish human comportment from animal behavior, he rigorously organizes his vocabulary in such a way as to segregate animality from humanity. Whereas human beings adopt a stance toward beings, *taking hold* of them and of themselves, *sich verhalten*, dumb animals are dazed, bedazzled, and *benumbed* by their world: *benommen*. (Descartes would have said *hébété*, thinking of dullwitted creatures whose pineal glands are corrugated and rutted with traces.) What in *Being and Time* constitutes the most human of all human possibilities, namely, *Benommenheit*, a *giving* taking, is two years later predicated of a deprived and impoverished *animality*. Anxiety, crouching on the verge, utterly motionless, poised to spring, is both daimon and beast.[7]

(4) I have by no means exhausted the problem of memory and oblivion in *Being and Time*. One would have to continue to confront "the power of *forgetting*" (SZ, 345), the "waxing oblivion" (SZ, 347, 354) of inappropriate dailiness, tracing the *experience* of such oblivion in Heidegger's writings both before and after (but also within) *Being and Time*.

Both the public lecture of 1924, "The Concept of Time," and the Freiburg lecture course of 1921–22, "Introduction to Phenomenological Research," betray the need to recover what has been, to resist a kind of *ruination* in which the past sinks into oblivion. "History can wind up in oblivion; the tradition we bring to expression can break off" (61, 42). Recovery is therefore everything: " *'Wiederholung'*: everything hangs on its meaning. Philosophy is a fundamental manner [*ein Grundwie*] of life itself, so that in each case it properly fetches life back [*wieder-holt*], guiding it back from its decline. This guiding back, as radical research, is life" (61, 80). Recovery alone produces phenomenological evidence, repeats the "primal decision" by which alone life escapes the play of masks, the carnival in which it is caught up; recovery alone resists the plunge (*ruina, Ruinanz*) by means of a counterthrust, a movement *within* life yet *counter to* life's own tendency to fall. Heidegger calls such recovery *counterruinance* (61, 80, 88, and 153–54). *Counterruinance* would be Heidegger's first word for the overcoming of complacency and oblivion, his first word for commemorative thinking.

Furthermore, we would have to follow the transformations of the temporal analysis in chapter five of Division II of *Being and Time*. For "Temporality and historicity" brings Heidegger to confront our "being toward the beginning," our *birth* as well as our *death*, and the stretch of time between commencement and end (SZ, 373). The "emphatic function" of the past in the historical happening that is Dasein would also take us to those passages that try to transform what is bygone (*Vergangenes*) into what—as the perfect of being-there, *Da-Gewesenes*—still has an impact on the present and future (SZ, 379–80). Here we might be able to rescue from oblivion the earlier and more modest forms of those brave words in *Being and Time* (SZ, 384–85) that so disturb us: readiness for anxiety—forgetting for a moment that without a covert voluntarism anxiety can never temporalize—becomes readiness to assume a national identity and destiny (*Geschick*), to invoke the historic happening of a people (*Geschehen . . . des Volkes*), thus transforming finitude and even impotence (*Ohnmacht*) into a surfeit of power (*Übermacht*). The fundamental ontologist goes to join his "generation" in "communication" and "struggle," chooses his "hero," elects a murky liberation of "struggling successors" and an equally murky "fidelity to what is recoverable." No doubt Heidegger means it all *spiritually* rather than nationalistically, politically, or brachial-brutally. In which case it would simply be a matter of remembering what *spirit* has meant.[8]

Remembering spirit, animality, and anxiety in the context of Heidegger's account of historicity in *Being and Time,* let me now expand my fourth point of insertion and focus on one intriguing passage in which the fundamental ontologist goes to confront Nietzsche. At the end of section 76, which relates the scholarly discipline of history to the happening of Dasein in time, Heidegger recollects in some detail Nietzsche's *On the Use and Disadvantage of History for Life,* the second of his *Untimely Meditations.*[9]

REMEMBERING TIME

"The beginning of his [Nietzsche's second *Untimely*] *Meditation* allows us to surmise that he understood more than he was telling." Thus Heidegger on Nietzsche's *On the Use and Disadvantage of History for Life.* By the "beginning" he presumably means not Nietzsche's Preface but the following:

> Observe the grazing herd as they pass before you: they do not know what yesterday and today are; they frisk, feed, doze, digest, and frolic again; they do so from morning to night and from day to day, taciturn about their pleasures and unpleasures; that is to say, fettered to the peg of the moment [*Augenblick*] and therefore never melancholy or world-weary. This is a hard thing for a man to see, because he boasts of his humanity in the face of the animal and yet gazes jealously upon the latter's happiness—for that alone is what he wants: like the animal neither to be world-weary nor to live with pain; and yet he wants it in vain, because he does not want to be like an animal. (*1,* 248–49)

Does not want to be *benumbed* like an animal. Heidegger too insists that human beings are separated from animals by an abyss of essence, *ein Wesensabgrund.* Animals are more like stones than human beings, "life" to the contrary notwithstanding. Nietzsche too apparently knows that animals are in a daze as they graze; although he always knows more than he tells, always "ruminates." The bucolic fable he is now spinning has a dazzling quality about it; one is stunned by the beauty of the prose and the gentle, lowing irony. Nietzsche's bovine "beginning" continues as follows:

> The human being once asked the animal, "Why don't you tell me of your happiness, why do you only gaze at me?" The animal did its best to answer and to say, "That's because I always forget straightway what I wanted to say," but then it forgot this answer too and was silent: so that the human being stood in amazement.

The cow would make a bad phenomenologist, but a marvelous writer. It is caught up in what Hegel, Husserl, and perhaps Heidegger too would call "the natural attitude." Yet while Nietzsche's human being is capable of bracketing the natural attitude, thus indicating his or her solidarity with the human beings of Hegel, Husserl, and Heidegger, that is not what causes amazement, not at the moment when we are confronting the herd:

> Yet he is also struck by amazement at himself, at his being unable to learn how to forget, at his clinging always and everywhere to the past: no matter how far or fast he travels, he drags his chain with him. It is a wonder: the moment, whoosh! it's here, whoosh! it's gone, previously a nothing, afterwards a nothing; yet it returns as a ghost to disturb the tranquillity of a later moment. Again and again a sheet is separated from the roll of time, slips out, flutters on—and suddenly flits back into a man's lap. Then the man says, "I remember" ["*ich erinnere mich*"], and is envious of the animal, which forgets instantly and sees each moment actually die, sinking back into fog and night, extinguished forever.

Humanity is thus a child at play, whose aeon is interrupted by the dominion of time. The genesis of time fascinates Nietzsche, not only in this early text but also in the second treatise of his *On the Genealogy of Morals*, to which I shall turn at the end of the chapter. For the moment, let me return to the playing child   *not knowing any better*   and the fatal interruption:

> And yet his play will have to be disturbed: well before his time [*nur zu zeitig*] the child is summoned out of oblivion. Then he learns to understand the phrase "it was," an incantation that unleashes struggle, suffering, and weariness upon man, in order to remind him of what his existence at bottom is—an imperfect that is never to be brought to completion.

We recognize the *es war,* the "it was" of time, as that which will present the gravest obstacle to the will and spur the thought of eternal return.[10] Here the *imperfect* introduces time to the living creature, and the resulting interruption is humankind. To be sure, Nietzsche also introduces the perfect. Yet the perfect is by no means an improvement on the imperfect. It is instead, as we shall now witness, a monument to human finitude, an "uninterrupted has-been" that is sealed by death: "If death finally brings the oblivion for which we yearn, it also at the same time embezzles both the present [*Gegenwart*] and existence [*Dasein*]; it thereby sets the seal on the insight that existence is but an uninterrupted has-been [*ein ununterbrochenes Gewesensein*], a thing that thrives on denying, devouring, and contradicting itself."

So much for the "beginning" that   *I went to the dresser and took up the watch, with the face still down. I tapped the crystal on the corner of the dresser and caught the fragments of glass in my hand and put them into the ashtray and twisted the hands off and put them in the tray. The watch ticked on. I turned the face up, the blank dial with the little wheels clicking and clicking behind it, not knowing any better* knows more than it lets on. Perhaps its duplicity hinges on the ambiguity of *Gewesenheit, Gewesensein:* for Heidegger, not only in *Being and Time* but also in his later writings, "having-been" rescues Dasein from an absolute past and secures for it a significant future; for Nietzsche, "has-been" suggests the irremediably bygone, which *Beyond Good and Evil* (numbers 269 and 277) calls *das ewige leidige* "Zu spät!"—the wretched, eternal "too late!" (5, 223, 229). The resonance of Nietzsche's "perfect" is thus eminently imperfect. (Heidegger comes closer to that resonance in his 1924 lecture, *Der Begriff der Zeit*, than he does in *Being and Time*—as we shall see later in the chapter. The lecture emphasizes *I passed a jeweler's window but I looked away in time* the time of Dasein as an experience of the *Vorbei!*—"gone," "over and done with," "bygone.")

Nevertheless, Heidegger's use of the Nietzschean text in *Being and Time* is a far more "constructive" one than readers could have anticipated: it attempts to integrate the second *Untimely Meditation* into the essential structures of existential-ontological analysis. Because oblivion and remembrance are crucial to fundamental ontology, we might well examine the entire passage (SZ, 396–97), interrupting only in order to comment briefly. Heidegger begins: "The possibility that the discipline of history can in general be either of 'use' or a 'disadvantage' 'for life' is grounded in the fact that life is historical [*geschichtlich*] in the root of its being; so that, as factically existing, it has always already decided for appropriate or inappropriate historicity." We might well wonder what sort of "decision" life has in each case already made (noting the perfect), inasmuch as the temporalization of the shift from (inappropriate) fear to (appropriate) anxiety is precisely what the ecstatic analysis could *not* demonstrate. In section 9 Heidegger introduces the structures of appropriateness and inappropriateness by insisting that Dasein "has always already somehow decided [*hat sich schon immer irgendwie entschieden*] in what way Dasein in each case is mine" (SZ, 42). We need only remind ourselves of the familiar and much-discussed circular "grounding" of *Uneigentlichkeit* in *Eigentlichkeit* (SZ, 189, 259) and vice-versa (SZ, 130, 179, 317). If the primal, perfect decision has been in favor of oblivion, how will appropriateness spring from it? Further, if the factical ideal of self-possession and assumption of responsibility for one's own living and dying is itself a *traditional* ontotheological ideal, what can prevent the thorough contamination of the appropriate by the inappropriate? Would one not have to be always *on the verge* of a decision? And is this not the tendency of Heidegger's own later thought on the *Ent-scheid*, which treats decision not as a matter of the individual or collective *will* but as a kind of watershed (cf. *Wasserscheide*) where one willy-nilly finds oneself?

A second region of problems awaits us in Heidegger's reference here to "life," the use or disadvantage "for life." Life is little in evidence in *Being and*

Time. Whatever problems Jaspers's philosophy of existence may have had, it seemed to rescue fundamental ontology from the *embarras* of philosphy of life. "Life is a mode of being all its own, even though it is accessible for essential reasons only in Dasein," namely, by way of a "privative interpretation" (SZ, 50, 58, 194). Yet the meaning of "just-plain-life," which is neither a being at hand nor Dasein, hounds the analysis of Dasein from beginning to end. Each time human embodiment   *There was a clock, high up in the sun, and I thought about how, when you don't want to do a thing, your body will try to trick you into doing it, sort of unawares. I could feel the muscles in the back of my neck, and then I could hear my watch ticking away in my pocket and after a while I had all the other sounds shut away*   is discussed (although it is discussed rarely and from a vast height: see SZ, 56, 97, 346) or an effort is made to distinguish animal "demise" from human "dying" (see SZ, 240–41, 316) it is always with reluctance and discomfiture. Indeed, the problem of "life" and "nature" lies at the heart of the ontological problem of the "reality of the external world"; and even before the splendid but failed effort of 1929–1930 Heidegger knows that "the fundamental ontological analysis of 'life' cannot be inserted subsequently [*nachträglich*]" into analysis of Dasein "as a substructure [*Unterbau*]" (SZ, 210). All of which induces us to ask the following question of Heidegger's interpretation of Nietzsche's "*Leben*": By what right can Heidegger claim that "life" itself is *geschichtlich,* historical in the profound sense? (See also 29/30, 386.) Is he not merely assuming that by *Leben* Nietzsche here means human life, the life of Dasein? As long as the question of life, "just-plain-life," is not raised explicitly, Heidegger has no basis for his reading of *Vom Nutzen und Nachteil.* Nevertheless, I continue to cite:

> Nietzsche recognizes what is essential concerning the "Use and Disadvantage of History for Life," in the second of his *Untimely Meditations* (1874), and says it unequivocally and compellingly. He distinguishes three kinds of historical discipline; the monumental, the antiquarian, and the critical, without however explicitly demonstrating the necessity of this trinity and the ground of its unity. *The threefold character of the discipline of history is prefigured in the historicity of Dasein.* Such historicity enables us to understand how the proper discipline of history must be the factically concrete unity of these three possibilities. Nietzsche's distribution is not contingent. The beginning of his *Meditation* allows us to surmise that he understood more than he was telling.

Heidegger does not explicitly cite the opening of the second section of Nietzsche's text (*1, 258*) in which Nietzsche sets up the threefold structure of the monumental, antiquarian, and critical, relating it expressly to the three ways in which history pertains to life. History belongs to the living as "acting and striving" (monumental), as "preserving and esteeming" (antiquarian), and as that which "suffers and is in need of liberation" (critical). Nietzsche's analysis of the monumental or memorable would conduct us to one of the first limnings of the thought of eternal return and also to Heidegger's emphasis on the being of the *possible* (*1, 260–61*). Nietzsche's analysis of the antiquar-

ian   *The place was full of ticking, like crickets in September grass, and I
could hear a big clock on the wall above his head.* *"I broke my watch"*
would conduct us to Heidegger's emphasis on the *preservation* of the work of
art in the third and final section of *Der Ursprung des Kunstwerkes* (1935), but
also to the sense of preservation in the very hold (*halten*) or keeping (*behalten*)
emphasized in fundamental ontology. Finally, Nietzsche's analysis of the critical would conduct us to Heidegger's *deconstructive* style of philosophizing:
when Nietzsche criticizes contemporary historiography for its attempts "to
adapt the past to timely trivialities" (*1*, 289), we sense what Heidegger will
soon call the "depresentification of what is today," *Entgegenwärtigung des
Heute.* Heidegger will affirm Nietzsche's avowal that "the genuine historian
must have the force to transform 'what everyone knows' into 'what is unheard
of' " (*1*, 294). It is even possible that Nietzsche's references to Hölderlin here
(*1*, 300) and in the notebooks (*7*, 680–81) will be instructive for Heidegger's
own uses of that poet, and plausible that Heidegger's lifelong sense of being a
"latecomer," a "late arrival," has much in common with this "untimely" meditation and its "eventide mood" (*1*, 303; 312). In the end, however, one must
wonder whether Heidegger was able to absorb the core of Nietzsche's account
of critical history: "momentary forgetting" (*1*, 305), "the art and the energy
that enables forgetting" (*1*, 330), quite beyond the compulsion to remember
and the addiction to *Wissenschaft,* surely do not inform Heidegger's own
project of fundamental ontology as a "science of being." In a moment we shall
turn to the second treatise of Nietzsche's *Genealogy of Morals,* where Nietzsche tells more about what he knows of forgetting and the genesis of time; for
the present we continue with Heidegger's adaptation of *The Use and Disadvantage of History for Life,* for that adaptation now turns explicitly to the question of *temporality.*

"As historical [*geschichtliches*], Dasein is possible only on the basis of
temporality. Temporality temporalizes in the ecstatic horizonal unity of its
raptures [*Entrückungen*]." One must interrupt in order to remind oneself that
precisely this account of the raptures of time is riddled with difficulties.
*There were about a dozen watches in the window, a dozen different hours and
each with the same assertive and contradictory assurance that mine had, without any hands at all. Contradicting one another. I could hear mine, ticking
away inside my pocket, even though nobody could see it, even though it could
tell nothing if anyone could.*   The putative primacy of the future, except
for the temporalization of anxiety, where having-been is primary; the ostensible equiprimordiality of all three ecstases; the rapture of the instant or ecstatic
moment as both horizon and rupture of horizon, as both overture and closure,
as both revelation and radical concealment alike—we have already rehearsed
these problems here and elsewhere.[11] The sole question now is whether the
Nietzschean modes. of historiography—"monumental," "antiquarian," and
"critical"—will aid our understanding of the ecstases of time. "Dasein exists as
properly futural in the resolutely open disclosure of a chosen possibility. Resolutely coming back to itself, it is by way of repetition open for the "monumen-

tal" possibilities of human existence. The historical discipline that springs from such historicity is 'monumental.' "

Whether resolutely open disclosure (*entschlossenes Erschliessen*) ever temporalizes we have good reason to doubt. Whether it temporalizes as heroism—as the "elevated procession of humanity through millennia" (*1, 259*)—might with good reason disconcert us. Whether for Nietzsche the "chosen possibility" is freedom unto death and nothing else we cannot yet say. It is worth noting, however, that that *possibility* is the crucial modality for both thinkers. Nietzsche writes:

> What good is it for one who lives in the present [*dem Gegenwärtigen*] to observe the monumental past, to be concerned with what is classic and rare in earlier ages? He will take from it encouragement that the magnificent things that once occurred there were *possible* at least once and therefore may well be possible again. He treads his path more confidently, because now the doubt that infected him in his hours of weakness—the doubt that he might be willing the impossible—has been soundly thwarted. (*1, 260*)

It is the possibility of a monumental history that now (*1, 261*) evokes one of Nietzsche's earliest formulations of his "thought of thoughts," eternal recurrence of the same. To think through that possibility as an eminently *mortal* possibility, as the closure of the ring of eternity, would take us to the heart of Heidegger's 1937 lecture course on eternal recurrence: the thought of downgoing. That thought in turn would take us back to *Being and Time*. While Nietzsche would be reluctant to assert that freedom unto death is *the* chosen possibility of human existence, he does employ the phrase himself (*10, 21*) and, more importantly, he devotes his every energy to the destruction of hinterworlds and subterfuges of all kinds. Add to this Pierre Klossowski's emphasis on eternal return as amnesia and anamnesis, and we are brought back to forgetting and remembering as the very possibility of mortality.[12]

No doubt the impassable possibility of mortality is the possibility on which we verge. Such verging would be what Nietzsche calls recurrence, *Wiederkehr;* Heidegger, recovery, reprise, recapitulation, or repetition, *Wiederholung.* However, what remains unclear is the Heideggerian sense of, and commitment to, *life,* which for Nietzsche is the ultimate horizon for any discussion of use and disadvantage. Not being unto death, but being unto life. (As if after Freud one could set them in simple opposition, outside of every economy, and beyond all contamination.) Nietzsche apparently opposes Heidegger by taking the present (*Gegenwart*) as the scene of life; yet for Nietzsche too much of the present is but the deformed and degenerate legacy of a forgotten past.   *Because Father said clocks slay time. He said time is dead as long as it is being clicked off by little wheels; only when the clock stops does time come to life.* "Critical" history is as much *Entgegenwärtigung* as *Gegenwart.* Nietzsche would therefore be sympathetic to Heidegger's analysis, perhaps because his untimely meditation informs Heidegger's own in *Being and Time*—which continues as follows:

As having-been [*gewesendes*], Dasein is made answerable to its thrownness. In the recapitulating appropriation of the possible, we find prefigured at the same time the possibility of an esteeming preserving of an existence that has been [*dagewesene Existenz*], an existence in which the possibility that is taken up has become manifest [*offenbar geworden*]. As monumental, proper history is thus "antiquarian."

The words "esteeming preserving," *verehrende Bewahrung*, are taken directly from Nietzsche's text (1, 258), indeed from that part in which Nietzsche lays out the tripartite structure of history, the part which I accused Heidegger of neglecting: Nietzsche attributes the antiquarian type of historical discipline to *dem Bewahrenden und Verehrenden*, "the preservers and esteemers." One cannot help suspecting, however, that Nietzsche, as a philologist and a "pupil of more ancient ages" (1, 247), is more relentlessly reproving of his colleagues and brothers, Melville's sub-sub-librarians, than is Heidegger: the piety of esteem and preservation is dearer to Heidegger than it is to Nietzsche, just as Heidegger will be harder on the active ones and strivers than Nietzsche will be. Heidegger writes:

> Dasein temporalizes in the unity of future and having-been as present. The present [*Gegenwart*] properly discloses, as the moment [*Augenblick*], what is today [*das Heute*]. If what is today is interpreted on the basis of the futural-recapitulative understanding of a possibility taken up from existence, proper history becomes the depresentification of what is today [*Entgegenwärtigung des Heute*]; that is to say, it becomes a painful release [*leidendes Sichlösen*] from the ruinous publicity of what is today [*von der verfallenden Öffentlichkeit des Heute*]. Monumental-antiquarian history, as the proper historical discipline, is necessarily a critique of the "present." Proper historicity is the fundament of the possible unity of the three kinds of historical discipline. But the *ground* of the fundament of proper history is *temporality* as the existential meaning of the being of care [*Seinssinn der Sorge*].

The "painful release" no doubt refers to Nietzsche's *dem Leidenden und der Befreiung Bedürftigen*, "the one who suffers and needs liberation." The need for such release and liberation has already been sketched out in the preceding section of *Being and Time*, where the word *Entgegenwärtigung* appears terminologically for the first time. In its inappropriate historicity, Dasein is dispersed and distracted in the present, oblivious of its destiny. "Ready for the next novelty, it has also already forgotten the old" (SZ, 391). As its public self, Dasein avoids choices, evades possibilities. It theorizes and speculates on "world history" by presentifying the past in terms of the trivialized present. "As opposed to this, the temporality of proper historicity, as the moment that runs ahead and recapitulates, is a *depresentification* of what is today and a weaning from the customary ways of the They." Yet the secret of such painful release is well-kept. What the moment or glance of an eye may be which grants insight once and for all into the finitude of Dasein remains as recalcitrant for Heidegger's temporal interpretation—his remembering time—as Nietzsche's doctrines concerning the "health of life" and a "culture" that would be "a new and improved *physis*" remain for his thought on will to power and eternal return (1, 331; 334).

Inasmuch as the three Nietzschean modes refer to history, the ecstasis of having-been embraces them all. Their tripartite structure bears no identifiable relation to the three temporal ecstases. Both the monumental and the critical modes have to do with the future and the present as well as with the past; the musty antiquarian has as much to do with an oblivious "today" as with a sentimentalized past. In short, these modes of history cannot be inserted into an account of ecstatic temporality; or at least if they are so inserted they will resolve none of the difficulties of that analysis. For the threefold ecstatic character of time continues to be bisected by the impossible line of *Eigentlichkeit/Uneigentlichkeit,* which is the organizing axis of Heidegger's fundamental ontology. How the preeminently inappropriate antiquarian mode would *temporalize* from the appropriate monumental-critical modes, or how the latter could *in time* have degenerated into the first, remains inexplicable. Once more we are tossed back onto the insoluble quandaries of the ecstatic analysis. The truncated temporalization of anxiety out of having-been and resolute openedness out of the future remains precisely that, truncated, throughout the fifth and sixth chapters of *Being and Time,* Division II. However informative Heidegger's reading of Nietzsche's second *Untimely Meditation* may be for Heidegger's own hermeneutic of history and his later "history of being," it does not help us to bridge the abysses   *in darkness in silence the bridge arching into silence darkness sleep the water peaceful and swift not good-bye*   of Heidegger's *magnum opus.*

MNEMOSYNE

It is surely no accident that in the lecture courses immediately following the publication of *Being and Time* Heidegger describes his project as "metaphysical remembering," *metaphysische Erinnerung* (26, 186). The thinking of being is *anamnēsis,* remembering back to the forgotten horizon of time. Time is the a priori condition of the possibility of something like being: as such it reposes beyond being, *epekeina tēs ousias.* Time is not merely the "earlier," the a priori of traditional metaphysics; it is "the earliest without qualification" (24, 401–5; 463–64; 26, 284). Hence one could depict Heidegger's thinking of the 1930s and 1940s as metaphysical remembrance, or "remembrance back into metaphysics."[13]

I shall nevertheless forego discussion of Heidegger's work during the 1930s and 1940s, and turn directly to a text from the early 1950s, *Was heisst Denken?* "What is it we call thinking, and what calls for our thinking?" Heidegger opens his 1951–52 lecture course, the first course he was permitted to teach after the Freiburg University Senate required him to retire, as follows (WhD? 1):

> We come to know what it means to think when we ourselves are thinking. If our attempt is to be successful, we must be ready to learn thinking.
>
> As soon as we allow ourselves to become involved in such learning we have admitted that we are not yet capable of thinking.

Yet man is called the being who can think, and rightly so. Man is the rational animal. Reason, *ratio,* evolves in thinking. Being the rational animal, man must be capable of thinking if he really wants to. Still, it may be that man wants to think, but cannot. Ultimately he wants too much when he wants to think, and so can do too little. Man can think in the sense that he possesses the possibility to do so. This possibility alone, however, is no guarantee to us that we are capable of thinking. For we are capable of doing only what we are inclined to do. And again, we truly incline toward something only when it in turn inclines toward us, toward our essential being, by appealing to our essential being as what holds us there. To hold genuinely means to heed protectively, for example, by letting a herd graze at pasture. What keeps us in our essential being holds us only so long, however, as we for our part keep holding on to what holds us. And we keep holding on to it by not letting it out of our memory. Memory is the gathering of thought. To what? To what holds us, in that we give it thought precisely because it remains what must be thought about. What is thought is the gift given in thinking-back, given because we incline toward it. Only when we are so inclined toward what itself is to be thought about, only then are we capable of thinking.

The grazing herd passing by at pasture returns from Nietzsche's text to haunt Heidegger's thinking. As a herd must be herded, heeded, and *held* from danger (*hüten/halten*), so our thoughts must be shepherded by and in memory. Memory, *Gedächtnis,* is the "gathering of thinking," *Versammlung des Denkens.* Such "holding," "keeping," or "retaining," *halten* and *be-halten,* proved to be particularly elusive for Heidegger's existential-ontological analysis of having-been. We will remind ourselves of these difficulties once again, as soon as we have glanced quickly through the remainder of the passage.

It is constructed on a series of word-associations, plays, and puns; yet nothing here is contingent, nothing has been left to chance. *Heissen* is of course the guiding play, for it means "to mean" as well as "command" and "call." Thinking, commemorative thinking, will have to do with a call or invitation. *Er hiess mich niedersetzen,* says Heinrich's father of the hospitable innkeeper in his dream. The call or invitation to which Heidegger refers is recollected later in the *Zuspruch,* "appeal" or "address," that "holds us in our essence." The call is a call to think, a call to learn thinking. Readiness to learn is as important to this project as readiness for anxiety was to fundamental ontology. And every bit as enigmatic. To be sure, thinking is a capacity, *Vermögen,* of human beings, the rational animals, as distinguished from the herd. Thinking is possible, *möglich,* for us; perhaps even like-ly, *mög-lich.* Thinking belikes us. We incline to it.[14]

What wrecks the playful relationship between possibility and likelihood is a certain willfulness, the very will to *be* the rational animal, a certain inflexibility and inability to respond—in a word, a voluntarism. Is it not easy, almost inevitable, to confuse resoluteness and decisiveness with inflexibility? As long as we resist the sense of *ent-schlossen* as unlocked, open, "resolutely opened," such confusion is indeed all that is "likely." Response to the *Zuspruch,* the claim, address, or appeal of what calls on us to think, cannot itself be rigid. A stiff upper lip belikes a thick head. And yet Heidegger here—

as earlier in the project of fundamental ontology—is driven, as it were, to be rigid in his opposition to that sheer dispersion and distraction, *Zerstreuung*, that he invariably associates with humanity's lapsing, falling, and ruination in the world. To the flux of dispersion he would contrapose containment, retention, and keepage—*halten, das Haltende*—a holding action that draws on the gathering power of memory. *Das Gedächtnis ist die Versammlung des Denkens.* No doubt the genitive is subjective as well as objective: it is thinking that does the gathering, not "us," and what it gathers is the to-be-thought, *das zu-Denkende.* Heidegger appeals to the language of gift-giving and bestowal to describe the gathering of thinking. We keep what holds us by not letting it slip into oblivion, by bestowing on it commemoration, *Andenken*, and recollective meditation, *Nachdenken.* Such bestowal is not an intuition of names after the manner of Hegel; it is not *Gedächtnis* as the transition to conceptual thinking. Holding, embracing, gathering, and bestowing or gift-giving are the graces of Mnemosyne.

Behalten, retaining, we remember, designates in section 68 of *Being and Time* the essential mystery of escape from perfect oblivion. If oblivion is an autochthonous, positive, ecstatic mode of having-been, it *must* be the ground of retention. Dasein retains the beings it takes care of in its daily routine on the basis of a thoroughgoing forgetting of its own being as possible, *möglich*. It belikes Dasein, at first and for the most part, to forget.[15] What bedevils fundamental ontology, and so intrigues us, is the relation between oblivious retention—the proclivity of Dasein to forget its own being precisely by clinging to beings unlike itself—and that memorious hold, *halten,* that prevents utter dispersion. Anxiety is said to temporalize as a hold on the present (*Gegenwart*) as having-been (*Gewesenheit*). It holds the moment poised, poised for a decisive leap. Resolve is that impossible poise verging on openedness. Yet if neither anxiety nor resolve can temporalize as such, if the analysis of ecstatic temporality cannot show how *halten* springs from *behalten*, one can understand why Heidegger's later thinking about thinking continues to ponder this tenuous hold. *Was uns in unserem Wesen hält, hält uns jedoch nur so lange, als wir selber von uns her das Haltende be-halten.* "What holds us in our essential unfolding, however, holds us only as long as we ourselves for our part retain [or be-hold] what does the holding." As in *Being and Time*, neither the holding nor the retaining yields up the secret of its essential unfolding.

What holds us, as what is most to be pondered, and what we dare not let slip from memory, is the fact, according to Heidegger, "*that we are not yet thinking*" (WhD? 2). What we must hold onto is the diversion or slipping away, the withdrawal   *The half-hour went. Then the chimes ceased and died away*   of what calls for thinking. Withdrawal   *While I was eating I heard a clock strike the hour. But then I suppose it takes at least one hour to lose time in, who has been longer than history getting into the mechanical progression of it*   is what we must own, is what propriates us, claims us: withdrawal is the propriative event of our time, *Entzug ist Ereignis* (WhD? 5). Preposterous. Perverse. Plausible. Persuasive.

Mortals are those who point toward the self-withdrawal of that which grants time and being, those who are caught in the wake   *The chimes began again, the half hour. I stood in the belly of my shadow and listened to the strokes spaced and tranquil* . . . , *with that quality of autumn always in bells even in the month of brides*   of withdrawal, tugged along by it. *Zeigen, ziehen, Zug, Entzug, Zeichen:* human being is a sign undeciphered. No en-grammatology can glean and decode the traces of this withdrawal. The undeci-phered sign appears in Hölderlin's drafts to that hymn entitled (or having as *one* of its titles) *Mnemosyne.* Heidegger takes some trouble to note that the German translation of the word as *das Gedächtnis* is problematic; on the model of *die Erkenntnis,* he suggests adoption of the feminine gender, *"die Gedächtnis."* Preserving the feminine gender of the word will allow him to retain the mythic and poetic valences of memory, reminiscent of a time *"Hear them swimming, sister? I wouldn't mind doing that myself."* If I had time. When I have time   when *logos* and *mythos* said "the selfsame":

> Mnemosyne, daughter of Sky and Earth, bride of Zeus, in nine nights becomes the Mother of the Muses. Play and music, dance and poetry are of the womb of Mnemosyne, Dame Memory. It is plain that the word means something else than merely the psychologically demonstrable ability to retain [*behalten*] a mental repre-sentation of something that is past. Memory [*Gedächtnis*] thinks back to [*denkt an*] what is thought [*das Gedachte*]. Yet as the name of the Mother of the Muses, "Memory" does not mean an arbitrary thinking of just anything that might be thought. Memory is the gathering of thought unto what everywhere and from the start would like to be thought. Memory is the gathering of commemorative thought [*Andenken*]. It harbors and conceals that to which at any given time thought must be given, in everything that essentially unfolds and appeals to us as having being [*Wesendes*] and having-been [*Gewesendes*]: Memory, the Mother of the Muses: thinking back to what is to be thought—this is the source and ground of poesy. (WhD? 7)

The gift of Mnemosyne, Mother of the Muses, returns. Returns and enters into circulation, not as a slab of wax, nor as a shapeless receptacle, but as the call to thinking. The incentive for thanking. Yet it *is* a return. For when Heidegger invokes the Mother of the Muses he is doubtless quoting Socrates, the *purest* thinker of the West, the thinker who incises nothing in wax, stains no papyrus sheet with ebon ink (WhD? 52). Also the thinker who, in Hölderlin's words, "loves what is most alive," the erotic thinker who, Nietz-sche says, nonetheless killed poetry with philtres of dialectic. Nietzsche and Socrates are the thinkers we shall have to remember as we invoke the following extracts from the third lecture hour of Part II of "What Calls for Thinking?" (WhD? 91–95). Here I shall let them stand without much comment, inasmuch as they too will return in chapter 7 under the aegis of memory and *affirmation.* For the moment, it is simply a matter of identifying the lineage of *Behalten,* "retention," in a thinking that is a thanking. Heidegger asks: "What is named with the words 'to think,' 'something thought,' 'a thought'? Toward what sphere of the spoken word do they direct us? Something thought—where is it, where does it stay? It [*Gedachtes*] needs memory [*Gedächtnis*]. To that which is thought and its thoughts, to the "*Gedanc*," belong thanks [*Dank*]" (WhD? 91). At this point the translators insert remarks on the parallel to *Gedanc, Gedanke, Dank* in English: "The old English *thencan*, to think, and *thancian*, to thank, are closely related; the Old English noun for thought is *thanc* or *thonc*—a thought, a grateful thought, and the expression of such a thought; today it survives in the plural *thanks*." Heidegger's own text continues:

> But perhaps these intimations of memory and thanks in the word "think" are merely superficial and contrived [*ausgedacht*]. In any case, they still do not show what is designated by the word "thinking."
>   Is thinking a thanking? What does thanking mean here? Or do thanks consist in thinking? What does thinking mean here? Is memory no more than a container [*Behälter*] for the thoughts of a thinking, or does thinking itself consist in memory? How do thanks relate to memory?

Heidegger turns to "the history of these words" in order to seek guidance and direction for his own thinking. *Gedanc,* the root of *Gedanke,* "thought," means not merely an idea or representation but "primordially" and "incipiently" (*anfänglich*) "the gathered, all-gathering thinking that recalls [*das gesammelte, allesversammelnde Gedenken*]." He notes that *Gedanc* "says as much as" the German words *Gemüt, der muot, das Herz:* perhaps (although Heidegger does not say so) what the Greeks called *thymos*, a kind of depth through the heart, or perhaps even *kēr*, the heart itself. One is reminded of Mentor, in *The Odyssey* (2, 233), who addresses the suitors who plague the house of Odysseus: "Do none of those he ruled think thankfully on godlike Odysseus?" The German translation says, *Denkt und dankt es keiner?* in order to render the word *memnētai*. Eumaeus, the faithful sowherd, does remember. With thanks—and in mourning. Still believing that Odysseus is lost, and most probably dead, he tells the returned but disguised hero: "My heart is sad when anyone puts me in mind of [*mnēsēi*] our suffering master" (14, 169–70). After decrying the loss incurred when *Gedanc* becomes *Gedanke,* "the degeneration of the word" in academic philosophy and techno-science, Heidegger *what have I done to have been given children like these*   continues:

> However, the word *der Gedanc* does not merely mean what we call *Gemüt* and heart, the essence of which we can scarcely fathom. In *Gedanc* memory as well as thanks reside and essentially unfold. "Memory" does not at all initially mean the faculty of remembrance [*Erinnerungsvermögen*]. The word "memory" [*Gedächtnis*] names our entire *Gemüt* in the sense of a steadfast [*steten*], intimate [*innigen*] gathering unto what essentially speaks to us [*zuspricht*] in every thoughtful meditating. Memory originally suggests as much as a devoted thought to something [*An-dacht*], an uninterrupted, gathered remaining-with-something; indeed, not only with what is bygone [*dem Vergangenen*], but likewise with what is present and what may come. The bygone, the present, and the coming appear in the unity of an essential unfolding *toward* [or coming *to* presence: An-*wesen*] that is in each case unique.

Heidegger now follows the thread of *An-dacht* and *An-wesen*, devotion *to* what comes *to* presence in past, present, and future, toward the crucial notion of *hold* and *retention*. Such holding and retaining do not limit themselves to the past (*dem Vergangenen*), but encompass the three dimensions of time. To think the gathered holding without cease   *Then it was past*   is the very gift or talent (*Gabe*) for which the mortals must be thankful, for it is *Done in Mother's mind, though. Finished. Finished. Then we were all poisoned*   their endowment, the dowry (*Mitgift*) thanks to which they *are*. One final, extended excerpt: "Inasmuch as memory, the gathering of *Gemüt*, devoted thought-toward, does not let go of that to which it is gathered, memory is imbued not merely with the trait of essential thinking back to something [*An-denken an*] but equally with the trait of an unrelinquishing and relentless retention [*Behalten*]." Memory may not be a *Behälter*, a mere container, but its function is *Behalten*, a dogged, incessant retaining. But to continue, for the passage now sends us back to those strange thesauruses and memory theaters about which Frances Yates (cited at the outset of chapter 2) has written so eloquently:

> Out of the memory, and within the memory, the soul then pours forth its treasury of images; that is to say, of visions by which the soul itself is espied. Only now, within the widely and deeply grasped essence of memory, the contrast emerges between that firm hold on things [*Festhalten*], which the Romans called *memoria tenere*, and evanescence [*Entgleiten*]. The firm hold by means of *memoria* refers as much to what is bygone as to what is present and to come. It is mostly occupied with the bygone [*das Vergangene*], because the bygone has fled [*entgangen*] and in a certain way no longer affords a hold [*nichts Haltbares mehr bietet*]. . . .

Let the extract end here. Mnemosyne's gift will continue to occupy us as the call for thanks and affirmation, but also as   *A face reproachful tearful an odor of camphor and of tears a voice weeping steadily*   the call for caution and hesitation. The gift is a capital *Gift,* and we will not have left behind the danger of poison wherever the remedy is so confidently promised. Nostalgia for the *hold* permeates Heidegger's Mnemosyne, in opposition to the ephemeral, the evanescence of things. Tenacious memory occupied with what has passed and is past, absent, bygone; occupied, preoccupied, perhaps even obsessed   *All right I wonder what time it is what of it*   by it: *Dem Festhalten macht vorwiegend das Vergangene zu schaffen.* . . . The *firm* hold, *Festhalten,* so reminiscent of *Festmachen* (see note 12 of chapter 4), exceeds mere retention, *Behalten,* as though the cornucopia of Mnemosyne were after all a *Behälter,* a bin or bowl. Containing what? Icons or images (*Bilder*) that are themselves views   *There was something terrible in me sometimes at night I could see it grinning at me I could see it through them grinning at me through their faces, it's gone now and I'm sick*   on the soul: *Anblicke, von denen sie selbst [die Seele] erblickt ist.* Is the soul, *die Seele*, that which is always thought *to*, the term of all devotion? Byzantine devotion (*An-dacht*) to presencing (*An-wesen*), whether of what is past, passing, or to come? Are the intimations (*An-klänge*) devoted to steadfast, intense, and intimate (*innig:* Hegel's word, Hölderlin's word) securities? Securities for which the heart gives thanks, about which it gathers, to which it clings? *Das gesammelte, alles versammelnde Gedenken,* a memorial that gathers relentlessly   *Not that blackguard, Caddy*   into a unity, never relinquishing its hold, never forgetting? Carved typographically, iconographically, and engrammatologically in granite? Which *none* of us yet, none of us, and   *Father I have committed*   me first of all, is remembering to think?

LET BYGONES BE BYGONES

Nietzsche is Heidegger's "star-witness" in the inquiry into commemorative thinking, Nietzsche being the *last* thinker of the West (WhD? 61). Yet it is not Nietzsche's genealogy of memory in treatise two of *On the Genealogy of Morals* that Heidegger turns to in lectures IX and X of the first part of *Was heisst Denken?* Instead, he offers an interpretation of the "It was" of time as it appears in *Thus Spoke Zarathustra* II, "Of Redemption." (He says nothing, incidentally, about the "it was" of the second *Untimely Meditation.*) I will offer a brief account of Heidegger's interpretation of time's imperfection, its "It was," and then turn to Nietzsche's most explicit remarks on memory and time past in the *Genealogy.*

Perhaps the most important point to be made about Heidegger's account of the "It was" in *Was heisst Denken?* and in the contemporaneous article "Who Is Nietzsche's Zarathustra?" is that it is missing from the 1936–1941 lectures and essays gathered up into his *Nietzsche* and published in 1961. Why should the most thought-provoking and stellar thought of Heidegger's star-witness be a *supplement* to Heidegger's major inquiry into that thinker? Even the 1937 lecture course, on the eternal recurrence of the same, neglects to cite "Of Redemption" and its discussion of the "It was" of time.[16] The supplement of the 1950s still retains the core of the earlier thesis on eternal return: that Nietzsche's thought of thoughts designates the *existentia* of beings—what Heidegger here calls the primal being (*Ursein*) of beings, on the model of Schelling's dictum *Wollen ist Urseyn,* "Willing is primal being." Yet Heidegger's emphasis on the transiency of time and time's imperfect(ion), the "It was" of time, is new, and so is his discussion of the spirit of revenge (*Rache*) as the regnant genius of metaphysics. Revenge as the will's ill-will toward time and its "It was," as the stumbling block to all willing, appears now (that is to say, in Heidegger's Nietzsche interpretation of the 1950s) as the culmination of a tradition that commences with Aristotle and Augustine. It is as though Nietzsche's were an Aristotelian proposition touching the "essential determination of time" elaborated in *Physics* IV, 10–14 (WhD? 38–40; 78). For both Aristotle and Augustine, the essential unfolding of time, *das Zeitwesen,* is infected by nothingness: time is the not-yet-now (future) and no-longer-now (past). Only the cyclical motion of the aeon, the *nunc stans* of   *shabby and timeless patience, of static serenity*   eternity, appears to escape time's vengeance—until Nietzsche shows that "eternity" is the very expression of the will's ill-will toward time, the cindered heart of vengeance exacted upon time.

Heidegger's account of ill-will apparently speaks from the *persona* of Nietzsche, or of Western ontotheology from antiquity through Nietzsche, but perhaps also *in propria persona*.[17] He writes:

> How do matters stand with time "as such" (*mit "der" Zeit*)? They stand in such a way that time goes. And it goes by passing away [*geht/vergeht*]. The going of time is of course a coming, but a coming that goes by passing away. Whatever of time is to come never comes to stay but to go. Whatever of time is to come is always already inscribed [*gezeichnet*] by the sign of passing by and passing away [*Vorbeigehen/Vergehen*]. The temporal is therefore taken to be the transitory [*das Vergängliche*] without qualification. Hence the "It was" does not merely designate one division of time alongside the others. Rather, the proper endowment [*Mitgift*] that time dispenses and leaves as a legacy is what-is-past [*das Vergangene*], the "It was." Time dispenses only what it has. And all it has is what it itself is.

The passing away of what passes in time   *One day you think misfortune would get tired, but then time is your misfortune Father said*   constitutes the temporal. The temporal is what a human being "blesses" when he or she departs from the world: *das Zeitliche segnen* (cf. WhD? 78). It is the Heidegger of *Being and Time* who more than any other thinker confronts without subterfuge this blessing of the temporal and who affirms Zarathustra's desire: "That your dying be no blasphemy against humanity and earth, my friends: this I beg of the honey of your souls" (ASZ I, "Vom freien Tod"). It is Heidegger more than any other thinker who affirms the being of time as the radical past, the *Vorbei!* That is his message to the Marburg theologians in the lecture, "The Concept of Time," delivered on July 25, 1924.

Dasein is a going ahead into its being bygone, *ein Vorlaufen zu seinem Vorbei*. The word *Vorbei* designates the possibility of Dasein that is ownmost and utmost, certain and undetermined at once: it will have been a matter of my own being bygone, *als Vorbei von mir*, that the "how" of my existence discloses itself. For the nonce, I am "tossed back" (*zurückgeworfen*) to the fact that I am still-being-there, *Noch-Dasein*. Being thus tossed back, I am "held" by the "how"   *and then I was hearing my watch and I began to listen for the chimes*   of my existence, running ahead to my own being bygone. There is something "Mephistophelean" about such "being bygone," no doubt, which is a being tossed backward, thrown forward, and "held," all at (or in, or as) the same time; and Goethe's *Faust* (II, v, "Grosser Vorhof des Palasts," lines 11,595–11,603) may be as important for this early notion of Heidegger's as it is for the ontological meaning of *Sorge*, "Care" (cf. *Faust*, II, v, "Mitternacht"). In the mouth of Mephistopheles, *Vorbei!* proclaims the end of engrammatological "gleaning" and becomes a shadow of eternal return in its most dismal guise:

> Vorbei! ein dummes Wort.
> Warum Vorbei?

> Vorbei und reines Nicht, vollkommenes Einerlei!
> Was soll uns denn das ew'ge Schaffen!
> Geschaffenes zu nichts hinwegzuraffen!
> "Da ist's vorbei!" Was ist daran zu lesen?
> Es ist so gut, als wär es nicht gewesen,
> Und treibt sich doch im Kreis, als wenn es wäre.
> Ich liebte mir dafür das Ewig-Leere.
>
> Bygone! a stupid word.
> Why bygone?
> Bygone, purest nothing—altogether one!
> Why our eternal efforts to fashion!
> Snatching to nothingness all our creation!
> "Now it's bygone!" What sense do you glean?
> Just as well, say I, it had never been,
> And yet it moves in a circle, as though it were withal.
> I'd trade it all in for the Empty-Eternal.

Yet the word *Vorbeigehen,* "passing by," reminds us of quite a different context. In the mid-1930s Heidegger comes to associate what Hölderlin calls divinity and the holy with *Vorbeigang,* passing by. In the very lectures we are considering (WhD? 67) he reminds us of the importance of this theme for him. When Hölderlin in his late hymns sings the fraternity of Christ with Heracles and Dionysos   *that Christ was not crucified: he was worn away by a minute clicking of little wheels. That had no sister*   he is announcing "a still unspoken gathering [*Versammlung*] of Occidental destiny in its entirety." It is precisely that historic destiny of the West, its *Geschick* and *Geschichte,* that Heidegger tries to think in the 1930s as the passing, *Vorbeigang,* of "the last god," *des letzten Gottes.* It is also worth recalling that the fundamental mood that dominates the "futural ones" who contemplate the approach and departure of "the last god" is *Verhaltenheit,* not merely an awful reserve, an amalgam of joy and mourning, but a "holding," *Ver-halt;* it is related to the *Hineingehaltenheit* by which Heidegger in 1929 characterizes the mood of anxiety and no doubt to the *Halten* of *Being and Time,* as well as to the *Behalten* of *Was heisst Denken?* What the thinker must hold to, and hold out in, is the deathly silence of the *Vorbeigang* of the last god. Whether that passing by passes in review before us, so to speak, so that we can observe it; or passes on by us, and thus is forever behind us, as it were; whether like Zarathustra's dwarf we squat on the sidelines and merely observe, or stand frontally in the gateway called the "Moment"; this unanswered question is what constitutes the stillness (*die Stille*) of the passing by of the ultimate god.

To what extent "passing by" recuperates what has been, *das Gewesene,* of Western history and destiny is the question we must now ask. No doubt Heidegger remains confident that even in our age of downgoing, *Untergang,* the arrival and departure of gods is removed from what is simply bygone, *vergangen,* and rescued to the perfect, *gewesen. Vorbeigehen* thus would decidedly not be *vergehen.* Passing by would not be passing away. By virtue of the perfect, *das Gewesene,* the end and commencement of our essential history would be bound in their essence, *im Wesen.* A path of retreat from being's abandonment of beings would thus be located, surveyed, and paved, in accord with hints or signals (*Winke*) granted by the last god. Even if the principal signal should be *Verweigerung,* the refusal to arrive and become present, the very pace and footfall (*Gang*) of the god   *majestical in the face of god gods. Better. Gods. God would be canaille*   will lend a certain consistency (*Beständigung*) to beings as a whole. No god of redemption, the last god will nevertheless provide a certain *hold* for the truth of being as *Ereignis.* Whether and how that "consistency" might differ from the "permanence of presence" (*Beständigkeit des Anwesens*) that has characterized traditional ontotheological systems of metaphysics remains an arresting question. If the *Augenblick* is no longer the glance of a resolute Dasein in the face of its own bygone destiny, but the site of the last god's passage, it nonetheless provides a *hold* for historical existence and a support for the thinker's readiness, intensity, and steadfastness. If the last god overpowers mortals, mortals supersede the god. They bear the torch   *Now and then the river glinted beyond things in sort of swooping glints, across the noon and after*   of the truth of being. They are the blessed.[18]

In the 1951–52 lectures, "What Calls for Thinking?" passing by, *Vorbeigehen,* is once again invoked, this time as the very essence of time as transiency, *Vergehen.* "It is time, high time, finally to meditate on this essence of time and its provenance" (WhD? 40). The avowal that in our time we are *still not thinking* points to time as the unthought ground of metaphysics. For metaphysics, being is presencing (*Anwesen*), hence, the present (*Gegenwart*). It is the unthought eminence of the *Gegenwart* that allows future and past to be marked and marred by the nothing, the not-yet and no-longer. Heidegger cites Augustine's commentary on Psalm 38 (Migne, IV, 419a; WhD? 41): *Nihil de praeterito revocatur, quod futurum est, transiturum expectatur.* "Nothing of what is to come is called back from the past; rather, it is expected as what passes by [*als Vorbeigehendes*]." The temporal is the transitory, whereas being belongs to the constantly standing present. Heidegger now (WhD? 42–43) tries to get closer to the object of vengeance, the target of the will's ill-will. "The ill-will [*Widerwille*] does not go to oppose mere passing away [*Vergehen*]; it advances against passing away insofar as passing away lets what has passed be nothing more than past [*nur noch vergangen*], lets it congeal in the paralysis of finality [*die Erstarrung des Endgültigen*]." Heidegger's question is: What sort of bridge   *I began to feel the water before I came to the bridge*   can rescue us from the raging flood of vengeance? He knows that Nietzsche's answer is the eternal return of the same. He also knows that Nietzsche's thought of thoughts does not mean to repulse time as such: "For human beings time will not be cast aside." Rather, the will is liberated from revenge against time and its "It was" when it becomes free for "the passage that is in passing away," *das Gehen im Vergehen.* Such passage would not be sheer evanescence; rather, it would somehow bring back what is gone. The will constantly wills (*ständig will*) the going and coming again of what passes. "The will becomes free of what is repulsive in the 'It was' when it wills the continuous recurrence [*die ständige Wiederkehr*] of the 'It was'." By shifting the modifier *ständig* from the willing to the being of the willed, to recurrence as such, the thought of eternal return—through a kind of *trompe d'oeil*—achieves the Schellingian project of primal being. *Wollen ist Urseyn*. And the essential predicate of primal being (or of the absolute) is "eternity." "The eternal recurrence of the same is the supreme triumph of the metaphysics of the will," concludes Heidegger.

There are two questions that one will want to put to Heidegger's supplement. First, if he acknowledges that eternal return is Nietzsche's "most burdensome thought" (WhD? 46), and that one merely flees from it when one traces it back to earlier thinkers, can one be satisfied by Heidegger's own carefully plotted Schellingian reading? Second, if *ständiges* willing of *ständiger* recurrence betrays the fatal tie that binds Nietzsche's thought to the spirit of revenge in Western metaphysics, how does such *Ständigkeit* relate to Heidegger's own will to rescue the bygone in what has been, his own passion for *Ständigkeit* and *Stätigkeit* (SZ, 322; 378–82; 390–91; 423–24; cf. 427 n. 1), as well as for "consistency," "constancy," "permanence," *Beständigung?* Is Heidegger's the ancient dream   *That's where the water would be, heading out to sea and the peaceful grottoes*   of the perfect(ion) of the imperfect? One could scarcely overestimate the consequences of such an affinity between the Heideggerian "hold" and metaphysical constancy and consistency. For holding is a challenging, ordering, and framing of beings. If *Gestell* is, as Philippe Lacoue-Labarthe reminds us, a word for the essence of the oblivion, seclusion, or withdrawal of being, then the Heideggerian "hold" on an essential "coinage of being" (*die Prägung des Seins*) is itself onto-typological, hence a remnant of the thinking of memory that I have been calling *typographic*.[19]

Heidegger says that in Nietzsche's view the imperfect "It was" is the proper endowment, *Mitgift*, of time. Time's dowry is that of the wicked fairy, however: *Mit-gift* is the dose of benumbing *poison* that causes all that passes *by* to pass *away*. Heidegger would counteract the poison with gifts parcelled out by the Mother of the Muses, who like "a proper mother," *eine rechte Mutter* (WhD? 19), teaches her son to obey. Dame Memory, *die Gedächtnis*, the gathering of thought, would be the balm to imperfection. However, in his essay for Ernst Jünger, "Toward the Question of Being," Heidegger writes: "The human being, in his or her essence, is the memory of being—but of ̶B̶e̶i̶n̶g̶."[20] The poison is thus felt to do its work within memory itself, insofar as memory is the gathering of thought to the question of being. Commemorative thinking must be not a hold on beings—or even on ̶B̶e̶i̶n̶g̶—but a letting be, even if the hope expressed in the continuity of having-been remains buoyant in it. And if the devastation of our own times can be described as the "high-velocity expulsion of Mnemosyne" (WhD? 11), as we heard at the end of chapter 2, Heidegger dare not be too quick to consign his star-witness to oblivion. The thought of eternal return is thought by the thinker in transition, *der Hinübergehende*, who is eminently the one who goes down, *ein Untergehender* (WhD? 26). The one who goes down knows of transition   *and the caverns and the grottoes of the sea*   and transiency.   *A quarter hour yet. And then I'll not be. The peacefullest words. Peacefullest words. Non fui. Sum. Fui. Non sum.*

Before we abandon the time of forgetting and remembering to too sanguine a perfect, too recuperative a *Gewesenheit,* too matronly a Mnemosyne, let us review one further Nietzschean text, not on the "It was" of time but on the provenance of memory and of time as such. If Heidegger's description of the traditional metaphysical conception of time (see WhD? 40 and 78) seems to embrace Nietzsche's fable about the roll of time that spins and releases a sheet of remembrance, nothing seems more foreign to that description than Nietzsche's account of time in the second treatise of *Zur Genealogie der Moral* (5, 292–97; sections 1–3). Here Nietzsche mingles with the grazing herd that passes by at pasture, in order to meditate on the breeding of an animal that is able *to promise.* For that is the paradoxical task that nature sets itself when producing humankind. Human beings must have shared as fully as other animals in that *active forgetfulness* which dominates life. Not a mere *vis inertiae,* oblivion "is rather an active and in the strictest sense positive faculty of inhibition." It ensures that we know as little of our wonted experience as we do of alimentation and ingestion: human beings are as little conscious of how things enter the psyche, *"Einverseelung,"* as they are of how they enter the body, *"Einverleibung."* Only in blissful ignorance of what rules in their own bodies, only with "a bit of tranquillity, a bit of *tabula rasa* in consciousness," can the human organism survive. In the language of *Being and Time,* remembering is a modification of forgetting, and not the other way around. Active forgetfulness is thus the Cerberus of the psychic order. One of the products of its guardianship, the only one that Nietzsche emphasizes, is the present, *Gegenwart.* However, rather than being the bearer and avatar of oblivion (as in Heidegger), the present is grounded in oblivion in a very different sense for Nietzsche. The human animal is not the resolute keeper of a lapsing and ruinant world; he or she is rather the "necessarily oblivious animal" whose forgetting has in a moment of exuberant health created a counter-faculty. Memory is a pendant to pervasive oblivion. "With its help, forgetfulness is to be suspended for certain cases—for cases in which a promise is to be made." Memory is   *Don't touch me just promise*   therefore "by no means a merely passive inability to get rid of an impression once it is incised in us [*des einmal eingeritzten Eindrucks*]." Memory is not typography—except as the prehistory of pain. Rather, it is "an active *willing* not to get rid of something . . . , a proper *memory of the will.*" In this way, concludes Nietzsche, the human being promises something; in this way, he or she becomes futural.   *Not until tomorrow, remember.*   If human existence is preeminently cast into a future and is a vector of possibilities, it is only because the mysterious faculty of active forgetfulness has interrupted the flux with an instant of *Gegenwart,* and consequently an instance of *memory.* How does that interruption occur? That is the genealogical question.

In section 2 Nietzsche asks about the provenance (*Herkunft*) of responsibility, about the creation of a breed of animal sufficiently uniform and regular to be accountable to itself and to others. What Hegel calls *die Sittlichkeit der Sitten* is the proper work of human phylogenesis over vast aeons of time, "its entire *prehistoric* work" (5, 293). However, if the ripe fruit of that maturation process is the sovereign, autonomous individual who (ironically) has transcended ethicality and is "free" to give his or her word, must one not say that the free human being is nonetheless a slave to conscience (*Gewissen*)? Section 3 finds Nietzsche pausing over the phenomenon of conscience in the sovereign individual: *Sein Gewissen?* . . . During this pause the very myth of the sovereign individual is undone, just as the fabulous "blond beast" vanishes in the genealogy of the ascetic priest. For the history of autonomy is linked genealogically to the prehistory of inflicted pain. In his own way, in the dramaturgic-genealogical theater of prehistory, Nietzsche   *told me the bone would have to be broken again and inside me it began to say Ah Ah Ah and I began to sweat*   recreates the story of memory as typography (5, 295): " 'How shall a memory be made for the human animal? How shall one imprint something on this somewhat dull, somewhat flighty intellect-of-the-instant [*Augenblicks-Verstand*] and bit of embodied oblivion, so that it will remain present [*gegenwärtig*]?' " Heidegger would no doubt insist that it is Aristotle who speaks here, enjoining the selfsame typography of metaphysics, for which being is the presence of what is presently present. Yet Nietzsche too is struck by the antiquity—even proto-antiquity—of the scene of memory:

> This primeval [*uralte*] problem, as one can imagine, is not resolved with the gentlest of means and responses. Indeed, perhaps nothing is more terrible and uncanny [*furchtbarer und unheimlicher*] about the entire prehistory of mankind than its *mnemotechnic*. "One has to brand it in, in order for something to remain in memory: only what does not stop *hurting* perdures in memory"—this is the first principle of the very oldest (and, unfortunately, the longest-lasting) psychology on earth.

One is no doubt reminded here of the outrage   *and my mouth saying Wait Wait just a minute through the sweat ah ah ah*   that directs the first reminiscences—and first repressions—envisaged in psychoanalytic theory, not only in the 1895 "Project" but also in the last writings on "civilization." Nietzsche writes: "The past, the longest deepest hardest past, breathes on us and wells up in us whenever we grow 'serious'." "Serious" here means "memorious," and memory remains incisive and violent:

> It never happened without blood, martyrdoms, sacrifice, whenever human beings found it necessary to form a memory. The most horrific sacrifices and gages (among which belong the sacrifice of the firstborn), the most repulsive mutilations (for example, castrations), the cruellest forms of ritual in all religious cults (for all religions, in their deepest substratum, are systems of cruelties)—it all has its origin in that instinct which senses in pain the mightiest means of mnemonics.

We are apparently in a theater quite different from that of Heideggerian "Mnemosyne." Yet a "proper mother," *eine rechte Mutter,* "a right mother," according to Heidegger, is the one who says to the son, to "her little boy, who does not want to come home": "Just wait, I'll teach you what it means to obey [*was Gehorchen heisst*]" (WhD? 19). Doubtless, the less she scolds, the more authority her teaching will have, and the more seriously *you will remember that for you to go to harvard has been your mother's dream since you were born and no compson has ever disappointed a lady* she will be taken. "In a certain sense," writes Nietzsche, "all asceticism belongs here: a few ideas are to be made inextinguishable, omnipresent, unforgettable, 'fixed'...." He thereby locates within the prehistory of mnemonics his own (unforgettable!) third treatise in the *Genealogy,* "What Do Ascetic Ideals Signify?" He also writes a few lines of the horrific history that will unite him with Heidegger, genealogical lines, painful lines, incisions never to be forgotten:

> We Germans surely do not take ourselves to be a particularly cruel and hard-hearted people; even less do we take ourselves to be particularly carefree, the sort who just-take-it-as-it-comes. Yet one only has to examine our old penal codes to get a glimpse of the trouble it takes on this earth to breed a "nation of thinkers" (which is to say, *the* nation of Europe in which one finds even today the maximum confidence, seriousness, bad taste, and devotion to the matter at hand [*Zutrauen, Ernst, Geschmacklosigkeit und Sachlichkeit*], a nation whose qualities grant it the right to breed every species of mandarin in Europe). These Germans have made themselves a memory by virtue of terrible means, in order to master their squalid basic instincts and the brutal coarseness of those instincts [*um über ihre pöbelhaften Grund-Instinkte und deren brutale Plumpheit Herr zu werden*].

Nietzsche now catalogues these Germanic punishments. For our part, we perhaps need only recall again—as we did in the discussion of Hobbes—Kafka's *In der Strafkolonie* and the machine that incises the flesh with the Law and the encouragement, "Be just!" We need now only take up one phrase from Nietzsche's conclusion of section 3, not so much a conclusion as an apostrophe:

> —and really! with the help of this kind of memory one finally came "to see reason"!—Ah, reason, seriousness, mastery over the affects, the whole grim affair we call meditation [*diese ganze düstere Sache, welche Nachdenken heisst*], all these perquisites and treasures of mankind: how dearly we had to pay for them! how much blood and horror lie at the ground of all "good things"!...

Well, then, *Was heisst Nachdenken?* What calls on us to think back and remember the titanic, Teutonic cruelty that Heidegger's mythic invocation of Mnemosyne appears to suppress? "Presuming we did not *have to* think back," Nietzsche would say, reminding us of the genealogy of the genealogist, for whom interiorized cruelty is a way of life. If memory is the gathering of thought, that gathering is not without its prehistory of pain, and perhaps its painful posthistory as well. Mnemosyne is a right mother. A jagged bosom *We have sold Benjy's pasture so that Quentin may go to Harvard*   whether in full-front or lateral view.

Not that father and fatherland fare any better. Not if we remember the gynephobia of *Timaeus* and the task of thinking called *khōra.* To the extent that Heidegger resists the *Vorbei!* that announces the finitude of being and time, resists it by conjuring a *perfect,* a *Gewesenheit* that would be the inexhaustible font of the future and a "constant" source of presence, he seals the oblivion   *I put on my new suit and put my watch on . . . and wrote the two notes and sealed them*   he is struggling to escape. Or at least *risks* sealing it. The matter is hardly certain. For Heidegger tries to abide by the judgment of Saturn, who in the Cura fable settles the question of humanity's "*temporal metamorphosis in the world* [*der* zeitliche Wandel (*des Menschen*) in der Welt]" (SZ, 199). No amount of will or willfulness can make mortal transition and transience perfectly recuperable. The call to readiness, wakefulness, resolute openedness, and to an "other" kind of thinking dare not become a command to wreak vengeance on the "It was"   *there is nothing else in the world its not despair until time its not even time until it was*   of time.

The hold ventured by thinking slips. Already in Hegel, we recall, where the "content" or "holding-in" (*In-halt*) slackens. The gathering power of memory is unequal to passing by, *Vorbeigehen,* and even the most anxious and earnest endeavors of thinking leave us on the verge. Of what? Not of laughter and forgetting, nor of mirth and mischief, but   *Then I remembered I hadn't brushed my teeth*   of mirth and mourning.

SEVEN

Of Ashes

The Promise of Memory in the Recent Thought of Jacques Derrida

Can one be satisfied to remain on the verge of affirmation?

To renounce the typography, iconography, and engrammatology of memory and surrender the dream of full restoration of what is bygone to perfect presence—nothing easier, now that the ruse no longer works. However, to muffle the unstinting affirmation of eternal recurrence; to let the cry *da capo! da capo!* be stifled; to reject celebration and settle for bovine contentment or agnelline consent; or, turning the tables, to forget the century in which we (barely) live and to bray like an ass, *pulcher et fortissimum, J-a! J-a!—nein, nein,* impossible, all of these.

Affirmation redeems—"Yes-saying . . . unto redemption of everything past"—said Nietzsche. Redemption is decadent—"The morbid hedonism of the Redeemer-type"—said Nietzsche. Right on both counts. Is it possible to affirm without dreaming of redemption? Is it possible to remember without being trapped in the miasma of nostalgia and sentimentality? Has not mirth always served to explode the pomp of redemption? If not a burst of Bataillean laughter, at least a spray of chuckles? *Con brio.* Has not mourning always been the promise of a fidelity of memory that does not swoon in nostalgia? Not black crêpe and funereal melodrama, but an ineluctable sadness? *Ma non troppo.* Might mirth and mourning together be the *Janus bifrons* of human beings on the verge?

I shall begin by examining Pierre Klossowski's thinking of eternal recurrence as a cycle of anamnesis, amnesia, and affirmation. I will then take up Derrida's three lectures on "impossible mourning" in *Mémoires: For Paul de Man,* the second and third lectures being in memory of Hegelian *Gedächtnis* and Heideggerian *Andenken.* I shall then proceed to examine the contrapuntal structure of the double-yes of mourning and mirth in the two lectures that constitute *Ulysse gramophone.* Finally, I will try to say something about the leitmotiv of *la cendre,* the trace of ashes, in these and other recent texts.[1]

ANAMNESIS, AMNESIA, AFFIRMATION

If the affirmation of eternal recurrence dreams of redemption, that affirmative thought is itself decadent: such is one of the vicious circles of Nietzsche's "thought of thoughts." Another circle is that of remembering and forgetting, as Pierre Klossowski demonstrates in the third major section of his book (CV, 89–112). Not that anamnesis and amnesia can be neatly distinguished on the circumference of the circle or the declination of the spiral. The very act of *thinking* the thought—Klossowski's question is in essential proximity to Heidegger's—risks at each instant the loss of lucidity, as though it were caught in a vortex of simultaneous ascent and descent: "*That a thought rises only by descending, progresses only by regressing*—inconceivable spiral whose 'pointless' description proves to be repugnant" (CV, 14).

The very act of thinking on the helix, as it were, is radically dependent on the pulsional life of the body—its drives, humors, migraines, neuralgias, its ups and downs. "The act of thinking comes to be identical with suffering and suffering with thinking." Suffering at the hands of what Nietzsche in "The Wanderer and His Shadow" calls "the closest things" will nevertheless ultimately make thinking as such *impossible* for him (CV, 47–48). The very brain is menaced, wholly in consonance with the phylogenetic process of cephalization, which is inevitably linked with hazard, effraction, violence, and pain. In the case of Nietzsche, physical suffering can be endured only through a "voluptuous lucidity," a delirium that allows thought to reside *alla breve* alongside ecstasy. Yet ecstasy and delirium are as closely linked to *oblivion* as to lucid thought, to *amnesia* as to a gathering anamnesis. The mirror of reflection has a tain, thin and fragile, on which reflexive lucidity depends: "No mirror without a tain: the tain forms the base [*fond*] of 'reason.' Thanks to the opacity of impulsions, oblivion is possible. No consciousness without forgetting. Yet as soon as consciousness 'scratches' the tain, it confuses itself in its very transparency with the flux and reflux of impulsions" (CV, 53).

Such confusion is lodged in the erect and vertical human being, who measures high and low, front and back, with mindless confidence. What Merleau-Ponty in the final chapter of the *Phenomenology of Perception* calls the "absolute generality" and "double anonymity" of the body here betrays its most sinister aspect: even though "the cohesion of the body is the cohesion of the self," defining the "irreversible course" of a life, that very body, one's *own* body—here, *Nietzsche's* body—is "no more than a *fortuitous gathering* of temporarily reconciled, contradictory impulses" (CV, 54–55). Nietzsche's experience of eternal return, of the *vicious circle*, announces a rupture with the unilinear sense that dominates the erect and oblivious body. By conjoining commencement and end, direction and goal, the circle confounds the history of thought, for which the body is a *property* of the self. The body, as the site and the product of contradictory pulsions, *reversible* pulsions in the sense that they prevail, bide their time, pass, and return, gains a new centrality for thought.

The thought of thoughts, eternal return, is thus a bodying thought, *une pensée corporante* (CV, 55–56). Klossowski attempts to secure a new "cohesion" for the Nietzschean body through a "memory that ultimately detaches itself from the cerebral self, a memory that no longer *designates itself* except according to *the most remote* motifs" (CV, 57). He elaborates that cohesion in the most traditional of possible terms: *par des traces d'excitations antérieures . . . ; la trace des excitations antérieures . . . qui assure la permanence de l'identité du moi*. And yet the quotidian code of "traces" compels the question: "How will the *memory subsist* if it is to be borne back to all the things that are no longer the self: *how to remember without becoming that which remembers everything save itself?*" Nietzsche's doctrine of the vicious circle, his "invention" of eternal return, challenges lucidity by virtue of its impossible demands on memory. The vicious circle is the very emblem of oblivion. It is founded on "the *forgetting* of the fact that we were and will be, not only numberless times but always, different from what we now are: *other,* not somewhere else, but *always* in this *same life*" (CV, 86). In short, the very *thinking* of the affirmative thought, eternal recurrence of the same, revolutionizes memory, reminiscence, and writing. So much for the vestibule of Klossowski's structure: it is time to enter the vicious circularity of his labyrinth (see Plate 8).

In the "lived experience" of the eternal return of the same, Nietzsche undergoes a "sudden revelation," a revelation based on a *Stimmung* or "certain tonality of soul"; even after the experience detaches itself from the float of experience and assumes the form of a "thought," one that Nietzsche will try to

PLATE 8

demonstrate scientifically and deploy for purposes of pedagogy and "selection," eternal return remains "a brusque awakening," "a sudden unveiling"
(CV, 93). Yet does not *oblivion* have to play an essential role in the revelation?
Is not forgetfulness in fact "the source as well as the indispensable condition"
of the thought? How else account for the always startling character of the
revelation? Does not eternal return challenge the very *identity* of the one to
whom it is (eternally recurrently) revealed? And if the affirming individual
suffers fragmentation, does not the individual *affirmation* suffer likewise? Instead of *da capo! da capo!*—da-da? Klossowski accentuates the willed loss of
identity in the thought of return:

> From the instant eternal return has been revealed to me, I cease to be myself *hic et
> nunc* and am susceptible of becoming innumerable others, knowing that I am
> going to forget this revelation once I am outside [*une fois hors de*] the memory of
> myself; this forgetting forms the object of my present will; because the very forget-
> ting would be equivalent to a memory outside my proper limits: and my current
> state of consciousness will be established only in the forgetting of my other possi-
> ble identities. (CV, 94–95)

The memory of eternal return is thus the vicious circularity to which I must
yield, precisely because it excludes me, expulses me. If the revelation makes any
sense at all, it must cause me to lose consciousness of my self. The thought
banishes me once and for all from my self, in order to embrace me as its
fortuitous moment. Except that precisely this "once and for all," *une fois pour
toutes,* is the very thing I must surrender:

> Yet to re-will oneself as a fortuitous moment is to renounce being oneself *once and
> for all:* inasmuch as it is not once and for all that I renounced it there, not once and
> for all that I must will it: and I am not even this fortuitous moment once and for
> all, if it is the case that I am to re-will this moment: *one more time!* For nothing?
> For myself. "Nothing" being here the *circle once and for all.* It is the valid sign of
> all that has happened, all that happens, all that will happen in the world. (CV, 95)

Renunciation of one's self, for oneself! Once and for all, one more time! How
can these conflicting shibboleths abide one another? Must they not rather
decapitate one another? Derrida's *Shibboleth: For Paul Celan* is an extended
reflection precisely on the impossibility of *une seule fois,* the absolute resistance
of the unique time and place to thought, and I shall digress a moment now in
order to consider it.

If the *datability* of an event appears to circumscribe and circumcise the
event once and for all, locking it in the historical archive of the tribe, the very
comprehension of its date necessitates a liberation and dispersion of the event.
If every event appears to be as unique and impassable as death, utterly
unüberholbar, it nonetheless appears as eminently repeatable, *wiederholbar,* at
least in terms of commemoration. To be sure, datability first comes to the fore
as an enigma, a conundrum (SH, 13): "How date that which does not repeat
itself, if dating also appeals to some form of return, if it calls us back [*rapelle*]
to the readability of a repetition? But how date anything else than the very

thing that never repeats itself?" If Celan dates his poems, and incorporates dates into his poems, it is in order to commit events to memory, to a memory that still disposes over and commands a future (SH, 20). The date *of* the poem *in* the poem effaces itself in order to let the memory of the event(s) circulate one more time. If the date is cryptic, scarcely decipherable, it is only in order that the trauma never be forgotten, that the incision or wound remain in memory and return to haunt us *Mit Brief und Uhr,* "With Letter and Clock":

> Wax,
> To seal the unwritten things
> that guessed your name,
> that encoded
> your name.[2]

The traumas—political oppression, fascism, antisemitism, genocide, extermination—are commemorated by their dates, yet also put at risk by the hazards of inversion (56) and oblivion (40):

> Yet if readability effaces the date, effaces the very thing it gives to read, this strange process will have begun with the very inscription of the date. The date must in some way dissimulate the stigma of singularity in itself in order to last longer: this is the poem, and what it commemorates. That is the only chance to assure its returning to haunt. Effacement or dissimulation, the annulation [both annullment and anniversary] proper to the ring of return [*l'anneau de retour*], pertains to the movement of dating. That which is to be commemorated, gathering and repeating *at once* [à la fois], is from thence *at once* annihilation of the date, a sort of nothing, or ash.
> The ash awaits us.

Every date is thus a future anterior, a future perfect, inasmuch as it grants from its bourn the anniversaries that will have commemorated it (48). Yet those anniversaries will never restore the full presence of the encrypted event, just as no absolute witness will ever have deciphered the poem exhaustively: the future of poet and poem alike remain imperfect, and each is radically isolate (60). If the poem should seem perfectly readable, eminently decipherable, its ideality "bears oblivion in its memory," "the memory of oblivion itself, the truth of oblivion" (65).

That ideality remains bound to the sheer chance and chances of the body: the tongue and buccal orifice of an entire tribe unable to wrap around the *sh-* of *shibboleth*. Legend has it that 42,000 Ephraimite soldiers were put to the sword by Jephtha as they tried to escape to their homeland on the West Bank. The memory of the event and the place, the bloodred riverbank, Shibboleth, is scorched by the solar annulation that commemorates it. Any specific date and signature that one might attribute to such an event would soon incinerate, as Locke would affirm, burning to cinder and ash (72–75). Paul Celan's poems are such incinerations, ashen benedictions in the face of horror, appeals broadcast to chance. From *Engführung* Derrida cites these few lines on return and nonreturn, "amnesia without remnant," the "return of nonreturn":

Go, your hour
has no sisters, you are—
are at home. A wheel, slowly,
rolls by itself, the spokes
clamber (. . .)

Years.
Years, years, a finger
touches down and ahead (. . .)

Came, came.
Came a word, came,
came through the night,
wanted to shine, wanted to shine.

Ashes.
Ashes, ashes.
Night.
Night-and-night. (. . .)[3]

However different the tonality of both Derrida's *Shibboleth* and Paul
Celan's poetry may be from Klossowski's *Vicious Circle*, they share the task of
thinking the circle *once and for all, one more time*. In Klossowski's labyrinth,
the circle of recurrence (once and for all) is reaffirmed by an act of will (one
more time!) beyond the self and thus becomes the sign of *chaos*. Chaos is
neither the Hesiodic gap between sky and earth nor the swamp of a contemporary malaise. It appears by virtue of "traces of signifying fluctuations" in the
"code of everyday signs" (CV, 99). Chaos is the sign by which the thinking (or
remembering) self falls outside the circle into incoherence. No longer is the
circle delineated by the radius of *lucid* experience, by an Aristotelian thought-
thinking-itself. No longer is the circle the radial, radiant path of the absolute
within an autonomic system, as it is for at least one of the Hegels. No longer is
the circle the sign of essential being, the *grammè* of *ousia*.[4] "The circle opens
me to inanity and encloses me in this alternative: *either* everything recurs
because nothing ever had any meaning, *or* the meaning never returns to anything except through the return of all things without beginning or end" (CV,
101). Reaffirmation as an act of the *will* both executes and eliminates the very
meaning of (re)willing, sacrificing deliberation to chance and metaphysical
recollection to a vicious circuitry of anamnesis *with* amnesia. The result, according to Klossowski, is a flux and reflux of contradictory pulsions—
bitterness, laughter, and silence:

Re-willing, pure adherence to the vicious circle: to re-will *the entire series once
again* [encore une fois]—to re-will all these experiences, all these acts, but not
insofar as they are *mine:* precisely *this* possessive no longer makes sense, nor does
it represent a goal. The sense of direction and goal are liquidated by the circle.
Whence Zarathustra's silence, the interruption of his message. Unless his message
is a burst of laughter that bears all its own bitterness.[5]

To be on the verge of the thought of eternal recurrence is to sacrifice both cool deliberation and ardent will to chance. To be on the verge of affirmation is to find oneself within the vicious circle of anamnesis-with-amnesia—which is to say, outside the circle of self-sufficient thought. It is perhaps to be abashed in the face of Zarathustra's laughter and bitterness both, and to understand better than anything else the interruption of messages, the intermittent silences.

IMPOSSIBLE MOURNING POSSIBLE

It breaches the bounds of discretion to cite a work of mourning as though it were a work like any other, and as though its wounds were not being continually prodded, reopened, salted, and insulted. Yet Derrida's *Mémoires: For Paul de Man* is so rich a text on memory, reminiscence, and writing that I cannot afford discretion. Its three parts—three lectures delivered not long after Paul de Man's death in December 1983—touch on various topics that are central to my own undertaking. Hegel's *Gedächtnis* and *Erinnerung,* Hölderlin's "Mnemosyne," and Heidegger's *An-denken,* the gathering of thinking in memory, emerge there as thoughts that induce mirth and mourning, yes-saying and promise, but also contamination and hesitation. Hesitation—as though on the verge.

The first lecture, "Mnemosyne," begins with the confession of a certain incapacity on the lecturer's part, a confession that may well be a parody, full of Odyssean ruses, or a straightforward lamentation about gifts withheld:

> I have never known how to tell a story.
> And since I love nothing better than remembering and Memory itself—Mnemosyne—I have always felt this inability as a sad infirmity. Why am I denied narration? Why have I not received this gift? Why have I never received it from Mnemosyne, *tēs tōn Mousōn mētros,* the mother of all the muses, as Socrates recalls in *Theaetetus* (191d)? The gift (*dōron*) of Mnemosyne, Socrates insists, is like the wax in which all that we wish to guard in our memory is engraved in relief so that it may leave a mark, like that of rings, bands, or seals. We preserve our memory and our knowledge of them; we can then speak of them, and do them justice, as long as their image (*eidōlon*) remains legible.

To suffer the memory but lose the narrative is no personal failing, one might well insist, but the failure of typography, iconography, and engrammatology. Simulacra displace the icon, and a straightforward reading of typed marks becomes impossible. Engravement in relief, the gravemarking of all hermeneutics, instead of producing monuments to eternity now signals a default of mourning. Derrida cites Hölderlin's "Mnemosyne," from which one might extract these telling lines, lines that with some variations conclude all three drafts of the hymn:

> . . . For the celestial ones
> Balk when one has not guarded his soul, not

> Held himself together, for even so he must; like him,
> Mourning is in default.[6]

Mourning is as indefinite and as overdetermined as the *Gleich* and the *Zusammengenommen* of Hölderlin's recalcitrant verses, as remote as Achilles and Patroklos both, as distant as God and the gods, with furious Ajax deep in the grottoes of the sea. We are therefore justified in securing aid and counsel wherever we can find it. *The Oxford English Dictionary* reminds us—as does Edward S. Casey's *Remembering* (273; 353 n. 17–22)—that mourning and memory are scions of the same semantic vine. *Mourn* has as its Indogermanic root *smer-,* "to remember," a root that yields the Greek *merimna,* "care, sorrow, solicitude"; perhaps there is no real disagreement with those scholars who emphasize the Old Nordic root *morna,* "to pine away," apparently de-rived from the Indogermanic *mer-,* "to die." One would hardly be surprised to find that mourning and *morior, mourir* are related. What may surprise us is the way in which *merimna* lends a kind of fundamental-ontological force to the conjunction of memory and mourning: in *Being and Time* (SZ, 199 n. 1) Heidegger refers to the Stoic term *merimna,* translated in the Vulgate as *sollicitudo,* as an important stepping-stone on the way to his notion of *cura, Sorge,* "care," as the existential-ontological designation of human being. Memory-and-mourning would not simply be a contingent and distressing way to bring a book about memory, reminiscence, and writing to a close; rather, whatever our skepticism concerning the temporalization of anxiety and the purported *hold* that "appropriate care" ought to lend our existence, mourning would remain in memory of being. Yet can we be sure of even this remnant of fundamental ontology? Can we hold onto mourning, or can it hold us? Is mourning a *possibility* of Dasein? Is it *possible* at all—or is precisely mourning in default? Derrida asks:

> What is an impossible mourning? What does it tell us, this impossible mourning, about an essence of memory? And as concerns the other in us, even in this "distant premonition of the other" [*Par son pressentiment lointain:* Armel Guerne's transla-tion of line 33 of the third draft of "Mnemosyne": *Fern ahnend* . . .], where is the most unjust betrayal? Is the most distressing, or even the most deadly infidelity that of a *possible mourning* which would interiorize within us the image, idol, or ideal of the other who is dead and lives only in us? Or is it that of the *impossible mourning,* which, leaving the other his alterity, respecting thus his infinite remove, either refuses to take or is incapable of taking the other within oneself, as in the tomb or vault of some narcissism? (MPM, 29/6)

These questions haunt Derrida's *Mémoires,* whether Paul de Man, Hölder-lin, Hegel, or Heidegger is the personage in question, whether deconstruction, memory, or affirmation is the theme under scrutiny. For that reason we would do well to recall the basic features of Freud's account of the *work* of mourning, *die Trauerarbeit,* in "Trauer und Melancholie" (StA 3, 193–212). The thematic arrangement whereby mourning should simply be the "normal" counterpart of "pathological" melancholy or depression is disturbed by the fact that Freud's earliest reference to mourning places it at the heart of neurosis and the Oedipus complex. Indeed, one of Freud's earliest references to mourning is also the first reference to the Oedipus complex: it appears in the third set of notes from the Fliess period, published as Manuscript N, mailed to Fliess as an appendix to letter 64, dated May 31, 1897 (*Aus den Anfängen*, 221). The first note of the appendix bears the title "Impulses":

> Inimical impulses toward one's parents (the wish that they should die) are likewise an integral component of neurosis. They come into the daylight of consciousness as compulsive representations. In paranoia they correspond to the most severe delusions of persecution (pathological mistrust of rulers and monarchs). These impulses are repressed whenever compassion for the parents predominates, during the periods of their illness and death. Then it is an expression of mourning to blame oneself for their death (so-called melancholia) or to punish oneself by means of hysteria, suffering the very same symptoms they suffered, as though by way of retribution. The identification that takes place in this instance is, as we can see, nothing other than a mode of thought, and it makes the search for a motive superfluous.

The word *identification* (as elsewhere *introjection*) betrays the fact that mourning touches the very heart of ego-formation. Freud is exercised by the problem of ego-formation from the 1890s through *The Ego and the Id* (1923), especially from the time of the "Narcissism" essays (1914). If we dare to simplify Freud's accounts of an extremely complex set of processes, we can say that "successful" mourning manages to withdraw its libidinal "occupation" of every "memory and expectation" connected with the mourned person. No doubt, a great deal of time and effort goes into this withdrawal. The sole compensation for the loss is provided by "the sum of narcissistic satisfactions" that one attains by being the survivor (3, 209). However, even though Freud would like to contrapose successful mourning to depression—"With mourning the world has become poor and empty; with melancholy it is the ego itself that becomes so" (3, 200)—their similar symptomatology becomes ever more compelling as "Mourning and Melancholy" proceeds. Unsuccessful mourning seems the likelier fate, with its concomitant outrages: clinging to the lost object in well-nigh psychotic, hallucinatory desire (as though regressing to the earliest possible mistake), lacerating the self with accusations of guilt, identifying fully with the lost object (so that the self becomes a flitting "shadow" of the beloved), and regressing to the most primitive form of object-choice in "original Narcissism" (3, 203). Such primitive "choice" occurs as the desire to devour and ingest the other, the "ambivalent" consumption, destruction, and preservation of the other (cf. "Drives and Their Vicissitudes," StA 3, 101). True, a discussion of the *manic* phase of depression leaves Freud without a corresponding "economic" explanation for mourning, unless it be sheer renunciation of the (lost) object, "declaring the object dead and offering the ego the prize of survival [*die Prämie des Amlebenbleibens*]. . . ." And yet the meager prize does not compensate for the effraction suffered when the reality principle breaks through: whether the work of mourning is successful or collapses into depression and melancholy there will inevitably be the severe pain of loss—*Schmerz*.

Perhaps it is the unassuaged pain of mourning, whether "successful" or not, that enables Derrida to ask about the greater injustice: if one should pull back from the departed one, having snatched up the laurel of survival, or if one should inter the other in oneself either as an intimate idol or as a shade at an "infinite remove," that is to say, either in the communion of a complacent Narcissism or the encystation of a wretched one—is not the pain equal in intensity? Whether mourning is possible by means of obsequy, obsequience, or some other strategy of the interpreting ego; or impossible, whereupon the second best's a gay good night and quickly turn away; the questions of fidelity and faithlessness haunt the logic of the living and the logic of the dead.[7]

No totalizing answer to such questions concerning mourning, fidelity, or betrayal seems possible. No narrative can exhaust them, no semiology encode and decipher them, no memoir absorb and defuse them. Mourning is   *I have said, that I minutely remember the details of the chamber—yet I am sadly forgetful on topics of deep moment; and here there was no system, no keeping, in the fantastic display, to take hold upon the memory*   and remains cryptic.

In "Fors: Les mots anglés de Nicolas Abraham et Maria Torok," Derrida investigates the psychoanalytical-anasemiological concept of *cryptonymy*. Developed in articles and books by Abraham and Torok since 1961, cryptonymy focuses on the distinction between *introjection* (related to the situation of *mourning*) and *incorporation* (related to the interment of phantoms of pleasure and prohibition in the self, more closely related to unsuccessful mourning, *melancholy* or *depression*). Their analysis of Freud's Wolfman case combines linguistics and mythopoetics with more traditional psychoanalytical approaches. Derrida focuses on the various kinds of *interiors* that may be constructed, according to Abraham and Torok, *within* the walls of the psyche, within the *forums* and *fortresses* of the unconscious—in a word, within *fors*. (*For*, a masculine noun derived from *forum*, public place or tribunal, is in its literary usage *le for intérieur*: the tribunal of conscience, located at the very foundation [*fond*] of oneself. However, by writing the word in the plural, *fors*, Derrida produces its antonym, the preposition *fors*, from *foris* "outside the walls" [*concordia domi foris pax*], as suggested by the English phrases "except for, apart from, outside of." The interior place is no doubt related to impregnable strength and force [cf. the adjective *fort*], as long as that place is protected from the piercing and perforating action of *forer, forage,* from the outside.—*Robert.*) The crypt in which the traumatic event (or dual event involving pleasure/prohibition) is sealed becomes an interior *for*. Yet the *for* thereby becomes "an outside excluded from the internal interior of the inside" (*Fors*, 13). The crypt seals off its contents from the outside—but from the inside of the psyche as well. (This difficulty of distinguishing inclusions from exclusions arose for us when we tried to understand how Descartes' interior gland *H* could have had an *exterior,* and how the icons engraved on that *interior* exterior could ever be engrammatologically identified as figures or objects on the *exterior* exterior; it also arose in Hegel's account of the nocturnal shaft of signs that spirit appears to be able to mine, inasmuch as the shaft is *interior* to the interiority of spirit, and is hence a kind of encrypted exteriority—in a word, a kind of crypt.) Because the crypt in which the traumatic event remains sealed is barred to *me*, it is both within me and without me. It is an effraction, a violence, for it keeps alive in me something extraneous, something dead, something of the father which was never enjoyed and yet which never perishes (14). Unlike the steady, progressive, laborious work of mourning, defined by Torok as the work of introjection, *incorporation* imposes itself with alacrity—through a kind of foreign invasion into the cryptic heart of the self. Imposes itself as the phantom invasion of a foreign body: ". . . phantasmatic, nonmediated, instantaneous, magical, sometimes hallucinatory" (17). A phantom invasion inasmuch as the incorporated desire was never anything but excluded desire: "What the crypt commemorates, as the 'monument' or 'tomb' of the incorporated object, is not the object itself but its exclusion; exclusion of the desire outside the process of introjection, its portal to the interior of the self condemned, the excluded *for*" (18).

Cryptonymy—no doubt uncomfortably housed in the long tradition that extends from Plato's aviary, Augustine's cavern, and the mnemonist's *theatrum mundi* to Descartes' tubes, Hegel's shaft, and Nietzsche's cave haunted for a thousand years by the shade of the dead god—does not spell the end of lucidity. (An end that haunts Klossowski's vicious circle, insofar as his book begins and ends with the challenge of lucidity.) Yet its lucidity is that of a votive candle, flickering uncertainly in the rarified air of the crypt. Such lucidity "illumines the inside wall of a cracked symbol" (23). It is the lucidity of a cryptic communication *within* the unconscious, one that inverts the egological maxim of psychoanalysis, as follows: *Wo ich war soll Es werden.* The *Es* invokes not only the Id but also incorrigible imperfection—*Es war,* "It was." Absorption through incorporation is thus never entirely successful, and is never fully achieved (25). The phantom (father or sister, or both, in the Wolfman's case) occupies its own encrypted place *Caddy's head was on Father's shoulder. Her hair was like fire, and little points of fire were in her eyes, and I went and Father lifted me into the chair too, and Caddy held me. She smelled like trees* in the self, heterogeneous both to the self and to the other (41–42). The role of *signs* in cryptonymy—signs as a kind of *mortgaged* desire—and especially the role of the Wolfman's secret sign (*tieret*) cannot detain us here. Neither the ingestion of such signs nor the "satisfactions of the mouth" can be explained sufficiently in a few lines; enough if we recall the importance of quality signs and reality signs in overcoming the primal hallucination analysed by the 1895 "Project." That such signs are encrypted means that they are somehow both incorporated and excluded at the same time, vomited, as it were, into an interior receptacle or pocket (56), indeterminately dead and alive, undecidably within and without. Cryptonymy is therefore the science of the signs of an impossible mourning.

The very linguistic multivalence of the word *mémoire*—to pick up the thread again of Derrida's *Mémoires*—whether masculine or feminine, singular or plural, preserves the cryptic quality of mourning. "These entanglements are multiple; they meet nowhere, neither in a point nor in a memory. There is no singular memory" (MPM, 38/14). Mourning does not (allow) rest. It pushes ahead. The desire to think and speak *in memory of* a departed friend is the intense desire for and affirmation of the future. It engages the bereaved in an alliance, not for purposes of progress or power, but toward an uncertain future to which one nevertheless must say "yes":

> . . . the "yes," which is a non-active act, which states or describes nothing, which in itself neither manifests nor defines any content, this *yes* only commits, before and beyond everything else. And to do so, it must repeat itself to itself: *yes, yes.* It must preserve memory; it must commit itself to keeping its own memory; it must promise itself to itself; it must bind itself to memory for memory, if anything is ever to come from the future. This is the law, and this is what the performative category, in its current state, can merely approach, at the moment when "yes" is said, and "yes" to that "yes." (MPM, 42/20)

Again and again in Derrida's recent work we confront this series of imperatives. Here too his precursor (". . . if anything is ever to come from the future") appears to be Heidegger, however different the tone of "memory" in the two thinkers may be. The difference in tone doubtless has to do with both mourning and mirth—and thus perhaps with the role that Nietzsche plays in the thinking of each. Be that as it may, *mourning* is in ascendancy for the moment:

> What do we mean by "in memory of," or, as we also say, "to the memory of"? For example, we reaffirm our fidelity to the departed friend by acting in a certain manner *in memory of* him, or by dedicating a speech *to his memory.* Each time, we know our friend to be gone forever, irremediably absent, annulled to the point where he himself knows and receives nothing of what takes place in his memory. In this terrifying lucidity, in the light of this incinerating blaze where nothingness appears, we remain in *disbelief* itself. Never will we believe in either death or immortality; and we sustain the blaze of this terrible light through devotion, for it would be unfaithful to delude oneself into believing that the other living *in us* is living *in himself:* because he lives in us and because we live this-or-that in his memory, in memory of him. (MPM, 43/21)

The lucidity that so challenges and goads Klossowski returns here to haunt the obscurity of the phrase *in his memory. He,* the dead one, has no memory; *he,* Nietzsche would say, *war.* To know that he is gone forever, *es ist mit ihm vorbei!,* and not to take comfort too quickly in his having been or being *gewesen,* is the doleful mark of such lucidity. No resurrection. No narcissistic fantasy of inclusion by incorporation or even introjection. "Already installed in the narcissistic structure, the other so marks the self of the relationship to self, so conditions it, that the being 'in us' of bereaved memory becomes the *coming* of the other. . . . And even, however terrifying this thought may be, the *first* coming of the other" (MPM, 44/22). How the *first* coming? Inasmuch as advenience to full presence *never takes place* in life, but only in the infinite distance that is opened by death, when a proper name sets the seal on a life by the typography of a final date: December 21, 1983   *June 2, 1910.*

Yet the law of *mémoire* sees to it that a twist and turn of memory prevents the full gathering of any being into an epitaph or any trope of personification. "This specular reflection never closes in on itself; it does not appear *before* this *possibility* of mourning . . ." (MPM, 49/28). If the friend lives only in us, we ourselves never live comfortably there. Friends know of such mortality, such finitude, not as a limit situation (such as anxiety, perhaps), but as radical alterity:

> If there is a finitude of memory, it is because there is something of the other, and of memory as a memory of the other, which comes from the other and goes back to the other. It defies any totalization and directs us to a scene of allegory, to a fiction of prosopopeia, that is, to tropologies of mourning: to the memory of mourning and to the mourning for memory. This is why there can be no *true mourning*, even if truth and lucidity always presuppose it. . . . (50/29)

Truth as revealing/concealing or as self-showing and withdrawal would have to remain in mourning and sustained imperfection: a perfect typographical error, if error it was, demonstrates this when in *Mémoires: For Paul de Man* (page 30, line 8) Nietzsche's question "What then is truth?" appears as "What then is *Warheit*?" What then is was-ness? *Es war.* It was. He *war*.

"True" mourning is "the tendency to accept incomprehension, to leave a place for it" (51/30). Proust's Marcel slips into the place of such incomprehension when he returns (in *Sodome et Gomorrhe*) to his grandmother's haunts over a year after her death. He finds the very "anachronism" of his sudden paroxysm of mourning the most shocking aspect of the *bouleversement*. It is the very infidelity of his memory, which he traces back to "the intermittences of the heart," that make his mourning so profoundly painful. "Incomprehensible" is his own word for the "strange contradiction of *survivance* and nihilation" in him. ". . . The brusque revelation of death had like lightning hollowed out in me [*creusée en moi*], in line with some supernatural and nonhuman graphics, a mysterious double furrow" (*Recherche*, II, 755–63). Such graphic doubling is the doleful "truth" (*War-heit*) of mourning: the one who lives on also bears the prize of nihilation, *la douloureuse synthèse de la survivance et du néant*.

In the final pages of "Mnemosyne," Derrida brings his reflections on the death of a friend to the question of *being* as gathering and as the *law* of memory. I shall reproduce a number of extracts, with very little commentary:

> This terrible solitude which is mine or ours at the death of the other is what constitutes that relationship to self which we call "me," "us," "between us," "subjectivity," "intersubjectivity," "memory." The *possibility* of death "happens," so to speak, "before" these different instances, and makes them possible. Or, more precisely, the possibility of the death of the other *as* mine or ours in-forms any relation to the other and the finitude of memory. (53/33)

No resolute openedness or readiness for an anxiety that is poised for the leap could prepare us for such solitude. Or for such companionship. No choice of or election to this possibility. No brave mustering of "our generation" to struggle and heroism. Impossible mourning is not possible anxiety. Nor is it a gathering, unless as a persistent focusing on what has slipped through the fingers, as Heidegger's Stefan George writes: "*Worauf es meiner Hand entrann,*" "Whereupon it slipped from my hand" (US, 220). Such slippage, or seepage, or loss Heidegger calls *der Schmerz,* "pain," and we shall some day have to return to Heidegger's own sense of mourning (*Trauer*) and joy (*Freude*). Such pain, in Heidegger too, remains unfamiliar. It is not the repeatable-insurmountable, not the possible impassable possibility of "my own" death that initiates mourning, but the otherness impacted in "my" "own" living beyond and surviving the other. The prize of survival. Congratulations.

Derrida writes:

> We weep *precisely* over what happens to us when everything is entrusted to the sole memory that is "in me" or "in us." But we must also recall in another turn of memory that the "within me" and the "within us" *do not* arise or appear *before* this terrible experience. Or at least not before its possibility, actually felt and inscribed in us, signed. The "within me" and the "within us" acquire their sense and their bearing only by carrying within themselves the death and the memory of the other; of an other who is greater than them, greater than what they or we can bear, carry, or comprehend, since we then lament being no more than "memory," "in memory." Which is another way of remaining inconsolable before the finitude of memory. We know, we knew, *we remember*—before the death of one we loved—that being-in-me or being-in-us is constituted out of the possibility of mourning. We are ourselves only from the perspective of this knowledge that is older than ourselves; and this is why I say that we begin by *recalling* this to ourselves: we come to ourselves through this memory of *possible* mourning. (53/ 33–34)

Derrida calls such memory of *possible* mourning an *allegory* in de Man's sense and in de Man's memory, an allegory of *im*possible mourning, of the *un-readability* of mourning, of the double-bind of successful/unsuccessful labors of mourning. "The possibility of the impossible commands here the whole rhetoric of mourning, and describes the essence of memory." Such a rhetoric is no doubt stamped powerfully by both Hegel and Heidegger: because the other is nowhere to be found outside, mourning is *interiorization* of the other's memory; yet the other resists closure within me precisely by being *nothing,* and we experience the failure of our appropriation as "the dark light of this noth-ing," which Heidegger in "What Is Metaphysics?" calls *die helle Nacht des Nichts.* The dazzling night releases not intimations of my own mortality but the impossible *intimation* (Derrida suggests this word as a translation of *Erinnerung:* MPM, 54/35) of the mourned other. Even if we should interiorize and idealize the body and voice of the other, devouring them, incarnating, assimilating, and mimicking them, such interiorizing has at all events always already happened, catching us by surprise, so that everything begins by re-membering. Yet nothing fails like success. We bear the dead alive—yet also defunct or stillborn—into our own future. Failure alone succeeds. We tenderly eject or release the other, "outside, over there, in his death, outside of us." The infertile dialectic of mourning seems an inexorable law, a decree of Anankē, beyond being.

And yet Derrida doubts whether we can acquiesce in it. "Can we accept this schema? I do not think so, even though it is *in part* a hard and undeniable necessity, the very one that makes *true mourning* impossible." He thereby points beyond impossible mourning to something possible, outside of *acceptance* and beyond *consent,* but also without a tinge of bitterness. Perhaps it is closer to a kind of *affirmation,* not as a resounding celebration of success, but as an inevitable reiteration—a kind of anniversary—of the failure. For "the other will have spoken first" (56/37), and will have had effects only as a *trace*. The trace that nevertheless regulates all our relations with others, with the other "*as other,* that is, as mortal for a mortal, with the one always capable of dying before the other" (57/39). "Our 'own' mortality is not dissociated from, but rather also conditions this rhetoric of faithful memory, all of which serves to seal an alliance and to call us to an affirmation of the other." Even if faithful memory is precisely always and only on the verge of remembering.

GEDÄCHTNIS AND ANDENKEN: IN MEMORY OF HEGEL AND HEIDEGGER

Perhaps it comes to the same: whether one emphasizes the exteriority that attaches itself to thinking memory (*Gedächtnis*) in Hegel's system of subjective spirit (and this is the emphasis of Paul de Man: see Notes, chapter 5, note 15); or whether one stresses the eminence and immanence of *Erinnerung,* which is everywhere and nowhere in the system, all-consuming and all-excreting at once (as I have stressed "interiorizing remembrance" throughout chapter 5); in either case it is a matter of unsuccessful sublation and the failure of dialectic. In his central lecture on de Man, Derrida takes up de Man's thesis on *Gedächtnis* in "Sign and Symbol in Hegel's *Aesthetics*." I will not pursue the lines of either de Man's or Derrida's argument, but will consider the nature of the failure of dialectic—which is a failure of recollective memory—and de Man's and Derrida's strategies for successfully keeping the failure in mind. These strategies involve (1) establishing the relation of the *name* to mourning; (2) interpreting memory as allegory and irony; and (3) envisaging a "nonarchitectonic" gathering of memory.

Derrida has long been intrigued by the relation of the *name* and the *signature* to death and mourning. Whether in chapter seven of *Voice and Phenomenon* (VP, 104–8), which considers what Husserl calls the "essentially occasional" expression "I," a supplement to the zero-point of subjectivity in the soliloquy of mental life, along with the written, testamentary "I" as a transcendental ideality ensconced in the very possibility of my death, or in "The Logic of the Living" of *Otobiographies,* where Nietzsche's signature is read as a mark of his absence, an obsequy, Derrida has pursued the question of the proper name and death.[8]

In "The Art of *Mémoires*" (MPM, 62–63/49) he defines *memory* as the "name" that has to do with the very *possibility* and *preservation* of names—as though in a nocturnal shaft or crypt. Derrida qualifies the nature of such preservation as follows:

> Not preservation as what conserves or maintains the thing named: we have just seen on the contrary that death reveals the power of the name to the very extent that the name continues to name or call what we call the bearer of the name, who can no longer answer *to* or answer *in* and *for* his name. And since the possibility of this situation is revealed at death, we can infer that it does not wait for death, or that in *it* death does not wait for death.

Because "I" could not stop for death, "he" kindly stopped for "me." Stopped well ahead of time. Stopped in the name, in *my* name—monumentalized, for example, on the title-page of a book. In "Interpreting Signatures," Derrida reflects on Heidegger's insistence that the name *Nietzsche* stands for the matter of Nietzsche's *thinking,* as opposed to the mere *person* of Nietzsche, *Herr* Nietzsche, whom Nietzsche himself (in the Foreword to the second edition of *The Gay Science: 3, 347*) encourages us to ignore.[9] But to continue:

> In calling or naming someone while he is alive, we know that his name can survive him and *already survives him;* the name begins during his life to get along without him, speaking and bearing his death each time it is pronounced in naming or calling. . . . [The name] is from the outset "in memory of." We cannot separate the name of "memory" and "memory" of the name; we cannot separate the name and memory. (MPM, 62–63/49)

Thus "the ambiguity of memory," which encompasses what we bear within us in mourning and what is forever outside us, like an epitaph on a stele or monument (MPM, 63–64/50–51). To be "in memory of" is thus "the most ambiguous fidelity."

The "ambiguity of memory" *Let the ambiguous procession of events* *reveal their own ambiguousness* expresses the ultimate failure of interiorizing remembrance. Whether one chases *Erinnerung* or champions *Gedächtnis,* the result is "rupture, heterogeneity, disjunction," rather than dialectical resolution or speculative reconciliation. In Derrida's view, such disjunction arises from the ineradicable alterity of the other—and also of the other-in-me as narrated in the allegory of mourning (69/56). Derrida cites Paul de Man's study of Georges Poulet, which speaks to (and from) an experience of the verge:

> The *instant de passage* supplants memory or, to be more precise, supplants the naive illusion that memory would be capable of conquering the distance that separates the present from the past moment. . . . Memory becomes important as failure rather than as achievement and acquires a negative value. . . . The illusion that continuity can be restored by an act of memory turns out to be merely another moment of transition. Only the poetic mind can gather scattered fragments of time into a single moment and endow it with generative power.[10]

Passage as both *Vorbeigang* of the last god and the *Vorbei* of a human existence cast toward its future; as the "moment of transition," *Übergang,* in Heidegger's interpretation of the moment of recurrence, transition as downgoing, *Untergang;* passage as absolutely resistant to the recuperative powers of memory; passage as the failure of recollection, the "negative value" of memory. Yet the negativity and finitude of memory, Derrida emphasizes, must also be recognized as "the very opening of difference," a difference somewhere between the *ontological difference* between being and beings and the difference that occupied us in chapter 4, a difference that has to do with the *rhetoric of memory* insofar as it involves traces and tracings. Derrida reiterates his effort to remove from that rhetoric the Hegelian (and Heideggerian?) heritage of an "essential past," *Wesen* and *Ge-wesen.* "Memory stays with traces, in order to 'preserve' them, but traces of a past that has never been present, traces which themselves never occupy the form of presence and always remain, as it were, to come— come from the future, from the *to come*" (MPM, 70/58). Ironically, or allegorically, such a memory would be not of the past, as Aristotle avows, but of the present; of the present not as the guarantor of presence but as the site of difference. "What if there were a *memory of the present,* and what if, far from fitting the present to itself, it divided the instant?" (72/60). The very duplicity of Mnemosyne/Lethe sunders presence and opens the space of memory as mourning. Such a memory would be "already 'older' than *Gedächtnis* and *Erinnerung*" (81/71). Derrida portrays it as a "nonarchitectonic *Versammlung*" (83/73), a force of both allegory and irony which, gathering *and* disseminating "over the dead body" of Hegelian reconciliation, leads to "disjunction, dissociation, and discontinuity" (84–85/74–75). Only a long and careful detour through the work of Paul de Man, as Derrida reads it, could show how the combination of *allegory* and *irony* produces the rhetoric of memory—"the common discovery," writes de Man, "of a truly temporal predicament" and of "an *authentic experience of temporality* which, seen from the point of view of the self engaged in the world, is a negative one."[11]

It is perhaps sufficient for our purposes to note Derrida's identification of "the allegorical Mnemosyne and the ironic Lethe," and his own ironic identification with one of these rather than equally with both. He refers to de Man's discussion of a novelist who "manages to be at the same time an allegorist and an ironist" (92–93/85). Such a novelist would "know how to tell a story" (remember: "I have never known how to tell a story"), "but he would refrain from doing so, without one ever being able to know whether he were telling the truth." Such a novelist would be very much like a verger, a two-faced *Janus bifrons,* a Gemini, his manner hesitant but his face full of mirth and mischief. A Socrates so embellished and modernized that he does all the writing for Plato.

However, because we have invoked Mnemosyne as well as Lethe; because allegory accompanies irony, granting irony the chance to work its effects; and because Derrida himself has spoken of a nonarchitectonic gathering of memory; it will not do simply to let Heidegger sink into oblivion. Derrida's third lecture in memory of Paul de Man concentrates on the enigma of memory as both gathering and disjunction. It begins (98/91–92) by citing that long passage from "What Calls for Thinking?" that ties memory (*Gedächtnis*) to thought (*Gedachtes, Gedanke*), and thought to thanks (*Gedanc, Dank:* see pages 265–66, above). The passage encompasses in a strange way the thought of *promise,* "probably today the most profound, most singular, and most necessary thought; probably, too, the most difficult and disconcerting" (99/ 93). Again, it will not be possible here to reduce de Man's texts on the promise to a brief report. Derrida cites the concluding lines of de Man's (revised version of) "Promises," on Rousseau's *Social Contract:* "The error is not within the reader; language itself dissociates the cognition from the act. *Die Sprache verspricht (sich);* to the extent that it is necessarily misleading, language just as necessarily conveys the promise of its own truth. This is why textual allegories on this level of rhetorical complexity generate history."[12]

Die Sprache verspricht (sich). The parody is multifaceted. The first essay of Heidegger's *Unterwegs zur Sprache* ("Die Sprache") has as its refrain, "*Die Sprache spricht,*" "Language speaks." It is a refrain that Derrida, as we shall see, does not scorn. Yet he also values de Man's "discreet parody" of it: de Man alters *spricht* to *verspricht* ("Language promises"), but then adds the reflexive pronoun *sich* in parentheses—*die Sprache verspricht (sich).* Language promises itself, but lapses, makes slips of the tongue. Language slips into promises. Language gives its (false) word. Language commits (errors). Language always tells the *War-heit.* A light touch of mockery here, one that suggests a difference in the styles of thinking: "Heidegger does not laugh often in his texts" (101/96). Yet the important points to be made are that "language is not the governable instrument of a speaking being" and that "the essence of speech is the promise" (101–2/97). The first point is of course Heidegger's own in his essays on language. That Derrida takes it seriously—and in the direction of the second, language as promise—becomes clear in a long note from *Of Spirit: Heidegger and the Question* (DE, 147–54), to which we must now turn, by way of a digression.

The "question of the question," which spurs Derrida's thinking about Heidegger, "veers into the memory of a language, the memory of an experience of language that is 'older' than the question, always anterior and presupposed, so old that it has never been present in an 'experience' or an 'act of language'— in the current sense of these words" (DE, 147). An experience that is not an "experience," an act ("Acts" is the title of Derrida's third lecture on de Man) that is not an "act." And both of these involving a moment that is not a "moment"—yet one that is marked in Heidegger's own text. The text in which the question of the question "turns" in Heidegger's thought is "The Essence of Language" (US, 174–76), a text to which Derrida was led through discussions with Françoise Dastur (DE, 154). Here Heidegger concedes that to pose the *question* of language is already to be caught up in language. Language must always already speak *to* and *for* us; in it we are spoken to and addressed, *zugesprochen.* Precisely this *Zuspruch* of language precedes any inquiry or investigation into language. Language thus *precedes* and *exceeds* interrogation. Its precedence constitutes "a sort of promise or originary alliance" in which we have always already acquiesced, to which we have said *yes,* handing hostages to fortune, as it were, the (mis)fortunes of our future discourse. Such acquiescence Heidegger calls *Zusage,* and it is the pendant to *Zuspruch.* Heidegger affirms *Zusage* as the "ultimate instance of the questioning attitude" (DE, 148). His most candid statement of the preeminence of language-as-promise over language-as-questioning now appears (US, 175; DE, 148): "What do we experience when we ponder this sufficiently? That questioning [*das Fragen*] is not the appropriate gesture of thinking [*nicht die eigentliche Gebärde des Denkens ist*]; rather, [the appropriate gesture is] hearing the assent [*die Zusage*] of what is to come into question." Before the word, in a perhaps unspoken *yes,* mortals are engaged to language, en-gaged in the sense that they have always already paid a gage or forfeit to speech. Questioning is thus a response, is engaged to a responsibility that it has not, and never can have, chosen.

The gage will have been given prior to all other events. However, in its very antecedence the gage is an *event,* but one whose every remembrance [*souvenir*] memory [*la mémoire*] has left behind, and to which a faith that defies all telling [*tout récit*] binds us. No erasure is possible with regard to this kind of gage. No getting back behind it.

Derrida's note goes on to demonstrate the overwhelming consequences such a subordination of questioning to the appropriate gesture of assent might have for Heidegger's thought—for example, for the very question of being, posed by that ostensibly exemplary being (Dasein) which poses questions. And yet if the *Zusage* cannot be circumscribed, if it is always already "behind" every questioning, what sense would it make to recommence or to insist that Heidegger expand and radicalize his "immanent critique" of *Being and Time?*[13] Derrida's strategy is to discern those "strata" traversed by Heidegger's path of thinking which, although "less massive" than the themes commonly discussed, restructure the landscape of his discourse. For example, the stratum of *responsibility*—which is much more than an example. That strategy would search for "another topology, for new tasks." Ethical and political tasks, to be sure, but also tasks involving Heidegger's relation to other discourses—the sciences, linguistics, poetics, psychoanalysis, and so on. There is no need here and now to pursue these various strata and topologies, which Derrida outlines with typical meticulousness. (At this point in the note Derrida introduces [in brackets] a "pause." He pauses for a daydream, an admittedly perverse and wicked fantasy: he tries to imagine what the Heideggerian *corpus* would look like if one were to apply quite literally and across the board all the strictures that Heidegger himself at one time or another enforces on his readers. What would happen if one ranged over Heidegger's text like a voracious rat, gnawing, ruminant, and ravenous, a mechanical animal   *The machines clanked in threefour time. Thump, thump, thump. Now if he got paralyzed there and no-one knew how to stop them they'd clank on and on the same, print it over and over and up and back. Monkeydoodle the whole thing. Want a cool head*   obedient to the following instructions: avoid the word *Geist;* at the very least, place it always in quotation marks; erase all the words that relate to *world* and *worldliness* whenever discussing forms of life other than Dasein; cross out the word *Sein;* finally, erase all the question-marks in the text whenever *language* is under discussion, which is to say, just about everywhere. Concerning his daydream about obsessive obedience Derrida concedes this: "It would not simply be 'unspirited' and 'witless' ['*sans esprit*']; it would be a figure of evil. The perverse reading of Heidegger. End of pause.")

Heidegger's emphasis on "hearing" and "assent" in the essays underway to language is not an invitation to docility or "hearsay." (Such hearsay, *ouï-dire,* will nevertheless soon occupy us.) It is rather testimony to Heidegger's experience of the commitment of mortals, who are *always already engaged* to language. At the moment language addresses us (*zuspricht*), it has already elicited our assent (*Zusage*), ". . . and this past never returns, never again becomes present . . ." (DE, 153). Rather, ". . . it reverts always to an older event, which will have engaged us ahead of time in this subscription of en-gagement." Engagement to the address marks the essential unfolding of language, *Das Wesen der Sprache: Die Sprache des Wesens* (US, 181; DE, 154). The colon serves to erase the copulative *ist,* while preserving and intensifying *Wesen* as "essential unfolding." Erasure of being thus introduces the thinking of *Ereignis,* and Derrida's note ends as follows:

> Thought of *Ereignis* measures itself upon this acquiescence that responds—engages itself—to the address. And what is proper to the human being advenes only in this response or in this responsibility. It does so at least only when man acquiesces, consents, renders himself to the address of that which addresses him; that is to say, to *its* address, which properly becomes his own only in this response. After having named *Ereignis* in this context, Heidegger reminds us that the *Zusage* does not err in the wilderness. "It has already struck home [*Sie hat schon getroffen*]. Who else than the human being? *Denn der Mensch ist nur Mensch, insofern er dem Zuspruch der Sprache zugesagt, für die Sprache, sie zu sprechen, gebraucht ist* [For human beings are human only to the extent that they assent to the address of language and are needed and used for speaking language]." (US, 196; DE, 154)

The context of Derrida's note in *De l'esprit* is the selfsame *promise* and *lapsus* of language that we have been discussing in the context of *Mémoires: For Paul de Man.* Derrida calls that context "the dysymmetry of an affirmation, of a *yes* prior to all opposition of *yes* and *no*" (DE, 147). We shall soon take up discussion of this dysymmetry. Yet not before noting that the word *consent* has just now fallen—as a translation of *Zusage.* Is Heidegger's piety or docility (*Frömmigkeit* as *Fügsamkeit*), whether expressed toward being, propriation, essential unfolding, or the speaking of language, tainted by a nostalgia for restoration of the lost dreamworld of presence? The *homesickness* (*Heim-weh = nost-algie*) that Nietzsche diagnosed at and as the heart of German philosophy? Would such nostalgia be essentially altered in the French heart, or in any other, if engagement to language is a matter of "consent"?

That it is not nostalgia is at least suggested by the intensity of *pain* in the *Zusage,* precisely in these essays that are underway to language. Derrida himself introduces the theme of pain when he writes about the flame and ash invoked in Heidegger's essay on Trakl (see DE, 173–75). Yet as I suggested some pages back, *der Schmerz* requires far more detailed treatment: it gathers (nonarchitectonically) Heidegger's thinking on thought *as gathering*, on poetic language and song, on the *Riss* that is both the rift or fault in being and the outline of the work of art, and on the gathering of humankind into one *Geschlecht*. If early in *Unterwegs zur Sprache* it is a matter of the pain that turned the threshold to stone ("*Schmerz versteinerte die Schwelle*"—Georg Trakl, "*Ein Winterabend*"), it is later the pain associated with death that becomes increasingly explicit in Heidegger's reflections on language:

> Yet as the joy grows more joyous still, mourning slumbers all the more purely within it. As the mourning grows more profound, the joy that resides in it calls all the more. Mourning and joy engage in interplay. The play that attunes the two to one another, letting what is remote come near and what is near lie afar, is itself *pain* [der Schmerz]. Thus both supreme joy and profoundest mourning are painful, each in its own way. And pain tempers the sensibility [*mutet das Gemüt*] of mortals, so that they derive from pain their center of gravity. That center holds mortals—for all their vacillation—in the tranquillity of their essential unfolding. (US, 235)

To be sure, it is still a matter of the *hold*, to prevent vacillation. Yet the vacillation Heidegger is referring to is the ever-inventive craving for subter-fuges of one kind or another. Nostalgia being not the least of these. So that precisely when we are ready to consign Heidegger to the ranks of the homesick, hoping in that way finally to be rid of him, purged of all his Teutonic failings and Titanic failures, spared the entire enigma of Heidegger, these words of pain and mourning stop us. Unless we are *very* good at subterfuges, mourning and pain make it difficult to lose Heidegger.[14]

Even enjoying a laugh at Heidegger's expense—*Die Sprache (ver)spricht (sich)*—brings us back to mourning. And to debts that Derrida has never ceased to acknowledge, however great the pain. The promise of language itself exacts this unacquittable debt, inasmuch as the "fatal drift" of language itself accompa-nies even the most fervent promise. "The promise is impossible but inevitable" (MPM, 102/98). We are engaged to language even as it slips and slides and makes of our "pure promise" something considerably less pristine than we had hoped. We are engaged to it, engaged in it, even when we read. Yet the "allegory of unreadability" does not result in resignation or dogmatism. Rather, it ac-knowledges the abyss of yes-saying: "You cannot read without speaking, speak without promising, promise without writing, write without reading that you have already promised even before you began to speak, and so on. And you can only take note of this—in other words, take a note as *acte*—before every act. You can only say and sign: yes, yes in memory of yes" (MPM, 103–4/100). Such *notatio* and *notio* do not secure the promise typographically, by way of contract, but only indicate a kind of rupture or interruption: a signature, signed and sealed, if not delivered, "can only promise itself, and can only (inevitably) prom-ise itself insofar as the path toward its destination is barred, within a no-exit, without end, a dead-end, the impasse of the aporia" (MPM, 103–4/100). *Die*

Sprache verspricht (sich): language promises itself to itself, and in so doing misspeaks itself. Derrida calls it "the aporetic event": the shadow of *Ereignis,* the withdrawal or expropriation "of a promise which never occurs, which never happens, but which cannot not occur . . ." (104/101).

These reflections—redolent of paradox—on the aporetic event of promise lead to Derrida's most detailed remarks on the overdetermined *Mémoires* in which he is engaged. He does not cite Heidegger's gesture toward a "gyne-morphic" *Gedächtnis,* his invocation of the mother, Dame Mnemosyne, *die Gedächtnis.* Nor, when discussing the many senses of the English *memento,* from the Sanscrit *manmi,* Latin *Memini,* "I know, I remember," does he ponder one of the most extraordinary scions of *mnēmē,* one that no doubt has to do with memory as affirmation. Affirmation in the face of every dead-end or impasse. The Middle High German word *minne,* "love," remembered today because of the Minnesingers, springs from "keeping in mind," "dwelling on," remembering. Yet such remembering, apparently from early on in the history of the word, is *philia,* "brotherliness in the community." The word "community" (*Gemeinde*) is itself related to loving memory. *Mnēmē* as *minne* comes to have during the thirteenth century the sense of both love of God and sexual love, both *agapē/caritas* and *erōs/amor,* thanks to   *What a mnice old mness it all mnakes!*   the writings of the mystics, although even in Old High German the sense of sexual love is never altogether absent. Nor is the erotic sense of *minne* deprived of the mnemic senses of "friendship, dedication, and good will" until quite late, well after the great poets, Walther von der Vogelweide and Gottfried von Strassburg.[15]

Nor is *minne* without its ancient counterpart. The "suitors" who assemble at Penelope's palace during Odysseus' absence are called in Greek *mnēstēres* (*Odyssey 14,* 81; *17,* 65 passim). They would gladly "minister" to Penelope's every need; she wishes they would "mind" their own affairs. Their courting or wooing (*16, 391; 21, 161: mnasthō; 14, 91: mnasthai*), their "ministry," as it were (cf. *16, 294: mnēstu*), is less a being mindful of and doting on a much sought-after woman (*14, 64: polymnēstē*) than a calculated plundering of the household. To say the least, these ministers are not thinking thankfully on their host (cf. *15, 54: mimnēisketai*). It is therefore ironic, and even gruesome, when the leader of the suitors—and the first to be slaughtered—assures the others that he remembers Odysseus: *kai gar mnēmōn eimi,* "For I am still very much in mind of him" (*21, 95*). Finally, the lover's keepsake or memento brings together love and memory in unforgettable ways. When Helen gives Telemachos the peplos she has woven for him she says—perhaps a bit coyly, perhaps to irritate Menelaos—that it is to be "a memento of the hands of Helen" (*15, 126*). The keepsake that Nausicaa presents to Odysseus is nothing more than the vision he has of her at the banquet prior to his departure, and these words of hers: "I hope that when you are in your homeland you will, every now and then, dwell on me (*8, 462: mnēsēi emei*).

If Derrida fails to draft a specific memo on the *minne* in *mnēmē,* Heidegger will surely be unable to remind him. Yet *minne's mnēmē* is vital to Heidegger's thought of *Gedanc* and *Dank,* the "heart," and Dame Mnemosyne, as well as the thought of *Geschlecht* and "the more gentle twofold." And however manic it may seem, *minne* should be vital to both mourning and mirth in Derrida's thinking. Perhaps it will be.

Bypassing now Derrida's remarks on Rousseau, Hölderlin, and Nietzsche, "the three madmen of Western modernity," who brought Derrida and Paul de Man together (MPM, 126/128); bypassing them even though they would enable me to rejoin Pierre Klossowski's "mad lucidity" and "light of lunacy" (126/129); bypassing "the madness of the promise and the madness of memory" (129/132); bypassing the aporias and disjunctions of a promise that retains irony, its incalculable and fickle other; bypassing a memory that "*does not* lead us back to *any anteriority*" (133/137); I wish only to summarize Derrida's own account of the differences in the "style of promise" found in Heidegger's and in his own texts. Derrida tries to dispense with Heidegger's insistence on the "originality" of the *Gedanc,* as *das anfängliche Wort,* the matutinal word; with the gesture of gathering, *das gesammelte, alles versammelnde Gedenken;* with the more originary, *ursprünglichere,* thought of the heart—all this encompassed in the original essence of memory, *das ursprüngliche Wesen des Gedächtnisses* (MPM, 136/141; WhD? 91–93; see above, pages 265–77). However, as we saw in chapter 4, the "indispensable reference to originality" is as attributable to Derrida's early work as it is to Heidegger, and even here in *Mémoires, Versammlung* has been admitted with the proviso that it not be "architectonic," that it perhaps be only *quasi*-transcendental. Not only that. Derrida's own note on the future tasks of a reading of Heidegger insists on an originary, antecedent *yes, Zu-sage,* or *gage* to language, which would be anterior to questioning and secure from all erasure.

What Derrida continues to affirm in Heidegger's thinking of memory is its *call,* its invitation and command, its *promise* to respond affirmatively to the call of thinking. Nevertheless, the *mortal* promise traces out a tentative and precarious future rather than recollecting or hoarding a past. It responds to the call of an absent friend, responds to a *mourning*—rather than to a *being*—in default. It changes its shape in Derrida's lectures on memory and mourning, differs from Heidegger's text more than it can know, whatever the undeniable debts and confessed loyalties. Before passing on to the second trait of memory as affirmation, the joy or mirth that Heidegger—after Hölderlin, yet more sternly than he—would call *Heiterkeit,* these final words from *Mémoires:*

> What is love, friendship, memory, from the moment two impossible promises are involved with them, sublimely, without any possible exchange, in difference and dysymmetry, in the incommensurable? What are we, who are we, to what and to whom *are we,* and to what and to whom are we *destined* in the *experience* of this impossible promise? Henceforth: what is experience?
>
> These questions can be posed only after the death of a friend, and they are not limited to the question of mourning. What should we think of all this—of love, of memory, of promise, of destination, of experience—from the moment a promise, the instant it pledges, and however impossible it appears, pledges beyond death,

beyond what we call, without knowing of what or of whom we speak, death. It involves, in reverse, the other, dead *in us,* from the first moment, even if no one is *there* to respond to the promise or speak for the promise. What does *"in us"* mean if such an impossible promise is *thinkable,* that is to say, possible in its impossibility? This is perhaps what thinking gives us to think about; this is perhaps what gives us to think about thinking. (143/149)

MIRTH

The two long lectures that constitute *Ulysse gramophone: Deux mots pour Joyce* arise from and speak to an essentially comic situation: in both cases the Philosopher has been invited by the most formidable scholarly machine at work in literary studies today, the machine of *Etudes joyciennes,* in order that he might address the machine on the matter of its own expertise. Derrida comes to the Joyce experts as Elijah, though with less prophetic dignity than fear and trembling, "at an angle of fortyfive degrees over Donohoe's in Little Green Street like a shot off a shovel."[16]

The Philosopher, to whom the gift of narration has ostensibly been denied, regales the assembled Joyce Scholars with tales of his recent travels—his odysseys to Tokyo and Ohio, for example. Like Scheherezade, he hopes thereby to postpone the moment when he will have to lose his head and beg for acknowledgment or at least a stay of execution from the Sultans of Joyce Scholarship. And yet the most serious of Derrida's recent preoccupations are to be found here among all these jimmyjokes: memory, mourning, and the yes-saying of affirmation. If it breaches the bounds of discretion to have commented on Derrida's lectures on Paul de Man, my account here will no doubt stultify the humor, verve, and trenchancy of his "two words for Joyce."

HE WAR. These *are* the two words, extracted from the penultimate page of the first section of Book II ("Feenichts Playhouse") of *Finnegans Wake* (258.12). The context? Only the Joyce Scholar knows for sure whether there is (n)one. From the penultimate page of II, 1:

> Yip! Yup! Yarrah! And let Nek Nekulon extol Mak Makal and let him say unto him: Immi ammi Semmi. And shall not Babel be with Lebab? And he war. And he shall open his mouth and answer. I hear, O Ismael, how they laud is only as my loud is one.

"And he war." "And he deed." Derrida also cites the final lines of the final page of II, 1 (259.3–4; 7–10):

> O Loud, hear the wee beseech of thees of each of these they unlitten ones! Grant sleep in hour's time, O Loud! (. . .)
> Loud, heap miseries upon us yet entwine our arts with laughters low!
> Ha he hi ho hu.
> Mummum.

The infinite Babel of Joyce's archive and the infinite Yahwism of I-am-who-am are Derrida's two preoccupations throughout. "He" wars, that is to say, the

Loud prosecutes war and commits all the acts of violence and outrage that constitute the nightmare of human history. And yet, because *war,* pronounced somewhat differently, is also the past tense, the imperfect, of the German *bin,* "I am," and *ist,* "he/she/it is," Joyce's phrase suggests that He *was.* In other words, the Loud is inextricably bound up with *Vorbeigang,* the "It was" of time—even though Derrida does not explicitly mention the (possible) connection with Nietzsche. Further, the German *war* is gramophonically bound up with *wahr,* "true," with the truth of being as preserving (*wahren, bewahren*) and, one would have to add, with *gewähren,* the "granting" of time and being in and through the propriative event, *Er-eignis.* Yet who is He?

In the first place, argues Derrida, He is the James Joyce of the Joyce Scholars, the Joyce who is not unalloyed joy to Derrida: "I am not sure I like Joyce." "More precisely, I am not sure that he is well liked. Except when he laughs—and you will tell me that he laughs all the time" (UG, 20/146). It will therefore be a matter of distinguishing among various tonalities of laughter: for example, the laughter of one who like a Universal Spider spins a web that neither Scholar nor Philosopher will be able to flee, a weft of writing designed to be all-embracing and all-consuming, permitting no escape, paralyzing all who enter its silky mesh. Web of Atropos. The laughter of one who has the laugh of all those he will cause to be indebted to him—cause to be in *memory* of him (UG, 21/147). Perhaps the laughter of a writer or thinker who imagines that university chairs will one day be endowed for the purpose of encyclopedic research into his own texts; so that future generations will be consigned to a memory larger than their own, trapped in a hypermnemic tissue that gathers all it can (*rassembler;* cf. Heidegger's *Versammlung*) of "cultures, languages, mythologies, philosophies, sciences, histories of spirit or of literatures" (UG, 22/147). "He" would thus "war" against all future generations of readers and scholars, never allowing them to forget "the sadistic demiurge" looming at the origin of it all.

Finnegans Wake is no doubt but one book; yet it is a book with "the greatest possible memory" (UG, 26/149). Nevertheless, or precisely for this reason, Derrida remembers his own debt to the memory of Joyce, extending from his 1962 Introduction to Husserl's "Origin of Geometry," in which Hegelian *Erinnerung* and Husserlian *Epoche* are made to spin about the Joycean axis, through the 1968 "Plato's Pharmacy," where the *apotheca* as a whole is brought under the spells of Bataille and Joyce, to the 1977 *Carte postale,* in which the "he war" explicitly resounds.[17] The memory of debts, the entire economy of promise and contract as delineated in the second treatise of Nietzsche's *Genealogy,* spins a web of incredible complexity and density. Such is the archival system of computations and accounts to which the memory of Joyce—*genitivus subiectivus et obiectivus*—appears to commit and condemn us. The Joyce who laughs up his sleeve *ironice* at generations to come; the Joyce who, understandably, Derrida does not like to like. He war. YHWH bristling with omnipotence, weaving all the webs, weaver of the wind.

Yet he *war* is also a sign of fall and ruinance, as we have seen, a sign of the *vorbei* and of bygones. YHWH is *gttrdmmrng*, deathly consonants without the breath of vowels. The imperfect tense of *ist* invokes "a past without appeal," a past which, "before being, and before being present, was" (UG, 40/154). Derrida relates the was, the *fut*, to the *fuit*, and thence to the fire of Spinoza's jealous (*zelotypic*) God. Let us pray. One could also relate it to the *fui* of Quentin Compson and, rather than to any zelotypography, to the eternally wretched "Too late!" *Es war.* Signature of God and memory of the whole world (UG, 48/157), he war ultimately only in mourning and mirth, only with "laughters low" (FW, 259.7–8; UG, 51/158). However, if Derrida worries about "Joyce's vengeance vis-à-vis the God of Babel" (UG, 52/158) in a way that the verger does not, it is nonetheless a question of the *tonality* of laughter, and of *giving* according to the fine arts of laughter. Calling upon the counter-signing goddess, Molly, who says *yes* and thus issues Bloom's passport to eternity, Derrida concludes his two words for Joyce with a kind of invocation and prayer: "Countersigned God, God who signs yourself in us, let us laugh, *amen, sic, si, oc, oï*" (UG, 53/158). *Oc, oï.* Hoc illud, "here and there," presumably the origin of the French *oui*. The theme of Derrida's second lecture on Joyce, "Ulysse gramophone: Ouï-dire de Joyce," is Joyce's hearsay and yes-saying. *Ouï-dire* and *oui, rire:* Joyce's hearsay is also, yes, laughter. Let us play.

Derrida begins his Frankfurt lecture with the double assurance *oui, oui;* yes, yes. A "particle," a particle of language that particularly in French likes to double itself, as though under contract with itself. In English, *yes* appears to have been formed by the affirmation *yea* and the third person singular of *beon* "to be," *si.* "Yes" would thus be the contraction of the form that appears so often in *Ulysses* as a form of assent, "Ay," "It is," "Ay, it is." Before he discusses the import of the double-yes (in ways already familiar to us through our discussion of *Mémoires*), Derrida relates two tales concerning the yes as dysymmetrical with the no, hence as outside the oppositional or dialectical pair, yes/no. He swears the tales he tells are true, *Ja, wahr.* He reports visiting the state of Ohio—"A perfect cretic! the professor said. Long, short and long" (U, 105. 369), the name of that great state itself obviously being a play on *oï, oui-oui*—and finding in a supermarket there a brand of yogurt called *Yes.* Beneath the grand affirmation of the brandname on the cap an advertising jingle teases, "Bet You Can't Say No to Yes" (UG, 61; in American in the original). He then recounts an incident in the newspaper shop of the Hotel Okura in Tokyo, where he is looking for postcards to buy. He sees a business-man's "self-help" book on the shelf entitled *16 Ways to Avoid Saying No* and recalls that the Japanese always avoid saying no (out of courtesy) even when they *mean* no. "Beside this book, on the same shelf, another book by the same author, once again in English translation: *Never Take Yes for an Answer*" (UG, 70).

The double-yes can doubtless take a servile or an obstreperous, a reassuring or an impatient form. Derrida does not dream of barring contamination or parody from the repetition. Nevertheless, he stresses "the *yes* of affirmation, assent, or consent, of alliance, engagement, signature, or giving," which must bear repetition in itself "if it is to be taken in the way it wants to be taken" (UG, 89). The double-yes "must immediately and a priori confirm its promise and promise its confirmation." As we heard Derrida say in *Mémoires,* the yes can be said only if it "promises to itself the memory of itself," so that affirmation of the yes "is affirmation of memory." This is the gramophone-effect that attaches itself to the yes. It seems to contradict in the strongest possible terms the amnesia that as Pierre Klossowski's *Vicious Circle* insists must intervene in the re-willing of eternal return. Are we to take it that the double-yes does not emanate from that high tonality of the soul, the *Stimmung* of ecstasy, of which Klossowski and Nietzsche write? Is the repetitious *yes* prosaic?

That this need not be the case—and that the yes of consent need not be cloying—is suggested by Derrida's insistence on parody and mimicry, as well as on "the mourning of the yes" (UG, 90). For the yes appeals to an *other* yes, the yes of *an other.* Derrida speaks of "the distress of a signature that demands *yes* of the other, the suppliant's injunction for a countersignature . . ." (UG, 99). And what is true of the yes is true of the entire corpus over which the Joyce Scholar would attain mastery: hypermnemic interiorization, like the yes, can never close in on itself once and for all. If only for the reason that the countersignature may come in the form of a very nervous guest speaking in foreign tongues—speaking French to a German audience that is expert in Joyce's Hibernian English—as follows:

> For a very long time the question of the *yes* has mobilized or traversed all that I apply myself to think, write, teach, or read. To mention only readings—I have devoted seminars and texts to the *yes,* the double *yes* of Nietzsche's *Zarathustra* ("Thus spake Zarathustra," as Mulligan also says [19.727–28]), the *yes, yes* of the hymen, which is always the best example of it, the *yes* of the grand affirmation of midday, and then the ambiguity of the double *yes:* the one reverting to the Christian assumption of a burden, the *"Ja, Ja"* of the donkey laden like the Christ with memory and responsibility; the other *yes,* a light, airy, dancing, solar *yes,* also a *yes* of reaffirmation, promise, and profession of faith, a *yes* to eternal return. The difference between these two *yeses,* or rather between the two repetitions of the *yes,* remains unstable, subtle, sublime. One repetition haunts the other. (UG, 108)

It would be necessary (though impossible) to distinguish, between two repetitions of the *yes.* There can be no doubt that both Nietzsche and Joyce place—or find—the precarious yet persistent *yes* in the mouth of a woman. Not simply woman as mother, flesh, and earth—the attributes of Tellurian Penelope in the secondary literature surrounding *Ulysses* and in Joyce's own utterances. Derrida therefore rereads the novel with the aim of providing a *typology* of the yeses, especially those of Molly Bloom, who commences with a suspicious confirmation ("Yes because he never did a thing like that before . . .") and concludes with an eschatological signature of affirmation doubled and trebled (". . . and yes I said yes I will Yes"). Molly's affirmation occupies the site of Joyce's own signature, above the place and date that mark the period of the novel's gestation. These two signatures of affirmation "appeal to one another, appropriately, across a *yes* that always sets the scene of appeal and demand: confirm and countersign" (UG, 110). Affirmation calls forth the "*a priori* confirmation, repetition, retention, and memory of the *yes.*" Such eschatological affirmation is merely the more dramatic appearance of a certain "narrativity" at the "heart" of the simplest *yes:* "I asked him with my eyes to ask again yes and then he asked me would I yes to say yes . . ." (U, 644.1605–6).

Because laughter is as infectious as the *yes,* and because the possible differences in tone are vital in both, Derrida now (re)turns to the theme of laughter. And to the man who laughs. In French in the original, in caricature of Victor Hugo, as follows:

THE HOBGOBLIN

(*his jaws chattering, capers to and fro, goggling his eyes, squeaking, kangaroohopping with outstretched clutching arms, then all at once thrusts his lipless face through the fork of his thighs*) Il vient! C'est moi! L'homme qui rit! (U, 413.2156–60)

The apocalyptic epiphany of the man (not the *vache*) who laughs transpires between the raucous, repetitious bellowings of the gramophone in Nighttown. It occurs quite a few pages after Bloom has rescued himself from the nastiest sorts of incriminations by virtue of a shibboleth—a passage of the mocking Joyce which Derrida does not cite:

BLOOM

(*behind his hand*) She's drunk. The woman is inebriated. (*he murmurs vaguely the pass of Ephraim*) Shitbroleeth.

But back to the apocalyptic *homme qui rit!* Derrida distinguishes between the written (gramo) and the spoken (phonic) *yes:* the *oui* that is heard (*ouï*) does not differ from the *oui* that is written. Although unrelated etymologically, the homophonic *oui* and *ouï* (the *trema* marks the written word as "heard," even though no one can hear it) captivate Derrida. Hearsay, *ouï-dire,* becomes a "*yes for the ears,*" and the *dire* induces laughter, *rire.* Yes, laughter (*oui-rire*) could have been Derrida's title as readily as hearsay (*ouï-dire*), especially given the series of accidents that went into the arrangements preceding his Frankfurt lecture. (Whose arrangements? Dire-rire-da's, no doubt.) After having informed Jean-Michel Rabaté by long-distance telephone from Tokyo of the title of his proposed paper for the Ninth International James Joyce Symposium, "L'ouï-dire de Joyce," he received the following confirmation from the chairman, Klaus Reichert (in English in the text): "I am very curious to know about your Lui/Oui's which could be spelt Louis as well I suppose. And the Louis' have not yet been detected in Joyce as far as I know. Thus it sounds promising from every angle" (UG, 77).

Why laughter, when it is a matter of yes, yes, double affirmation in the face of mourning? One hopes in vain that *mirth* and *merriment* will prove to share the roots *smer-* and *mar-,* so that they can be etymological cousins to *merimna* and *mourning.* Derrida speaks nevertheless of the *rire* as a remnant, a *reste,* not unrelated in fact to mourning. It is the *Stimmung* or *pathos* of the yes-laugh (*l'oui-rire*) that intrigues him, just as the challenge to sustain the high tonality of the experience of return obsesses Klossowski (UG, 116). Derrida now carries out the typology (not typography) of laughter that was envisaged in the lecture on *Finnegans Wake*. "With one ear, and for a certain hearing [*ouïe*], I hear a yes-laugh [*oui-rire*] resonating that is reactive, negative" (UG, 117). (Derrida employs the Deleuzean genealogical category of the *reactive*, even though his recent work takes greater distance from the genealogical project than does *Of Grammatology*.)[18] The reactive laugh is a laugh of defiance: let herhim disentangle himherself from this web who can. Again Derrida calls it "hypermnemic mastery," a fortress as "impregnable as an alpha and omegaprogramophone," to which "all histories, stories, discourses, forms of knowledge, and all signatures to come" must address themselves. Thus there is a James Joyce *polytropos*, as cunning and as *rusé* as Odysseus himself, master of the Grand Tour, yet also cautious—remembering his former toils, confronting a novel choice. "A triumphant, jubilant laughter, to be sure, but a jubilation that always betrays a sense of mourning [*quelque deuil*]; the laughter is also one of lucid resignation." *Ulysses* and *Finnegans Wake,* "supercharged with a savvy that is as impatient to show itself as it is to hide itself" (UG, 118), are but *two* tomes in the Library of Congress. Even if they contain the universe (of discourses), one may still fail to find them on sale in the *souterrain* newspaper shop of the Hotel Okura. Derrida has already recounted this part of the chronicle of "my experiences," and again he swears that it is true, or was true, *ja, er war wahr:*

> As I was taking note of these titles [16 *Ways to Avoid Saying No,* and *Never Take Yes for an Answer*], an American tourist of the most typical sort leaned on my shoulder and sighed, "So many books! Which is the definitive one? Is there any?" It was a tiny bookshop, a newspaper kiosk. I refrained from telling him, "Yes, there are two of them, *Ulysses* and *Finnegans Wake.*" Instead, I kept this *yes* to myself and smiled stupidly like someone who did not understand the language. (UG, 71)

That sighing American was of course Melville's Pierre, feigning garrulousness, and we can be sure that he knew who he was talking to and what he was asking for.

The laugh of hypermnemic mastery, waxing sardonic, mocking, engorges itself "on all memory," *de toute la mémoire* (UG, 119). It assumes, resumes, and exhausts perfect presence or *parousia*. By a curious operation of anagram, its OUI becomes an I.O.U., and the donation of laughter an impressment or indenturing of the reader:

> There is no contradiction in putting it this way: such yes-laughter is that of Nietzsche's Christian donkey, the one who cries *Ja ja,* the Judeo-Christian animal who wants to make the Greek laugh now that he has been circumcised of his own laugh: absolute knowing as the truth of religion, arrogated memory, culpability, literature burdened by the *summa* and become what one might think of as "a beast of burden," a literature of summation, moment of the debt: A, E, I, O, U, *I owe you,* whereby the "I" is constituted in the very debt and comes to itself only where it gets into debt.

OUI, I.O.U., I owe you. The anagrammatical operation dots the i into the
bargain. When the jackass of "The Awakening" and "The Ass Festival" (ASZ
IV: 4, 388–90) screeches his hee-haw litany of pure affirmations   *the
long, ardently protracted lovecry of the ass*   it takes the orthographic
form I-A, i-a, in order better to approximate the music. Dotting the i in the
inane litany of I.O.U.s—this is precisely the function of the monarch in Hegel's
sovereign state (*Grundlinien der Philosophie des Rechts, §281, Zusatz: 7,*
451):

> One often hears the complaint raised against the monarch that he puts the fortunes
> of the state at risk, inasmuch as he may be poorly educated to the task and may not
> be worthy to occupy the summit of the state; and that it is a nonsense that
> *precisely for that reason there was perhaps no second heroism of love as disconso-*
> *lately sweet as his*   such a situation should exist as a rational one. The
> complaint's premise—that what matters is the particular character of the person
> involved—is invalid. In a consummately well-organized state, matters at the top
> require merely formal decision-making; for a monarch one needs only a human
> being who says "Yes" and dots the I [*einen Menschen, der "Ja" sagt und den Punkt*
> *auf das I setzt . . .*].

When at the end of Hegel's treatise (§352) all the peoples of the Earth "throng
about the throne" of the regal *Weltgeist,* one must wonder whether the universal spirit of world history is a capital long-ear dotting the j's of all the asinine
ja-ja's. I.O.U. U.O.me. Yes, yes. Yet one must also wonder whether wondering
so is not the reactive laughter of frustrated mastery. Brood of mockers. Mock
mockers after that, for we traffic in mockery.

Yet there is a second kind of yes-laugh, an affirmation not of recuperation
but of potlatch. The eschatological tonality of *l'homme qui rit* is "worked,"
"traversed," and even "haunted" by another kind of music, a jinglejoyous
ventriloquy. "I also hear, close to the other, as the yes-laughter of a gift without
debt, the light-winged affirmation [*l'affirmation légère*], almost amnesiac, of a
gift or an event abandoned . . ." (UG, 120). Almost amnesiac: a burst of laughter that bears all its own bitterness, or, at least, a generous spray of chuckles.
Not Elijah despatched from some celestial Central Telecom, but the unexpected
expected guest, Elie. Yet the contamination of these two figures—Elijah as
master of the chair *and* vagabond Elie—is the very rule of laughter: one courts
the risk of mockery and masterful appropriation in the very celebration of a
laughter that does not indebt. Laughter signs on the dotty line, but its signature
remains unassignable. "Thus if laughter is a fundamental or abyssal tonality of
Ulysses, if analysis of that book is not exhausted by any of the branches of
knowledge available to us precisely because *Ulysses* laughs knowingly at knowledge, then laughter explodes in the very event of signature" (121).[19]

Not that the explosion of signatures precludes the signing. Far from it.
Assent is always already engaged, as in the instance of Heideggerian *Zu-sage.*
"If the signature does not recur in order to manipulate or mention a name, it
does presuppose the irreversible engagement of the one who confirms—by

saying or *doing yes*—the hostage of a mark that has made its mark [*le gage d'une marque laissée*]." What happens when the *yes* makes it mark? In the first place, it need not be spoken or written at all; something the French translations of *Ulysses* demonstrate when they render many words and phrases as *oui*. Especially in French, as I have mentioned, but also in English (ja ja OK OK auf deutsch auch sí sí), the yes inclines of itself to reaffirmation, reconfirmation, doubling. For example, in telephonic exchanges: ". . . the *yes* comes from me to me, from me to the other in me, from the other to me, confirming the first *hello?* over the telephone: yes, that's it, that's just what I'm saying, in effect I'm speaking, yes, here I am, speaking, yes, yes, you hear me, I hear you, we are here to talk, there is language, you understand me well, that's just how it is, it's taking place, it's happening, it's writing itself, marking itself, yes, yes" (124). No doubt, it is difficult to find a referent for *yes*, difficult to make proper use or even mention of it. Scarcely an adverb, an "affirmative particle," reiterate the dictionaries. Yet more than any other adverb, *yes* exhibits "transcendental adverbiality"; it is "the ineffaceable supplement" of every *verbum*, an interjection, almost "an inarticulate cry"; *yeah, oui, ja* is something like a "preconceptual vocalization," "the perfume of a discourse" (125). *Yes* is less a performative than a perfumative (129). A Bloom, as it were, in the pharmacy. Disconsolately sweet. Every constative seems to need and presuppose it: Yes, I can confirm that . . . ; yes, it is the case that . . . ; Ay, S *is* p. Nor can the fragrance of the yes be captured by the words *approbation, affirmation, confirmation, acquiescence,* and *consent.* When a bombardier confirms over the radio his orders to waste this or that supply depot, village, or hospital, he replies, "Affirmative." Yet his reply presupposes this: "Yes, you hear me, I'm saying 'Affirmative,' and we both know what that means." *Yes* performs rather than constates:

> What does it call on us to think, this *yes* that names, describes, designates nothing and that has no reference outside the mark? not outside language, because the *yes* can dispense with words, at least with the word *yes.* In accord with its radically nonconstative or nondescriptive dimension, even if a description or a narrative says *yes,* the *yes* is from top to bottom and *par excellence* a performative.

However, the Heideggerian question, which is also Klossowski's question, is insufficiently answered by such talk of performatives. Performance, at least in a well-defined situation, always produces a determinate effect. Derrida again has recourse to the classic philosophical discourse through which we saw him *passing* in chapter 4: yes is "the transcendental condition of every performative dimension" (126). Any promise, declaration, order, or engagement occupies the dimension of a "*Yes, I'm signing.*" Such a *yes,* Derrida affirms, again with recourse to the classic philosophical discourse, is *anterior to* affirmation and denegation, "anterior," in scare-quotes, to all symmetries and dialectics. Even if one should go on to say *no* and do *no,* even if one should say, Yes, I'm going in there wasting, the "affirmation" of me-here responding cannot be eradicated. It is marked as a site *there* occupied by me-here, "*je-là,*" performing or constating a "yes"-there. *Là* is of course the inaudible site of ashes (*Il y a là cendre*), ashes of Plato's Second Letter, burned by the Philosopher in the backroom of "Plato's Pharmacy." We shall soon have to return to those cinders. Yet because Derrida has now invoked the transcendental dimension of the *yes*, we confront once again all the questions of memory, reminiscence, and writing on the verge. Does the *yes* grant time and being, is it equivalent to being as such, as opposed to beings; equivalent to propriation; is *yes* a new principle of sufficient reason; a co-responding to the speaking of language; is it the condition of all conditions, the be-thinging of things, the worlding of world; are *yes, yes* the raptures or ecstases of time and space? Derrida replies:

> I had to cede to the rhetorical necessity of translating this minimal and indeterminate address, almost virginal, into words. Into words like "I," "I am," "language," and so on, where the position of the *I*, of being, and of language still remain derivative with regard to the *yes*. That is precisely the difficulty for one who wants to say something on the subject of the *yes*. A meta-language will always be impossible on this subject, inasmuch as it will itself presuppose an event of the *yes* that it will not be able to comprehend. The matter will fall out the same way for all accountability and computation, all calculation aiming to order a series of *yeses* according to the principle of reason and its machines. *Yes* marks the fact that there is address to the other [*qui'il y a de l'adresse à l'autre*].
>
> Such address is not necessarily dialogue or interlocution, for it presupposes neither the voice nor symmetry. Yet from the outset it presupposes the precipitation of a response that already is demanding. For if there is something of the other [*s'il y a de l'autre*], if there is something of the *yes*, then the other can no longer be produced by the same or by the self. *Yes*, condition of all signature and of every performative, is addressed to the other, which it does not constitute, and with respect to which it can commence only by *asking*, in response to a demand that is always anterior, *asking it to ask it* to say *yes*. Time appears only after this singular anachrony. (127–28)

Molly's "monologue" is therefore anything but monologue. It is rather "a discourse embraced by two forms of 'Yes,' two capital 'Yeses,' hence two gramophonic 'Yeses.' " At least two, inasmuch as a certain confusion of Leopold Bloom, Marion Bloom, and James Joyce occurs here, to say nothing of Henry Flower, Bartell D'Arcy, Boylan, Mulvey, Gardner, Paul de K. or Poldy B. A second yes, an *other* yes, comes to augment the first. Yet the second yes is, in its turn, "a *yes* that *recalls itself* [*un oui qui se rapelle*]." Molly herself commences with the other Yes. "The *yes* says nothing but *yes*, an other *yes* that resembles it, even if it says *yes* to the coming of an altogether other *yes*" (128). The yes "addresses itself to the other and can only appeal to the *yes* of the other; it begins by responding" (130). And if we insist on recalling once again the classic philosophical discourse, as perhaps we must, Derrida replies that the apparent self-positing of the yes "keeps open the circle it inscribes" (132). It is neither strictly performative nor strictly transcendental, even if performativity presupposes the yes. It is "pre-ontological"—a category to which Heidegger too appeals, incidentally, when it is a matter of situating the understanding-of-being in being-there between the nearest and the farthest reaches of being (SZ,

15–17 and 65). During the final moments of "Ulysse gramophone," in a "telegraphic" style, Derrida situates the possibility of the yes and of yes-laughter "in this place where transcendental egology, the onto-encyclopedia, grand speculative logic, fundamental ontology, and the thought of being open upon a thought of the gift and a thought of the envoy that they presuppose but can never contain" (UG, 132). In order to ensure nonclosure of the circle—if such can ever be ensured—he recalls the essentially comic situation of a sending that can never cease even if it can never arrive, even if it must be always only on the verge of arriving: "Molly says to herself (apparently talking to herself all alone), recalls to herself, that she says *yes* in the course of asking the other to ask her to say *yes*, and she begins or ends by saying *yes* in the course of responding to the other in herself, but in order to tell him [*pour lui dire*] that she will say *yes*, if the other asks her, yes, to say *yes*" (133). *L'oui-dire. Pour lui dire.* The sending is always a being sent, love's old sweet song, Sam Cooke's *minnesang,* "Darling, you send me."

Yet if the yes is consigned "to the memory of the other," if it has to take its chances, if it can be menaced, then mirth inevitably reverts to mourning. Memory is not hypermnemic reappropriation but a kind of faithful dissemination or dispersion, a return of nonreturn, as we heard earlier.

> With or without words, apprehended in its minimal event, a *yes* demands *a priori* its repetition, its being placed in memory [*sa mise en mémoire*]; and it requires that a *yes* to the *yes* inhabit the arrival of the "first" *yes*, which is therefore never simply originary. One cannot say *yes* without promising to confirm and remember it, retain it, countersigned in another *yes;* one cannot say it without promise and memory, the promise of memory. Molly recalls. (UG, 136–37)

That the yes can readily collapse back into the circle of automatic or technical repetition and dissimulation cannot be denied or prevented. Countersignature opens up, and is open to, absolute risk. Countersignature is not iconography. The "quasi-transcendental" situation of yes-laughter requires that it remain suspended between the *Stimmungen* of restitution and gift-giving. Somewhere between poisonous mockery and the milk of mirth.

ASHES

as though one could conclude a book on the verge   *Nothing crowded her, no clinging to the past, no striving toward the future; when her gaze fell upon something in her surroundings it was as though she were calling to a baby lamb: either it approached quietly, to be near her, or it paid her no mind—but she never grasped it by way of an intention, with that inner seizing movement that lends to all chilly understanding something both violent and vain, inasmuch as it dispels the happiness that is in the things*   of memory, reminiscence, and writing by reminding oneself of what happens when the materiality of the matrix for typography, iconography, and engrammatology alters irreversibly from stone or wood or wax to ashes. Locke's granite tombstone calcined to powdery ash. So that while *traces* or *tracings* would be at issue in both kinds of materials—ashes themselves containing trace elements and so preserving microscopic monuments to what was—the solidity, durability, and duration of the marks of memory would be radically reduced for us. Us who in passing say yes to the passing of what was. Yes to a vortex of ashes   *In this way everything around Agathe seemed to be much more comprehensible than usual; but it was still her conversations with her brother that occupied her above all*   in the wind. And this swirl of cinders should satisfy a concluding chapter on memory and affirmation? Yes

In 1980 friends invited Jacques Derrida to write on the unpromising theme of ashes for a now defunct journal, *Anima*. "Feu la cendre" appeared in *Anima* 5 in 1985, and was then released in 1987 as a slim volume by *Des femmes* and simultaneously as a cassette in "La Bibliothèque des Voix," read by Derrida and Carole Bouquet.   *In accord with the peculiar nature of her unusually faithful memory, a memory that did not deform its material by any kind of bias or prejudice, once again there emerged all about her the living words, the little surprises in the tone of voice and in the gestures of these conversations; they were not altogether coherent, were more after the manner in which they had occurred before Agathe properly grasped them and knew what they wanted.*   The title, *Feu la cendre*, resists translation. "Fire, the ash," yes; but also "the smoldering ash," "the extinguished and expired ash," taking *feu* as the invariable adjective meaning "recently dead," as in the phrase *feu la mère de Madame*, Madame's mother, who recently passed away, Madame's mother, *of recent memory. Feu la cendre.* Ashen fire, defunct ash; fiery cinder, clinkered ash. The book and the recording hover or shift and feint in this ambiguity: the polylogue of voices male and female, a *minnesang* of ardor and a chronicle of chill.   *Nevertheless, everything was meaningful in the highest degree; her capacity for remembrance, dominated so often by rue, this time was full of tranquil fidelity, and in a graceful way time past clung closely to the warmth of her body, instead of losing itself as it usually did in the frosty obscurity that swallows everything lived in vain.*

"Animadversions" or fragments from "Plato's Pharmacy," *Glas*, and *La Carte postale* themselves mark *Feu la cendre* with traces of Derrida's work. Among these traces is the phrase that has already resounded here as well as in chapter 4: *il y a là cendre*, "There there is ash," heard in the backroom of "Plato's Pharmacy" and in the "dedication" at the end of *Dissemination*. The fifteen years of Derrida's career that separate these first appearances of the phrase from its mirrorings   *On the very morning of her brother's departure Agathe had observed herself minutely: it had begun with her face, begun by accident, for her gaze fell upon it and then never came back from the mirror*   in *Feu la cendre* testify to the memory of the trace and the trace of the memory. The phrase *il y a là cendre* returns, returns to haunt. Its "author" responds to it, is engaged to it, but by no means does he command it.   *She was held fast, as when one has no intention of walking but repeatedly takes a hun-*

dred more steps toward a thing that has only at that moment become visible, at which point one then firmly proposes to turn back, but then once again declines to do so.   Yet the phrase itself, with the *là* dissimulating *la* to the ear and the very word *cendre* so close to *tendre*, seems an "immemorial image" of something unspeakably remote, something "there" rather than "here," "down there" or "back there" as a lost memory   *From out of the mirror the somewhat uncanny feeling of the indeterminate hour returned*   of something that never was present. Ash both preserves and loses the trace. Preserves it through all the heat of incineration, holocaust, immolation, and passion; loses it in the chill of all things ill-fated, fugitive, fled, defunct.   *A quarter hour yet. And then I'll not be. The peacefullest words. Peacefullest words. Non fui. Sum. Fui. Non sum.*

Nevertheless, *Feu la cendre* is not without fire. A certain pyrification, if not purification, assures us that something has taken place, that there *is* a place   *She came to her hair, which was still like bright satin; she unbuttoned her collar to her mirror image and, brushing back her dress, bared her shoulders; finally, she undressed completely that image and brought it all to attention, down to the pink lacquer of the nails, where in hands and feet the body comes to an end and but barely belongs to itself*   in which something takes place. And is remembered. Or is on the very verge of being remembered. Intensely. Like the late-morning or midday sun, approaching the moment of the shortest shadow, when   *It was all still like the brightly blazing day as it nears its zenith: ascendant, pure, precise, and permeated by the becoming that is fore-noon, the becoming that expresses itself in a human being or young animal in the same indescribable way it does in a ball that has not yet reached its apogee but is only a tiny arc below it*   the flame is invisible, effaced, but more intense than ever:

> —but that is precisely what he calls the trace, this effacement. I now have the impression that the best paradigm of the trace, for him, is not (as certain people have believed, and perhaps he himself as well) the animal's tracks, effraction, the rill in the sand, the wake in the sea, the affinity of a footstep for its imprint, but the ash (that which remains without remaining of the holocaust, the conflagration, incense ablaze) (LAC, 27)

As the flame annihilates and annuls, it opens up the ring of annulation, anniversary, and   *"Maybe the ball is passing through its apogee at this moment," thought Agathe. This thought startled her*   recurrence to memory: the sun in Hegel's account of the religion of the sun, or in Bataille's thought of solar *extravagance* (LAC, 30). What moves the voices of *Feu la cendre* is not the labor of mourning ("How could we agree to work for Monseigneur Mourning?") but the history of the very *refusal* to incorporate and incarnate the other   *Her body, uninfluenced by sport instructors and masseurs, unaltered by childbearing and motherhood, had been formed by nothing other than its own waxing and flourishing*   as the wolf does the grandmother or the Wolfman his father and sister.

If you no longer recall, it is because incineration follows its course and consumma-
tion goes without saying, down to the very ash. Trace destined to disappear
*Had one been able to transpose it naked to one of those vast and lonely landscapes
that great chains of mountains show in the face they turn to the sky, she would
have been borne on the swollen and barren surge of such heights like a heathen
goddess*   all by itself, like everything else, in order to open up the way, rather
than to rekindle a memory. The ash is fitting [*est juste*]: because it is without trace,
precisely ash traces more than one other, and as the other trace(s) [*elle trace plus
qu'une autre, et comme l'autre trace*]. (39)

   Feu la cendre memorializes the trace   *In a terrain of this kind, midday
pours no streams of light and heat to the earth; it merely seems to climb apace
to its summit and pass indiscernibly over into the declining, hovering beauty of
afternoon*   of the other, reproducing the animadversions of "Plato's Pharmacy," distinguishing, between two repetitions, the "Two knocks . . . four . . ."
of the later version (here reprinted *first*) from the "Three knocks . . ." of the
earlier version published in *Tel Quel* (LAC, 40–43; 60). Marcel remembers *les
trois petits coups* he would give the wall that separated his bedroom from his
grandmother's, three knocks every morning that she would answer *par ces
autres coups* as though saying, "Don't worry, little mouse, I know you are
impatient, but I'm coming soon." Yet these reassuring "three knocks" have
been silenced forever, and the knocks on the pharmacy door—"They seem to
be coming from outside this time, these *coups*"—are more disconcerting. *Feu la
cenfre* does not account for them, neither for the three nor for the two and four.
It does not explain. It allows the other the last word. Not "the" other of an
inflated ethical pretension—which is the pretension to full recovery and totalizing restitution through one judgment once and for all—but the other(s)
who are or were loved.   *But in some mode of fantasy she heard—before
she could call her memories of it to account—behind everything she had experienced, the long, ardently protracted lovecry of the ass, a cry that had always
excited her in a strange way: it sounded infinitely ridiculous and odious, yet
precisely for that reason there was perhaps no second heroism of love as
disconsolately sweet as his.*
   With these final, remarkable animadversions from *La Carte postale* (CP,
46/40 and 211/196; LAC, 46 and 58), *Feu la cendre* moves toward its own
evanescence: " 'The symbol? A great holocaustic fire, a conflagration, really,
into which we would throw—along with our entire memory—our names, the
letters, the photographs, the little objects, keys, fetishes, etc.' (. . .)" One
sentence-fragment from the original passage in *La Carte postale* is missing
from its reproduction in *Feu la cendre*. After ". . . keys, fetishes, etc." in the
original version appear the words: *Et s'il n'en reste rien,* "Even if nothing
should remain of them." In *Feu la cendre* there are remains. Ashes. Reminiscences. Reveries. The final animadversion reads:

Before my death I would give these orders: if you are not there, they are to recover
my body from the lake [*mon corps du lac*], burn it, and send you my ashes, with
the urn well-protected ("fragile") but not sent registered mail, not to tempt fate.

This would be an envoy of mine that would no longer come from me (or an envoy coming from me—who will have ordered it done—but more like or no longer an envoy of mine, as you like). You would then want to mix my ashes into the food you eat (morning coffee, brioche, five o'clock tea, etc.). Once a certain dosage were taken, you would begin to go numb, fall in love with yourself; I would watch you advancing slowly toward death; you would approach me within yourself, with a serenity we have never known, absolute reconciliation. And you would give orders. . . . Awaiting you, I am going to sleep; you are always there, my sweet love.

as though one could yes finish a book with the likes of such yes lugubrious lakes of cinder   *She shrugged her shoulders on the subject of her life and turned once again with firm purpose to her image, seeking to discover there a place where her appearance betrayed signs of aging*   and ash; as though Derrida himself finished this way, because of course   *There are the little places near the eyes and ears that are the first to change, and when it starts they look like something had slept on them, or the curve beneath the inner sides of the breasts that so readily loses its transparency: it would have satisfied her at this moment, and promised her peace, had she noticed a change; but as yet there was nowhere such to behold, and the beauty of her body hovered almost uncannily in the depths of the mirror*   he does not. *Feu la cendre* ends and evanesces with one of the interlacing interlocutory voices objecting to the uses made there of *LAC* and *LA Cendre*, the lake of capital recovery and restoration:

—No, you are treating the phrase like the accumulation of a surplus value, as though it were speculation on some capital *cendre*. It is rather a matter of *retrait* [a redrawing and reinscribing as well as a retreat],[20] in order to enable a gift to take its chances, without the least memory of itself, after all the accounts have been drawn up; not[21] a corpus, but a pile of ashes careless of its form, merely a *retrait* without any relation to what I now through love have just done and am on the verge of telling you [*je m'en vais vous dire*]—

as though a musical idea   *"I am a bit dead"—this feeling Agathe often had, and precisely at moments like this when she had just become conscious of the health and contours of her young body, conscious of this tensed beauty, as groundless in its mysterious cohesion as in the dissolution of elements in death, moments when she easily slipped from a state of happy security into a state of fright, astonishment, taciturnity, as happens when one steps out of a noisy, crowded room to confront the shimmer of stars*   were constantly in retreat from itself, retracing itself in its own ashes only to shift and veer away from itself, shunning every resolution to its own tonic: Sibelius's Seventh and last symphony, Opus 105 in C, composed between 1918 and 1924, originally entitled *Fantasia Sinfonica*, with its four scarcely isolable or identifiable movements (*Adagio, Rallentando al . . . Adagio, Allegro molto moderato, Presto-Adagio*) fused into one relentless *kinēsis* of sound, announcing itself forthrightly as being in the key of C, the most common and chantable of keys, without sharps or flats, absolutely candid (*Il y a là cendre*); and yet from the perfunctory opening in the tympani   *For in accord with the original, uncomplicated way of thinking that*

was hers, Agathe felt her disposition to be warm, vital, happy, easy to please—a
disposition that had accompanied her into life's most diverse situations and
made them bearable; never had there been a collapse into indifference, as hap-
pens to women who can no longer bear their disappointment: but in the midst of
her very laughter or the uproar of some sensuous adventure, which continued in
spite of all, there dwelled the devaluation that made every fiber of her body
slacken and yearn for something else, something that might best be described as
Nothing   all is modulation, gliding on by, *Vorbeigang,* evading and avoiding the tonic, as though the Seventh were locked under seven seals, fleeing the
tonic every instant and retreating into a kind of crypt; as though the somber
strings ascending and descending, their melodies mildly elegiac and unpreten-
tious, then the frivolous woodwinds in scherzo hurrying and worrying the stately
tempo lento, and finally the bursts of brass piercing the mounting turbulence—
as though each of these were colluding in retardation and postponement, frus-
trating again and again each irresolutely proffered resolution; even the evoca-
tion of Northern woods and invigorating winds in the third movement (*Allegro*
molto moderato), even the most homespun of chants unable to still the shifting
tonal clusters, clusters based on semitones rather than whole tones, approximating minor keys, always merely on the verge of C, then gliding on the oblique
away from the very place toward which it is presumably all tending; as though
the crisis precipitated *in rondo* by steadily mounting waves of strings in tandem
with or striving against (impossible to say which) the horns, trombones, and
trumpets, ascending finally to a vast plateau of calm, meant   *A terrifying*
expanse of emptiness suddenly oppressed her, a shoreless glare occluded her
spirit, and her heart was swept away in anxiety   something like nothing; as
though the final plaintive cries and distended harmonies in the string section
were trying to remember the point of origin that was never there from the outset;
and as though a series of false resolutions glancing off of C, hitting it, clutching at
it, while a semitone seventh drags it down from below, succumbs to it finally,
surrenders, rising at the very end to the tonic as though to say, "Yes, yes, this is
where we will have been heading all the while, here is where we shall never have
arrived, certainly not now, certainly not as you are now hearing it now end
now"; as though such deferral were nonetheless always mindful of what it most
loves, mournfully letting what it loves slip irretrievably into passing away; as
though shouting   *Throw everything you have into the fire, down to your*
shoes. When you have nothing left, think of nothing, not even your shroud, and
leap naked into the fire!   yes yes to eternal recurrence, laughing to the
point of tears, mirth and mourning alike spurning the triplicate blows of typography, iconography, engrammatology; as though in the end it were enough to say
that repetition, recollection, recall, reminiscence, remembrance, revery, and all
the motions of memory were on the very verge of being written on the verge

Notes

INTRODUCTION

1. Readers will find a more comprehensive survey of mnemic phenomena in Edward S. Casey, *Remembering: A Phenomenological Study* (Bloomington: Indiana University Press, 1987); cf. my review article, "On the Verge of Remembering," in *Research in Phenomenology* XIX (1989), 251–72.

2. See Jacques Derrida, *De la grammatologie* (Paris: Minuit, 1967); translated as *Of Grammatology* by Gayatri Chakravorty Spivak (Baltimore: Johns Hopkins University Press, 1974). I will cite Derrida's texts throughout the book by a code letter (here, G), with the page numbers of the French and English editions. I have not used the available translations for my own work, but have translated Derrida's texts afresh; this is not because I dream of improving on the work of expert translators, but because such close work with the texts—commencing with the effort to translate—is the only way I am able to proceed. A final checking of my own efforts against the published translations (when available) has saved me from many crimes and abominations, and I am grateful to Derrida's translators for that, and for more than that.

3. The principal text here of course is Jacques Derrida, "La pharmacie de Platon," in *La dissémination* (Paris: Seuil, 1972), pp. 69–197; translated as "Plato's Pharmacy" by Barbara Johnson, in *Dissemination* (Chicago: University of Chicago Press, 1981), pp. 61–171. Cited throughout my book as: D, 69–197/61–171.

4. See Martin Heidegger, *Sein und Zeit*, 12th ed. (Tübingen: M. Niemeyer, 1972). I shall cite this work throughout as SZ, with the page number. Here again, as with Hegel, Nietzsche, and Freud, I have ventured my own translations.

ONE. SLABS OF WAX

1. *Peri mnēmēs kai anamnēseōs*, in *Parva naturalia*, 449b 4 to 453b 11. I have used the Loeb Classical Library edition, vol. VIII, trans. W. S. Hett (Cambridge, Massachusetts: Harvard University Press, 1975 [1st ed. 1936]), pp. 285–313, and the translation with copious notes and discussion by Richard Sorabji, *Aristotle on Memory* (Providence, Rhode Island: Brown University Press, 1972). I have also used the Loeb edition when referring to other Aristotelian treatises such as "On the Soul." For references to Plato I have used the Oxford Classical Texts, ed. Ioannes Burnet (Oxford, England: Oxford University Press, 1973 impression), along with the German translation by Schleiermacher and the English translations in Plato, *Collected Dialogues*, eds. Edith Hamilton and Huntington Cairns (New York: Bollingen, 1961). For *Theaetetus* and *Sophist* I have referred to vol. III of the Loeb Classical Library edition of Plato, trans. H. N. Fowler (Cambridge, Massachussetts: Harvard University Press, 1977 [1st ed. 1921]).

2. See Sorabji, p. 35, for this and the following. I shall refer to his text in the body of my chapter by page number in parentheses.

3. "Out of something, into something," Aristotle's description of the "now" of time as discussed by Martin Heidegger, *Die Grundprobleme der Phänomenologie* (Frankfurt am Main: V. Klostermann, 1975), pp. 343–48; *Basic Problems of Phenomenology*, trans. Albert Hofstadter (Bloomington: Indiana University Press, 1982), pp. 242–47. I will cite the *Grundprobleme*, which is vol. 24 in the *Martin Heidegger Gesamtausgabe*, simply as 24, with page number. See also Krell, *Intimations of Mortality: Time, Truth, and Finitude in Heidegger's Thinking of Being* (University Park, Pennsylvania: Pennsylvania State University Press, 1986), chap. 3.

4. Aristotle's argument is terribly complex: it involves the assimilation of magnitude, change (or motion), and time to the primary or common power through the

medium of the image (which *has* magnitude), so that memory is imagic both in terms of its objects and in terms of its "perception" of time. Sorabji unravels the several strands of the argument on pp. 74–75. Furthermore, Sorabji is surely right when he argues that *time* is somehow *between* thought and perception (cf. pp. 72 and 77), that it cannot be attributed to one or the other exclusively. The problematic nature of time will not be resolved when Kant refines but essentially duplicates these structures in the Schematism of *The Critique of Pure Reason.*

5. Cf. *On Sense and Sensible Objects*, 449a 8–10 and 17–20.

6. See Sorabji's comments on pp. 75–76, which are plausible.

7. By stressing the sense of *kinēsis* as a movement of self-showing and presencing, I am of course elaborating on Heidegger's understanding of it in "Vom Wesen und Begriff der *Physis*: Aristotle's *Physik* B, 1," in *Wegmarken* (Frankfurt am Main: V. Klostermann, 1967), esp. pp. 367–71.

8. See Sorabji, pp. 31–34. Perhaps Aristotle is only following the advice of Plato's *Philebus.* At 16c Socrates stresses that in relating forms to things and in all the problems of dialectic the crucial matter is to avoid rushing from any given "one" to an unlimited "many"; we must contemplate all the forms that are intermediate or in-between, *to metaxy, ta mesa.* One of Socrates' examples is the alphabet and its relation to the infinite possibilities of sound. We shall consider *Philebus* later in the chapter.

9. Robert Musil, *Der Mann ohne Eigenschaften*, 2 vols. (Hamburg: Rowohlt, 1978), I, 530–31.

10. On "deliberation," see *Nicomachean Ethics* 1112a 18–1113a 14.

11. I should also record here at least two indications of the lasting power of *ho typos.* See Philippe Lacoue-Labarthe, "Typographie," in *Mimésis des articulations* (Paris: Flammarion, 1975), pp. 165–270, which is merely one of a series of his *Typographies.* Lacoue-Labarthe's principal inspiration here comes from Heidegger's remarks on *typos* as *das Prägende;* see Martin Heidegger, "Zur Seinsfrage," in *Wegmarken*, p. 223.

12. Lawrence Sterne, *The Life and Opinions of Tristram Shandy*, vol. V, chapter 42. The helpful editor of my edition (Harmondsworth: Penguin, 1967) renders Sterne's graceful phrase (quite correctly) as "slogging it."

13. See G. S. Kirk and J. E. Raven, *The Presocratic Philosophers: A Critical History with a Selection of Texts* (Cambridge, England: Cambridge University Press, 1966), pp. 413–14, 416, and 421.

14. *To sēmeion* (cf. also *to sēma*) means a mark or sign, trace or track; an omen, wonder, or portent; a signal (to put to sea, engage in work or battle, etc.); a standard or flag (cf. *hē sēmeia*); a landmark, boundary or limit; a device on a shield or figurehead on a ship; a signet on a ring; a figure, image, written character, etc. I shall generally render the word as "sign" or "trace."

15. The following discussion, however abstruse it may appear to be, does not touch on the truly complex issues of the latter half of the *Sophist*, e.g., the matters of being, oneness, and the "indeterminate dyad," nor does it mention the peculiar outcome of the first half, namely, the discovery of the "sixth" sophist, who in fact resembles the philosopher Socrates. For a full treatment of these and other issues, which do have an impact on the question of likeness, see John Sallis, *Being and Logos: The Way of Platonic Dialogue*, 2nd ed. (Atlantic Highlands, New Jersey: Humanities, 1986), chap. 6, esp. pp. 472–78 and 519–32.

16. *Sophist*, 236e. John Sallis, *Being and Logos*, pp. 482–83, refers to the ambiguity of *phainō*, used to refer to any and every bringing to light or self-showing, but also the root of semblance, *phantasma*, and comments: "The point is that in images as such (whether they are like the original or are only semblances) nonbeing is involved: an image lets the original appear, lets it show itself in some degree; but the image *is not* the original, and it is the negativity expressed in this 'is not' that constitutes the problem. . . . What is important is that this problem arises not only with regard to

semblance-making and, specifically, sophistry, but with regard to all image-making. We recall (from our reading of the *Republic*) that even Socrates, the philosopher, practices image-making, and so we again get a glimpse of the philosopher beside the sophist— very close beside him."

We shall take up this issue in *Republic* in a moment. And although I cannot enter into discussion of so complex a matter here, it will not do to ignore the importance of the issue we are now confronting for Jacques Derrida's demonstration of the "double inscription" of *mimēsis*. See *La dissémination*, pp. 159 n. 58 and 211–13 n. 8. For Derrida it is a matter of discerning all those aspects *"within* philosophy and mimetology" from Plato to Hegel that "exceed the oppositions of concepts in which Plato defines the phantasm" (159). Especially important for memory, reminiscence, and writing will be the *duplicity of all duplication,* the failure of every effort to separate off "mere seeming" from "really looking like"; that is, to divide all self-showing into two and to exclude the Other in order to embrace the One; that is, to banish absence for the sake of presence. For memory, always on the verge, is duplicitous. See also Jean-Luc Nancy, "Le ventriloque," in *Mimésis des articulations*, pp. 271–338, esp. 305–9. Finally, see chapter 4, below.

17. See Liddell-Scott, p. 1970a, III. 2. c. For some Homeric uses, see *Iliad* 24, 706; *Odyssey* 8, 461; 20, 199; 24, 402; cf. *13, 39.*

18. Martin Heidegger, *Nietzsche,* 2 vols. (Pfullingen: G. Neske, 1961), I, 207; see *Nietzsche, Vol. I: The Will to Power as Art* (San Francisco, Harper and Row, 1979), p. 178. See the entire discussion of section 22, but especially pp. 176–78. I shall refer to the English translation by page number in parentheses within the body of my text.

19. On the entire problem of *eikasia,* and especially dianoetic *eikasia,* the thinking that knows an image *as* image (that is to say, within difference), see Jacob Klein, *A Commentary on Plato's "Meno"* (Chapel Hill: University of North Carolina Press, 1965), chap. V, esp. pp. 166–67. Note that Klein's "digression" (from a dialogue we are leaving out of account here!) begins with a discussion of Aristotle's treatise on memory and then touches on the dialogues we are considering here. Even though Klein's focus is on the difference between mere memory and active, recollective learning, there are moments—such as the last full paragraph on p. 168—when he confronts problems of iconography and engrammatology.

20. I have tried to interpret *Timaeus* as comedy—to A. E. Taylor's posthumous delight and F. M. Cornford's posthumous horror—by concentrating on one important theme in the dialogue; see Krell, "Female Parts in *Timaeus,*" *Arion,* New Series 2/3 (Boston University, 1975), pp. 400–21, from which the following paragraphs derive.

21. Pursuit of this matter would lead us from Aristotle, *Physics* IV, 10–14, to Hegel, *Encyclopedia,* sections 254–61, to Heidegger, *Sein und Zeit,* section 82 (pp. 432–33n.), to Derrida, "Ousia and Gramme: Note to a Footnote in *Being and Time,*" in *Marges de la philosophie* (Paris: Minuit, 1972), pp. 31–78, an itinerary we cannot now follow, lest we entirely forget memory.

22. Hieronymus Müller mistranslates, here, adding an *euch* to the phrase *"das will ich [selber] übergeben."* See Platon, *Sämtliche Werke,* tr. F. Schleiermacher, H. Müller, ed. Walter F. Otto, Ernesto Grassi (Hamburg: Rowohlt, 1959) 6, 164.

23. See 202e–207b; cf. *Sophist,* 253a and 262d 8 as Bury reads it: *grammata* instead of *pragmata.* Engrammatology is not simply grammatology, but is the full-blown science of memory.

24. For *ameletēsiai,* cf. *Symposium* 208a 4, where *meletē,* "rehearsal" or "pursuit," the German *Nachsinnen,* is a crucial word for remembering. Note the opening line of the *Symposium,* where Apollodorus, who must *remember* the tale recounted to him by Aristodemus, declares himself "not unprepared" (172a 1: *ouk ameletētos*). In case we miss the point, he repeats the claim not many lines later (cf. 173c 1).

25. That is perhaps the simplest way to formulate the basic prescription of "Plato's

Pharmacy." See Jacques Derrida, "La pharmacie de Platon," in *La dissémination* pp. 69–197, discussed in chapter 4, below.

26. For the moment there seems to be no compelling reason to belabor the sexual connotations of Socrates' story, whatever the lessons of *Timaeus,* inasmuch as Phaedrus himself remarks that Socrates is telling Egyptian tales (275b 3). Although it is far afield in terms of centuries, one might do well to compare Socrates' metaphor here with that rather bizarre passage in Hegel's *Phenomenology of Spirit* which contrasts the piddling of representational consciousness with the procreative act of infinite judgment. See G. W. F. Hegel, *Phänomenologie des Geistes,* "Philosophische Bibliothek" (Hamburg: F. Meiner, 1952), p. 254; and Krell, "Pitch: Genitality/Excrementality from Hegel to Crazy Jane," in *boundary 2,* vol. XII, no. 2 (Winter 1984), 113–41.

27. See F. W. J. Schelling, *Über das Wesen der menschlichen Freiheit,* in *Sämtliche Werke* (Stuttgart, 1860), VII, 363–64. Schelling's importance for this tradition is reflected in his realization that no word can be spoken without consonants, even in the mouth of God.

28. Ibid., pp. 404–8. See Krell, "The Crisis of Reason in the Nineteenth Century: Schelling's Treatise on the Essence of Human Freedom (1809)," in *The Collegium Phaenomenologicum: The First Ten Years,* ed. John Sallis, Jacques Taminiaux, and Giuseppina Moneta (Dordrecht: Kluwer, 1988), pp. 13–32. For the following quotation from the *Stuttgarter Privatvorlesung,* see VII, 478.

TWO. WAXEN GLANDS AND FLESHY HOLLOWS

1. I have used the Loeb Classical Library edition of the *Confessions* (Cambridge, Massachusetts: Harvard University Press, 1979 [1st ed. 1912]). While referring to the William Watts translation of 1631, along with that by John K. Ryan (Garden City, New York: Doubleday-Image, 1960), I have made my own translations. I will cite the *Confessions* in the body of my text by Book (in Roman numerals) and chapter (Arabic).

2. See Krell, "Engorged Philosophy: A Note on Freud, Derrida and Differance," in David Wood and Robert Bernasconi, eds., *Derrida and Différance* (Evanston, Illinois: Northwestern University Press, 1988), pp. 6–11. See also Krell, "Engorged Philosophy II," in *Postmodernism and Continental Philosophy,* ed. Hugh J. Silverman and Donn Welton (Albany: State University of New York Press, 1988), pp. 49–66.

3. Frances A. Yates, *The Art of Memory* (Harmondsworth: Penguin, 1969 [1st ed. 1966]), pp. 61–62. I will cite Frances Yates's wonderful book in my text by page number in parentheses.

4. See *Summa theologiae, prima pars,* q. 78 a. 4, which refers to the *vis memorativa* (but also the *phantasia* or *imaginatio*) as a *thesaurus* (or *quasi thesaurus*) of forms (or *intentiones*); cf. q. 79 a. 7, ". . . thesaurus vel locus conservativus specierum." For Locke, see the remarks on the "Repository of Memory," below, p. 76.

5. I have used the Pléiade edition of Descartes' *Oeuvres et Lettres,* ed. André Bridoux (Paris: Gallimard, 1953), but I also refer to the thirteen-volume Adam and Tannery edition (Paris, 1891–1912), by volume and page number, after the *slash solidus* in each reference. I have tried wherever possible to compare my own translations with those by E. S. Haldane and G. R. T. Ross, *The Philosophical Works of Descartes,* 2 vols. (Cambridge, England: Cambridge University Press, 1967 [1st ed. 1911]), and to the new Cambridge translations (1985) by John Cottingham, Robert Stroothoff, and Dugald Murdoch. The latter however appeared only after my work had been completed. My account of Descartes on memory owes an enormous amount to Véronique M. Fóti, "Presence and Memory: Derrida, Freud, Plato, Descartes," in *The Graduate Faculty Philosophy Journal,* vol. XI, no. 1 (New School for Social Research, 1986), 67–81, esp. 74–77.

6. Compare both Leibniz's view that writing liberates the *imagination* rather than

memory and Leroi-Gourhan's paleoanthropological account of writing as a "liberation of memory." Both views are discussed in detail and with reference to the literature in Jacques Derrida, *De la grammatologie*, pp. 116/78 and 125/84. Note too that Kant's *Anthropologie in pragmatischer Hinsicht* (1798) confirms the supplementary relation of writing and memory: "It is truly a great convenience, by having a writing tablet securely in one's pocket, to be able to come back precisely and effortlessly to everything one wanted to keep in one's head; and the art of writing remains a masterful art, because, even if it were not used to communicate one's knowledge to others, it still stands in for [*die Stelle vertritt*] the most extensive and most faithful of memories [*des ausgedehntesten und treuesten Gedächtnisses*], whose lacks it can supply [*dessen Mangel sie ersetzen kann*] (185)." As we shall see in chapter 3, Freud remains wholly within this mnemotypographical tradition.

7. See esp. the letters to Meyssonnier, January 29, 1640 (1066–7); to Mersenne, April 1, 1640 (1070–2) and August 6, 1640 (1083); to "Hyperaspites," August, 1641 (1130–1); to Huyghens, October 13, 1642 (1148); to Mesland, May 2, 1644 [?] (1164–5); and to Arnaud, June 4, 1648 (1303). I am grateful to Véronique Fóti for these references, and for her commentary on them, in "Presence and Memory," which I shall cite in what follows by page number in my text.

8. My account focuses on the following sections of the *Treatise:* on the general physiology of the blood, brain, and animal spirits, pp. 812–15 and 841–46 of the "Pléiade" edition, Adam-Tannery XI, 127–31 and 165–71; on sense-perception and memory, pp. 850–63 of "Pléiade," corresponding to XI, 174–89.

9. See 85/180. I have not been able to corroborate in contemporary anatomical studies this off-center situation of the pineal gland: see the discussion in Theodore W. Torrey, *Morphogenesis of the Vertebrates* (New York: John Wiley & Sons, 1962), pp. 508–9: "These structures [the parietal and pineal bodies] have had a unique history in vertebrates, a history linked to the fact that in ancestral vertebrates the conventional bilateral eyes were supplemented by one or two median dorsal eyes. . . . Yet the fossil evidence usually indicates the presence of a single eye alone. . . . The pineal body [in contrast to the parietal] does appear in all vertebrates but appears to be glandular in nature. It has been suspected of being an endocrine organ, but its properties have not been established with certainty." See the remarkable photograph of the pineal body (called *pineal* because of its ostensible *pinecone* shape) by Lennart Nilsson and Jan Lindberg, *Behold Man* (Boston: Little, Brown, 1974), p. 170. This singular evagination of the brain, somewhere between a gland and a visual organ, fascinated Georges Bataille as much as it had Descartes before him. See Bataille, *Visions of Excess*, ed. Allan Stoekl (Manchester, England: University of Manchester Press, 1985), pp. 73–90. Whether *Descartes* was aware of the tradition of the pineal *eye* I am uncertain. In sections 32 and 35 of the *Treatise on the Passions of the Soul* (1645–46), where, to be sure, he drops the word *environ* and locates the gland squarely *au milieu du cerveau*, as well as in letters to Meyssonnier (January 29, 1640) and Mersenne (April 1, 1640), he describes as the principal attraction of the gland its being the only part of the entire brain that is not dual, bicameral, bilateral, etc. The gland is a kind of *chiasm* where two images converge in one. Yet there are five other characteristics that induce him to declare it the seat of the soul: (1) it occupies "the most appropriate position" in the midst of the brain (*au milieu;* but cf. the *Traité de l'Homme's* "about" in the middle, and a "bit removed from the center" [855/180], to which we shall have to return), "between all the concavities"; (2) it is served by the carotid arteries, ducts that transport the animal spirits, and is lightly supported, hence highly elastic and mobile, in the sense that it can readily lean in all directions; (3) it is exceedingly soft in substance, and although it must somehow be affected by folds and convolutions, these dare not be excessive; (4) it is the only part of the brain that is *smaller* in humans than in animals, so that it is meet and just that it should be the seat of intellection; (5) the gland is so soft that not only in "lethargics" but

also in human beings generally it disappears soon after death; it is not so much corruptible as volatile, one might say, and Descartes urges Meyssonnier not to wait three or four days to examine the pineal gland of a corpse, but to go in search of it while the cadaver is as fresh as possible. I have commented on these matters in more detail in "Paradoxes of the Pineal: From Descartes to Georges Bataille," in A. Phillips Griffiths, ed., *Contemporary French Philosophy*, a special issue of the journal *Philosophy* (Cambridge University Press, 1988), vol. XXI, 215–28. Finally, it may not be entirely otiose to report that *not all philosophers* rest content with Descartes' choice of the pineal gland as the seat of the soul. For example, Jack Shandy, in *Tristram Shandy*, II, 19, p. 162:

Now, as it was plain to my father that all souls were by nature equal,—and that the great difference between the most acute and the most obtuse understanding,— was from no original sharpness or bluntness of one thinking substance above or below another,—but arose merely from the lucky or unlucky organization of the body, in that part where the soul principally took up her residence,—he had made it the subject of his enquiry to find out the identical place.

Now, from the best accounts he had been able to get of this matter, he was satisfied it could not be where Des Cartes had fixed it, upon the top of the *pineal* gland of the brain; which, as he philosophized, formed a cushion for her about the size of a marrow pea; though, to speak the truth, as so many nerves did terminate all in that one place,—'twas no bad conjecture;—and my father had certainly fallen with that great philosopher plumb into the centre of the mistake, had it not been for my uncle Toby, who rescued him out of it, by a story he told him of a Walloon officer at the battle of Landen, who had one part of his brain shot away by a musket-ball,—and another part of it taken out after by a French surgeon; and, after all, recovered, and did his duty very well without it.

10. Cf. Michel Foucault on the changing etiology of hysteria and hypochondria with the decline of the theory of "humours" and the emergence of the physiology of specialized "parts": for the evaporation of the animal spirits throughout anatomical space would represent or mimic the very motion diagnosed since time immemorial as *hysteria*. See Foucault, *Histoire de la folie à l'âge classique*, 2nd ed. (Paris: Gallimard, 1972) II, 3, iii, esp. pp. 306–7; see also Krell, "Female Parts in *Timaeus*", pp. 401–6, 414–16, and note 5 on p. 419.

11. *Frapper*, to strike with one or more blows. Cf. the noun *frappe* (f.): "Choc qui fait entrer le poinçon [puncturing point, cutting edge] formant la matrice d'un caractére ou d'une monnaie; empreinte ainsi obtenue. . . . Pression du cylindre d'une machine à imprimer sur la forme" (*Le Petit Robert*, 1984).

12. Descartes comments on foetal memory in some detail in his letter (1303–4) to Arnauld of 4 June 1648. The context is that "double power of memory" we have already examined; that is, in addition to corporeal memory, "a certain reflexion of the understanding or of the intellectual memory." Descartes emphasizes that the second cannot be practiced by the infant in the womb. In the child's soul generally, even after birth, there are only "confused sensations," never "pure intellection." And even though certain of these earliest traces perdure throughout a person's lifetime, they do not suffice to enable us to remember, especially if they are traces inscribed during the time we were in our mothers' wombs, a time when intellectual memory was certainly not yet active. Yet because *thinking* is the *essence* of the soul, it must be supposed that, even though we remember nothing of it, we must have been thinking all the time *in utero*. It is in the Cartesian womb precisely as it was in Aristotle's heaven—we simply do not remember. Or in Schelling's hell—whence the smiles of contentment.

13. In his "Notes Directed Against a Certain Program" (Haldane-Ross, p. 442; Adam-Tannery, VIII B, 358) Descartes defends himself against the "charge" of innate ideas by reducing them to *dispositions*. A certain family may be disposed to generosity, a

particular individual prone to this or that disease. Precisely with dispositions, it is difficult to distinguish between nature and nurture. Dispositions are like those laws that God imprints in the mind of man or that a monarch "would imprint in the heart of all his subjects, if he had sufficient power to do so" (letter to Mersenne, April 15, 1630 [933], cited by Véronique Fóti, "Presence and Memory", p. 75). One thinks of Rousseau's persistent use of this metaphor a century later.

14. Laurence Sterne, *Tristram Shandy,* II, 2, pp. 106–8.

15. I have used the edition by Peter H. Nidditch (Oxford, England: Oxford University Press, 1975). I cite the *Essay* by Book (Roman numeral), chapter (in Arabic), and section (§), in order that readers using other editions can check the references.

16. Thomas Hobbes, *Leviathan,* ed. C. B. Macpherson (Harmondsworth: Penguin-Pelican, 1968 [1st ed. 1651], Part I, chap. 1, "Of Sense." I shall refer to *Leviathan* in the body of my text simply by part (in Roman) and chapter (Arabic). A more detailed account would of course have to include Hobbes's *Short Tract on First Principles* and *Elements of Philosophy: The First Section, Concerning Body,* something I do not undertake here.

17. *Ignis fatuus,* a will-o'-the-wisp or jack-a-lantern. *The Oxford English Dictionary* notes: "A phosphorescent light seen hovering or flitting over marshy ground, and supposed to be the spontaneous combustion of an inflammable gas. . . . When approached, the ignis fatuus appeared to recede, and finally to vanish, sometimes reappearing in another direction. This led to the notion that it was the work of a mischievous sprite, intentionally leading benighted travellers astray."

18. Martin Heidegger, *Was heisst Denken?* (Tübingen: M. Niemeyer, 1954), p. 11; English translation by J. Glenn Gray and Fred D. Wieck, *What Is Called Thinking?* (New York: Harper & Row, 1968), p. 30; and *Vorträge und Aufsätze* (Pfullingen: G. Neske, 1954), p. 264; English translation by Frank A. Capuzzi in *Early Greek Thinking* (New York: Harper & Row, 1975), p. 108.

19. See David Hume, *A Treatise of Human Nature,* ed. L. A. Selby-Bigge, 2nd ed. by P. H. Nidditch (Oxford, England: Oxford University Press, 1978); and *Enquiries Concerning Human Understanding and Concerning the Principles of Morals,* ed. L. A. Selby-Bigge, 3rd ed. by P. H. Nidditch (Oxford, England: Oxford University Press, 1975), pp. 1–165. The Coleridge story which follows appears on p. 165 of the *Biographia literaria,* cited with full publishing information in note 20.

20. In *The Selected Poetry and Prose of Samuel Taylor Coleridge,* ed. Donald A. Stauffer (New York: Modern Library, 1951), pp. 109–428, esp. pp. 164–68. On David Hartley, see Basil Willey, *The Eighteenth-Century Background: Studies on the Idea of Nature in the Thought of the Period* (Boston: Beacon, 1961 [1st ed. 1940]), chap. 8, esp. pp. 136 and 141–42.

21. One would no doubt have to take up the problem in Henri Bergson's terms—something I cannot do here—especially in *Essai sur les données immédiates de la conscience* (1889) and *Matière et mémoire* (1896). (I shall refer to both by page number in Henri Bergson, *Oeuvres* [Paris: Presses Universitaires de France, 1963].) Particularly in the latter, Bergson tries to show the limits of a neurophysiological account of the body through an analysis of "pure perception" and "action" in the present. "Pure memory," in his view, "opens a perspective on what one calls spirit"; whereas pure perception allows us to take up a position between realism and idealism, "pure memory" opens a gap between materialism and spiritualism (218). Whether his doctrine and descriptions of the "two forms of memory" are truly helpful in *closing* the gap remains doubtful. Yet his description of the "myriad, myriad" systematizations of long-term memories (308–12), his thorough criticisms of associationism, and his detailed discussions of pathologies of the body, aphasias, etc. point clearly in the direction of Merleau-Ponty, and they merit renewed and detailed study. In the following paragraphs I shall refer to Maurice Merleau-Ponty, *La structure du comportement* (Paris: Presses Universitaires de France,

1942; English translation by Alden L. Fisher, *The Structure of Behavior* (Boston: Beacon, 1963), parts I and II. See also his "Study Project on the Nature of Perception" (1933) and "The Nature of Perception" (1934), presented by Forrest Williams in *Research in Phenomenology*, vol. X (1980), pp. 1–20.

22. R. B. Malmo, in *Handbook of Psychophysiology*, ed. N. S. Greenfield and R. A. Sternbach (New York: Holt, Rinehart and Winston, 1972), p. 971.

23. See Karl Pribram's remarks in *Memory Mechanisms*, ed. K. H. Pribram (Harmondsworth: Penguin, 1969), p. 295. Cited in the body of my text by page number in parentheses.

24. William Faulkner, *Light in August* (Harmondsworth, Penguin, 1960 [1st ed. 1932]), chap. 10, pp. 173–74.

25. See Edward S. Casey, *Remembering: A Phenomenological Study*, pp. 15–17; 269–72; and elsewhere. See also my review article, "On the Verge of Remembering," cited in the Introduction, above.

26. Erwin Straus, *Phenomenological Psychology* (New York: Basic Books, 1966), chaps. 3–4, pp. 59–73 and 75–100. I shall refer to the text by page number in parentheses.

27. For a critical account of Husserlian phenomenology of memory, see Krell, "Phenomenology of Memory from Husserl to Merleau-Ponty," in *Philosophy and Phenomenological Research*, XLII (June 1982), 492–505; see also my "On the Verge of Remembering."

28. Jean-Paul Sartre, *L'être et le néant: Essai d'ontologie phénoménologique* (Paris: Gallimard, 1943), p. 146; translated by Hazel Barnes as *Being and Nothingness* (New York: Philosophical Library, 1956), pp. 107–8.

29. Maurice Merleau-Ponty, *Le visible et l'invisible*, ed. Claude Lefort (Paris: Gallimard, 1964) p. 263; English translation by Alphonso Lingis, *The Visible and the Invisible* (Evanston, Illinois: Northwestern University Press, 1968), p. 210. I shall cite the work as VI, with page numbers, in parentheses.

30. Maurice Merleau-Ponty, *Phénoménologie de la perception* (Paris: Gallimard, 1945), pp. 490 and 492. I shall cite the work by the letters PP, with page numbers, in parentheses.

31. Marcel Proust, *Swann's Way*, trans. C. K. Scott-Moncrieff (New York: Vintage, 1970 [1st ed. 1928]), pp. 5–6, with minor changes. Page numbers after the *slash solidus* refer to *A la recherche du temps perdu*, 3 vols., "Pléiade" edition (Paris: Gallimard, 1954). For the passage in question, see vol. I, p. 6. See also Casey's fine pages on Proust, in *Remembering*, pp. 169–72; 192–93; 206–7.

32. See Marcel Proust, "Projects de Préface," in *Contre Sainte-Beuve*, written in 1907–1908, "Pléiade" edition (Paris: Gallimard, 1971), pp. 211–17. See also the final part of *Le temps retrouvé* in *A la recherche du temps perdu*, III, 870–73. I am indebted to Jonathan Krell for these references and for discussions about Proust.

33. No doubt one of the things to remember is that the writer is an artificer of *images*, images that are never icons in the sense we have elaborated, but idols that are never the same. See Walter Benjamin, "Zum Bilde Prousts," in *Illuminationen* (Frankfurt au Main: Suhrkamp, 1961), pp. 335–48, and the excellent discussion by Carol Jacobs, *The Dissimulating Harmony: The Image of Interpretation in Nietzsche, Rilke, Artaud, and Benjamin* (Baltimore: The Johns Hopkins University Press, 1978), chap. 4.

34. Martin Heidegger, *Der Ursprung des Kunstwerkes* (Stuttgart: P. Reclam, 1960), pp. 70–72; English translation by Albert Hofstadter in *Basic Writings*, second, revised and expanded edition (San Francisco: Harper & Row, forthcoming).

35. For the following, see Maurice Merleau-Ponty, *Résumés de cours: Collège de France, 1952–1960* (Paris: Gallimard, 1968), pp. 66–73. References will be designated R, with page number. The pages of VI that are most relevant here are 137–41.

36. Because it is unavailable in English, as far as I know, I cite here in translation a

portion of the *Nachschrift* to that course presented by Alexandre Métraux in the German edition of the résumés: Maurice Merleau-Ponty, *Vorlesungen I* (Berlin: W. de Gruyter, 1973), pp. 303–4, no. 15.

THREE. WAX MAGIC

1. See the 1895 *Psychologie* and the Freud-Fliess correspondence in Sigmund Freud, *Aus den Anfängen der Psychoanalyse*, ed. Ernst Kris (New York: Imago, 1950), the former on pp. 379–466. I will refer to this crucial sourcebook by page number in parentheses in the body of my text. I will not be able to refer to the enormous literature that has gathered about the "Project" and will be reading the latter solely for the purposes of a discussion of typography, iconography, and engrammatology. For an excellent bibliography, see Adolf Grünbaum, *The Foundations of Psychoanalysis: A Philosophical Critique* (Berkeley: University of California Press, 1984), pp. 3–4 and 287–96. I have found particularly useful Robert R. Holt, "A Review of Some of Freud's Biological Assumptions and Their Influence on His Theories," in Norman S. Greenfield and William C. Lewis, eds., *Psychoanalysis and Current Biological Thought* (Madison and Milwaukee: University of Wisconsin Press, 1965), pp. 93–124; Mark Kanzer, "Two Prevalent Misconceptions about Freud's 'Project' (1895)," in *Annual of Psychoanalysis*, vol. I (1973), 88–103; and especially Karl H. Pribram and Merton M. Gill, *Freud's 'Project' Re-Assessed* (New York: Basic Books, 1976), also with extensive bibliography. Again, I will not try to adjudicate the traditional (neurological) *vs.* revisionist (mentalistic) debate surrounding the "Project," but merely point to the remarkable concluding pages of Pribram and Gill (pp. 168–69): here a third voice intervenes to note that "Pribram" and "Gill" ultimately disagree about whether they ultimately disagree. Far more interesting than any of these however will be the paper by Alan Bass, to be published in Richard Rand, ed., *Mochlos in America: Our Academic Contract*, by The University of Nebraska Press in 1990.

2. Jacques Derrida has painted such a picture (not a tableau) in "Freud and the Scene of Writing" in *L'écriture et la différence* (Paris: Seuil, 1967), pp. 293–340; English translation, *Writing and Difference*, by Alan Bass (Chicago: University of Chicago Press, 1978), pp. 196–231. The number *after* the slash solidus in my references will refer to the English translation. I shall refer to this text in parenthesis as ED, with page numbers of the French and English editions.

3. Sigmund Freud, *Darstellungen der Psychoanalyse* (Frankfurt am Main: Fischer, 1969), p. 58. He repeated the claim in the 1920 *Jenseits des Lustprinzips;* see Sigmund Freud, *Studienausgabe*, 12 vols. (Frankfurt am Main: Fischer, 1969ff.), 3, 223. I shall cite this edition as StA, with volume and page numbers.

4. Sigmund Freud, StA Ergänzungsband, pp. 101–6.

5. Sigmund Freud and Josef Breuer, *Studien über Hysterie* (Frankfurt am Main: Fischer, 1970 [1st ed. 1895]), p. 90. I shall refer to this text as SH, with page number, in parentheses.

6. See StA 2, esp. 512–19 and 569–77; and 3, esp. 217–21 and 234–43. References to the dual or tripartite neural or psychic systems are of course to be found throughout the so-called metapsychological writings. Derrida's "Scene" has commented perceptively on these survivals of the principal propositions of the 1895 sketch. See ED, 302–5/203–5, passim. One such survival is identified by Robert Holt ("Biological Assumptions," p. 94), who relates the opening pages of the "Project" with David Hartley's conviction "that nerve impulse was a mechanical vibration of 'the material particles in question . . . [,] the neurons'." See chap. 2, above, pp. 83–85.

7. *Anfängen*, p. 386, line 15. Derrida adopts the statement as the epigram to his "Scene," ED, 296. See Freud's similar formulation in chapter 4 of *Jenseits* (twenty-five years after the "Project"!), StA 3, 236.

8. While one finds a certain amount of support in contemporary neurophysiology for Freud's effort to distinguish between external (or somatic) neural functions and internal (or visceral) functions, there can be no doubt that his binary account vastly oversimplifies the picture: the autonomic, sympathetic, and parasympathetic systems each combine somatic/visceral and sensory binaries, and all involve spinal gray in the dorsal and ventral columns of the spinal cord as well as the cerebellum and cerebrum, so that in higher mammals the whole nervous circuitry is constituted as a bewilderingly complex "feedback" system that no simple binary distinction can portray. See chapter 18 of Torrey, *Morphogenesis of the Vertebrates*, esp. pp. 490–91, 505, and 514–31. None of this however prevents Karl Pribram from enthusiastically endorsing Freud's "Project" as a remarkably prescient neurophysiology. See Pribram and Gill, 1976, passim. Commenting on the two principal postulates of Freud's sketch, the theory of neurons and of neural inertia, neurophysiologist Pribram writes: "Contemporary neurophysiology could find little to fault in this outline of nervous system function" (34).

9. In addition to the new formulations in chapter 7 of *Traumdeutung* and in the later metapsychology, one would have to mention a number of very early letters to Fliess, especially no. 39, dated January 1, 1896 (see esp. 152–54). Freud congratulates his friend for advancing through medicine to his genuine goal, physiology, taking medicine as a kind of "detour." (I presume that *Unweg* [= "impossible path"] is a typographic slip for *Umweg* [detour]!) Freud confesses that his use of medicine would conduct him toward his own "initial goal," which he cites as *Philosophie*. There is no doubt that with the discussion of quality, sensation, and perception, we are in the thick of *philosophical* problems. We shall no doubt have to revert to this letter and its highly technical discussion of the intermediate W system in just a moment.

10. Before proceeding, we might note that it is in this vicinity that Derrida's account of the 1895 sketch breaks off; about here, where Freud introduces his account of the sources of pleasure and unpleasure (*Lust- und Unlustempfindung*). Precisely these emerge to play a role in the final pages of Derrida's account, so that the bulk of the essay (ED, 306–38/206–29) may be viewed as an immense grammatological parenthesis or detour within the breach of Freud's own sketch.

11. See *Sein und Zeit*, section 43b, esp. pp. 209–10, and refer back to pp. 50 and 194. See the comments by D. F. Krell and Jacques Derrida on Heidegger and the philosophy of life in *Research in Phenomenology*, XVII (1987), esp. pp. 23–53 and 171–85. Finally, on Heidegger and "drives," see 29/30, §§58–61.

12. Ernst Kris notes (409 n. 1) that we are here witnessing the earliest formulation of Freud's abiding conviction that the ego has the function (in the psychic system) of testing reality, *Realitätsprüfung*. See, for example, *Traumdeutung* (StA 2, 76n., 540–42) and "On the Two Principles of Psychic Occurrence" (StA 3, 17–19). However, on the *unconscious* as the source of the probe, see below. It would be fruitful to compare to the Freudian reality probe Husserl's efforts to distinguish among perception, memory, and fantasy. See, for example, Edmund Husserl, *Phantasie, Bildbewusstsein, Erinnerung: Zur Phänomenologie der anschaulichen Vergegenwärtigungen. Texte aus dem Nachlass, (1898–1925)*, ed. Eduard Marbach (The Hague: M. Nijhoff, 1980). The reference to Husserl will seem less strange once we recall the importance of Franz Brentano's "act psychology" for both Husserl and Freud. For the latter, see Pribram and Gill, pp. 17–18.

13. See *Cours de linguistique générale* (Paris: Payot, 1972 [1st ed. 1915]), pp. 97–113 and 155–69, on the nature of the linguistic sign, the immutability and mutability of the sign, and linguistic value. See also Derrida, *De la grammatologie*, pp. 46–69. On the entire question of linguistic association in Freud, see John Forrester, *Language and the Origins of Psychoanalysis* (New York: Columbia University Press, 1980), esp. chap. 2, pp. 40–49.

14. See Jacques Lacan, *Ecrits* (Paris: Seuil, 1966), pp. 501–2; on the 1895 *Entwurf*

see also Lacan, *L'éthique de la psychanalyse* (Paris: Seuil, 1986), pp. 45–53. The latter focuses less on the question of language than on *ethics*—the ethics of satisfaction, hallucination, *Nebenmensch*, and the principles of pleasure and reality.

15. Freud's account of language here is highly dependent on that of his 1891 monograph on aphasias. An illuminating extract of that work appears as Appendix C to "Das Unbewusste" in StA 3, 168–73. The two preceding Appendices, on Freud's relation to the neurologies of Ewald Hering and Hughlings Jackson—involving Freud's early commitment to fundamentally unlocalizable unconscious representations and a general psycho–physical *parallelism*, and by no means a *reductionism*—are also enlightening. They make it even more difficult to read the *Entwurf* as anything but a massive, tortuous, and tortured regression.

FOUR. OF TRACINGS WITHOUT WAX

1. See Rodolphe Gasché, *The Tain of the Mirror* (Cambridge, Massachusetts: Harvard University Press, 1986), chap. 9, "A System beyond Being." I will refer to Gasché by page number within parentheses in the body of my text.

2. See Krell, "Engorged Philosophy II," cited in note 2 of chap. 2, above, for the modest beginnings of such a review.

3. Martin Heidegger, *Unterwegs zur Sprache* (Pfullingen: G. Neske, 1959), p. 244; see the English translation in the revised, expanded edition of *Basic Writings*, forthcoming.

4. See Jacques Derrida, "Différance," in *Marges de la philosophie*, pp. 1–29, esp. pp. 8–9; 13–14. English translation, *Margins of Philosophy*, by Alan Bass (Chicago: University of Chicago Press, 1982), pp. 1–27, esp. pp. 7–8; 12–13.

5. See Krell, "The Perfect Future: A Note on Heidegger and Derrida," in *Deconstruction and Philosophy: The Texts of Jacques Derrida*, ed. John Sallis (Chicago: University of Chicago Press, 1987), pp. 114–21.

6. Bergson's inclusion here may seem odd, inasmuch as his *Essai sur les données immédiates de la conscience*, published in the year of Heidegger's birth, resists Kant's thesis concerning time. Yet even if for Bergson *space* is "the fundamental given," so that time is merely "the phantom of space which obsesses reflexive consciousness" (67), Bergson's is nonetheless a *transcendental* inquiry. Which is no doubt why Heidegger's copy of *Les Données* was so heavily marked. (We shall be hearing some day from Sabine Mödersheim of the Husserl Archive, Freiburg-im-Breisgau, about those marginalia.) Finally, when one hears Bergson say (70) that "the instant one attributes the least homogeneity to duration one surreptitiously introduces space," one cannot help speculating on the radicalized Bergsonism of Derridean *espacement*.

7. F. de Saussure, *Cours de linguistique générale*, p. 30.

8. See Martin Heidegger, *Hegels Phänomenologie des Geistes*, Gesamtausgabe vol. 32 (Frankfurt am Main: V. Klostermann, 1980) section 5, "The presupposition of the *Phenomenology* [*of Spirit*], its absolute beginning with the Absolute."

9. On *creux, se creuser* in Merleau-Ponty, see chap. 2, above. With regard to "trace" in Levinas, cf. the following from "Violence and Metaphysics: Essay on the Thought of Emmanuel Levinas" (ED, 194/132): "The notion of a past whose meaning could only be thought in the form of a (past) present marks the *impossible-unthinkable-unsayable* not only for a philosophy in general but also for a thinking of being that would like to take a step outside of philosophy. This notion nonetheless becomes a theme in the meditation on the trace that announces itself in the most recent writings of Levinas." Derrida is presumably thinking of Levinas's "The Trace of the Other" (1963). On this entire subject, see Robert Bernasconi, *Between Levinas and Derrida* (Bloomington: Indiana University Press), forthcoming.

10. See Derrida, "Chôra," in *Poikilia: Etudes offertes à Jean-Pierre Vernant* (Paris:

Ecole des Hautes Etudes, 1987), pp. 265–96, cited by page number within parentheses in the body of my text. I am aware that virtually every point I will be making here, or have already made in chapter 1, would have been sharpened and clarified by more attention to Ronna Burger, *Plato's 'Phaedrus': A Defense of a Philosophic Art of Writing* (University, Alabama: University of Alabama Press, 1980), esp. chap. VI, "The Art of Writing," pp. 90–109.

11. *Phaedrus*, 278a; G, 26–27/15–16; see chap. 1, above, pp. 42–44.

12. The selfsame ambiguity within fixing or fixating constitutes the principal enigma of Heidegger's third lecture course on Nietzsche. According to Heidegger, the question for Nietzsche—the question that requires a confrontation with Western metaphysics in its entirety—is whether and how *artistic transfiguration* differs decisively from *perspectival knowing* with regard to fixation (*Festmachung*). If the *cognitive* project petrifies and paralyzes becoming and all life, the *artistic* project should be in harmony with the chaos of becoming and thus should enhance life. Yet both projects appear to involve fixation of appearances—and there is no doubt that such fixation is continuous with Plato and Platonism. See Martin Heidegger, *Nietzsche*, I, 616 passim; *Nietzsche, vol. 3: The Will to Power as Knowledge and as Metaphysics* (San Francisco: Harper & Row, 1987), pp. 123ff. and throughout.

13. D, 99/87, and Krell, "Body Spaces: Merleau-Ponty and Georges Bataille," an unpublished lecture presented in 1987 to the Architectural Association, London.

14. See Jacques Derrida, "Logique de la vivante," in *Otobiographies* (Paris: Galilée, 1984), pp. 33–69; English translation, *The Ear of the Other: Autobiography, Transference, Translation*, ed. Christie V. McDonald (New York: Schocken, 1985), pp. 3–19; and Krell, "Consultations with the Paternal Shadow," in *Exceedingly Nietzsche*, ed. D. F. Krell and D. Wood (London: Routledge, 1988), pp. 80–94.

15. John Llewelyn, *Derrida on the Threshold of Sense* (London: Macmillan, 1986), pp. 81–82. The quotations appear in *La Carte postale: de Socrate à Freud et au-delà* (Paris: Aubier-Flammarion, 1980), pp. 209 and 212; *The Post Card: From Socrates to Freud and Beyond*, tr. Alan Bass (Chicago: University of Chicago Press, 1987), pp. 194 and 197. See also Llewelyn's excellent account of Derrida on *Timaeus* and *Sophist*, pp. 74–80. Other pages in the "Envois" of *La Carte postale* of particular relevance to memory are: 17/12, 28–31/23–26, 39/34, 59–60/52–53, 70–73/63–65, 133/121, 191/177, 214/199, and 263–65/246–48.

16. L. A. Post, *Thirteen Epistles of Plato* (Oxford: Oxford University Press, 1925); reprinted in Hamilton and Cairns, p. 1567. See Derrida's "Envois," passim, esp. pp. 65–66/58 and 91–92/82–83.

FIVE. OF PITS AND PYRAMIDS

1. I have used the *Philosophische Bibliothek* edition throughout, ed. Otto Pöggeler and Friedhelm Nicolin (Hamburg: F. Meiner, 1969). I will cite this edition as E, with section (§) number. I will not attempt a careful reconstruction of the three editions (1817, 1827, 1830) and all their variants. See also the "Appendices" (*Zusätze*) to the relevant paragraphs in the *Jubiläumsausgabe* of Hegel's *Encyclopedia*, "System der Philosophie," ed. Ludwig Boumann (Stuttgart-Bad Cannstatt: F. Frommann, 1965 [1st ed. 1845]), *10*, 328–58. In the edition by M. J. Petry, *Hegel's Philosophy of Subjective Spirit*, 3 vols. (Dordrecht, Holland: D. Reidel, 1978), see esp. *3*, 144–217 and 401–36. Finally, see the useful collection of Hegel's own notes to the first (1817) edition of the *Enzyklopädie*, "Hegels Vorlesungsnotizen zum subjektiven Geiste," ed. Friedhelm Nicolin and Helmut Schneider, *Hegel-Studien*, Band 10 (1975), esp. the notes to §§ 372, 375–6, 378, 381, and 383, pp. 59, 61–64, and 67–69.

2. Jacques Derrida, *Marges de la philosophie*, pp. 79–127/69–108. For an excellent account of *imagination* in these pages of the *Encyclopedia*, see John Sallis, *Spacings—*

Of Reason and Imagination in Texts of Kant, Fichte, and Hegel (Chicago: University of Chicago Press, 1987), pp. 132–57.

3. Quoted in John C. Greene, *The Death of Adam: Evolution and Its Impact on Western Thought* (New York: New American Library, 1961), p. 86.

4. M. J. Petry, ed. and tr., *Hegel's Philosophy of Nature*, 3 vols. (London: Allen & Unwin, 1970), II, 24.

5. See Jacques Derrida, "Différance," in *Marges de la philosophie*, pp. 1–29/1–27.

6. ". . . schwächere Umbildung zur Seite." My reading differs from that of Petry at II, 25.

7. Quoted in Greene, p. 69.

8. G. W. F. Hegel, *Werke in zwanzig Bänden* (Frankfurt am Main: Suhrkamp, 1970), 4, 39. We will return to the *Propaedeutics* when we take up the psychology of memory and remembrance.

9. See Krell, "Pitch: Genitality/Excrementality from Hegel to Crazy Jane," referred to above in note 26 of chap. 1.

10. Hegel's metaphor sparks a recollection of Freud's astonishing remarks on the origins of fabric weaving. See his second set of introductory lectures on psychoanalysis, *Neue Folge*, StA 1, 562.

11. See F. W. J. Schelling, *Sämtliche Werke*, VII, 360; and Georges Bataille, *Visions of Excess*, p. 13. See also Krell, "The Crisis of Reason in the Nineteenth Century: Schelling's Treatise on Human Freedom (1809)," and Krell, "Paradoxes of the Pineal: From Descartes to Georges Bataille," cited in note 28 of chap. 1, above.

12. Derrida's "Pit" must be supplemented by remarks in *De la grammatologie*, p. 40/ 25. Here Derrida discusses what is perhaps the most revealing reversal in §459, one that tends to modify Derrida's own thesis on the suppression of writing and the privilege of speech in metaphysics. Hegel celebrates alphabetic script as an "educational" or "formative" device for spirit's developing interiority. He identifies "the resounding word" with the "more formal" and abstract element of thought thinking itself. However, the peculiarity of the alphabetic script, that is, its phonetic character, is itself suppressed "in the interest of vision." *In the act of reading, alphabetic script itself becomes a kind of hieroglyphics.* While reading we no longer need to be conscious of the sounds, the phonemes. The transformation of alphabetic into hieroglyphic script results from a "capacity for abstraction" that is essential to thought. Hegel speaks (that is, writes) of a "hieroglyphic reading" that is "for itself a deaf reading and a mute writing." True, in a final reversal Hegel reasserts the privilege of the audible: "visible language" comports itself to resonant language "merely as a sign," and intelligence expresses itself "immediately and unconditionally" through speech. Yet it is a mutilated speech, tongueless, ripped from the gorge, and speaking to readers who have no ears; and it is a mutilated reading and writing, groping its way about the verge. I have commented briefly on the suppression of the voice in metaphysics in "Engorged Philosophy," and also in "Engorged Philosophy II," both cited in chapter 2.

13. See §464. Cf. Hegel's *Grundlinien der Philosophie des Rechts* (7, 146 and 161) on the mysterious exteriority of "spiritual production" in book printing and in signs generally. See also Derrida's careful analysis of mechanical memory: *Marges*, 123–27/ 105–8. Lest we decide too quickly that Hegel's celebration of mechanical repetition or rote memorization as the summit of intelligence is a mere quirk on his part, consider the researches of Hermann Ebbinghaus at the University of Berlin in the 1880s, researches that undergird not only the empirical psychology of memory but also the modern testing of intelligence. Ebbinghaus designed series of nonsense syllables, reading them aloud to scores of subjects until they could reproduce them without hesitation. He searched for statistical constants involving the relation of retention to (1) the speed in learning syllables of various lengths; (2) the number of repetitions; (3) elapsed time; (4) repeated learning; and (5) the associative sequence of members in the series. Perhaps

those who in the modern world prove to have excellent memories—and who are presumed (as the very title of Jean Piaget's *Mémoire et intelligence* [Paris: Presses Universitaires de France, 1968] suggests) to have high intelligence—are precisely those who through docility or credulity conform to the examiner's short-term demands. Perhaps, on the contrary, they are merely destined to become confirmed Hegelians. Perhaps, finally, these two possibilities are not as distinct as one might have liked. See Krell, "Phenomenology of Memory: Some Implications for Education," in *Phenomenology and Education,* ed. Bernard Curtis and Wolfe Mays (London: Methuen, 1978), pp. 138–42.

14. In the penultimate section of his critique of aesthetic judgment (*Kritik der Urteilskraft,* §59, "On Beauty as Symbol of Ethicality"; B 254–60), Kant introduces *hypotyposis.* Any thorough study of typography would have to take it into account, even though Kant does not relate the notion specifically to memory—about which in general he has very little to say. Hypotyposis has to do with the subsumption of intuitions (as examples) under empirical concepts or of schemata under pure concepts of the understanding. (Of course, hypotyposis cannot *properly* be performed for concepts of reason, to which no intuition can be assigned.) Kant writes: "All *hypotyposis* (presentation [*Darstellung*], *subiectio ad adspectum*), as a making sensible [*Versinnlichung*], is twofold: either schematic, when the corresponding intuition is given a priori to a concept grasped by the understanding; or *symbolic,* when such an intuition [*eine solche*] is subsumed under a concept that can only be thought by reason and to which no sensible intuition can approximate [*angemessen sein kann*]; an intuition in which the process of judgment is only analogically related to what it observes when it schematizes; that is, an intuition by which only the rule of the process, not the intuition itself, and therewith only the form of reflection without regard to content, accords with the concept." The nightmarish syntax of symbolic hypotyposis and the bewildering analogical intuition which is not properly an intuition suggest the crucial importance of hypotyposis in the *Kantian* hierarchy of cognition. Both schematic and symbolic modes of representation-via-intuition are subsumed under the subsuming power of hypotyposis: both are *exhibitiones* not of mere characters or word-signs but of represented reality (*Realität*). Here Kant is no doubt close to the iconographic repetition of intuition, first as *things* and then as *names,* in Hegelian psychology. The fact that symbolic hypotyposis is the very mechanism that expresses the analogical relation between ethicality and the beautiful, between intelligibility and the sensuous, between the freedom of imagination and the lawfulness of understanding, and between particularity and universality makes one wonder whether this sophisticated grandchild of typography is somehow meant to achieve the unity of the Critical project as a whole. How both *Erinnerung* and *Gedächtnis,* the very *sites* of traditional typographies up to and including Hegel, can be absent from the three critiques (when, after all, *tantum scimus, quantum memoria tenemus* [*Anthropologie,* 184], why they must be relegated to pragmatic anthropology, are questions that would detain us long on the verge.

15. Jacques Derrida, "De l'économie restreinte à l'économie générale, *Un hegelianisme sans réserve,*" in ED, 406/276. See also Paul de Man, "Sign and Symbol in Hegel's *Aesthetics,*" in *Critical Inquiry* 8 (Summer 1982), pp. 761–75. De Man is right to complain that Hegelian *Denken* about *Gedächtnis* seems "as remote as can be from the sounds and the images of the imagination or from the dark reach of words . . ."; but whether one can say that in Hegel's system *Gedächtnis* utterly "effaces" *Erinnerung* is open to question (772–73). After all, as we shall now insist (as also below, in chapter 7), the very illimitability and ubiquity of remembrance removes it from the grasp of *Denken* and *Gedächtnis.* This matter, crucial to the verge, apparently plays no role in the Geuss–de Man "debate" (*Critical Inquiry* 10 [December 1983], 375–90).

16. M. Merleau-Ponty, *Résumés de cours,* p. 81.

17. *L'être et le néant,* II, 1, iii, p. 129. In a similar vein, Merleau-Ponty writes: "Thus

all consciousness is unhappy, since it knows it leads a double life and regrets the innocence from which it feels itself expelled." Not merely for Sartre, but for all contemporary thought, "the dialectic is truncated." See Merleau-Ponty, "L'existentialisme chez Hegel," in *Sens et nonsens* (Paris: Nagel, 1966), p. 120.

18. Friedrich Nietzsche, *Sämtliche Werke: Kritische Studienausgabe in 15 Bänden,* ed. Giorgio Colli and Mazzino Montinari (Berlin and Munich: de Gruyter/DTV, 1980), 12, 476. Hereinafter cited in the body of my text by volume and page.

19. See Krell, "Lucinde's Shame: Hegel, Sensuous Woman, and the Law," in "Hegel and Legal Theory," *Cardozo Law Review,* vol. 10, nos. 5–6 (March/April 1989), 1673–86.

20. See *Sämtliche Werke,* VII, 375 and 394–99.

21. Jean Hyppolite, "Hegel's Phenomenology and Psychoanalysis," in W. Steinkraus, ed., *New Studies in Hegel's Philosophy* (New York: Holt, Rinehart and Winston, 1971), p. 58. Eugen Fink feels his way toward that trauma of spirit as he interprets those very lines of Hegel's *Phenomenology* (PG, 86–87) to which we referred a page or two ago—on the remembering and forgetting of phenomenological and natural consciousness (respectively!). Fink understands such trauma, amnesia, and anamnesis in terms of *Heidegger's* question of being, which we shall take up in the next chapter. Yet Fink's comments on Hegel are highly suggestive and worth quoting at length—see Eugen Fink, *Hegel: Phänomenologische Interpretationen der "Phänomenologie des Geistes"* (Frankfurt am Main: V. Klostermann, 1977), pp. 88–89.

Hegel observes that sensuous certainty always has this experience of itself, to be sure—but that it always forgets the experience. The power of oblivion enables us to abide, as we usually do, in sensuous certainty. The power of oblivion permeates our entire existence. Human beings are creatures that are aware of being, although for the most part they forget about it. Oblivion of being is as originary as the inchoate openness of being. If Hegel explicitly designates oblivion as that counterforce, then the path of knowing, from sensuous certainty all the way to absolute knowing, loses its compelling character, a character that is often attributed to it. The path is a necessary one, yet its necessity does not take the form of a process regulated by some law of nature. It is a historical necessity. The dialectic of sensuous certainty is an experience that such certainty must have of itself, but that it can also forget again.

Does Fink here endeavor to step back from the radicality of his statement that oblivion deprives the path of knowing (or, for that matter, the hierarchy of transition) of its compelling character by inserting *kann* into the dialectic, instead of allowing the *muß* to retain its compelling power? Does he not slack the tension of Hegel's dialectic in order to diminish the monstrous power of the negative? Does not the reduction of oblivion to a mere possibility enable him to pursue the established itinerary of spirit? Would not such pursuit be under the sway of oblivion? Ever only on the verge of phenomenological remembrance? But to continue:

The oblivion can be so profound that human beings are assured that with sensuous certainty they have taken the measure of the actual, that what the senses show them they may safely take to be being, indeed, being [*das Seiende*] in the proper sense. Only human beings can forget themselves so profoundly, elevating the inconstant and ephemeral-nugatory to the truly actual, thus comprehending even less than the brute animals. Hegel says of the animals that in their desperation they immediately approach the reality of sensuous things and, completely certain of their nothingness, devour them. The human being who is trapped in the sensuous, having forgotten being, no longer catches a glimpse of the profound meaning of the ancient mystery of bread and wine, that sacrament of the Earth whereby nontransient or perdurant being [*Sein*] is celebrated in the annihilation of the nugatory sensuous/sensible [*des nichtigen Sinnfälligen*] and in the metamorphosis of transiency. Hegel, in his magnificent language, interrupting the arduous path of his disciplined thought from time to time with a poetic image, says: ". . . to those who assert the truth and certainty of the reality of sensuous objects it [can] be said that they must be sent back to the most elementary of the schools of wisdom, namely, that of the ancient Eleusinian mysteries of Ceres and Bacchus, where they can for the first time learn the secret of eating bread and drinking wine; for the initiate who knows these mysteries comes not only to doubt the being of sensuous things but also to despair of such being." (PG, 87)

Dionysian wine as an elixir of remembrance rather than oblivion? Remembrance of the nothingness of its own spirit? The nothingness of a mere image interrupting rigorous prose? A mere image of animals and Bacchants consuming and being consumed by a nothing? Dreaming of perdurance and sustenance as they swallow and are swallowed? If Hegel espies "all nature celebrating these open mysteries" (open? mysteries? *diese offenbaren Mysterien,* PG, 88), no wonder Fink concludes his commentary (352) by counterposing to Hegel the *mythos* of Nietzsche's Zarathustra: "Remain true to the Earth!"

22. "The Rhine," in Hölderlin, *Werke und Briefe,* ed. F. Beissner and J. Schmidt (Frankfurt am Main: Insel, 1969), p. 150:

> Es haben aber an eigner
> Unsterblichkeit die Götter genug, und bedürfen
> Die Himmlischen eines Dings,
> So sinds Heroen und Menschen
> Und Sterbliche sonst. Denn weil
> Die Seligsten nichts fühlen von selbst,
> Muss wohl, wenn solches zu sagen
> Erlaubt ist, in der Götter Namen
> Teilnehmend fühlen ein Andrer,
> Den brauchen sie. . . .

23. "Mnemosyne," first version, p. 198:

> . . . Nicht vermögen
> Die Himmlischen alles. Nämlich es reichen
> Die Sterblichen eh an den Abgrund. Also wendet es sich
> Mit diesen. Lang ist
> Die Zeit, es ereignet sich aber
> Das Wahre.

24. M. Merleau-Ponty, *Résumés de cours,* p. 81.

SIX. OF HAVING-BEEN

1. I will not repeat here my discussions of ecstatic temporality and the vicissitudes of fundamental ontology. See Krell, *Intimations of Mortality,* chapters 2 and 3; "The Perfect Future," in *Deconstruction and Philosophy: The Texts of Jacques Derrida,* pp. 114–21; and "Beneath the Time of the Line," in *Writing the Future,* ed. David Wood (London: Routledge, 1989), pp. 106–11.

2. See Martin Heidegger, *Schellings Abhandlung über das Wesen der menschlichen Freiheit (1809)* (Tübingen: M. Niemeyer, 1971), p. 229.

3. See William McNeill, *The Modification of 'Being and Time',* Ph.D. Thesis, University of Essex, 1987.

4. I say "virtually" because of the important statement in section 65 (SZ, 330)—to which I referred only briefly above—that comes at the culmination of Heidegger's initial sketch of temporality as the ontological meaning of care: "The original and proper

future is the toward-itself, toward its *self*, existing as the impassable possibility of nullity [*die unüberholbare Möglichkeit der Nichtigkeit*]. The ecstatic character of the original future consists precisely in the fact that the future closes our ability to be [*schliesst das Seinkönnen*]; that is to say, that the future is itself closed [*selbst geschlossen ist*], and that as such it makes possible the resolutely un-closed [*entschlossene*] existentiell understanding of nullity." Such closure, the essential finitude of temporality, haunts fundamental ontology in all its transformations. Again, I refer readers to chapters 2 and 3 of *Intimations of Mortality*, esp. p. 60. And I remember to thank John Sallis, who first pointed out to me the importance of the above passage on *schliessen*.

5. In his 1927 lecture course on the "fundamental problems of phenomenology" (24, 411), Heidegger poses the problem of oblivion, *Vergessen*, as an autonomous, positive, ecstatic mode of temporality (*ein eigener positiv ekstatischer Modus der Zeitlichkeit*) with even greater radicality: "The ecstasis of forgetting something has the character of disengagement vis-à-vis one's ownmost having-been, indeed in such a way that this disengagement-in-the-face-of closes off what it faces. Because forgetting closes off having-been—such is the peculiar nature of that ecstasis—it closes itself off to itself [*verschliesst es sich für sich selbst*]. Oblivion is characterized by the fact that it forgets itself. It lies in the ecstatic essence of forgetting that it forgets not only the forgotten but also the forgetting itself. The vulgar prephenomenological view of things is that forgetting is nothing at all. Oblivion is an elementary mode of the temporality in which at first and for the most part we *are* our own having-been." *Are* it, to be sure, by having always already forgotten it. Such oblivion appears to be perfect.

6. A second example, a second sighting of the same gorge. At the top of SZ, 260 two kinds of *holding* are juxtaposed: first, Heidegger raises the *question* as to whether Dasein can ever *properly understand* its "ownmost, nonrelational and impassable, certain and as such undetermined possibility," that is, whether it can "*hold itself* in an appropriate being toward its end [my emphasis]"; second, some eight lines later, the opening words of §53, "Existential projection of an appropriate being toward death," read as follows: "Factically, Dasein persists [*hält sich:* holds itself] at first and for the most part in an inappropriate being toward death." The slippage that occurs between these two *holds* runs through the entire second division of *Being and Time*, which must show that an appropriate being toward death is possible both *existentielly* and *existential-ontologically* without jettisoning its own hold on the essentially "indifferent" structure of the average everyday *zunächst and zumeist*. And, finally, a third sighting of the same abyss. In §58, "Understanding the call [of conscience], and guilt," to which I referred earlier, Heidegger's effort to achieve *ontic* attestation of the *ontological* possibility of a resolute openedness that runs ahead into an appropriate future confronts the nothing, *das Nichts*. "Being the (null) ground of a nullity" expresses the *guilt* of Dasein (SZ, 285). Yet guilt sleeps, and must be called to wakefulness; the meaning of the call is understood when "the existential sense" of guilt is "held." "Held" by being "heard aright," "heard aright" through "readiness for being able to be called" (SZ, 287). Dasein *is* ready, insists Heidegger, slipping now into the perfect, because "it has chosen itself [*Es hat sich selbst gewählt*]." Willing to have a conscience, *Gewissen-haben-wollen*, we learn in §60 (SZ, 296), is "readiness for anxiety." Which, we remember, is always on the verge of waking, always on the very verge of remembering. And which therefore does not temporalize, does not propriate, does not rescue.

7. See Krell, "Daimon Life, Nearness and Abyss: An Introduction to Za-ology," in *Research in Phenomenology*, XVII (1987), 23–53, esp. note 14; and Jacques Derrida, *De l'esprit: Heidegger et la question* (Paris: Galilée, 1987), pp. 75–90 passim.

8. See, again, Jacques Derrida, *De l'esprit*, throughout. I have discussed Derrida's extraordinary text in "Spiriting Heidegger," *Research in Phenomenology*, XVIII (1988), 205–30.

9. See SZ, 396–97. Heidegger apparently taught a semester-long course on this

text, although we do not know precisely when he did so. See my note to "Plan of the English Edition" in Martin Heidegger, *Nietzsche, Vol. 3: The Will to Power as Knowledge and as Metaphysics,* pp. xi–xii, along with pp. viii and 248–49. Otto Pöggeler still argues that 1928 is the more likely date than the date stated in the *Gesamtausgabe* prospectus, i.e., 1938–39.

    10. See "Of Redemption," in *Also sprach Zarathustra,* Part II, 4, 177–82; Martin Heidegger, *Nietzsche, Vol. 2: The Eternal Recurrence of the Same* (San Francisco: Harper & Row, 1984), pp. 223–27. See also *Intimations of Mortality,* chap. 8, pp. 132–35. Finally, see the many rich sketches in Nietzsche's unpublished notes contemporaneous with *Untimely* and relating to memory: *Studienausgabe,* 7, 636ff.

    11. Again, see chaps. 2 and 3 of *Intimations of Mortality.*

    12. See Pierre Klossowski, *Nietzsche et le cercle vicieux* (Paris: Mercure de France, 1969), pp. 93–103. I shall return to this theme in chapter 7, in the context of memory and affirmation.

    13. See Martin Heidegger, "Die Erinnerung in die Metaphysik," in *Nietzsche,* II, 481–90. The tone of this brief piece resounds throughout the "intimations" of Heidegger's vast *Beiträge zur Philosophie* of 1936–38 (Frankfurt am Main: V. Klostermann, 1989), especially its second part, *Anklang.*

    14. The play on *Vermögen, mögen, möglich* is already familiar to us from Heidegger's "Letter on 'Humanism'." See *Basic Writings,* 1st ed., p. 196.

    15. See Heidegger's use of *Behalten* in his 1927 lecture course *Basic Problems of Phenomenology,* 24, 367, 375, 412, 432 and all of section 21a on absence, *Abhandenheit,* and the nothing.

    16. To be sure, Heidegger knows of the passages in question: see *Nietzsche, Vol. II: The Eternal Recurrence of the Same,* section 6, opening paragraph; see also my commentary, pp. 253–59; and 268–81. On this important shift in Heidegger's thinking between 1937 and 1951, see Wolfgang Müller-Lauter, "Das Willenswesen und der Übermensch: Ein Beitrag zu Heideggers Nietzsche-Interpretation," in *Nietzsche-Studien,* Band 10/11 (1981–1982), 132–92.

    17. In my brief remarks on the very similar passage in "Who Is Nietzsche's Zarathustra?" (cf. WhD? 39 and *Vorträge und Aufsätze,* p. 116) I assumed that Heidegger's account had all the force of his own voice behind it. My student and friend Joel B. Shapiro convinces me that Heidegger may well wish to distance himself from that account. Let us then put in abeyance any attempt to identify the voice that speaks in the following account; let us take it as a matter of memory, reminiscence, and writing from Aristotle through Nietzsche—and *perhaps* Heidegger. The "brief remarks" I refer to appear in John Sallis, ed., *Deconstruction and Philosophy,* p. 119, lines 14ff. from the bottom.

    18. To confront the puzzle of "passing by" as an epochal *recuperation* of what-has-been in Western history is to broach the question of Heidegger and practical philosophy—Heidegger and political philosophy. As Reiner Schürmann struggles to provide an introductory characterization of the "anarchy principle," he invokes "a deposing of the very principle of epochal principles, and the beginning of an economy of *passage.*" See Reiner Schürmann, *Heidegger on Being and Acting: From Principles to Anarchy* (Bloomington: Indiana University Press, 1987), p. 9; my emphasis. I sense here a filiation with my own preoccupations with the transcendental *parcours,* the existential *Vorbei,* ontotheological *Vorbeigang,* and Nietzschean *Übergang/Untergang.* Whether and how an economy of passage can sustain "deposition" of the "very principle of epochal principles" remains the stinging nettle. But there we are. In memory of *a time of transition,* our time, shared by many, one has to regret the narcissism and egoism impacted in discourses on memory, including my own. If there is a collective memory, and if (as Casey argues in his chapter 10, "Commemoration") there is an essentially public space of memory, are we not always on the verge of a *politics* of memory? On *Vorbeigang,* see the *Beiträge,* pp. 393–417.

19. See Philippe Lacoue-Labarthe, "Typographie" in Sylviane Agacinski et al., *Mimésis des articulations* (cited in note 11 of chap. 1), pp. 173–90, esp. p. 185. For a number of reservations concerning Lacoue-Labarthe's reading of Heidegger's *Nietzsche,* see Krell, "A Hermeneutics of Discretion," *Research in Phenomenology* XV (1985), 1–27.

20. Martin Heidegger, *Wegmarken* (cited in chapter 1, note 7), p. 239.

SEVEN. OF ASHES

1. See Pierre Klossowski, *Nietzsche et le cercle vicieux,* cited in note 12 of chap. 6; I shall refer to this text as CV in the body of my text, with page number; an English translation of one of its chapters, "L'expérience de l'Eternel Retour" appears in David B. Allison, ed., *The New Nietzsche: Contemporary Styles of Interpretation* (New York: Delta, 1977; reprinted in 1987 by MIT Press), pp. 107–20. Jacques Derrida, *Mémoires: For Paul de Man* (New York: Columbia University Press, 1986), French edition (which I shall cite first) by Galilée, 1988, cited as MPM; *Ulysse gramophone: Deux mots pour Joyce* (Paris: Galilée, 1987), cited as UG; the first half of this volume has been translated by Geoff Bennington in *Post-structuralist Joyce: Essays from the French,* ed. Derek Attridge and Daniel Ferrer (Cambridge, England: Cambridge University Press, 1984), pp. 145–59, and I shall refer to it by page number; *Schibboleth: pour Paul Celan* (Paris: Galilée, 1986), cited as SH; *Feu la cendre* (Paris: Des femmes, 1987), cited as LAC; *De l'esprit: Heidegger et la question,* cited in note 7 of chap. 6, above, and quoted here as DE; "Fors," Preface to *Le verbier de l'Homme aux loups,* by Nicolas Abraham and Maria Torok (Paris: Aubier-Flammarion, 1976), cited as *Fors;* these are by no means the only works that treat of affirmation, the double-yes, mourning, and ash, but they will serve as this chapter's principal sources.

2. SH, 32, 36–38. See Paul Celan, *Gesammelte Werke,* 5 vols. (Frankfurt am Main: Suhrkamp, 1986), *1,* 154:

> Wachs,
> Ungeschriebnes zu siegeln,
> das deinen Namen
> erriet,
> das deinen Namen
> verschlüsselt.

3. SH, 83; Celan, *Gesammelte Werke, 1,* 197–99: Derrida's extracts are from the first third of this long poem:

> Geh, deine Stunde
> hat keine Schwestern, du bist—
> bist zuhause. Ein Rad, langsam,
> rollt aus sich selber, die Speichen
> klettern, [. . .]
>
> Jahre.
> Jahre, Jahre, ein Finger
> tastet hinab und hinan, [. . .]
>
> Kam, kam.
> Kam ein Wort, kam,
> kam durch die Nacht,
> wollt leuchten, wollt leuchten.
>
> Asche.
> Asche, Asche.
> Nacht.
> Nacht-und-Nacht. [. . .]

4. See Jacques Derrida, "Ousia et Grammè," in *Marges*, pp. 59–61/52–53; see also note 21 of chap. 1.

5. CV, 107. On Zarathustra's silence and laughter, see the final twenty lines of "On Redemption," ASZ II (4, 181–82): "—But at this point in his speech it happened that Zarathustra suddenly grew taciturn [*innehielt*] and had the look of someone who is terrified utterly. . . ." For the impact of Klossowski's "vicious circle" on a reading of Heidegger's interpretation of eternal return, see my "Analysis" to Martin Heidegger, *Nietzsche, Vol. 2: The Eternal Recurrence of the Same*, pp. 268–81, esp. p. 279.

6. Hölderlin, *Werke und Briefe*, I, 198–202:

> . . . Himmlische nämlich sind
> Unwillig, wenn einer nicht die Seele schonend sich
> Zusammengenommen, aber er muss doch; dem
> Gleich fehlet die Trauer.

7. See Derrida, *Otobiographies*, pp. 65–66; also Krell, "Consultations with the Paternal Shadow," in *Exceedingly Nietzsche*, pp. 88–89.

8. Jacques Derrida, *La voix et le phénomène* (Paris: Presses Universitaires de France, 1967), pp. 104–8; English translation, *Speech and Phenomena*, by David B. Allison (Evanston, Illinois: Northwestern University Press, 1973), pp. 93–97. Derrida's "Logique de la vivante" is cited in chap. 4, note 14.

9. See Jacques Derrida, "Interpreting Signatures (Nietzsche/Heidegger): Two Questions," in *The Gadamer-Derrida Encounter: Texts and Commentary*, ed. Diane Michelfelder and Richard Palmer (Albany: State University of New York Press, 1989), pp. 58–71.

10. Paul de Man, *Blindness and Insight: Essays in the Rhetoric of Contemporary Criticism*, 2nd, revised ed. (Minneapolis: University of Minnesota Press, 1983), pp. 89–90; cf. MPM, 70/57.

11. Paul de Man, "The Rhetoric of Temporality," in *Blindness and Insight*, pp. 222 and 226; cf. MPM, 91/82–83. A nagging doubt persists, to be sure, that de Man's emphasis on the *instant de passage* and on the *failure* of memory as constituting the "authentic experience of temporality" may cripple what one might call *political memory*. Although the tendency to compare the "cases" of de Man and Heidegger is usually the familiar tendency to rush to judgment, at least one aspect remains troubling: if "authenticity" serves as an attempted *hold* on things, and ultimately a kind of desired hegemony over them, a terrible sort of oblivion may well infest it. Yet the remedy—if there is one—is surely not an even more desperate hankering after an authentically authentic theory of an authentic politics, dressed up in the vogue rags of emancipatory discourse. I find Geoffrey Hartmann's response to the political issue thoughtful (see "Blindness and Insight," in *The New Republic* for March 7, 1988, pp. 26–31), and I cite its concluding sentence: "De Man's critique of every tendency to totalize literature or language, to see unity where there is no unity, looks like a belated, but still powerful, act of conscience." Derrida's own response, "Like the Sound of the Sea Deep within a Shell: Paul de Man's War," appears in *Critical Inquiry 14* (Spring 1988), 590–652, translated by Peggy Kamuf. In the French edition of MPM, pp. 147–232. It too emphasizes de Man's resistance to totalizing discourse, a resistance put to rout by the very professors and journalists who are ardent to condemn de Man and all the works of "deconstruction." De Man's own memory, Derrida suggests, must have remained a site of ordeal, mourning, and even agony for him. They are certainly such now for his doubly bereaved friends and readers.

12. Paul de Man, *Allegories of Reading: Figural Language in Rousseau, Nietzsche, Rilke, and Proust* (New Haven, Connecticut: Yale University Press, 1979), p. 277; cf. MPM, 100/94–95.

13. DE, 150. Heidegger invokes the project of an "immanent critique" in the lecture,

"The End of Philosophy and the Task of Thinking," in *Zur Sache des Denkens* (Tübingen: M. Niemeyer, 1969), p. 61; see *Basic Writings*, 1st ed., pp. 370 and 373.

14. Little has been written on *Schmerz* in Heidegger's language essays, as far as I am aware. I expect to hear more on it from Philippe Lacoue-Labarthe and Christopher Fynsk, as well as from Derrida's work on the third generation (of) *Geschlecht*, still to come. And I look forward to the reflections of James Urpeth, at the University of Essex, who is now writing on the topic.

15. See Gottfried von Strassburg, *Tristan: Text, Nacherzählung, Wort- und Begriffserklärungen*, ed. Gottfried Weber (Darmstadt: Wissenschaftliche Buchgesellschaft, 1967), pp. 849–51; G. F. Benecke *et al.*, *Mittelhochdeutsches Wörterbuch* (Hildesheim, 1963), vol. II, pp. 177–82. My thanks to Ursula Willaredt.

16. I shall cite James Joyce's *Ulysses* by page and line, as though by chapter and verse, in the edition by Hans Walter Gabler, Wolfhard Steppe, and Claus Melchior (New York: Random House, 1986). Here: U, 282.1917–18. I shall cite *Finnegans Wake* in the 8th printing ("With the author's corrections incorporated in the text") published by The Viking Press (New York, 1971), again by page and line numbers.

17. See Edmund Husserl, *L'origine de la géométrie*, translated and introduced by Jacques Derrida (Paris: Presses Universitaires de France, 1962), pp. 104–5; Derrida, *Dissémination*, p. 99 n. 17/88 no. 20; and *La Carte postale*, esp. pp. 257–58/240–41.

18. On the concept and uses of genealogy, see *Of Grammatology*, 26/14, 52–55/35–37, 149–50/101–2, 182/125, 196/135, and 202/140. For recent hesitations with regard to genealogy, see "Interpreting Signatures (Nietzsche/Heidegger): Two Questions," in Michelfelder-Palmer, passim; cf. MPM, 38/15, 88/78.

19. The burst of laughter signals Derrida's own debt to Bataille, as the spray of chuckles signals mine. See "From a Restricted to a General Economy: An Hegelianism without Reserve," in ED, 369–407/251–77, esp. 376/255–56.

20. See "Le retrait de la métaphore," in *Psyché* (Paris: Galilée, 1987), pp. 63–93; see also "Télépathie," also related to *Feu la cendre* and *La Carte postale*, in *Psyché*, pp. 237–70; finally, for further discussion of the double-yes of affirmation, see "Nombre de oui," in *Psyché*, pp. 639–50.

21. The word *par* (LAC, 61, line 3), should be *pas*, in accord with the text in *Anima 5* and as spoken in the "Bibliothèque des Voix" version.

Index

absence, 16–20, 32, 48–49, 76–77, 159, 161, 165–66, 169–70, 186, 236, 267, *317*
affirmation, xii, 9, 277, 282, 301–309 *passim.* *See also* yes.
alētheia (truth), 2, 33, 35, 63, 159, 169
anxiety, 8, 237, 247–48, 250–54, 257, 262, 264, 288, *331*
Aquinas, Thomas, 55, 67, 82, *318*
Aristotle, 3–4, 8, 13–29 *passim*, 42, 45, 47–48, 75–77, 82, 90, 142, 168, 170–71, 182, 210, 240-51, 268, 274, 282, *315–16*
arkhē kinēseōs (the principle of motion), 19, 22, 77, 96, 142–45, 148, 157, 182, 210, 224
art, 17, 33–34, 96; as imagination, 198; of memory, 54–55; of philosophy, 190; of weaving, 48, 190–92, *327*; of writing, 60, *319*
Augustine, 52–56, 62, 75, 89, 92, 100–102, 127, 177, 188, 219, 241–42, 268, 271
aviary, the, 27, 48, 51, 66, 169, 223, 229, 286
Avicenna, 66

Bacon, Francis, 58
Bataille, Georges, 217, 301, 311, *319–20*, *327*, *335*
Benjamin, Walter, *322*
Bergson, Henri, 180, *321*, *325*
body, 5, 22, 25–26, 58, 66, 68, 90, 93, 168, 177–79; separation of soul from, 45–46, 50; Socrates' "etymology" of, 51–52; as tomb and engraved sign, 77
Borges, Jorge Luis, xi, 79
Boyle, Joseph, 83
Breuer, Josef, 149; Freud and, 106–108
Bruno, Giordano, 56

Camillo, Giulio, 56
Capella, Martianus, 55
Casey, Edward S., 283, *322*; mnemic phenomena, *315*
cathexis (*Besetzung*), 120, 125–38 *passim*, 141, 147, 156; and desire, 124, 132–33; lateral, 126–28, 138–43 *passim*, 145, 209; satisfaction by way of, 123
Cicero, 55
Claudel, Paul, 97
Coleridge, Samuel Taylor, 5, 167, *321*
commemoration, 253, 263–72 *passim*
consciousness, 6, 93–94, 125, 138–60 *passim*, 183, 186–87, 212, 278; ego-consciousness, 107–108, 137, 157; experience of, 230–34; and intelligence, 215; natural, 231–33, 237, 247, *329*; origin of, 156; and perception, 118–22, 135, 154–58; phenomenological,

329; reflexive, *325*; representational, *318*; and time, xi, 214; as unhappy, 237, *328*

de Man, Paul, 282, 284, 290–92, 296, 298, *328*, *334*
Democritus, 23–24
Derrida, Jacques, 7, 49–50, 67, 94, 104–105, 112–14, 141, 148–59 *passim*, 165–204 *passim*, 205, 219–21, 277–312 *passim*, *315*, *318–19*, *323*, *325-27*, *331*, *334–35*; on cryptonymy, 285–86; demonstration of "double-inscription" of mimesis, *317*; on Joyce, 299–306 *passim*
Descartes, 3, 5, 54, 56–73 *passim*, 82, 85, 90, 92, 101, 149, 165, 172, 177, 254, 286, *318–19*; on foetal memory, *320*; his account of memory, 69; theory of "memory traces," 88, 134
différance, 7, 49, 67, 159, 172, 174–75, 182–83, 187, 208. *See* trace
difference, 7, 30, 31, 36, 39–40, 48–49, 80, 101, 111, 114, 167, 174–76, 179, 186, 207, 217, 299; between fear and anxiety, 250; in Cartesian physiology, 66; ontological, 176, 292; as *pharmakon*, 198
Dilthey, Wilhelm, 19, 122
Diogenes Laertius, 36
dream, 42, 50, 129–45 *passim*, 194–97, 199, 203–204, 263; Plato's, 7, 166, 186–87, 196–97, 201–203; Derrida's, 201
Driesch, Hans, 122

ecstases of time, 8, 96, 243–53 *passim*, 257–64 *passim*, 307
ego, 6, 107, 124–41 *passim*, 184; ego-consciousness, 107–108, 137, 156–59; ego-formation, 284–85
eidōlon, 25–36 *passim*, 168, 196–97, 283
eikōn, 17, 23, 28–41 *passim*, 48–49, 51, 76, 89, 168, 173, 201–202
Erasistratus of Chios, 64
eternal recurrence, xii, 9, 277–82 *passim*, 314
eternity, 301
Exner, Sigmund, 110
eye, the, 68, 80. *See also* pineal eye

father, the, 101, 172, 192–95, 199–201
Ficino, Marsiglio, 56
Fink, Eugen, 174, *329*
Fliess, Wilhelm, 105, 111, 122, 150–51, 158, 284, *322–24*
footprints, 25, 54, 62, 77, 90, 167. *See* vestiges
forgetting, 50, 106–107, 149–50, 214, 240–54 *passim*, 259–60, 264, 272–73, *329*, *331*. *See also* oblivion

Index

DAVID FARRELL KRELL is Professor and Chair of Philosophy at DePaul University. He is the author of *Intimations of Mortality: Time, Truth, and Finitude in Heidegger's Thinking of Being* and *Postponements: Woman, Sensuality, and Death in Nietzsche*. Krell has edited and translated numerous works by Martin Heidegger.